A SHORT HISTORY
OF INTERNATIONAL
AFFAIRS
1920-1939

A SHORT HISTORY
OF INTERNATIONAL
AFFAIRS
1920–1939

By

G. M. GATHORNE-HARDY

Of revolutions and intrigues,
The War, its causes, course, and crime,
The ups and downs of pacts and leagues,
And wounds as yet unhealed by time ;

Such are the themes you treat, who dare
(A risk which many a heart dismays)
To stir hot ashes, which may flare,
At any moment to a blaze.

HORACE, Odes, II, I.

FOURTH EDITION

Issued under the auspices of the
Royal Institute of International Affairs

OXFORD UNIVERSITY PRESS
LONDON   NEW YORK   TORONTO

Oxford University Press, Amen House, London, E.C.4

GLASGOW   NEW YORK   TORONTO   MELBOURNE   WELLINGTON
BOMBAY   CALCUTTA   MADRAS   KARACHI   LAHORE   DACCA
CAPE TOWN   SALISBURY   NAIROBI   IBADAN   ACCRA
KUALA LUMPUR   HONG KONG

First Edition 1934
Second Edition 1938
Third Edition 1942
Fourth Edition 1950
Reprinted 1952, 1960 and 1964

Printed in Great Britain by Butler & Tanner Ltd., Frome and London

PREFACE TO THE FOURTH EDITION

SIXTEEN years have now passed since the first appearance of this 'Short History'; in the meantime the infant has grown considerably, till I have sometimes wondered whether the epithet in the title was any longer appropriate, and, measured by a book's average expectation of life, I suppose that this one should now have reached maturity. Indeed, it may be said to have come of age with the publication of the third edition in 1942, when its scope was extended to include the whole inter-war period. Up to that date, however, the rapid progress of events which it was necessary to cover afforded little opportunity for reflexion, or for consulting fresh sources of knowledge to supplement or correct the earlier portions of the narrative. In these circumstances, the time now seems ripe for a much more thorough revision of the whole work than has hitherto been undertaken. The lapse of more than ten years since the end of the period covered has brought it into a truer historical perspective. Up to now, the greater part of the work has necessarily been no more than an attempt to record contemporary and extremely fluid events, and even the earlier portions have been mainly of that character. When the book was originally published, in 1934, the First World War was a living memory to practically all its readers, and a very recent memory to a large proportion of them. But I have come to realize, with a certain sense of shock, that to the present generation of students 1914 is a date as far antecedent to the birth of most of them as 1863 is to my own. When I think how abysmal would be my ignorance of the events and personalities of that year without the assistance of historians, it is clear to me that very little knowledge of the pre-war world can any longer be taken for granted and that even the events of somewhat later years, such as the rise of Italian Fascism, call for considerably fuller explanation than was originally felt necessary.

Some matters, too, have undergone changes in importance and significance. The intention, for example, to prosecute the German Emperor, and the Leipzig trials of war criminals in 1921, were points to which, in 1934, it only seemed necessary to make very brief allusion, but the bearing which these precedents have upon the extension of the same policy at Nuremberg and elsewhere, after the Second World War, has made a more detailed treatment desirable.

An even more cogent reason for revision lies in the mass of official documents dealing with the period which have been published since 1945. Never before, I suppose, have the recent *arcana* of our own and other Foreign Offices been so fully or quickly disclosed to the world, thus enabling detailed knowledge to be substituted for conjecture or to supplement what was previously known. While errors calling for definite correction have proved to be satisfactorily rare, it is hoped that the information provided in the present edition will be found to rest on firmer foundations.

The opening chapter of my book has been recast and expanded in the light of the longer perspective now available, and I have also yielded to the temptation to indulge in some personal reflexions, in a final epilogue, on some of the lessons to be drawn from a study of the period as a whole. I am not vain enough to imagine that my conclusions are likely to commend themselves to all my readers; many of my opinions I know to be at present unfashionable and even heretical. It can do no harm, however, to place them on record, and may even do good by stimulating discussion of the points raised. Facts, I hope, have been fairly, accurately, and impartially set down; I have indeed taken particular trouble to do full justice to the motives actuating policies with which I have found myself in disagreement. My experience has convinced me that the *intentions* of statesmen are very rarely as foolish or reprehensible as they are apt to be represented by contemporary critics, and I think it is important for students of history to do their best to see political action, however disastrous, from the point of view of those responsible for it. But in view of the mounting debt of gratitude which I owe to the members and staff of the Royal Institute of International Affairs, for much generous and expert assistance and constructive criticism, I must make it perfectly clear that all opinions expressed are my own, and that no-one else has any responsibility for them.

G. M. GATHORNE-HARDY

April 1950

PREFACE TO THE FIRST EDITION

By THE RT. HON. LORD EUSTACE PERCY

THE first original contribution which the Royal Institute of International Affairs made to the study of international relations has been Professor Toynbee's Annual *Survey.* That is an attempt, and may claim to be a successful attempt, to apply the art of the historian and the methods of historical scholarship to the chronicling of contemporary events. It is in this form that contemporary history must be written for serious students, whether actors on the scene of international relations or merely observers. Provisional conclusions, hints of failure or possible success, suggestions of trend and rhythm, which are all that Today can hope to gather from the memory of Yesterday, come home to such students with most force when they emerge from current narrative. But there are many others interested, as all thinking people must today be interested, in the course of international affairs, to whom intensive and progressive study of this kind must be possible. The question arises whether we have not now reached a point when some kind of retrospect is possible over the events of the last fifteen or sixteen years, and when those events can be focused in one book neither too long nor too detailed for the general reader. It appeared to the Institute that the attempt was at least worth making; Mr Gathorne-Hardy undertook the task, and this book is the result. As with all publications issued under its auspices, the Institute takes no responsibility for any views expressed by the author; and the character of the task undertaken by Mr Gathorne-Hardy makes this book peculiarly his own.

The writing of such a book raises an interesting problem of method. How is the focus to be secured? Obviously, it cannot be secured by the mere piling up of accumulated facts; the grouping of facts is of the essence of history. Yet how can they be grouped? The historian of the remoter past gets his focus by the completeness of the story which he has to tell. He knows how it ends. The end is, of course, never a final one and, in modern history especially, the historian must avoid the assumption that it is the best end in the best of all possible worlds. But, though it is not an absolute standard by which he may judge the wisdom, still less the nobility, of men's acts, it inevitably determines the form of his study. The achievement of a united Italy justifies no final judgement on Metternich, or Mazzini, or Cavour, but it gives at least one point on which their lives may be seen to converge. But the contemporary historian cannot with any certainty discern even one temporary halting place at which the course of events which he is tracing will debouch. If he is to provide a focus, he must find it, not in the end, but in the beginning of his narrative. He must take a compass bearing and estimate the direction in which events were moving at the outset. But such an estimate must be a mere hypothesis and it must, therefore, be explicitly stated, in order that the reader may have no cause to fear some hidden grouping of facts, some tacit process of selection and arrangement. In other words, the contemporary historian must borrow for the nonce the method of hypothesis used in scientific research. To some extent that method must be used even by the chronicler, but to the retrospective summarizer it is indispensable.

This is the method adopted by Mr Gathorne-Hardy. In his first chapter he has stated clearly his estimate of the direction taken by the policies of statesmen in the Peace Settlement. It is not, of course, by any means the only estimate that can be put forward; indeed, it is not the one most commonly put forward by writers on these subjects. That may, however, be an advantage. These last fifteen years have presented in politics some of the features of a period of rapid advance in scientific discovery, when experiment tends to outstrip the hypotheses from which it started. At the end of the war we felt that we were discovering a new world; and we have, in fact, made many novel and exciting political experiments. We have been stimulated in this course by certain assumptions as to the character of our new world, and by the belief that these assumptions would prove true if we only brought courage and goodwill to the task of political construction. In the last two or three years, however, we have begun increasingly to doubt whether these sanguine hypotheses entirely fit the facts. The new order of political society seems to be very different from what we had been led to expect. The time may well have arrived when, if we are to see clearly, we should look again at the facts of the modern world

from a slightly different angle, always provided that the change
in the point of view does not conceal any of the facts of the past
or obscure any of the issues of the present. And here Mr
Gathorne-Hardy seems to have done his work with great
candour and judgement. The reader who rejects from the outset the point of view set out in the first chapter will find the facts
of the past set out in the subsequent chapters, fully and without
bias, in objective and dispassionate narrative; and he will find
the issues of the present set out in the last pages in terms which
will probably satisfy him, whatever may be his own point of
view. A hypothesis which thus covers the facts and illuminates
the issues is not necessarily true, but it fulfils all the requirements
of scientific method, and it avoids the greatest danger which
threatens the historian and the student of contemporary events
—the danger of unconscious bias and tacit assumptions.

EUSTACE PERCY

CONTENTS

PART I
THE PERIOD OF SETTLEMENT
1920 to 1925

1

THE WORLD IN 1920

Introductory Considerations

HISTORIANS are rarely presented with so clearly defined
a starting-point—or, for that matter, conclusion—as
characterizes the period with which this volume will
deal. By most of those who grew to manhood in or before the
first decade of the twentieth century, the War of 1914–18 has
from the first been felt as the definite close of an epoch—a great
gulf fixed between two different worlds. Experience has confirmed the correctness of this intuitive recognition, which,
nevertheless, does not appear, on reflexion, to have been by any
means natural or obvious. The map of Eastern Europe had,
indeed, been almost unrecognizably transformed, and there was
an important difference in the new attitude to war as an institution; but even this was hardly fundamental, seeing that the
prevention of war had long been recognized as the principal
function of international diplomacy. Many of the changes
most striking to a nineteenth-century Englishman were of an
extremely trivial character—such things as the disappearance
of gold coinage from general use, the reintroduction of passports,
hitherto regarded as a relic of barbarism, or the substitution of
female for male service in clubs and the households of the rich.
Looked at broadly, the new order established in 1920 involved
no radical change of policy—it seemed but a logical application
of well known nineteenth-century principles and expedients,
with such modifications as the situation seemed to demand.
The most striking innovation—The League of Nations—applied,
as we shall see, to the maintenance of peace the traditional
alternatives of conference and the mobilization of decisive force
as a deterrent to aggression, though control of this mechanism,
hitherto mainly restricted to European Powers and European
problems, was now, in theory at least, world-wide. Apart from
this, the principles of democracy and its corollary, nationalism,
had been given a new and insistent emphasis, but they remained
familiar principles of nineteenth-century Liberalism.

Looked at from the perspective of the present day, the point which calls especially for explanation is the apparent paradox of the death of the spirit of the nineteenth century in what looked at first sight like the climax of its triumph. To all appearance, the peace settlement of 1920 marked the decisive victory of those Liberal principles which had dominated the preceding epoch. Yet in fact, as was soon to be demonstrated, Liberalism was on its deathbed. Within a few years, the majority of Englishmen who sympathized in their hearts with the Liberal outlook were deterred from recording a Liberal vote by the conviction that it would be a vote for a corpse. Elsewhere in Europe a similar process was at work. There was a large transfer of allegiance to Socialism; alternatively or simultaneously there was a widespread repudiation of democracy. But Liberalism, the force which had won the war and made the peace, was completely out of fashion. Such a paradox certainly merits investigation.

Yet, on second thoughts, while the problem remains, the paradox seems to be a phenomenon regularly recurrent at the close of every large-scale war. As already suggested, the spirit animating the nineteenth century was that democratic Liberalism which originated in the French Revolution of 1789. In 1815 the decisive victory of the forces inimical to that revolution was apparently consummated, and the Congress of Vienna proceeded logically upon that basis. None the less, it was the defeated principle which coloured the succeeding century. Again, there are plenty of indications at the present moment that we are experiencing another example of the same phenomenon. Ostensibly victorious over the forces of totalitarianism, we seem to be entering an age in which the features of that system are likely to be increasingly manifest.

In a work of this scale we can do little more than indicate the existence of this phenomenon; the explanation must be left to others. It has in fact been attributed to widely divergent causes. Professor E. H. Carr suggests that such large-scale wars as those here in question are both the product and the cause of a revolution, which may be expected to 'break up and sweep away the half-rotted structure of an old social and political order, and lay the foundations of a new'.[1] This view, which seems to imply

---

[1] Carr, E. H., *Conditions of Peace*. London, Macmillan, 1942, p. 3.

invariable approval of the vanquished cause, may no doubt be
acceptable in relation to the Napoleonic wars, for the French
revolution had manifestly shaken the foundations of the old
order before the advent of Bonaparte. It could conceivably be
true of the war from which we have lately emerged—though
such a conclusion would be highly unpalatable to most of us—
since the totalitarian challenge to democracy was actively
present long before 1939. But no obvious ideological issue was
presented by the War of 1914, and Liberalism at that date was
still too vigorous and too widely accepted to be convincingly
described as a 'half-rotted structure'. In this instance, at any
rate, the alternative explanation propounded by Sir Norman
Angell,[1] that 'the change . . . has been a largely unconscious
adaptation to the ends of war', carries more conviction.
Developing this point, he says:

We did not abandon the relative freedom and toleration, the
democracy, the respect for life, for order which we possessed in the
pre-war years because we deliberately decided that they were poor
things. We abandoned those things because they got in the way of
our 'winning the war', which demanded autocracy, 'action',
violence, ruthlessness; and we acquired a taste for those methods,
preparing the way for acceptance of Fascism and its cousin Dictatorship of the Left. These vast changes in moral and social values are
a by-product, an unanticipated and unintended by-product, of
military needs.

The fact that war is a forcing ground for state regimentation
inconsistent with Liberal aspirations must, indeed, be generally
recognized. It was foreseen by Sir Edward Grey (Lord Grey of
Fallodon) at the very outset of the First World War, when, in
August 1914, he regretfully prophesied, 'It is the greatest step
towards Socialism that could possibly have been made. We
shall have Labour Governments in every country after this.' [2]
Sir Norman's interpretation of the phenomenon has at all
events the advantage that it does not involve a complacent
acceptance of the change which has taken place, as something
either beneficial or ultimately inevitable. It only means that
the final victory of the principles for which we have fought has
still to be won. Professor Carr's alternative theory may indeed

[1] *Preface to Peace.* London, Hamilton, 1935, p. 56.
[2] *Twenty-Five Years.* London, Hodder & Stoughton, 1925. Vol. 2, p. 234.

contain an element of truth. What has happened may, to some extent, be an instance of the proverbial results of putting new wine into old bottles. The stiff and desiccated fabric of the wine-skins is incapable of controlling the exceptional ferment produced by a great war. But this does not mean that it should be left uncontrolled, but merely that something more supple and elastic, not something altogether different, is required. The real criticism of the Liberal doctrines applied to the peace settlement of 1919 is not that they were wrong or obsolete, but that they were applied in a too rigid and unyielding form. The lesson most surely inculcated by the rise and fall of the pre-War system is that political spirit should never be swallowed neat. The prodigious success of the nineteenth century was developed, like a satisfactory photograph, by a process in which accelerator and restrainer were suitably balanced. The spirit with which the age was permeated, irrespective of the forms of government or political parties actually in control, was unquestionably the spirit of Liberalism, whose characteristics may be summarized as respect for individual and national freedom, a humane desire for social amelioration, the rule of law—interpreted as the controller of power rather than its instrument—and what were known as democratic institutions. These principles, admirable as they are, are all capable of being carried to vicious extremes. Individual liberty in excess means anarchy and the negation of government; national freedom tends, as we shall see, to a sub-division of sovereignties which exacerbates international suspicions and jealousies, and to an encouragement of aspirations of independence among racial units neither politically competent nor economically viable; enthusiasm for social reform may run to lengths which pamper and spoil a single section of the community, subject the national finances to crippling burdens and artificially stimulate class antagonisms; the rule of law becomes the instrument of arbitrary power, and democracy culminates in the tyranny of the majority or the alternative evils of totalitarianism. But, before the First World War, no Liberal principle was anywhere applied in an undiluted form. Nothing was pressed to a disastrously logical conclusion. Alike in the domestic and the international sphere, compromise was recognized as a cardinal political virtue. Thus, the principle of reform in social conditions, with perhaps

some exceptions towards the end of the era, was harmonized
with the demands of economy and retrenchment. Sympathy
with nationalist aspirations fell far short of applying the post-
war doctrine of self-determination. Democracy meant no more
than parliamentary government on a broadly representative
basis; in this form it existed, theoretically at any rate, in almost
every country before the close of the period. But before the
First World War, democracy carried to its logical conclusion as
the rule of a class-conscious proletarian majority was unknown;
indeed, as Lecky has pointed out, such full-blown democracy
and representative parliamentarism are contrasted and even
incompatible conceptions.[1] As recently as 1927 it was possible
for an acute and intelligent foreign observer to remark:
'Englishmen often speak with pride of their democratic institutions, but in certain respects they are the least democratic
nation I know'.[2] However this may be, in 1914 the executive
and legislative functions of the State were still in the hands of
a governing class, broadly similar throughout Europe in outlook
and social standing; this at any rate precluded the existence of
any such pronounced ideological cleavage as characterizes the
present day. The rulers of different countries might govern, or
even misgovern, their subjects as they pleased; there was no disposition to insist on conformity to a single Procrustean standard.

The Pre-War World

It is tempting to dwell on the vanished delights of that pre-
war world to which we, who grew up in it, look back so wist-
fully. The temptation must be resisted, though it must be
emphasized that its happiness was not, as is often suggested,
confined to the wealthier sections of the community. Happiness
depends on comparison with accustomed standards, and this
was pre-eminently an age when there was a continuous extension of political power and improved standards of living to all
classes of the people. 'Material enjoyments were alike vastly
more numerous and better distributed than ever before.'[3]
Though no single homogeneous Labour Government had yet

[1] Lecky, W. E. H. *Democracy and Liberty*. London, Longmans, 1899. Vol. 1,
chap. 2, p. 143.
[2] Westermarck, E. *Memories of my Life*. London, Allen & Unwin, 1929, p. 104.
[3] Fisher, H. A. L. *History of Europe*. London, Eyre & Spottiswoode, 1935.
Vol. 3, p. 792.

attained to power, the immense numerical preponderance of the industrial proletariat ensured ever-increasing consideration of its interests. The world was moreover a consumer's paradise, in which the natural and manufactured products of every country were available to all, at prices which, in spite of tariffs, were on the whole kept low by competition. Though the world had not fulfilled the expectations of the early British free traders and was for the most part more or less protectionist, the barriers imposed by economic nationalism to the flow of international commerce were at this time by no means impassable. Of the forces of industrialism and nationalism which conditioned the period, the first was for the present by far the more potent; indeed, in the only striking successes hitherto won by the second, the two forces had been allies rather than antagonists. In the unification of Italy and the consolidation of the German Empire, nationalism served industrialism, since in both places the racial and linguistic unity was wider than pre-existing frontiers, and the substitution of large for small economic units obviously furthered industrial progress by the reduction of obstacles to the flow of international trade. Economically, at any rate, it was a step in the right direction, since industrial efficiency called for large areas, such as those controlled by Great Powers with their satellite colonies and spheres of influence. In regions like those of Eastern Europe, where nationalism was to prove a disruptive force, it was not as yet operative.

Turning to the purely political sphere, power was still concentrated in the European continent in the hands of a limited number of Great Powers. In the early part of the nineteenth century the Great Powers of Europe numbered no more than five—Austria, France, Great Britain, Prussia, and Russia. A new Power was added by the unification of Italy, and the consolidated German Empire in due course took the place of Prussia. Politically, the advantage of this triumph of nationalism was not so unquestionable as it was economically, since it seriously affected the existing balance of power. But since in the domain of foreign affairs Great Britain spoke for her whole Empire, and since the seas of the world were controlled by the unchallenged strength of the British navy, the influence of Europe was predominant over the whole globe, while at the same time no world war was possible without British intervention. It is true that America, with the exception of Canada, stood outside the system, by virtue of the Monroe Doctrine, but this doctrine, as the famous phrase of Canning testifies, was, in its inception, quite as much an extension of the European policy of balance as a unilateral declaration by the United States. It meant that the American continent was thenceforth a forbidden field for the aggrandizement of a European Power, much as Constantinople became during the progress of the century; the policy, from the standpoint of Europe, was directed to prevent a disturbance of the balance of power, on exactly the same principle which had aroused combined opposition to a Franco-Spanish Anschluss in the days of Louis XIV. The European system, therefore, may be said to have dominated and controlled the world.

Down to the outbreak of the First World War, the situation remained substantially unaltered, though symptoms of impending change were already perceptible. During the course of the century, the hegemony of the European Great Powers became apparently challenged both at home and abroad. Outside Europe, two new Powers acquired first-rate importance—the United States and Japan. The authority of a purely European combination was further weakened by the fact that the oversea partners in the British Commonwealth, and the Latin-American republics, had relatively increased in strength, and become involved more closely than before in the main system of political relations. Nationalism, moreover, was already displaying disquieting activities by which Austria-Hungary was internally weakened and externally disturbed to a point which threatened her with a dissolution which could not but prejudicially affect the existing equilibrium. Meanwhile, the progress of industrialism had so far advanced that it no longer supplied an economic justification for the existence of the Great Powers, as the scope of commerce and industry overflowed all frontiers and assumed a world-wide character.

Concert of Europe

The tendencies referred to above were not, however, sufficiently strong before 1914 to produce any change in the pre-War system. The control of international crises liable to disturb the peace remained in the hands of the European Great

Powers, meeting in conference, like self-constituted prefects of Dame Europa's school. Like many arrangements which work well in practice, this 'Concert of Europe' had no acknowledged constitutional basis, but had evolved naturally out of the necessities of the situation. The Concert was based on the aristocratic theory that a crisis could be most effectively dealt with by consultation between those Powers which had the widest and longest experience of international relations, and, while possessing the force to support their decisions, had a vital stake in the avoidance of disorder, since each of them had attained a position where far more was risked than gained in a disturbance of the *status quo*. War, to each of them, involved so serious a dislocation of national life, so doubtful a result, and such a wasteful expenditure of life and treasure, that its avoidance had become far more necessary to them than to more primitive nations. Even if one of them was disposed to venture on a breach of the peace, the rest could be relied upon to exert great pressure to dissuade it. The preservation of world peace rested, in fact, upon a basis of enlightened self-interest.

This system, which it has become the fashion to denounce as 'international anarchy', was in fact extremely efficacious, and succeeded, as the late Professor Mowat rightly pointed out, in preventing 'at least seven great European wars'[1] between 1871 and 1914. There was always, however, a danger that the self-interest which normally averted and avoided war might assume another and less wholesome form in the eyes of any Power or group of Powers which saw a chance of establishing an unquestioned supremacy. It was to meet this danger that the political expedient was designed which has long been known as the 'Balance of Power'.

The Balance of Power

The principles underlying this expedient are now so widely misunderstood, and the term so misapplied, that it is of fundamental importance to start with clear notions on the subject. The idea may be traced back to the earliest times, and, though sometimes wrongly or imperfectly applied, was a generally accepted principle in international relations right down to the

---

[1] Mowat, R. B. *The European States System*. London, Oxford University Press, 1923, p. 80.

First World War. The war, however, was thought to have discredited it irretrievably, and it is quite true that the system which went by that name in 1914, though capable for some time of postponing the evil day, led to such an accumulation of power in two armed camps that the eventual explosion was fraught with unprecedented catastrophe. But when the opinion is constantly quoted with approval that the war for ever discredited the great game of the Balance of Power,[1] it is permissible to suggest that the situation is wholly misconceived, and that in fact the First World War and its agonies were the inevitable effects of the abandonment, at an earlier date, of this time-honoured policy.

The Balance of Power, as it was understood from the days of Polybius to Castlereagh and even later, is correctly defined in the *Encyclopaedia Britannica* as the maintenance of 'such a "just equilibrium" between the nations as shall prevent any one of them being in a position to dominate the rest'. Reduced to practical politics, it involved collective action against such a threat to the security of the community as was involved in the disproportionate strength of a potential aggressor. Thus regarded, it had manifest points of resemblance to the machinery for collective security envisaged in the Covenant of the League of Nations. It was therefore one of the points wherein the pre-war and post-war worlds were nearer together than at first sight appeared. Both systems, indeed, relied on sanctions, but the law which the sanction was directed to enforce was different in each case. The Balance of Power said, 'Thou shalt not grow formidable'; the post-war system said, 'Thou shalt not resort to war'. In fact the essential differences were that the older system attempted to meet the peril at an earlier stage, and that it did not invoke the community to prevent all wars, but only those wars which involved unpleasant consequences to the community as a whole. The question which method is the more practical is distinctly arguable.[2]

---

[1] 'The great game, now for ever discredited, of the Balance of Power.' The phrase originates with Wilson, and is used in connexion with the second of his 'Four Principles'—speech of 11 February 1918.

[2] The Balance of Power, says Lord Hankey, 'kept the peace in Europe before the First World War for the longest period since the age of the Antonines'. Royal Institute of International Affairs: *Atomic Energy, its International Implications,* London and New York, 1948, p. 112.

Now the Balance of Power broke down, like its post-war
substitute, through isolationism and reluctance to join in collective action. Bismarck launched the German Empire on the
course leading to disproportionate power by means of three
wars, with none of which was there any general interference.
It grew so great that, like the mass of the sun, it attracted
satellites into its system, and the final stage before the First
World War was not the application, in any real sense, of the
principle of the Balance of Power, but a frantic and hopeless
attempt to catch up with a lost opportunity, and to redress a
balance for which no sufficiently powerful counterpoise was
then available. The essence of the situation was the might of
Germany. If we imagine the rest of the world neutral, and
think in terms of Germany single-handed against the Triple
Entente, we must now confess that the issue would still have
been in doubt, and the struggle probably long and calamitous.
What the First World War really discredits is not the Balance
of Power, but short-sighted isolationism.

Great Britain, indeed, remained blind or indifferent to this
threat to European equilibrium until, in 1900, Germany embarked on the creation of a large navy. Up to this point,
though the disadvantages of 'splendid isolation' were already
apparent, there was no tendency towards an anti-German
orientation. In 1899, indeed, Mr Joseph Chamberlain publicly
expressed the view that while 'we should not remain permanently isolated on the continent of Europe . . . the natural
alliance is between ourselves and the great German Empire'.
At this time, the danger to our peace and security was generally
held to come from France and Russia, and the Anglo-Japanese
alliance in 1901 does not seem to have been in any way inspired
by the recent change in German policy but by quite different
considerations. In the following years, however, we trace the
beginnings of an approach to France which gradually developed
into the Entente. A stage was soon reached when the preservation of peace was felt to be no longer permanently possible, and
the main consideration of the Great Powers was that the
inevitable contest should not find them unprepared. Two or
three more dangerous crises were successfully negotiated by the
old diplomacy—Algeciras, Bosnia, Agadir—and then the end
could be no longer postponed.

The Post-War World

We have now said enough to be able to contrast the world, as it appeared to observers in 1920, with that of 1914. In some important respects, as can be seen from the viewpoint of 1950, this appearance differed from the reality. But it was by observers in 1920 that the peace settlement had to be evolved. The development of industry had converted a large-scale atlas into a small-scale globe. The growth of two extra-European Great Powers, the United States and Japan, had diminished the importance of the old Continent, as had the increase in individual importance of the Dominions of the British Empire and the Latin-American republics. At the same time, the three great empires which had contributed half the membership of the former Concert of Europe had fallen into ruins, and, of these, Germany was for the moment impotent, and Austria-Hungary dissolved into its component fragments; while from Russia, which had also partially disintegrated, co-operation in the ordering of world affairs was neither sought nor proffered. The remaining Great Powers were politically and economically exhausted. As a corollary, President Wilson had achieved that decisive influence in the evolution of the new order which he had contemplated even in the earliest stages of American neutrality. The policy pursued at the Peace Conference had effected another no less important change in the European situation. The casualties in the ranks of the Great Powers had been compensated by a remarkable increase in the numbers of the smaller. The new map contained some names which were entirely unfamiliar, others, like Poland and Finland, were new in the list of independent sovereign States, the mutilated remains of Austria-Hungary now formed two separate nations, and, though Montenegro had been absorbed, the number of States in Eastern Europe had risen from seven to fourteen.[1]

It seemed that the predominance of Europe and its Concert

---

[1] Excluding Turkey from both lists, since after 1913 she was mainly an Asiatic Power, and Albania from 1914, since her independence had hardly been consummated.

1914: Russia, Austria-Hungary, Serbia, Montenegro, Bulgaria, Roumania, Greece.

1920: Russia, Finland, Estonia, Latvia, Lithuania, Poland, Czechoslovakia, Austria, Hungary, Yugoslavia, Albania, Bulgaria, Roumania, Greece.

was at an end, and that the future basis of international government must be world-wide. The system of conference previously
employed should continue, but the seats on the board previously monopolized by five or six European Great Powers must
now be thrown open to representatives of some ten times that
number of States, small and great, collected from every corner
of the earth. Simultaneously with the adoption of this world-
wide democratic internationalism, the war, with the deliberate
encouragement of the American President, had resulted in the
complete and apparently final triumph of nationalism. The
problem was to harmonize these two inconsistent principles.

Changed Attitude to War

Apart from the apparent change in the situation which called
for the substitution of a world order for the previous European
system, a revolutionary change had taken place in the general
attitude to war as an institution. War had hitherto been universally accepted as a legitimate instrument of national policy, an
ultima ratio, indeed, to which resort should only be had in
extreme cases, but nevertheless a natural and eventually inevitable incident of human existence. The principal heroes of
history were distinguished by their military prowess, and they
earned this place in our school-books irrespective of whether
this prowess had been displayed in aggression or defence.
Pacificism was a voice crying in the wilderness; in fact, abhor-
rence of war was far more keenly felt by responsible statesmen,
conscious of the expense and uncertainty of the expedient, than
it was by the general public. Wars in the nineteenth century
were, in their inception, usually popular; the view that war was
a curse and a crowning calamity was held by a negligible
minority, and that resort to it was a crime was held by hardly
anyone. It must be remembered in justification that the war
of 1914–18 was a portent to which no previous war afforded a
parallel. Its colossal expenditure of blood and treasure, with
lasting effects on the life and economy of victor and neutral
hardly less than of vanquished, its monstrous inventiveness and
efficiency in the field of scientific devastation, were things quite
outside the experience of the pre-1914 generation. Only five
years before (1909), the successful transit of the English Channel
by Blériot in his monoplane had been a sensational feat of

aviation. In the most recent campaign in which a Great Power
had been engaged, the South African War of 1899–1902, conditions were still so primitive that a few thousand farmer-
riflemen had been able to protract resistance for nearly three
years. These instances may suffice to point the contrast with the
subsequent situation, when successful belligerence called for
such wealth and industrial equipment as only the greatest
Powers could dispose of, and when aircraft, ignoring physical
obstacles of sea or land, could involve distant and defenceless
non-combatants in the dangers and terrors of the campaign.
The year 1914 so transformed the whole nature of war as to
create a new problem, which naturally produced a revised
outlook.

The League of Nations

The changed attitude to war produced by the terrible experience of 1914–18 found expression in the Covenant of the League
of Nations, which was incorporated in the Treaty of Versailles.
This instrument was an admirable illustration of the attempt to
harmonize nationalism and internationalism to which allusion
has already been made. But this was not the only conflict of
ideas which it sought to reconcile. A great authority has
declared that 'the Covenant embodies five different systems',[1]
and the League was in any case the offspring of a marriage of
two separate lines of thought. In one of these, which was
developed by Mr Taft and others in the United States even
before President Wilson became its advocate, the stress was on
organized force; there was to be a 'League to *enforce* peace'.
This aspect found support, at the Peace Conference, in the
French desire for organized security. On the other hand, the
typical British attitude to the problem was extremely hesitant
in its approach to the notion of enforced peace, and even in its
acceptance of the principle of compulsory arbitration. The
British solution was rather an extension of the method of the
former Concert of Europe, through wider international consultation and co-operation. It was thus more evolutionary than
the other. If the 'Fourteen Points' are consulted, we find that
a general association of nations is projected 'for the purpose of

[1] Zimmern, Sir A. *The League of Nations and the Rule of Law, 1918–1935*. London,
Macmillan, 1936, p. 264.

affording mutual guarantees of political independence and territorial integrity'. It is noteworthy that in this proposal the word 'peace' is not mentioned and international co-operation is restricted to one limited object; the proposal described might well be a wide system of alliance for the forcible protection of the *status quo*. If, on the other hand, we look at the preamble to the Covenant, the purpose placed in the forefront is 'to promote international co-operation', and the preservation of peace is almost equally prominent. The League was thus, from one point of view, emphasized in Article 10,[1] the bulwark of a territorial settlement constructed on extremely nationalistic lines, and from another the instrument of the new internationalism. Thus the two inconsistent principles, the harmonizing of which has already been indicated as the crucial problem of the settlement, were incorporated in the fabric of the League itself, and the questions arose—would such a harmony be found possible, and, if not, which of its two parents would the offspring eventually be found to resemble? The success of the project further depended upon the validity of the assumption that the whole world was now, or was capable of becoming, for major purposes, a co-operative unit. The withdrawal of the United States, and their interpretation—embodied in the Covenant—of the Monroe Doctrine as a 'regional understanding' (Article 21), at once tended to make the organization of the world hemispherical as opposed to global. Apart from this, it remained questionable whether a world organized on a national basis could display a sufficiently unselfish spirit of collaboration to implement the provisions for security, or even whether such impromptu collaboration between scattered units of vastly different strength could ever be really effectual. Failing this, or even if the possibility of failure was suspected, the formation of alternative regional alliances, which President Wilson rightly saw to be almost incompatible with his system, was really inevitable. The complicated exigencies of the Peace Settlement, moreover, introduced from the first a sort of dual control in international affairs. Many of the most important issues,

---

[1] Article 10 was, in President Wilson's view, the heart of the Covenant. 'Anybody,' he said, 'who proposes to cut out Article 10, proposes to cut out all the supports from under the peace and security of the world. . . . Do not let anybody persuade you that you can take that article out and have a peaceful world.'

related as they were to the carrying out of the terms of the Treaties, necessarily remained under the control of the Supreme Council of the Allies, and a succession of conferences between the members of this body, from which America was now dissociated, at once took place, thus reviving in effect a Concert of Europe. The same method of independent conference was inevitable in any case with which a Power outside the League, for example, the United States, was concerned. There was thus from the first a danger or likelihood that this institution of diplomacy by conference apart from Geneva would grow in popularity, till the Great Powers, who already had a predominant influence in the League through their permanent seats on the Council, succeeded in making the League itself of secondary importance, a mere alternative field for their diplomacy. This would mean a progressive return, for good or ill, to the old decried system.

The League, however, was the great constructive idea of the Peace Conference, fully international in spirit, and capable of becoming a magnificent instrument of peace in the hands of members determined to use it disinterestedly. It was the other, or nationalistic, side of the Peace Treaties which contained the seeds of future trouble. It is necessary to emphasize that this side was as deliberately introduced as the other.

The Peace Settlement—Myth and Reality

Before developing this point, something must be said as to the character of the settlement as a whole. Since the first edition of this book was published, a myth relating to the Peace Treaties, and with least justification but widest circulation to the Treaty of Versailles, has won so extensive an acceptance that it seems necessary to deal with it in somewhat greater detail. A sedulous propaganda put out by the vanquished Powers, and by Germany in particular, has led even responsible writers on international affairs constantly to condemn the settlement as a whole, and the Treaty of Versailles in particular, as a vindictive and fraudulent departure from the principles on the faith of which Germany had laid down her arms. This legend that the peace was ruined by the substitution of Machiavellian principles of the 'Old Diplomacy' for the ideals on which it purported to be based must emphatically be denied. On the contrary, there has surely never been constructed a peace of so idealistic a character.

The conditions accepted by Germany are set out in President Wilson's note of 5 November 1918. By this, the Allied Governments 'declare their willingness to make peace with the Government of Germany on the terms of peace laid down in the President's address to Congress of 8 January 1918 (i.e. the Fourteen Points) and the principles of settlement enunciated in his subsequent addresses', subject to two qualifications, the first of which practically eliminated the second of Mr Wilson's points—'freedom of the seas'—while the other stipulated that 'compensation will be made by Germany for all damage done to the civilian population of the Allies and their property by the aggression of Germany by land, by sea, and from the air'. The latter stipulation established a clear, though limited, claim for reparation which is further dealt with in Chapter III of this work.

From the standpoint of Austria-Hungary, the military situation after the enunciation of the Fourteen Points had deteriorated so far that President Wilson (18 October) refused to 'entertain the present suggestion of that Government'—proposing peace on the Fourteen Points and subsequent Wilsonian dicta—leaving it to the Czechoslovaks and Yugoslavs to 'be the judges of what action on the part of the Austro-Hungarian Government will satisfy their aspirations'. Later, the Austrian surrender of 3 November was made unconditionally: the terms accepted by Germany were thus not in this case legally binding, and though the Allies might be expected, from motives of consistency, to follow the same principles as far as possible, they had incurred an inconsistent and binding obligation under the Treaty of London, 25 April 1915, on the faith of which Italy had entered the war on their side.

Reverting to Germany, it seems to be hardly realized by critics of the settlement how few of the 'Fourteen Points' concerned that country at all. Points 1 to 4 and Point 14 were general provisions relating to a new world order, Point 6 dealt with Russia, and Points 9–12 with Austria-Hungary and Turkey. The Points of substantial interest to Germany were no more than four—5, 7, 8, and 13. Put in the practical form of what Germany might expect from surrender on this basis, they meant an overwhelming probability that she would lose her colonies (5), the evacuation and restoration of Belgium and France and the cession of Alsace-Lorraine (7 and 8), and the creation, from former German territory, of a Polish state with access to the sea (13). Germany would also, by virtue of the stipulation added by the Allies and accepted by herself, have to pay a reparation claim which, in the critical judgement of the late Lord Keynes, might fairly be put as high as £3,000 million. She must also count on being drastically disarmed, both as a preliminary to the general reduction in armaments adumbrated in Point 4, and also in conformity with the first of the 'Four Ends' (speech of 4 July)—destruction or reduction to virtual impotence of every arbitrary power. The rule of self-determination laid down in the 'Four Principles' and elsewhere in Mr Wilson's pronouncements covered the transfer under plebiscite of North Schleswig to Denmark, and, rather less certainly, the small adjustments of territory made in favour of Belgium. The temporary provisions with regard to the Saar fell under the head of reparation, and the military occupation of the Rhineland was a general guarantee for the fulfilment of the Treaty. Less clearly, perhaps, within the agreed framework were the provisions for the trial of the Kaiser and of war criminals (see final section of Chapter II), but if these constituted a grievance, it was personal rather than national. On the other hand, the free use of plebiscites in determining doubtful questions of territorial adjustment, and the strenuous and successful resistance offered to the French demand for a Rhine frontier, show how conscientious an attempt was made to confine the terms of the Peace Treaty to the conditions accepted.[1]

All those who accept the fashionable imputation of vindictiveness and perfidy by the 'Big Four' should study the memorandum presented by Mr Lloyd George to the Conference on 25 March 1919,[2] and contrast it with the vituperation to which he and his colleagues were at that time exposed in press and parliament on the ground of their leniency to the enemy.

Even if it be granted that, in the difficult and heated circum-

---

[1] For a fuller treatment of the question above discussed, see my pamphlet, *The Fourteen Points and the Treaty of Versailles* (Oxford Pamphlets on World Affairs, no. 6). G. M. G-H.

[2] Cmd. 1614 of 1922.

stances of the time, a strained interpretation was in some
instances given to the series of pronouncements made by the
American President which Germany accepted as a basis for
surrender, no better result could reasonably have been anticipated by the vanquished Powers. As a contributor to the
History of the Peace Conference of Paris points out, 'political
speeches . . . necessarily possess a vagueness and a generalized
aspect which unsuit them for diplomatic interpretation'.[1] Yet
it may be claimed that the Treaties, broadly considered, were
in fact permeated by Wilsonian principles, and further, that it
is not in any departures from those principles that grave and
lasting dangers to international understanding were to be found.
Indeed, it may well be argued that the seeds of future discord
lay precisely in those decisions which most faithfully implemented the 'Fourteen Points', and their associated 'particulars',
'principles', and 'ends'.

Mr Wilson's share in the responsibility must not, of course,
be exaggerated. Nationalistic aspirations, as we have seen, were
in any case present, and the weakening of their former masters
would inevitably have secured to the Succession States a large
measure of autonomy. It is often pointed out that the dissolution of Austria was a *fait accompli* before the victors met in
Paris. It must also be acknowledged that, by the beginning of
1917, 'the liberation of the Italians, as also of the Slavs,
Rumanes, and Czecho-Slovaks from foreign domination' was
a declared part of Allied war policy.[2] It should not be forgotten,
however, that the Note, in which the phrase above quoted
occurs, was written in reply to an inquiry from the American
President a month before the United States severed diplomatic
relations with Germany, and when there was already a prospect
of their intervention in the war. It was natural, therefore, that
it should reproduce, in general terms, the known ideas of the
President. Its actual meaning must be read in the light of such
declarations as that of Mr Lloyd George, on 5 January 1918,
which disclaimed an intention to 'alter or destroy the Imperial
Constitution of Germany', and stated that 'the break-up of

[1] Temperley, H. W. V., *ed.*, *A History of the Peace Conference of Paris*. London,
Frowde and Hodder & Stoughton for the British [Royal] Institute of International
Affairs, 1920–24. Vol. vi., p. 540.

[2] Allies' reply to Wilson, 10 January 1917. *History of the Peace Conference of Paris*,
vol. i, p. 428.

Austria-Hungary is not part of our war aims'. We may fairly assume, therefore, that, in the first place, the hopes and efforts of subject nationalities were materially encouraged by Mr Wilson's utterances, and also that the Allies, if left to themselves, would have carried the principles of democracy and self-determination no further than was necessary to foment a useful disaffection in the enemy countries. And, even if the break-up of the Austro-Hungarian Empire was inevitable, there is a wide difference between mere acquiescence in this situation, and making the secession of discontented subject-races the guiding principle of the settlement. The main credit, or responsibility, therefore, for the principles applied at Versailles may fairly be assigned to the American President.

Universal Democracy

The leading ideas underlying Mr Wilson's policy may be reduced to two. The first was a bias against the form of government which had hitherto directed the affairs of the Central Powers. He believed and insisted that permanent peace was incompatible with the existence of any regime which was not fully democratic. As late as 23 October 1918,[1] he refused to accept as sufficient the constitutional changes which had been authorized in Germany, and hinted that nothing but complete surrender would satisfy him, so long as 'the power of the King of Prussia to control the policy of the Empire is unimpaired'. The effect of this concern for forms of government was that, in a time of unprecedented upheaval, peace could only be secured by revolution, and that large parts of Europe became committed to a political regime in the working of which they were wholly without experience, and which ran counter to all their historical traditions. It may further be suggested that democracy violates its own central principle—government by the choice and in accordance with the will of the people—when it is forced upon a nation as a consequence of military defeat, to create a Government charged with the fulfilment of peace terms highly distasteful to the majority.

In all countries in which democracy has worked satisfactorily, it has been created by a process of gradual evolution, giving time for the expansion of political experience and capacity on

[1] *History of the Peace Conference of Paris*, vol. i, p. 131.

which it depends for success. The effects of carrying its principles to their logical conclusion had not, in 1920, been tested in practice on any important scale; in the United States, where the lines of party cleavage run vertically through all sections of a community which is relatively classless, where circumstances have fostered an exceptional respect for individual liberty, and where an elaborate system of constitutional checks and balances protects the fundamental rights of the citizens from the dangers of majority rule, the conditions under which democracy has developed have been unusually favourable, but in Europe, where lack of widespread political training was destined to make the workings of popular government either inefficient or one-sided, experience was soon to confirm the thesis of Socrates, 'that democracy may all too easily become the parent of tyranny'.[1]

Self-Determination

The right of racial self-determination, the second strand in the thread of Wilsonian policy, seems, no doubt, a logical application of democratic theory—a corollary from its fundamental dogma that sovereignty rests on the choice of the people. The validity of this argument has, however, been contested by so representative a Liberal as Lord Acton,[2] and in any case this is a capital instance of the disastrous results of a rigid insistence on logic in politics. Like other principles to which the maxim *corruptio optimi pessima* applies, it is sound enough when not carried too far. The trouble was that in the President's mind it was the key to the whole situation, and an infallible, universal panacea. As adopted by the other Allies, it was something quite different. Italy, indeed, did not adopt it: the principle was an obstacle to her claims, which she strenuously contested throughout the Conference. France, no doubt, saw in the doctrine a useful pretext for dismembering her enemies; to her and to England it also appeared in the light of a price to be paid, with due caution and reservations, for the advantage attained by fostering disaffection among the suppressed minorities of the Central Powers, but the pledges given under this head ranked no higher than those comprised in the secret

[1] Plato. *The Republic*, Book 8, final passage.
[2] Dalberg-Acton, J. E. E. *The History of Freedom and Other Essays.* London, Macmillan, 1909, p. 288.

treaties, in the promises to the Arabs, or the Zionist declaration by which it was sought to win the sympathy and support of Jewish opinion. All these promises must be kept, and so far as possible—which was more difficult—reconciled; but no illusion was entertained as to the efficacy of self-determination as an instrument of peace. Left to themselves, the European Allies could have been trusted to push the doctrine no further than was reasonable. English opinion as a whole had never accepted the principle: under the terser synonym of 'home rule', it had long been vigorously repudiated by a large section of the population: the British ideal was to give to a wide diversity of races so just and impartial a government that they should become loyal and contented citizens; it was not her practice to admit the claims of each subordinate fraction to independent sovereignty. It is fair, then, to lay the major share of responsibility at the door of the American President.

Yet by no means all of it. Governments may sometimes be suspected of lack of scruple, but the public opinion, without which such a struggle as the First World War cannot be carried on, must be emotionally satisfied by a noble aim and a high ideal. The sanctity of treaties, and its violation by the German invasion of Belgium, had provided this stimulus in the early stages of the contest. Something more was now needed, and in the liberation of races striving for freedom it was generally felt that this ideal war aim had been found. This fact gave to the eloquence of Mr Wilson a far-flung influence which it would not otherwise have attained. For the inspiration was a noble one, free from any taint of self-seeking, and only rendered harmful by the limitations of the President's knowledge of European conditions. His error may in fact be compared to that committed by Mr Gladstone in 1862, when he occasioned embarrassment by the statement that Jefferson Davis had 'made a nation' out of the Southern secession. Mr Gladstone interpreted American federation in the terms of European nationalism; Mr Wilson reversed the process by attempting to apply to the sovereign States of Europe the principles upon which his own country had been successfuly built up. Each speaker suffered from a fatal ignorance of the conditions obtaining across the ocean. But the spirit which prompted each utterance must be acknowledged, even while we deplore its consequences.

As a basis of European settlement, the principle was assailable from a number of standpoints. In an age when much depended on a demonstration of the futility of war, it was surely misguided to stress its effectiveness as an instrument of national or racial liberation. It is also clear that the division of territory on racial lines must often override not only strategic considerations—which in a peaceful world might perhaps be disregarded—but also economic considerations. The idea of self-determination, moreover, causes unrest by the fatal fascination of its appeal to primitive races quite unfitted, except in their own estimation, to play the part of sovereign States. But the cardinal inherent vice of the doctrine lies in the fact that to apply it in practice inevitably involves its violation. In the racial and linguistic jig-saw of Eastern Europe there are no clear-cut lines of demarcation.[1]

The Allied and Associated Powers did what they could to secure, by means of the Minority Treaties, that the effects of such violation should be mitigated, but the fact remained. However impartially the principle might be applied, millions of Europeans would necessarily be left with a rankling grievance, which they could justify by an appeal to that principle itself. From this situation there was no escape. Finally, the extent to which the doctrine was carried into effect, by the creation of entirely new sovereign States, almost precluded the possibility of peaceful alteration, where the danger had become apparent. The old policy of 'bartering peoples and provinces like pawns in a game' had at least the advantage that a fresh barter could take place, or the pawns be moved into a position of greater safety. But, under the principle applied at Versailles, the problem was wellnigh insoluble. Not much help could be derived from the much-quoted Article 19 of the Covenant, relating to the reconsideration of treaties 'which have become inapplicable', a phrase which seems to rule out grounds of criticism applicable from the first. Punitive provisions, or conditions based on defensive strategy, may indeed be so described

[1] With the actual situation in those regions, President Wilson was, as he subsequently admitted, imperfectly acquainted. 'When I gave utterance to those words', he said ('that all nations had a right to self-determination'), 'I said them without the knowledge that nationalities existed, which are coming to us day after day.' (*Hearings*, Committee of Foreign Relations, U.S. Senate, 66th Congress, no. 106, p. 838.)

when relations grow more friendly, but no such reason for revision could be advanced in such a case as the Polish Corridor, the population of which grew not less but more Polish than at first, and where the interest of the possessors was strengthened by such new ties as the construction of the port of Gdynia. Its existence might, in the further words of the article, be 'a condition whose continuance might endanger the peace of the world', but if, to create this condition, a claimant had only to threaten aggression, what became of Article 10? The real difficulty arose from the fact that the territorial clauses of the Treaties were based, not on practical considerations of strategy, economics, or even punishment, but on a solemn principle which endowed the possessors with an increasingly incontrovertible title. Almost any proposal for revision thus assumed the appearance of an attack on the principle on which the sovereignty of a number of new States was based. It therefore filled every successor State with outraged alarm. Thus it came about that the nations upon whose friendly co-operation the new order was based tended at once to be divided into two main groups— revisionist and anti-revisionist—ominously suggestive of the combinations which had brought the pre-war world to ruins.

On the fringe of these groups stood Italy, an ambiguous Power whom the Peace Settlement had partly satisfied and partly disappointed, a serious threat to their ultimate equilibrium. To the east lay Bolshevist Russia, a still unsolved enigma, at best non-cooperative and credited with international aspirations which the rest of the community repudiated with horror. And to the west Great Britain, whose commerical interests called for a restoration to strength of one of the opposing forces which could not but arouse the suspicion and resentment of the other. Such was the situation which the idealism of the world and the eloquence of the American President had created, and which Mr Wilson hoped would be 'sustained by the organized opinion of mankind', but for which his country promptly disclaimed all responsibility.

The destination which the world was to reach at the conclusion of the story which these pages record was in fact foreshadowed in the good intentions with which the road had been paved.

II

WESTERN EUROPE: THE ALLIES AND GERMANY
TO THE OCCUPATION OF THE RUHR

Relations between the Allies

INTERNATIONAL history in Western Europe during the years
immediately following the conclusion of peace was almost
completely dominated by the relations between the Allies
and Germany. For even where the degree of solidarity attainable between the Allied Powers themselves was not directly
affected by differences of policy in regard to their late enemy,
the decisions, whether in the Supreme Council or on such
subordinate bodies as the Reparation Commission or the Rhineland High Commission, were liable to depend, to an important
extent, on the degree of concord existing between any two or
more of the countries represented. The withdrawal of the
United States had reduced the membership of these bodies to
a point where agreement between two nations was enough to
produce an impassable obstruction to views opposed to their
policy, if not an actual majority in favour of it. On the Rhineland High Commission, indeed, there remained only three
Powers, Belgium, France, and Great Britain; on the other
bodies which have been mentioned the Italian vote also entered
into the question. In regard to the fundamental difference in
point of view which developed between Great Britain and the
rest in their attitude to Germany, the American defection
probably deprived our country of a vote on which she could
usually have counted, while the settlement of any question
which might have strained the relations between France and
Belgium had, as things had turned out, a far greater international importance than might otherwise have been imputed
to them.

Belgium, France, and Luxembourg

Such an apple of discord was apparently provided, in
October 1919, by the situation in Luxembourg. The war had
inevitably severed the connexion of the Grand Duchy with the

German *Zollverein*, but, since it was impossible for this small but heavily industrialized territory to remain in economic isolation, the alternatives of a new customs union with either Belgium or France naturally presented themselves. By a plebiscite held in October 1919 the question was decided in favour of France by a considerable majority, contingently upon the arrangement of satisfactory terms between the two countries. This decision offended Belgium to the point of causing her to suspend diplomatic relations with Luxembourg, but at this point the withdrawal of the United States, in November, and the consequent cancellation of the British-American guarantee against German aggression, opened the eyes of France to the importance of friendly relations with her Belgian neighbour, with whom she concluded a defensive military agreement in September 1920; she consequently retired from the field, and a treaty of economic union between Belgium and Luxembourg was signed in July 1921. For the same reason, a *surtaxe d'entrepôt* which had been imposed by France on German goods transported through Antwerp, to the grave dissatisfaction of Belgium, was abolished in April 1921, and the way was thus cleared for the economic agreement which was signed some two years later.

This *rapprochement* with France was viewed with some distrust by the Flemish-speaking Belgians, who had fostered a linguistic national movement since the early days of Belgian independence. The opposition of this section at one time seemed serious, but it was conciliated by far-reaching concessions on the part of the Belgian Government in regard to the status and use of the Flemish language. Although, therefore, there were elements in her situation which still made Belgium nervous of too intimate a dependence upon France, and she became a strong supporter of the League of Nations, the principal obstacles to a co-operation in policy between Belgium and France were, almost at the outset, removed.

French and British Attitudes to Germany

It was, however, almost inevitable that between Great Britain and France a wide divergence of aim and outlook would shortly develop. The readiness of the Englishman to forget and forgive, while perhaps hardly a reason for self-congratulation, combined as it is, in continental opinion, with a proportionate inability to remember past favours and friendships, is a quality the existence of which is everywhere recognized. Moreover, in a nation to which the widest extension of international trade was a paramount interest, the ultimate recovery of Germany was not merely to be contemplated as an inevitable evil, but looked forward to as a desirable consummation. In the third place, Britain, from her world-wide responsibilities, was naturally prone to take a broad view in international affairs, which her chief ally, preoccupied with the narrower objective of her own security, could hardly be expected to share. France was rather in the situation of a boxer who has laid out the former champion by a well-planted blow, but is still too dazed to be certain whether his opponent has been or will be 'counted out'. The terms of the ring are perhaps inappropriate, for, without apportioning blame to one side rather than the other, it must be admitted that the recent contest had been one in which 'Queensberry' rules had been conspicuously disregarded. From France, forgetfulness of past injuries, even if desirable, was scarcely to be expected. Searching vainly, in a chaos of water-logged shell-holes, for a brick to indicate where a smiling village had previously stood, she would have been less or more than human if her thoughts had not concentrated on reparation for her injuries and permanent security against their repetition. The late war was, moreover, the second round which she had fought, within living memory, against the same opponent, who had renewed the struggle with a flagrant disregard of treaty obligations and his plighted word, and by whose unprecedented adoption of poison as a weapon the lungs of many a French soldier were still affected. We may dispute the soundness of French policy in the calm light of reason, but we cannot feel either surprise or indignation if to France for some years a German was still the *sale Boche*, a creature to be feared, to be hated, and never to be trusted.

Administration of the Saar

Apart from the fundamental cleavage of opinion on the main question of reparation, the friction betweenFrench and British points of view was destined to be stimulated by two other factors arising out of the Peace Settlement—the administration of the Saar, and the Rhineland occupation. Under the Treaty, the coal, mines and plant of the Saar territory were transferred to France as her absolute property,[1] the ultimate sovereignty of the region was left to be determined by a plebiscite in the year 1935, and, in the meanwhile, the Government of the territory was entrusted to a commission under the auspices of the League of Nations, to whose trusteeship it had been assigned. The chairman of this Commission was a Frenchman, M. Rault, there was a German local representative, and the remaining three places were filled by a Belgian, a Dane, and a Canadian.

This arrangement might seem calculated to ensure an impartial administration, but, since the Danish member was criticized in some quarters for being unduly subject to French influence, and the Belgian representative might be expected to agree with the French view, there was, in fact, some suspicion, whether well grounded or not, of the machinery of government thus constituted. The German member soon resigned, and his successor did not meet with universal approval, while the Canadian, who frequently found himself in a minority of one, relinquished his position in 1923. At the time when the Commission entered upon its duties, a French garrison was still in occupation of the province, and this was retained, pending the formation of a local gendarmerie, the slow materialization of which was the subject of protests from the German Government to the League. On pressure being brought to bear by the Council, a reduction in the garrison from 7,977 in 1920 to 2,736 was reported in 1922, but the numbers were again considerably increased by 7 April 1932 in consequence of the disturbances in the area in the early part of that year.

The question whether the maintenance of the French garrison was consistent with the Treaty was raised in an acute form as early as July 1920, when a strike of officials, who were dissatisfied with the system of pay and pensions arranged by the Commission, was broken by military intervention. The administration by the Commission gave rise, perhaps unavoidably, to various minor grievances, but a critical state of affairs developed in the spring of 1923, owing to the measures taken to

---

[1] Subject to a right of re-purchase by Germany, in the event of the return of the territory to her, at a price to be fixed by three experts, nominated respectively by France, Germany, and the League of Nations: the decision to be made by a majority vote.

cope with a miners' strike, which was largely connected with the tension created by the Franco-Belgian occupation of the Ruhr. In his criticism of these measures the British delegate on the Council of the League was brought into conflict with the French representative, and some strong words used in a debate in the British Parliament served to increase the tension between the two countries.

The Rhineland Occupation

Apart from the differences which arose during the period of the occupation of the Ruhr and over the question of the Separatist movement, both matters which call for later treatment, the divergence between the French and British attitudes was mainly shown, in the Rhineland occupation, by the marked difference in the spirit in which the occupation was carried out. With regard to this point in the peace settlement, it is necessary to realize that, though the occupation was justified in the Treaty as a guarantee for its performance by Germany, the question was in fact intimately bound up with the negotiations between France and the other Allies in respect of French proposals for security. This aspect must continually be borne in mind, and we shall have occasion to recur to it later, in connexion with the encouragement by France of Separatist movements in the Rhineland in 1923.[1]

Internal Situation in Germany

There can be no just appreciation of the policy which it was desirable for the Allies to pursue towards Germany without some understanding of the internal situation in that country. The revolution of 1918 had the effect of placing political power in the hands of men who were altogether unprepared to exercise it. The change was too sudden. Up to the resignation of Hertling, on 1 October 1918, no progress had been made in the direction of establishing responsible parliamentary government, though the matter, particularly since President Wilson's speech of 8 January and those which followed it, had become a live political issue, and promise of some measure of reform had been held out by the Imperial rescript of 11 July 1917. Prince Max of Baden, whose succession to the Chancellorship marked the

---

[1] Page 53. See also Tardieu, A. *La Paix*. Paris, Payot, 1921, pp. 201–24.

beginning of the armistice negotiations, introduced on 22 October
1918 his proposals for constitutional change in a democratic
direction, and had treated the adoption of these changes as a
foregone conclusion in the note dispatched to the American
President two days earlier. The alterations proposed, however,
were entirely constitutional. It was Mr Wilson's reply to this
note on 23 October, with its marked insistence on 'the power of
the King of Prussia to control the policy of the Empire', and its
refusal to deal with 'monarchical autocrats' on any other terms
than those of surrender, which rendered revolution inevitable.
Except for the naval mutiny at Kiel on 28 October, there was
no revolutionary outbreak until 7 November, when it took place
in Bavaria; there were thus but two days before the Kaiser's
abdication and flight on 9 November, Prince Max's resignation,
and the proclamation of a republic on the same day.

Control suddenly passed into the hands of the Socialists,[1]
only an extreme section of whom was in any real sense revolutionary. These, the Spartacists, with their approximation to
Bolshevism and proneness to methods of violence, inaugurated
an era of street-fighting, ironically confined to the political
parties of the Left, an irony enhanced by the fact that the only
force on which the Government could rely was composed of
relics of the old army officered by avowed reactionaries. That
the scale turned in the direction of bourgeois control, and the
menace of Bolshevism was repelled, was largely due to the
authoritarian training received by the German people under the
regime which President Wilson had deliberately overthrown.
But, though disturbances continued for some time, the elections
of January 1919 placed a coalition of moderate parties in power.

Upon these, and their successors, for in spite of changes the
Government continued to be of the same character, rested the
responsibility and the necessary odium of accepting, and
attempting to fulfil, the peace terms imposed at Versailles.
Their position, opposed by Nationalist extremists on the one
hand and by revolutionary Socialists and Communists on the
other, was obviously very precarious, and it might appear to
have been in the interests of the Allies to show sympathy with
their difficulties and give support to their administration. Both

[1] See on this, Bonn, M. J. *Crisis of European Democracy*. New Haven, 1925,
pp. 48-9.

the dangerous factions had been joined, in accordance with their different political leanings, by disbanded officers, non-commissioned officers, and men from the army, whom the peace had thrown upon the world discontented and without prospects. These were organized into what were known as *Frei Korps* by self-appointed leaders. The attempted disbandment of one of these was the cause of a serious incident in March 1920, the Kapp *Putsch*, when the Government was temporarily ejected from Berlin and an immediate election demanded, in the hope, apparently, of a monarchist majority. Though this movement quickly collapsed, largely through the organization of a general strike, which proved that public sympathy was on the side of the recognized administration, it was immediately followed in the industrial region of the Ruhr by disturbances of a communistic complexion, which brought the question of Allied policy prominently forward. The disturbed area was within the demilitarized zone, and to deal with the danger the German Government requested permission to introduce troops into the district, additional to those which they had been allowed to retain there for a period which was shortly due to expire. The British were inclined to favour the request, but the French were opposed to it; and, on the Germans taking matters into their own hands, the French, without consultation with their Allies, occupied the towns of Frankfurt and Darmstadt. This incident, which increased the tension between the Allies, was, however, satisfactorily settled in the month of May. But the effect was felt in the ensuing German elections, when both extremist parties were considerably strengthened, with the result that a series of weak and unstable administrations followed for the next few years.

War-Guilt Clause

Of the principal sources of grievance to the German people which stimulated extremist tendencies, those connected with disarmament and reparation will be dealt with separately. Apart from these, the War-Guilt Clause in the Versailles Treaty (Art. 231) created a surprising degree of resentment. It might have been regarded merely as a characteristic expression of a transient emotion, and, having been accepted under duress, could not be considered a genuine admission of respon-

sibility. But standing as it did at the head of the Reparation
section of the Treaty, it might be interpreted as being the
ground on which the demands which followed stood or fell;
Mr Lloyd George, indeed, gave support to such an interpretation in a statement made during the London Conference in
March 1921. Such a theory is not, however, tenable, since the
actual claim to reparation was clearly referable to the conditions agreed before the Armistice (see p. 37), and the War
Guilt Clause was in fact just as out of place in a formal statement of terms imposed upon an enemy as the corresponding
statement, in the Disarmament section, of the Allies' desire and
intention to reduce their own armaments. (See Chapter V,
p. 62.) Nevertheless, the imputation of war-guilt, which
represented, no doubt, the sincere conviction of all the Allies,
and which still remains, in the minds of many impartial
persons, substantially if not literally true,[1] was the cause not
only of an abiding irritation in Germany, but of most laborious
and voluminous documentary efforts to disprove it.

War Criminals

The provisions in the Treaty of Versailles for the surrender
and prosecution of the Kaiser and of persons charged with
violation of the laws and customs of war have recently acquired
a greatly increased importance, owing to the application and
extension of the same procedure after the Second World War.
It is therefore more essential now, particularly in view of
prevalent misconceptions, to treat this question historically than
it was when the first edition of this book was published. At the
time, in spite of the prevalence of the slogan 'Hang the Kaiser!'
during the 1918 election in Great Britain, the suggestion of
proceeding against the ex-Emperor was widely regarded as a
harmless method of allaying popular feeling, which would not
have been officially adopted had not the defendant already
removed himself to the sanctuary of a neutral country. In spite
of high legal opinion in favour of the existence of a case, the
idea was very generally questioned and even derided in the
purlieus of the Temple. The most favourable interpretation of
this clause in the treaty (Art. 227) seemed to be that it was a

---

[1] See a letter from Professor Zimmern, *Journal of the British [Royal] Institute of
International Affairs*, 1923, p. 87.

gesture significant of a new attitude to aggressive war. It is now clear, however, that the intention of the principal Allied Powers to arraign the Kaiser was quite serious, and the dicta of the 'Big Four', as reported by Mr Hunter Miller, indicate that the Dutch Government was not expected to persist in refusal to surrender the fugitive, in spite of the unassailable correctness of such an attitude.[1]

The Commission on Responsibilities and Sanctions set up by the Peace Conference reported, subject to reservations by the American and Japanese members, that offences against the laws and customs of war, and those of humanity, could properly be made the subject of judicial proceedings, from which not even the heads of States were immune. They even extended this doctrine to include those who, with knowledge of the intention and authority to intervene, had abstained from preventing the commission of such offences. But they held that the acts which brought about the war could not be made the subject of such proceedings, stating specifically that 'a war of aggression cannot be considered as an act directly contrary to positive law, or one which can be brought, with any chance of success, before a tribunal such as the Commission is authorized to contemplate', and that, in particular, 'no criminal prosecution can be undertaken against the authorities or individuals responsible, and especially the ex-Kaiser' in relation to the deliberate infringement of treaties involved in the invasion of Belgium and Luxembourg. These matters, they considered, should be the subject of a formal condemnation by the Conference, though they went so far as to suggest that the Conference might consider, in this unprecedented situation, the advisability of adopting special measures to enable those responsible for the acts in question to be subjected to the treatment they deserved.

The representatives of the United States on the Commission, in their statement of reservations, demurred to the doctrine of 'negative criminality' attaching to a mere omission to prevent the perpetration of war crimes, and to the extension of 'offences against the laws and customs of war' to include infractions of 'those of humanity'. They drew a sharp distinction between legal and moral offences, holding that the latter, 'however

[1] Miller, D. H. *My Diary at the Conference of Paris.* 21 vols. Privately printed, 1924–6. Vol. 19, pp. 262–3.

iniquitous . . . were beyond the reach of judicial procedure'. They also condemned, as inconsistent and illogical, the tentative suggestion that the Conference might consider special measures to get round the legal difficulty. Finally, they held that the head of a State was not responsible to any foreign sovereignty. The Japanese reservations agreed with the Americans on the last point, and also in challenging the doctrine of 'negative criminality'.[1]

The Treaty of Versailles, however, overrode both the majority and minority views of this Commission. Instead of arraigning the ex-Kaiser for war crimes in the strict sense, Article 227 directed the charge to 'a supreme offence against international morality and the sanctity of treaties'. As originally prepared by the drafting committee of the Conference, the repudiation of the Commission was even more emphatic. It ran: 'The Allied and Associated Powers publicly arraign William II of Hohenzollern, formerly German Emperor, *not for an offence against criminal law, but*' for the charge as cited above. Though the words in italics were eventually omitted, it seems clear that they expressed the deliberate intention of the Conference to emphasize the extraordinary character of the contemplated proceedings. Thus, the Allied and Associated Powers, in their reply to German comments on the Treaty, state that 'they wish to make it clear that the public arraignment under Article 227 framed against the German ex-Emperor has not a juridical character as regards its substance but only in its form. The ex-Emperor is arraigned as a matter of high international policy, as the minimum of what is demanded for a supreme offence against international morality, the sanctity of treaties and the essential rules of justice'. Though the proposed trial was frustrated by the sanctuary accorded to the defendant in Holland, the principles which it was sought to apply are not thereby deprived of permanent interest.

The prosecution of persons accused of violating the laws and customs of war was covered by ample authority and precedent and was therefore a comparatively straightforward matter.

---

[1] The report of the Commission will be found, in English, in the *American Journal of International Law*, vol. 14 (1920), pp. 95 *et seq.* For the French text, see La Documentation Internationale: *La Paix de Versailles*. Paris, Editions Internationales, 1930–36. Vol. 3.

For the course originally proposed in the Treaty, whereby the aggrieved parties would have been judges in the case, a trial before a German tribunal was eventually substituted. Twelve test cases were selected, and the trials, which took place in Leipzig in 1921, resulted in six convictions, the British charges, at any rate, being satisfactorily vindicated by a record of only one acquittal. Though there has been adverse comment on the lightness of the sentences, this termination to the assertion of this claim in the Treaty may therefore be said to have been, on the whole, satisfactory.

III

THE REPARATION PROBLEM: TO THE OCCUPATION OF THE RUHR

The Moral Aspects of Reparation

CONSIDERED from an academic standpoint, there can hardly be a doubt as to the well-established right of a victor to recover, if he can, and in the absence of agreement to the contrary, the whole costs of a war from his defeated antagonist. This right is completely independent of any question as to the moral or legal responsibility of either party for the hostilities; the question of war-guilt is, therefore, wholly irrelevant. But the immense scale of the War of 1914–18 rendered it obvious at the outset that a claim of this description would be beyond the power of any nation to satisfy, and the Allies therefore restricted themselves, in the course of the armistice negotiations, to a claim for[1] 'all damage done to the civilian population of the Allies and their property by the aggression of Germany by land, by sea, and from the air'. It was upon the basis of this claim that the Germans laid down their arms, and it is repeated textually in Article 232 of the Versailles Treaty. In respect, then, of any claim, however large, falling strictly within the terms agreed upon, Germany had no justifiable grievance. And in fact it seems probable that an unimpeachable claim of this description would have taxed Germany's capacity to pay to the limit.[2]

Unfortunately, however, the question was made to assume a more doubtful form. Very possibly the leading statesmen concerned considered from the first that what they were in fact agreeing to amounted in practice to a claim for the cost of the war to the limit of German capacity, since she could not in any

---

[1] Wilson's Note of 5 November 1918. *History of the Peace Conference of Paris,* vol. i, p. 136

[2] The damage falling strictly under the agreed formula was estimated by Lord Keynes at between £2,120 million and £3,000 million. Mr R. H. Brand, addressing a meeting of the Royal Institute of International Affairs on 26 February 1929, stated that he originally put Germany's capacity to pay between £2,000 and £3,000 million, which was 'much higher than I should put it now'.

case pay a larger amount than that covered by the heads of damage properly included in the armistice agreement. Two doubtful steps which were taken thereafter may in that case have been regarded as justifiable. In the first place, it would follow that the detailed definition of the heads of damage was a matter of no consequence to Germany, though the inclusion of something which did not appear to have been originally contemplated might affect the division of the receipts as between the Allies themselves, and perhaps remedy the rather arbitrary incidence of the criterion adopted. This would explain the acceptance of the much-criticized argument put forward by General Smuts,[1] as a result of which the cost of pensions and separation allowances was added to the bill. It would further explain how Mr Lloyd George and his supporters, in the general election of 1918, should have considered themselves entitled to state that they intended to exact from Germany the cost of the War to the limit of her capacity. In a sense, though calculated to mislead the public, it was true. The prevarication, however, came home to roost in the Peace Treaty, where it affords a reason for the presence of the 'War Guilt' Clause (Art. 231). Articles 231 and 232 may, in fact, be paraphrased as follows: 'We have a moral claim against Germany for the whole cost of the war, but since complete reparation was obviously beyond her power, we consented at the Armistice to limit our claim to a particular class of damage (which it is anticipated will exhaust the uttermost available farthing).' It afforded an explanation to an otherwise outraged British public as to why the claim for the cost of the War had not been further pressed. The inclusion of the 'war-guilt' claim in the Reparation section of the Treaty is otherwise as inexplicable as it is irrelevant. The reparation actually claimed rested upon a clear contractual basis, on which even the doubtful inclusion of pensions and separation allowances was definitely founded.

The course adopted in the Peace Treaty was, however, unfortunate in several respects. It obscured the justice of the claim, and appeared to increase the amount to be paid by a strained interpretation of the criterion agreed on. It also fostered exaggerated ideas of the amount which would be forthcoming, and therefore encouraged on the one hand a degree of

---

[1] *History of the Peace Conference of Paris*, vol. **v**, p. 372.

pressure on Germany and on the other an obstinate resistance
on her part which were destined to prove disastrous to the
economic welfare of the world. The degree to which public
expectation had been aroused rendered it impossible to set
down a sober estimate of the total, and the Treaty therefore left
the amount of the claim for future settlement, laying down
not what Germany was to pay, but what she was to pay for.
The satisfactory settlement of the matter was thus unduly
postponed.

Economic Aspects of the Problem

The economics of the reparation problem form far too complicated a subject to be dealt with in a volume of this size,
except in the most superficial way. All that can be done is to
indicate a few of the more obvious features, of a kind readily
intelligible to the 'man in the street'. As a preliminary observation it may be pointed out that the capacity of Germany to pay
was a matter on which widely different estimates could be
formed, according to whether the ultimate recovery of the
country was a factor to be recognized and encouraged, or
whether this was a matter of indifference or even that the
economic break-down of the nation was contemplated from
ulterior motives. A relatively self-supporting nation, such as
France, mainly preoccupied with the preservation of her own
defensive security, was likely on such a question to take a very
different view, and to pursue more ruthlessly the task of
exacting the maximum, than a people so dependent on
external markets and the prosperity of world trade as Great
Britain. In this fact lay the reason for the fundamental divergence of policy which soon developed between the two principal
Allied nations. Another point to be borne in mind is that the
resources of Germany after the Peace Settlement were by no
means comparable with those which she previously enjoyed.
Impoverished by the war, and temporarily ostracized in
foreign markets by the prevailing state of public opinion, she
had also been deprived of her colonies, and shorn of large
portions of her most productive industrial districts. But the
cardinal consideration, after all, is the effect of an international
payment of this kind upon the recipients. Broadly speaking, the
payment can be made in three ways only, by the transfer of

gold, commodities, or services. Gold is in the first place out of the question in connexion with so large a liability. There is not enough of it, and if the debtor country procures it from outside, she does so either by immensely stimulated competitive trading in the markets of the world, or by borrowing, which not only leaves the real liability undiminished but, by depreciating the value of her currency, enables her cheaply to meet or even extinguish her internal debt, thus giving her a competitive advantage against her rivals which they can hardly contemplate with equanimity. Moreover, except to the extent that it may be used to meet other liabilities such as inter-Allied War debts, gold is not wealth unless it is converted into commodities. On the other hand, payment in commodities on the scale required so dislocates the economy of the creditor countries that it is in practice regarded as 'dumping', and as such is not likely to meet with favour, or be accepted without obstruction, in a world given over to economic nationalism. The third alternative, payment by services, was open to much the same objections in the minds of the recipients, and its possibility had been materially lessened by the confiscation of a part of the German mercantile marine. Finally, whichever form the payment takes, while damaging the recipient it impoverishes the payer, who is therefore not able to continue to purchase the exports of other nations, so that the market of the world is disastrously contracted. It has, indeed, been argued that an indemnity does not differ in principle from the revenue received from a foreign investment. But this surely overlooks the fact that a foreign investment has the effect of developing production in the country where it is invested; it consequently creates an asset which enables the debtor to pay, and expands the market, which an indemnity payment tends to destroy or restrict.[1]

This statement of economic considerations of course suffers from extreme over-simplification; it is, however, felt to be essential as a preliminary to an intelligent grasp of the history of German reparation.

Early Attempts to Fix the Total

The desirability of an early settlement, and the disadvantage of leaving the extent of Germany's liability indeterminate, was

[1] See the *History of the Peace Conference of Paris*, vol. ii, p. 47, para. 7.

recognized by the Allies during the session of the Peace Conference. An opportunity was therefore afforded for Germany to
present proposals for a settlement within four months from the
signing of the Treaty. Failing the submission or acceptance of
such a proposal, the task of formulating the amount of Germany's liability was entrusted to a Reparation Commission,
which had the duty of reporting by 1 May 1921. Meanwhile,
there were certain payments on account, both in cash and in
kind, which fell due in the intervening period. An instalment
of 20 milliards of gold marks or their equivalent [1] had to be paid
in the interim, out of which the costs of the armies of occupation
were to be met before the balance could be reckoned as a
reparation payment, while, besides the arrangements made for
the replacement of destroyed shipping, there were, for example,
to be deliveries of coal to France, Belgium, and Italy which
were to begin immediately. As the question of the 20 milliards
was cleared out of the way at a comparatively early stage, it
may be convenient to begin by tracing its short and unsatisfactory history.

As the Reparation Commission was not unanimous as to the
legal situation with regard to a possible method of realizing
some part of this sum, and since the policy pursued by the
Allies rendered it likely that the whole question of reparation
might be settled before the spring of 1921, the Commission was
for some time disposed to let the matter rest. The question was,
however, brought to a head in January 1921, by the receipt of
a memorandum from the German Government purporting to
establish that over 21 milliard marks of their liability had
already been discharged by that date. On examination, however, the Reparation Commission decided that at least 12
milliards of the first 20 were still owing; they therefore demanded payment of 1 milliard by 23 March, and on the 24th
of that month notified the Allies that Germany was in default.
This notification must be borne in mind in relation to the
general history of the question, but we may here pass on quickly
to 1 May, the date by which the total sum of 20 milliards
was due under the Treaty. On that date the Reparation
Commission found that the amounts hitherto paid were no
more than sufficient to cover the costs of the Rhineland

---

[1] A milliard gold marks may be reckoned as equivalent to £50 million.

occupation, exclusive of the United States forces, and that therefore Germany was in default to the full extent of her indebtedness.

Policy of the Allies

We must now return to the efforts made independently by the Supreme Council of the Allies, to secure a satisfactory settlement of the whole problem.

The first step was taken at the San Remo Conference of April 1920, when it was decided to invite the German Government to a direct conference, with a view to fixing the total liability. This Conference took place at Spa in July of the same year, and, though it did not succeed in its main objective, it settled some complicated questions of inter-Allied accounting and apportionment, and arranged a protocol with Germany on the subject of coal deliveries, default in which had been notified by the Reparation Commission on the preceding 30th of June. In the conclusion of this agreement, the Allies showed a more lenient and conciliatory spirit than they usually exhibited, which produced, during the six months for which the agreement was in force, a satisfactory improvement in coal deliveries, though this was not subsequently maintained. On the main question, however, the German proposals proved unacceptable, and they are therefore of merely academic interest.

Between the dates of the San Remo and Spa Conferences, there had been another Allied Conference, at Boulogne, at which a counter-proposal had been formulated by which Germany should pay 42 annuities of 3 milliards for the first five years, 6 milliards for the next five, and 7 for a further thirty-two, with discretion to the Reparation Commission to modify the scheme after the first five years. This suggestion had an unfortunate influence on a conference of Allied and German experts which met at Brussels in December 1920, for the Allied experts, in spite of private misgivings, 'could not take the responsibility of suggesting a lower total than that indicated in the Boulogne agreement'. This conference, therefore, also proved abortive, and at the Paris Conference of January 1921 the Allies put forward substantially independent proposals of their own, under which Germany was to pay two series of forty-two annuities, one series fixed, the other variable. In the fixed series, the first two annuities were to be of 2 milliard marks (gold), the next three of 3 milliards, the next three of 4, the next three of 5, and the remainder of 6. In addition to these the second series of annuities were to amount to 12 per cent of the annual value of the German exports.

This proposal was confronted at the ensuing London Conference (1 March 1921) by a German counter-proposal, which suffered from a baleful lack of diplomatic tact. The German Government would have been on strong ground in altogether ignoring the Allied proposals, and either making an independent offer of its own or falling back on the Versailles Treaty, for, in accordance with the arrangement made in June 1919, it was for Germany, rather than the Allies, to make proposals. Instead, however, of adopting either of these courses, Germany proceeded to consider the Allied proposal, and to scale it down in a decidedly disingenuous manner. Having done so, the Germans brushed aside the 12 per cent levy on German exports contemplated in the second series of annuities, and the whole offer was made conditional, not only on the withdrawal of the Armies of Occupation 'as soon as the sum fixed in para. 1 had been paid in full', but also upon the retention of Upper Silesia by Germany.

The Allies promptly took the questionable step of issuing an ultimatum on 3 March 1921, which was followed on the 8th by the occupation of Ruhrort, Duisburg, and Düsseldorf, and the imposition of further sanctions. The negotiations on both sides had probably been injuriously influenced by the necessity of propitiating public opinion, but it is difficult to find any legal justification for the procedure adopted by the Allies. The sanctions were, however, fortunately covered with a cloak of *ex post facto* legality by the Reparation Commission's notice of default on 24 March.

The Schedule of Payments

Germany appealed fruitlessly, first to the League of Nations, and then for the mediation of the United States, but by this time the question was entering on another phase, for on 27 April 1921 the Reparation Commission published its decision, fixing the total, exclusive of sums payable under Articles 232 and 238 of the Treaty,[1] at 132 milliard marks (gold), or approximately £6,600 million. On 2 May, the Supreme Council, after making preparations for the military occupation of the Ruhr in the event of German recalcitrance, decided to invite the Reparation Commission to transmit to Germany a schedule prescribing the time and manner for discharging her obligations. This was accordingly forwarded on 5 May, accompanied by an ultimatum from the Allied Governments. The details of the schedule must be studied elsewhere,[2] but they included a demand for the immediate payment of £50 million (1 milliard marks) by the end of the month. The ultimatum reached Germany in the midst of an internal crisis, which had occasioned the fall of her Government. Another ministry was, however, formed in time to accept the terms; by the end of August the last of the treasury bills delivered in payment of the first milliard had been redeemed in approved foreign currencies, and the first phase of the reparation problem was thus brought to a conclusion.

Divergence of Allied Policy

It soon began to be apparent, however, that the prospects that Germany would be able to conform to the scheme laid down in the schedule were far from bright. The payment of the first milliard had only been achieved through a loan provided by a number of London financial houses. By August 1921 the exchange value of the mark was showing serious signs of depreciation, and in November the effort to repay the loan caused a sudden further fall, which, judged by previous standards, might be called catastrophic. Though Germany's failure to meet her obligations had brought about a stricter measure of financial control, under a Committee of Guarantees set up by the Reparation Commission, this did not avail to check an impending collapse. Meanwhile, the solidarity of the Allies was not improved by the disputes which developed over the question of the allocation of the milliard obtained. The schedule of payments had paid no regard to two charges which ranked before reparation—the claim of Great Britain for costs

---

[1] Art. 232 provided for reimbursement of Allied loans to Belgium, Art. 238 for restitution of cash and property seized or sequestrated by Germany.

[2] See Toynbee, A. J. *Survey of International Affairs*, 1920–3. Oxford University Press for British [Royal] Institute of International Affairs, 1925, pp. 146–7.

of occupation and the Belgian right to priority. On 31 July 1921, the Reparation Commission provisionally allocated the sum received to Belgium, conditionally on her transferring any sum in excess of her final allocation to any Power entitled to it on account of cost of occupation. Under this arrangement France would receive no part of the milliard obtained, and she refused to consent to an arrangement whereby the value of the Saar mines should be debited to her under Article 235 of the Treaty, and the reparation instalment divided equally between Belgium and Great Britain.

This proposal in fact was more favourable to France than her strict rights under the Spa agreement of July 1920, but French public opinion could not easily be reconciled to receiving no part of the first substantial reparation payment. Further difficulties were produced by the Loucheur-Rathenau agreement signed at Wiesbaden in August 1921, which, while it rightly facilitated the direct reconstruction of the devastated areas through deliveries of German plant and materials, imposed additional financial burdens upon Germany, and, by deferring the date at which the value of some of the deliveries was to be debited to France, indirectly gave her a priority to which she was not entitled. This matter was still under negotiation between the Allies when the November collapse of the mark occurred.

This, foreshadowing as it did a serious risk of a further default, brought the question of a moratorium prominently forward, and occasioned a discussion between M. Briand and Mr Lloyd George in London in the third week of December, at which a comprehensive project was drawn up which was accepted as a basis for discussion by the five Powers at the Cannes Conference in January.

Its main feature was increased control over the internal finances of Germany, in return for a partial moratorium, or a limitation of the reparation claims during the ensuing year. It also adjusted, by an elaborate bargain, the outstanding differences between the Allies on the subject of apportionment and priority. In spite of French and Belgian criticisms of the scheme, the Conference at Cannes was making good progress, and a better understanding between England and France was being promoted by an important proposal for a British guarantee of French security, when M. Briand was suddenly recalled, and the difficulties were left unsolved. For the moment the situation was met by the Reparation Commission, which granted a conditional postponement of the January and February instalments of reparation, subject to a payment in approved currencies of 31 million gold marks every ten days, and the submission by the German Government of a scheme of budget and currency reform.

The control of French policy had meanwhile passed into the hands of M. Poincaré, who, though unable to reverse the decisions previously arrived at, submitted a memorandum severely critical of Germany's past conduct, and maintaining her complete ability to discharge her entire obligations. His concrete suggestions adopted the limitations agreed on for 1922, but greatly increased the severity of the supervision and control to be exercised. These suggestions were adopted as the basis of two notes which were addressed to the German Government. Since Germany, though protesting, complied with the stipulations, the Reparation Commission, at the end of May, confirmed the partial moratorium.

Relation between War Debts and Reparation

On the question of the relationship between Reparation and war debts, a fundamental difference of opinion existed on the two sides of the Atlantic. Looked at from a somewhat narrow point of view, the American attitude was logically defensible. In so far as the right to reparation was really a right possessed by Allied civilians to compensation for damage to their property, its relation to a debt payable by Great Britain to the United States would appear remote. Because the Mayor of Les Bœufs had a right in tort against the German Government for the destruction of his house, there seemed no reason why this should affect a contractual obligation between the United Kingdom and America. If, however, as the wording of the Treaty suggested, the Allies had merely accepted a particular limitation of an inherent right to be indemnified against war costs because of the inability of the enemy to pay in full, then reparation was to them a satisfaction of their general claims *pro tanto*, and into the cost of the war the element of their borrowings of course entered: and, as a matter of economic fact, the cash payments received could best be utilized in discharging such liabilities, leaving the damage to the civil population to be dealt with in other ways. But the connexion became more obvious and intimate when the economic situation pointed to the advisability of remitting Germany's obligations. For the effect of doing so, if war debts remained, would be to leave the victors paying a virtual indemnity while their defeated enemy was absolved from anything of the kind, a state of things which the public opinion in no country could be expected to accept with equanimity. For these reasons it was really clear that the question of reparation and inter-Allied debts was an indissoluble whole.

This issue was first raised in a concrete form when a Committee of Experts was appointed to consider the feasibility of the raising of foreign loans by Germany with which to meet her obligations. The Committee reported that in existing circumstances the plan was not practicable, and laid down four conditions for its realization, the most important of which linked intimately with the uncertainty regarding Germany's liabilities the further uncertainty connected with inter-Allied debts. These it regarded as an essential element in the problem, and the matter was followed up, on 1 August 1922, by a Note from Lord Balfour to the representatives of Allied Powers owing war debts to Great Britain. After pointing out that the amount which Great Britain must require from them depended on the amount for which the British debt to the United States was settled, he added that His Majesty's Government

content themselves with saying once again that so deeply are they convinced of the economic injury inflicted on the world by the existing state of things that this country would be prepared (subject to the just claims of other parts of the Empire) to abandon all further right to German Reparation and all claims to repayment by Allies, provided that this renunciation formed part of a general plan by which this great problem could be dealt with as a whole and find a satisfactory solution.

Unfortunately, this statesmanlike proposal did not meet with the reception it deserved. The Allied debtors saw only the refusal to set off inter-Allied debts against reparation unconditionally, while the American interpretation of the proposal has been accurately summarized as being, 'We will pay you if we must, but you will be cads if you ask us to do so'.[1]

M. Poincaré and 'Productive Guarantees'

The opposing policy of France was almost immediately launched at the ensuing London Conference on 7 August 1922, when M. Poincaré brought forward, as conditions of a moratorium, a series of 'productive guarantees', which included the appropriation of 60 per cent of the capital of German dye-stuff factories on the left bank of the Rhine and the exploitation and contingent expropriation of the state mines in the Ruhr basin. The British delegation responded by proposing a total moratorium on cash payments for the remainder of 1922 and certain guarantees which included the supervision, in case of default in wood and coal deliveries, of the forests of the public domain and of the Ruhr coal mines. These suggestions were, however, wholly unacceptable to M. Poincaré, and this Conference, like so many others, achieved nothing. The situation was more or less repeated at a second London Conference on 9 December 1922, when Mr Bonar Law went farther than the Balfour Note by stating that

if he saw some chance of a complete settlement with a prospect of finality he would be willing to run the risk in the end of having to pay an indemnity, that is to say, of paying more to the United States of America than Great Britain would receive from the Allies and Germany. But he was sure that all would agree that it would be foolish to make such a concession if the whole question were going to be raised again.

M. Poincaré, on the other hand, after a severe criticism of a German plan submitted to the Conference, elaborated his scheme for 'productive guarantees' and made it clear that he would consent to no moratorium without the adoption of the pledges which he proposed. This Conference was therefore adjourned, with the idea that the discussion should be continued at a subsequent meeting, in Paris, at the beginning of the new year; but before the proposed date the whole situation had become vitally altered.

In the circumstances then existing, since the question of the

[1] Mr Wickham Steed, at a meeting of the Royal Institute of International Affairs, 26 February 1929. *Journal*, 1929, p. 219.

moratorium requested by Germany was in suspense, there could be no question of applying M. Poincaré's policy so long as his 'guarantees' were merely put forward as conditions for the stay required. The experiment could only be tried if Germany were declared in default by the Reparation Commission. In consequence, mainly, of difficulties in payment to the contractors owing to the fall in the mark, there had been a temporary cessation of timber deliveries to the German Government, to be used in reparation. There was therefore a technical default in timber deliveries to the French Government, the shortage being, however, comparatively trifling. At the meeting of the Reparation Commission on 26 December, M. Barthou, the French representative, moved for the official notification of the default. His proposal was violently opposed by Sir John Bradbury, who exposed its true implications and purpose. 'This trumpery accusation', he said, 'was only before the Commission at the moment as a preparation for an offensive in other fields. Since ... Troy fell to the stratagem of the wooden horse, history recorded no similar use of timber'. He was, however, out-voted by the French, Belgian, and Italian members of the Commission, and the default was officially notified. Though on this occasion the British representative was in a minority of one, the result might well have been different but for the repudiation of the Peace Treaty by the United States. The Reparation Commission had been deliberately constituted with a membership of five, to ensure a majority vote on every occasion. The withdrawal of the United States produced exactly the effect which it had been desired to avoid—an even number of members on the Commission. To meet the imminent possibility of deadlock, a provision from Article 437 of the Treaty, giving the Chairman a casting vote, had been prayed in aid, though the application of this article to the Reparation Commission does not seem to have been originally contemplated. This arrangement gave a second vote, in case of necessity, to the French representative, who presided. 'It was rarely if ever cast; but the knowledge that it was there in reserve necessarily underlay all these discussions'.[1] Italy, whose attitude was somewhat hesitant, might well have decided differently had the United States been present.

[1] Salter. Sir Arthur. *Recovery : the Second Effort.* London, Bell, 1933, p. 133.

Armed with the notification thus secured, and with the prospect of an early declaration of default in coal deliveries also, M. Poincaré, at the Paris Conference of 2 January, felt himself on strong enough ground to venture upon a complete breach with his British Allies, to reject their proposals and to proceed with the execution of his own plan. The expected notification on 9 January of default in coal deliveries gave him his opportunity, and two days later the French occupation of the Ruhr basin began.

IV

THE REPARATION PROBLEM: FROM THE OCCUPATION OF THE RUHR TO THE DAWES PLAN

Legal Aspects of the Ruhr Invasion

IT is open to question whether the Franco-Belgian occupation of the Ruhr could be legally justified under the Versailles Treaty. 'The highest legal authorities in Great Britain had advised His Majesty's Government that the contention of the German Government was well founded, and His Majesty's Government had never concealed their view that the Franco-Belgian action in occupying the Ruhr, quite apart from the question of expediency, was not a sanction authorized by the Treaty itself'.[1] There were three main questions involved: (i) Was the question of default which arose in this case one which the Reparation Commission was entitled to decide by a majority vote? (ii) Were France and Belgium entitled to take separate action, or must any action be taken jointly by all the Governments represented on the Reparation Commission? (iii) Was the sanction applicable in this case limited to 'economic and financial prohibitions and reprisals', or was the action taken permissible under the Versailles Treaty? For the arguments on either side of the question, the student must consult other sources;[2] having regard to the political unwisdom and disastrous consequences of the course taken, the legal aspect is of minor importance.

Economic Importance of the Ruhr

The industrial resources of post-war Germany were concentrated in the Ruhr basin to an extent which rendered any disturbance of the normal activities of that region a step which was bound to react deleteriously upon the financial stability of the Reich and consequently upon its capacity to meet the Allied demands. Eighty to eighty-five per cent of Germany's

---

[1] British Note of 11 August 1923. Cmd. 1943 of 1923.
[2] *History of the Peace Conference of Paris*, vol. ii, p. 40.

coal, 80 per cent of her steel and pig-iron production, and 70 per cent of the goods and mineral traffic on her railways were dependent upon the Ruhr. It is only fair, however, to point out that the action originally contemplated by the French and Belgian Governments did not in itself materially impede the normal working of industry; the dislocation which actually followed was a result of German resistance to the policy which does not appear to have been foreseen or expected. In their Note to the German Government of 10 January 1923, France and Belgium proposed to send into the Ruhr, under military protection, a mission—known as the Mission Interalliée de Contrôle des Usines des Mines, or M.I.C.U.M.—to supervise the action of the local *Kohlensyndikat* and to take the measures required to secure the payment of reparation. The normal life of the local population was not to be disturbed.

Passive Resistance in Germany

The first interference with the smooth working of the plan occurred before the arrival of the French troops on 11 January. The *Kohlensyndikat* withdrew its headquarters from Essen to Hamburg, thus placing itself outside the range of direct control. The German Government immediately afterwards ordained a policy of passive resistance, suspended all reparation deliveries to France and Belgium, thereby placing itself in general default, and by undertaking the financial support of strikers and recalcitrant officials, while at the same time prescribing severe penalties for all German citizens who assisted the plans of the enemy, it fostered and promoted the non-cooperative movement which arose spontaneously in the occupied area. The invaders were consequently at once confronted with the necessity of working the intricate railway system of the Ruhr with a greatly restricted staff, drafted from their armies, which of course was totally unfamiliar with local conditions. The M.I.C.U.M. had also to staff a number of the mines with its own personnel, as a result of German refusals to work them. The volume of goods carried over the railways consequently dropped to considerably less than a third of its normal figures.

In these difficult circumstances, the French and Belgian Governments, with whom the Italians were technically associated though they played no active part, resorted to severe measures of reprisal. They extended the area of their occupation, and exploited the majority which they now commanded on the Rhineland High Commission, owing to the withdrawal of the United States, by the promulgation of ordinances of extreme severity directed against all attempts to impede the success of their operations. These ordinances were applied not merely to the Ruhr, but throughout the whole Rhineland area under military occupation; in the British zone, however, they were treated as a dead letter, and this region consequently became a sort of oasis of peace in the desert created by the struggle, a fact which did not improve Franco-British relations during this unhappy period. A continuous customs cordon was drawn, from Wesel to Düsseldorf, between occupied and unoccupied German territory, and an almost complete embargo, except in relation to foodstuffs, was placed on the transit of goods to the parts of Germany beyond the Allied control. Except, therefore, for such amounts as the invaders could transfer to France and Belgium on account of reparation deliveries, stocks continued to accumulate without being profitably disposed of.

The Separatist Movement

A further weapon of which the French availed themselves was the support of Separatist movements in the occupied territory. In extenuation of their conduct in this matter, it must be pointed out that it was the logical continuation of a policy which they had persistently though fruitlessly urged during the Peace Conference, which they sincerely considered essential not only to their own but to the general security, and which they had ranked among their war aims at an even earlier date. In February 1917, a secret exchange of Notes between France and Russia, disclosed by the Bolsheviks after the revolution, had secured the support of the Tsarist Government to a proposal to include in the terms of peace 'the political separation from Germany of her trans-Rhenish districts and their organization on a separate basis in order that in future the River Rhine might form a permanent strategical frontier against a Germanic invasion'. It is important to observe that this scheme did not contemplate the annexation to France of the territories on the left bank of the Rhine, but the establishment there of an autonomous and neutral State, freed from economic and political dependence upon Germany. At the Peace Conference, the case for this policy was elaborately argued in a memorandum prepared by M. Tardieu on the instructions of M. Clemenceau.[1] In view of what subsequently occurred, it is of interest to quote from this document the following prophetic passage:

Suppose, in fact, that Germany was mistress of the Rhine and wished to attack the Republic of Poland or that of Bohemia (Czechoslovakia). Established defensively on the Rhine, she will keep in check—for how long?—the western nations who have come to the aid of the young republics, and these will be crushed before it has been possible to help them.

In the course of a subsequent discussion between M. Tardieu and Mr Philip Kerr (afterwards Lord Lothian) at the Conference, the former made a remark destined to be repeated many years later by Mr Baldwin, who has since been popularly regarded as its originator:

She [England] knows that her frontier is not at Dover. Now the late war has taught her that her European frontier is on the Rhine, and that the Rhine is even more important to her than the Suez Canal and the Himalayas.[2]

On 14 March the issue was discussed between President Wilson, Mr Lloyd George, and M. Clemenceau. The representatives of the United States and Great Britain were obstinately opposed to the French proposal, but in order to secure its abandonment they at once offered their joint guarantee of immediate military assistance in the event of a renewal of German aggression. Even this offer did not, however, win the immediate approval of M. Clemenceau. Further negotiations followed, as a result of which changes were made in the terms contemplated in the Treaty, in respect of German disarmament, the demilitarization of the Rhineland and other matters, and eventually the Rhineland occupation was conceded in the form which it eventually took in the Treaty of Versailles. Still, however, the compromise was stubbornly opposed by Marshal

---

[1] The full text of this document is set out in Tardieu, A. *La Paix*. Paris, Payot, 1921, pp. 165–84.
[2] ibid., p. 192. M. Tardieu's book was published in 1921.

Foch, who, as late as 25 April, argued that a military occupation limited to fifteen years was a guarantee of security 'equivalent to zero, while involving us in increasing military expenditure'.[1] His arguments, however, were rejected, and M. Clemenceau gave up the French demand for the Rhine frontier in consideration of the Anglo-American guarantee of immediate military assistance. This vital consideration was completely destroyed by the refusal, in November 1919, of the United States Senate to ratify the work of their President. The British engagement stood and fell with the American, and France was therefore reduced to the position of having surrendered her cherished scheme for nothing. It is in the light of this situation that we should judge the action of the French in encouraging Separatism on the left bank of the Rhine. That they did so is really indisputable, though they continually denied it, representing the movement as a spontaneous expression of the wishes of the local population, which they were not concerned either to defend or prevent. In reality, however, the Separatist movement in the Rhineland was carried on in the teeth of local public opinion; its leaders were largely foreign to the district, and its rank and file included convicted criminals and other undesirable characters. Moreover, not only was French support of Separatism incontrovertibly attested by the speedy collapse of the movement when such help was not forthcoming, but there is abundant evidence of acts which are capable of no other explanation. The insurgents were transported upon Franco-Belgian *Régie* trains to the scene of their operations; arms confiscated from the German civil population were distributed to them, and those of which the German police had deprived the Separatists were restored to them by the French authorities. The police were disarmed and their resistance was otherwise impeded, and the 'Rhineland Republic' proclaimed by the leaders of the movement was recognized by the French High Commissioner as the *de facto* Government wherever its authority was regarded by him as effective.[2]

In Belgian occupied territory, where similar assistance was

[1] ibid., p. 209.
[2] For a convincing and vivid account of the Separatist occupation of Düsseldorf, 30 September 1923, see *The Uneasy Triangle* by 'Apex' (Captain R. G. Coulson). London, Murray, 1931, pp. 39–43.

not forthcoming, the movement swiftly collapsed, but in the Bavarian Palatinate, hemmed in between French Alsace-Lorraine and the provisionally French territory of the Saar, events took a peculiarly serious turn, involving at one point the danger of a complete breach between France and Great Britain. On 24 October 1923, the Palatinate was recognized by a representative of General de Metz, the delegate of the Rhineland Commission, as an autonomous State with a Provisional Government, and the General himself, on the following day, prohibited all the Bavarian officials from the exercise of their functions. Thus encouraged, the Separatists seized by force the public buildings of every town in the Palatinate, and deported the officials wholesale, to the number of 19,000. On 2 January 1924, the Rhineland High Commission decided (against the vote of the British representative) to register the decrees of the 'Autonomous Government', thus according to it official recognition. At this point the British Government demanded that ratification should be suspended pending an inquiry, and the subsequent investigations of Mr Clive, the British Consul-General for Bavaria and the Palatinate, conclusively established that the overwhelming majority of the population was opposed to the Separatist Government. On the strength of this report, the British Government proposed a reference of the question to the Permanent Court of International Justice, with the result that the French resistance gave way. In February, their support having been withdrawn, the true state of public sympathy was disclosed at Pirmasens, by the massacre of fifteen Separatists, who had been driven by fire from the building which they were defending. At Durkheim the same story was repeated, and there was a further clash, attended by loss of life, at Kaiserslautern, though on this occasion the Separatists seem to have taken the offensive. After these events, the Rhineland High Commission proclaimed a state of siege, and ordered the dissolution of the local nationalist organization. By the end of February 1924 the last Separatists had disappeared from the scene.

The disturbances, however, which resulted from the French policy on the Ruhr, were not confined to the occupied territory. On 9 November 1923, a rising promoted by General Ludendorff broke out in Bavaria, which, though promptly suppressed, is of

some historical importance, as one of the leaders was a native of
Austria, named Adolf Hitler, of whom the world was destined
to hear more in a few years' time. Hitler was condemned, for
the part he had played in the disturbance, to imprisonment in
a fortress, which provided him with the leisure to write the
book, *Mein Kampf*, in which the National Socialist doctrine is
explained and elaborated.

Losses of the Struggle

Apart from the bloodshed caused by the Separatist movement in the Rhineland, the virtual state of war existing between Germany and the Powers in occupation of the Ruhr was
not free from casualties. French sources admit a loss of 20 killed
and 66 wounded on the side of the Allies, and of 76 killed and
92 wounded on that of their opponents, while German measures
in enforcement of the policy of passive resistance involved a
casualty list of 300 dead and more than 2,000 injured. But the
financial consequences to both sides were far more disastrous.
The franc had lost nearly a quarter of its value, and the mark,
depreciated a billion-fold, had become to all intents and purposes worthless. In these circumstances, saner counsels had an
opportunity of being heard; in September 1923, Germany
unconditionally abandoned passive resistance and withdrew the
ordinance suspending reparation deliveries. But Germany's
actual capacity to pay had been so impaired that France was
also ready to listen to reason. From October 1923 she had
adopted the policy of negotiating arrangements for coal deliveries and other payments in kind directly with a committee
of the Ruhr industrialists, but the standard agreement of
23 November 1923 was due to lapse, if not renewed, in April
1924, and there seemed small prospect that it would be continued, while this system of exacting a local tribute from
private industry, in lieu of reparation from the Government,
bade fair to complete the ruin of Germany.

Genesis of the Dawes Plan

Fortunately the Allied Powers, while they had all rejected
proposals put forward by Germany in May 1923, had, from
that date, been engaged in more or less continuous negotiations
with each other and with their former enemy, and, after the

cessation of German intransigence, Mr Baldwin appealed to the Government of the United States to collaborate in an investigation into Germany's capacity to pay.[1] The reply was favourable, and resulted in the appointment, at the end of the year, of a Committee presided over by the American General, Charles G. Dawes. The Committee met in Paris in January 1924, and presented its report on 9 April. Basing itself upon the slogan 'Business not politics', the report went on to emphasize Germany's need for the resources of her whole territory, and the interdependence of the two requisites of a stabilized currency and a balanced budget. Permanent stability was to be secured to the new 'Rentenmark'[2] by the reorganization of the bank of issue, free from government interference and under the supervision necessary to protect foreign interests. Germany was to pay amounts rising in five years from 1,000 million gold marks or £50 million to 2,500 million gold marks (£125 million), to be raised partly in the German budget, and partly from State railway bonds and industrial debentures, together with a transport tax. To guard against collapse of the exchange owing to transfer difficulties, payments were to be made in German currency, the operation of transfer resting with the recipients. To cover the gold reserve requirements of the new bank, and internal payments for treaty purposes in 1924–5, a foreign loan of 800 million gold marks was regarded as an essential condition of the scheme.

Fortified by this report, the interested Powers continued their negotiations, and eventually arranged a conference which met in London on 16 July 1924. The prospects of a successful result had meanwhile been improved by the fall of M. Poincaré's Government (11 May). Though the French Premier had of late become considerably more conciliatory in his attitude towards his former Allies, discussions between M. Herriot and Mr Ramsay MacDonald held greater promise of agreement than those of the previous year, in which M. Poincaré and Lord Curzon had been the protagonists. The Conference in fact proceeded smoothly; on 5 August it was ready to welcome the

---

[1] The first suggestion of such collaboration had been made in the United States in a speech delivered by Mr C. E. Hughes to the American Historical Association in December 1922.

[2] Introduced as an emergency currency in November 1923.

participation of the German delegates, and on the 16th the necessary agreements for carrying out the Dawes Plan were signed. By the end of the month the legislation required had passed the Reichstag, and in October the proposed loan was floated with complete success. The largest portion ($110 million) was raised in the United States.

Improvement in International Relations

The favourable atmosphere created by the London Conference and the adoption of the Dawes Plan inaugurated an era of improved understanding, not only between the Allies and Germany, but between Great Britain and France. The subordinate question of apportionment of the reparation payments was quickly and happily settled during a conference of Allied Finance Ministers which took place in January 1925. The payments themselves were punctually made for several years, though the plan itself had never been intended as more than a temporary arrangement, pending a definite settlement of the problem. This point was emphasized from the first in the annual reports of the Agent-General for Reparation Payments.[1] But for the moment the question of reparation was allowed to rest, and the statesmen of Europe were enabled to direct their attention more exclusively to the permanent organization of world peace. The 'Locarno Spirit', which did much in the ensuing years to encourage a more hopeful sense of security, was thus a logical outcome of the Dawes settlement, and, since the appeal to American co-operation of which this was the culmination was occasioned by the catastrophic experiences of the Ruhr occupation, and it was this sharp lesson which brought the protagonists nearer together, it appeared, for the moment at any rate, that good had been born out of evil.

[1] 'The results achieved . . . do not by themselves mark a final readjustment. They are rather the starting-point from which readjustment must proceed. *Reparation Commission: Report of the Agent-General for Reparation Payments*, May 1925.

V

THE PROBLEM OF SECURITY: TO THE LOCARNO TREATIES

THE close of 1924 marks a stage when most of the problems involved in the Peace Treaties appeared either to have been liquidated or in a fair way to become so, and the statesmen of Europe were free to direct a more undistracted attention to the constructive work of the new regime in laying the foundations for a durable tranquillity. The territorial adjustments had been completed, not only in Europe but also in the Near East, and if the problem of reparation could not be regarded as finally settled, a *modus vivendi* had at least been arrived at which could be relied upon to shelve the question for some time. Finally, though the international activities of the Russian revolutionaries still continued to disturb harmonious relations, this side of their policy had become, since the death of Lenin in January 1924, increasingly incompatible with the designs of the Soviet Government, and while the latter could claim a substantial measure of success in the recognition accorded to it by the principal European Powers, the efforts of the Third International had only served to discredit it by a record of continual failure.[1]

Conditions, in fact, seemed ripe for substantial progress in the consolidation of a new system from which the fear of war could be eliminated. There can be no doubt that this was the objective which the authors of the Peace Settlement had principally in mind, and which indeed at first they dreamt that they had achieved. In Great Britain, at any rate, for some years after the signature of the European Treaties, it was regarded as almost blasphemous to hint at the possibility of another war. The struggle from 1914 to 1918 had, at its close, become in the minds of most people in Great Britain a 'war to end war': unless this aim had been realized, the effort had been wholly fruitless. What was confidently expected, or at least not openly questioned, was the inauguration of a new era, in which nations and

[1] See Chapter VII.

races, under governments of their own choosing, would un-
selfishly and automatically co-operate in the suppression of the
first signs of an appeal to force.

In such a golden age, disarmament was hardly at first
expected to present any serious difficulties. It was the natural
corollary of restored confidence, satisfied ambitions, and a
general will to peace, and the removal of any temptation which
might remain to revert to militarism and aggression. It is true
that difficulties and dangers had been foreseen by some of the
negotiators before the conclusion of the Peace Conference. Mr
Lloyd George, for instance, not only perceived the elements of
future discord which lay in the territorial settlement, but clearly
realized and advocated the advantages of striking while the
iron was hot. The time for achieving a satisfactory limitation
of armaments was, he saw, the present moment, before doubts
as to the efficacy of the collective machinery for peace had time
to develop: for this reason he argued strenuously that an agreement for the limitation of their armaments, concluded between
the principal Powers, should precede the signature of the
Covenant.

The first condition of success [he urged] for the League of Nations
is, therefore, a firm understanding between the British Empire and
the United States of America and France and Italy that there will
be no competitive building up of fleets or armies between them.
Unless this is arrived at before the Covenant is signed the League of
Nations will be a sham and a mockery. It will be regarded, and
rightly regarded, as a proof that its principal promoters and patrons
repose no confidence in its efficacy. But once the leading members
of the League have made it clear that they have reached an understanding which will both secure to the League of Nations the strength
which is necessary to enable it to protect its members, and which at
the same time will make misunderstanding and suspicion with
regard to competitive armaments impossible between them, its
future and its authority will be ensured. It will then be able to
ensure that not only Germany, but all the smaller States of Europe
undertake to limit their armaments and abolish conscription. If the
small nations are permitted to organize and maintain conscript
armies running each to hundreds of thousands, boundary wars will
be inevitable and all Europe will be drawn in.[1]

---

[1] Memorandum of 25 March 1919. Published in Cmd. 1614 of 1922.

The favourable occasion was, however, permitted to pass. Indeed, reflexion in the light of subsequent events may induce doubts as to whether the policy proposed or the arguments adduced were sound. The danger to world peace did not in fact arise from the conduct of the small States, and it is questionable whether the reduction of their armaments by the victorious Great Powers in the glow of optimism created by the immediate flush of triumph would have been either prudent or beneficial. Yet it is clear that in 1920 a general limitation of armaments was contemplated by all the Allied and Associated Powers. Reduction 'to the lowest point consistent with national safety and the enforcement by common action of international obligations' figured in the 'Fourteen Points'—Point 4, and in Article 8 of the Covenant, and the same intention ('to render possible the initiation of a general limitation') is given in Part V of the Versailles Treaty as the reason for requiring the drastic disarmament of Germany, and was repeated, even more explicitly, in the reply to the German delegates of 16 June 1919. These utterances have, indeed, been misrepresented by German propaganda, with an unwarranted degree of success even outside the frontiers of the Reich, as establishing a contractual relationship between the disarmament of the vanquished and that contemplated by the victors. Such a contention cannot, of course, be accepted.[1] The Allies never said, 'If you will disarm, we will'. Their attitude may be more appropriately likened to that of a group of householders thus addressing a convicted burglar: 'Patent locks and a large police force are expensive luxuries which we should like to escape, but we cannot until we know that you are safely put out of harm's way'. There is nowhere any indication that the victors contemplated a reduction commensurate with that imposed on Germany, but the criterion 'the lowest point consistent with national safety' is manifestly a variable standard which is lower if the principal potential disturber of the peace has been rendered innocuous.

This criterion, embodied in Article 8 of the Covenant, is another way of saying that security is everything. Inflated

[1] Cf. British Statement of Policy, 18 September 1932, 'To state what the object or aim of a stipulation is, is a very different thing from making the successful fulfilment of that object the condition of the stipulation' (Wheeler-Bennett, J. W., *ed.*, *Documents on International Affairs*, 1932. London, Oxford University Press for the Royal Institute of International Affairs, 1933, p. 196).

armaments are not so much a cause of war as a symptom indicating a dangerous situation: given complete freedom from the risk of attack, real or imaginary, there can be few nations so mad as not spontaneously to reduce the crushing and unproductive expenditure involved in their forces to a universally satisfactory minimum. On the other hand, it would clearly be impossible to persuade any State to reduce its armaments if it felt that its national security was thereby imperilled. It is therefore rather surprising that, in its earlier efforts to cope with the problem, the League of Nations tended to concentrate narrowly on schemes for disarmament on a statistical and mathematical basis, which paid little or no attention to this controlling factor. A Permanent Advisory Commission, consisting of military, naval, and air experts, was constituted, in accordance with Article 9 of the Covenant, in May 1920, and this step was followed, nine months afterwards, by the creation of the Temporary Mixed Commission.[1] These bodies, however, spent much time at the outset in the collection and exchange of statistical and other information on existing armaments, while the assembly, at each of its first four sessions, recommended a preliminary form of limitation based on the restriction of expenditure on armaments to the current figure in each national budget. The scheme proposed in 1922 by Lord Esher, the British representative on the Temporary Mixed Commission, was also of the mathematical type, proposing an allocation to each European Power of a fixed number of units of 30,000 men in a defined ratio.

The Washington Conference, 1921–2

Lord Esher's plan was admittedly based on the precedent applied to naval disarmament at the Washington Conference of 1921–2, but the circumstances which enabled agreement to be reached on that occasion had little resemblance to those in which the reduction of European land forces had to be attempted. In the first place, the United States, by whom the invitation to the Washington Conference was issued on 11 August 1921, enjoyed at the time so unassailable a financial superiority that no other Power was in a position to compete with them if unrestricted ship-building was allowed to continue.

[1] *Survey of International Affairs*, 1920–3, p. 104.

Of the four Powers associated with the United States in the
agreement, neither France nor Italy was threatened by the
naval superiority of the British Empire, the United States, or
Japan, and Italy, as a comparatively poor nation, was bound to
welcome any limitation proposed, on a basis of her parity with
France. The relations between Great Britain and the United
States were such that she had nothing to fear from parity in
battleship strength with America, while the agreement left her,
in this respect, in a ratio of 5 to 3·5 to the next two naval Powers
of Europe.[1] The numerical limitations imposed were restricted
to large battleships,[2] a form of armament the necessity for which
is open to dispute and to which a mathematical ratio is more
clearly applicable than to any other; one, moreover, which it is
impossible to provide in secret or without a very great financial
outlay. The parties to the agreement were comparatively few,
and its duration was limited in time, since the Treaty was
capable of being terminated in 1936. But, above all, agreement
was not arrived at without prior consideration of possible
danger-points and of the security of the parties.[3] Collateral
negotiations between Japan and China settled, as it was
thought, the outstanding differences between them, while
American grounds for alarm were allayed by the recognition of
her rights in the Japanese mandated island of Yap. The
requirements of security were to some extent dealt with by the
conclusion, in December 1921, of a Four-Power Treaty between
the British Empire, the United States, Japan, and France,
which pledged the parties to a policy of co-operation, consultation, and mutual help in the Pacific area, and by the Nine-
Power Treaty of February 1922, recognizing the sovereign
independence and territorial and administrative integrity of

[1] 'A position we have not held in Europe for the last seventy years.' Sir Frederick
Maurice, in an address to the British [Royal] Institute of International Affairs,
published in its *Journal*, vol. i, 1922, p. 103.

[2] There was a total *tonnage* limitation applied to aircraft carriers, and a maximum
size was fixed (as some think, too high) for capital ships, aircraft carriers, and
cruisers, as well as for their guns, but the only restriction of numbers was in respect
of battleships.

[3] Doubts are still entertained as to whether the consideration was sufficient. It is
contended, for instance, that France embarked upon submarine construction
largely because an assignment of five capital ships was considered inadequate. The
Washington Treaty attempted to scale down from the top, instead of building
upon the requirements of the lesser Powers.

China. In these circumstances, while the achievement was substantial, it is obvious that the problem was one of far greater simplicity than that confronting the League of Nations in relation to the land forces of Europe.

France and Security

Outside the genial influences of the 'Geneva atmosphere', there had, from the first, existed little doubt as to the preliminary necessity for a sense of security. France, as already stated (p. 55), had only been persuaded, at the Peace Conference, to renounce her darling plan of keeping the German frontier behind the Rhine in consideration of an Anglo-American Treaty of Guarantee, and, when this broke down owing to the retirement of the United States, she lost no time in safeguarding the position by the conclusion of a treaty with Poland in February 1921. The states of the Little Entente had simultaneously acted on a realistic view of the situation, and their system of alliance was linked with the French, long before such a bond was formally completed, by the fact of a common interest in the preservation of the Peace Settlement. But even these precautions were insufficient to allay the anxieties of France; negotiations for the renewal of an Anglo-French pact continued until 1922, and appeared, indeed, on the brink of realization during the Cannes Conference, when they were interrupted by M. Poincaré's advent to power in succession to M. Briand. The project eventually broke down owing to the unwillingness of Great Britain to regard the violation by Germany of Articles 42 and 43 of the Treaty of Versailles (fortifications or armed forces in the demilitarized area near the Rhine) as a *casus belli*, or to enter into any engagements, other than her obligations under the Covenant, in respect of the countries on the eastern frontiers of Germany. The British argument is summarized in a memorandum prepared by Lord Curzon in February:

In so far as British public opinion will endorse our guarantee, it will be in the belief that it can only become operative in the event of a German army actually crossing the French frontier . . . [As to obligations elsewhere] the two Powers, not waiting for any one else, are 'to examine in common the measures necessary to ensure speedily a peaceful and equitable settlement'. Of course, this might

mean that they would jointly refer the case to the League of Nations.
But, if so, the provision is unnecessary. On the other hand, it . . . is
probably intended by the French to mean that the settlement of the
future European disputes is a matter primarily for Great Britain and
France, and that the rest of the world is to look on until our two
Governments have made up their minds what they will do. . . . A
military alliance of this description between Great Britain and
France could only result in rival and, it might be, hostile combinations between other Powers . . . and it is inconsistent with the theory
upon which it has hitherto been assumed that the post-war polity
of Europe is to be based.

The Flight from Sanctions

Meanwhile, the confidence which had been reposed in the
provisions of the League Covenant for collective action was
being rapidly undermined. The most vital factor in bringing
about this change was, no doubt, the withdrawal of the United
States. But for a time there was still a general belief that peace
had been established on durable foundations. Now this was
waning. Undertakings cheerfully assumed in the optimism
which followed the conclusion of the War took on a graver
aspect when it became apparent that they might actually have
to be fulfilled, and a large number of signatory nations took
early steps to qualify them. At the First Assembly, in 1920, the
Canadian Delegation proposed the elimination of Article 10
(preservation of territorial integrity), and further developed its
point of view in 1922, by proposing, *inter alia*, that 'no Member
shall be under the obligation to engage in any act of war
without the consent of its parliament, legislature, or other
representative body'. At the Fourth Assembly, in 1923, an
interpretative resolution was proposed, which after adopting
another Canadian amendment, to the effect that the Council,
in advising on action to be taken in fulfilment of the obligation
under Article 10 should take account of the geographical and
general situation of each State, laid it down that

It is for the constitutional authorities of each Member to decide,
in reference to the obligation of preserving the independence and
the integrity of the territory of Members, in what degree the
Member is bound to assure the execution of this obligation by
employment of its military forces.

Though the resolution was opposed by Persia, and therefore not carried, it was thereafter generally regarded as expressing the accepted interpretation of the Article, and the principle which it laid down was also applied in many quarters to the sanctions imposed under Article 16. Meanwhile the Second Assembly, in 1921, had adopted a series of nineteen resolutions bearing upon Article 16, the effect of which was generally to weaken the provisions of the Covenant in regard to sanctions. As a French critic expressed it:

The result which we are in danger of having obtained is to have ruined the strength of the original Article 16, without putting anything in its place.[1]

A school of thought was, in fact, rapidly growing up, more especially in Great Britain and the British Dominions, which valued the League purely for the opportunities it afforded for consultation and the development of an international public opinion, and regarded the machinery of the Covenant designed to guarantee its signatories against aggression as not only of minor importance but positively dangerous. As a result, the security which the League was intended to afford was increasingly believed to be illusory, and States were thrown back upon a reliance on their own forces and those of such allies as they might be able to attract.

The Draft Treaty of Mutual Assistance

These developments, which seemed to threaten a relapse to the pre-war system, brought into rather unexpected alliance the French with their insistence on guaranteed security and the more zealous champions of the League as the last bulwark of civilization. In 1922 Lord Robert Cecil (now Viscount Cecil) submitted four propositions to the Temporary Mixed Commission:

i. That reduction of armaments, to be successful, must be general.
ii. That such reduction depended upon satisfactory guarantees of security.
iii. That these guarantees should be general.
iv. That the provision of such guarantees should be conditional on an undertaking to reduce armaments.

[1] Ray, J. *Commentaire du Pacte de la Société des Nations*. Paris, Recueil Sirey, 1930, p. 519.

A discussion followed in the Assembly, as a result of which two drafts were submitted to the Temporary Commission by Lord Robert Cecil and Colonel Requin, who had been the principal critic of his third proposition, and from the co-ordination of these texts was produced the Draft Treaty of Mutual Assistance, which was circulated to the members of the League, and also to non-members for their observations.

The Draft Treaty was a highly ingenious attempt to combine the respective advantages of a general guarantee and a local system of alliances, while obviating their defects. While a joint and several obligation was to rest upon all signatories to assist any of their number against a war of aggression, which was stigmatized as 'an international crime', the duty to engage in military, naval, or aerial action was restricted to States situated in the continent in which such operations took place. While the allocation of such duties, as well as the function of determining the aggressor, was laid upon the Council of the League, voluntary local alliances were permitted, and their immediate intervention was sanctioned, subject to the risk of incurring the penalties of aggression if this power was, in the opinion of the Council, wrongfully used. Thus the risk of a regional group combining for purposes other than the maintenance of peace was minimized, while self-interest might be counted on to stimulate the action which the general obligations of the Treaty required. It was, however, the careful way in which the obligations of signatories were limited which caused the rejection of the scheme. The apportionment of liability on continental lines cut fatally across the structure of the British Commonwealth with its world-wide responsibilities. Either some parts of the Empire might be at war while others remained at peace— a situation regarded at that date as intolerable—or Great Britain and her Dominions would be subjected to a wholly disproportionate share of the burden of resisting aggression in all parts of the world. In any case, no continental exemption could apply to the British Navy, and the arrangements contemplated seemed likely to raise in an acute form the difficult question of the constitutional relationship between the nations in the British Commonwealth. For these reasons, as well as because of the large executive functions which the Treaty conferred on the Council of the League, the scheme was rejected by the Government of the United Kingdom as well as by the Dominions. There were objections and criticisms from other quarters, especially the European ex-neutral Powers, but it was the rejection by Great Britain and the Dominions which was decisive.

The Geneva Protocol

The defunct proposal had, however, set the feet of European statesmen on the right path. The paramount importance of security, not only as a preliminary step to any considerable limitation of armaments, but also as the only foundation on which a durable peace could be established, had been generally recognized. If the Draft Treaty had to be sacrificed, it was felt that some acceptable alternative method of establishing the security at which it aimed must rise from its ashes. The method chosen was a return to the Covenant, and an endeavour to improve the machinery of the League as an instrument to preserve peace and deter aggression. It was sought to achieve this result in two ways—by supplying a satisfactory test of aggression, and by closing the 'gap in the Covenant' which still left war legitimate in the event of a failure of the machinery for settlement laid down in Article 15. The key to both difficulties was sought in compulsory arbitration. The utility of this expedient as a test of aggression was emphasized by Mr Ramsay MacDonald in his opening speech at the Fifth Assembly of the League, in September 1924:

The one method by which we can secure, the one method by which we can approximate to an accurate attribution of responsibility for aggression is arbitration. . . . The test is: Are you willing to arbitrate?

But it was also clear that the acceptance of an award in all cases of dispute would close the door upon all private war. With these leading ideas in their minds Mr MacDonald and M. Herriot presented a joint resolution which started M. Politis and M. Beneš on the labour of drafting the Geneva Protocol, in which these principles were embodied.

It is impossible to enter into the details of this historic document, which are, in any case, easily accessible. Broadly speaking, it relied on establishing unescapable means of identifying the aggressor, mainly by applying the test above referred **to,** and it applied the machinery of arbitration to all disputes except those arising out of matters solely within the domestic jurisdiction of one of the parties. Even in such cases, the Council or the Assembly might still consider the situation under Article 11 of the Covenant. The sanctions to be applied against the aggressor were identical with those laid down in Article 16 of the Covenant.

The real objection to this procedure is that disputes leading to war are often of a nature which is not susceptible of arbitral adjudication. The Polish Corridor problem is a good example. Juridically, the title of Poland was incontestable. The only alternative to a judicial decision is a compromise, but here it was difficult to conceive a compromise acceptable to one party which would not be inevitably unsatisfactory to the other. To connect the German Reich with East Prussia, which was the minimum of the German aspirations, obviously cut off Poland from the sea and merely created a corridor from east to west instead of from north to south. In such cases the Protocol made no new contribution to the problem of security, but threw the nations back upon the old question—were the sanctions of the Covenant an adequate or a trustworthy safeguard? Yet it was not an objection of this character which brought about the ultimate rejection of the Protocol. Indeed, for the moment, in the favourable atmosphere of Geneva, the success of the policy which it proposed seemed assured.

Rejection of the Protocol

On 2 October 1924, the Protocol was unanimously recommended to the acceptance of the Governments of its member states by the Assembly of the League of Nations. Within a few days the representatives of some seventeen States had signed the instrument, and before the end of the month it had been not only signed but ratified by Czechoslovakia. Yet in the spring of the following year the project was dead. Its sudden demise seems to call for some explanation.

Some writers [1] have laid great stress on the fact that the Labour Government of Mr Ramsay MacDonald, who had

---

[1] See S. de Madariaga, *Disarmament : the Role of the Anglo-Saxon Nations.* Oxford University Press for Geneva Institute of International Relations, 1927, p. 18.

played a leading part in formulating the views of which the Protocol was the outcome, had fallen in November 1924, and had been succeeded by a Conservative administration. No doubt, the exigencies of party politics in the heat of a general election tend to subject the whole policy of opponents to a criticism which makes the subsequent acceptance of any part of their programme difficult, but it is impossible to contend that the Protocol was simply scrapped on account of its origin. Continuity in foreign policy has been a tradition in Great Britain which Conservatives, perhaps more than any other party, have been inclined to follow, and, though the majority in the new Parliament contained a certain number of men who favoured isolationism, this was certainly not the attitude of the Foreign Secretary, Mr Austen Chamberlain.

We are too near [he said in the House of Commons on 5 March 1925] to the Continent to rest indifferent to what goes on there. At periods in our history we have sought to withdraw ourselves from all European interests . . . but no nation can live, as we live, within twenty miles of the Continent of Europe and remain indifferent to the peace and security of the Continent . . . nor is it in that spirit of selfish, and, at the same time, short-sighted isolation, that we shall exercise now, when we speak in consultation with the free self-governing Dominions of a great Empire, our mission and our influence in the world.

The most that can be claimed as a result of the political situation in Great Britain is that it delayed the formation of an immediate and possibly precipitate judgement: the new Government was faced with urgent problems in Russia, arising out of the 'Zinoviev letter' (see p. 107), and in Egypt, consequent upon the murder of Sir Lee Stack in November 1924 (see p. 137). It consequently asked, with every justification, for further time to consider its attitude to the Protocol, and it is possible that in the interval objections not at first apparent may have become increasingly evident.

The chief reason, however, for the rejection of the Protocol lay undoubtedly in the attitude of the British overseas Dominions. Their opposition was partly due to fear of interference with their domestic sovereignty in such matters as immigration, in view of modifications made in the text of the document at the instance of the Japanese. But fundamentally it was based on a growing aversion from the whole idea of becoming involved in the application of sanctions in consequence of the Imperial tie connecting the Dominions with Great Britain. Geographically remote, as they at this time appeared, from the probable danger-spots of the world, the Dominions viewed with increasing distaste a prospect of European entanglement. In Canada, whose proximity to the United States encouraged sympathy with American isolationism, this attitude had long been apparent. It had coloured her policy at Geneva, as we have seen, from the days of the First Assembly, and it was voiced in the rather ominous remarks with which her delegate, M. Dandurand, had marred the unreserved acceptance of the Protocol in the debates of the Assembly:

In this association of mutual insurance against fire, the risks assumed by the different States are not equal. We live in a fireproof house, far from inflammable materials.

South Africa, too, was already inclined to adopt the view of the true functions of the League subsequently expressed by General Smuts at a meeting of the Royal Institute of International Affairs (January 1930):

There are a few traces still of the old order in the Covenant. They will disappear; opinion is hardening against them—Clause 10 and the section of Clause 16 referring to military and naval force— they have never been put into force; public opinion is hardening against those clauses.[1]

India also feared a disproportionate share in the burden of sanctions in the event of trouble in Asia, and Australia and New Zealand, while more afraid of inroads upon their domestic sovereignty than of the possible calls upon their military resources in the enforcement of sanctions, were equally uncompromising in their opposition to the Protocol. In short, disguise it how we will, the demise of the Protocol really meant that a number of countries which had willingly accepted the obligations of the Covenant in 1919 would have refused to do so in 1924. The sanctions were identical; their burden was the same; but what they entailed had become more apparent. In these circumstances, the rejection of the Protocol was inevitable,

[1] *Journal*, 1930, p. 150.

and the *coup de grâce* was administered by Mr Chamberlain in his address to the Council of the League on 12 March 1925.

The Locarno Agreements

Yet it remained evident, and was universally agreed, that some form of guarantee against the main dangers threatening European peace was indispensable, more especially if that which the Covenant had been supposed to supply was increasingly regarded as illusory. With minor occasions of conflict, indeed, the League might still be presumed able to cope, but to deal with the menace, which could not be indefinitely postponed, of a revived and powerful Germany, something more definite and specific was required before France or her Eastern Allies could be expected to co-operate in disarmament. A general system of sanctions having apparently broken down, attention was re-directed to the possibilities of regional agreements. The objection to such a system of local groupings is that it tends to promote counter-alliances, and that, once formed, the alliances on both sides will probably persist, irrespective of the merits of the policy pursued by their members, and may even become a formidable instrument of aggression. These objections are largely met if both parties to a possible dispute are combined in the same group, by a system of mutual guarantee against aggression, and agreements for the peaceful solution of their differences. A solution of this kind, so far as the Rhineland frontier was concerned, was suggested by Germany as early as 1922. Germany then proposed to France to enter into mutual pledges with the Powers interested in the Rhine to abstain from war for a generation, another disinterested Power being included in the pact as trustee. M. Poincaré, then in power in France, had, however, rejected this advance as 'a clumsy manoeuvre'. The offer was twice repeated in 1923, with no better success, but at the close of 1924 a hint was conveyed by Lord D'Abernon, the British Ambassador in Berlin, that the time was ripe for a renewal of the proposal. While British opinion had usually been reluctant to enter into general commitments in unpredictable circumstances, a guarantee limited to the frontiers of France and Belgium was more in line with the traditional policy of this country, and more obviously restricted to meeting a direct threat to British strategic interests,[1] and the approaching rejection of the Geneva Protocol was likely to turn the mind of France to the favourable consideration of an alternative, though less general, method of attaining security. The German proposal was consequently revived, and transmitted to Paris on 9 February 1925.

French opinion was not immediately favourable, and decision was delayed by governmental changes in France, Belgium, and Germany. The death of President Ebert, in February 1925, and his succession in the Reich by Field Marshal von Hindenburg seemed at first unpropitious to a policy of reconciliation. The fall of the Theunis Cabinet in Belgium prevented that country from immediately devoting its attention to the question, and the defeat of M. Herriot in April caused a further interruption. The new French Foreign Secretary, M. Briand, was, however, a man with whom Mr Austen Chamberlain was able to establish particularly cordial relations, and a provisional welcome was given to the proposal by the middle of May.

There were, however, difficulties on the German side as well, though Germany had initiated the proposal. M. Briand stipulated, as a condition, that Germany should enter the League without reservations, and this was difficult for a Government resting on a precarious majority derived from a coalition peculiarly dependent on Nationalist support. The Reich wished to make its entry into the League conditional on the evacuation not only of the Ruhr but of the first Rhineland zone, and also claimed a special status in regard to Article 16 of the Covenant.[2] Germany also desired to keep the question of a Rhineland pact completely severed from that of a settlement of her eastern frontiers, while France not unnaturally saw a vital connexion between the two problems.

However, negotiations progressed favourably enough to permit of the assembly of the Conference of Locarno on

[1] 'All our greatest wars have been fought to prevent one great military Power dominating Europe, and at the same time dominating the coasts of the Channel and the ports of the Low Countries. . . . The issue is one which affects our security.' Speech by Mr (afterwards Sir) Austen Chamberlain, House of Commons, 24 March 1925.

[2] Germany probably feared that public opinion at home would not permit of her co-operation in sanctions directed to preserve Poland from Russian aggression.

5 October, and in the genial atmosphere of that charming locality agreement was speedily reached. The difficulty relating to Article 16 of the Covenant was met by the incorporation of a passage from the Protocol, limiting co-operation 'in the degree which geographical position and particular situation as regards armaments allow', and this was interpreted in Germany as extending, in her case, to a refusal to allow the transit of troops. The German delegates yielded on the point of simultaneously concluding the eastern arbitration treaties, while the question of the Rhineland evacuation had been eliminated, by agreement, from the agenda. Understandings were, however, arrived at at Locarno for the alleviation of some of the conditions of the occupation; a German Commissioner for the occupied territories was to be appointed, forces were to be reduced to 'a figure approaching the normal', and the evacuation of the first zone, which actually began in December 1925, and was finished by 1 February 1926, was indicated as an immediate prospect. On 15 October the Conference was brought to a happy conclusion by the initialing of the whole complex of documents constituting the Locarno Pact. These comprised, in addition to the final protocol:

i. A treaty of mutual guarantee of the Franco-German and Belgo-German frontiers between Germany, Belgium, France, Great Britain, and Italy.
ii. Arbitration conventions between Germany and Belgium and between Germany and France.
iii. Arbitration treaties between Germany and Poland and Germany and Czechoslovakia.
iv. A Franco-Polish and Franco-Czechoslovak treaty for mutual assistance in case of aggression by Germany.

The difficulty, arising from the reluctance of the British Dominions to accept commitments for the preservation of European security, was avoided by a clause (Article 9), exempting the British Dominions and India from obligations under the Treaty, unless specifically accepted. The passage of the Pact through the German Reichstag was not achieved without considerable difficulty, but the support of President Hindenburg enabled a majority of 291 to 174 to be secured. The Treaties were signed in London on 1 December.

The immediate effect on international relations in Europe

was undoubtedly most favourable. The sense of improved security which the British guarantee implanted in the minds of Frenchmen and Germans had an importance far outweighing that of the question whether, on occasion arising, it would prove possible for Great Britain to fulfil her obligations. A democracy can hardly resort to war without the support of national opinion, and, while it is comparatively easy to enlist this on the side of a known ally, the existence of two alternative allies or opponents complicates the situation. During the crisis preceding an outbreak of war, sympathy may very well have rallied to the side which eventually proves to be the aggressor; a sudden *volte-face* is then difficult. It is still more probable that, in such a case, public opinion would be hopelessly divided on the merits. So long, however, as British intervention was feared by the potential aggressors of both sides, it seemed unlikely that the reality of the Pact would be put to the test. To scare the war-maker from his purpose is a more useful task than to arrest or defeat him when his offence has been committed. At the time of its adoption, at any rate, the Locarno Pact was a most effective and formidable looking scarecrow, which went far to justify the opinion of its creator, Mr Austen Chamberlain, that its erection marked 'the real dividing line between the years of war and the years of peace'.

VI

THE SETTLEMENT IN EASTERN EUROPE

IN Eastern Europe, the devastating processes of war, revolution, and self-determination had shattered the pre-existing structure like a vast earthquake. The history of this region, for four or five years, was a record of the final shocks and convulsions of this volcanic disturbance, and, when it subsided, the rents which it had made in the political landscape were traceable from the Arctic Ocean in the north to the Black Sea and Adriatic in the south of the continent. Each of the two main centres of upheaval, operating respectively upon the Russian and Austro-Hungarian Empires, had its peculiar and distinct characteristics. In Russia the sundering force was, in ultimate analysis, the lateral tension exercised by the conflicting political ideals of the East and the West: its effect was to sever the semi-Asiatic Power of Russia more completely from Europe by a single fissure, continuous except for the short break between Estonia and Finland, where the Union of Soviet Socialist Republics still maintained contact with the Baltic and Western civilization.

The Baltic States and Finland

In this Baltic sector a condition of stability was soon attained, for the Soviet Government at this time recognized in principle the right of the seceding states to self-determination, though it aimed at penetrating them with its political ideals, and thereby bringing them within the Soviet system as a federation of autonomous communities. In Finland, though its independence had been formally acknowledged as early as January 1918, the Soviet propaganda led to civil war, and ultimately to a 'White' reaction, which, during the Allied occupation of the Archangel region and Murmansk, started an advance against the Russians, animated by hopes of the fall of Bolshevism. The withdrawal of the Allies, however, in the spring of 1920, forced the Finnish Government to negotiate for peace, and terms were arranged at Dorpat, on 14 October, by which the former boundaries of the

ARCTIC OCEAN

.... Pre-war frontiers
        done away with
——— Post-war
        frontiers

English Miles
0   100 200   400

ATLANTIC
OCEAN

The Faeroes
(Danish)

GREAT BRITAIN

NORTH SEA

London
The Hague
HOLLAND
BELGIUM
Brussels
Paris

FRANCE

NORWAY
SWEDEN
FINLAND

Oslo
Stockholm
Helsinki (Helsingfors)
Leningrad
Aaland Is. (Finnish)
Tallinn
ESTONIA
Riga
LATVIA
Klaipėda (Memel)
LITHUANIA
DANZIG
East Prussia
Kaunas (Kovno)
Wilno (Vilna)

DENMARK
Copenhagen

GERMANY
Berlin
Upper Silesia
LUXEMBOURG
THE SAAR
Prague
CZECHOSLOVAKIA
Vienna
SWITZERL?
Bern
AUSTRIA
HUNGARY
Budapest

POLAND
Warsaw

U.S.S.R.

Moscow

ROUMANIA

Bucharest

BLACK SEA

Istanbul (Constantinople)

Trieste
Fiume
Belgrade
YUGOSLAVIA
Sofia
BULGARIA

ITALY
Corsica (French)
Rome
Sardinia (Italian)

ALBANIA
Tirana
GREECE

TURKEY
Ankara (Angora)

MEDITERRANEAN SEA

AFRICA

Malta (British)

Sicily (Italian)

Crete (Greek)

Athens

78

Grand Duchy were confirmed, except for the addition of a narrow strip between Murmansk and Norway, which gave Finland an outlet to the Arctic Ocean. Further disputes arose, however, in consequence of the situation in east Karelia, where the population, which was of Finnish nationality, rebelled against the Soviet Government in November. As the Treaty of Dorpat had made provisions for the autonomy, under Russian sovereignty, of this region, which the Finns alleged to have been violated, the matter was submitted by Finland to the League of Nations and the Permanent Court of International Justice. The Court, however, decided that it had no jurisdiction, and the Finnish efforts on behalf of their Karelian kinsmen were therefore ineffective.

The only other question which brought Finland within the purview of international history was that of the Aaland Islands. These islands, which had been ceded to Russia, with Finland, by Sweden in 1809, were desirous of exercising the right of self-determination by a reunion with Sweden. The question was referred to the League of Nations in June 1920, and was decided in favour of Finland, subject to a number of guarantees to safeguard the rights of the population. The case is of importance, not only as the first instance in which the League intervened in a question of the allocation of territory, but also because of the important principles which it laid down, regarding the practice of self-determination.

Break-up of Austria-Hungary

The seismic disturbance to the north was, therefore, comparatively unimportant in its international reactions until a considerably later date, except where, in combination with the convulsion which had wrecked Germany and the catastrophic eruption in the former domains of the Habsburg Monarchy, it had resulted in the re-emergence of Poland upon the map, like some forgotten volcanic island. It was in the Danubian basin that the political earthquake had produced its most complex and spectacular results, where it amounted, indeed, to an explosion which had blown the whole area to unrecognizable fragments.

The form which these fragments assumed upon the map had a suggestive likeness to the jaws of a hungry dog closing upon an already well-gnawed cutlet, which was following another morsel down the animal's throat: the cutlet represented the meagre remains of Austria, Hungary was the meat already swallowed, the upper and lower jaws were respectively Czechoslovakia and Yugoslavia, while the muscles which worked them were comprised in Roumania, the third member of what was shortly to be known as the Little Entente. Outlying portions of the vanished Empire were included in Italy and Poland, bringing the total number of pieces to seven.

Economic Effects

The economic dislocation produced by such a cataclysm beggars description. The pre-war system constituted a single customs area, the external trade of which was directed by elaborate and costly railway communications to the Adriatic ports of Trieste and Fiume, for, though the natural outlet for its commerce was by the navigable system of the Danube to the Black Sea, the remoteness of this waterway from the main centres of European economic activity and the political uncertainties connected with a passage through the Straits to the Mediterranean had directed the flow to the west. The financial and commercial heart of the region was centred in Vienna: the country drew its supplies of industrial material predominantly from Bohemia, where a large proportion of its manufacturing industry was also situated, while from the agricultural plain of Hungary, and the districts now included in Yugoslavia and Roumania, came abundant supplies of essential foodstuffs. Now the lines of communication, both natural and artificial, were blocked, impeded, or diverted, the balance between agriculture and manufacturing industry destroyed, and the reciprocal flow of the internal trade of a great commercial unit dammed in every direction by the tariff walls of a jealous economic nationalism.

Austria

In this predicament it was Austria which fared the worst. The factories which lay within her territory had drawn their oil from Galicia, their coal and many of their material resources from what was now Czechoslovakia, which was, in any case, the centre of her former industrial activity. Vienna was a metropolis which had lost its *raison d'être*; a heart from which every vital artery had been ruthlessly severed. Constructed to serve as a financial and commercial centre for a great and thriving Empire, it stood meaningless among the mountains of Austria, almost like those ruins of a bygone civilization over which the traveller wonders in the desert. But for such semblances of life as might be evoked from her by the galvanic stimulus of foreign charity, Austria appeared to be dead.

It was fortunate for her that her helpless plight was not destined to appeal in vain to the sympathy of her neighbours. It was manifest, indeed, that this was a case in which charity and self-interest coincided. If the Austrian people were not to be driven by sheer desperation into the chaos of Bolshevism, or irresistibly impelled towards that Anschluss with Germany which the Allies feared and their treaty prohibited, it was necessary that the country should be subsidized. But the help which was to be afforded to her was also dictated by a genuinely altruistic sentiment, into which no thought of political advantage entered. It may appear strange at first sight, since the proximate cause of the war was an Austrian ultimatum, that she should never have been regarded, even in the bitterest days of the struggle, with the feelings of hostility and detestation which had been aroused against Germany. It was German aggression which had for years been anticipated both in Great Britain and in France. These anticipations had not only been stimulated by a succession of actual crises, but by the universally accepted and probably justified belief that 'Der Tag' was habitually toasted in German military circles; they were fostered by a continuous flow of satire in the columns of *Punch* since the days of the Kaiser's telegram to Kruger (1896), and are even implied in so pacifist a work as Sir Norman Angell's *Great Illusion*, published in 1909. Moreover, from the outbreak of the war to its close, hostile sentiment had been concentrated upon Germany by such actions as the violation of Belgian neutrality, the introduction of poison gas, the sinking of the *Lusitania*, and the execution of Nurse Cavell. Austria had escaped all this. In thinking of Austrians, most Englishmen thought of the gay social life of Vienna, of mountaineering friendships with the Tyrolese, of Austrian gentlemen with a kindred passion for sport, and, if only the dispute with Serbia could have been isolated, there can be little doubt that the prevailing sympathies in Great Britain would have favoured the chastisement by Austria of a people regarded, however unfairly, as a horde of uncivilized banditti. France, too, entertained no grudge against Austria, from whom, apart from her alliance with Germany, she anticipated no danger, and with whom she had no outstanding quarrel. Even Italy, in spite of traditional animosities, had been, until the war, Austria's ally: her territorial ambitions were now satiated in Austria proper, and what remained of them was concentrated on Croatians, who by the part they had played in Austrian service had always been the special object of Italian hatred, and who now formed part of the distinct and even unfriendly State of Yugoslavia. For these reasons, the part played by Austria was as easy to forget as to forgive, and there was no obstacle to prevent the assistance dictated alike by pity and policy from being immediately mobilized in a practical form. By the irony of fate, the first steps towards the necessary assistance devolved upon the Reparation Commission, which was requested by the Supreme Council, in May 1919, to take up the question, not of reparation but of relief. In April 1920, the basis of relief was broadened to include the support of ex-neutrals, by the constitution of an International Relief Credits Committee, in consultation with which the Reparation Commission authorized the issue of bearer bonds charged upon the assets and revenues of Austria, and vested with priority over the costs of reparation under the Treaty. In February 1921, the four principal Allied Powers agreed to suspend their claims, both for reparation and the repayment of relief bonds, if their example were followed by the other creditors, and they took the important step of referring the further solution of the problem to the League of Nations. Meanwhile it became apparent that the recovery of Austria necessitated not only relief but drastic financial reconstruction, a complete collapse being only staved off, in February 1922, through advances made from public funds by Great Britain, France, Italy, and Czechoslovakia. Later in the year a complete scheme of reconstruction was put forward by the Financial Committee of the League, and adopted in October 1922.

This aimed firstly at the effective control and reform of Austrian finances, and secondly at the facilitation of loans in the

private market, through the guarantee of the four signatory
Powers, Great Britain, France, Italy, and Czechoslovakia, and
of any other countries willing to participate. It instituted a
Committee of Control composed of representatives of the
guaranteeing Governments, and appointed a Commissioner
General, representative of the League, and purposely drawn
from a neutral Power (the Netherlands), to supervise the programme of reform. It further instituted a new Bank of Issue,
vested with the sole right of issuing notes, and independent of
government control.

The necessary legislation was passed by the Austrian Parliament in November 1922. Inflation ceased, and the situation
was so far improved as to admit of the flotation of the two loans
in February and April 1923, the first guaranteed by the four
Powers above mentioned and Belgium, while, for the second,
additional guarantees were obtained from Sweden, Holland,
and Denmark. Both issues were extremely successful, the
second being everywhere over-subscribed within a few hours.
For the time being Austria appeared to have good prospects of
recovery.

The Burgenland Dispute

During the period which elapsed between the signature of
the Treaty of St Germain and the reconstruction of Austria
under the auspices of the League, the apparently hopeless
position of the country depressed its inhabitants into a state
of political apathy, out of which they were temporarily aroused
on one occasion only. This was in connexion with the dispute
which arose with her companion in misfortune and former
associate, Hungary, over the question of the Burgenland. The
Burgenland was a strip of territory in western Hungary, the
frontier of which was, at the nearest point, within fifteen miles
of Vienna. This district had been transferred by the Treaties
of St Germain and Trianon from Hungary to Austria on racial
grounds, which were reinforced by strategic considerations,
during Bela Kun's Bolshevist regime in Hungary. Of its
330,000 inhabitants, 235,000 were German, while of the
remainder only about 25,000 were of Magyar stock. The
region was also of economic importance to Austria, being an
important source of food-supplies, and has been described as

the 'kitchen-garden of Vienna'. The Allies therefore determined upon the transference of the territory to Austria without the formality of a plebiscite, which they considered superfluous, though it was in fact at first requested by both the parties concerned. At the date of ratification of the Treaty of Trianon, however, the Burgenland was still in Hungarian occupation, and, when the day arrived for its evacuation, control was assumed by bands of Hungarian irregulars, who ejected the Austrian gendarmerie, and defied the Commission appointed to supervise the transfer. An impasse was thus created which was met by an offer of Italian mediation in October 1921. The principal bone of contention was the town of Sopron or Ödenburg, near the new Hungarian frontier, which was said to contain a large Magyar element. It was agreed to decide the ultimate fate of this town and the surrounding villages by a plebiscite, which was held on 14 and 15 December and resulted in a decisive vote for union with Hungary being returned by some 87 per cent of the registered voters. But too short a time had been allowed for the satisfactory revision of the registers, and, two days before the plebiscite, the Austrian delegation had resigned in protest. The Conference of Ambassadors, however, which seems to have imperfectly appreciated the grounds for Austrian dissatisfaction, decided to recognize the plebiscite, and Sopron was handed over in January 1922. Considerable feeling was thus aroused, though in February the Austrian Government accepted the inevitable and agreed to recognize the transfer.

Events in Hungary

The history of this incident illustrates the fact that the Magyars of Hungary, though placed by the Treaty in an almost equally depressing situation, were folk of a less acquiescent temperament than the Germans of Austria. This morsel, in fact, though even more securely enclosed within the jaws of its enemies, was considerably more difficult of digestion. Permission, on military grounds, to Roumania to occupy temporarily a considerable sector of Hungarian territory gave rise, in March 1919, to the militant Communist regime of Bela Kun, which carried on for some time an unequal struggle on two fronts, not only with Roumania but also with Czechoslovakia.

This episode was followed, after a Roumanian occupation which sowed the seeds of a lasting bitterness, by a 'White' counter-revolution of a monarchist complexion which had set up a Habsburg archduke as 'administrator' of the Hungarian Crown during its abeyance, the abolition of the Monarchy having never been recognized in Hungary nor, indeed, stipulated in the Treaty of Trianon. The Allies, however, refused to permit the return of a Habsburg administration, and the archduke acquiesced in this decision. But in March 1921, and again in October, the dovecotes were fluttered by the arrival in Hungary of the ex-King Charles. On the first of these occasions, Charles withdrew to Switzerland in response to protests from the Allies and an ultimatum from Czechoslovakia, but the second *Putsch* created a more serious situation. Taking advantage of the disturbances in the Burgenland, the ex-King arrived there by aeroplane on 20 October and began a march upon Budapest. In this emergency, the Hungarian Government acted correctly, and the *coup* was successfully opposed by troops under their orders, with the result that, on the 28th, the monarchist forces were defeated and their leader arrested on the following day. This, however, did not allay the excitement and alarm occasioned in the surrounding Succession States, and especially in Czechoslovakia: Yugoslavia and Czechoslovakia mobilized, and M. Beneš adopted so threatening an attitude that a curious situation arose, wherein Hungary was appealing to the protection of the Allies against the militant insistence of Czechoslovakia. On 7 November the ex-King was safely conveyed to Madeira, where he died in the following year, but the energetic pressure of M. Beneš by no means ceased with the removal of the main cause of the crisis. He insisted, under threats of military intervention, not only on the deposition of Charles and the legal exclusion of the Habsburgs from the throne, but also upon an indemnity for the costs of mobilization. This last demand was rejected, but his policy was otherwise successful, for in November legislation was passed which, while retaining Hungary's right to monarchical government, formally excluded Charles and changed the right of succession from a hereditary to an elective basis, while, by a separate declaration, the Hungarian Government bound itself to exclude the Habsburgs, and to make no election without the consent of the

Conference of Ambassadors. The matter therefore terminated
in a substantial victory for the forceful diplomacy of M. Beneš
and his associates.

The Austro-Hungarian Succession States

It was, in fact, fear of their neighbours, and of Hungary in
particular, as the only State with grievances against all of them,
which bound the three 'satiated' Succession States, Czechoslovakia, Yugoslavia, and Roumania, in a close understanding.
It may even be said that the association of different elements
within the borders of two of these States was partially attributable to the same motive. As the name itself implies, Czechoslovakia was made up of two distinct if kindred peoples, differing in culture, speech, historical traditions, and economic
outlook, and geographically divided by a range of mountains
from which all the natural communications on the Slovak side
led southward into Hungary. But the Serb-Croat-Slovene
Kingdom of the Yugoslavs was a still more precarious unity.
It represented, as a contributor to the *History of the Peace Conference of Paris* [1] points out, an ideal 'conceived by literary men and
visionaries', and precipitately adopted in the abnormal conditions of war. Perhaps it would be more exact to say that it
represented the fusion of two ideals, a Greater Serbian movement from Belgrade, and a project for the union of the Serb,
Croat, and Slovene peoples within the boundaries of the former
Habsburg Empire into an autonomous State with its capital at
Zagreb. The latter appears to have been the solution contemplated by the resolution of the Croatian National Parliament,
passed on 20 October 1918. But though the credentials of the
Committee which offered the crown to King Alexander on
1 December have been called in question, it seems probable
that the union with Serbia had at the time the general support
of Yugoslav opinion, though it must be remembered that the
advantage of presenting a united front to the Italian claims
under the Treaty of London played an important part in the
decision. But Croat and Serb are an ill-mated couple, with
fundamental differences in mentality. The Serbs are a nation
of primitive peasants, but lately emerged from 350 years of
Turkish domination; the Croats have European memories of

----

[1] Vol. iv, p. 171.

a kingdom dating as far back as the tenth century; the influences by which they have been moulded have been Roman rather than Bvzantine. The Croats are Catholics, the Serbs Orthodox, and though the two peoples speak the same language, they use different alphabets. The Yugoslav nation was in fact held together in a state of tension by external pressure, and there was danger that, like the bulb of annealed glass known as a Rupert's drop, it might altogether disintegrate when the pressure was relaxed.

Roumania and the Little Entente

The third member of what was known as the 'Little Entente' was impelled to a policy of alliance by a far more serious combination of irredentist dangers than either of her two associates. From Bulgaria she had retained the Dobrudja, as spoils of the Balkan War of 1913, though on ethnic grounds it was indisputably Bulgar. Hungary had not only been deprived in her favour of Transylvania, but was embittered by the recollections of the Roumanian occupation occasioned by Bela Kun's regime, which had been accompanied by acts of spoliation not easily forgotten or forgiven, and had brought Roumania into open collision with the Supreme Council of the Allies. Besides this, Roumania had a precarious hold on Bessarabia, which the Soviet Government refused to recognize, and which, grounded as it was on the vote of an irregularly constituted Bessarabian Council, was not recognized by the Allies until March 1920, when the collapse of Roumanian recalcitrancy induced them to adopt a more favourable attitude. Even then the Treaty of 28 October, implementing this recognition, was not supported by the United States or ratified by the Powers except Great Britain, while it evoked immediate protests from the Russian Government. Roumania was thus sorely in need of friends, and M. Take Jonescu's policy was consequently directed towards a general defensive alliance between the five 'victor' States of the region, i.e. with Greece and Poland as well as between the three who subsequently formed the Little Entente. Czechoslovakia and Yugoslavia, however, were determined not to enter into an anti-Russian combination, both because of the sentimental tie between Slavonic peoples, and because they believed in Russian recovery and consequently regarded the existing frontier with Russia, either in Poland or elsewhere, as danger-ously unstable. The real initiator of the Entente was therefore M. Beneš of Czechoslovakia, who began by entering into a purely bilateral convention with Yugoslavia, in August 1920, which was directed towards the maintenance of the Treaty of Trianon and mutual defence against Hungarian aggression. Preparations were at once made for the conclusion of a similar agreement between Czechoslovakia and Roumania, but before it had gone farther the first *Putsch* of the ex-King Charles increased the urgency of the step proposed, and on 23 April 1921, a second bilateral agreement of substantially the same kind as the first was signed by Czechoslovakia and Roumania. The triple nexus of treaties was completed on 7 June by a convention between Yugoslavia and Roumania, which differed from those concluded with Czechoslovakia in being aimed not only at Hungarian but also at Bulgarian aggression. Thus, when Charles made his second appearance, the Little Entente was really in being, and this no doubt accounted for the energy with which M. Beneš pursued his policy, and the success which he achieved. Roumania, however, showed during the crisis comparatively little solidarity with the remaining members of the Entente.

Effects of Hungarian Reconstruction, 1923-4

A glance at a map will emphasize a point to which allusion has already been made—the paramount importance of the Hungarian danger in uniting the Little Entente. Czecho-slovakia is geographically a part of central Europe; a natural ally of France and Poland,[1] on guard against the threat of German expansion; Yugoslavia and Roumania have common Balkan affiliations, facing a possible Bulgarian irredentism; in the meanwhile, if Hungary is discounted, Roumania is mainly preoccupied with Russia, and Yugoslavia with Italy and the question of the Adriatic. The three members of the Entente shared of course a general interest in the maintenance of the territorial settlement; on a broad classification they belonged to the anti-revisionist grouping; but for the moment the individual preoccupations of each were likely to become

---

[1] This natural alliance was in fact impeded by a traditional antipathy between Czechs and Poles.

prominent if the tension created by fear of Hungary were relaxed. In 1923 this effect was produced by the discovery that Hungary, like Austria, was financially dependent upon the goodwill of her neighbours and ready to submit to a scheme of reconstruction modelled closely upon that which had proved so successful in the case of Austria. The necessary arrangements, which were completed in May 1924, won the approval and support of the Little Entente, and the relief to their anxieties brought about, to some extent, a new orientation of each member's policy. When France, whose adventure in the Ruhr had alienated British support and increased the risk of disturbance in Germany, made advances in January 1924 with the object of extending the system of alliance which had begun with the Franco-Polish Treaty of 1921, the immediate reactions of the separate members of the Little Entente differed from one another. France secured at once a treaty with Czechoslovakia (24 January 1924), but Roumania, for the moment, refused the overture; while Yugoslavia was actually engaged at the time in signing a treaty with Italy, in circumstances to which our attention must now be turned.

Italo-Yugoslav Relations

If the external policy of Yugoslavia had been directed against the possible irredentism of Hungary and Bulgaria, her internal unity was largely maintained by the pressure of Italian claims on the Adriatic coast-line. Based as these were upon promises made by Great Britain and France in the Treaty of London (26 April 1915), they had the substantial support of three out of the four Great Powers who controlled the Peace Conference. President Wilson, indeed, would have disregarded the Treaty, of which he said that he had never heard until his arrival in Paris, but the British and French memorandum of February 1920 [1] shows clearly that these Powers considered themselves bound to give at least partial effect to its obligations. In contesting the Italian claims, it was obvious that a Yugoslavia which included a former belligerent ally, Serbia, stood in a stronger position than a new State carved exclusively from the possessions of a defeated enemy. And circumstances prolonged the struggle with Italy far beyond the termination of the Peace

[1] *History of the Peace Conference of Paris*, vol. v, p. 423.

Conference. Though the main question of the frontier was settled in February 1921 by the Treaty of Rapallo, the fili-bustering of the poet D'Annunzio, who seized and occupied Fiume in September 1919 and was not finally ejected until January 1921, brought a new difficulty into the situation, since the port still remained in Italian hands and was the scene of repeated nationalist disturbances. The problem was, indeed, not completely solved by the signature of an Italo-Yugoslav agreement on 23 October 1922, for this was followed on the 30th by the commencement of Mussolini's dictatorship in Italy, an event which did not seem to augur well for the continuance of a conciliatory foreign policy. The frontier remained un-delimited in its most contentious sector, and the appointment of General Giardino as Governor of Fiume in March 1922 gave rise to serious misgivings, for he appeared from his actions to be obeying instructions to incorporate the town in Italy in every respect; more especially since his arrival coincided closely in date with the Corfu incident.[1] The question was, however, finally settled by an agreement signed in Rome on 27 January 1924, together with a useful 'Pact of Friendship and cordial Collaboration' between the parties, which was executed simultaneously. By this arrangement the original solution creating a Free State of Fiume was abandoned, and the greater part of the disputed territory was incorporated in Italy, leaving Yugoslavia in possession of the adjacent Port Baros and provided with satisfactory economic facilities in the main harbour. Though the question of Fiume was thus settled, the terms were more palatable to the Serbian than the Croatian and Slovene sections of Yugoslav opinion, and the internal tension was not diminished. The Serbian requirements of access to the sea had been satisfied in May 1923, by a conven-tion with Greece, affording to Yugoslavia a 'Free Zone' in the port of Salonika, which, however, was not formally handed over until 1925.

Albania

'Friendship and cordial collaboration' did not, however, show much promise of permanence. A state of affairs in which one nation looks at the sea while another controls most of its

[1] See p. 92.

THE SETTLEMENT IN EASTERN EUROPE 91

ports is hardly conducive to harmonious relations. But a phase of the Adriatic question specially calculated to bring into conflict the rival interests of Italy and Yugoslavia was that connected with the status of Albania. Although, prior to the grant of autonomy in 1912, that country was politically a part of Turkey, it was sufficiently a separate region to be an object of interest not only to the neighbouring Balkan States, but in particular to Italy and Austria-Hungary. Both these Great Powers are believed to have expended considerable sums in subsidizing the local politicians, and, from the date of its existence as an autonomous unit, it may be described as a sort of Adriatic Constantinople, whose continued existence was preserved by the conflicting jealousies of its neighbours. During the Balkan War of 1912, the resistance of both Italy and Austria-Hungary to the emergence of a third Power on the Adriatic defeated the attempts of the Balkan allies to dismember it, and in July 1913, the Conference of Ambassadors in London declared Albania an independent sovereign State. Parts of the country were, however, eyed covetously by Serbia, Montenegro, and Greece; Austria-Hungary regarded it as a special sphere of her interest, while Italy was nervous of the occupation by any important Power of the fine harbour of Valona, sixty miles from the Italian coast, which controls the access to the Adriatic. Even before her intervention in the War, Italy occupied the Island of Sasseno, at the entrance to the harbour, and from November 1914 she occupied Valona itself. By the Treaty of London, April 1915, the Allied Powers contemplated the partition of Albania between Italy,—who was to retain Valona, Sasseno, and the adjoining region—Montenegro, Serbia, and Greece, but in 1920 it was proposed to give Italy a mandate over the whole of Albania, with full sovereignty over Valona. She had, however, an uncomfortable time at the hands of the surrounding population, and in August 1920 an agreement was signed between Italy and the Albanian Government, providing for the independence of the territory and the evacuation of the Italian forces. Meanwhile, Yugoslavia had inherited both the Austrian and the Serbian outlook, Greece and Yugoslavia were demanding the revision of the frontier defined in 1913, complaints of Yugoslav incursions came repeatedly before the League of Nations, and, thus stimulated, the

Conference of Ambassadors, on 9 November 1921, confirmed the 1913 frontier, subject to the further delimitation of certain portions.

On the same day a remarkable declaration was signed in Paris by the British, French, Italian, and Japanese Governments. This instrument recognized in an emphatic way the paramount interest of Italy, and declared that in the event of an appeal to the League by Albania for the preservation of her territorial integrity, their representatives on the Council would recommend that the restoration of the frontiers should be entrusted to Italy. This declaration was the subject of some criticism as a derogation from the principles of the League.[1] Enough has here been said to indicate to the reader the explosive possibilities of a situation of which more will be heard at a later stage.

The Corfu Incident

It was out of the work of delimitation ordered by the Conference of Ambassadors in November 1921 that an incident occurred which may be regarded as an early test of the working of the post-war system. On 27 August 1923, an Italian General with three other Italian companions and an Albanian were murdered on Greek soil in the neighbourhood of Janina while carrying out the work of delimitation. After an ultimatum vividly reminiscent of that delivered by Austria to Serbia in 1914, and a submissive reply of much the same tenor as the Serbian, the Italian Government sent a squadron to the Greek island of Corfu, which it occupied after a bombardment which caused casualties among some unfortunate Greek and Armenian refugees from Anatolia, who were housed in the obsolete fortress. On 1 September two Notes were delivered, one from the Greek Government to the Council of the League calling attention to the Italian ultimatum—though not the bombardment—and another from the Conference of Ambassadors to the Greeks, protesting against the Janina outrage and demanding an inquiry. In answer to the second Note, the Greek Government submitted in advance to any decision by the Ambassadors' Conference, and thus the case was unfortunately in the hands

[1] See paper by Mr Wickham Steed, *Journal of the Royal Institute of International Affairs*, May 1927.

of two distinct authorities. The Council of the League acted with vigour and promptness, but its activities were impeded not only by Signor Mussolini's threat to occupy Corfu indefinitely if the League intervened, but by the refusal of the Italian representative at Geneva to assent to action by the Council. After Articles 10, 12, and 15 of the Covenant had been read aloud as a comment on the Italian attitude, a plan of settlement was drawn up at an informal meeting of the Council, and sent to the Conference of Ambassadors. Since this proposal, with unimportant amendments, was accepted by the Conference of Ambassadors and, within forty-eight hours, by both parties to the dispute, the incident appeared to have ended satisfactorily. Under the terms agreed upon, a sum of 50 million lire was to be deposited by Greece to await the decision of the Permanent Court of International Justice. A few days later, however, the Conference of Ambassadors receded from their position, and, alleging negligence by Greece on the strength of a preliminary report by the Inter-Allied Commission of Inquiry, peremptorily insisted on the payment to Italy of the Greek deposit. This denouement, which looked painfully like paying the aggressor to evacuate Corfu, was not calculated to discourage the recurrence of similar incidents.

Graeco-Bulgarian Relations

The mention of Greece in this connexion renders it convenient to digress for a moment from consideration of the concerns of the Little Entente, and to transfer our attention from the Danubian basin to the Graeco-Bulgarian frontier. During the earliest stages of the post-war period, Bulgaria, like Austria, was too much exhausted to constitute a serious danger, while the attention of Greece was concentrated upon her disastrous adventure in Anatolia (see Chapter VIII). The repulse of the Greeks by the Turks created, however, a new situation which had important reactions upon the Macedonian frontier. The flight of Greek refugees from Anatolia made it necessary to find space to accommodate them in Greece: this question was complicated by simultaneous attempts to repatriate Greek and Bulgarian minorities respectively across the Macedonian border. While the influx of Anatolian Greeks could be partially met by the transfer of Turks to their own country, the effort to induce Bulgarians to withdraw was also stimulated, with the result that continual complaints arose as to the treatment of this section of the population. Moreover, since most of the transferred Greeks and Bulgars settled in the frontier regions where communities of the opposite race were most numerous, relations progressively deteriorated, and acts of violence together with *komitadji* raids and other frontier incidents were increasingly the subject of complaints.

A particularly serious incident occurred at Tarlis, on the Greek side of the frontier, in July 1924, when a number of Bulgarian prisoners, arrested for supposed complicity in a *komitadji* raid, were massacred by their escort in circumstances found by the Mixed Emigration Commission to be completely without justification, though the Greek Government was exonerated from responsibility. An attempt was made to arrive at a satisfactory settlement of the minority problem by the signature of two protocols in September 1924, as a result of negotiations which took place during the session of the League Assembly. This effort was, however, frustrated, mainly owing to pressure from the Yugoslavs, who felt that the Greek admission of the existence of a Bulgarian minority in Macedonia was prejudicial to their own claims in the part of Macedonia which was under Serbian rule. The Greeks abandoned the protocol, and matters remained as before. A crisis developed in October 1925 as the result of a frontier incident at Demir-Kapu, where a Greek soldier was killed and the Greek commandant of the post was shot dead in an endeavour to mediate under cover of a white flag. The Greeks began a serious invasion of Bulgarian territory, and war was only stopped by the intervention of the League of Nations, whose supporters rightly claim this episode as perhaps the most strikingly successful instance of the efficacy of its machinery for the preservation of peace. In this case, aggression was not only checked but signally penalized, for the League Commission of Inquiry recommended the payment of reparation by Greece to Bulgaria to the amount of about £45,000, and the sum was paid in full by the beginning of the following March (1926). Another aspect of the question is, however, stressed by a historian of modern Greece: 'It was not unreasonably felt in Athens, that Greece had been sacrificed a second time to save the prestige of the League, which turned the left cheek to Great Powers and demanded the uttermost farthing from small States'.[1]

Poland and her Neighbours

The reluctance of the Czechs and Yugoslavs to include Poland in their system of defensive alliance was, as already indicated, partly due to their sympathy with Soviet Russia and belief in her ultimate recovery, and also to their appreciation of the exceptionally risky position which Poland occupied, between two Powers of the size and potential strength of Germany and the Soviet Union. In the first years following the peace, a *rapprochement* between these two countries was a danger very generally feared—witness the concern occasioned, in April 1922, by the signature of a Russo-German Treaty at Rapallo. Apart from this, there were outstanding differences between Poland and Czechoslovakia, which maintained rather strained relations for some time. The question of Teschen had, in February 1919, brought the two countries into actual collision, while the boundary dispute in the Zips region over the Javorzina district dragged on unsettled until 1924, and had ultimately to be referred from the Conference of Ambassadors to the League of Nations.[2]

The new Poland, indeed, seemed more distinguished by a reckless and almost fanatical patriotism, leading her to pursue a policy of liberation to the farthest limits occupied by her scattered people, than by the diplomatic prudence which her precarious situation demanded. During the Peace Conference, for example, she had carried on hostilities against the Ruthenians of East Galicia in open defiance of the Supreme Council, and it must be admitted that the *fait accompli* with which she thus confronted them led ultimately to her acquisition of a stretch of territory to which she had a most questionable claim on racial grounds. Having, as a compromise, been originally allotted a mandate over East Galicia for twenty-five years, after which the question was to be reconsidered by the League of Nations, Poland was eventually, in March 1923, assigned the whole region.

[1] Miller, W. *Greece*. London, Benn, 1928, p. 94.
[2] For details of this dispute see *History of the Peace Conference of Paris*, vol. iv, p. 364, and *Survey of International Affairs*, 1924, p. 457.

Relations with Lithuania

A similar—and similarly successful—intransigence characterized the relations of Poland with her new neighbour, Lithuania,
though in this case, perhaps, the Poles had more excuse.
Lithuanian separate independence had previously had a
history of little more than a century, from the middle of the
thirteenth to the last quarter of the fourteenth century, when
the country became united with Poland under the Lithuanian
king, Jagiello, a union which was further consolidated in 1569
and lasted till the partition of Poland in 1793, when Lithuania
was absorbed, with the eastern provinces of Poland, in the
Russian Empire. This long association had naturally brought
about a considerable intermixture of the Polish and Lithuanian
peoples, and in the historic capital of Lithuania, Vilna, and the
surrounding district, there was a large preponderance of Poles,
the proportions in the town itself being about 56 per cent Polish
to no more than 2·5 per cent Lithuanian. There can be no
doubt that the Poles were disappointed by the decision of
Lithuania to adopt an independent existence; it must also be
recognized that in 1920 Poland regarded herself as engaged in
a crusade for the rescue of her own people and her neighbours
from the horrors of Bolshevism, a danger which an independent
Lithuania was far too weak to withstand alone. The self-
determination of Lithuania had however been proclaimed,
during the German occupation of 1917, by a Taryba or
national council sitting at Vilna, though, since this body
coupled its declaration of independence with an acknowledge-
ment of permanent ties of alliance with the German Reich,
it is charitable to assume that it was hardly a free agent. The
selection of Vilna as the seat of the assembly, though intelligible
on historical grounds, was naturally unpopular with the Polish
majority in the town and district. The Lithuanian claim to
independence was recognized, with some qualifications, by the
Germans in January 1918 and conceded by the Kaiser in
March. The German withdrawal after the Armistice was the
signal for the retreat from Vilna of the provisional Lithuanian
Government which had been established there. For the return
of the Russians was imminent, and in January 1919 the defence
of the city by a Polish force under General Wejtko failed to

prevent its capture by the Bolsheviks, though it was retaken by the Poles in April. On 12 July 1920, when Vilna was still in Polish occupation, the Lithuanian and Soviet Governments signed a treaty of peace, which ceded to Lithuania not only Vilna, but also territory near Suvalki which had been declared to be Polish by the Supreme Council on 8 December 1919, though the decision had never been communicated to the Lithuanians. Two notes annexed to the treaty gave permission to the Russians to occupy Lithuanian territory in the course of their military operations against Poland. On 14 July 1920, the Bolsheviks recaptured Vilna, but the tide of war turned in August, and, when they perceived their withdrawal to be inevitable, the Russians allowed the Lithuanians to occupy the town, with the rest of the territory transferred to them by the treaty. During the new Polish advance, a collision occurred between Polish and Lithuanian troops near Suvalki. Poland thereupon appealed to the League of Nations, alleging that the Lithuanians were actively collaborating with the Bolsheviks, an allegation which was vigorously contested by the other party to the dispute. In the course of the ensuing negotiations, the Polish Minister of Foreign Affairs gave a positive assurance, on 3 October, that the Poles would not occupy Vilna, and suggested a plebiscite to settle the frontier dispute. This assurance was rather less definitely repeated on the following day by Marshal Pilsudski, himself a native of Vilna, who occupied the dual position of Commander-in-Chief and Chief of State. He confirmed that an advance against Vilna was 'not intended', but added that, if he were not Chief of State, as a soldier he would have occupied it a week ago. The next stage was the signature by the disputants of an agreement for a provisional *modus vivendi*, at Suvalki on 7 October. The object of this arrangement, which was expressly stated to be without prejudice to the territorial claims of either party, was to interpose a barrier between the Lithuanian and Polish forces. For this purpose, however, it was regrettably incomplete, since the eastern portion of the line of demarcation was not to become operative until after the complete withdrawal of the Soviet troops to the east of the railway approaching Vilna from the south, and even then it was not to extend east of the station of Bastuny on that railway. Vilna was therefore, so far as the

Suvalki agreement was concerned, left wide open to an advance from the south. The agreement was timed to come into force on 10 October, but on the previous day Vilna was forcibly occupied by General Zeligowski, a semi-independent commander, allied with and paid by Poland. His action was officially disowned by the Polish Government, but the town remained in Polish occupation. Since force was unavailable, and negotiations were fruitless, the efforts of the League of Nations to handle the situation were unsuccessful: the Poles retained possession, which in this case proved more than nine points of the law. After two years, in February 1923, the Polish Government appealed to the Conference of Ambassadors, and on 15 March they were awarded an official title to the town and district of which they had been so long in *de facto* occupation.

Memel

Thus instructed in the advantages of 'direct action', the Lithuanians proceeded to apply the same methods to the determination of another problem—the status of Memel. This German town and territory, on the right bank of the Niemen, had, up to the end of 1922, been administered on behalf of the Allies by a French High Commissioner. Though it was clearly essential that the port should have special relations with Lithuania, the project appears to have been under consideration of creating it a self-governing territory, on the model of Danzig. Fearing such a solution, the Lithuanians, in January 1923, invaded Memel, and compelled the surrender of the French garrison after some street fighting. As this incident occurred on the eve of the French occupation of the Ruhr, the Allies had no troops to spare for the restoration of their authority; they consequently took refuge in negotiations which eventually left the juridical sovereignty in the hands of Lithuania. Though a convention suggested by a Commission of the League, which was accepted in March 1924, secured a measure of autonomy to the inhabitants and rights of transit for Poland, it cannot be said, in this case either, that the position of the aggressor was in any way prejudiced by his high-handed action.

Upper Silesia

In the settlement of the Upper Silesian problem, we observe the same tactics employed on behalf of Poland, though the measure of success achieved is, perhaps, more disputable. The Treaty of Versailles, in its original form, had proposed to transfer, without consulting the wishes of the inhabitants, the greater part of the former German province to Poland.[1] In response to protests, however, it was decided to hold a plebiscite in the area in question and this was accordingly done (30 November 1921), to the marked disappointment of the Poles. The announcement of the plebiscite figures, which resulted in a majority in favour of Germany of 717,122 votes against 483,154, excited a fear in Poland that the whole district might be restored to its former owners, Mr Lloyd George, in particular, being believed to favour this solution. In consequence, a serious rising broke out on 3 May 1922, under the leadership of the Polish plebiscite commissioner, M. Korfanty. For the time being, the Allied control of the district was rendered impotent, a feature of the situation being the almost undisguised support which the Polish claims received from the French garrison. On 11 May *The Times* correspondent reported that 'the first marching in of the insurgents met with friendly greetings from the French soldiers', and further,

In Beuthen there is a battalion of French chasseurs with tanks to preserve order. The armed insurgents can parade with impunity past the French barracks, and keep the town awake at night fusillading down the streets.

Owing to this dissension between the Allies, it is impossible to say how much the eventual solution of the problem owed to these violent methods, but in August 1922 the Supreme Council referred the matter to the League of Nations, who suggested the partition eventually adopted. This solution, while probably the best available in the circumstances, has been stigmatized as 'the easiest compromise between justice and the interest of the stronger',[2] and it is difficult to resist the conclusion that Poland was certainly not penalized, and probably gained, as the result

[1] A small portion was also destined for Czechoslovakia.
[2] *Journal of the British [Royal] Institute of International Affairs*, vol. i, 1922, p. 28.

of her tactics. In any case, a 'judgement of Solomon', while providing a satisfactory test of the validity of conflicting pretensions, loses much of its effectiveness when executed, and tends to promote some dissatisfaction on the part of each claimant, neither of whom is likely to be content with part of a baby from whom some vital organs have been severed.

Alliances with France and Roumania

Though Polish policy was characteristic of the spirit of her people, it need not be imagined that she would have pursued the same course in isolation. From the first, her resurrection had been looked upon with particularly friendly eyes by France, who welcomed the return of her historic ally, for whom Russia had only in comparatively recent times been substituted. Since the days of Richelieu, if not earlier, France had pursued a policy of balancing the central European power by means of alliances on its eastern frontiers, and among these allies, so long as she existed, Poland had usually been prominent. It is therefore intelligible, if scarcely excusable, that in all the questionable steps which have been outlined above Poland should have been able to rely on French support, and as early as 18 February 1921, the situation had been regularized by the signature of a definite treaty of alliance. This was followed, a few weeks later (3 March 1921), by the conclusion of a treaty between Poland and Roumania, who faced an even greater danger from Russia than her prospective ally, and was consequently not deterred by the same considerations which influenced the other members of the Little Entente. This treaty, however, did not constitute a general defensive alliance, but was restricted in its scope to the defence of the two countries on their eastern frontiers. The further development of relations between France, Poland, and the members of the Little Entente belong more properly to a later chapter. This period is concerned principally with the conclusion of the territorial settlement, and at this stage matters were as we have left them.

The moral likely to be drawn from the circumstances narrated in this chapter augured ill for the prospects of a new world based on the renunciation of force and the general acceptance of arbitral decisions. In practically every instance in which a nation had resorted to force or the threat of it, its ends had been promoted if not wholly achieved. Violence and disorder had restored Sopron to Hungary, the retention of Fiume by Italy had been facilitated by the inexcusable filibustering of D'Annunzio, without force it seems unlikely that Poland would have obtained possession of Vilna, or Lithuania have achieved the position in Memel which she was permitted to enjoy. Upper Silesia seems to point the same deplorable moral; and the Corfu incident constituted no exception. The Graeco-Bulgarian incident may seem to be one, but in this case it is at least doubtful whether war was commenced as an instrument of policy. It must anyhow be confessed that in no case but the last did a resort to 'direct action' compromise the prospects of the aggressor. Allowance must of course be made for the dissensions of the Supreme Council and their lack of available power in a period of war-weariness. But the fact unfortunately remains, and the hitherto unsolved difficulties connected with the establishment of an era of peace and security owe not a little to its existence.

VII

THE EXTERNAL POLICY OF SOVIET RUSSIA

BEFORE the close of 1920, all attempts at external interference with the revolutionary Government of Russia had broken down. British and other Allied support had been withdrawn from the 'White' commanders, Denikin had been defeated in 1919, Kolchak in the beginning, and Semenov and Wrangel before the end, of 1920, and, though the Japanese still occupied Vladivostok, Siberia east of Lake Baikal was not at this time under the direct rule of the Soviet Government in Moscow, which had recognized the proclamation of an independent federated republic in this region. This was only formally reunited with Great Russia after the Japanese evacuation in 1922.

It was essential, however, for the Soviet Government to endeavour to break through the economic ostracism to which European disapproval of its tenets had condemned it. If man cannot live by bread alone, the Russian famine of 1921 made it evident that the principles of Communism, in a capitalistic world, were no satisfactory substitute. The relaxation of those principles by the adoption of the New Economic Policy in April 1921 was symptomatic, and it was combined with repeated and determined efforts to re-establish commercial relations with the outside world. As early as May 1920 a trade delegation under M. Krassin had visited England, but though his mission bore some fruit in the shape of the Anglo-Russian Trade Agreement of March 1921, this did not effect any substantial improvement, since it was unaccompanied by *de jure* recognition, and made no provision for the re-establishment of that credit which the Russians had forfeited by the confiscation of foreign property and the repudiation of external debts. The British Government at this time was fully alive to the necessity of promoting the resumption of international trade, and it was due to the action of Mr Lloyd George at the Cannes Conference of January 1922 that Russia was enabled to attend the general Conference which succeeded it in Genoa in April of the same year. But the only tangible result of this meeting was the conclusion of the Treaty of Rapallo between Germany and the Soviet Government, which accentuated the suspicion and distrust of the other Powers participating. Apart from this, the negotiations broke down on the question of compensation for private property nationalized by the Revolutionary Government, a point on which Belgium and France opposed all suggestions for compromise, insisting upon full restitution. The attitude of the Russians, after their success with the Germans, was also far from conciliatory: they stood out in the later stages of the Conference for complete cancellation of war debts, and stipulated for the grant of extensive direct credits to their Government. They also claimed compensation for the results of the Allied support of the 'White' counter-revolutionaries.

A further difficulty which continued to impede the conclusion of satisfactory arrangements lay in the persistent Communist propaganda by means of which the Russians sought to foment revolutionary movements in all parts of the world. The original leaders of Soviet policy, indeed, regarded themselves as the missionaries of a world-wide economic and social revolution, and to them Russia was merely the instrument by which their ultimate objects could be promoted. Nationalism was irrelevant to their creed: it was for this reason that they were willing to subscribe to the doctrine of self-determination and to permit the existence of a large number of outwardly autonomous communities within the confines of Russia itself. Near the frontiers, such contented racial units which had adopted the Communist faith were politically a safeguard against counter-revolutionary invasion and a base for the extension of Bolshevik influence. Viewed from this standpoint, the republics of Karelia on the Finnish border, Moldavia confronting dissatisfied members of its own race within the confines of Roumania, and the Ukrainian and White Russian republics on the Polish frontier might have met with the approval of a national diplomat of the ordinary type. The method of Bolshevism was that of the Böig in *Peer Gynt*, to win without fighting; it was for this reason that the Soviet Government had been prepared to offer to Poland, in the summer of 1920, far better territorial terms than the Allies at the time were contemplating. By thus conciliating nationalistic aspirations they hoped to rally to their cause the workers of

Poland, and thus to bring another country within their political orbit; and it may well be that their object would have been achieved but for the unexpected success of the Polish army. In the neighbourhood of the Russian frontiers there was therefore no inconsistency between the national interests of the former Empire and those of Communism as a world-movement. The revolutionary movements which the Soviet leaders fostered in Bulgaria after the fall of M. Stambulisky's Government in 1923, and in Estonia and Latvia in 1924, were in no way disadvantageous to Russia, and, had they succeeded, as they had in Transcaucasia in 1920–1, they would have resulted in a valuable extension of the Russian sphere of control.

It was otherwise with the propaganda and intrigue conducted in Communist circles at a greater range. The Soviet Government was forced by circumstances to seek the financial and commercial assistance of the capitalist world, and their efforts in this direction were bound to be handicapped by the missionary activities of the Third International. During the lifetime of Lenin, there was little or no distinction between the organization of the International and that of the Russian Government. The same small hierarchy directed both, and there was therefore little possibility of divergence between their respective policies. They were two parts of the same machinery, both operated by the driving force of that numerically small *corps d'élite* which constituted the Communist Party. But, since Russia was an essential instrument in the international campaign, it was necessary to preserve its efficiency, and a natural cleavage soon grew up between those whose business it was to look after the tool and those who were concerned to use it, even if they damaged it, as part of a wider task. Thus arose a situation, most confusing to external students, wherein certain Communists in positions of authority constantly affirmed the essential identity of the Third International and the Soviet Government, while others, equally entitled to be heard, as strenuously denied it.

With Lenin's death, in January 1924, this divergence of outlook became clearly perceptible. The Kommissars entrusted with the internal and external affairs of Russia, Krassin and Chicherin, developed an increasingly specialized interest in their tasks. The latter, as Kommissar for Foreign Affairs, became, in language and action, hardly distinguishable from a conventional diplomatist of the old school. Zinoviev, on the other hand, who presided over the activities of the Third International, was quite undeterred in his task of permeating the world with Communist principles and propaganda, by any consideration of its reactions upon Russian prosperity. His methods were explained in public speeches with an engaging candour. While he continued openly to revile and ridicule the constitutional Socialism exemplified by such an organization as the British Labour Government in 1924, in diatribes described by Mr MacDonald as 'of great assistance to me and the Government', he yet valued it as an organism in whose constitution the red bacillus of Communism might hopefully be injected.

A Labour Government [he said] is the most alluring and popular formula for enlisting the masses in favour of a dictatorship of the proletariat. We must make the most of opportunities offered by such 'Labour' Governments as, for instance, MacDonald's. . . . The worker, peasant, and railwayman will first do their revolutionary 'bit', and only afterwards realize that this actually is 'the dictatorship of the proletariat'. [1]

In this view, he was doubtless encouraged by the rapidity with which the bourgeois-democratic revolution of March 1917 had developed into the proletarian-Bolshevik revolution of November. Indeed, since Communism does not rely upon majority support, this method of making the masses the unwitting instrument of a policy destined to enslave them possesses distinct advantages over a direct frontal attack. The failure of mass-revolution in Germany, Hungary, and elsewhere had only led to a violent reaction against Bolshevik tenets and propaganda, and the Third International had consequently come to rely, to an increasing extent, on the introduction of Communist 'cells' into the political organism. So proud, however, were the Russian revolutionaries of their methods, that they largely neutralized their effects by the extreme frankness with which they were in the habit of discussing them. Indeed, the 'cell' method was not regarded as essentially secret; [2] in Russia the minority admitted to the Communist Party was itself

---

[1] Speech to the Congress of the Third International, July 1924.
[2] Marx was particularly opposed to all forms of secret action.

looked upon as a nucleus of the same character. Zinoviev and his associates, therefore, were not only in the habit of expounding their *modus operandi* in public speeches; their correspondence with Communist organizations in other countries, which they made little attempt to conceal, was also couched in terms likely to arouse the liveliest protests from any constitutional government.

Authentic letters of this description came to light in 1923 and 1924, addressed to Norwegian, German, and American disciples. But disclosures of this kind naturally affected all efforts towards recognition and commercial *rapprochement* most prejudicially.

In Great Britain, especially, these tactics showed an astonishing degree of political ineptitude. The early date at which a trade agreement had been secured, during the tenure of office of a Coalition Government containing a strong Conservative element,[1] augured well for the prospects of full recognition and closer and more profitable relationships, but abstinence from propaganda was an essential part of the undertaking upon which the agreement was based, and with this undertaking the activities of the Third International were wholly incompatible. The British Government displayed great patience and forbearance: repeated violation of the terms of the undertaking was met with nothing stronger than protests; when, in February 1924, a Labour Government came into power, one of its first acts was to announce the *de jure* recognition of the U.S.S.R., and in April a conference was convened in London, having as its object the conclusion of treaties for the settlement of outstanding differences and the restoration of Russian credit by means of a loan guaranteed by the British Government. After the negotiations appeared to have broken down, agreement was eventually reached at the eleventh hour, but it soon became apparent that the treaties had little chance of being accepted by Parliament, owing to the opposition which they aroused not merely in Conservative but also in Liberal circles. At this point, therefore, Mr MacDonald decided to appeal to the country, though the actual issue on which Parliament was dissolved was not the treaties themselves, but the cognate

[1] The agreement was actually signed by a Conservative Chancellor of the Exchequer, Sir Robert Horne (16 March 1921).

matter of 'The Campbell Case', which had itself involved allegations of Soviet propaganda. It was therefore above all things necessary, from the standpoint of Russian diplomacy, that nothing should be done to alienate or alarm the public opinion of Great Britain.

Five days before the date fixed for the election England was startled by the disclosure of the notorious 'Zinoviev Letter'. Its authenticity remains in doubt, but there can be no dispute that it was in any case *ben trovato*. Such letters had in fact been written by Zinoviev, as we have seen, on numerous occasions, and the tactlessness involved in choosing this particular time was no more than the world's previous experience might lead it to expect of him. The inevitable result of the disclosure, coming when it did, was to ensure the return of a Conservative Government to power, and the treaties were incontinently scrapped.

De jure recognition, however, remained, and in the course of the year 1924 the Soviet Government was able to congratulate itself on having achieved important progress in this respect. Its desire to secure recognition had led it to promise specially favourable terms to the first Power to concede it. Italy, which had no serious outstanding claims against Russia, was accordingly first to open negotiations, and, though British recognition actually preceded Italian recognition, a commercial treaty, which included this advantage, was concluded in March 1924. M. Herriot's Government in France followed suit in October, and by the end of the year the number of European States which had accorded *de jure* recognition had risen from six to fifteen. The United States of America, however, continued to withhold recognition.

Meanwhile, the exponents of the international side of Russian Communism had been entertaining great hopes of winning the masses of Germany to their cause. Such a success would have been of profound importance, owing to the central position occupied by Germany among the countries of Europe; and the provocative action of France in occupying the Ruhr in January 1923 appeared to afford an opportunity which could not be neglected. The Third International consequently dispatched M. Karl Radek to Germany to maintain contact with the German Communist Party, and there seems a strong probability that a serious revolution would in fact have broken out in the course of 1923 had not the Russian emissary, who regarded such an outbreak as premature, exerted his influence to restrain the movement. For this action M. Radek was severely censured by the Central Committee of the Russian Communist Party. Owing, however, to the feelings aroused by the occupation of the Ruhr, the situation remained critical as late as October 1923, and disaster seems to have been but narrowly averted.

In Oriental countries the Russian propaganda was of a somewhat different type. In these parts of the world there were signs of a close co-operation between the political diplomacy of the Soviet Government and the missionary zeal of the Third International. It was, from the Communist point of view, quite unscientific to apply the same methods of propaganda to un-developed Oriental countries as to Western European ones. In the former the bourgeois revolution had not yet taken place, and they were not therefore in any sense ripe for the proletarian revolution and the collapse of capitalism. In these circumstances the Communists did not consider that they were in any way inconsistent in carrying on propaganda in those countries on nationalist rather than anti-capitalist lines. In India and the Far East, the enmity of the masses was directed rather against the alleged 'imperialism' than the 'capitalism' of Western Powers. The leaders of anti-European movements were Nationalists rather than Communists, and were, in fact, largely drawn from capitalist classes. For this reason, the contacts established by Soviet propaganda in these regions seemed rather to serve the interests of traditional Russian diplomacy than to attract converts to the cause of Communism.

At the end of 1924 the international revolutionary activities of the Russians had been discredited by a number of failures, while the diplomatic successes of the Soviet Government had been considerable, and would have been more so but for the obstacles to its policy created by the Third International. The revolutionary movements in different parts of Europe had been checked or defeated, in spite of unusually favourable circumstances, while in Great Britain the persistence of Bolshevik propaganda had proved an unrelieved disaster. In 1926 the miners' strike and the general strike of May had appeared to create a fresh opportunity for the encouragement of revolutionary Communism: large sums of money contributed by the Russian trade unions for the support of the strikers were therefore permitted by the Soviet Government, in spite of its control upon the export of currency, to be transmitted to Great Britain: but the British Trades Union Congress, fearing to be discredited, refused the sum sent for the support of the general strike, and the sums contributed to the miners merely gave rise to energetic protests from the British Government and increased the prevailing tension. Public opinion, both within and outside of Parliament, became increasingly critical of the supposed advantages to be derived from a continuance of trade relations, and it was pointed out that the balance of trade was increasingly in favour of Russia, while the value of British exports transmitted to that country formed a comparatively insignificant proportion of the national trade. Complaints of Soviet propaganda within the British Empire continued, and in February 1927 a Note, in the nature of a solemn and final warning, was dispatched by the British Government to Moscow, in which charges of subversive activities were made and substantiated. The reception of this ultimatum in Russia was not conciliatory, and in May matters reached a climax in consequence of a police raid on the premises occupied conjointly by the Soviet Trade Delegation and the Russian commercial organization known as Arcos Ltd. The formal ground for this action on the part of the police was information that a stolen document of a confidential nature had been conveyed to these premises. No evidence was found to substantiate this, but a quantity of compromising material bearing upon the question of the Soviet's anti-British activities was discovered. As a result of this the Trade Agreement of 1921 was abrogated, and the Soviet diplomatic staff and Trade Delegation were requested to leave the country. In June the expulsion of Zinoviev and Trotsky from the Central Committee of the Russian Communist Party, a decision finally confirmed in October, and followed in November by their expulsion from the party itself, suggested that efforts to promote world revolution were no longer regarded as an immediate objective by the Soviet authorities.

VIII

THE ISLAMIC WORLD

THE classification suggested by the title of this chapter, which is borrowed from the *Survey of International Affairs*, is adopted purely for reasons of convenience. Outside the main topic with which it will deal—the situation consequent upon the defeat of the Turks in the war and their subsequent recovery—there remain a certain number of events in other countries which cannot readily be treated in any other connexion, and which are not of sufficient importance in themselves to justify a separate chapter in a work of this scale. It is necessary to mention occurrences in Persia, in Afghanistan, in Morocco, and in Libya, the only connexion of which with the main subject to be treated is that they all took place in Mohammedan countries. Egypt, from its technical though insubstantial connexion with the Ottoman Empire, occupies an intermediate position. But it may well be questioned, in relation to the events recorded, how much reality attaches to the concept of an 'Islamic World'. Would not history have taken very much the same course if the religious creeds in these regions had differed from each other, and even if none of these people had been adherents of the Islamic faith? Islam, in theory, is a universal, potentially world-wide community, both in its political and religious aspects, and was presided over by a Caliph whose functions in relation to both these spheres was one and indivisible. It is true that this political theory of a unitary State was in practice abandoned long ago by Islamic thinkers. But in any Islamic conception there is no place for the modern European ideal of national States. With the progressive 'Westernization' of politically-minded Muslims—a phenomenon which was not confined to them—it was the unity of Islam which was defeated in the clash between the incompatible ideals. The history recorded here is essentially that of the triumph of nationalistic aspirations. The ineffectiveness of the pan-Islamic appeal was brought out, as early as November 1914, when the proclamation of a *Jihad*, or Holy War, in the

name of the Caliph, was generally disregarded. In the British
and Russian armies, Muslim troops fought loyally against the
Ottoman forces, while in Arabia the Sherif of Mecca, the Amir

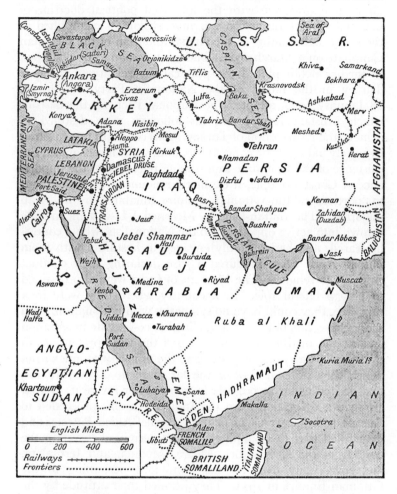

of Nejd, and other local potentates, cast off their allegiance to
Turkey, and embarked in what was to them a war of national
liberation against their co-religionists.[1]

[1] It is not of course denied that there are certain aspects in which the conception
of an 'Islamic World' has reality; it is merely questioned whether this unity was an
operative factor in the international reactions here described.

Abolition of the Caliphate

But the impossibility of reconciling the postulates of Islam on its temporal side with the imported political doctrine of national self-determination was most strikingly exemplified in the events culminating in the virtual abolition of the Ottoman Caliphate on 3 March 1924. The matters soon to be described in further detail placed the political sovereignty of the new Turkey in the hands of the Nationalist Party, which, on 28 January 1920, adopted the National Pact, on the basis of which Mustafa Kemal and his followers were destined to achieve the resurrection of Turkey. This covenant was inspired by purely nationalistic conceptions, and, while it recognized the existence of the Caliphate in a passing reference to the importance of Constantinople, it explicitly renounced Turkish claims to 'portions of the Ottoman Empire inhabited by an Arab majority'. The Sultan-Caliph, Mehmed VI, was meanwhile thrown into active opposition to the Nationalists, whose control he feared, and had not only engaged in hostilities with them but, in April 1920, procured a *fetva* declaring their conduct contrary to religion. The Muslims of India were also destined to play a fateful role. In a country where they were in a minority, they could have no sympathy with nationalism, even though a section of them was inclined to co-operate in agitation against the British *Raj*. They valued the wide pretensions of the Islamic Caliphate as a solace to the minority complex from which they suffered *vis-à-vis* the far more numerous Hindus, and desired as far as possible to maintain or revive its glories. In 1920 a delegation from the Indian Muslims proceeded to Europe to lay their views before the chief Allied Powers, and demanded that the Caliph should be permitted to retain the custody of the Holy Cities, Mecca, Medina, and Jerusalem, and sovereignty over all the dominions pertaining to the Ottoman Empire in 1914. They justified their attitude by the technically valid argument that in Islam the distinction between religious and temporal power was non-existent, and that the temporal power of the Caliphate was therefore of the essence of the office. The pretensions of the Caliphate came, therefore, into conflict with the aims of the Kemalists from two distinct quarters.

On 1 November 1922, the National Assembly voted a law in which they definitely renounced allegiance to the Constantinople Government; the Sultan-Caliph, Mehmed VI, left his country on 17 November, and on the following day the Assembly elected Abdul Mejid, the son of a former sultan, to the Caliphate in his place. Not only was this choice obnoxious to certain sections of the Islamic community, but the Westernized minds of the Nationalists evidently shared a prevalent European misconception as to the true nature of the Caliph's office. They had regarded it as possible to dissociate its religious functions from temporal authority, and were at once exposed to the charge of apostasy for the attempt to deprive the Caliphate of political power which was no less essential to it in the eyes of orthodox Muslims. The Angora Assembly had no intention whatever of recognizing any sovereignty but their own, and in October 1923 they defined their attitude by an enactment proclaiming Turkey a republic, and by the election of Mustafa Kemal to the Presidency. In March 1924, having meanwhile become painfully aware of the difficulties in the existing situation, through a well-meaning intervention by the Aga Khan and Mr Ameer Ali, the Assembly finally came down on the side of national independence as opposed to religious orthodoxy, by decreeing the expulsion from Constantinople of their puppet nominee, Abdul Mejid, and withdrawing recognition from the line hitherto holding the Caliphate. This action was followed by a drastic policy of secularization, which still further emphasized that Islam was no longer a controlling factor in the regime of the new Turkey. The effect of this policy was to leave the rest of the Muslim community free either to regard the Caliphate as in abeyance or to put forward alternative candidates. The Caliphate Congress of 1926 practically decided upon the former alternative.

Problems of Reorganization in Asiatic Turkey

The foregoing sketch of the circumstances leading to the abolition of the Caliphate, with its bearing on the preliminary question of the existence of an 'Islamic World' as a factor in international relations, has carried us away from the main theme of this chapter, and to some extent anticipated matters to which we must now return. The settlement of the problems connected with the former Ottoman Empire was complicated by a number of different factors. Overriding all was the circumstance that the Allied and Associated Powers had, in the terms of the fable, partitioned the bear's skin while the animal was still living. No Peace Treaty had been concluded with Turkey at the date when this history begins: the Treaty of Sèvres, the terms of which were settled in April 1920, was torn up by an unexpected resurrection of the Turkish nation, and a final settlement was delayed for three more years. But, even apart from the confusion thus occasioned, the problems to be faced were in any case sufficiently formidable. Part of the difficulty was traceable to the unregenerate days at the beginning of the war, when nations still thought in terms of annexation, and when practically all the participants entertained frequently incompatible hopes, based on a complex of treaties, promises, and understandings, of acquiring a share in the spoil. The Russian revolution, while it had removed one of these competitive interests, had created its own complications by altering the basis on which some of these arrangements rested.

But all this was as nothing compared with the confusion which arose when, in the later stages of the war, the world adopted, at least outwardly, an entirely new principle of settlement. The races released from Ottoman control added their clamour to that of disappointed annexationists by appeals to the 'blessed word' self-determination, and the compromise which the Peace Conference sought to effect by the institution of mandates was involved in a battle on at least two fronts. If the native races could be entrusted with independent sovereignty in an enlarged Arabia, why not, it was asked, in Syria, Palestine, or Mesopotamia? There was, in fact, good ground for differentiation in the heterogeneous character of the races and creeds included in the mandated areas, though this argument made a more cogent appeal to the European than to the Asiatic mind. But, even if this question could be satisfactorily answered, ought not the appointment of the mandatary to depend upon the free choice of the inhabitants, rather than upon an arbitrary decision of the Supreme Council, which sought thereby to implement as far as possible its previous treaty engagements? Such a question, indeed, was bound to follow from the Anglo-French declaration of 7 November 1918,

which defined the policy of the two Powers towards the peoples
emancipated from Turkish control as being 'the establishment
of National Governments and administrations deriving their
authority from the initiative and free choice of the indigenous
populations', expressed the intention of 'encouraging and
assisting the establishment of indigenous governments and
administrations in Syria and Mesopotamia', and disclaimed the
wish 'to impose on the populations of these regions any particular institutions'. Moreover, in Article 22 of the Treaty of
Versailles, and of the League Covenant, it was clearly laid down
that the wishes of the native communities, not the treaty claims
of certain European Powers, were to be the criterion. On the
other hand, these claims were still urged, insisted on, and in
many instances enforced; and sometimes the distinction in the
mind of the Power concerned between its rights and obligations
under the new and old arrangements was not very apparent.
Before, however, these difficulties could reach their acutest
stage, it was necessary to arrive at a definitive settlement with the
Power whose territory was the bone of contention.

The Settlement with Turkey

There is at first sight a strange paradox in the fact that of all
the Powers allied with Germany in the First World War, the
first to recover from defeat, the last to make peace, and the only
nation on the beaten side with whom terms were negotiated
rather than imposed was Turkey. In spite of the high fighting
quality of its soldiers, Turkey, in the estimation of Europe, had
been for considerably more than a generation the 'sick man',
whose survival was only due to the agreement of the European
Great Powers that he must not be too roughly handled, or
rather to their mutual jealousies. The Turkish collapse, moreover, appeared to have taken place at an earlier date than that
of any of the nations on the same side, with the possible exception of Bulgaria, whose signature of an armistice coincided with
the decisive victory of Allenby in Palestine. The armistice with
Turkey was signed at Mudros on 30 October, and thus preceded
by some days the cessation of hostilities with Germany and
Austria-Hungary. If anyone had predicted, in November 1918,
that definitive terms of peace with this apparently moribund
Power would not be concluded until after a lapse of nearly five

years, it is safe to say that his prophecy would have been received with amused incredulity.

Yet so it turned out. How did it happen? There was a multiplicity of causes, and it is probable that no one of these in isolation could have produced so surprising a result. It is historically as well as dramatically justifiable to make the whole issue hang on so accidental a circumstance as the bite of a monkey which killed King Alexander of Greece in October 1920.[1] This may well have been a *causa sine qua non*, though far from being a *causa causans*. There is also truth in the suggestion that the delay occasioned by President Wilson's determination to ascertain the wishes of the inhabitants by means of a Commission on the spot afforded a fatal opportunity to the forces of disorder to gather strength. The phenomenon has also been attributed, by Professor Toynbee, in a letter to the writer, to the fact that 'primitive organisms do not suffer so badly from shock as more complicated ones. . . . It was no accident that, of all the defeated Powers, Turkey and Russia, which collapsed most ignominiously during the war, were also each able to fight a war-after-the-war almost immediately. A low organism is incompetent, but you cannot stun it or kill it as easily as a higher one.' With due respect to such an authority, I doubt myself whether this argument can fairly be applied to the Turkish organism. But the fundamental reason was the increasing weakness of the forces behind the Allied demands, due partly to demobilization and war-weariness, and partly to the jealousy and dissension which grew among the Allies themselves. The chief ground for such dissension lay in the varied and scarcely reconcilable commitments with regard to the partition of Turkish territory into which the Allies had been driven by the necessity for purchasing the support of additional auxiliaries.

First of these in point of time was the bribe offered for Italian co-operation by the Secret Treaty of London of April 1915. By this, in addition to the compensation at the expense of Austria-Hungary which created difficulties in the application of pure Wilsonian doctrine to the Treaty of St Germain, Italy

---

[1] Cf. Churchill, W. S. *The World Crisis.* 5 vols. London, Butterworth, 1915–29, vol. v, p. 386: 'It is perhaps no exaggeration to remark that a quarter of a million persons died of this monkey's bite.'

was promised, in regrettably vague language, 'a just share of the Mediterranean region adjacent to the province of Adalia'. Her disappointment in the realization of her anticipated claims in Europe was not likely to render more modest the Italian interpretation of this elastic phraseology. But from an even earlier stage, Great Britain had been dangling the bait of an independent Arab Empire before the eyes of the Emir Husein, Sherif of Mecca, and though the sweeping claims which this ruler's ambition dictated could not be accepted without important reservations, it was necessary that these reservations should not be so emphasized or defined as to obscure the lustre or risk the effectiveness of what was promised. Here, too, therefore, there was a certain vagueness.[1]

In these circumstances, while deeming it politic to associate herself with the inducements held out to the Arabs, France felt the need for some more precise definition of her own share of the prospective spoils, a claim to which had been generally reserved as early as 18 March 1915, in the 'Constantinople Agreement' between Great Britain, France, and Russia. Her desire was gratified by the Sykes-Picot Agreement concluded, behind the backs of Italy and of Mecca, between France, Russia, and Great Britain in May 1916. This agreement is of importance, since it became the basis, with certain minor adjustments, of the settlement proposed by the abortive Treaty of Sèvres.

A further attempt was made to define the Italian share in Asia Minor, at St Jean de Maurienne in 1917, but, owing probably to Russian objections, this arrangement never attained a fully recognized validity.

At the Peace Conference a new claimant to territorial acquisitions in Asia Minor turned up, in the shape of M. Venizelos, under whose inspiration Greece had abandoned neutrality and performed conspicuous services for the Allies in the closing phase of the war. It is right to say 'M. Venizelos' rather than Greece, since it was only that part of the Greek population which supported the Cretan statesman which had earned the gratitude of the Entente: the bias of the ex-King Constantine and his partisans had been definitely on the side of the Central Powers. Venizelos's claim on behalf of his country

---

[1] The late Dr Hogarth in *History of the Peace Conference*, vol. vi, p. 121, says: 'the wording [of our pledge] justified Husein's interpretation.'

to the Smyrna area was resisted by the Americans on grounds of principle, and bitterly opposed by the Italians, who alleged that the territory in question had already been ear-marked, in whole or in part, for them under the Treaty of London, and/or the agreement of St Jean de Maurienne. It received, however, the support of Great Britain and France, and unfortunately at this juncture the Italian delegation temporarily retired, in umbrage, from the Conference. During the interval before they returned, the Italians began to extend the military occupation which they had already begun in Adalia, north-westwards in the direction of Smyrna. A resort to the pressure of a *fait accompli* appeared to be in contemplation, and the French and British were thus enabled to persuade Mr Wilson to consent to steps to forestall it.

The Mudros armistice permitted the Allies to occupy strategic points in Turkish territory in the event of a situation arising which threatened their security. Under cover of the guns of Allied warships, a Greek force was landed in Smyrna on 14 May 1919. We need not reopen the bitter controversy raised by reciprocal charges of atrocities brought by Turkey against Greece and vice versa, since the disastrous policy of entrusting the maintenance of order among Turks to their traditional enemy and former vassal was inevitably calculated to fan the flames of Nationalist indignation, while the resentment of a tricked and disappointed Italy would just as certainly have followed in any event. For the real motive of the step was too transparent for either the Turks or the Italians to be deceived.

Immediately after landing, the Greek force became involved in a bloody conflict with the inhabitants, which was followed in a few days by an advance for some distance into the interior. Though the military situation now remained unchanged for some time, the forces which were to wreck the schemes of the Allies were already in motion. Turkish Nationalism had found its Man of Destiny. As early as 9 June Mustafa Kemal began his agitation in Anatolia. Before the end of the year the control of affairs beyond the Bosporus had passed, *de facto*, from the Constantinople Government, and the British General Staff had warned the Cabinet that 'the acquisition by Greece of any portion of the Pontus', or her 'permanent occupation of any part of the Aidin vilayet' (of which Smyrna was the capital), were among the measures which could not be pursued without greater military resources than the Allies seemed to have readily at their disposal.[1] Before this, in October, the illness of President Wilson and the first rejection of the German Treaty in the United States Senate foreboded the imminent withdrawal of support from the Greeks by one of the nations on whose authority they were acting.

In January 1920 revolt was spreading to Constantinople itself. On the 28th the Nationalists in the new Chamber of Deputies adopted the 'National Pact', soon to be the basis of the Kemalist programme. In March the Allies were forced to occupy Constantinople, and eject the Kemalists, though in February the final decision had been announced that the city was to be left by the Treaty in Turkish hands.[2] By the end of April the full terms of the Treaty of Sèvres were settled, and in May they were announced.

We are for the moment concerned with its provisions purely from the Turkish point of view, and need not go into arrangements made between the Allies with regard to the ceded territory. By the Treaty of Sèvres, then, Turkey was to lose Arabia, Palestine, Syria, and Mesopotamia, including in the two latter the length of the Baghdad railway east of the Gulf of Iskanderun. She renounced all rights in Africa and the Mediterranean islands; Armenia, with a frontier to be decided by the President of the United States, was to be free and independent; and autonomy was to be granted to Kurdistan. Then came the bitterest drop of all. Smyrna and its hinterland were to be left under Greek administration for five years, after which their fate should be decided by a plebiscite.

Though the Treaty was not finally signed until 10 August, its terms, as has been said, were made known in May. In June, Kemalist forces attacked the British positions on the Ismid Peninsula. It was not a serious engagement, and the Turks were quickly induced to retire out of range, but it was a threat with unpleasant possibilities. France, meanwhile, under

---

[1] Churchill, *The World Crisis*, vol. v, p. 371.

[2] The occupation of Constantinople could be justified under the terms of the Armistice. A number of prominent Turkish Nationalists were, however, arrested in their private houses and conveyed by British warships to Malta. It is difficult to contend that this action was covered by the Armistice provisions, and it certainly had important reactions upon Turkish national feelings.

circumstances later to be described, had her hands pretty full in Syria. The two Allies, with some misgivings, thereupon accepted an offer from M. Venizelos to send a Greek force to cope with the situation. The Greek advance began at once, and was at first unexpectedly successful. The Kemalist forces were driven back, the Treaty of Sèvres was signed in Constantinople (10 August 1920), and for the moment the outlook seemed promising. But the war went on.

In October the fateful monkey bit the young King Alexander, and his death from the effects brought about a general election in Greece. Venizelos was defeated, and resigned, and the ex-King, Constantine, returned. Greece thereby forfeited all claims to Allied consideration, and was left friendless, except for the personal sympathy and trust of Mr Lloyd George. Though for a considerable time the Greek troops continued to progress, and even reached within some forty miles of Angora by the end of the following August (1921), the Italians had begun to withdraw from Asia in April 1921. In September 1921 the tide turned, with the defeat of the Greeks at Sakaria River. All attempts by the Allies to mediate between the belligerents failed, and in October M. Franklin-Bouillon, on behalf of France, secretly negotiated a separate peace with the Angora Government.

The announcement of this agreement called forth a vigorous protest from Lord Curzon. Not only had France, in consideration of valuable commercial concessions, withdrawn from Cilicia and made peace with the Turks, but she had surrendered ground allotted to Syria under the Treaty of Sèvres, and brought the greater part of the railway line, running through the north of the mandated area, within the Turkish frontier. But the mischief was done, and Great Britain had to be content with a French admission that the territorial clauses of this agreement, as of the others, were subject to adjustment in the final settlement with Turkey.

The position of the Greek army was now desperate. Of the Powers at whose invitation it had entered Anatolia, the United States had retired, France had not only made peace but, in Mr Winston Churchill's words, 'was now ardently backing and re-arming the Turks',[1] and Great Britain, almost completely

---

[1] Churchill: *The World Crisis*, vol. v, p. 413.

demobilized, was in no position, even if she so desired, to render effective assistance. Italy, with no reason from the first to favour the Greek adventure, had, as we have seen, withdrawn almost entirely, and in April 1922 had followed the French example by concluding, for commercial advantage, an agreement with the enemy. Only the neutral zone protecting the Straits remained in Allied occupation. The end was at hand. In the last days of August 1922 the Greek army was in precipitate retreat towards the coast, and at the beginning of September 1922 the victorious Kemalists entered Smyrna.

The danger was now no longer addressed to the ill-fated and abandoned soldiers of Greece; there was a pressing risk that the weakness and lack of cohesion of the Supreme Council would be exposed with incalculable results. If Kemal and his army, swollen with triumph, were to obtain a footing in Europe, it was hardly too much to say that the whole settlement achieved by the blood and sacrifice of the First World War might be endangered.[1]

Between Europe and such a catastrophe stood but a few battalions of the Allied forces, guarding the approaches to the Straits at Chanak and across the Ismid Peninsula. They were supported by the guns of the British Mediterranean fleet, stationed in the Sea of Marmora; but they were sorely in need of reinforcement. At this critical juncture, the unhappy dissensions of the Allies produced their most deplorable results. The French and Italian Governments issued orders for the withdrawal of their forces, and on 21 September 1922, these troops evacuated Asia. It must be remembered to the everlasting credit of Mr Lloyd George that in this apparently desperate isolation he stood firm. He had already issued an appeal to the British Dominions for support, in circumstances of haste which poignantly illustrated the necessity for improved machinery in the Commonwealth for the co-operation in foreign policy which is essential. Nevertheless, the Dominions, though protesting, responded to the call. Before,

---

[1] Such was the apparent position, though it must be remembered that the Turkish war aims were, in fact, strictly limited under the National Pact. But 'l'appétit vient en mangeant', and it is possible that such overwhelming success would have increased Mustafa Kemal's demands. In any case, the blow to the moral authority of the Supreme Council in Europe would, it seems to me, have been extremely serious.

however, their assistance could be forthcoming, the bold stand
of the British had achieved its purpose. Mustafa Kemal was
fortunately not only a successful military leader, but a man
great and wise enough not to push his advantage to extremes.
He agreed to a Conference with the Allies which assembled on
3 October at Mudania. Once more the attitude of the French
and Italians was unhelpful, and the armistice agreed upon on
11 October was due exclusively to British firmness, in contact
with Kemal's statesmanship. But the crisis was ended, and the
way at last cleared for the final settlement, which was embodied
in the Treaty of Lausanne (23 August 1923).

Having regard to the circumstances, the losses to which the
Allies submitted in this Treaty were remarkably few and small.
The Turks had made up their minds to renounce the Arab
provinces, and they stuck to their decision. British and French
interests were probably most seriously affected by the abolition
of the Capitulations, upon which the Turks firmly insisted.
The main loss fell upon Greece, who was, throughout, the
catspaw of the Allies. Turkey, of course, recovered Smyrna,
and in Europe her territory was extended to include eastern
Thrace, with Adrianople and Karagach. Of the islands, she
retained Imbros, Tenedos, and the Rabbit Islands near the
entrance to the Dardanelles. But two zones were demilitarized,
one on the Thracian frontier, and the other in the area of the
Straits. The Anatolian frontier remained as defined in the
Franklin-Bouillon agreement. All things considered, a contributor to the *History of the Peace Conference of Paris* [1] is probably
justified in predicting that the Treaty inaugurated a more lasting settlement than any other which followed the war. It was
not imposed but negotiated, and in that fact lay hopeful
prospects for its permanence.

Mosul and Iraq

By the Treaty of Lausanne the declared aims of the Angora
Turks were achieved, with one exception. The claim of the
National Pact to territories inhabited by the non-Arab Muslim
majorities logically extended to the vilayet of Mosul, in a large
part of which the Kurdish element was predominant. Hence,
as a matter of sentiment and prestige, the Turks were unwilling

[1] Vol. vi, p. 115.

to assent to leaving the northern boundary of Mesopotamia at the line laid down in the Treaty of Sèvres. This sentimental objection was reinforced by the practical consideration that the Kemalist policy of absorbing and 'Turkifying' the Kurds was likely to be hampered if a large Kurdish element, enjoying a greater degree of freedom and autonomy, was established immediately outside the Turkish frontier. For these reasons, the Turks held out, at Lausanne, against the incorporation of the Mosul vilayet in the new territory of Iraq, for which a mandate had been provisionally allocated to Great Britain by a decision of the Supreme Council in May 1920. At Lord Curzon's suggestion, the Treaty laid down that the question should be referred to the League of Nations, in the event of no agreed solution having been found within a period of nine months. In August 1924, therefore, the matter came before the Council of the League, which appointed a strictly neutral commission of inquiry to investigate the problem on the spot. In October, in consequence of complaints by both parties of attempts to encroach on the line representing the *status quo*, an extraordinary session of the League of Nations Council was held in Brussels, which laid down a provisional frontier, thereafter known as 'the Brussels Line', which approximately corresponded to the northern boundary of the former vilayet.

While the question was still undetermined, the Turks prejudiced their position in the eyes of the League by the repressive measures which they adopted in consequence of a Kurdish revolt in 1925, towards non-Turkish minorities, especially the Chaldean Christians living immediately to the north of the 'Brussels Line'. Iraq was flooded with refugees, and the atrocities perpetrated by the Turks were incontestably established by the neutral report of a League representative, the Estonian General Laidoner. The award of the League consequently adhered substantially to the 'Brussels Line', and thereby included in Iraq practically the whole of the Mosul vilayet. The question was finally settled, though after some delay and not without considerable hesitation on the part of the Turks, by the signature, in June 1926, of a tripartite Treaty between Turkey, Iraq, and Great Britain, which adopted the frontier thus determined.

But the settlement of the status and frontiers of Iraq was

complicated by other factors besides the recalcitrance of the Angora Government. The most formidable of these was the attitude of the inhabitants to the proposed mandate, but there were also difficulties resulting from the claims of other Western Powers to interests in the territory. By the Sykes-Picot agreement, Mosul had been allotted to France, but this arrangement had been founded on the fact that Russia also contemplated territorial acquisitions in Asia Minor, since it was therefore considered advisable to interpose a third Power, as a buffer, between the Russian zone and the British. With the Russian revolution the reason for such a policy disappeared; this was recognized by France as well as by Great Britain, and the transference of Mosul to the British zone consequently met with no serious objection; in fact, as early as the beginning of 1919, this modification had been accepted by M. Clemenceau. But a further complication was introduced by the desire of other Powers for a share in the oil resources of the district, though the importance of this factor has often been exaggerated. The British Government consistently repudiated any intention of establishing a monopoly over the oil of Iraq, and indeed rejected, in 1925, an offer from the Angora Government of a concession to a British company of all the oil in exchange for the return of the Mosul vilayet to Turkey. The only rights which we claimed to the oil of Iraq were dependent on a concession granted by the Turks before the war to a British company—the Turkish Petroleum Company. In this the Deutsche Bank had held 25 per cent of the shares, and the claims of France were satisfied by the transfer, under the San Remo agreement of April 1920, of this German interest to a French group. The United States, however, objected to the condition in the San Remo agreement that the Turkish Petroleum Company should be under permanent British control, and delayed the completion of the mandate for Mesopotamia by contending that equality of treatment for all nations, whether members of the League or not, was an essential principle of the mandatory system. Their objections were, however, ultimately removed by the offer of shares in the Company to the Standard Oil and other American interests.

Meanwhile, the mandate had been repudiated by the natives of Mesopotamia themselves. The assignment of the mandate to

Great Britain had hardly been announced when a serious rising broke out in Iraq. As a writer in the *History of the Peace Conference of Paris* puts it,[1] 'new American wine was fermenting in old Arabian bottles', and the inhabitants were indulging in premature hopes of complete national independence. As a conciliatory step, the British Government procured the election of Feisal, son of the King of the Hijaz, to the throne of Iraq (August 1921), and shortly afterwards concluded a treaty with him which sought to retain the control envisaged by the mandate, while abandoning its form. To the League the Treaty was represented as the machinery by which the duties pertaining to the still inchoate mandate could be performed, while to the Iraqis it was given, as far as possible, the appearance of a title deed to independent sovereignty.

The Mandate for Palestine

As has been hinted earlier in this chapter, the mandates allotted in respect of Iraq, Palestine, and Syria could only be justified as a practical compromise designed to satisfy a number of conflicting claims, and partially to reconcile the main principles adopted at the close of the war with undertakings made at an earlier stage. They were hardly consistent with the language of the Anglo-French declaration of November 1918, and it is impossible seriously to contend that they obeyed the conditions of Article 22 of the League Covenant. No candid person can admit that 'the wishes of these communities' (formerly belonging to the Turkish Empire) were in fact 'a principal consideration in the selection of the mandatary'. The origin of the choice imposed by the Supreme Council is in each case clearly to be found in the secret treaties concluded in the early stages of the war, and, in particular, in the Sykes-Picot agreement of May 1916. That agreement conceded to France her foothold in Syria, and gave to Great Britain Baghdad and southern Mesopotamia; moreover, while it vaguely suggested some form of international regime in the Holy Land, it recognized the special interests of Great Britain in that region by reserving to her the ports of Haifa and Akka (Acre). It is possible to argue, in spite of the Mesopotamian revolt of 1920, that, if compelled to accept any tutelage at all, the choice of the

[1] Vol. vi, p. 184.

Iraqis would have fallen upon Great Britain; the same may be said of Palestine; but the inhabitants were not, in fact, consulted. With regard to the allocation of the Syrian mandate to France, there is good reason to believe that the Power chosen was peculiarly unacceptable to the majority.[1] There was, perhaps, no alternative mandatary available, for the United States had withdrawn to her own continent, and Great Britain, through Mr Lloyd George, had expressly declined the responsibility in advance. Since, however, the reason given for this refusal was the suspicion and odium which the acceptance of the mandate by this country would create in France, the case is not materially altered.

In Palestine, however, it was not primarily the fact that the territory was subjected to external control, nor any antipathy to Great Britain as the mandatary, which were the real sources of trouble. Though the King of the Hijaz seems to have interpreted British promises as including Palestine within the confines of the Arab Empire, such a solution would have been no more consistent with self-determination than that actually adopted; moreover, some special regime for the impartial safeguarding of the different religious interests in this territory had in fact been contemplated at least as early as 1916, and the inhabitants, recognizing England's reputation for fair play, would probably have been more content to see such a regime administered by her than by any other European Power or combination. The factor which gave rise to discontent was the British pledge to the Zionists.

This pledge, as expressed by Mr (afterwards Lord) Balfour in the House of Commons on 2 November 1917, was in the following terms:

His Majesty's Government views with favour the establishment in Palestine of a national home for the Jewish people, and will use its best endeavours to facilitate the achievement of this object, it being clearly understood that nothing shall be done which may prejudice the civil and religious rights of existing non-Jewish communities in Palestine or the rights and political status enjoyed by Jews in any other country.

[1] Though, so far as the mandate was originally intended to apply directly to the coastal zone only, a certain justification might be found in the undoubted preference of the Lebanese Maronites for France.

The motives behind the adoption of this policy, though including, no doubt, an element of disinterested idealism, were to a great extent definitely strategic. It was in the first place advantageous to cover the approaches to the Suez Canal by a territory favourable to British interests. But the immediate object was to enlist on the side of the Allies the sympathies of Jewry, which, being naturally anti-Russian, tended by reason of our alliance with that country to gravitate to the side of the Central Powers, who were also making bids for its support. In particular, in 1917, it was desirable to check the pro-German activities of the Russian Jews, who were already believed to have done much to bring about the disintegration of the Tsarist power.

If these were the objects of the policy, it may be doubted whether they were completely achieved. The situation in Russia was certainly not improved, and, throughout the world, a considerable section of influential Jewish opinion has always been hostile to Zionism. On the other hand, Arab and Syrian sympathies were alienated from the outset, the latter by the subdivision of the boundaries of Syria, and the former by fears, based partly upon a misunderstanding of the terms of the pledge, that Arab interests would be subordinated to Jewish, and the balance of the population gravely disturbed by Jewish immigration. The policy was certainly in direct opposition to the wishes of the indigenous majority, about 90 per cent of the inhabitants being, at the time, of non-Jewish origin. Time alone could show whether the two main obligations of the mandate, the establishment of a Jewish national home and the development of self-government, were in fact compatible.

The idealistic or sentimental side of the policy, shared in common by its Jewish and Christian promoters, must engage the sympathy of every one who has been impressed by the poetic prophecies of a return to Zion which adorn the Old Testament. But it seems an ideal at best only capable of partial achievement, and, having regard to the difficulties to which even this partial realization gives rise, this may well be considered a conspicuous example of the dangers of introducing excessive idealism into a peace settlement.

Having regard to these difficulties, the British administration of the mandate must be acknowledged to have been at first comparatively successful. From the point of view of the industrial and agricultural development of the country, Zionist colonization, though carefully restricted in numbers, could claim a remarkable measure of achievement. If the choice of Sir Herbert Samuel as the first High Commissioner was expected in any quarter to result in any undue favouring of the Jews, the expectation was certainly belied by his strictly impartial administration, and though the announcement of the mandate in April 1920 was immediately followed by anti-Jewish riots in Jerusalem, and there were other disturbances in 1921 and, outside Palestine, on the occasion of Lord Balfour's visit in 1925, Sir Herbert's tenure of office was sufficiently peaceful to admit of the reduction of the British garrison, by 1925, to insignificant proportions. The conciliatory intentions of the Government towards the Arabs were demonstrated by the grant, in 1923, of autonomy to Transjordania under the sovereignty of Husein's son, Abdullah. On the other hand, in Palestine itself, as later events were to prove, the irreconcilable antagonisms of Arab and Jew remained a permanent source of anxiety, the non-cooperative policy pursued by the Arabs rendered the creation of the Legislative Council, originally contemplated, impossible, and it was necessary to continue semi-autocratic control. In the circumstances, however, the measure of peaceful progress achieved was highly creditable to the British Administration.

The Syrian Mandate

Very different was the progress of events in the neighbouring territory entrusted to France. French rule bore too close a resemblance to that annexation for which it was a substitute, and the limits of the mandate, as originally contemplated, were in fact soon extended by a process of military conquest.

At the outset, indeed, considerable efforts were made by Great Britain to restrict the French trusteeship to the coastal territory which alone had been allocated to France by the Sykes-Picot agreement. This compact had envisaged, between the French and British territories, a confederation of Arab States or one independent Arab State, which would have included the towns of Damascus, Homs, Hama, and Aleppo. Of this region the Emir Feisal, Britain's faithful ally, was in actual occupation at the time of the Armistice. On 3 October 1918, Feisal had galloped into Damascus at the head of his troops, and had there hoisted the Arab flag, with the authority of General Allenby and the British Government. He had immediately announced the formation of an independent government, and had done much by a conciliatory policy to consolidate his position. At a meeting of the Supreme Council held on 20 March 1919, Mr Lloyd George expressly contended that to admit a French claim to Damascus, Homs, Hama, and Aleppo would be a breach of faith with the Arabs. This position, so far as words went, was consistently maintained. When, in September 1919, it was agreed that the British garrison should be withdrawn from Syria, it was stipulated that in the area reserved for the Arabs by the Sykes-Picot agreement Arab troops and not French should take its place.

Feisal, however, had good reason to doubt whether, in the absence of his British friends, the French would long acquiesce in the situation. In March 1920 he took the false step of accepting the crown of Syria and Palestine, an action necessarily repudiated not only by France but also by Great Britain, the prospective mandatary for the Holy Land. At the Conference of San Remo, on 24 April, the Supreme Council definitely assigned the mandates for Syria, Palestine, and Iraq, the first to France, the two latter to Great Britain. The announcement of these decisions caused sufficient unrest in Syria to favour the French design. On 14 July General Gouraud, the French High Commissioner, dispatched an ultimatum to Feisal, which, though its requirements were wholly incompatible with any approach to Arab sovereignty, was immediately accepted. The inevitable disorders, however, broke out; a French outpost was attacked by some Arab horsemen; and the French seized the opportunity to launch a general offensive and to drive Feisal out of the country. Their action was of course not approved in Great Britain. Mr Bonar Law had to explain to a critical House of Commons that he was officially assured that the occupation of the disputed territory by the French would be only temporary. This expectation, however, proved unduly optimistic. The future situation was destined to be regulated, once again, by an act of violence and a *fait accompli*.

It would, of course, be unjust to condemn the action or

inaction of the British Government in these difficult circumstances. They did what they could to compensate Feisal, by promoting his election to the throne of Iraq, and they recognized his brother, Abdullah, as ruler in Transjordania, though this step was partly directed to dissuading him from a threatened attack upon the French in Syria. But the methods by which the French attained their object inevitably suggested that, in the post-war as in the pre-war world, the possession of preponderant military power was an asset, and that equal justice for small and great was still only to be found in an unrealized Utopia.

The French administration of the territory over which their mandate now extended was not calculated to allay the disaffection which their presence was in any case likely to arouse. The administrative staff was generally inexperienced and for the most part ignorant of Arabic, while those officials who did not suffer from these defects were military officers from the African colonies and protectorates, whose methods tended to be autocratic. Behind a façade of native self-government set up by the appointment of docile nominees of the mandatory Power, France exercised an all-pervasive legislative and administrative control. A regime of martial law, characterized by frequent deportations, continued to be enforced. It was natural, perhaps, that the Lebanese Christians, who had long enjoyed French protection and constituted the element of the population most friendly to the mandate, should be specially favoured, but the extension, in September 1920, of the Lebanon territory to include a large accretion of non-Christian inhabitants complicated the problems of self-government while arousing unrest through the suspicion of favouritism which it created. Elsewhere, French policy suffered from vacillation and lack of continuity. The whole mandate was first subdivided into five separate States—Greater Lebanon, the territory of the Alouites or Alawiyin, Aleppo, Damascus, and the Jebel ed Druse. This step was in itself open to criticism, as being based rather on the maxim *divide et impera* than on an intention to facilitate that co-operation upon which progress towards complete autonomy depended. An attempt was, however, almost immediately made to reverse this policy, by decreeing the federation of three of the five units. But this was thwarted by the particularist agitation which the original subdivision had promoted, though the States of Aleppo and Damascus were fused into a single unit. The uncertainty which these repeated and rapid changes of policy produced was subsequently held, by the Mandates Commission, to have materially conduced to the trouble which ensued. Other points which aroused complaint were the excessive encouragement of the French language in schools and law courts, and the substitution of a note issue, based on the rapidly depreciating French franc, for the stable Syrian currency which had previously existed. Matters, however, did not reach a critical stage until after the recall of the just and popular High Commissioner, General Weygand, in November 1924, and the arrival of his successor, General Sarrail, in 1925. Further developments may therefore be deferred to a later chapter.

Events in Arabia

In Arabia, until 1914, the interests of Great Britain had been mainly confined to Aden and the coast of the Persian Gulf, but the possibility of Turkish intervention on the side of the Central Powers at once gave rise to negotiations with the principal Arabian rulers. Persuasion, based upon financial subsidies, was brought to bear by both sides, with the result that the Turks retained the support of Ibn Rashid of Jebel Shammar in central Arabia, and the Imam of Sana in the neighbourhood of the Aden protectorate. England was more successful. She was already in treaty relations with the coastal chiefs of the Persian Gulf, and these she maintained. The Sheikh of Kuweit, at the head of the Gulf, was induced, in November 1914, to co-operate in the capture of Basra in return for the recognition of his territory as an independent principality under British protection. The Idrisi Sayyid of Sabya was brought into nominal if not active alliance by a subsidy and a similar guarantee of independence in the following year. Of far greater importance, however, were the relations established with the Wahhabi chief, Ibn Saud of Riyad, and the Emir Husein, who, as ruler of the Hijaz, controlled the Holy Cities of Islam.

Wahhabism was a militant puritanical movement in Islam which, in the early years of the nineteenth century, had established a dominant influence in the peninsula. Acting as its agent, the house of Saud had, by 1806, captured Mecca and Medina, and thus become the masters of most of Arabia. It was then overthrown by the Egyptian Pasha, Mehemet Ali, and reduced to impotence till, in 1901, it recovered Riyad from the rival house of Al Rashid, a gain which was consolidated by further territorial acquisitions up to the date of the First World War, when its authority extended to the shore of the Persian Gulf. Ibn Saud had thus recovered an influence sufficiently important to attract the notice of the Government of India, within whose sphere fell the negotiations dealing with the eastern side of the peninsula. As he had been engaged in hostilities with the Turks as recently as 1913, and his hereditary enemy, Ibn Rashid, had adhered to the opposite side, the prospects of enlisting his help in the British cause were hopeful from the first, and in December 1915 a treaty was concluded with him engaging his assistance, or at least his neutrality, in return for a subsidy of £5,000 a month, and the recognition of his hereditary right to his existing possessions. During the war, Ibn Saud did little more than hold in check the activities of his rival, Ibn Rashid, but his services, such as they were, were no doubt fully worth the comparatively slight expenditure in which they involved Great Britain.

Meanwhile, the British Foreign Office had arrived at an understanding, less precise in its terms, but of far greater immediate assistance, with the Emir Husein of the Hijaz. The course which British interests led the Government to encourage Husein to pursue was independently prompted by his own ambition. Negotiations had begun in 1914, and elicited, immediately after Turkey's entry into the war, a promise that the enemies of the Allies would not, in any event, be assisted. In August 1915 a letter from Husein disclosed the grandiose scope of his dreams of empire. He aimed at an independent Arab State extending from the Mediterranean to the Persian border as far north as the 37th parallel of latitude, thus including, outside the borders of Arabia, nearly the whole of Syria, as well as Palestine and Mesopotamia. The scale of his requirements placed the British authorities, already cognizant of rival claims in much of this area, in a difficult predicament, and it was fortunate that the Emir's own precipitancy dispensed with the necessity for a strict formulation of the limits of British concession. Without waiting for the conclusion of a treaty, Husein launched his revolt against the Turks in May 1916.

It does not fall within the province of this history to describe the ensuing campaign. As is well known, to the end of the war, Arab and British troops co-operated closely in the Turkish field of operations, and while Husein and his son Feisal were freely supplied with arms and munitions, as well as with a financial subsidy amounting to some £2,400,000 a year, the services which they rendered left them, whatever interpretation might be put on promises actually made, with substantial claims on British gratitude. Some of the complications arising out of our pledges to the Arabs are considered elsewhere. We are here concerned with the Emir's relations with his Arabian neighbours, and the fate which ultimately overtook him.

The first false step taken by the Emir Husein was to cause himself to be proclaimed 'King of the Arabs' by the notables of Mecca in October 1916. His pretensions could not be accepted by Great Britain, which, as we have seen, had guaranteed the independence of a number of other Arab protégés, and the European Allies would only recognize his title to be styled 'King of the Hijaz'. His claim was especially provocative to the rising power of the Wahhabis, and though Ibn Saud was for the moment restrained from open hostility by the fact that both he and his rival were in the pay of the same European Power, he began by systematic proselytization to wean some of the minor tribal leaders from their allegiance to the Hijaz. In 1917 he won over the chief of the oasis of Khurmah, a defection which led Husein injudiciously to attempt the occupation of the oasis in the following year. Strained relations followed, which culminated, in May 1919, in the battle of Turabah, in which the forces of Ibn Saud victoriously encountered those of the King of the Hijaz. A humorous element was introduced into this episode by the fact that each belligerent was in receipt of arms and money from a different British department: the Foreign Office and the India Office might be considered as being at war, and the theoretical possibilities of this situation are of a kind to which only a Gilbert and Sullivan opera could do justice. Intermittent hostilities continued, though Ibn Saud was for the time being deterred from pursuing his advantage to extremes, partly by fear of losing his British subsidy, and partly because he had not yet finally settled accounts with his hereditary antagonist, Ibn Rashid. In November 1921, however, he decisively defeated this enemy, and annexed his territory, and, in March 1924, the second reason for delay was removed by the termination of his subsidy.

Meanwhile, Husein had carried his intransigence still further, to the point of alienating all possible allies. The disappointment of his hopes by the creation of the Syrian and Palestinian mandates led him to refuse to ratify the Treaty of Versailles, or to enter into treaty relationship with Great Britain. He also offended Egypt by his attitude in disputes which arose in connexion with the Mecca pilgrimage. In March 1924, just when his rival's hands were free, he filled up the cup by assuming the title of Caliph, which had become vacant on the abolition of the Ottoman Caliphate by the Angora Government. This injudicious step, which Husein seems to have taken with considerable reluctance, gained for Ibn Saud the open encouragement of the Indian Muslims of the Khilāfat Committee, and, in August 1924, he started to deal conclusively with his rival.

The ensuing campaign rapidly completed the ruin of Husein. After a vain appeal for British support, he abdicated in October 1924, and was temporarily succeeded by his son, Ali. But this change brought no improvement; on the 13th of the month the Wahhabis occupied Mecca, and for the next fourteen months the new King was closely invested in the port of Jidda. On 22 December 1925, Ali abandoned hope and left the country, and on Christmas Day the war was declared at an end. In January 1926 the *de facto* situation was regularized by the vote of the Mecca nobles, who conferred the vacant Kingship of the Hijaz upon Ibn Saud, who had thus regained the commanding position in Arabia which his house had held at the beginning of the nineteenth century.

His difficulties, however, were by no means at an end. In spite of their claims to primitive orthodoxy, the Wahhabis were not a sect whose occupation of their holy places the rest of the Muslim world could view with complete equanimity. A report, apparently greatly exaggerated, that the tomb of the Prophet in Medina had been damaged by Ibn Saud's bombardment, in the course of his military operations, raised a storm which was not calmed without some trouble, and the obstacles which the campaign in the Hijaz had placed in the way of the annual pilgrimage had not strengthened the position of the conqueror. His attempts to conciliate religious opinion by convening an Islamic Congress in Mecca met at first with disappointing rebuffs, and when at length it was opened, in June 1926, it was at first but sparsely attended by official delegates, and some of the questions raised proved extremely delicate. The pilgrimage of that year also occasioned some unfortunate collisions between the Wahhabis and the Egyptians, and the efforts of those Muslims who were working for Islamic solidarity continued to be somewhat embarrassed.

Difficulties of a political nature were also created by Ibn Saud's accession to power. The successive conquests of the Jebel Shammar and the Hijaz had brought the Wahhabi power into continuous contact with Transjordania and Iraq, both of which territories were ruled, under the auspices of Great Britain, by the sons of Husein. It would in any case have been difficult for Ibn Saud to restrain the raiding propensities of the border tribes. The subdivision of the Turkish dominions had in fact both stimulated and facilitated such activities, for the new international frontiers ignored the facts of economic geography, and interposed obstacles to the customary migrations of the nomads, while the lawless could easily evade control by crossing the dividing lines between different jurisdictions. It was, however, particularly necessary that order should be preserved in the country lying to the north of Ibn Saud's dominions, since it was rapidly becoming an important motor-route connecting Baghdad and Persia with the Mediterranean. Serious raids continued to occur, and during Ibn Saud's attack on the Hijaz he had deliberately created diversions against the territory of both his neighbours, which had called for the stern interference of British aeroplanes and armoured cars. He appeared, indeed, at this time, to be contemplating the extension of his frontier as far north as the Syrian border, thus seriously threatening the communications between Palestine and Mesopotamia. Eventually, however, matters were arranged by the conclusion of two agreements, in November 1925, defining the frontiers with Iraq and Transjordania respectively, laying down rules for the control of the border tribes, and setting up mixed tribunals to deal with cases of infringement. The situation was thus safeguarded as far as the signature of documents could achieve that object.

Egypt

The position of Egypt, both in relation to Turkey and Great Britain, differed widely from that of any of the regions which have so far been considered. The theoretical suzerainty of the Sultan had continued to exist up to the date of Turkey's intervention in the First World War, but it had ceased to be a factor of practical importance from the days when Mehemet Ali acquired the hereditary title to the pashalik in 1841. From that date until the intervention of Great Britain in 1882, the country had enjoyed—if the verb can be considered appropriate to the prevailing regime—a substantial measure of autonomy. The British intervention did not juridically modify the national status of Egypt, and was at first declared, and indeed believed, to be temporary. In 1887 an evacuation after the lapse of three more years was very nearly arranged, the proposed convention only breaking down through the opposition of the Sultan. Egypt, in law, was governed by the Khedive with an Egyptian Cabinet, an Egyptian Legislative Council, and an Egyptian Assembly, though in practice Great Britain exercised a decisive measure of administrative and military control.

Even before the First World War this anomalous situation, in which the theoretic limitation of Egyptian independence by the Turkish suzerain was negligible, while that imposed by Great Britain under the colour of 'advice' amounted in practice to a protectorate, had not remained wholly unchallenged. A Nationalist movement was in being at least as early as 1905, though it was, in this early phase, largely confined to the intelligentsia. Pan-Islamism undoubtedly played an important part in the agitation at this stage. After the war the movement acquired a more popular character, and, though no doubt its leaders made what use they could of the religious factor, it became mainly a struggle for political independence, encouraged, like others, by the slogan of 'self-determination', and the opposition of Muslims to Christians was a comparatively unimportant incident in it.

Almost at the outset of the war Great Britain announced

unilaterally the termination of Turkish suzerainty and proclaimed a protectorate over Egypt. The claims of Turkey were not indeed juridically extinguished until the ratification of the Treaty of Lausanne, but they were from the date of the British declaration hardly an operative factor in the situation. The deportation of the Nationalist leader, Zaghlul, in March 1919, caused disturbances which led to the investigations and report of the Milner Mission, which proposed a treaty recognizing the independence of Egypt subject to safeguards of British interests and the conclusion of a protective alliance with Great Britain. Negotiations on this basis proved abortive. In 1921 Lord Allenby, the Special High Commissioner, reported that the continuance of the protectorate entailed serious risk of revolution. In February 1922 the protectorate was consequently abolished, and the independent sovereignty of Egypt provisionally recognized. At the same time the restrictions which the safeguarding of British interests imposed upon Egyptian sovereignty proved an insuperable bar to Nationalist acquiescence in the situation. A series of violent crimes took place, culminating, in November 1924, in the murder of Sir Lee Stack, Sirdar of the Egyptian Army and Governor-General of the Sudan. An ultimatum was consequently presented to the Egyptian Government, and a fine of £500,000 exacted. Zaghlul resigned, and a new Cabinet was constituted under the President of the Senate, Ahmad Ziwar Pasha. The Egyptian Parliament sent a protest to the League of Nations, but it was decided that the Anglo-Egyptian conflict was not strictly an international affair, and the League declined to intervene. The main issues in dispute were not, however, settled by agreement between the parties, in spite of repeated attempts. The most difficult questions in issue were those relating to the protection of the Suez Canal and the status of the Sudan, which involved that of the control and allocation of the Nile waters. It will be more convenient, however, to revert to these matters at a later stage.

Morocco

The disturbances in the remaining Islamic regions of North Africa are even less capable of being assigned to religious motives, or even to antagonism to Western domination as such.

In Libya the reaction against the Italians, which continued to give trouble, was merely the recrudescence of a situation which had arisen prior to the First World War. It was a clear case of simple and natural resistance to aggression, which had gone on more or less continuously since the act of militant imperialism by which Italy invaded Libyan territory in October 1911. In Morocco, as well as in the other portions of North Africa under French control, there was, until the successful rising of Abdul Krim against the Spaniards, no serious sign of discontent, and a large part of the area remained permanently quiescent, except for some Nationalist agitation on parliamentary lines. Abdul Krim no doubt based his eventual pretensions on the doctrine of self-determination, but it is clear that a more diplomatic handling of the situation in its earlier stages would have left the Rifis and their leaders content with Spanish protectorate: it was an extraordinary combination of political and strategic inepti- tude on the part of the Spaniards which must be held respon- sible for the long and calamitous campaign which began with the disaster of Anwal in July 1921, and was only ended at a vast cost with French co-operation in 1926.

Persia and Afghanistan

In completing this rapid survey of the reactions of the Islamic world to the First World War and its aftermath, it only remains to consider the effects in Persia and Afghanistan. In both countries, the circumstances and their results show a consider- able similarity. The rulers of each also shared a zeal for internal reform, though Western ideas played a more prom- inent part in the policy of the Amir than in that of the Shah, whose less sweeping programme was probably on that account the more successful.

Persia before the war had occupied the unenviable position of a buffer, upon which impinged the rival interests of Russia and of Great Britain. The latter was strategically interested in the south eastern frontier, bordering on Baluchistan, and com- mercially in the Persian Gulf. Her interest in the Anglo-Persian oil concessions had involved a certain amount of economic penetration in the south west. More disturbing to Persia was the control exercised by Russia in the northern half of the country. The Anglo-Russian agreement of 1907, assigning bounds to the respective spheres of influence of the two European Powers, had been suspected, not without reason, of covering Russian designs of annexation, which might necessitate similar tactics on the part of Great Britain.[1] In any case, Persia's soul was not her own. The agreement interfered with her traditional policy of playing off her rival masters one against the other, she had to face such facts as that the northern and southern divisions of her army were largely officered by Russians and Englishmen respectively, and an American financial adviser whom she had chosen was driven from the country by Russian diplomatic pressure.

As was to be expected, during the war, with Russia and Great Britain in alliance, Persian neutrality had worn a distinctly pro-German tinge, a fact which was countered by the presence of Russian troops in the northern area, and a British force at Bushire. When the Russian troops were withdrawn in consequence of the revolution, the British took their place, marching through the country and occupying the north and east. In 1919 an Anglo-Persian agreement was signed but not ratified, which provoked widespread protest in Persia by its proposal to employ British advisers in all branches of Persian administration. In 1920 a Bolshevik invasion resulted in the withdrawal of the British forces, and the Russians, by a parade of disinterestedness, managed to leave to England alone the stigma of appearing to seek the exploitation of the country. In February 1921 a *coup d'état* led by Riza Khan, a soldier from the Persian Cossack division, brought a Nationalist administration into power, which promptly denounced the Anglo-Persian agreement. The spectacular rise of Riza Khan after this date, to become successively Commander-in-Chief, Minister of War, Prime Minister, and finally, at the close of 1925, Shah of Persia, belongs to the domestic history of the country and must be studied elsewhere. The fact of international importance is the complete liberation of Persia from the foreign influences by which she had so long been dominated, and the consolidation of this position by an energetic internal policy, which made the new Shah, in a more real sense than any of his recent predecessors, master of the whole country.

The sovereignty of the Amir of Afghanistan had similarly

[1] See Sykes, Sir P. *Persia*. Oxford, Clarendon Press, 1922, p. 148.

been interfered with by the converging pressure of the same European Powers, Russia and Great Britain. Fear of the former had induced the Afghan Government to consent to accept British control of its foreign policy. The collapse of the Russian Empire in 1917 removed the sole inducement to remain under British tutelage, and though long-standing friendship restrained the hand of the Amir Habibullah, yet his murder in 1919 was immediately followed by an attack on British India by his son and successor, Amanullah. Though this impudent act of aggression ended in his speedy and complete defeat, Afghan intrigues continued to play an important part in the subsequent risings in Waziristan, and in the terms of peace the British control over Afghan foreign policy, which had previously been exercised, was renounced.

The two countries, Persia and Afghanistan, celebrated their newly-won liberty in remarkably similar ways. In 1921 both countries entered into a nexus of treaties which created in the Near and Middle East a kind of Little Entente in the interests of Soviet Russia. In February treaties were concluded by the U.S.S.R. with Afghanistan and Persia respectively, and these were followed in March by a Russo-Turkish and Turco-Afghan treaty. The process was completed in 1926 by the conclusion of a treaty between Turkey and Persia.

In his review of events in the Islamic world comprised in the first volume of the *Survey of International Affairs, 1925*, Professor Toynbee suggests as a connecting thread a paradoxical contrast, everywhere perceptible, between the acceptance of Western ideas and the rejection of Western tutelage. The reader of the foregoing may perhaps be inclined to doubt the existence of any paradox. It may rather be urged that the nationalistic aspirations with which a number of Islamic peoples became independently imbued were themselves a part of the Western ideology which they were tending increasingly to absorb, and that the process was therefore quite logical. The example of the Arabs shows that there was in the movement no antagonism to the West as such: any suzerainty, even that of co-religionists, was equally obnoxious. In Arabia, indeed, the leaders evinced imperialist rather than nationalistic aims, in the furtherance of which they were ready to engage in internecine conflicts and to welcome the assistance of a Western and

Christian Power. It is, in fact, difficult to apply one common denominator to all the occurrences described in this chapter; in so far as there is one, it may be extended beyond the circle of Islam to the post-war world in general. For democracy, in defence of which the war was alleged to have been fought, upholds the educational principle of that celebrated expert, Mr Squeers, 'when the boy knows this out of book, he goes and does it'. And the word with which the rising generation had been most sedulously familiarized was—'self-determination'.

PART II

THE PERIOD OF FULFILMENT

1925 to 1930

IX

THE WORLD IN 1925

THE punctuation of events, which allows to the historian and his readers a breathing-space, is unfortunately seldom so synchronized as to be applicable all over the world. At best there is but a comma in one place to correspond with the colons and full stops of others. But the year of Locarno affords a better opportunity than most for looking round and even back—like Lot's wife—without incurring her fate of being snowed under by the unchecked onrush of events. In Europe it marks definitely the conclusion of a period of preliminary settlement, and the start of a 'policy of fulfilment' which promised at least a temporary stability. In the Far East, the Shanghai and Shameen incidents of May and June 1925 inaugurate a phase when the disturbed affairs of China, hitherto a matter mainly of domestic concern, begin to occupy a place of increasing importance in the drama of international affairs. On the American continent, Chamorro's *coup d'état* in Nicaragua, almost exactly contemporaneous with the signature of the Locarno Treaties in October 1925, is the commencement of an episode leading to far-reaching modifications in the policy of economic imperialism hitherto pursued by the United States in Latin America, and provoking such active opposition to her claims to hegemony as is exemplified in the refusal of Panama in January 1927 to ratify the treaty signed at Washington during the previous summer. In the history of British Imperial relations, Article 9 of the Locarno Treaty, exempting the Dominions and India from its obligations, indicates that the stage has already been reached which the epoch-making Imperial Conference of 1926 is to endeavour to reduce to a constitutional formula. Finally, in the Islamic world, the Druse revolt against the French mandate in Syria breaks out in July 1925 and assumes critical importance during the later half of the year. Everywhere we seem to be entering upon new developments, and the temporary lull in the affairs of Europe may therefore profitably be utilized in considering the progress, if any, which had hitherto been attained.

If the reader will cast his mind back to the opening chapter of the book, he will recall that the policy inaugurated at the Peace Conference was founded upon a number of assumptions, which form a convenient basis of comparison with the situation which had actually developed. It will be found in practically every case that the expectation of 1920 had been belied.

1. *The European system was to be superseded by a world-wide system, in which Europe no longer retained a predominance.*

This was a natural conclusion to draw from the exhaustion of Europe consequent upon the war, and the corresponding growth in prosperity and importance of Japan and the United States. It was most emphatically expressed by General Smuts, in addressing the Imperial Conference of June 1921:

> Our temptation is still to look upon the European stage as of the first importance. It is no longer so . . . these are not really first-rate events any more. . . . Undoubtedly the scene has shifted away from Europe to the Far East and to the Pacific. The problems of the Pacific are to my mind the world problems of the next fifty years or more.

This opinion might well be tenable in its positive aspects at a later date, though the possibilities of a major crisis in Europe would still have seemed unduly belittled, but up to the end of the year 1925 it would have been generally admitted that Europe was still occupying the centre of the stage. Nor had the world system materialized according to expectations. The defection of the United States and the jealous hegemony which they exercised over the Western hemisphere through the 'almighty dollar' and the Monroe Doctrine, had placed the control of international affairs, for the most part, once more upon a regional basis.

2. *The dominance of the Great Powers in the Concert of Europe was to give place to a democratic system, in which it would be counterbalanced by the increased numbers of the smaller States.*

The affairs of Europe, if not of the world, were still under the control of the Great Powers of that continent. Whether as 'the

Supreme Council of the Allied and Associated Powers' or as the permanent members of the Council of the League of Nations, the Concert of Europe was still playing the decisive part. On major political issues the deliberations at Geneva were more and more yielding pride of place to conferences held elsewhere, and even at the meetings of the League there was a tendency, particularly marked during the convocation of the Special Assembly of March 1926 (see p. 176), for the tea-parties of the great to settle matters over the heads of the common herd.

3. *A general automatic co-operation, impartially exercised against all aggression, was to be substituted for the old system of local alliances.*

The third of the 'five particulars', expressed in President Wilson's speech of 27 September 1918, was as follows:

There can be no leagues or alliances or special covenants and understandings within the general and common family of the League of Nations.

This principle had in a sense been violated by the American President himself, in the abortive Anglo-American guarantee to France, but this exception had not, perhaps, the obvious defects of local alliances between the nations on the continent of Europe. Such understandings might well be felt to be incompatible with the impartial and general co-operation for which the League stood, however carefully they might be expressed to be 'within the framework of the League'. Was it possible to contemplate France applying sanctions against Polish aggression, or Poland co-operating against France? What had occurred throughout the period under consideration was, in ultimate analysis, a reversion to the old system. The members of the League had recoiled, from the first, from their collective obligations for the maintenance of peace; the sanctions article had been watered down more and more; peace and security had been preserved by what may well have been thought to be more effective and trustworthy means, but the system really amounted to an alliance of the old type between the satisfied Powers, aimed against the revisionists, who were so far not in a position to complete the return to the pre-War system by a counter-understanding. Even the engagement entered into by Great Britain at Locarno was a pact of local scope, consistent with her traditional policy; it was analogous to her guarantee of Belgian neutrality, and was limited to that protection of the Channel coasts and the ports of the Low Countries which, historically, she had long regarded as vital to her own interests. The machinery of the League could no doubt be used effectively in minor crises, such as that between Greece and Bulgaria, and Geneva had abundantly proved its utility as an instrument of international co-operation and a forum for the stimulation and expression of a world opinion, but the fate of the Draft Treaty and of the Protocol indicated pretty clearly how lightly the obligation to collective action sat upon the minds of those who had signed the Covenant.

4. *A world safe for democracy.*

This aspect was especially emphasized by President Wilson in his speeches. 'The people of this world . . . have determined that there shall be no more autocratic governments', 'The League of Nations sends autocratic governments to Coventry', and, most surprising of all, the following interpretation of the League Constitution, which occurs in a speech delivered at Oakland, California, on 18 September 1919:

One of the interesting provisions of the Covenant of the League of Nations is that no nation can be a member of that League which is not a self-governing nation. *No autocratic government can come into its membership; no government which is not controlled by the will and vote of its people.*

Of this interpretation, the American President seems to have been the only exponent: certainly no attempt was made to apply such a test as a qualification for membership of the League: but the outcome of the war was very generally regarded as a triumph for democracy, and the League as an essentially democratic piece of machinery, the palladium of the smaller and weaker nations. Both these expectations were destined to rapid and progressive disappointment. The most favourable conditions for popular government exist in periods of tranquillity, when the economic machine is working smoothly and profitably, and when political issues are few, simple, and mainly domestic, and are gradual in development. It is, more-over, a system which functions best in nations where it has

grown slowly and naturally, affording to their populations an
adequate opportunity for political education. All these conditions were conspicuously absent from the post-war world.
It was an age calling for quick decisions by adaptable and
unprejudiced minds, an age of hardships in which the suffering
masses saw only the inevitable failure of any political party to
provide immediate alleviation, and consequently tended to
vent their disappointment and impatience in rapid changes of
political allegiance, to demand the impossible from any government which it was in their power to threaten with defeat, while
at the same time they realized their blindness and bewilder-
ment, and were ready to surrender their powers to any leader
who promised to bring them out of the wilderness. It was an
age too when economic problems of baffling complexity,
altogether unintelligible to the man in the street, clamoured
for instant solution. Above all, the efficient functioning of
democracy depends on the existence of a large measure of
common assumptions, with a consequent willingness to co-
operate and to accept compromise. Where men are divided by
conflicting ideological conceptions held with the fanaticism of
a religion, or where the demands of the dominant majority
mean or seem to mean the extinction of life worth living for
their opponents, a democratic system becomes unworkable.
These unfavourable conditions were now increasingly present
in the world. In these circumstances democracy wilted even
where it was securely rooted, and could not hope to thrive in
new and unfamiliar soil. Unexpectedly but inevitably the
world swung back to autocracy in a new form. In 1925 the
tendency had only begun: in Russia, with the 'dictatorship of
the proletariat', which meant in effect the despotism of the
Bolshevik oligarchy; in Italy, with the Fascist dictatorship of
Mussolini; in Spain, with General Primo de Rivera; and
temporarily in Greece, under General Pangalos. But it was
everywhere already in the air, and destined to spread with
astonishing rapidity in the course of the next few years. A
League of Nations with President Wilson's democratic qualifications for membership would soon have dwindled into
numerical insignificance. For the same reasons international
affairs more and more depended upon the leadership of a few
Great Powers, and Geneva was less of a parliament of equal

nations than a convenient field for the diplomatic manoeuvres of the new Concert of Europe.

5. *That the satisfaction of Nationalist aspirations would prove the best foundation for peace and co-operation.*

In an earlier chapter the difficulty has been pointed out that the application of the principle of self-determination inevitably involved its own violation. But even if the territorial settlement could have been faultless in this respect, there would still have remained the potential antagonism of States which had never practised or believed in a doctrine of 'home rule all round'. The redistribution of territory would still have been liable to be challenged wherever opportunity permitted, on historical, economic, and even strategic grounds. Moreover, the disintegrating force of Nationalism harmonized but ill with a scheme based upon unselfish co-operation. Canada, for example, was encouraged by the doctrine to think rather of her private security in a 'fire-proof house', than of her wider loyalties as a member of the British Commonwealth or a signatory of the League Covenant.

In fact, perhaps the most disquieting feature of the situation was a general tendency to ignore the most solemn obligations if, on second thoughts, they appeared disadvantageous to those who had entered into them. No doubt there have been numerous instances throughout history when nations have failed in an emergency to implement treaty obligations, but there has at least hitherto been a general expectation that such duties will normally be fulfilled. And in the case of the League sanctions under Article 16 such an expectation was the all-important factor. No aggression could take place if it was anticipated that the act would automatically confront the offender with an overwhelming combination; so long as this remained even reasonably probable it was extremely unlikely that the guarantors of world peace would ever be challenged to redeem their pledge. But a situation had now arisen when no trust was placed in any engagement which was not based on obvious and immediate self-interest, and the bluff was therefore increasingly likely to be called. Better, it was felt, the old system with all its disadvantages than 'inky blots and rotten parchment bonds' to which no-one appeared to attach any really binding significance. Yet, now that no stigma appeared to attach to the repudiation of inconvenient liabilities, it was not easy to feel safe even with regional treaties of an earlier type. These, too, seemed to rest not upon the signature but upon the interests of the parties, which further developments might all too easily modify. Thus pact might be piled on pact, and treaty on treaty, without creating any trustworthy sense of security.

Apart from this, for the moment the old system of regional alliances was safe enough. The revisionist Powers were not only deficient in force, but separated by differences of policy, interest and outlook too wide to permit of the formation of an opposing group. But there were dangerous possibilities for the future. The normal tendency towards a reversal of combinations after a great war in itself suggested an ultimate *rapprochement* between Russia, Germany, and Italy: the first two had fluttered the dovecotes of Europe as early as 1922 by the conclusion of the Treaty of Rapallo, while the opposition between France and Italy was becoming increasingly acute, and the dissatisfaction of the latter at her treatment during the Peace Conference tended inevitably to bring her into the revisionist camp. With each reconciliation of existing differences between these three Powers, and with the ultimately inevitable recovery of Germany, a situation could therefore be seen approaching in which the worse as well as the better features of the pre-war system might easily be reproduced. The possibilities of this danger must be considered in greater detail in later chapters.

X

THE FOREIGN POLICY OF ITALY AND SOUTH EASTERN EUROPE

The Genesis of Fascism

IN the longer perspective of history, the event which will probably be regarded as that of greatest international importance in the recent history of Italy will be the establishment of the Fascist regime in October 1922. In the earlier years after its introduction, however, the movement was generally regarded as of mainly domestic importance, and, in spite of the intermittent truculence of Mussolini's utterances and actions, faith was put in the remark which he only tardily repudiated in 1930, that Fascism was not a commodity for export.[1] In its purely ideological aspects, indeed, Fascism was for some time of subordinate international importance, and the earlier editions of this work unduly ignored it, regarding it in its domestic aspects as irrelevant to the theme of the book, while the general facts were matters of sufficiently recent recollection to be taken for granted. The ideology of totalitarianism, however, must now be recognized as a factor which has played so prominent a part in world history that its origins and nature should be explained and examined in any work dealing with the international affairs of the period.

In particular, it seems necessary to challenge the prevalent misconception, which regards this and similar totalitarian movements as a Conservative reaction. It should, on the contrary, be clearly realized that in all the most typical cases the totalitarian dictator came from circles associated with Socialism and the political left. In relation to the Russian prototype this is a truism requiring no demonstration, but it is equally true of the movements which achieved power in Italy and in Germany. In the latter country, Hitler started his demagogic career as a

---

[1] 'Il Fascismo non è un articolo di esportazione': speech on the Alto Adige, 3 March 1928. *Scritti e Discorsi.* 12 vols. Milan, Hoepli, 1934, vol. vi, p. 151. Mussolini repudiated it on 28 October 1930, saying: 'la frase che il Fascismo non è merce d'esportazione, non è mia'.

'down-and-out' member of the working class: his closest associates were rabid anti-capitalists like Gottfried Feder, who actually drafted the official Nazi programme, the economic clauses of which were essentially socialistic; the original name of the party was simply the German Labour Party (Deutsche Arbeiterpartei), and it maintained the same association in its revised title—N.S.D.A.P. or Nationalsozialistische Deutsche Arbeiterpartei. Throughout *Mein Kampf* it is emphasized that the appeal of the movement is to the masses of the industrial proletariat rather than the bourgeoisie.

Incidentally, it may be useful to recall how in our own country the British Fascist, Sir Oswald Mosley, represented the Labour Party from 1924, and was a member of the Socialist Government in 1929-30; while the Norwegian exponent of the totalitarian ideology, the traitor Quisling, made his political debut with an approach to the extreme left, offering his assistance in the creation of 'red guards' to be used for revolutionary purposes.

But above all, Mussolini, as we shall see, was a product of revolutionary Socialism. It is in Socialism, in fact, that most of the typical features of the movement are to be found—the subordination of the individual to the State, a preference for violent methods, and reliance on the arts of the demagogue. The last point is important, for it is precisely because of their dependence for ultimate success on a substantial measure of popular support that such dictators suppress freedom of speech and opinion and pervert education into a system of one-sided propaganda. It is in this dependence on public opinion that the twentieth century tyrant differs essentially from earlier autocrats.

It is true, no doubt, that the unsatisfactory working of parliamentary democracy in several European countries gave rise to dictatorial regimes of a more simply reactionary type, controlled in most instances by army generals. This is not surprising, since the training of a military officer is a training for the application of force to the settlement of doubtful issues and the maintenance of order, while it inculcates reliance on authority and discipline: in a political tangle, it is natural for a soldier to try to cut the Gordian knot; but the whole bent of mind of such men is so remote from that of the politician that they are for the most part incapable of formulating a political philosophy, and indeed they frequently regard their own intervention as a merely temporary expedient. Political changes through military *pronunciamientos* are no novelty in history, and these exceptions, though through lack of originality they tend to follow the current pattern of similar governments, do not affect the general character of the totalitarian movement.

The circumstances under which Fascism developed in Italy, though in a sense peculiar to that country, confirm the thesis that this form of autocracy is the product of a situation when democratic sentiment proves incompatible with effective parliamentary government. In Italy, conditions have always been unfavourable to the development of a united public opinion, or to that mutual tolerance between political parties which enables a parliamentary system to work smoothly. The history of the peninsula, from the collapse of the Roman Empire until the second half of the nineteenth century, was that of a number of separate petty sovereignties, frequently under foreign control, and rent by civil wars which divided city from city. The national unification of the country, which was not finally consummated before 1870, was achieved by the confluence of a number of forces differing widely both in method and objective. The aim of some was at first a federation of the existing sovereignties, others favoured a united Italian republic, a third school thought in terms of a more or less gradual expansion of the Piedmontese monarchy. Yet another alternative was dreamed of by Gioberti—federation, on a Catholic basis, under the presidency of the Pope. The means advocated and applied were equally diverse, varying from the secret conspiratorial methods of Mazzini to the statesman-like diplomacy of Cavour. The one real common factor was hatred of the alien domination of Austria, applied directly in the north and indirectly elsewhere, where the different local tyrants survived through Austrian protection. When the reason for this temporary solidarity was removed, the patchwork nature of Italian unity was quickly manifested. This diversity was accentuated by two later developments, the hostility of—and towards—the Catholic Church resulting from the forcible occupation of Rome in 1870, and the growth of industry in the north, which contributed a new local element of political cleavage. Poverty and heavy taxation, the legacy of the Risorgimento, further complicated the problems of government. In these circumstances, the successful conduct of a parliamentary system depended more and more on the dexterous manipulation of a heterogeneous majority gathered from a large number of more or less discordant parties by a system of balanced concessions and electoral bargains, which left in each a discontented but politically impotent minority, and by the control of constituencies by even less reputable methods. Under the cynical management of Giolitti, who dominated Italian politics during the decade immediately preceding the First World War, these tactics resulted in the virtual dictatorship of a masterly parliamentary 'boss', in which no consistent principle was discernible. In these circumstances, the temper of Italian Socialism, despairing of parliamentary triumph, grew increasingly violent and revolutionary.

Benito Mussolini, whose Spanish first name significantly commemorates the anti-Clerical Mexican President, Benito Juarez, who was responsible for the execution of the Emperor Maximilian, was the son of a politically-minded blacksmith in the notoriously turbulent region of the Romagna. He first came into prominence as a Socialist of the extreme revolutionary type, in violent agitation against the Libyan war launched by Giolitti in 1911. His activities on this occasion earned him some months in gaol, whence he emerged to be promoted to the editorship of the leading Socialist paper, *Avanti*, and to push from power that moderate section of his party which had favoured collaboration with Giolitti.

The outbreak of the war of 1914 led to a startling change in Mussolini's attitude, which has been variously interpreted by friends and enemies. After a short period of hesitation, he came out strongly in favour of Italian intervention in the war. Such intervention, on the side of the Western Allies, had been decided on in 1915 by the Premier, Signor Salandra, upon purely mercenary grounds. After negotiations with both sides, he sold his country's services to the highest bidder. That he was uninterested in the ideological aspects of the struggle is demonstrated by the fact that his declaration of war was confined to Austria. There existed, nevertheless, a more reputable argument for intervention on the side of liberal democracy and the rights of small nations, which appealed to a growing section of Italian opinion. Italian Socialism, however, maintained for the most part a consistent opposition to this as to every other war, which brought it into a rather curious association with the Vatican and with Giolitti. Mussolini's defection, therefore, had the immediate result of his ejection from the party and from his editorial post. He left with deep resentment and undisguised threats of revenge.

Mussolini's motives have been interpreted as an unprincipled lust for power, which saw no outlet for further distinction in the incongruous association with former opponents which the opposite course would have involved. Alternatively, a reconciliation with such enemies was too bitter a pill to swallow. Possibly, too, Mussolini may have foreseen the possibilities of such a war as a forcing-ground for revolutionary sentiment. We may, however, give him the benefit of the doubt and the credit for sincere conviction, applauding his decision to advocate participation in a just war, one of the objects of which was claimed to be the abolition of war as an institution.

Whatever his reasons, he now threw himself energetically into the congenial task of a violent agitation, which played its part in the decisive explosion of popular opinion which thwarted Giolitti's schemes and endorsed Salandra's policy in May 1915. It was in the course of this campaign that the future Duce, in alliance with a prominent Syndicalist, Corridoni, mobilized bands of proletarian sympathizers under the title Fasci di Combattimento, or Fighting Groups.[1]

The course of the war disappointed expectations. The intervention of Italy did not succeed, as had been hoped, in speedily turning the scale. The struggle was long and costly, and stained by such inglorious and even disgraceful episodes as the collapse at Caporetto. The peace, in which the full exaction of the stipulated price of intervention was frustrated by the intrusion of Wilsonian principles, only served to increase the popular discontent. Thus the cause of official Socialism at first profited enormously by its opposition to the war. The Socialists became

---

[1] The derivation of the term *Fascisti* from the *fasces* of the Roman lictors, alleged in Fisher's *History of Europe*, vol. 3, p. 1193, appears to be incorrect. *Fasci* had long been used in Italy as a term descriptive of political combinations. Etymologically, no doubt, there is a relation between rods and individuals united by a common bond.

the strongest political unit in the country. In the elections of 1919, 156 Socialist candidates were returned, while no other single party could claim a comparable figure. At the same time, this did not give them a parliamentary majority, and the recent example of the Russian revolution suggested a way of exploiting military disaster in the interests of proletarian dictatorship. The advantages of 'direct action' as compared with constitutional dilatoriness were further advertised by such events as D'Annunzio's filibustering in Fiume. On the opening of the new parliament, the Socialist deputies rose together and left the chamber. Shortly afterwards, the National Council of the party carried a resolution for the erection of Workmen's Councils on the Bolshevik pattern.

Parliamentary democracy broke down; the Government of Signor Nitti was forced to legislate by decree. Meantime, the general unrest led to widespread cases of land-grabbing by the agricultural peasantry, and encouraged much sporadic pillage, which, though not officially sponsored, was naturally attributed to the prevalent Bolshevism. In September 1920, occurred the well-known incident of the occupation of the factories by the workers in Milan and elsewhere.

These excesses, while closely resembling Mussolini's own methods, were perpetrated under the aegis of a party with which he had irrevocably broken and against whose leaders he had sworn vengeance. The Fascists found a vent for their activities on the other side, and their use of the bludgeon and castor oil bottle thus won support and approval in unexpected quarters. In the elections of 1921 their hooliganism was enlisted in the service of Giolitti. Mussolini, however, was still thinking less in terms of parliamentary government than of revolution. 'Our revolution,' he said, 'is one which sweeps away the Bolshevik state in the expectation of a later reckoning with the Liberal state which will remain'.[1] He had in fact discovered, as Hitler was to discover later on, the power to be derived from coupling the force of Socialism with that of Nationalism. From the adventurers who had contributed to the momentary prestige of D'Annunzio he recruited no insignificant body of supporters. Naturally, in the chaotic conditions which

[1] Quoted in Sprigge, C. J. S. *The Development of Modern Italy*. London, Duckworth, 1943, p. 194.

prevailed, the propertied class also welcomed the appearance of this paradoxical saviour.

> Cet animal est très méchant;
> Quand on l'attaque, il se défend.

But it is normally too handicapped by lack of numbers to seek a trial of force, and too dependent on the protection of established law to relish the anarchy of revolution.

The tide of sympathy was in fact by this time turning against the Socialists, and the contention is largely correct that before the Fascists' *coup d'état* in the march on Rome in October 1922 their opponents had shot their bolt and their own *raison d'être* had disappeared. It is a moot point how far Fascism was entitled to the credit for the failure of the final Socialist effort in the general strike of the preceding August. Nevertheless, the bankruptcy of parliamentary democracy in Italy had become a generally-held belief throughout the country, and it was too late to expect that a man of Mussolini's forceful and ambitious character would abstain from reaping his reward. But it is noteworthy that the first stage of his access to power was cautiously constitutional in form. Not until 1924 did he ensure his power by a manipulation of the electoral law through a so-called reform; not till a year later was the totalitarian system, with its concomitant abolition of all individual freedom, openly proclaimed.

A final word may perhaps be devoted to explaining the bitter antagonism to Marxist Communism which is a feature common to Italian Fascism and its German counterpart. In Mussolini's case it was, as we have seen, partly attributable to personal rancour. But this antagonism was necessarily fortified by an alliance with Nationalism, for Marxism is essentially international; it is for this quality rather than its economics that it is ceaselessly arraigned by Hitler in the pages of *Mein Kampf*. This opposition to Communism was the one feature of Fascism and Nazism which appears to justify the popular misconception that these movements have Conservative affinities. It is true that the supporters both of the Duce and the Führer included men of the Right who welcomed these leaders as the two generals in 'The Knights' of Aristophanes welcome the 'tripe merchant' as an effective ally against a hated demagogue.

But both leaders were essentially men whose outlook was that
of the proletarian Left, and the accurately descriptive name for
both their movements is not Fascism but National Socialism.

Italy and the Peace Treaties

During the earlier years, however, of the period treated in
this history, ideological considerations played a very subordinate part in Italian foreign policy. The main factor in the international situation was Italian dissatisfaction with the peace
settlement. Although by the Peace Treaties Italy had realized
territorial gains in Austria considerably in advance of the line
demanded, as the price of non-intervention, in her negotiations
with the Habsburg Empire in 1915, the total effect of the settlement was to leave her dissatisfied, disappointed, and considerably wounded in her self-esteem. The result was to place her
in a special intermediate position between the revisionist and
anti-revisionist Powers. A strict application of the principle of
self-determination would have deprived her of the coveted
Brenner frontier, which indeed had only been conceded to her
on the clear understanding 'that the Italian Government proposes to adopt a broad liberal policy towards its new subjects
of German race, in what concerns their language, culture, and
economic interests'.[1] In reliance on the declaration of her
Ministers to which the passage above quoted refers, Italy had
also been exempted from the measures of control imposed on
other nations by the Minorities Treaties. But, elsewhere, the
application of Wilsonian principles had considerably impeded
the realization of what she regarded as her just demands. The
Italians contended, with some technical justification, that the
Armistice concluded with the Habsburg Empire was free from
the conditions which the Allies had accepted as a basis of
peace with Germany: but, however correct this contention
may have been, consistency demanded the application of
similar principles,[2] and the American President himself informed the Italian delegation, in April 1919, that he did not
feel free to differentiate in the principles to be applied to the
German and Austrian treaties.[3] The French and British

[1] Reply of the Allied and Associated Powers, 2 September 1919.
[2] See Notes of 17, 18, and 27 October 1918, between these parties. *History of the Peace Conference*, vol. i, pp. 449, 452, and 456, and cf. chapter I, p. 18.
[3] *History of the Peace Conference*, vol. v, p. 397.

Governments occupied a somewhat uncertain position between those of Italy and America. They worked hard for an acceptable compromise, but at the same time 'regarded themselves as being bound by the Treaty of London in the event of a voluntary agreement not being arrived at'.[1] Relations at the Paris Conference were, however, difficult and strained, and at one time resulted in the temporary withdrawal of the Italian delegation. The frontier with Yugoslavia was eventually settled by direct negotiations between the two nations concerned, which were embodied in the Treaty of Rapallo of 2 February 1921.

Attitude of Mussolini

This Treaty, however, was generally unpopular in Italy, and the weakness imputed to the Italian Government in the handling of the peace negotiations contributed not a little to the growth of the Fascist movement. On Signor Mussolini's advent to power in October 1922, the Duce did not conceal his opinion that the Treaty of Rapallo was a 'lamentable transaction', and he expressed from the first his conviction that the settlement, in this respect as in others, was 'not eternal or unchangeable'. But for the moment it was impossible to denounce the Treaty of Rapallo without risking the reopening of the whole settlement, a step which, apart from its dangers to general peace, was obviously disadvantageous to Italy in the region which she had secured in the Tyrol. The dictator had, in fact, in his early speeches, to steer a rather difficult course between the pacific sentiments necessary to allay European alarm at his accession to power, and the attitude which his followers expected of him in view of his previous utterances. His first efforts were directed to re-establishing Italian prestige and influence, and to advertising that his country could not be ignored or slighted, but he was too good a realist to pursue objectives not immediately attainable. He continued, therefore, to gratify Fascist opinion by truculent words and such actions as the bombardment of Corfu (see p. 92), but on the other hand he took the line that treaties once signed must be executed, and he applied this principle even to the Italo-Yugoslav Conventions which had been signed in Rome only

[1] *History of the Peace Conference*, vol. v, p. 426.

a few days before his accession to power. If, however, at this stage the more bellicose utterances of Signor Mussolini were usually neutralized by others, and by an unexpected moderation in action, it was not safe to assume that the latter, rather than the former, represented the true direction and ultimate aims of Fascist policy.[1]

Causes of Franco-Italian tension

The creation of the Fascist dictatorship inevitably tended to throw Italy and France into opposing camps. France was a prototype of democratic government, loyal to the principles of her great revolution; Italy was now the exponent of a new despotism, the antithesis of popular government, a possible source of infection to other democracies, whose ideals she repudiated with scorn. This ground of friction was intensified by the fact that a large proportion of the anti-Fascist refugees had sought asylum in France, which thereby became a base for propaganda hostile to the Italian Government, and even for plots and attempts against the life of the Duce. France might urge that this was her misfortune rather than her fault; that these émigrés had been thrust upon her, in spite of protests, together with an even more undesirable element of professional criminals; but the fact remained that the enemies of the Italian regime were very largely concentrated in this neighbouring country. On the main issue of post-war policy, too, France and Italy were in fundamental opposition. France was the protagonist of the *status quo* Powers, the uncompromisingly rigid upholder of the Treaty settlement, while Italy, in spite of her interests in the Tyrol, showed herself from the first sympathetic to the revisionist cause. But, in addition to the antagonism of contrasted political ideals and aims, there existed also definite causes of rivalry in North Africa and the western Mediterranean, and also, to an increasing degree, in the Balkans and the Danubian basin, a region where history suggested a peculiar danger in any competition for hegemony on the part of external Powers.

[1] Cf. Mussolini's speech of 26 May 1927: 'We shall be in a position then—tomorrow—when, *between 1935 and 1940*, we shall find ourselves at a point which I should call a crucial point in European history—we shall be in a position to make our voice felt, and to see, at last, our rights recognized.'

Colonial Questions

The colonial aspirations of Italy are founded not merely upon the question of prestige, but also upon a real need both for a supply of essential raw materials and for an outlet for her excessive but at the same time continuously increasing population. Since the war the last problem had been rendered more acute by the restrictions imposed upon immigration by several countries, notably the United States of America. Fascism never looked with favour upon an emigration to foreign countries which reduced the number of Italians who owed allegiance to their native land, and its solution of the problem was sought partly in domestic developments calculated to absorb and support a larger population at home, which fall outside the province of this work. But an effort was also made to check, so far as possible, the assimilation of Italian elements by foreign States, and Fascists also admitted an aspiration towards further territorial acquisitions. 'We are hungry for land', said the Duce in 1926, 'because we are prolific and intend to remain so'.

The colonial possessions of Italy were not in themselves adapted to meet the demand, either of her excess population for land or of her industrialists for material, to any adequate extent. They might ease the situation, however, and they were in any case a matter in which Italy took serious interest from the standpoint of her prestige. By the Treaty of London of 1915 it had been agreed that any increase in French or British colonial territory resulting from the war should be compensated by extension of the Italian frontiers in Eritrea, Somaliland, and Libya at the expense of France and Great Britain. The British redemption of this pledge was carried out in principle during negotiations which took place at the Peace Conference itself, whereby the cession of British Jubaland was agreed upon. The final settlement, which was delayed by linking it up with the dispute between Greece and Italy over the Dodecanese, did not take place until 1924, when it resulted in the transfer of a substantial area to Italy. In this region, Italian desires were satisfied, but the negotiations with France were more disappointing. The French might claim the benefit of the proverb 'Bis dat qui cito dat', since their concessions, such as they were, were agreed upon as early as September 1919. They amounted, however, to no more than a slight rectification of frontier to the south west of Libya, and were represented by Italian speakers as merely a 'restitution' of Italian territory occupied by French troops at the beginning of the war.[1] The agreement indeed spoke of reserving further points for future examination, but no additional steps had at this stage been taken in the matter.

The African interests of Italy were not, however, confined to territory under her own sovereignty or control. In the French protectorate of Tunisia, the numbers of Italian residents exceeded by about 30,000 those of French nationality. Having regard to the covetous eyes cast on Tunisia by the Italians, and to the fact that the establishment of the French protectorate in 1881 was represented as having forestalled Italian aspirations in the same region,[2] the situation was considered by France sufficiently serious to call for adjustment. By a Franco-Italian agreement of 1896 the descendants of Italian residents were enabled to retain their nationality: in 1918, however, France denounced this agreement, and it had since been precariously maintained in existence by renewals for periods of three months, pending fresh negotiations. Meanwhile, in 1921, the nationality decrees promulgated by the French and Tunisian authorities, which also gave rise to controversy with Great Britain, threatened the Italian status of the second generation born in the protectorate, if the agreement of 1896 was finally repudiated. The agitation aroused over this question served to intensify the feeling between the two Great Powers. This was aggravated when Italy was not invited to participate in the negotiations with regard to the international status of Tangier, which took place after the war. It was felt as a slight that the new statute, which was officially brought into force in June 1925, had been worked out in conference by Great Britain, France, and Spain; Italy, as a protest, withheld her recognition of its validity.

Competition in South East Europe

The causes of rivalry in the western Mediterranean led Italy to endeavour to strengthen her position by a *rapprochement* with

---

[1] See paper by Dr G. Paresce, *International Affairs*, May 1931, p. 352.
[2] This stroke had a great deal to do with the adhesion of Italy to the Triple Alliance a few years later.

Great Britain and Spain, but she felt no immediate hope of any adequate expansion in this quarter. Her attention was therefore directed to the possibilities latent in south eastern Europe, where a number of new or reconstructed States promised an opportunity of economic penetration, to which the door was opened through the newly-acquired ports on the Adriatic. This was admittedly the reason which led Mussolini to cultivate the unexpectedly friendly relations with Yugoslavia which were embodied in the pact of 'Friendship and Cordial Collaboration' of 27 January 1924.

For too long [he explained] the Fiume question has been a kind of portcullis impeding . . . direct and immediate contacts with the immense Danubian world. Now Italy can only move in an easterly direction, the fact being that on the west there are national states which have taken definitive form, and to which we can send nothing except our labour—though even our export of that may be prohibited or restricted any day. Therefore the lines for the pacific expansion of Italy lie towards the east.

This policy meant that Italy proposed to look upon the Balkan and Danubian countries as a sphere of influence peculiarly her own. To Yugoslavia, on the other hand, the conclusion of a treaty with Italy did not exclude an equally close relationship with another Great Power. The policy of the Little Entente, and of its separate members, was at this time aimed at the ultimate creation of a Danubian bloc independent of external influences, but this policy was for the moment impeded by the irreconcilable differences between the States of this region, an obstacle which the good offices of Italy might assist to remove. Apart from this, an alliance with France was recognized as more natural than a *rapprochement* with Italy, and the one was not conceived as excluding the other. In the same spirit, M. Beneš followed up the Franco-Czechoslovak treaty of 25 January 1924, by a treaty with Italy in July, frankly explaining that the multiplication of agreements with Great Powers was a guarantee against the exclusive hegemony of any one of them. Thus the tendency of the Little Entente Powers was to encourage a competition for their friendship, of which Italy desired a monopoly.

The competition, however, had begun. The first round was slightly in favour of Italy, who had concluded treaties both with

Czechoslovakia and Yugoslavia, while France, in 1924, had only succeeded in her negotiations with the former, though Yugoslavia, in January, accepted a French advance of 300 million francs for the purchase, in France, of munitions and military equipment. So matters remained at the date of the Locarno agreements in 1925, the eastern pacts with Germany being confined to France, Poland, and Czechoslovakia.

In 1926, however, the next round commenced in France's favour with the conclusion, in January, of a treaty with Roumania. Negotiations with this object had failed in the early part of 1924, but the break-down of the Russo-Roumanian conference on the question of Bessarabia in April put the advantages of French support in a more favourable light, and France improved the occasion by ratifying the Bessarabian treaty of October 1920 (see p. 87). For the moment the project for a defence alliance broke down owing to the unwillingness of Yugoslavia to co-operate, a condition on which France was insisting.[1] But Italy was, from 1924, concerned to keep on good terms with Russia; her ratification of the Bessarabian treaty was therefore withheld until 1927, with the result that her relations with Roumania were somewhat cool until after the signature of the Franco-Roumanian treaty. By this time, Italian penetration of the Danubian basin and the Balkans had become a cardinal point in Signor Mussolini's foreign policy, but he was only able to cap the French treaty with a pact of friendship and collaboration with Roumania some eight months later.

It appears that the competition, on the French side, was not so far deliberate, but that France was prepared to welcome Italian participation in the arrangements concluded: it was Italy alone who was adopting an exclusive attitude. This was clearly brought out in the history of the third treaty between France and the Little Entente States, that concluded with Yugoslavia. For agreement had been reached with regard to this document during the winter of 1925, but signature was deferred in the hope that a tripartite arrangement, to which Italy would be a party, could be negotiated. The suggestion was, however, unfavourably received in Rome, and the

---

[1] The Yugoslav attitude was possibly affected by the misbehaviour of some Roumanian troops, on the occasion of an evacuation of territory in April 1924, consequent upon the definitive regulation of the Temesvar frontier.

Franco-Yugoslav treaty was consequently initialed in March 1926, though even then some hope remained, which deferred the formal signature of the instrument until 11 November of the following year.

This refusal to entertain the idea of a tripartite agreement marks a point at which the 'forward policy' of Italy in south eastern Europe became much more vigorously pursued. Fresh friendships were everywhere cultivated. Since the Corfu incident in 1923, relations between Greece and Italy had been naturally strained at first, though in January 1924 a proposal to appoint an Italian minister to Athens had been well received. But 1926 saw a notable *rapprochement*. Bulgaria, who was in constant difficulties with her neighbours owing to the activities of the Macedonian Revolutionary Organization, owed much to Italian support, and the good offices of Italy were also of service in connexion with the raising of a loan for refugee settlement, for which Bulgaria had appealed to the League of Nations. But this Italian influence was inimical to a Bulgar-Yugoslav understanding. In October, approaches were also made to Hungary, suggesting an outlet on the Adriatic for Hungarian export trade, though the Italian offers in this case were interpreted in some quarters as an endeavour to frustrate similar overtures which had been made by Yugoslavia. The conciliatory policy towards Italy which had been hitherto pursued by the Yugoslav Foreign Minister, M. Ninčić, was nevertheless maintained until the end of November, when the signature of a treaty by Italy and Albania at Tirana produced reactions in Belgrade which permanently changed for the worse the relations between Yugoslavia and Italy.

Italy and Albania

As was pointed out in an earlier chapter, the traditional policy of the Albanians was to play off against one another the rivalries of external Powers. After the war the two nations principally involved were Italy and Yugoslavia. The latter was dissatisfied by the decision of the frontier delimitation commission, which had awarded to Albania the monastery of Sveti Naum, on the south eastern shore of Lake Ochrida, and the district of Vermosha, about thirty miles north north east of Skutari. The confirmation of this decision, in September 1924,

had given rise to frontier disturbances which were the subject
of complaint when, in December, a revolutionary movement
commenced against the existing Albanian administration presided over by Mgr Fan Noli, the Orthodox Bishop of Durazzo.
The revolution was promoted and led by Ahmed Bey Zogu, the
Muslim head of the previous government, which had been
driven from power in June. Ahmed Zogu had taken refuge in
Belgrade, and the Yugoslav Government was accused by that
of Fan Noli of complicity in the rising. The charge was officially
denied, and the success of the revolution within a month precluded the necessity for its investigation: Fan Noli and his
supporters in their turn left the country, and Ahmed Zogu was
naturally ready to withdraw the imputations of his predecessor.
The fact remains that the election of Zogu to the presidency of
the Albanian Republic, in January 1925, was immediately
followed by the cession to Yugoslavia of the disputed territories
of Sveti Naum and Vermosha.

Ahmed Zogu, who subsequently became King, 1 September
1928, was ambitious and imbued with Westernizing ideas, and
the determining factor in his policy was the need of money for
economic development. Though he appears to have begun by
applying to his former friends in Yugoslavia, the necessary funds
were not forthcoming from that quarter, and this placed a
powerful lever in the hands of Italy, who was only too ready
to engage in the economic penetration of the country. In
September 1925 a National Bank of Albania was founded in
Rome, and in the same year a Society for the Economic
Development of Albania (the S.V.E.A.) was organized in Italy,
which in 1926 financed a loan of 50 million francs to the
Albanian Government, the service of which was subsequently
guaranteed by a royal decree of the Italian State. Ahmed Zogu
had therefore golden reasons for modifying his external
relations. On 23 November 1926, an armed revolt against his
authority broke out, under the leadership of a Catholic priest,
Don Loro Tzaka, which was said to have been planned by Fan
Noli's supporters from the Italian enclave of Zara in Dalmatia.
It was in these circumstances that the Italo-Albanian treaty of
27 November 1926 was signed at Tirana.

The terms of this treaty, though represented in Italy as a mere
confirmation of the diplomatic engagements of 1921, aroused

lively concern elsewhere, and intense excitement in Yugoslavia, whose Government, as well as the nation, were completely taken by surprise. The agreement was construed as creating a virtual protectorate over Albania, and, taken with the other evidences of Italian activity in south-eastern Europe, completely changed the orientation of Yugoslav policy. The Italo-Yugoslav pact of 1924 was not renewed when it fell due for reconsideration, five years later.

The situation was rendered more critical by the occurrence of a series of incidents connected with Albania during the year 1927. In March Italian allegations of Yugoslav preparations directed against Albania were made and denied. In May fresh excitement was occasioned by the arrest of an employee of the Yugoslav Legation in Tirana, on a charge of espionage, which led temporarily to a diplomatic rupture. In October the Serbophil Albanian Minister in Belgrade was assassinated in Prague by an Albanian who had been educated in Italy, and who had travelled from Belgrade to the scene of the crime with an Italian visa. The cumulative tension produced by all these occurrences doubtless helped to determine the step taken by Yugoslavia on 11 November, when the long-suspended treaty with France was finally signed.

This was followed eleven days later by the signature of a second Treaty of Tirana between Italy and Albania, to which the latter acceded with some signs of reluctance. This was definitely a military alliance for defence, by which mutual assistance was promised in the event of war, while each party was bound not to conclude a separate peace. Though the close coincidence in time between the conclusion of the French and Italian agreements was represented as fortuitous, it created an unfortunate impression, and the chief delegate of Yugoslavia took occasion to comment adversely upon the terms of the new treaty before the special Committee on Security of the League of Nations. The situation bore, indeed, the ominous appearance of a definite attempt to counterbalance the ascendancy of France in the western Mediterranean by an anti-French combination in the east, and this aspect was more or less openly admitted by Signor Mussolini and by the comments of the Italian press. A statesman-like attempt to relieve the tension was made by M. Briand in a speech delivered in the French

Chamber on 30 November, and this was followed, a few days later, by the signature of a *modus vivendi* for the reciprocal regulation of the position of nationals of each country in the territory of the other. But the cloud was not altogether removed.

Yugoslav Suspicions of Encirclement

Meanwhile, in Yugoslavia the impression grew that the approaches made by Italy to her neighbours implied a deliberate policy of encirclement. For this suspicion there were some grounds. Wherever she turned, traces of Italian influence seemed perceptible. A visit of Count Bethlen to Rome, in April 1927, was followed immediately by the signature of a treaty of amity and arbitration with Hungary, and the speeches delivered on this occasion breathed a mutual desire for the closest understanding, while these events interrupted negotiations in which Yugoslavia herself was engaged with her neighbour. Towards Bulgaria, too, she was bent on maintaining a conciliatory attitude, but great difficulties were placed in the way of this policy by an intensive campaign of outrage launched in September by the Macedonian Revolutionary Organization, in which, though the evidence was not convincing, the hand of Italy was suspected even by responsible Yugoslav politicians. There could in any case be no doubt that Italy was a competitor for Bulgarian friendship. The effects of Italian reconciliation with Greece were apparent in the latter country's calm reception of the first Treaty of Tirana, though this was possibly due in part to another cause. During the years 1925–6 negotiations had been in progress for the renewal of the old Graeco-Serbian alliance of 1913, which Yugoslavia had denounced towards the close of 1924. These were coupled with questions connected with the Yugoslav Free Zone in the port of Salonika, in regard to which the Yugoslav claims were somewhat exacting. An agreement reached in August 1926, during the dictatorship of General Pangalos, was rejected a year later by the Government which replaced him. Some of the difficulties of Yugoslavia were no doubt due to the defects of her own diplomacy, but her suspicion that Italian policy was responsible for the situation in which she found herself appears to have been partially justified.

Roumania and the Optants

Roumania was in treaty relations with France, as well as being associated with Yugoslavia as a fellow-member of the Little Entente. Her treaty with Italy was therefore in any case of minor importance, but she also viewed with disfavour the *rapprochement* between Italy and Hungary, not only on general grounds, but because her relations with the latter country were particularly strained at this time. At the beginning of 1927 the question of the expropriated lands of the Hungarian optants had been revived, and during the year became an important subject for consideration at the sessions of the League of Nations. In the space available it is impossible to give more than a brief outline of the main features of the dispute.

By the Treaty of Trianon, residents in former Hungarian territory were entitled to opt for Hungarian citizenship. By Article 250 of the same treaty, property of Hungarian nationals situated in Roumania was not to be subject to 'retention or liquidation'. Immediately after the coming into force of the Treaty of Trianon (July 1921), an agrarian law was passed in Roumania, expropriating the rural land of absentees; this was not at first extended to the property of foreigners, but in August 1922 this exemption was abolished. The Hungarians contended that the consequent expropriation of their land in Roumania was a breach of the Treaty. The Roumanians replied that it was part of a general piece of domestic policy, and the Hungarians could not be placed in a privileged position as compared with other aliens. The intervention of the League of Nations in 1923 failed to settle the dispute, but in January 1927 a new issue was raised by the decision of the Mixed Arbitral Tribunal (constituted by the Treaty of Trianon), to which a number of Hungarian optants had meanwhile referred the matter, that it came within its jurisdiction. Roumania retaliated by withdrawing its judge from the Tribunal, and the question therefore came again before the League. It remained a subject of acrimonious discussion throughout the years 1927–8, at the end of which period a conference of the parties met to undertake direct negotiations for a settlement. These conversations, however, also proved abortive, and matters were not finally adjusted until the meeting of the second Hague

Conference in January 1930, when they formed an item in the general settlement of claims and counter-claims in eastern European countries in respect of reparation and post-war debts.

The Szent Gotthard Incident

In January 1928 some misgivings were occasioned by the discovery of a large consignment of machine-gun parts, contained in five trucks, at Szent Gotthard, on the Hungarian side of the Austro-Hungarian frontier. The discovery was made by Austrian customs officials. The consignment, which had been misdescribed as machinery, had been dispatched from a firm in Verona, its immediate destination being Slovenské Nové Mesto, on the Hungarian-Czechoslovak border. It was alleged by the Hungarians that the goods were ultimately intended for Warsaw, and a joint inquiry by the local customs officials of Austria and Hungary was stated to have established this fact: it was, however, denied by the Polish Government. The matter came before the League, on the application of the Little Entente Powers, and an inquiry was instituted, with inconclusive results. The question of the final destination of the machine-gun parts was never cleared up.

Franco-Italian Relations, 1928

On the whole, however, the situation cleared, at any rate for the time, during 1928. There was, in particular, a marked improvement in Franco-Italian relations. This was partly due to the friendly gesture made by M. Briand on 30 November 1927, and the signature of the *modus vivendi* of which mention has already been made (p. 169). But it was greatly assisted by the revision of the Statute of Tangier which had come into force in 1925, and had proved generally unsatisfactory. As already stated (p. 163), Italy had not been consulted in the previous negotiations, and had therefore withheld her recognition from the arrangement. Spain was also dissatisfied, and the conclusion of a treaty of amity with Italy on 7 August 1926, immediately emboldened her to reopen the question.[1] To the subsequent discussions Italy was a party, and the new Statute,

---

[1] Spain linked her claims in this matter with the question of her seat on the League Council (see p. 202), as a condition of her continued membership of the League.

which gave her representation in the Legislative Assembly and on the Committee of Control, was satisfactorily arranged, the exchange of ratifications taking place on 14 September 1928.

Relations with Yugoslavia

At the same time Italian diplomacy was in a measure successful in its dealings with Yugoslavia. The Yugoslavs had hitherto persistently refused to ratify the technical Conventions relating to Fiume, Zara, and Dalmatia, which had been signed at Nettuno in July 1925. But they were not in a position to hold out any longer against Italian pressure. The efforts of Italian diplomacy also affected their relations with Greece. An Italo-Turkish pact, and a similar pact between Italy and Greece, was concluded in 1928, and negotiations—which eventually bore fruit in the Graeco-Turkish treaty of 30 October 1930—were simultaneously being carried on, with the active encouragement of Italy, between Greece and Turkey. In the settlement of the question of the Salonika zone, which was made in 1928 and finally ratified in 1929, Yugoslavia was forced to abandon the extreme claims which she had previously advanced. Her main source of weakness was to be traced in the internal conditions of the country, where the cleavage between Serb and Croat had reached a critical stage. On 20 June 1928, Radić, the Croat Peasant Leader, was murdered in the Legislative Assembly, with his nephew and another Croat deputy, by shots fired from the Government benches by a Serbian member, Puniča Račić. There seems to be evidence tending to prove that the outrage was planned and pre-meditated.[1] After this occurrence the Croat deputies withdrew in a body from the Assembly, and it was in these circumstances that the Nettuno Conventions were passed for ratification, on 13 August, by the 'Rump Parliament' which remained. The anti-Italian riots which the proposal had occasioned earlier in the year showed, however, that the decision did not reflect the popular attitude. The internal conditions of Yugoslavia led the King, in January 1929, to suspend the constitution and inaugurate autocratic government.

[1] See address by C. D. Booth, *Journal of the Royal Institute of International Affairs,* vol. viii, 1929, p. 332.

Italianization in the Tyrol

The existence of causes of antagonism between Italy and France, and the growing inclination of the former to associate herself with the cause of treaty revision, gave her relations with Germany a bearing of great importance on the prospects of lasting peace. For some time after the inauguration of the Fascist regime, any close understanding between these two Powers seemed to be precluded by the policy which Italy was pursuing towards her subjects of German race, inhabiting the region of the Upper Adige, in what had formerly been the Austrian Tyrol. With the advent to power of Signor Mussolini, a deliberate policy of forcible Italianization, which the Fascists had pursued from an earlier date, was vested with legislative sanction. The pretext was an allegation that advantage had been taken of the indulgence of former governments to make the whole district a centre of German irredentism. But it should be remembered that this was in flagrant violation of promises repeatedly made by responsible Italians at the time of the Peace Conference in Paris: this indeed had been explicitly declared to constitute the understanding on which the region had been transferred to Italian control (see the quotation on p. 159 of this chapter). These pledges were now openly ignored. Local autonomy was first excluded by the erection of the whole territory, German-speaking as well as Italian, into a single province. Within this area the exclusive use of the Italian language was progressively enforced. From official documents, place-names, and public inscriptions—including tombstones—it spread to the courts of law and then to the schools, where from October 1924 even kindergarten instruction was compelled to be given in Italian, and by teachers approved by the Education Office, who had frequently no knowledge of German. This deprived the children of any effective education, and when the inhabitants sought to meet this difficulty by private schooling, a fresh decree forbade this expedient when applied to more than three children from different families. In these circumstances, illegal 'catacomb schools', as they were called, came into existence all over the South Tyrol, but these were remorselessly hunted down and suppressed.[1] These measures were

---

[1] It was announced in *The Times* of 28 June 1934, that private schools for the teaching of German might be reopened in the Alto Adige.

combined with steps of a more normal nature, such as a ban upon the local German press.

With the improvement in the status of Germany consequent upon the Locarno agreements, this policy was subjected to vigorous criticism throughout the Reich, where a general boycott of all things Italian was widely suggested by way of reprisal, though this was deprecated by the Tyrolese themselves, as calculated to subject them to an even fiercer persecution. The suggestion was in fact met by Signor Mussolini with threats of 'a boycott squared and reprisals cubed', the assertion that 'the Germans of the Alto Adige are not a national minority, they are an ethnical relic', and an ominous hint that 'Fascist Italy can, if necessary, carry her tricolour further'.[1]

Yet in spite of the feeling necessarily created by these exchanges, the question had a surprisingly small and transient effect upon Italo-German diplomatic relations. In December 1926 a treaty of conciliation and arbitration was signed by the two Powers, and a new protocol added to the commercial agreement of 1925. This was followed, indeed, by some temporary alleviation of the situation, when the German portion of the region was separated administratively from the Trentino, but the benefits anticipated from this modification did not materialize. Yet relations between Italy and Germany grew steadily closer during the ensuing years. It may seem paradoxical to see in friendly *rapprochement* a danger to peace, but Europe seemed one step nearer a relapse into its pre-war arrangement of two opposing alliances. Coupled with the rivalry in the Balkans of two Great Powers, one from each combination, it presented a picture which was ominously familiar.

[1] Speech of 6 February 1926.

XI

THE PROBLEM OF DISARMAMENT, 1925–30

The Preparatory Commission

WITH the conclusion of the Locarno agreements the prospects of disarmament assumed a more hopeful appearance. The French demand for security against German aggression seemed for the moment to have been effectively met, and the contracting Powers, in the concluding paragraph of the final protocol, had undertaken 'to give their sincere co-operation to the work relating to disarmament already undertaken by the League of Nations and to seek the realization thereof in a general agreement'. Animated by the prevailing optimism, the Council of the League made a fresh start by the appointment, in December 1925, of a Preparatory Commission, which, it was anticipated, would clear the way for the meeting of the final Disarmament Conference in a comparatively short space of time. The hope was widely entertained that before the end of 1927 the Conference would be in session.

It was true that the menace of war was not confined to the danger of a German revival. To Poland, Roumania, and other states on the Russian border, substantial disarmament remained an impossibility so long as the U.S.S.R. was not a party to the arrangements. It was mainly the desire to secure the representation of the Soviet Government which occasioned an initial delay in getting to work. The first meeting of the Preparatory Commission was timed to take place at Geneva on 15 February 1926, but at this time there were differences, still unsettled, between the Governments of Russia and Switzerland, as a result of the murder of the Soviet delegate to the Lausanne Conference in 1923. In these circumstances, the U.S.S.R. was unwilling to be represented at a meeting on Swiss soil, but a satisfactory solution was expected in the course of negotiations then in progress, and a postponement until May was therefore proposed, with the object of securing the attendance of a Russian delegation. This step was further prompted by the expectation that, by the later date, the special Assembly of the

League would have performed its allotted task of admitting Germany to membership. But the postponement, however reasonable, cast an inauspicious shadow over the outset of the proceedings.

As it turned out, neither of its objects was achieved. The special meeting of the Assembly proved abortive, in consequence of the disputes which arose over the constitution of the Council (see p. 200), and the Russo-Swiss negotiations broke down in February, with the result that when the Preparatory Commission met for its opening session, on 18 May 1926, the U.S.S.R. was still unrepresented.

Apart from this difficulty, the hopes entertained of speedy progress proved illusory. In the minds of some of the States participating, the preliminary problem of security had not yet been sufficiently solved to permit of a direct and unimpeded approach to the question of disarmament. Efforts were at once made, by the French, Polish, and Finnish delegations, to secure priority for the question of security. Their proposals were forwarded to the Council, a committee of which was engaged in the investigation of the problem, but the Commission itself continued to attack its allotted task from the single angle of disarmament. Further obstacles of a serious nature were not long in making their appearance. There were numerous and important points of principle upon which the opinion of the Commission was sharply divided.

The French delegation viewed with complete mistrust any agreement on measures of disarmament which was not controlled by effective international supervision. Any such control the representatives of Italy and of the United States categorically refused to accept, and their view was adopted, less emphatically, by Great Britain, which was disposed to rely upon the good faith of the signatory Powers. The French moreover, with characteristic logic but ignoring practical difficulties, desired to import into the discussion the question of 'war potential' in all its aspects. Such a proposal at once exposed the rock upon which previous suggestions for a limitation of armaments had invariably foundered. What is an armament? The military efficiency of a country is affected by considerations as remote from the number of its guns or of its regular battalions as the possession of certain raw materials, the construction and course of a railway, or the rise or fall of its birth-rate.

For example, it has been pointed out that the control of the Panama Canal approximately doubles the naval strength of the United States. Thus the mathematical equalization of the armed forces and equipment of two countries may well have the effect of establishing the unquestionable supremacy of the one over the other.

But, in spite of the undeniable force of such arguments, it was felt by an influential section of opinion on the Commission, particularly by the United States and Great Britain, that such an approach was fatal to progress. It involved consideration of many factors over which a Disarmament Conference could not expect to exert control—for instance, the rise or fall of a birth-rate. For this reason, practical considerations demanded the restriction of the survey, as far as possible, to armaments in the usual sense of the word.

On the other hand, on one point the rival protagonists appeared to change their ground. It was the British delegation which pointed out the potentialities of trained reserves as a matter which ought to be considered, while France and other conscriptionist countries argued hotly that limitation should only be applied to troops actually with the colours. On this point, the British finally agreed to give way, subject to a provision for so limiting the proportion of officers and non-commissioned officers as to preclude a sudden expansion, but the question remained unsettled, and Germany still adhered strongly to the original British standpoint. Another point of acute controversy arose in connexion with naval disarmament, between the advocates of limitation of total tonnage and those who favoured limitation by categories. This issue, however, may be more conveniently discussed on its recurrence at a later stage.

It soon became apparent, therefore, that the hopes originally entertained of the early assembly of the Disarmament Conference itself had been unduly sanguine. In March 1927, the British delegation endeavoured to stimulate progress by depositing a draft convention, but this was immediately countered by the production of a French alternative, and comparison of the two served only to accentuate the existence of numerous and apparently irreconcilable divergences. These were further emphasized in April by the decision to issue a report, in which the rival proposals were set out side by side, together with any reservations submitted in regard to clauses as to which there seemed to be substantial agreement. By the close of 1927, the labours of the Preparatory Commission seemed threatened with deadlock.

The Three-Power Naval Conference

A similar failure characterized the efforts of the United States to complete the work of 1921–2 by arriving at an agreement as to the limitation of naval armaments in the categories excluded from the Washington agreement (6 February 1922). American opinion differed from that of the 'Continental School' in several important particulars, the contrast being clearly tabulated in a letter addressed by Mr Kellogg, the United States Secretary of State, to an American correspondent, on 11 January 1927. America still believed in a direct attack upon the disarmament problem dissociated from the question of security; she repudiated the continental contention as to the interdependence of all arms, and the necessity for considering 'war potential' in all its aspects; and she considered that naval armaments could most easily be dealt with on regional lines, by agreement between a limited number of naval Powers. This attitude was perhaps justifiable in considering the relations between the United States and Japan, where the area of possible conflict was indeed restricted, and the issue definitely limited to rivalry in sea-power. But it was unacceptable to France and Italy, who were committed to the thesis that all aspects of the problem were interdependent, and were averse from the consideration of one item in isolation, particularly at a time when it figured on the agenda of the League of Nations Commission which was simultaneously occupied with the question. An invitation issued by the President of the United States to a conference on naval disarmament in June 1927 was therefore declined by these two Powers.

The position of Great Britain was, as usual, intermediate. As Mr Ramsay MacDonald pointed out in relation to a later conference,[1] the five Powers principally concerned in naval matters resolve themselves into two groups of three, Great

---

[1] *Journal of the Royal Institute of International Affairs*, vol. ix, 1930, p. 430.

Britain being a member of both of them. It was therefore impossible for her to treat the problem in a purely regional spirit, since whatever might be agreed with the United States and Japan had to be considered in relation to the absent continental European Powers. Great Britain was, nevertheless, willing to participate in the proposed conference, even in the absence of France and Italy.

The ground had, however, been insufficiently explored, and the American and British representatives arrived at Geneva, on 20 June, with independent schemes which there had been no preliminary attempt to co-ordinate. The United States wished to treat the matter as one of pure relativity. They proposed to apply to the remaining categories of ships, with unimportant exceptions, precisely the same ratio as had been agreed upon at the Washington Conference with reference to large battle-ships. Great Britain, on the other hand, was concerned about her absolute needs, in the special circumstances in which the nation was placed, dependent upon the protection of supplies drawn from all quarters of the world. The limitation which she proposed consisted in a general reduction in the size of ships and the calibre of their guns, together with an extension in the accepted life of each class of vessel. This latter provision it was proposed to extend to the capital ships dealt with at the Washington Conference, a proposal which involved a recon-sideration of the agreement previously arrived at. Great Britain was ready to accept the suggested ratio only in reference to the class of 10,000-ton cruisers carrying 8-inch guns. Of smaller cruisers, it was contended that her special needs called for a large number; the minimum suggested being 70.[1] Under the American proposal, the tonnage limit for all ships in the cruiser class would be 400,000 tons each for Great Britain and the United States: the latter declared their intention of having 25 of the large 10,000-ton cruisers, thus leaving only 150,000 tons for the smaller class, or 20 cruisers of 7,500 tons, the limit of size proposed by Great Britain. Since the maximum size tends to become the standard, it was felt that it would be neces-sary to build in parity with the United States, and the result would be to leave Great Britain with a most serious deficiency in the numbers of cruisers thought essential for trade protection.

[1] See note at end of chapter.

There was, in short, a complete discrepancy between the doctrine of 'mathematical parity' and fixed ratios advocated by the United States, and the 'absolute' standard of requirement insisted upon by the British. This divergence probably coincided with the actual needs of the parties. The United States wished to have a comparatively small number of cruisers of large size; Great Britain required a large number of cruisers and, to secure these, needed a size limit as low as was compatible with the performance of their functions. But the crucial difference arose from the fact that one party thought purely in terms of numerical parity of forces, while the other, though recognizing the opposing force as an element in the problem, took other factors of security into consideration as well, and maintained in effect that to police a large area requires a certain minimum number of constables, irrespective of the quantity of disorderly characters in it.

There appears to be no doubt that, during the sessions of the Conference, a section of opinion was gaining strength in the British Cabinet which was fundamentally opposed to any concession of the principle of mathematical parity, which was regarded as equivalent to yielding to America a position of practical superiority. On 19 July the British representatives were temporarily recalled for consultation to London, and on their return Mr Bridgeman's attitude was definitely more uncompromising, while his colleague, Lord Cecil, resigned from the Cabinet after the failure of the negotiations, which he was inclined to attribute to the instructions received at home. The lack of diplomatic preparation played, perhaps, a more important part. It was, no doubt, a cause of some quite avoidable misunderstandings, though these seem to have been satisfactorily cleared up in the course of the proceedings. But the fundamental cleavage between the advocates of 'relativity' and those of 'absolute requirements' makes it probably unnecessary to search for further reasons for the breakdown of the Conference, which occurred on 4 August.[1]

The Naval Construction Bill

Though the failure of American diplomacy on this occasion was destined to be offset almost immediately by the Kellogg

[1] See also note at end of chapter.

Pact, which was perhaps the most outstanding contribution hitherto made to the twin problems of security and disarmament, the immediate sequel to the break-down was the submission to Congress, in November 1927, of a bill for increased naval construction. Its programme, however, called out unsuspected depths of antagonistic feeling among the people of the United States, as a result of which it was subjected to drastic reductions before the final passage of the bill in February 1929. Meanwhile, much had occurred to modify the situation.

The Kellogg Pact

In unofficial circles in the United States there had for some time been in progress a movement for what was called 'the Outlawry of War'. As was pointed out by a lecturer before the Royal Institute of International Affairs, in November 1928,[1] the term is strictly speaking a solecism. But the fundamental idea of the adherents of this school of thought was that no progress could be made towards the ending of war until the use of force was altogether renounced as a method for settling international disputes. Opinion outside the United States had meanwhile advanced some distance in the same direction. On 24 September 1927, the Assembly of the League of Nations unanimously adopted a resolution proposed by the Polish delegation, which in terms prohibited all wars of aggression, and declared that pacific means must be employed in all cases to settle international disputes. At the Sixth Pan-American Conference, held in February 1928, a similar resolution was adopted on the proposal of the Mexican delegate.

But, at an even earlier date, the first steps in negotiations leading to the adoption of the Pact for the Renunciation of War had been taken. In April 1927 M. Briand had addressed a personal message to the American people, in which he suggested that the tenth anniversary of the entry of the United States into the war might be appropriately celebrated by the conclusion of a mutual engagement renouncing war as an instrument of policy between France and the United States. This suggestion he followed up in June by the transmission to Mr Kellogg, the Secretary of State at Washington, of a draft

[1] Mr Philip Kerr (afterwards the Marquis of Lothian), *Journal*, 1928, vol. vii, p. 361.

treaty embodying this idea. Though the initiative thus appears to have come from France, the United States are really entitled to the share of the credit which they have since enjoyed through the popular name of the peace pact, for M. Briand had undoubtedly been inspired by an American citizen, Professor Shotwell, during a conversation held in the previous March.

Mr Kellogg was somewhat slow in responding to this overture, but on 28 December he addressed two notes to M. Briand, the second of which suggested that the proposed treaty should be made multilateral. This suggestion was not immediately acceptable to the French Minister. It was one thing to indulge in the gesture of renouncing war with a nation with whom France was extremely unlikely to have any dispute which could possibly lead to hostilities, and another for a member of the League and a signatory of a number of treaties providing for an ultimate resort to war to adopt, without mature reflection, an unrestricted extension of the principle involved. In April, however, M. Briand agreed to submit the Franco-American correspondence to the Governments of Germany, Great Britain, Italy, and Japan, and, on 13 April 1928, this course was adopted, by the issue of a circular note to these Powers from Mr Kellogg, including the draft of a multilateral treaty. The two substantive articles in this draft were identical with those of M. Briand's original suggestion, except that they were cast in multilateral form. In answer to an alternative draft, issued on 20 April by the French Government, Mr Kellogg, nine days later, delivered a speech before the American International Law Association, in which he gave an interpretation of various doubtful points, calculated to dispose of misgivings entertained in various quarters as to the effect of the treaty on existing obligations and the right of self-defence. These interpretations he reaffirmed, in a note addressed to fourteen governments, on 23 June. These governments included, in addition to the four Great Powers originally addressed, Belgium, Czechoslovakia, and Poland, together with India and the self-governing Dominions of the British Commonwealth.

The reception of the proposal by public opinion was overwhelmingly favourable. The governments themselves were naturally and rightly more cautious. Great Britain made a reservation with regard to 'certain regions of the world the welfare and integrity of which constitute a special and vital interest for our peace and safety'. This was generally held to refer principally to Egypt. France reserved her previous treaty obligations, and emphasized the right of self-defence, which Mr Kellogg had conceded. She also stipulated that the violation of the pledge by one country should involve the automatic release of all. With these and similar understandings, the Pact was signed by representatives of the fifteen original contracting parties on 27 August 1928, and was immediately declared open to the adherence of the other States. In a comparatively short time, acceptance of its terms was almost universal, the only self-governing States not invited to adhere being those in Arabia, the Nejd-Hijaz, and the Yemen. By 1930, the only other absentees of any importance were Argentina, Brazil, and Bolivia. The ratification of the Treaty by the United States took place on 17 January 1929, and during the first half of that year it had been finally accepted by nearly all the other signatories. Somewhat surprisingly, the Soviet Government, which had originally damned the Pact with faint praise as a product of capitalism, took immediate steps to anticipate its general ratification by securing the adherence of its neighbours to an independent protocol for bringing the terms of the Pact into force locally. This 'Litvinov Protocol', as it was called, was submitted to Poland and Lithuania in December 1928. The Polish Government was at first undecided, principally on account of its treaty relations with Roumania, with whom Russia had a still outstanding dispute over Bessarabia. M. Litvinov, however, expressed his willingness to include Roumania as an adherent to his protocol, which was also open for signature to the Baltic border States. In these circumstances, the instrument was signed by the U.S.S.R., Poland, Roumania, Latvia, and Estonia in February 1929, and by Lithuania shortly afterwards. By this time, however, the ratification of the Pact by the United States had been concluded, and the ostensible reason for M. Litvinov's independent action was therefore removed.

As a historical event, this almost universal repudiation of war as an instrument of policy seems to have a unique importance. As a gesture indicative of a new ethical attitude to war, it was undeniably impressive. It was particularly important in that it created a basis upon which the great nations outside the League, the United States and Russia, could take a direct interest in the collective organization of peace. Yet, as Mr Wheeler-Bennett has pointed out,[1] 'only war of aggression had been outlawed', and actually it therefore carried the outlawry of war no further than the Polish resolution adopted by the League Assembly in September 1927 (see p. 181). As might be expected from an instrument of Transatlantic origin, it served at the moment as a magnificent advertisement of the pacific disposition of the world, and might have been thought to constitute a great step forward on the road to international security. It depended, however, on nothing more solid than the good faith of the signatory nations, and imposed no sanctions upon those who disregarded its pledges. In an age which had learned to ignore inconvenient obligations, it was not destined to restore that measure of confidence necessary to induce the nations to disarm.[2] Each probably considered that war was not, in any event, an instrument of its own policy, but each continued to mistrust the bona fides of its neighbours. At the very moment when the Pact was put forward for signature, an episode occurred which emphasized in a striking manner the existence of these suspicions.

The Anglo-French Compromise

On the adjournment of the Preparatory Commission in March 1927, its President, Jonkheer Loudon, had suggested the value of external conversations between the Powers concerned, with the object of removing the deadlock revealed in the French and British draft conventions. With this laudable motive, France and Great Britain accordingly entered into negotiations. Two main points of disagreement had been the respective attitudes of the two nations in relation to the treatment of land and sea forces. In the estimate of the former, Great Britain wished to include trained reserves, a course to

---

[1] *Disarmament and Security since Locarno.* London, Allen & Unwin, 1932, p. 248.

[2] One of those to whom the manuscript of this chapter was submitted remarked: 'I think the most striking result of the Pact deserves mention, i.e. that signatories who wanted to violate it have merely adopted the simple device of going to war without a declaration, so that we have really relapsed into the primitive age before "civilized" warfare existed!'

which France was strongly opposed, while, with regard to naval limitation, the French favoured a limitation of total tonnage, whereas Great Britain, as she had shown in her abortive negotiations with America, held out for a limitation by separate categories. On these two matters, the two governments now succeeded in reaching a compromise. The gist of this was that in consideration of the withdrawal of the British opposition to the French standpoint in regard to trained reserves, France was prepared to accept a naval limitation by categories, from which surface vessels of 10,000 tons and under should be altogether exempt, if armed with guns of no more than 6-inch calibre. The difficulty was that both of the subjects for compromise were matters in which other Powers besides the negotiators were keenly interested. Germany retained the original British view on the subject of trained reserves, while the United States had, as mentioned above, definitely rejected proposals for the subdivision of the cruiser class, and also attached great importance to freedom to arm all their cruisers with 8-inch guns, which, under the conditions now proposed, would place them in the restricted class.

It seems, therefore, strange that the two Powers should ever have believed that the fruits of their private negotiations would be generally acceptable. The actual terms of the compromise, however, caused less ferment than the manner in which they were revealed. On 30 July 1928, Sir Austen Chamberlain announced the fact of the compromise in the House of Commons, without disclosing its terms: the text of the naval formula, without reference to the connected matter of the trained reserves, was telegraphed simultaneously to the American, Japanese, and Italian Governments, but, while public curiosity as to the nature of the agreement still remained unsatisfied and at the mercy of rumour, the French press broke out into paeans of jubilation calculated to produce the most exaggerated impressions of the importance of the arrangements arrived at. The aspect of the question relating to land forces was next extracted by inquiries from Germany, though the British Government continued to deny that this was an essential part of the negotiations, since it was 'an understanding with the French Government, made before the text of the compromise was actually drawn up'. Speculation became rife as to the existence of secret clauses and political understandings of a far-reaching character between the two governments. 'It was taken everywhere in Europe as proof that Great Britain had decided to support a permanent French military preponderance in Europe and that the policy of Locarno was at an end.' [1] To make matters worse, before the texts were officially published, an American newspaper printed a confidential letter of instructions regarding the compromise, which had been circulated, on 3 August, to various French diplomatic missions. Circumstances thus combined to put a false construction on the whole affair, and to invest it with an atmosphere of secrecy and intrigue which was enhanced by its coincidence in date with the signature of the Kellogg Pact—the compromise and the Pact being actually referred to by Sir Austen Chamberlain, on 30 July in the same sitting of the House of Commons. The methods of the old and the new diplomacy were thus brought in the public mind, especially in America, into powerful and poignant contrast. When the American and Italian official replies had duly condemned the arrangement arrived at, the incident terminated in a round of apologies, disclaimers, and criticisms.

Progress of the Preparatory Commission

When the Preparatory Commission had resumed its labours, on 30 November 1927, it was fortified by two resolutions of the Assembly. The first of these was the Polish proposal condemning wars of aggression which has been already mentioned; the second (26 September) reaffirmed the primary importance of adequate guarantees of security and collective action for the maintenance of peace, and suggested the formation of a Committee of the Commission, charged with considering this aspect of the subject. A further change had been brought about by the attendance on this occasion of a delegation from Soviet Russia (Turkey was also for the first time represented). The Russian representative, M. Litvinov, made his début with a sweeping proposal for the complete and immediate abolition of all armies, navies, and air forces, and the destruction of all warships, war material, and arms factories. This drastic

---

[1] Philip Kerr (afterwards Marquis of Lothian), in *Journal of the Royal Institute of International Affairs*, 1928, p. 370.

suggestion was not treated seriously, and indeed was probably
not so intended, its real object being presumably to discredit the
League and the capitalist Powers by drawing attention to the
slow and hesitant progress made in the field of disarmament.
It is true, however, that the Soviet Government, whose weapon
was subversive propaganda, would have lost little and gained
much from the adoption, if conceivable, of such a proposal.

Meanwhile, the German representative, Count Bernstorff,
lost no opportunity of pressing upon the Commission the right
of his country to expect more rapid progress in general disarmament. He achieved, however, little more than to arouse
a suspicion that he was anxious to force the pace with the idea
of ensuring the break-down of the Conference, so as to clear the
ground for the rearmament of Germany. M. Litvinov was also
suspected of wrecking designs, and a growing *rapprochement*
between Russia and Germany, indicated by an interview
between Count Bernstorff and M. Litvinov in Berlin, before the
reassembly of the Commission, was viewed with some uneasiness. It is fair to add that the tactics imputed to the 'heavily-
armed Powers' were a subject of no less sincere criticism and
misgiving to their opponents. The Commission, in any case,
continued to make no perceptible progress during the year 1928.

The General Act

The work of the Committee on Security was more fruitful.
On the basis of preliminary work carried out in Prague under
the chairmanship of M. Beneš, it succeeded in producing no
less than ten model draft treaties, in which the changes were
rung upon the various expedients of arbitration, conciliation,
non-aggression, and mutual assistance. Three of these treaties
were multilateral and the remainder bilateral. The former were
combined by the Ninth Assembly of the League in September
1928, into a General Act for the Pacific Settlement of International Disputes, which was opened for the general accession
of all States.

The object of the General Act was to implement the Kellogg
Pact by providing machinery for the pacific settlement of international disputes, applicable to all cases. The first chapter
provided for procedure by conciliation, the second for the reference of justiciable disputes to the Permanent Court or to an

arbitral tribunal, while the third extended the expedient of arbitration to disputes for which the machinery of the Permanent Court was not appropriate. A final chapter, dealing with general provisions, permitted adherence to the Act to be either complete or partial; States were left free to accept either the conciliation procedure alone, or conciliation and judicial settlement, without committing themselves to the principle of compulsory arbitration in all cases. Chapter IV also permitted reservations, and provided that if one party to a dispute had made a reservation the other parties might claim the benefits of it. There was, therefore, an obvious advantage in waiting to see the attitude of other nations, and it is hardly surprising that no accessions had been notified by the close of 1928.

In May 1929, however, Sweden accepted Chapters I and II of the General Act, together with the relevant general provisions, and Belgium, a few days later, notified her general accession, reserving only disputes arising out of earlier events. Since the Act was to come into force ninety days from the second accession (Article 44), it accordingly entered into operation on 16 August. By September 1930, Denmark, Norway, and Finland had acceded completely and Holland had accepted the chapters relating to judicial settlement and conciliation. The example of these countries was soon followed by Luxembourg and Spain. The signatories, however, included no Power of first-class importance by the end of 1930.

The Convention on Financial Assistance

A rather important decision was reached by the League Assembly during its eleventh session, September 1930, when a convention for the provision of financial assistance to States victims of aggression, or subjected to the threat of it, was thrown open for signature. The coming into force of this convention was, however, made conditional upon the conclusion of a disarmament convention at the forthcoming Conference. The scheme was originally put forward by the representative of Finland before the Preparatory Commission in 1926, and a long discussion preceded its provisional adoption in 1930. The notion of 'promoting peace by financing war' was exposed to some criticism, and considerable difference of opinion prevailed as to whether the expedient should be applied at a stage preceding the actual outbreak of war and also as to whether its application should be contingent upon the success of the Disarmament Conference. It was eventually agreed that the convention should only be applied in circumstances short of actual war 'if the Council . . . shall, in any international dispute likely to lead to a rupture, have taken steps to safeguard peace' which have been disregarded by one party, and also 'provided it [the Council] considers that peace cannot be safeguarded otherwise'. The second disputed point was decided, as already stated, in favour of the contingent adoption of the convention.

The Naval Conference, 1930

An important change—for better or for worse—came over the spirit of the scene with the advent to office of Mr Ramsay MacDonald, as a result of the British general election of May 1929. The divergence of policy in the matter of disarmament between the Conservative and Labour Governments was of course not so conspicuous as that of the views entertained by some of their supporters. If a man were heard inveighing against 'this disarmament nonsense', and clamouring for large increases in the armed forces of the Crown, he would not represent the view of the Conservative Government, but there can be no doubt that his vote, if recorded, would be Conservative. On the other hand, the extreme pacifist, advocating reckless unilateral gestures of disarmament, could with equal certainty be set down as of the Labour Party, though, with the possible exception of Lord Ponsonby, he could claim no official supporter for his views. The affiliations of extreme views of this kind are an indication of a more subtle distinction in the approach by responsible statesmen of each party to the question of disarmament. Though both desired the same end, the motive and emphasis were different. The Conservatives, of whom Lord Cushendun, their representative at Geneva, was a typical specimen, laid the chief stress upon the economies to be achieved by a limitation of expenditure on armaments, and upon the obligation to disarm inherent in the League Covenant, but were openly sceptical of the efficacy of disarmament as a preventive of war.[1] They considered that the reduction in the

[1] See address by Lord Cushendun, *Journal of Royal Institute of International Affairs*, vol. vii, 1928, p. 77.

British forces had already approached the limits of safety, and, while they regretted this premature throwing away of cards, were reluctant to make further sacrifices. They were opposed to a general commitment to submit British interests to the adjudication of foreigners, such as was involved in the signature of the 'optional clause' of the Statute of the Permanent Court of International Justice, or adherence to the General Act. To the Labour Party, on the other hand, the achievement of a substantial measure of general disarmament was a better safeguard of the national interests than any which could be attained through the armed forces of the country, and they were correspondingly more ready to make concessions. Mr MacDonald's Government came into power pledged to sign the optional clause, and this pledge was redeemed, with the reservation of domestic and inter-imperial questions, in September 1929, the self-governing Dominions and India following the example of Great Britain.[1] In 1930 the Government took steps towards accession to the General Act, and, after consultation with the Dominions at the Imperial Conference which met in that year, instruments of accession were deposited by all members of the Commonwealth, with the exception of South Africa, in the summer of 1931. As a further pacific gesture, the Government also suspended operations upon the Singapore naval base. Of more immediate importance, however, was the revival of negotiations with the object of arriving at a satisfactory solution of the problems of naval disarmament. This had been facilitated by some encouraging pronouncements from America in the spring of 1929, and the rest of the year was largely devoted by Mr MacDonald to Anglo-American conversations, as a result of which an invitation was issued in October to the United States, France, Italy, and Japan to attend a conference in London in January 1930.

The Naval Treaty in London

For this Conference, unlike that of 1927, the ground had therefore been well explored. A further advantage lay in the fact that France and Italy accepted the invitation, for though the solution of the problem was thereby complicated, it was

---

[1] The Irish Free State did not reserve inter-imperial disputes. As she stood alone, however, this difference is not of practical importance.

faced, at the outset, as a whole. The hands of the British negotiators were also freed by the adoption, on the part of the Admiralty, of a more modest estimate of the 'absolute needs' of Great Britain in the matter of cruisers, the minimum demand being reduced from 70 to 50. The ground for this reduction was stated to be the 'improved world political relationships' consequent upon the adoption of the Kellogg Pact. But it remained doubtful whether it was not based on an unduly optimistic view of the international situation. The First Lord of the Admiralty, indeed, represented the figure as having only a temporary validity 'up to the next date for conference and revision', in other words, until 1935. The optimism of the Prime Minister went even farther. Mr MacDonald told the Conference that 'as the British Government viewed the present outlook, the risk of war was practically nil'. He admitted, however, in the same speech, that 'if the approach were made on the assumption that war had to be prepared for within a comparatively short time, then the British programme was altogether inadequate'.[1] It was also stated to be contingent upon adequate limitation being agreed to by other Powers.

Having secured this expert reduction in the claims of 'absolute need', the new Government was able to abandon all opposition to the American approach to the problem as one of pure relativity. It was left to the French, ably represented by M. Tardieu, to continue the attack upon the fallacy of mathematical ratios. The naval requirements of France, he insisted, were governed by such considerations as the distribution of her coast-lines on three seas, and the extent of her oversea communications. The same arguments were used, upon another front, in opposing the Italian claim to parity. This claim the French representative was only willing to concede in return for adequate guarantees of security which none of the other negotiators was willing to grant. All-round parity with Italy, he urged, meant in fact inferiority in the Mediterranean. M. Briand reinforced M. Tardieu's arguments by a reference to the 'pocket battleship' recently constructed by Germany.[2]

The Italian delegation, however, while protesting their

[1] Woodward, E. L., *and* R. Butler (*ed.*). *Documents on British Foreign Policy, 1919-1939*. Second series, vol. 1. London, H.M.S.O., 1946, p. 215.
[2] ibid., pp. 216-17.

willingness to accept any figure, however low, which was not exceeded by any other Continental Power, continued to insist upon equality, and on this issue the attempt to secure complete agreement between all the five Powers eventually broke down.

In other respects, the difficulties proved more tractable. Between the limitation confined to aggregate—or 'global'— tonnage advocated by France, and the restriction by separate categories preferred by Great Britain, a basis of compromise was found in the so-called 'transactional proposal' put forward by the French in 1927. This combined the 'global' system with an allocation of the total tonnage between different categories, which might be modified by the transfer of a proportion from one category to another, after due notice to the other Powers concerned. By substantial agreement upon this arrangement, one of the most formidable obstacles was surmounted, though Great Britain insisted that the right to transfer should be restricted to certain categories. It was soon apparent, however, that the proportion available for transfer could not be fixed until the tonnage ratio between the different Powers had been settled.

The principal obstacles to progress in this respect were the assessment by France of her absolute requirements at a high level, and a demand by Japan for a 70 per cent ratio with the United States in the class of 8-inch gun cruisers. The Conference, however, attained at an early stage substantial agreement upon certain important points. While Anglo-American proposals for the total abolition of submarines were rejected, all parties were prepared to agree to regulation of the conditions of submarine warfare; all were also prepared to acquiesce in a five years' holiday from the construction of capital ships. The Japanese claims in relation to large cruisers were met by negotiations between Senator Reed and Mr Matsudaira, resulting in an agreement allocating to Japan 60 per cent of the American figure in this class, subject to an understanding with regard to building which left her with a 72 per cent ratio up to 1936. In numbers, as opposed to tonnage, Japan was more favourably situated, since four of her cruisers in the 8-inch gun category were of lighter tonnage than the American. In other cruisers and destroyers a 70 per cent ratio was conceded, and in submarines complete parity. The ground was thus cleared for a treaty, which was signed on 22 April 1930. The failure to secure complete agreement from France and Italy necessitated its division into two parts, one of which was accepted by three Powers only, the United States, the British Empire, and Japan. The portions accepted by all embodied the agreements as to capital ships and as to the regulation of submarine warfare; they also limited the tonnage and gun calibre of submarines, and contained provisions extending the limitations of aircraft carriers prescribed by the Washington Treaty of 1922. The British Empire, the United States, and Japan agreed further to scrap five, three, and one battleship respectively by 1933 instead of 1936 as provided in the Washington Treaty. The tonnage in other categories was allocated between the three Powers according to the following table:

					British Empire	U.S.A.	Japan
(a)	8-in. gun cruisers	.	.	.	146,800	180,000	108,400
(b)	6-in. „ „	.	.	.	192,200	143,500	100,450
(c)	Destroyers	.	.	.	150,000	150,000	105,500
(d)	Submarines	.	.	.	52,700	52,700	52,700
	Totals	.	.	.	511,700	526,200	367,050

The numbers in category (a) were: for the United States, 18; for the British Empire, 15; for Japan, 12. A clause much criticized in Great Britain limited the replacement tonnage of the cruisers in the case of the British Empire to 91,000 tons within the period covered by the treaty, without any corresponding provision in regard to the other Powers. In view of the uncertainty as to the action of the two European Powers, a so-called 'escalator' clause was included, permitting an increase in these figures, upon due notice, if the requirements of national security of any of the three signatories demanded it.

The provisions of the treaty were subjected to considerable criticism in the countries of each of the three Powers. In Japan, one member of the Naval General Staff committed suicide, and the Minister of Marine, who had signed the treaty, was presented with a dagger on his return, as a hint that he might well follow the same course. In Great Britain, the view that our naval security had been imperilled was widely held. During the Second World War, Admiral Richmond stigmatized the estimate of British requirements as 'gravely erroneous'.[1]   On the other hand, the Government was able to point to substantial economies, and to claim that the work of the Preparatory Commission had been considerably facilitated. The Treaty came into force, after ratification, on 1 January 1931.

The Draft Disarmament Convention

Encouraged by the measure of agreement secured in the Naval Conference, the Preparatory Commission succeeded in concluding its labours by the close of 1930 by the adoption of a draft disarmament convention. The way was thus at last prepared for the meeting of a Disarmament Conference, which was arranged by the Council of the League for February 1932. But a phase in the history of European relations had been finished, and a new chapter had been begun, even before the Preparatory Commission had completed its allotted task. On 3 October 1929, Herr Stresemann died. He lived to catch a sort of Pisgah sight of one of his objectives, the evacuation of the Rhineland by the Allied forces. Though this was not completed until June of the following year, the procedure had been agreed upon in August 1929, and the withdrawal had actually begun a few weeks before the death of the German statesman. With Stresemann passed away the 'policy of fulfilment', of which he had been the champion.

The change in the situation was clearly indicated by the results of the German general elections in September 1930. The spectacular rise of the Nazi party is a subject of such importance that it must be dealt with more fully elsewhere. But the trend of events was plainly shown, when a party which in the previous Reichstag held only 12 seats succeeded in gaining 107. Germany was no longer content to acquiesce in the conditions imposed upon her at Versailles so long as the rest of the world declined to disarm to the same level.

Even before this date, there had begun an ominous tendency for the chief Powers of Europe to form two groups, irreconcilably divided over the question of Treaty revision. This tendency was exemplified in the replies returned to M. Briand's proposal for a Pan-European union (see further

---

[1] Richmond, Admiral Sir H. *War at Sea To-day*, 1942, p. 25. (Oxford Pamphlets on World Affairs, no. 60.)

pp. 339-42) which was circulated on 17 May 1930. During the later sessions of the Preparatory Commission, there were traces of a growing *rapprochement* between Italy, Germany, and the U.S.S.R., in opposition to the point of view of which France was the protagonist. The Commission had to abandon the hope of an agreed conclusion, and to face the alternatives of a majority decision unacceptable to Germany or complete failure in its allotted task. This consideration accounts for the unexpected attitude of the British representative. Lord Cecil was evidently more concerned to secure a convention embodying the largest measure of agreement attainable than to insist on, or even support, propositions with which he had formerly appeared to be in sympathy. Thus, when Germany revived the question of including trained reserves, he abstained from voting, and when it was proposed to apply direct limitation to land war-material he not only adopted the same course with decisive effect (for the voting on the German resolution was equal, and it was only rejected for lack of a majority), but actually spoke against the proposal and in favour of the alternative of budgetary limitation. While his policy was misinterpreted in some quarters as indicative of a Franco-British *rapprochement*, it was really based upon a preference for what seemed practically attainable rather than for the theoretically desirable.

The convention, which was thus passed by a majority vote, met with the freely expressed disapproval of the representatives of Germany and of the U.S.S.R. The Swedish delegate also declared his disappointment at the results achieved, and Mr Gibson, for the United States, was not enthusiastic. Judged, however, as a skeleton basis on which the Disarmament Conference might work, it had achieved a considerable measure of agreement.

The principles adopted can only be summarized here in their main features. Personnel was to be limited, and where possible reduced, in the number of serving effectives in all formations organized on a military basis, without consideration of the size of trained reserves. The period of service with conscript forces was to be limited. Land war-material was subjected to budgetary limitation, and naval material was to be limited in accordance with the conclusions of the London Conference. The budgetary limitation was not applied specifically to air material, which was restricted by numbers and horse-power. But an over-head budgetary limitation was applied to the total expenditure on land, sea, and air forces. Chemical and bacteriological warfare were prohibited. Other articles provided for the exchange of information, and the setting up of a Permanent Disarmament Commission.

A clause peculiarly obnoxious to Germany preserved rights and obligations secured by previous treaties. While this was primarily intended by Great Britain and America to apply to the London and Washington Treaties, it was construed by France and other Powers as maintaining the strict application of the military clauses of the Treaty of Versailles. It thus brought out, in sharp conflict, the contrast between the French and German views. To France, the complete disarmament of Germany entailed no corresponding obligation on other Powers. It was merely an element in the security on which her own willingness to reduce her armaments depended. To Germany, the Versailles Treaty had created a quasi-contractual right to demand that other nations should disarm to her own level. The article in the convention appeared, on the other hand, to impose on Germany a continuance of her existing disadvantage, irrespective of the action of her neighbours. To this she was not willing any longer to submit.

The effectiveness of the work done by the Preparatory Commission was in fact prejudiced by the time which it had occupied. A new era was beginning, and what might have sufficed for the Europe of 1925 to 1929 might well prove inapplicable to the Europe of 1932.

NOTE

The British claim of 'absolute need' in cruisers

On this point, an argument often advanced in influential political circles ought perhaps to be noticed. It contended that the number—70—originally stipulated by the Admiralty would in fact be so inadequate that it might be disregarded, since four or five German raiders were able to do damage in the war, in spite of the existence of a far larger number, some 120, of British cruisers. The argument proceeded on the lines of a rule-of-three sum: if it took 120 odd cruisers to cope with four or five raiders, how many were needed to deal with a much larger number, usually stated loosely as 'hundreds', which a less easily blockaded enemy could provide? The answer was —it was urged—evidently far more than 70, and the conclusion was drawn that the resistance to the American thesis was mistaken.

To this, the naval expert had several points of reply:

1. The security aimed at is not absolute: a few raiders may still do damage: the object is the substantial protection of essential supplies.

2. The raiders in the First World War did not ever imperil the security thus defined.

3. The mathematical argument is fallacious; the same number of cruisers could have afforded security against a much larger number of raiders, had they existed. The ships utilized as raiders normally act singly, because

(a) they do more damage if scattered;

(b) they are more difficult to supply if massed;

(c) even two or three together would be no match for a properly armed cruiser, with speed enabling her to choose the range, &c.

The number of raiders therefore does not cause a proportional rise in cruiser requirements. If a convoy has to cross the ocean, and there is one raider about, the escort must accompany the convoy throughout, since the whereabouts of the raider is unknown. Acting thus, the same escort could cope with the hypothetical 'hundreds', acting singly, as our cruisers actually did cope with hundreds of privateers in the Napoleonic wars.

4. The figure 70, though opinions may differ as to its complete adequacy, was based on the scientific calculations always applied in such cases. It depends

(a) on the number of convoys needed to keep the country supplied;

(b) on the number of fixed patrol areas where, e.g., converging traffic suggests a probable point of attack;

(c) on the capacity of the enemy to employ cruisers in massed bodies, a capacity mainly dependent upon his possession of bases in the vicinity of lines of communication. This varies with different enemies, but an approximation to the numbers needed to meet it, in differing circumstances, can be arrived at.

This summary is of course not exhaustive, but it seems unwise to ignore a figure completely, merely because the reasons for it are unknown.

XII

AMERICA AND THE LEAGUE OF NATIONS

The League and the Monroe Doctrine

SOME of the difficulties caused by the withdrawal of the United States from the world organization which she had helped to create at the Peace Conference have been referred to elsewhere in the course of this volume. But on the American continent itself the disadvantages of this defection went much further than the loss of a single member to the League, however distinguished and influential: it went far to deprive a number of States which had taken a different course of much of the benefit of membership, and practically to exclude most of the Western hemisphere from the scope of the League's political influence. In a vain endeavour to satisfy the susceptibilities of the United States, Article 21 had been inserted in the Covenant, which assured them that the validity of 'regional understandings like the Monroe Doctrine, for securing the maintenance of peace', remained unaffected. The phraseology of this article is not strictly accurate, for the Monroe Doctrine is not a 'regional understanding' but a unilateral declaration of policy, which moreover is not directly aimed at 'securing the maintenance of peace'. The pronouncement of President Monroe, which had the approval and essential support of Great Britain, was intended to preserve the young, weak republics of America from interference or exploitation by any of the Great Powers, which, at that date, were to be found exclusively in Europe. This purpose it served admirably; but the irony of fate had now raised the United States themselves to the position of a Great Power which was inclined to interpret the doctrine not as the palladium of the Latin American Republics, but as conferring upon herself a monopoly of exploitation and control. At the period with which we are now concerned the Monroe Doctrine was tending to become the pretext of economic imperialism. It had not, indeed, proved possible to act upon this interpretation in dealing with the large republics of South America, but over the feebler States of the

Central American isthmus an effective hegemony was not only claimed but exercised. After the war even great South American republics such as Brazil and Argentina had reason to fear an increase in the dominant influence of the United States: before that time their principal commercial relations had been with Great Britain and Germany ; the capital necessary for their development had been derived mainly from British investment; thus, while the political hegemony claimed by the United States protected them from the dangers of their economic dependence on Europe, the converse was also true.

But the effect of the war was to place the economic and political levers in the same hands. The impoverished nations of Europe, whether victors or vanquished, no longer provided an adequate market or a supply of capital; their place was taken by the United States, whose percentage of the trade with Latin America showed an almost incredible increase.

Faced with this combination of political and economic dominance, most of Latin America had turned eagerly to the chance which membership of the League of Nations seemed to offer of establishing an effective counterpoise; the only important exception being Mexico, which was not invited to adhere (since her Government was not at the time universally recognized). Their expectations were, however, doomed to disappointment. At the first Assembly of the League in 1920 the Argentine delegation moved a proposal calculated to emphasize the universal character of the new organization and the equality of its members. This, however, was not accepted, and Argentina, while continuing to pay her subscription, retired in disappointment from active participation in the work of the League.

It was not long before the apprehensions created in the minds of Latin America by the obscure wording of Article 21 began to be strengthened. The United States took the first opportunity of indicating their jealousy of any intervention from Geneva in the affairs of the American continent. When the tripartite dispute over Tacna and Arica revived between Chile, Peru, and Bolivia in 1920 (see p. 208), the League was invoked by the last two parties; but Peru was immediately subjected to pressure from the United States, in consequence of which she withdrew her application; Chile from the first denied the competence of the Assembly; while the Bolivian request, which was for the modification of an existing treaty under Article 19, was rejected by the Committee of Jurists to which the League had referred it. Again, in 1921, an alleged case of aggression by Costa Rica was referred to Geneva by the Republic of Panama: but this step stimulated the United States to energetic action to preserve its exclusive authority, as a result of which Panama was compelled to submit, after recording a formal protest. Both these cases suggested that on the one hand the League would be chary of any interference which might offend the susceptibilities of the United States, and that even more certainly the United States would object to any such intervention as an infringement of Article 21. Costa Rica gave notice of withdrawal from the League in December 1924, since she felt disappointed in the degree of protection against domination by the United States afforded by membership of the League of Nations. The faith of Latin America in the utility of the new world organization was thus speedily shaken, and though Geneva did all in her power to honour her American representatives, the problems of settlement consequent on the war brought about an inevitable preoccupation with European affairs which could not but increase the impression that the League was a regional institution with which the Western hemisphere was not directly interested. Peru and Bolivia followed the example of Argentina in withdrawing from active participation in 1921, and thus, though the number of Latin American States members of the League remained imposing, they consisted for the most part of the small Caribbean republics, with the islands of Cuba and Haiti, over which the control of the United States was close and effective, while a large and important area of South America was virtually unrepresented.

Question of Germany's Seat on the Council: Withdrawal
of Brazil from the League

By Article 4 of the League Covenant, the Council, as originally constituted, was to consist of representatives of the principal Allied and Associated Powers (France, Great Britain, Italy, Japan, and the United States), as permanent members, with four non-permanent members from other States, these seats being originally filled by representatives of Belgium, Brazil,

Spain, and Greece. The majority contemplated in favour of the Great Powers was of course destroyed by the withdrawal of the United States, but the second paragraph of the article gave power to appoint further permanent members of the Council, subject to the approval of a majority of the Assembly. This clause was no doubt intended to provide for the inclusion of Germany (and possibly Russia) at a later stage, and, as part of the Locarno settlement, and a condition of the entry of Germany into the League, it had been agreed that she should be granted a permanent seat on the Council. In March 1926 a special session of the Assembly was summoned to give effect to these arrangements.

In order to understand the difficulties which now arose, it is necessary to recognize that the Council, as constituted, was definitely a compromise between the democratic theory of the League and the practical survival of a Concert of Great Powers, without whose approval the new order could not be expected to work. Though permanent and non-permanent members met in the Council on a footing of technical equality, the existence of a class distinction in the international hierarchy was implicit in the arrangement; it was, moreover, evident that the permanent members were far less dependent on international public opinion than those whose re-election depended upon a vote of the Assembly. At the Second Assembly a system of rotation for appointment to non-permanent seats had been approved, but its adoption remained in abeyance pending the ratification of an amendment to Article 4, which would enable the Assembly to establish this rule by a two-thirds majority. The number of non-permanent seats was, however, raised from four to six by a decision of the Third Assembly.

Of these six seats the first three had been held continuously by the original members, Belgium, Spain, and Brazil, who by the delay in the adoption of a system of rotation had thus come to occupy an intermediate relationship of semi-permanency. Moreover, once the existence of classes in the hierarchy of States was admitted, it became apparent that these classes could not be restricted to two, but that there was an even greater distinction between, for example, Poland and Haiti, than between the former and the Powers to whom permanent seats had been allotted. There was thus an opportunity for the display of considerable jealousy the moment that the question of a new permanent seat was raised by the proposal in regard to Germany. Claims to further permanent seats were put forward by Spain, Brazil, and Poland and—provisionally—China, and since the first two were members of the existing Council they were in a position to block the appointment of Germany failing the acceptance of their claim. In regard to Poland, it is fair to say that her claim was not based on a mere question of *amour propre*; she feared the influence of Germany in the Council on the question of treaty revision unless she could also be represented. But a deadlock was thus created which rendered the special meeting of the Assembly abortive, and the election of Germany had to be postponed. The question of the composition of the Council was then relegated to a committee, which eventually adopted a compromise suggested by Lord Cecil, raising the number of non-permanent seats to nine, of which a third should be re-eligible on a decision of a two-thirds majority of the Assembly, thus creating an intermediate class of semi-permanent members, which, it was hoped, would satisfy the susceptibilities of the claimants for superior status. In June 1926 the ratification of the amendment to Article 4 by France and Spain made it possible for the Assembly to adopt the new procedure by a two-thirds majority. Poland accepted the situation, and was thereafter rewarded by the possession of one of the semi-permanent seats. But Spain and Brazil maintained their intransigence, and, though they refrained from continuing to withstand the desires of the remaining States members, they voiced their dissatisfaction by notifying their withdrawal from the League. Spain was later induced to reconsider this decision, but Brazil remained obdurate and her resignation took effect after the prescribed lapse of two years. The proposed regulations relating to the election of the nine non-permanent members were thereupon adopted at the ensuing Assembly, and Germany was admitted to membership with a permanent seat on the Council.

The United States and the Permanent Court

Though the United States never ceased to maintain their opposition to the idea of associating themselves in the League of Nations, American public opinion for some time increasingly favoured the policy of adherence to the Permanent Court of International Justice, which the League had set up in conformity with Article 14. In 1924 such adherence had become a plank in the platforms of both the great political parties, and on 27 January 1926, the Senate consented to adherence subject to certain reservations. The outlook at this point was therefore generally regarded as promising.

Adherence to the Court without membership of the League had been rendered possible by the provision of a Protocol of Signature open to all States mentioned in the Annex to the Covenant, which included the United States and 'States invited to accede'. On the other hand, the opponents of adherence professed alarm at the intimate connexion between the Court and the League, and, in particular, at the obligation of the Court to render an advisory opinion on any question referred to it by the League Council or Assembly, which gave it, in their view, the character of the League's private attorney. For this reason, the reservations proposed by the Senate included, *inter alia*, a stipulation that the Court should not, 'without the consent of the United States, entertain any request for an advisory opinion touching any dispute or question in which the United States has *or claims* an interest'. This reservation, which purported to be based on the decision of the Court itself in the East Karelia case (see p. 79), went in fact considerably beyond it. For Russia in that case stood not only outside the League and the Court, but refused to submit to its jurisdiction, whereas, *ex hypothesi*, the United States, though not a member of the League, would be, so to speak, one of the fellowship of nations which had agreed on this method of resolving international issues. In any case the italicized words, *or claims*, went much further than the decision relied on would warrant. The United States, by the mere assertion of a quite unfounded claim of interest, would have been in a position to exercise their veto in questions on which the League and the parties directly concerned ardently desired an opinion.

The United States do not seem to have anticipated that the League itself would intervene in the question of their accession to the Court. They desired in every way to treat the Court and the League as separate and independent organizations, and intended to effect their accession by direct interchange of notes with the States signatory to the Protocol. They were therefore disappointed and annoyed when the Council referred the question of the reservations to a conference of the States signatory to the Protocol, thus asserting its interest in the matter. They protested that the language of the reservations was 'plain and unequivocal', and that the proposed conference was therefore unnecessary, and refused, on that ground, to attend it. The Conference, however, assembled at Geneva, and considered the reservations for a length of time which in itself suggested that their meaning was not so clear as their author imagined. Eventually it was unanimously decided that the reservations, in their existing form, could not be accepted. The United States refused to modify them, and their hoped-for accession to the Permanent Court did not, therefore, take place. The failure gave rise to a good deal of mutual recrimination, but it was ultimately traceable to an irreconcilable difference in points of view. 'The one party thought of the Permanent Court as a vital organ of a League representing *in posse* all nations of the world; the other thought of it as only incidentally and superficially connected with the League, which it regarded as a regional organization of a limited scope and, possibly, of a transient character'.[1] The United States had, however, themselves contributed to giving the League the regional character which they ascribed to it, by their own abstention and the interpretation which they applied to the Monroe Doctrine in relation to League intervention in the affairs of the American continent. It remains to add that the project of American adherence to the Permanent Court was not finally disposed of by these events, but was destined later to be revived.

[1] *Survey of International Affairs*, 1926, p. 95.

XIII

INTERNATIONAL RELATIONS ON THE
AMERICAN CONTINENT

American Conferences

IT is at least arguable that a regional subdivision of the world
is a better and more manageable system than that contemplated in the oecumenical conception of the League of
Nations. What the South American republics objected to in
the current interpretation of the Monroe Doctrine was that it
tended to reverse the original intention of that declaration by
subjecting them to the hegemony of a Great Power. Had it
been, as the Covenant of the League suggested, a 'regional
understanding', the Latin American States would probably
have preferred to regulate their affairs in accordance with it,
rather than to turn to Europe: this course they had only
adopted as a counterpoise to the increasing domination of the
United States.

There was already in existence a regional system which, re-
moulded to their heart's desire, the American republics were
all prepared to accept as an alternative to the League. This
instrument of international collaboration consisted of a series
of loosely organized Pan-American conferences, which had met,
generally at quinquennial intervals, since 1889. Pan-Americanism was thus an older and more established check upon international discord than the world-wide system inaugurated at
Versailles.

The first of these conferences to assemble after the war was
held in 1923, but, in spite of an ambitious agenda, its results
were on the whole disappointing. Its principal achievement
was the adoption of a convention for the submission of disputes,
which had proved insoluble through diplomatic channels, to
an independent Commission of Inquiry, pending whose report
the parties undertook to refrain from hostilities. Underlying
the comparative failure of the Conference were the irreconcilable conceptions of Pan-Americanism held by the United
States and the Latin American Republics; the latter desiring

to mould the movement so as to secure equality and liberty, while the former were bent on maintaining decisive control. Suspicion of the new interpretation of the Monroe Doctrine became more vocal immediately after the termination of the Conference.

A more solid result was achieved at a Conference on Central American Affairs which met in Washington, D.C., in December 1922. An attempted federation of the five republics of Central America, which had actually got as far as a Treaty of Union, had broken down in January and February, and the Conference, which was convened on the invitation of the United States to consider the situation, reached agreement upon a number of points which were embodied in twelve conventions and signed by all the republics participating. The most important of these were an agreement for limitation of armaments and a general treaty of peace and amity, under which the signatories bound themselves to submit differences to a Central American Tribunal or to a Commission of Inquiry, with some important reservations excepting disputes affecting their sovereign and independent existence, or their honour or vital interests, which went far to limit the practical effects of the instrument. Of more immediate importance, in the political circumstances usual in Central America, was an agreement not to recognize a revolutionary government which was not constitutionally authorized or elected, to abstain from interference in civil wars or the internal affairs of neighbours, and not to allow the territory of a signatory State to become the base of revolutionary activity directed against the government of another.

The sixth Pan-American Conference was held in Havana, in 1928, under the shadow of the events in Nicaragua which are narrated later in this chapter. It was natural, therefore, that some of the features on its agenda should suggest an endeavour to reduce the influence of the United States in the affairs of Latin America. The convention in which the constitution of the Pan-American Union was given a permanent basis emphasized the juridical equality of the member States, and considerable support was obtained for a motion condemning interference by one nation in the internal affairs of another. Yet the delegation of the United States contrived to emerge victorious from the encounter, and the Conference has more

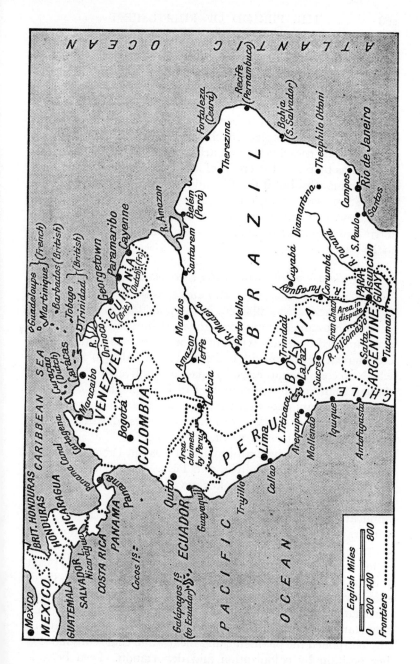

207

solid claims to be remembered on account of its resolutions, moved by the Mexican representative and unanimously adopted, prohibiting aggressive war, and expressing the intention to apply pacific means of settlement to all disputes which might arise. These resolutions were implemented, at a special conference called in December of the same year, by three instruments setting up complete machinery for the pacific settlement of disputes by conciliation and arbitration. The Pan-American Union has therefore the credit of anticipating the Kellogg Pact by some months, but it must be added that the signature of the arbitration convention, on 5 January 1929, was accompanied by reservations which effectively excluded practically all the territorial disputes to which the signatories were or were likely to be parties.

Boundary Disputes in Latin America: Tacna-Arica

This was the more unfortunate, inasmuch as South and Central America was afflicted, in the years following the European War, by an epidemic of boundary delimitations, frequently accompanied by quarrels of a more or less serious kind. Recent commercial developments had imparted a value to regions in which no country had hitherto taken a very lively interest, and, though many of these questions had been pending for a long time, it was only now that they assumed practical importance. Many of these matters were amicably adjusted without difficulty, but others proved more intractable.

Of these, one of the most important was the Tacna-Arica dispute, between Chile, Bolivia, and Peru. The abortive appeal of the last two parties to the League of Nations has been mentioned in the previous chapter. The rejection of the Bolivian application, which involved revision of a treaty, occasioned the withdrawal of that country from direct participation in the controversy. The facts, as between Peru and Chile, were briefly as follows: By the Treaty of Ancon (1883) it was stipulated that the provinces of Tacna and Arica, formerly held by Peru, should remain in Chilean occupation for ten years, after which their fate was to be settled by a plebiscite, the winner paying monetary compensation to the loser. Circumstances continually postponed the plebiscite, and meanwhile Chile consolidated her position by colonization and deportation. Peru became consequently less inclined to resort to the plebiscite in proportion as her neighbour came to favour it. In December 1921 Chile invited Peru to hold a plebiscite, and the latter, in refusing, suggested arbitration under the auspices of the United States. Chile, after some demur, accepted this proposal. In January 1922 an agreement was signed, referring the matters in dispute to the arbitration of the United States, including the question as to whether a plebiscite should be held. In March 1925 the arbitrator issued his award, deciding in favour of the plebiscite. This decision was received by Peru with consternation. Strangely enough, however, it was the Chilean Government which impeded the execution of the decision, by a resort to measures of intimidation and forcible deportation of Peruvian voters. As a result, the plebiscite was abandoned, and, after further endeavours on the part of the United States to arrange a settlement on other lines, the two parties were left to continue direct negotiation from October 1928. Eventually it was agreed to divide the territory in dispute, and a treaty was concluded in July 1929 embodying this solution.

Bolivia-Paraguay

An even more serious dispute, though later in coming to a head, was that between Bolivia and Paraguay. The bone of contention in this case was the Chaco Boreal, a wedge of territory, about 116,000 square miles in extent, in the angle formed by the confluence of the Paraguay and Pilcomayo rivers. The whole area had been included in the Spanish *audiencia* of Charcas, with which the republic of Bolivia claimed territorial identity, but there was some confusion in the title owing to administrative changes in 1776 and 1783, on which Paraguay based its claim to lands west of the Paraguay river. The main difficulty, however, here as elsewhere, arose from the fact that until recently the tract had been regarded as of little value, and that such penetration as had taken place had come from the Paraguayan side. But of late there had been rumours of oil, and other better authenticated natural resources had become an object of interest to foreign investors, some of whom had been granted concessions from the Paraguayan Government. At the date of the crisis of 1928 the territory was still mainly inhabited by Indians.

The boundary dispute was, however, of long standing, and a series of unratified agreements from 1879 onwards served only to confuse the issue by their variations of the frontier. Both sides had established a number of small forts, facing one another in the disputed territory. The situation was thus pregnant with explosive possibilities when, in 1927, Argentina offered her good offices with the object of achieving a settlement. Negotiations, however, broke down, and on 5 December 1928, the world was shocked, if hardly entitled to be surprised, by a Paraguayan attack upon the Bolivian Fort Vanguardia, which incidentally lay far to the north of any of the numerous frontiers which previous negotiations had provisionally awarded to Paraguay. The Paraguayan Government, to do it justice, hastened to repudiate the action of its soldiers, and to suggest the application of machinery for peaceful settlement. Bolivia refused this overture, severed diplomatic relations, and on 16 December retaliated by the capture of a Paraguayan post, Fort Boqueron. These events had occurred while the Council of the League and the Pan-American Conference on conciliation and arbitration were simultaneously in session. Both bodies promptly intervened, even before the date of the Fort Boqueron incident. The immediate effect was satisfactory, for on 18 December it was reported that both parties had accepted the good offices of the Pan-American Conference. For the time being, the League heaved a sigh of relief and gratefully relinquished the control of the matter to American hands.

Under the terms of a protocol signed at Washington on 3 January 1929, a Commission of Inquiry and Conciliation was set up, consisting of representatives of the parties and five neutral American countries. The Commission met in March, and in September settled the immediate controversy by the adoption of a resolution of mutual forgiveness on the basis of the *status quo ante*. The frontier question, however, remained unsettled, and fresh fighting occurred as early as January 1930. But both parties still professed pacific intentions, adopting the usual excuse of schoolboys detected quarrelling—'Please, sir, he began it'. Peace was for the time being restored, but in July 1931 there was a fresh rupture of diplomatic relations, and a year later the attention of the League of Nations was once more called to the existence of hostilities, which continued intermittently from this time forward. On 10 May 1933, the last veil was removed from the true character of the situation when Paraguay formally declared war on Bolivia. In July a commission was set up by the League to examine the dispute, the inquiry being subsequently transferred, at the request of the belligerents, to the governments of Argentina, Brazil, Chile, and Peru. In February 1934 this commission submitted a draft treaty of peace and arbitration to the parties, which, however, was rejected by both. On 24 May the Bolivians claimed a great victory and the infliction of some 18,000 casualties on their opponents, besides the capture of over 1,000 prisoners. A week previously, Mr Eden, on behalf of the British Government, proposed the imposition of an arms embargo on both belligerents, and, by the end of September, twenty-eight countries informed the League Secretariat that they had acted upon this proposal. A report adopted by the Assembly of the League on 24 November was accepted by Bolivia in December, but rejected by her opponent, with the result that, in January 1935, the Advisory Committee recommended the raising of the embargo so far as Bolivia was concerned, and its intensification against Paraguay. Whether owing to this or to the fortunes of war, the Paraguayans were driven from Bolivian territory by the middle of May, and hostilities ceased on 14 June 1935.

Peru and Colombia

Another frontier dispute which necessitated the intervention of the League was that between Peru and Colombia. In this case there exists no possibility of doubt as to the juridical rights of the parties. By a treaty signed in 1922, in return for reciprocal recognition of Peruvian claims north of the Putumayo river, Colombia became entitled to a strip of territory contiguous with the Brazilian frontier, a sort of Colombian corridor giving her access to the waters of the Amazon. This treaty, after many vicissitudes, was ratified by Colombia in 1925 and by Peru in 1928, and was registered with the Secretariat of the League on 29 May of the latter year. The final delimitation on the ground was completed in August 1930.

Within the new Colombian frontier, where the boundaries of Brazil, Peru, and Colombia meet on the Amazon, stood a collection of thirty or forty huts known by courtesy as the town of Leticia. The reader will have difficulty in finding it on any map constructed prior to 1932. On the night of 1 September of that year, some Peruvian filibusters made history by seizing the town and remaining in occupation. Their action was at once repudiated and condemned by the Peruvian Government, but the authorities of the Peruvian department of Loreto not only dissociated themselve from the official attitude, but contributed support and assistance to the raiders. Colombia took steps to evict them, but, owing to the impassable nature of the country, had to proceed by the Panama Canal and up the Amazon, a roundabout journey involving a delay of several months.

The Peruvian Government meanwhile changed its attitude, under pressure of public opinion, and began to talk of treaty revision and the right of self-determination. By November, the imminent prospect of war induced the republic of Ecuador to notify the League of Nations, which, however, took no action until January 1933, when these representations were reinforced by a communication from Colombia. On 14 January the President of the Council sent a telegram to both parties recalling their duty as signatories of the Covenant. A protracted discussion followed, during the progress of which the Colombian flotilla was bombed by Peruvian aircraft, but succeeded in recapturing the town of Tarapaca, which the Peruvian forces had also occupied (February 1933). The President of Peru sent a message to the force in Leticia, declaring that Peru would keep that town in face of any opposition. Colombia thereupon appealed to the League to summon a meeting of the Council under Article 15, and the Council accordingly met on 21 February. On 18 March the Council adopted a report, condemning the action of Peru, and recommending their immediate withdrawal from Colombian territory, the effect of which was to cause the Peruvian delegate to leave the Council room, after an ineffectual protest. Hostilities meanwhile continued.

On 30 April, however, the murder of the Peruvian President brought about an improvement in the atmosphere, and on 25 May an agreement was signed for the immediate cessation of hostilities, and for the administration of the territory in dispute by a League Commission for a period not exceeding one year, at the expense of the Colombian Government and with the aid of Colombian forces. The Commission took charge in June 1933, but negotiations between the parties broke down in April 1934, and both sides recommenced military preparations. On 24 May 1934, however, an agreement was signed by the parties which would appear to constitute a durable settlement. It included a protocol of friendship and co-operation, and an expression of regret by Peru for the strained relations which her conduct had occasioned. The future rights of the two countries were based upon the treaty of March 1922, and it was agreed that its conditions should only be modified by mutual consent or a decision of the Permanent Court of International Justice.

Relations between Mexico and the United States

The history of the Leticia dispute suggests that the United States had, in later years, somewhat modified the objections which it evinced at an earlier date to the interference of the League in America. Probably matters of this kind had been shown to be so intractable that the task of dealing with them was no longer coveted. It was, however, in Central rather than South America that the United States exercised a jealous and exclusive control. Over most of the States of the former region it tended to assert a virtual protectorate; Mexico, however, was able to maintain its independence, and constituted, therefore, an important exception.

The dictatorship of Porfirio Diaz, which had encouraged the penetration of foreign capital both from America and Europe, was ended in 1911 by a revolution of an extremely anti-capitalistic tendency. The new constitution of 1917, which vested the land and subsoil in the nation, brought the Mexican Government into immediate conflict with foreign concessionnaires and landowners. The Government took over the whole railway system, including lines which were foreign property, and ceased, for the time being, to pay its external debt. The oil industry came to a standstill, and there was agitation in the United States in favour of armed intervention. Negotiations, which had achieved some measure of success during the presidency of Carranza, had to be recommenced after his assassination, in 1920, with his successor, President Obregon. Though the latter showed an unexpected readiness to honour international obligations, and satisfactory agreements were reached in 1922 for the payment of interest and arrears on the foreign debt and the return of the railways to their owners, adequate protection of the interests of concessionnaires and landowners was not attained for some time; in 1923, however, the main legal difficulties were satisfactorily adjusted, and formal recognition was extended to the Mexican Government by the United States.

In spite, however, of this achievement of a *modus vivendi*, foreign interests remained a matter of acute controversy between the two Governments for many years, indeed the relations between revolutionary Mexico and so essentially capitalistic a Power as the United States continued to show a marked resemblance to the contemporary situation existing between Bolshevik Russia and Western Europe. A further problem was created through the marked increase in Mexican emigration to the United States which followed upon the restrictions imposed by the Acts of 1921 and 1924 upon immigration from overseas. As in the analogous case of France and Fascist Italy, this influx was not wholly industrial, but consisted to some extent of political *émigrés*, whose counter-revolutionary activities threatened to disturb the relations of the two countries. To some extent, however, the existence of this counter-revolutionary movement was an advantage to the United States, for the existing regime was only preserved through a prohibition placed by President Coolidge upon the export of arms to Mexico, except to the recognized Government. By lifting the embargo or suspending the exception, the Government of the United States was in a position at almost any moment to threaten the life of the Mexican administration; this fact gave to their negotiations an invaluable support. Yet the continuance of so many sources of friction, and the fundamental incompatibility of the political and economic ideals of the two countries left their relations in a state of considerable tension.

Events in Nicaragua

The antagonism of the two Powers was exposed in 1926 by events which took place on the soil of Nicaragua, a typical

Caribbean republic with a characteristic history of alternate dictatorship and revolution under a mask of democratic party government. Until 1910 Nicaragua had been left to enjoy these political institutions without external interference, but about that time she had the misfortune to become an object of special interest to the United States for two main reasons. The first, which was common to the whole Caribbean area, was the growing demand for tropical raw materials; the second was special, and due to a topographical feature of the country. Across almost the whole width of the republic from east to west was a natural waterway consisting of the great Lake Nicaragua and its outflow to the Caribbean; it formed, therefore, a possible route for a second inter-oceanic canal, alternative or supplementary to that through Panama. Such a canal was in contemplation, and it was a fundamental tenet of United States policy that, if and when constructed, it must be under United States control. These considerations may possibly have had something to do with the fact that in 1909 a revolution was fomented by a clerk in an American oil company, named Diaz, who contributed to the campaign fund a sum six hundred times as large as his salary, and who had the satisfaction of seeing the cause which he supported carried to triumph with the material assistance of United States naval forces. In 1910 Diaz himself was rewarded by becoming Vice-President of the Republic, and he was made President soon afterwards. His administration was, however, threatened with another revolution in 1912, which was put down by United States marines, a guard of whom remained from that date until 1925, ostensibly for the protection of American lives and property.

One good turn deserves another, and in 1914 a treaty was negotiated between the United States and Nicaragua whereby the former received in perpetuity the exclusive right to construct a canal across Nicaraguan territory and a ninety-nine years' lease (with option of renewal) of a site for a naval base on the Pacific coast bordering on the Gulf of Fonseca. It was at the same time agreed that an approved citizen of the United States should be appointed Collector-General of the Nicaraguan Customs, be made responsible for the service of the external debt, and be empowered to take over the collection of internal revenue if it fell below a specified figure.

In October 1924 a presidential election resulted in the return of a Conservative President and a Liberal Vice-President, Señor Sacasa. The withdrawal of the United States marines in August 1925 was almost immediately followed by a *coup d'état*, carried out by the Conservative General Chamorro, as a result of which the Liberal Vice-President fled the country, while the President, in January 1926, resigned in Chamorro's favour. This transaction, however, in accordance with the General Treaty of 1923 (see p. 206, was not recognized either by the United States or the adjacent Caribbean republics. In a few months, a Liberal revolution had imparted its familiar touch to the Nicaraguan political situation.

At this juncture General Chamorro telegraphed, on 27 August, to the League of Nations a complaint that the Mexican Government was assisting the Liberal revolutionaries. Three days earlier, however, the Secretary of State at Washington had requested the dispatch of a squadron to Nicaraguan ports 'for the protection of American and foreign lives and property'. The force requested arrived and landed 200 men at Bluefields in time to avert any interference by the League on Chamorro's behalf or the equally unpalatable alternative of a Liberal victory achieved with Mexican support. General Chamorro was simultaneously pressed to resign, in a note addressed to him by the United States State Department.

In November the good offices of the United States Chargé d'Affaires had succeeded in regularizing the Conservative administration by the withdrawal of Chamorro, and the election by a Congress, which appears to have been packed, of Señor Diaz to a new term of office as President. A constitutional point of some nicety was thereby raised, for an emergency candidate of this kind was only eligible in default of the Vice-President, who would otherwise succeed automatically to the presidential vacancy. Sacasa, the Vice-President of 1925, had never relinquished his office, but had merely been temporarily excluded from the country by *force majeure*. He had returned on 1 December, within a month of Diaz's election, and was proclaimed President by his Liberal supporters, his claim receiving official recognition from Mexico.

The juridical merits of the rival claims need not detain us, since the plain fact was that at this point Diaz and Sacasa had become pawns in a game played by the United States and Mexico on the soil of Nicaragua. The Mexican revolution of 1910 was, in essence, a revolt against precisely such a policy of economic imperialism as the United States was pursuing in Central America. As has appeared in a previous section, Mexico was not powerful enough permanently to resist her neighbour's claims on behalf of United States capitalists on Mexican soil, but the existence of competing factions in Nicaragua seemed to offer a favourable opportunity for interfering with the hegemony of the United States in an important sphere of influence. Such, at any rate, were the motives commonly imputed to Mexico in the course which she pursued.

The policy of both protagonists must, indeed, remain to some extent a matter of speculation, for the intervention of United States troops, which from this point increasingly hampered the efforts of Sacasa's party, was never officially admitted to have had any other purpose than the stereotyped 'protection of American lives and property'. Appeals for protection were certainly made, not only by Americans but by the representatives of other foreign Powers. But the progress which the Liberal forces made towards the close of 1926 resulted in a striking augmentation of those of the United States in the first three months of 1927.

Public opinion in the United States had meanwhile grown increasingly critical of these developments, and at the end of March President Coolidge dispatched Mr Stimson to Nicaragua to endeavour to secure a settlement. This he eventually achieved, by the middle of May, on the understanding that a free and fair election should be held, on the conclusion of President Diaz's term of office in 1928, under the supervision and control of the United States. On the strength of this agreement, the majority of the Liberal insurgents laid down their arms, but the provisions for United States control were criticized as unconstitutional both in Nicaragua and Washington, ratification of the electoral arrangements by the Nicaraguan Congress had eventually to be dispensed with, and the matter regulated, with questionable legality, by a presidential decree. In May 1927 a conference of the four remaining Caribbean republics condemned Mr Stimson's terms as irreconcilable with the General Treaty of Peace and Amity of 1923 (see

p. 206), and withheld, on that ground, their recognition from Señor Diaz: a step which, though of no practical importance, was a strong moral protest against the policy pursued by the United States.

The latter, meanwhile, were involved in fresh and more serious trouble. One of the insurgent commanders, General Sandino, had remained recalcitrant; and he now began a guerilla warfare against the United States troops, which necessitated considerable reinforcements, and continued for nearly two years. Indeed, though Sandino temporarily withdrew to Mexico during the later part of the year 1929, and the United States Marine Expeditionary Force was considerably reduced in numbers during the same year, there was a recurrence of trouble in April 1931, which necessitated the intervention of two United States warships. By 1929, however, the policy of Washington was to extricate itself as far as possible, and to leave the control of internal order in the hands of the Nicaraguan National Guards, under United States officers.

The elections of 1928 had meanwhile resulted in a decisive Liberal majority, and the new President, General Moncada, though personally on good terms with the United States Government, was actually one of Señor Sacasa's principal supporters in the previous struggle. In January 1919 Señor Sacasa himself was appointed Nicaraguan Minister in Washington, a denouement which, while indicating more friendly relations between his party and the United States, wore also the aspect of a rather ironic commentary on the situation. The episode concluded on 2 January 1933 when the last of the United States marines left the country.

The Panama Treaty

The Nicaraguan affair did not add to the prestige of the United States in Latin America, and indeed conduced to strengthening the resentment with which their claims to hegemony were regarded. A striking instance of these reactions was the gesture of independence made by Panama in refusing to ratify a treaty concluded with the United States in 1926. This little republic had perhaps been more completely divested of the attributes of independent sovereignty than any other. In regard to the canal zone, absolute sovereign rights were openly claimed by the United States as the result of the Treaty of 1903, by which the use, occupation, and control of the zone were secured. The Treaty of 1926, which was designed to make the situation clearer, went so far as to stipulate for the participation by Panama in any war in which the United States might be engaged, a provision difficult to reconcile with the status of Panama as a member of the League of Nations, and marked in other ways a considerable tightening of the United States control over this Central American republic. The treaty was, however, duly signed in July 1926, but the premature publication of its terms, at a time when the Caribbean policy of the United States was a special subject of suspicion and resentment, led to a refusal to ratify the instrument. Further negotiations were proposed, and the Finance Minister of Panama, in a public utterance, offered to submit the question of sovereignty over the canal zone to arbitration; to this, however, the Government of the United States was quite unwilling to agree, and for the time being the whole question remained in abeyance.

The United States and Haiti

The Nicaraguan experience, indeed, appeared to lead to a modification of policy on the part of the United States. After the arrival of Mr Dwight Morrow as American Ambassador in Mexico in 1927, the United States oil companies were warned that their differences with the Mexican authorities were likely to be left to the negotiation of the parties and the decisions of the Mexican courts without the assistance of diplomatic pressure. Generally, the U.S. State Department evinced less readiness than formerly to champion the cause of its citizens in other parts of America, and in 1931 it went so far as to advise them that the Government could no longer undertake their protection in Nicaragua. The beginning of this change of policy approximately synchronized with the publication, in December 1928, of a memorandum on the Monroe Doctrine prepared by an eminent American international lawyer, Mr Reuben Clark, at the request of the Secretary of State. This interpretation tended to restore to the Doctrine its original significance as a 'shield between Europe and the Americas', and repudiated the intention of using it as a pretext for intervention in the affairs of other republics on the continent. 'The

Doctrine', it said, 'states a case of the United States *versus* Europe, and not of the United States *versus* Latin America.'

A region hitherto particularly subject to the control of the United States, which was destined to derive a new freedom from the change in policy, was the black republic of Haiti. Since 1915, Haiti had been virtually a protectorate of the United States, who had found a pretext for intervention in the violation of the French Legation by a mob which had dragged out a Haitian ex-president from its sanctuary, and torn him to pieces. Interference was justified under the Monroe Doctrine as necessary to forestall similar action by France, though such action, in the middle of the First World War, does not appear to have been probable. Since 1915, the island republic had been governed by a United States High Commissioner, assisted by five other American officials, and supported by a force of marines. In 1929, however, dislike of certain aspects of United States policy, especially the removal of the ban on acquisition of land by foreigners, and the Americanization of educational methods, led to a disturbance, in consequence of which a Commission was appointed, in February 1930, to investigate when and how the United States should withdraw from Haiti, and their policy in the interim. This Commission reported in favour of the progressive Haitianization of the services, to fit the departments of the Government to assume responsibility in 1936, the abolition of the office of High Commissioner and the substitution of a non-military Minister to combine his duties with those of diplomatic representative, the gradual withdrawal of the marines, and the negotiation of agreements providing for less intervention in Haitian domestic affairs in the future. The grievances connected with the educational system were at the same time independently investigated by another commission. As a sequel to these investigations, the United States troops refrained from supervising the elections which took place in October 1930, and these passed off without serious disorder.

In November of the same year a Minister appointed by the United States arrived in Haiti, and the High Commissioner was withdrawn. This was followed up, in September 1932, by the signature of a treaty, which, however, the Haitian Assembly rejected on account of certain alleged ambiguities. On

7 August 1933 a new agreement was signed, which, while continuing the financial administration previously set up to ensure service on some outstanding bonds, provided for the complete withdrawal of American forces by October 1934.

The Philippines

The most ironical example of the conversion of the United States from imperialistic ideals was afforded by the Philippines, the annexation of which at the close of the nineteenth century had inspired Mr Kipling's poem, 'The White Man's Burden'. From 1929 onwards, a policy designed

> To seek another's profit
> And work another's gain

did not appeal to American industrial interests, who found their own products exposed to competitive exports from the islands. A Bill introduced in 1929, to confer independence, and consequent subjection to tariffs, upon the Philippines, was only rejected by the narrowest of margins, and between December 1931 and February 1932 ten Bills with the same object were introduced in Congress. One of these was passed at the end of 1932, but was vetoed by President Hoover in January 1933, on the ground of the injustice to the islanders involved in so sudden a change in the conditions of their economic life. The veto was, however, overridden by large majorities in both Houses, but the Bill was rejected by the Filipino legislature. There was thus a curious reversal of the policies originally advocated by the United States and the islanders respectively. The attitude of both parties was also doubtless affected by considerations of defence, in view of the menace of Japanese expansion. Simultaneously, the Filipinos began to realize the value of a powerful protector, and the Americans the disadvantages of an embarrassingly distant commitment. The will of the latter prevailed. In March 1934, the question was settled by the passage of an Act of Congress which, except for the abandonment of the military and naval rights originally reserved to the United States, was substantially identical with that previously rejected. This received the rather reluctant approval of the Philippine legislature on 1 May, and there

thus came into being, from November 1935, a transitional
period designed to culminate in complete independence ten
years later.

Cuba and the United States

The complete aversion of the United States from the policy
of intervention which they had formerly pursued was clearly
brought out by the attitude of the Roosevelt administration
during the disturbances which broke out in Cuba during the
year 1933. Cuba had long been ripening for revolution as a
result of a severe economic depression, connected particularly
with the decline of her trade with the United States. American
purchases of Cuban products had declined from 207 million
dollars in 1929 to 58·3 millions in 1932. This conduced to the
unpopularity of the existing administration, which, moreover,
kept itself in power by methods hardly calculated to enhance
its popularity. By the arrangement known as the Platt Amendment of 1901, the United States were fully entitled to intervene
in Cuban affairs 'for the maintenance of a government adequate
for the protection of life, property, and individual liberty'. Yet
when American efforts at conciliation proved unsuccessful, and
two revolutions broke out in quick succession in 1933, the
Government of the United States showed itself most reluctant
to intervene. Warships were dispatched on two occasions, but
were withdrawn as soon as possible, and active interference in
the fighting which took place on the island was carefully
avoided. President Roosevelt invited a conference with the
diplomatic representatives of the leading South American
states and Mexico, and expressed to them his extreme reluctance to engage in intervention. The non-existence of a government fit to be recognized placed great obstacles in the way of
the conclusion of a trade agreement with Cuba which was
calculated to ease the economic tension, and it was felt in many
quarters that the rights conferred by the Platt Amendment
were more of a hindrance than a help. At the close of 1933, the
President was reported to be considering the abrogation of the
Amendment as a step towards the improvement of relations,
and, on 9 June 1934, a treaty was ratified by which this arrangement was definitely terminated. The United States had, by
this time, enough to do to deal with their own internal situation,

but it had also become evident that any suggestion of pressure on their part in the affairs of other States in Latin America or the Caribbean islands tended to produce a widespread resentment which would defeat its objects.

XIV

NATIONALISM, ZIONISM, AND THE ARAB

Growth of Pan-Arabian Aspirations

As that great authority, the late Dr Hogarth, pointed out in his *History of Arabia*, 'Arabia, as a regional name, has different acceptations: some confine it to the Peninsula, some include the great wedge of desert prolonged to an apex between Syria and Mesopotamia far north of that thirtieth parallel which roughly subtends the peninsular mass.' Even this exclusion of Syria and Mesopotamia is, in a sense, artificial. To the Arab mind, the 'Jaziratu'l-Arab'—the island or peninsula of the Arabs—comprises the whole region as far north as the present frontier of Turkey, bounded on the east by Persia and on the west by the Mediterranean.

Before the First World War, the whole of this region, as well as Egypt, to which the cultural unity of the Arab-speaking world extends and from which it draws its inspiration from books and newspapers printed in Cairo, was subject to a single sovereignty, that of the Ottoman Empire. Yet, under the policy of *divide et impera* which actuated the Turkish regime, this superficial unity was counterbalanced by the fact that the Arab population comprised in the area was broken up into a large number of mutually hostile tribes, none of which possessed or claimed more than a very limited share of the territory. The idea of a united Arabian Empire first received overt expression in the claims which the Sherif of Mecca made in his negotiations with Great Britain in the early stages of the war.

In the situation apparent in 1925-6, there was an equal contradiction between the superficial and the essential position, but the contrast was reversed. The single sovereignty had been subdivided into the four States of the Syrian mandate—Great Lebanon, the Alawi, Syria proper, and the Jebel ed Druse; Palestine and Transjordania to the south of these, and to the east Iraq; while in the Arabian peninsula there were at least two independent sovereignties, the Nejd-Hijaz and the Yemen. There seemed at first sight to be no vestige of Arabian unity.

But, in fact, the combined effects of improved communications and the nationalist ideal encouraged by the Peace Settlement had given the conception of such a unity a reality which it had never had before. An Arab movement in Palestine or Syria was for the first time capable of producing immediate reactions as far away as Baghdad.

Risk of a 'Holy War'

At the same time, the traditional bellicose proclivities of the Arab had been diverted into more serious channels. Hitherto the constant and internecine raiding of nomad tribes had been, as Professor Toynbee has put it,[1] 'not so much a form of warfare as a wasteful redistribution of stock conducted with the amenities of a sport', a 'traditional method of easing . . . economic stresses', which the new conditions had rendered less practicable. The economic stresses remained, but the consolidation of the greater part of the Arabian peninsula into a single kingdom had familiarized its inhabitants with a larger and more scientific conception of warfare: they had absorbed some experience of Western military technique, and the acquisition and adoption of Western armaments seemed only to be a question of time. Taken with the growing sense of Arab homogeneity which the prevalent nationalism, the improvement in communication, and the diminution of tribal warfare promoted, there seemed a danger that for the comparatively harmless raids of the past would be substituted a 'Holy War', waged against the foreign control which had partitioned the territory of greater Arabia.

Relations with the Nejd-Hijaz

That this was not merely a theoretical possibility was soon rendered evident by the attitude of some of the subordinate chiefs of the Wahhabi Kingdom. The puritanical fanaticism of Ibn Saud's subjects combined with their cupidity and warlike propensities to reinforce economic motives with religious. In the autumn of 1926, Faysal ud Dawish, the most redoubtable of the Wahhabi captains, joined with the chief of another tribe to request from Ibn Saud permission to launch a Jihad against

[1] *Journal of the Royal Institute of International Affairs*, 1929, p. 367.

all non-Wahhabis, and in April of the following year he returned, in company with about 3,000 fighting men, to repeat the demand, suggesting on this occasion that his sovereign was 'allowing himself to be tempted by worldly interests into neglecting the interests of God'.

It was fortunate that Ibn Saud continued to maintain his friendship with Great Britain. As the result of negotiations with Sir Gilbert Clayton at Jidda, a treaty was signed in May 1927, superseding that of 1915 which had hitherto governed the relations between the two countries. This instrument, which recognized the complete independence of the Wahhabi ruler, and was drawn between the parties on an equal footing, in terms of reciprocity, provided for the suppression in each territory of unlawful activities directed against the peace of the other, and safeguarded the interests of Kuweit and the coastal chiefs under British protection. In February 1927 Ibn Saud had fortified himself with a legal opinion obtained from the 'ulamā of Nejd, which, while returning a reactionary answer on subordinate matters where Wahhabi puritanism was in conflict with the practice of laxer Muslims, diplomatically left the issue of the Jihad in the discretion of the sovereign. Ibn Saud was accordingly enabled to refuse, with authority, the demands of his subjects for a 'Holy War'. The less satisfactory decisions on minor religious matters brought him, however, into somewhat strained relations with the Government of Egypt.

Faysal ud Dawish, however, now proceeded to independent action. In the autumn of 1927 and the early part of 1928 he inaugurated several serious raids into Iraq and Kuweit, which necessitated the intervention of British aircraft and armoured cars; Transjordan was threatened with similar activities, and in both regions Wahhabi penetration induced several tribes to transfer their allegiance. In the later part of 1928 the situation improved, notwithstanding the breakdown of two conferences with Ibn Saud, which took place at Jidda and Haifa respectively at this time. The second of these was concerned merely with the status of the Hijaz Railway, which ran through the mandated territories of Palestine and Syria, as well as through Ibn Saud's dominions. But the first broke down over the question of the establishment of military posts within the Iraq frontier, which had served as a pretext for Wahhabi raids. Ibn

Saud regarded the construction of these posts as an infringement of his treaty rights, a contention which the British and
Iraqi representatives disputed, on the ground that the nearest
of the posts was sixty miles within the frontier. But in November 1928 Faysal ud Dawish threw off all pretence of allegiance
to Ibn Saud and resorted, to armed rebellion, which was
apparently terminated in March 1929 by the victory of the
King at Sabalah, in the course of which Faysal ud Dawish was
wounded. Ibn Saud thereupon departed upon a pilgrimage,
but the revolt not only broke out again but assumed more
serious proportions; in November, however, the forces of the
Nejd-Hijaz began a general advance, and in January 1930 the
rebels, including Faysal ud Dawish, surrendered unconditionally. This success greatly strengthened Ibn Saud's position, and
he was enabled not only to establish friendly relations with Iraq
and Kuweit, but to make some judicious progress in the introduction of those Western innovations which had hitherto
offended the puritan susceptibilities of his subjects. It was clear,
however, that the general situation owed much to the personal
prestige and diplomatic sagacity of the ruler, and that in the
event of his death or removal there might easily be a recrudescence of serious trouble.

The French in Syria

Such serious trouble had in the meantime broken out in the
French mandated territory of Syria.

After the recall of the just and popular General Weygand in
November 1924, a critical situation was not long in developing.
His successor, General Sarrail, a violent anti-clerical, managed
almost immediately to alienate the sympathies of the traditional
supporters of France, the Lebanese Christians. No sooner had
he done so than he was confronted with a critical situation in the
Jebel ed Druse. In that isolated mass of rugged mountains,
dividing the fertile Hauran from the Hamad desert, the feudal
community of the Druses had its principal stronghold. Under
every administration of Syria these Druse clans had proved
exceptionally formidable and difficult to control. They had
been induced to recognize the French mandate in return for an
agreement, signed in March 1921, which conceded to them a
wide measure of independence, under a native Governor elected

by themselves, with a French adviser. In 1923, however, in consequence of the death of Salim Pasha, the Governor, the elective Council of the Druses appointed the adviser, Captain Carbillet, as his temporary successor.

Captain Carbillet was an enthusiast for public works, and the modern improvements which he carried out in less than two years were really astonishing. Roads, reservoirs, and irrigation channels appeared as if by magic among the rocks of the Jebel, and these material benefits were accompanied by a number of decidedly useful administrative reforms. But the works were carried out by a system of forced labour to which the Turkish regime could show no parallel, and the administration was exercised with a heavy-handed severity which alienated chieftain and peasant alike. In April 1925 a deputation from the Druses laid before General Sarrail their complaints of this tyrannous regime, requesting that the condition of the agreement of 1921, which stipulated that the Governor should be a native, should now be fulfilled. The High Commissioner expressed his entire confidence in Captain Carbillet, treated the agreement as possessing 'a purely historic value', and brusquely dismissed the delegation. On receiving alarming reports of the local situation from the officer acting as the Governor's deputy during his absence on furlough, he not only disregarded them but ordered the supersession of his informant. Further representations from the Druses were summarily rebuffed. Finally, General Sarrail ordered that the leading chiefs should be invited to present their grievances in Damascus, and should, on arrival, be placed in confinement. In spite of protests from the French delegate in Damascus, this treacherous scheme was carried into effect, and the three Druse chiefs who were confiding enough to accept the invitation found themselves relegated to 'enforced residence' at Palmyra. Within a few days one of the remaining chieftains, Sultan el Atrash, had mobilized his followers, and a most serious revolt had commenced.

The military authorities seem to have been quite unprepared for this development, and the campaign opened with a disastrous defeat of the French forces, with heavy casualties, and the capture by the enemy of guns and munitions. Further reverses followed, and in October the insurgents were fighting in Damascus itself. The garrison retired to the citadel, and bombarded the town, causing much loss of life to the civilian population and immense material damage. Though the indignation aroused by this episode brought about the immediate recall of General Sarrail, the revolt spread, and the issue remained for a long time doubtful. The French adopted the dubious expedient of enlisting and arming irregulars from the minority communities, thus intensifying the internal dissensions which it was the duty of the mandatary to reconcile. The oasis around Damascus was laid waste by military operations, and the city itself was in a state of siege.

The arrival of the new High Commissioner, M. de Jouvenel, who in face of immense difficulties attempted to pursue a conciliatory policy, failed to bring the hostilities to an end before his resignation in August 1926.

By the summer of 1927, however, peace was substantially restored, and on 17 February 1928 the end of the insurrection was signalized by the proclamation of a general amnesty to all rebels who should surrender within a specified period, with thirty-nine named exceptions.

These events in the Jebel ed Druse had rendered impossible the due performance of one of the obligations of the mandate, which was to frame an organic law for Syria and the Lebanon within three years from its coming into force. A constitution for the Lebanese Republic was, indeed, promulgated in May 1926, within the prescribed period, but with regard to the remainder of the mandated territory an extension had to be obtained from the Council of the League. In July 1927 M. Ponsot, the new High Commissioner, took the first steps towards enabling the Syrians themselves to draw up a constitution. A provisional Government was formed under the presidency of a prominent Syrian nationalist, Sheikh Tuju'd Din, and elections were held in April 1928. The Assembly was assured that on the completion of its task the time would have come for regulating the relations between Syria and France, like those between Iraq and Great Britain, on the basis of a treaty.

Thus encouraged, the Assembly duly drafted a constitution which it adopted as a whole on 7 August. M. Ponsot, however, found many of its provisions unacceptable to the mandatory Power. Article 2 declared the Syrian territories detached from the Ottoman Empire to constitute an indivisible political unity. This was not only inconsistent with the subdivision of the mandated territory which had been made by France, but also, in M. Ponsot's opinion, with the status of Palestine. He accordingly declared reservations on this and a number of other points, which he suggested should be separated from the rest of the draft in its consideration by the Assembly. The suggestion was nevertheless rejected, and the Commissioner retorted by adjourning the Assembly. After further negotiations had resulted in a deadlock, M. Ponsot, in May 1930, promulgated a Constitution for Syria by his own unilateral act, accompanied by four other proclamations, regulating the administration of the other divisions of the mandate, and making arrangements for a conference on their common interests. The publication of these documents led to protests and demonstrations, but to no serious disturbance.

Palestine

In Palestine the problems created by the mandate were, as may have been gathered at an earlier stage, of exceptional complexity. Whereas the spirit of the age everywhere encouraged the creation of national States with a homogeneous racial composition, the Palestine mandate had as its declared object the preparation for self-government of a population consisting of two discordant elements, one native, the other deliberately introduced, and in the meanwhile the reconciliation of Jewish claims to a national home with the full preservation of the rights of the Arab inhabitants. Professor Toynbee has compared the *tour de force* attempted by Great Britain to the action of a small boy who has witnessed an accidental explosion of gunpowder in a neighbour's garden, and, finding only one of the necessary ingredients in his own, has bought a sackful of the necessary saltpetre and having mixed it well in is waiting for the wind to blow a spark that way.[1]

In August 1929 a partial explosion occurred, sufficiently serious to indicate the probable consequences of leaving the explosive ingredients without efficient and experienced supervision. Hitherto, the antagonism between the two races had been confined to economic and cultural grounds: it was the

[1] *International Affairs*, January 1931, p. 48.

rekindling, on this occasion, of the fires of religious fanaticism which produced the fatal spark. The heat was engendered by a controversy over a piece of ancient masonry, which had a peculiar sanctity, for different reasons, in the eyes of each community.

That which was the 'Wailing Wall' to the Jews on the ground that it was the last surviving vestige of their Temple was to Muslims the stable of the Buraq—the beast which had carried the prophet Mohammed to heaven on 'the Night of Power'. The scene of the Jewish devotions is part of the retaining wall of the Haram-esh-Sherif, an enclosure of special sanctity in Muslim eyes, as the starting-point of the Prophet's celestial journey, and as containing the Dome of the Rock and the Mosque of Aqsa. The inflammatory possibilities of the situation were increased by the fact that the Jewish fast in commemoration of the destruction of the Temple coincided with the date of the Muslim celebration of the birthday of Mohammed. Though the Jews had acquired by long prescription a right to perform their devotions at the 'Wailing Wall', the structure itself, as well as the pavement at its foot, was Muslim property. Under the Turkish regime, when the Jews realized that they enjoyed their privilege on sufferance, no serious trouble had arisen, but it was natural that a community encouraged to regard Palestine as a 'national home' should increasingly resent the fact that their most sacred building was in alien hands. In the early days of the British occupation fruitless negotiations had been started by the Jews for the purchase of the pavement abutting on the wall, but this encroachment on the *status quo* had alarmed the Arabs, and made them suspicious of even the slightest innovation in the procedure established by prescription. Any such innovations were consequently discountenanced and restrained by the mandatory authority, which had forbidden, in 1925, the bringing of seats or benches to the spot, and in 1928 had removed a screen erected to separate the male and female worshippers. The occurrence of such incidents had led to an increasing propaganda on both sides, and it may be said that in a small area of 120 square yards, constituting until very recently the only access to the adjacent dwellings of the Muslim inhabitants, the contest of the two world-forces of Jewry and Islam was concentrated around this provocative symbol.

In August 1929 demonstrations by both sides culminated in a most serious outbreak, as a result of which 133 Jews and 116 Arabs lost their lives, while a much larger number suffered injuries. The disturbances extended to other parts of the territory, necessitating the augmentation of the military and police forces, a stricter surveillance of the press, and the suspension of discussions on the subject of constitutional changes in Palestine. In May 1930, at the request of the British representative, the Council of the League appointed a neutral Commission to investigate the rights and claims connected with the Wall, and at the same time Sir John Hope Simpson was sent to Palestine to report on the wider questions of Jewish immigration and land-settlement, while the Labour Schedule, governing the admission of Jews to the country, was temporarily suspended.

The publication of the Simpson Report, in October 1930, was accompanied by the issue of a White Paper,[1] intended to define the policy of the mandatory Power. The latter document aroused a storm in Zionist circles, where it was interpreted as a departure from the pledges of the Balfour declaration, and as being anti-Jewish in tone and temper. The Simpson report, with its limited estimate of the possibilities for Zionist settlement, created considerable disappointment, demonstrating, as it did, the impossibility of looking forward to an eventual Jewish majority in the country. An attempt to allay the storm was made by Mr Ramsay MacDonald in a letter to Dr Weizmann, the ex-President of the Zionist organization, but this only served to arouse, in a similar manner, the suspicion and resentment of the Arab party. In spite of the announcement of a projected expenditure of £2½ million on the development of the productivity of the country, with a view to facilitating increased immigration, the situation continued to give little promise of that approach towards self-government which the terms of the mandate prescribed.

Iraq

In Iraq, meanwhile, the attempt to regulate the relations between the mandatory Power and the territory by a treaty which, while purporting to recognize independence should

[1] Cmd. 3692 of 1930.

retain the requisite measure of control, was giving some dissatisfaction to Iraqi politicians. The original treaty of 1926 contemplated the admission of Iraq to membership of the League of Nations in 1928, but this date was postponed to 1932 and made conditional upon continuous progress in the political development of the country. A new treaty, signed in 1927, remained unratified, and a new term, meaning in translation 'the perplexing predicament', was coined to cover the numerous and striking anomalies qualifying ostensible independence by practical control.

On the advice of the new High Commissioner, Sir Gilbert Clayton, who assumed office in March 1929, and unfortunately died in the following September, an unconditional promise was given to support the candidature of Iraq for League of Nations membership in 1932, and this had an immediate effect in clearing the atmosphere. In June 1930 a new treaty of alliance was concluded (ratified 26 January 1931), to take effect on the termination of the mandate by the election of Iraq to membership of the League. By the terms of this instrument, Great Britain was entitled to maintain forces at Hinaidi and also in Mosul for five years after the coming into force of the treaty, and subsequently at air bases to be leased in the vicinity of Basra and at a selected spot to the west of the Euphrates. Each party promised consultation and ultimately military support in the event of a dispute arising with third parties. The treaty was subjected to considerable criticism from a number of conflicting standpoints. To the Iraqi mind, the independence which it provided was still illusory; French opinion was perturbed on account of the stimulus which this early termination of the mandate was calculated to give to Syrian agitation in favour of a similar status; in Conservative circles in Great Britain, the safeguards to our communications appeared insufficient, while other critics felt a danger that the British forces might be utilized in maintaining internal order, to enforce an Arab policy, which it would have ceased to control, against minority communities.

The Fate of the Assyrians

From another angle, the danger to be contemplated by minorities in an independent Iraq was a subject of alarm to the minorities themselves, though it was the withdrawal of British influence which they feared, rather than the prospect that British force might be subservient to Arab policy. These fears were only too amply justified within a short time of the termination of the mandate by Iraq's admission to the League in October 1932. The victims were the Assyrian community, a group of Nestorian Christians originally resident in the mountains to the north of the Mesopotamian frontier. They had entered Iraq as refugees from the Turks, and their existence was the principal reason for the British claim to extend the frontier of the mandated territory sufficiently far north to include their home district (see Chapter VIII). The League, however, awarded this territory to Turkey, which refused to permit the repatriation of the fugitives. After the Arab revolt of 1920, numbers of them were enlisted by Great Britain in a fighting force, which acquired considerable prestige and did excellent work under British officers. This policy, however, tended to emphasize their alien status, and gave rise to jealousy through invidious comparison with the new Iraqi army, which the Levies regarded with undisguised contempt.

The problem of settling the Assyrians in their adopted country proved one of insuperable difficulty. There was no vacant accommodation in which to plant them as a homogeneous community. In June 1932, alarmed at the imminent prospect of the termination of the mandate, many of them adhered to an Assyrian National Pact, which made impracticable demands, in support of which the Levies mutinied, and were with difficulty persuaded to return to their duties. Their hereditary leader, both spiritual and temporal, the Mar Shimun, travelled to Geneva to present their claims, but was completely unsuccessful. The attempt, moreover, gravely incensed the Iraq Government, at a time when King Feisal, whose policy was more humane and conciliatory, was unfortunately absent in England. In July, under some misunderstanding, about 800 Assyrians left the country with the object of settling in Syria. The French authorities, however, refused to receive them, and sent them back, unfortunately without depriving them of arms. On 4 August they returned, and a collision took place with Iraqi troops, who suffered some casualties and retaliated by shooting all prisoners out of hand.

Exaggerated reports of the fighting led to panic in official circles in Baghdad, who encouraged the Iraqi army to severe measures. The result was a wholesale massacre of unarmed inhabitants in Assyrian villages, the worst episode being that at Simmel, on 11 August, where the male inhabitants were methodically exterminated, while the women and children were left without food for three days. A certain amount of murder and looting was also perpetrated by Kurds and Arabs, but the main responsibility attaches to the Iraqi troops, who may have exceeded their orders, though their commander, Bekir Sidky, was honoured on his return to Baghdad by driving through the streets with the Prime Minister to the applause of the inhabitants. The British did what they could, by organizing relief work and administering a refugee camp at Mosul, but they were deterred from intervention or the encouragement of League intervention by the fear of exciting further massacres, which were openly threatened in such an event. The prestige of Great Britain suffered a severe blow, and the incident was a grave warning against the danger of premature abandonment of any of the Arab mandates.

Egypt

The history of Anglo-Egyptian relations during this period is that of a series of unsuccessful attempts to employ the expedient which had achieved at least moderately satisfactory results in Iraq. When British diplomacy, with its native love of compromise, wishes to retain the substance of control while conceding the shadow of independence, it is apt to resort to the method of a treaty. This was the solution adopted not only in Iraq, but also in attempting to settle the Irish question. The difficulty is to find a formula reconciling the requirements of the one party with the nationalistic susceptibilities of the other. In February 1922, Great Britain had told Egypt that she was henceforth an independent sovereign State, and had proceeded to secure, by appropriate reservations, that her independence should be qualified. This had failed to meet with the acceptance of Egyptian Nationalist politicians, and in 1927–8, and again in 1929–30, attempts were made to render the appearance of independence more convincing by incorporating the essential reservations—which really were essential—in the clauses of a treaty ostensibly concluded between two parties of equal status. The history of both attempts shows remarkable points of resemblance. In both instances the initial step was taken by the Egyptian Prime Minister in the course of informal discussions with the British Foreign Secretary. In both cases agreement appeared to have been reached between the original negotiators. In both cases the ultimate break-down was due to the fact that the Egyptian Prime Minister did not enjoy the support of a parliamentary majority, the party in overwhelming superiority being that of the Wafd or nationalists, whose leader on the first occasion, Zaghlul Pasha, had refrained from taking office ever since his resignation following the murder of Sir Lee Stack in 1924. The success of the first attempt, in 1927, was further prejudiced by the death of Zaghlul in August of that year, since his successor in the leadership of the Wafd, Nahhas Pasha, could only judge the proposals on the general principles of the party, and was unable to be certain what would have been his predecessor's reactions towards them. The point on which the views of the parties proved impossible to reconcile was, however, different in each case.

The matters absolutely reserved to the discretion of the British Government by their declaration of February 1922 were as follows:

1. The security of the communications of the British Empire.
2. The defence of Egypt against foreign aggression or interference.
3. The protection of foreign and minority interests.
4. The status of the Sudan.

Of these, the two most important points of difference were the presence of British troops on Egyptian soil necessitated by (1), and the fourth point relating to the Sudan. The latter was eliminated on the first occasion by the expedient of omission, and an attempt was made to postpone the other main issue; it was, however, upon the question of the presence of the British Army in Egypt that the Wafd leader proved entirely uncompromising, and it was upon this that the negotiations broke down in March 1928. In the draft of 1930 the British forces were restricted to an area east of longitude 32° E. and this appeared to meet Egyptian susceptibilities. But on this occasion the Sudan proved to be the insuperable obstacle during the final negotiations, which were conducted by Nahhas Pasha, after his party, the Wafd, had been returned to power by an enormous majority in the elections of December 1929.

The Sudan, after its reconquest by the joint forces of Egypt and Great Britain in 1896–8, had been placed under an Anglo-Egyptian Condominium by an agreement made on 19 January 1899. In its subsequent development both nations had shared, though Great Britain had played the preponderant part in its administration. With the growth of Nationalism after the War was associated an agitation for the complete incorporation of the Sudan in Egypt, which increased in intensity and was accompanied by disturbances of a more or less serious character. There was at this time never any question of any British Government acceding to the demand: on this point the assurances of Lord Parmoor were as emphatic as those of Sir Austen Chamberlain. Great Britain was, however, content to let the Condominium continue, and even to enter into negotiations as to its future status, providing nothing was done by either side in the meanwhile to disturb the *status quo*. But this reasonable condition was never observed by the Egyptians, and after the murder of Sir Lee Stack the British Government took the step of evacuating all Egyptian officers and Egyptian units of the army, and converting the remainder into a Sudan Defence Force, owing allegiance purely to the Sudan Government, and under the orders and control of the Governor-General—an Englishman appointed by the King of Egypt on the recommendation of the British Government. This step, which led to a serious mutiny on the part of one of the Egyptian units, added fuel to the fire of Nationalist discontent, and tended to make Egyptian opinion more intransigent on the question. The most substantial ground for the Nationalist attitude lay in the fact that control of the Sudan involves potential control of the Nile water-supply. The allocation of the Nile waters was, however, separately examined by a Commission in 1925–6, and this issue was satisfactorily settled, on the lines of the Commission's report, by an agreement signed in May 1929.

The actual point on which the negotiations for a treaty in 1929–30 broke down was not the main question of the Sudan, which was reserved for future discussion, but the comparatively minor issue as to the right of unrestricted immigration of

Egyptian nationals into this territory. It is difficult to avoid the conclusion that the real obstacle to a settlement was a mutual mistrust, which was probably more or less justified on both sides, from the standpoint of each. Great Britain felt that her material interests could not be left to depend merely upon Egyptian good faith, and Egyptian nationalism suspected that there was no intention of allowing the independence at which it aimed to be anything but illusory. Though these difficulties of arriving at a permanent and trustworthy settlement were for some time enhanced by the domestic political situation in the country, where constitutional parliamentary government was repeatedly suspended by the act of the King, every obstacle was eventually destined to be overcome. At the time, however, it appeared surprising that agreement should have been so nearly attained, even though on each occasion success was only approached by postponing the most serious points of controversy.

In the field which has been surveyed in this chapter, the main conclusions which seem to emerge are—firstly, the great danger to peace and orderly government if the control of a Western Power was removed, and secondly, the growing difficulty of maintaining such control in a world which discountenances force and encourages the aspirations of racial nationalism. Taken with the increasing sense of Arab unity, and the emergence of a consolidated Power in the Arabian peninsula, the prospect might well arouse considerable anxiety.

XV

CHINA TO 1930

THE truth or falsity of the prediction by General Smuts, quoted in Chapter IX (p. 146), had not yet been established, but during the first four or five years following the termination of the Peace Conference of Paris it would have been difficult to point to any striking evidence in support of the view there expressed. Europe undoubtedly was the focus of attention and the seed-plot of international crises: such Pacific problems as had seemed to constitute a threat appeared to have achieved an early and satisfactory solution during the Washington Conference of 1921-2. Not until the summer of 1925 did the scene begin to change: but with the second period of our history, the Far East started to take a place in world affairs which promised to justify the prediction of the South African statesman.

The central factor in the situation—anarchy in China—had indeed existed from the first, but from 1920 to 1925 this was little more than a question of Chinese domestic politics. Strikes and trade disputes were numerous, and in these a political motive might generally be traced behind the economic pretext; Bolshevik propaganda, insidious and persistent, was working, even then, to influence the growing nationalism of China against the domination of Western capitalists; perpetual civil war hampered commercial relations; but no international crisis arose of a magnitude sufficient to divert attention from the menacing problems of Europe. Indeed, regarded as a whole, the trade figures of the country remained extraordinarily satisfactory.

Yet the moment that questions arose necessitating international negotiations, the internal state of China constituted a formidable obstacle; foreign countries, however accommodating and conciliatory in intention, found it difficult to achieve a lasting and satisfactory settlement when they could find no generally recognized government capable of speaking for the whole of China. Misrule and anarchy, combined with a spirit of nationalism which was the one feeling at all generally

shared by all sections of the Chinese population, were at once
a threat to peace and an obstacle to settlement. The internal
condition of the country cannot, therefore, be ignored: though
domestic politics should as far as possible be excluded from the

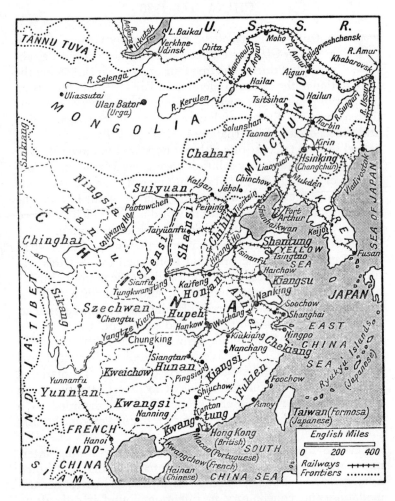

scope of this work, in dealing with the Far Eastern question it is
necessary to devote some space to its consideration.

For some 2,200 years, the constitution of China had remained
unchanged. The rule of the Emperor was technically autocratic,

but in practice his control over the provinces was confined to the appointment of the governing officials and the requisition of funds to meet the central expenditure. There was thus a large measure of local independence throughout the Empire, and the Emperor himself was the only real bond of union.

Through the revolution of 1911, a millennial tradition of government was subjected to a sudden and complete change. A republic with a parliamentary system of government based upon Western ideas was substituted overnight in a vast country about ninety-nine per cent of whose population was illiterate. It has been claimed that the adoption of parliamentary institutions was less difficult in China than in any other oriental country, since a crude popular control of oppressive taxation had long been intermittently exercised through the institution of a communal boycott.[1] The author referred to suggests that: 'In so acting the people unconsciously exercised the essential function of parliamentary government, the maintenance of the principle that taxation can only be imposed with the consent of the people', but it may be doubted whether so rudimentary and instinctive a reaction against oppression is any adequate evidence of political capacity.

The immediate effect of the revolution was anarchy and disintegration. The link which bound the vast Empire of China in some sort of unity had been destroyed. The new movement gathered its main inspiration from westernized intellectuals in the Canton area of the extreme south, of whom Sun Yat-sen was the leading spirit. This was exceedingly remote from the centre of government at Peking, and such liaison as was possible was removed at the outset of the revolution by the withdrawal of Sun Yat-sen from the position of President to which he had been elected, in favour of Yuan Shih-kai, a Conservative statesman of the old school, who had resisted the revolution as long as possible, and who had no intention of submitting to popular control. In 1913 he dissolved and proscribed the Kuomintang or National Party, and thenceforward ruled without Parliament. In 1915 he threw off all pretence and proclaimed himself Emperor, but was forced to postpone the change of constitution, and shortly afterwards died (6 June 1916). His successor to the

---

[1] Paper by Alfred Hippisley on 'The Chinese Revolution' read to the Central Asian Society in 1912.

Presidency, Li Yuan-hung, re-convoked the Parliament, but dissolved it again in the following year, after which the split between north and south was openly declared by the assembly of a rival parliamentary government in Canton, under the leadership of Sun Yat-sen. This political cleavage had, however, in fact existed throughout the revolution, and was, indeed, almost a permanent factor in the situation, reflected geographically by the bisection of China from east to west by the Yangtse river.

The Northern Civil War, First Stage

After the death of Yuan Shih-kai the government which his strong personality had succeeded to a large extent in holding together rapidly dissolved into its component fragments. In 1922 civil war broke out in North China, and its history became a bewildering kaleidoscope of continually changing alliances between the rival Tuchuns. Of these the most important at this stage were Chang Tso-lin, the Manchurian 'war-lord', and Wu Pei-fu, one of whose subordinates, Feng Yu-hsiang, 'the Christian General', was soon destined to achieve independent notoriety. The early operations of the civil war forced Chang Tso-lin and Sun Yat-sen into an unnatural alliance from which neither profited, for Chang was defeated by the Wu Pei-fu combination, and Sun, on his return to Canton, found it occupied by his former supporter, General Chen Chiung-ming, and was temporarily forced to retire to Shanghai. The immediate effect of Wu's victory was the reinstatement of the ex-president, Li Yuan-hung, and the reassembly of the Peking parliament, but this apparent restoration of constitutional government in the north was of short duration. The new President aimed at the unification of China through peaceful reconciliation, whereas the war-lords who had reinstated him were believers in force. In June, therefore, a fresh interregnum was caused by the eviction of Li Yuan-hung, pending the appointment to the presidency of Tsao Kun, a military colleague of Wu Pei-fu. In 1924 Wu started a campaign in pursuance of his ideal of forcible unification. But, owing to the desertion of Feng, who withdrew to Peking and assumed military control of the capital, he was easily defeated by Chang Tso-lin, and forced into temporary retirement.

Progress of the Kuomintang

Meanwhile, Sun Yat-sen had succeeded in getting back to Canton, in the spring of 1923. With him was an adviser from Soviet Russia, Michael Borodin. Though this liaison with Bolshevism was to prove a two-edged weapon, the policy had much to commend it in the eyes of a revolutionary like Sun, who saw the early fervour and enthusiasm of his associates fading into respectability. It was, moreover, natural to turn to Russia, since he could not expect much help from other Western Powers. In the year of his return he was destined to come into conflict with them through a misguided attempt to seize the Canton custom-house in order to secure a share of the surplus revenue, and in 1924 the action of his Government in dealing with a plot organized by the merchant volunteer corps brought him a warning from the representatives of Great Britain. But Russia could be and was of great assistance in strengthening the forces at Sun's disposal. It was with Russian advice and under Russian instructors that the Whampoa military academy was started in 1924, while Borodin and his associates also succeeded in thoroughly reorganizing the Kuomintang, giving it a relation to the government closely modelled on that occupied by the Third International in regard to the Moscow Government. Indeed, anyone seeing the word 'Kuomintang' for the first time at this stage might readily have taken it for a Chinese transliteration of 'Comintern'. Last but not least the Russian Communists were experts in propaganda. Nor was the help derived from the Soviet Government confined to China. In Moscow a university was founded, where hundreds of young Chinese were instructed in the Bolshevik gospel. Under these auspices the Kuomintang acquired a remarkable and rapid invigoration.

The next element in the progress of the National party was, paradoxically enough, the death of its leader. In March 1925 Sun Yat-sen died. As a practical leader and a man of action, he had exhibited many defects. All that was best of him, his political writings and the 'Three Principles' on which he had conducted his revolution, was equally available after his death. The Russian advisers, who had recently seen the effects of Lenin-worship in their own country, were quick to grasp the

possibilities. The body of Sun Yat-sen was embalmed. A cult
in his honour was sedulously propagated: his writings were
everywhere disseminated. From a rather precarious position as
the head of a local and unrecognized government he became
a rallying symbol for the Nationalist aspirations which were
the one thing which united Chinese opinion throughout the
Empire.

The Shanghai Incident

The Communist influence was not long in making itself felt
in an increase of ostensibly industrial disputes, which had a
political background in the anti-foreign movement created by
a growing nationalism, whose claims the absence of organized
government made it impossible to satisfy. The returns of the
Shanghai Municipal Council showed strikes in 1924 resulting
in a loss of 289,730 days. Other ports were similarly affected.
In February 1925 the dismissal of forty employees at a Japanese
mill in Shanghai led to a prolonged dispute accompanied by
violent agitation, sabotage, and even murder. On 14 May an
attempt on the part of strikers to force an entrance into a mill
was resisted by the Japanese occupants, who fired in self-
defence, killing one of the strikers. A memorial procession was
organized through the international settlement on 30 May,
which culminated in a riot, and an attack upon the police-
station, in the course of which the police opened fire, killing
twelve of the rioters and wounding seventeen.

This event was followed almost immediately by a similar
occurrence on the island of Shameen, a portion of Canton
containing the French and British concessions. On 23 June
a monster demonstration of protest was marching past the
concessions when one of its contingents, from the Whampoa
military academy, fired a volley at the island, its fire being
immediately returned by the European forces, with the result
that thirty-seven Chinese were killed and many more wounded.

The repercussions of these events were felt almost immediately
throughout China. A widespread boycott, directed mainly
against the British, followed, and the demands of the Chinese
for the abolition of foreign privileges were urged with increased
impatience and vehemence. The incident forms, in fact, a
landmark in the history of Chinese international relations.

Anarchy in the North

Yet, paradoxically enough, the international crisis provoked by the Shanghai and Shameen incidents was the first step towards the recognition of the southern Government by the foreign Powers concerned. For a stage had now been reached when it was necessary to come to an understanding upon the issues raised by Nationalist claims, and the difficulty did not consist in any unbridgeable gulf between the standpoints of the parties but in the impossibility of finding a responsible authority with which to negotiate. For example, the Conference convened in October 1925, in conformity with the Washington Agreements of 1922, to consider the future status of the Chinese Customs' tariff, broke down not because of any unwillingness on the part of the twelve nations represented to concede the demands of the Chinese for tariff autonomy and the abrogation of existing treaty restrictions, but because, before the termination of the Conference, the Peking Government had faded out of existence. The same obstacle alone prevented the completion of arrangements for the rendition of Wei-hai-wei, in accordance with undertakings which had also been given at Washington. The Commission on Extra-territoriality, another product of the Washington Conference, continued, however, its deliberations at Peking during eight months of the year.

The real trouble in Peking was due to the resumption of the northern civil war with a remarkable change of partnerships. After the defeat of Wu Pei-fu, owing to the defection of Feng Yu-hsiang, the victorious Manchurian leader, Chang Tso-lin, had endeavoured to purchase the friendly neutrality of Feng by a cession of territory, only to experience, within a month, the same perfidy of which his antagonist, Wu, had been the victim. In December 1925, taking advantage of a revolt by one of Chang's generals, Feng had attacked another of Chang's subordinates and driven him from Tientsin. Wu Pei-fu and Chang Tso-lin were, therefore, temporarily forced into an unnatural alliance by a common resentment, with the object of settling accounts with the treacherous 'Christian General'. Feng Yu-hsiang, faced by this new combination, found the moment opportune to depart on a visit to Moscow, but before his leaderless troops had withdrawn from Peking, in April 1926, they deposed the head of the Government, Tuan Chi-jui, whose departure to Tientsin left a complete interregnum behind him. At an earlier stage of the hostilities, the difficulties created for foreigners by the existence of the civil war had been exemplified by the Taku forts incident, when foreign shipping was fired on in the neighbourhood of Tientsin, and mines were reported to have been laid at the entrance to the harbour. A protest from the diplomatic body met with an almost abjectly conciliatory reply from the Government, but the episode only showed the impotence of the ostensible authority, and the hopelessness of attempting negotiations in that quarter.

Progress and Recognition of the Southern Government

In the South, on the other hand, though the situation in which foreigners were placed was far more serious, and therefore demanded more urgent attention, there was at the back of the agitation a solid, even if obnoxious, organization, with an intelligible purpose behind its policy.

The element of Bolshevism represented by the Russian advisers no doubt increased the difficulty of negotiation, for it was definitely set upon embroiling the relations between China and the Western Powers, but the claims of the Nationalists placed no insuperable obstacle in the way of settlement, and in any case there was a substantial authority rather than a shadow to deal with.

The star of the southern—or National—Government was in any case in the ascendant. Under the leadership of Chiang Kai-shek, formerly the commandant of the Whampoa Military Academy, its forces had succeeded in making a rapid advance in their campaign against the northern 'war-lords'. In August 1926 they received a notable recruit in Feng Yu-hsiang, whose visit to Moscow—or his characteristic opportunism—induced him to enrol himself as a member of the Kuomintang. By the end of the year Wu Pei-fu and his ally Sun Chuan-fang had been practically eliminated as serious factors in the situation, the southern armies were astride the Yangtse, in occupation of the province of Hupeh, and on New Year's Day, 1927, the National Government issued a mandate removing their capital to greater Hankow, which they renamed Wuhan.

In these circumstances the first steps towards negotiation

with the National Government were taken in December 1926, when Mr Lampson, the British Minister, met the Kuomintang Foreign Secretary, Mr Eugene Chen, and held conversations with him at Hankow. The Nationalists had displayed their readiness to negotiate since the beginning of June, when attempts were made to end the anti-foreign boycott in Canton, which was finally terminated in October. This improvement in the relations of the parties was not permanently disturbed by an incident in the British Concession in Tientsin in November, when fourteen persons connected with the Kuomintang were arrested on a charge of seditious activities and handed over to the authorities of the north. The occurrence excited protests from the National Government, but the action of the British had been diplomatically correct. The conversations at Hankow were immediately followed up by the communication of a British memorandum to the representatives in Peking of the Washington Treaty Powers, which spoke with sympathy of the Nationalist movement, and expressed readiness to negotiate on treaty revision and other outstanding questions; and in January 1927 a statement was sent to the Chinese Foreign Secretaries both in Hankow and Peking, outlining the measures for treaty modification which the British Government was prepared to consider.

Violation of British Concessions at Hankow and Kiukiang

Notwithstanding these evidences of *rapprochement*, the success of the Nationalist party had not unnaturally been accompanied by a good deal of agitation directed against the foreigners. After the occupation of greater Hankow in October 1926 the majority of the working population were at once enrolled in labour unions, a step which not only led to a ruinous rise in wages but was accompanied by a succession of strikes and culminated in a general foreign boycott, which, however, was actually enforced only against the Japanese. On the eve of Mr Lampson's arrival in December, matters took a new turn, specifically directed against the British, a change of policy in which M. Borodin was the protagonist and in which the hand of Russia was evident. As a result, on 3 January 1927, a large mob, incited by Borodin, attempted to enter the British Concession, and was only kept out by a cordon of British marines and other naval ratings, who displayed a heroic steadiness under a sustained fusillade of bricks and stones. Not a shot was fired; not a Chinese was killed; but the concession was nevertheless effectively guarded. Two days later, however, the defence of the Settlement having been entrusted to Chinese troops, the mob succeeded in effecting an entrance, and the same evening most of the women and children in the concession were evacuated. At Kiukiang a similar crisis had occurred on 4 January, though in this case the evacuation of women and children preceded the invasion of the mob. Evidence was not lacking, however, that these events were instigated and approved only by the left wing of the Kuomintang, which was already beginning to lose its controlling influence. Mr Eugene Chen, the Minister of Foreign Affairs, took immediate and energetic steps to secure the safety of the British Concessions and their inhabitants, and within a few days conversations were opened at Hankow between Mr Chen and Mr O'Malley, the Counsellor of the British Legation, who had been sent for the purpose by his chief, Sir Miles Lampson.[1] Shortly, however, after the conversations were started, the British Government, fearing for the security of the international settlement at Shanghai, ordered the dispatch of a defence force of three brigades to the town, under the command of Sir John Duncan. The National Government took umbrage at this step, which they construed as an act of coercion directed against them. After an agreement had been drawn up, therefore, Mr Chen refused to sign it, but after some delay negotiations were resumed, and an agreement was eventually signed on 21 February by Mr Chen and Mr O'Malley, resigning the care of the Hankow concession to a new Chinese administration, under regulations to be communicated to the British Minister. The agreement caused considerable dismay to the foreign community in other concessions and treaty ports, but was equally disliked by the extreme left wing of the Kuomintang, who had hoped for unconditional surrender.

Anti-Communist split in the Kuomintang

As has already been hinted, the Kuomintang party had been suffering for some time from internal dissensions, between a

[1] Mr Lampson had been made a K.C.M.G. on 1 January 1927. Created Lord Killearn 1943.

section which resented the Russian tutelage and was opposed to Communism, and a left wing which Borodin and his associates had effectively converted to Bolshevik principles. The most active opponent of Communist influences was the military leader, Chiang Kai-shek. As early as March 1926, during the temporary absence of Borodin from Canton, he had attempted the expulsion of the Chinese Communists and the Russian Mission from the city. Borodin, however, returned in time to thwart the *coup*, and succeeded in inducing Chiang to throw over his associates in return for a promise of support to the projected northern expedition. On 15 May, at a party conference, Chiang Kai-shek succeeded in carrying certain resolutions disqualifying Communists from service as heads of departments in the central organization, and otherwise controlling the activities of the Chinese Communist party. These resolutions, however, in practice merely saved Chiang's face, without materially hampering Borodin, who may thus be said to have won the first rounds in the contest. In the early part of 1927 the left wing of the Kuomintang continued its successes. The events at Hankow and Kiukiang have been interpreted as being primarily aimed at embarrassing Chiang Kai-shek and his associates by embroiling them with a great European Power. In meeting on 10 March at Hankow rather than at Chiang's headquarters at Nanchang, the Communist section of the party registered another victory, which they were able to follow up, owing to the boycott of the assembly by the Centre and Right of the party, by a resolution deposing Chiang Kai-shek from the post of Commander-in-Chief, a decision formally ratified by the Government on 17 April. In Shanghai, however, which had meanwhile fallen into his hands, the General took energetic steps to suppress the Communists by force, and on 15 April, at Nanking, he inaugurated an opposition Kuomintang Government. The Hankow Government retorted by expelling him from the party, and appointing Feng Yu-hsiang to the chief military command in his place. Yet the Nanking Government succeeded in obtaining the adherence of the provinces on the southern littoral, and the position of its rival appeared precarious, when the latter suddenly revised its policy, and associated itself with the movement for the expulsion of the Russian Mission and its converts. The first hint of this change was a telegram dispatched by General Feng to the Hankow Government, demanding the expulsion of the Communists, which is believed to have been sent in collusion with those to whom it was ostensibly addressed. But the real reason for it appears to have been the revelations of Soviet intrigue derived from documents captured and published by the Northern Coalition in Peking in the month of April, and the discovery, in June, of secret instructions issued to Borodin from Moscow, in which he was not only directed to foster the confiscation of land by the peasants, without reference to the Hankow Government, but also to take steps to secure that the Kuomintang should gradually be supplanted by the Chinese Communist party. These revelations converted the Hankow Government to a view identical with that of Chiang Kai-shek, and in the middle of July the Chinese Communists were arrested wholesale, and Borodin and his mission sent back to Russia.

An unexpected result of this change of front, which made possible a reunion of the party and the transfer of the seat of government to Nanking, was the temporary eclipse of Chiang Kai-shek, on whose retirement the Hankow leaders continued to insist; and in August he withdrew to Japan, after issuing two long proclamations explanatory of his action. In November, however, he returned to Shanghai, on 1 December he married the sister of Mr T. V. Soong, the Finance Minister, and of Mrs Sun Yat-sen, and on the 10th he was reinstated in the post of Commander-in-Chief.

His return to power was probably due, to some extent, to a general reaction against disturbances which had meanwhile been taking place in the south. Canton had from the first associated itself with the anti-Communist policy of Chiang Kai-shek, and had violently suppressed the movement locally as early as April. The sudden change of attitude at Hankow, however, did not suit the view of some military commanders in the service of that government, and in September some of them appeared in the south and set up a Communist regime in part of Kwantung province, from which they were not wholly dislodged. In December, a 'Red Army', led by one of these commanders, succeeded in entering the city of Canton, where it started a serious Communist rising, and created a temporary reign of terror, before the disturbance was ruthlessly suppressed, with a loss of life estimated at not less than two thousand. The emergence of the danger in so acute a form no doubt turned the minds of the Government to the strong man who had been the first to foresee it, and Chiang Kai-shek, on his reappointment, at once took energetic steps to complete the elimination of the Russian influence and its supporters.

The End of Chang Tso-lin

At the close of 1927, therefore, the National Government was once more united, and prepared to enter upon the final phase of the struggle with Chang Tso-lin, whose principal allies had by this time been eliminated. Shanghai was occupied by the National forces in March, with the exception of the International Settlement, which was protected by the Defence Force, fortunately without any serious clash. The occupation of Nanking, on the other hand, on 23–24 March, had been accompanied by serious outrages against foreigners, which appeared to have been deliberately instigated, probably with the idea of embarrassing Chiang Kai-shek, who had not arrived at the time, and who expressed regret for the occurrences. By the end of the year, the northern armies were more or less confined to the provinces of Shantung and Chihli, for Feng Yu-hsiang was in occupation of Honan, and the advance of the National forces had induced the governor of Shansi, Yen Hsi-shan, commonly known as 'the model Tuchun', to abandon neutrality and throw in his lot with the Kuomintang. A general advance began in April 1928, and on 9 May Chang Tso-lin announced his abandonment of the struggle. His departure from Peking was hastened by a note sent by the Japanese to both sides, on 18 May, warning them that the nearer approach of the disturbances to Peking and Tientsin might lead to their intervention to preserve order. They put further pressure upon Chang Tso-lin to withdraw to Manchuria, and at the same time strongly reinforced their detachment at Tientsin. Chang Tso-lin accordingly evacuated Peking on 2 June, and retired to Manchuria, but while crossing under the Japanese South Manchurian railway line near Mukden his train was blown up, and Chang himself was killed. The origin of the outrage is unknown, but in China it was freely attributed to the Japanese.

The Tsinanfu Incident

Chiang Kai-shek had, however, been prevented from achieving the glory of being the first to enter Peking, an honour which fell to Yen on 8 June. The Japanese, as indicated in the preceding paragraph, had become concerned by the transference of the theatre of operation into regions which they regarded as their special sphere of interest, and their policy had taken a decidedly more militant turn on the resignation of Baron Shidehara's Government in April 1927, and its succession by that of Baron Tanaka. In May 1927 a defence force had been dispatched to Shantung, which had not only occupied the treaty port of Tsingtao, but also Tsinanfu, the junction of the Tientsin–Pukow and Tsingtao–Tsinanfu railways, both of which were Chinese property. This action had given rise to Chinese protests and an anti-Japanese boycott in the summer of 1927, but no actual trouble had occurred on the spot, and in September the Japanese troops had been withdrawn from Shantung. With the revival of operations in April 1928, however, they had been replaced, and on the arrival of Chiang Kai-shek's forces on 2–3 May, a collision took place, the responsibility for which is strenuously contested. As a result, the Japanese commander launched a vigorous attack, drove back the main body of Chinese troops to a distance of about seven miles from the city, and ejected the remainder by shelling the town, causing numerous casualties to the civilian population. The incident evoked protest from the Nanking Government to Japan, and they also informed the League of Nations by telegram on 11 May. They exerted themselves, however, to restrain manifestations of anti-Japanese feeling.

End of the Civil War

On 6 July 1928 the three National commanders attended a ceremony in the Western Hills, near Peking, to announce to the spirit of Sun Yat-sen the successful termination of the war. The dead leader had laid down three stages for the progress of the nation towards democracy; the first or military stage was now over, and the second, that of tutelage, had now to be begun, before the time was ripe for the ultimate phase of popular government. In this spirit, a Government Organiza-

tion Law was promulgated by the Central Executive of the
Kuomintang in October 1928, setting up an executive Yuan,
or board, with four other boards, legislative, judicial, public
examiners, and censorship, under the presidency of Chiang
Kai-shek. The process of financial reconstruction was begun,
and the first steps taken in the demobilization of the armed
forces.

Status of Manchuria

There was now a unified government over the whole of China
proper, but the question of the inclusion of Manchuria aroused
immediate opposition from the Japanese. The son and successor
of Chang Tso-lin, the 'Young Marshal', Chang Hsueh-liang,
was from the first sympathetic to union with the National
Government, but on 18 July 1928, he was warned by the
Japanese that the union of Manchuria with China might
prejudice their interests. In the British House of Commons,
however, Sir Austen Chamberlain declared that His Majesty's
Government regarded Manchuria as part of China, and in
August Baron Tanaka repudiated the intention of opposing the
union, though he said that he could not endorse it. In these
circumstances, Chang Hsueh-liang was appointed in October
as one of the sixteen State Councillors, and at the end of
December 1928 the Kuomintang flag was hoisted in Manchuria.

Disturbances of 1929–30

Tranquillity had not, however, yet been attained. In the
spring of 1929, a quarrel broke out between Chiang Kai-shek
and Feng Yu-hsiang, who was expelled from the party by the
Central Executive of the Kuomintang on 23 May. Actual
warfare was averted during this year, but in April 1930 a revolt
against Chiang Kai-shek was started by his two former allies,
Yen and Feng, which was defeated before the end of the year
with the assistance of Chang Hsueh-liang. In both years,
trouble was caused in the south by the 'Kwangsi Group', led
by Chang Fai-kwei, and the disbandment of the troops used
during the civil war led to a great increase of banditry. Widespread famine occurred to increase the troubles of the Government, and its prospects of peacefully controlling the whole
country did not appear to be bright at the close of 1930.

PART III

THE PERIOD OF COLLAPSE

1930 to 1939

Gods of our land, and heroes of our race,
Ye guardians of each dear remembered place,
In this new reign vouchsafe us to assuage
The maladies of our distracted age.
Surely sufficient blood has long been spilt
To wash our history clean from stains of guilt.
Yet well may Heaven, in envy of our state,
Grudge us the leadership which made us great,
When wrong replaces right: these latest times
Have filled the world with nought but wars and crimes.
Neglected in the field the plough stands still,
And thistles thrive while conscript farmers drill.
Swords from their crooked scythes are forged, to meet
At once an eastern and a German threat.
Neighbours, their treaties broken, arm once more,
And cruel Mars runs wild from shore to shore.
As when, in chariot races, from the start
Out on the course the eager rivals dart,
The beasts take charge, the driver tugs in vain,
Whirled in a car that answers not the rein!

VIRGIL, *Georgic I*, lines 498–514.

XVI

THE WORLD IN 1930

IN the first edition of this work the title of the final part, beginning in 1930, was merely 'Period of Crisis'. When I started in 1938 to recast it and bring it up to date, with the experience of four additional and momentous years, I felt compelled to describe it definitely as 'The Period of Collapse'. I hoped, indeed, that better times might emerge, recalling that the terribly appropriate *sortes Virgilianae*, of which I have attempted a translation on the preceding page, were falsified in the event by one of the few periods of protracted peace in the history of Rome. Yet the settlement which followed the struggle of 1914–18, and the mechanism which it devised for the elimination of war, lay in irretrievable ruin. To call the period any longer 'the post-war era' would have savoured of bitter irony. War had already broken out in the East and in the West, while many nations still technically at peace were enjoying only the immunity of the victim who surrenders his property with the bandit's pistol at his head. In the sense insisted on by Hobbes, we were already at war.

For 'war' consisteth not in battle only, or the act of fighting; but in a tract of time wherein the will to contend by battle is sufficiently known. . . . For as the nature of foul weather lieth not in a shower or two of rain, but in an inclination thereto of many days together, so the nature of war consisteth not in actual fighting, but in the known disposition thereto all the time there is no assurance to the contrary.[1]

Yet when, at the conclusion of the labours of the Preparatory Commission for the Disarmament Conference, the world once more paused to draw breath, it seemed at first sight that a satisfactory measure of progress might be set to the credit of the preceding quinquennium. In Europe, the problem of reparation was believed to have been finally settled by the adoption of the Young Plan (May 1930; see Chapter XVII). A further indication of improved relations with Germany had been the

[1] *Leviathan*, chapter 13.

complete evacuation of the Rhineland by the military forces of the victor Powers. In the matter of disarmament, a draft convention had been produced—though unfortunately without unanimous agreement—which promised a useful basis for the forthcoming deliberations of the Conference in 1932. At the same time, a substantial advance towards limitation had been made by the three principal maritime Powers of the world in the naval treaty concluded in London. The general acceptance of the Kellogg Pact seemed to mark an important stage in the elimination of war from international relations, while a further contribution to the problem had been made by opening for accession the General Act for the Pacific Settlement of International Disputes, and by proposals such as the Convention for Financial Assistance. In Russia, the fall and expulsion of Zinoviev and his associates in 1927-8 suggested the definite abandonment of the policy of propagandist interference with the domestic affairs of other countries which had been carried on by the Third International, and, since 1928, the Soviet Government had been mainly preoccupied with the effort undertaken, in the Five-Year Plan, for the industrial development of the country. In their sphere of operations in the Far East, Communist propaganda had been simultaneously checked by the expulsion of the Russian agents, and the forcible suppression of their disciples. Lastly, through the presence of their representative on the Disarmament Commission from the end of 1927, the Russians had once more taken a co-operative place at the council table of Europe.

Events in America showed signs of a similarly satisfactory progress. The Kellogg Pact had been forestalled by the Mexican resolutions at the Sixth Pan-American Conference of 1928, and supplemented by the Conventions for Conciliation and Arbitration in 1929. The protracted and difficult negotiations over the Tacna-Arica dispute had ended in the treaty settlement of 1929, the Peru–Colombia boundary was delimited in August 1930, and the disturbances shortly to arise in that region were still in the womb of time. There had been a temporary pacification of the quarrel between Bolivia and Paraguay; the serious phase of open war was not to be reached until later. The Nicaraguan trouble was settled, and the United States had abandoned the policy of economic imperialism which had aroused misgivings in the earlier portion of the quinquennium. Up to the autumn of 1929 the United States had enjoyed an apparently unexampled prosperity, which had enabled them to ease, by lavish and welcome loans, the economic stresses of Europe.

In the Middle East, the surrender of Faysal ud Dawish in January 1930 had put an end to the serious threat of a Holy War directed against the European mandataries. The Syrian trouble seemed to be over, and the promulgation of a Constitution for this territory suggested a distinct advance. In Iraq, a new treaty had marked a further and final stage in the progress of that State towards freedom from mandatory leading-strings and qualification for membership of the League. In Egypt, the latest negotiations for a treaty were still in progress, with considerable hope of a satisfactory outcome. Palestine had recently given trouble, but was now again quiet.

Finally, in the Far East, there was at last the germ of a unified China. All over the world, then, there appeared at first sight to be solid material for satisfaction.

It may, therefore, occasion surprise that this year, 1930, the year when the British Prime Minister had described the risk of war as 'practically nil' (cf. p. 191), was the date when the shadow of a possible or probable recurrence of war first began to darken the world. All over Europe, as English travellers in that period reported, the imminence of war was a staple topic of conversation. This was not mere irresponsible rumour. Distinguished financiers, like Dr Somary of Zurich, arrived at a similarly serious diagnosis from the consideration of economic symptoms. In a lecture delivered at Chatham House in December 1930 this authority pointed to the high rate of interest offered in vain by the largest of German banks on guaranteed first mortgage bonds, and drew the conclusion, from this and similar phenomena, that, in the absence of effective steps for the restoration of political confidence, 'the present crisis will be but a prelude to a dark period to which the historian of the future will give the name "Between two Wars" '.[1] A year later the American journalist, Mr Frank Simonds, published his book with the ominous title—*Can Europe keep the Peace?*

[1] *International Affairs*, March 1931, p. 169.

What were the reasons for these forebodings? In the first place, some of the items which have been placed on the credit side of the situation must be subjected to qualifications which deprive them of much of their face value. The success of the three-Power naval treaty was equally the failure of the five-Power negotiations, and, by virtue of the 'escalator' clause (see p. 193), the real value of its provisions might depend upon the action taken by the two European Powers, France and Italy, who had failed to reach agreement. Subsequent Franco-Italian discussions on naval limitation, which took place in 1930–1, and which must be more fully dealt with hereafter, engendered, at various stages, a dangerous amount of heat. Thus, in Florence on 17 May 1930, the question inspired Signor Mussolini to perhaps the most hair-raising of his more truculent utterances:

Words are a very fine thing; but rifles, machine-guns, warships, aeroplanes, and cannon are still finer things. They are finer, Blackshirts, because right unaccompanied by might is an empty word. . . . Fascist Italy, powerfully armed, will offer her two simple alternatives: a precious friendship or an adamantine hostility.

Somewhat similar considerations apply to the conclusion of the draft Disarmament Convention. Attention has already (p. 195) been drawn to the fact that the final sessions of the Preparatory Commission showed a dangerous tendency to *rapprochement* between Germany, Italy, and the U.S.S.R., and, though the votes of these three countries were insufficient to prevent the adoption of the Convention by a majority, a minority consisting of these three Powers was really a much more formidable obstacle in the path of disarmament than a much larger opposition, consisting of less powerful States, could have been.

Apart from this, the mere fact that a Commission which had been appointed five years previously had only achieved a meagre and partial agreement on general principles of limitation by the end of 1930 was enough to make anyone despair of the prospects of eliminating armed force from international relations. The unwillingness of the nations to reduce their armaments was an indication that no one really placed much trust in the observance of pacts or covenants. 'Without which', to quote Hobbes again, 'covenants are in vain, and but empty words; and the right of all men to all things remaining, *we are still in the condition of war.* . . .'

By the year 1930, the hand had already begun to write upon the wall its forecast of doom to the post-war system, and indeed the same words, in the same order, which interrupted the revellings of Belshazzar, might soon be read by the discerning interpreter. 'MENE'—the force of arithmetic, exemplified in the economic crisis: 'TEKEL'—the practical tests, which exposed the deficiencies in the system of collective security: and finally, 'PERES'—the prospect of redistribution of territory through the agency of a newly arisen aggressive Power. The first word began to be traced in 1929, with the financial crash in the United States; the second in September 1931, with the failure to curb Japanese aggression in Manchuria; and the last in January 1933, with the accession of Adolf Hitler to the Chancellorship of the German Reich. It is with these three influences, and their reactions and interactions upon the course of international affairs, that the following pages must attempt to deal.

XVII

THE ECONOMIC CRISIS AND THE END OF REPARATION

The Young Plan

THE reader will have observed that in the preceding section of this work the subject of reparation has not been mentioned. Logically, there is no doubt a stage in the history of this topic between the adoption of the Dawes and Young plans, but in practice there was nothing to record. The payments due under the Dawes Plan were made punctually, smoothly, and with apparent ease, and, since the Young Plan did not supersede them until 17 May 1930, this happy state of things continued during the whole 'period of fulfilment' with which Part II is concerned. All was quiet on the Reparation front.

The Agent-General, Mr Parker Gilbert, had, notwithstanding, continually pointed out that the Dawes Plan was not, either in intention or in fact, a final settlement of the problem. It was described by its authors as 'a settlement extending in its application for a sufficient time to restore confidence' and 'framed to facilitate a final comprehensive agreement as to all the problems of reparation and connected questions, as soon as circumstances make this possible'.

One of these 'connected questions' was, of course, the occupation of the Rhineland, to the termination of which Herr Stresemann's 'policy of fulfilment' was mainly directed: so long as it continued, the resumption of cordial relations between Germany and her former opponents was evidently impeded, and, as time went on, the German people evinced increasing impatience at the postponement of this reward of good behaviour. The unexpected ease with which the conditions of the Dawes Plan seemed to have been carried out produced, moreover, a widespread impression that the time was now ripe for a final settlement.

Accordingly, during the session of the League Assembly in September 1928, an agreement was announced, as the result of informal discussions between the Powers concerned, for the opening of official negotiations in regard to the early evacuation of the Rhineland, and for the appointment of a Committee of financial experts to work out a complete and definitive settlement of the Reparation problem. On this Committee, unlike that which had produced the Dawes Report, Germany herself was to be fully represented. In January 1929 the experts were accordingly appointed, and in the following month the Committee assembled, under the chairmanship of the leading American representative, Mr Owen D. Young.

Since the settlement which it was charged to evolve was to be a final one, the task of the Committee was not only to assess the total amount payable by Germany, and the period over which it was to be paid, but also to arrange for the abolition of the foreign controls which had so far been imposed. Under the Dawes Plan, the responsibility for transferring the payments into foreign currencies had been laid upon the creditor countries, but, as a corollary, they had been given extensive powers of control. The unsuitability of incorporating such provisions in a final arrangement had been emphatically pointed out by the Agent-General in several of his reports, especially in that for 1927.

The removal of the responsibility of transfer from the shoulders of the recipients to those of Germany was in fact the fundamental distinction between the proposals of the Young Report, which was completed on 7 June 1929, and those of the Dawes Commission. But this change introduced an element of uncertainty as to the amounts which the debtor would be able to pay over a long period, and, in order to obtain agreement upon an amount sufficiently large to satisfy the demands of the creditors, it was considered essential to divide it into two categories, of which one alone would be unconditional.

The unconditional annuities corresponded to the mortgage interest derived from the German State Railways under the Dawes Plan. In the case of the conditional annuities, the German Government was entitled to postpone *transfer* into foreign currencies for a period not exceeding two years; the sums payable were, nevertheless, to be paid in Reichsmarks to the Bank of International Settlements which had been created, as an integral part of the scheme, to perform such financial functions of the agencies existing under the Dawes Plan as it was necessary to continue. In fact the reparations issue served as an opportunity for setting up an international banking institution which had been for some time an aspiration in many quarters. In times of exceptional stress, *payment* to half the amount of the conditional annuity might likewise be postponed, if transfer had already been postponed for one year.

Notwithstanding the provision of these safeguards, the Young Committee does not seem to have entertained any doubt as to the capacity of Germany to continue the payment of the whole of the annuities, which represented indeed an average reduction of RM. 500 million a year on what she had hitherto been paying with apparent ease. To us, at the present day, the optimism of the Committee may appear strangely short-sighted, but it was none the less sincerely entertained and expressed in the Report. As a result, it was not considered essential to renew the safeguard provided by the Dawes Plan against the effects of a fall in gold prices and the consequent increase in the real burden. In view of subsequent events, this omission was important.

In the course of the Committee's proceedings, a number of contentious points had emerged. The first was a claim on the part of Belgium to cover the loss on the depreciated German marks left in that country after the war. This claim, which had been discussed and rejected in Paris in 1919, was left to be settled by separate and direct negotiations. The second difficulty arose over the relation between reparation payments and inter-Allied debts. Though the *de facto* connexion played an important part in the calculation of the sums to be paid and accepted, it could not, in view of the attitude of the United States, be recognized in the Report itself: it was, however, acknowledged in a concurrent memorandum, signed by the members of the Committee other than the American representatives. This memorandum provided for an apportionment between Germany and her creditors of any reduction in the latter's payments to the United States. But a dispute was also occasioned by the question of distribution. There was a complete departure, to the detriment of Great Britain, from the percentages agreed upon at Spa in 1920 (see p. 42). In respect of the unconditional annuities in particular, the arrangement was peculiarly disadvantageous to Great Britain. Of these, roughly five-sixths had been allotted to France, and Great Britain was thus mainly put off, as was subsequently observed by Mr Snowden, with 'ordinary shares of a perhaps not very sound concern, whereas the unconditional payments might be regarded as first-class debentures'. Nor had due allowance been made for arrears owing to Great Britain on account of the fact that she had started paying the United States before receiving anything on war debts account from her Allies.

The Hague Conferences

At the Hague Conference of August 1929, called to settle the question raised by the Young Report, Mr Philip Snowden took an early opportunity of expressing his complete dissatisfaction with the proposals. In the firm attitude which he assumed, he was reinforced by a telegram from the Prime Minister, stating that he was supported by the whole country, without distinction of party. In these circumstances, he ultimately secured the greater part of his claim. Mr Snowden had further objected to the proposal to permit deliveries in kind in diminishing degrees for a period of ten years; and to permit the re-exportation of such deliveries. Under this head, also, he succeeded in obtaining some satisfaction.

The first Hague Conference was followed, on 3 January 1930, by a second in the same place, which was mainly concerned with the question of establishing wilful default now that the Reparation Commission was to be abolished, and with the imposition of sanctions in such an event. These questions were solved, from a technical point of view, by an agreement to submit the question of default to the Permanent Court of International Justice, with a power to the creditors to reserve full liberty of action in the event of a decision in their favour. The Conference further dealt with the problems of safeguarding the assigned revenues, and of dates of payment. A number of outstanding questions connected with the payment of non-German reparations were settled at the same time.

Meanwhile, the opposition to the Young scheme by the German Nationalist party under Herr Hugenberg had been defeated, both in the Reichstag and on a subsequent referendum, by overwhelming majorities. Ratification of the plan, after the second Hague Conference, proceeded smoothly, and on 17 May it came into force. The importance of this event, as of Mr Snowden's victories at The Hague, depended, however, on the correctness of the assumption as to Germany's capacity to pay. In fact, though the closing stage of the reparation problem was now in sight, the end was to take a very different form from anything hitherto contemplated.

Fall in Prices of Raw Materials

Even before the occurrence of the world economic crisis, signs had not been lacking to suggest that the optimism of the Young Committee was ill founded. A catastrophic fall in the prices of foodstuffs and other primary products, such as wool and cotton, had already begun. In spite of the unexampled prosperity which the United States appeared to be enjoying in 1929, there was, even in that country, a serious agricultural depression. The causes of this phenomenon have been much discussed, and variously diagnosed, and it is no part of the functions of this book to go deeply into them. The maldistribution of gold, leading to shortage in most countries of the world, no doubt played its part in lowering prices. The main cause, however, would seem to have been over-production in relation to effective demand. It is often observed that there was at no time absolute over-production, and the phenomenon is usually presented as a paradox, since great distress was associated with the existence of unprecedented plenty. There is, however, no true paradox. What the bulk of mankind have to offer in exchange for their daily bread is the services of their brain and muscle, and these things are obviously of less value in conditions of over-production. Unemployment and consequent distress follow logically when the stocks in existence are greater than can readily be disposed of. Under conditions of *laissez-faire*, the over-production is automatically corrected by the ruin of a large number of producers, but agriculture is a factor of such vital importance, both politically and economically, in most countries of the world, that it tends to be artificially supported. The national farmer is encouraged to go on producing, while his market is restricted by the imposition of tariffs and other measures calculated to exclude the competition of his foreign rivals. Thus the over-production continues, accompanied by a shrinkage of markets and a decline of purchasing power. It is much easier, too, in the case of agriculture, to reach the saturation point of demand than in the case of manufacturing industries. A prosperous and wealthy man can expand his demand for industrial products almost indefinitely, but his capacity for food is limited, and not greatly larger than that of a poor man. There is a tendency, too, for a farmer to increase his production in bad times. If one litter of pigs will not pay the rent or the mortgage interest, he sells two. Hence the disease of glut is not corrected, and a large section of the world's population loses its purchasing power, with reactions upon the whole community. This process had already begun in 1929, but its inevitable effects were to some extent masked because, so far, credit and loans were easily come by. The main source of these alleviating supplies was, at this time, the United States of America.

The Slump in America

At the date when the Young Report was signed, the United States was apparently enjoying an unexampled prosperity. The Americans are a highly impressionable people, and this state of things had gone to their heads. Readers old enough to have read *The Golden Butterfly*, by Sir Walter Besant and James Rice, will recall the remarkable geological theories of Mr Gilead P. Beck, the fortunate oil-striker, who regarded the world as a vast pumpkin pie, the crust of which covered a juice consisting entirely of petroleum. ' "At Rockoleaville," he went on, "I've got the pipe straight into the middle of the pie, and right through the crust. There's no mistake about that main shaft. Other mines may give out, but my Ile will run for ever." ' In a similar spirit, the public of the United States, in the early part of 1929, imagined themselves to have tapped the springs of an inexhaustible and eternal prosperity.

The ordinary slump of a trade cycle is usually attributed to the unco-ordinated optimism of manufacturers, each of whom over-estimates the extent and duration of his market. Where there is a demand for ten hats, each of ten mad hatters estimates his share at ten rather than one, and a hundred hats are produced, which have to be disposed of at a loss. This sort of thing was now happening in America on a vastly exaggerated scale. In

1929 the United States produced 5,358,000 motor-cars, 55 million tons of steel, and about three pairs of boots per head of the population. The capacity of the plant, in the last example, was three times that quantity.[1] Other production was proportionate. The home demand was obviously no longer even approximately adequate. The success of operations on this scale depended on the continuance of purchasing power in the outside world. At the same time, the tradition of a nation till recently self-supporting, with huge domestic resources and an exalted standard of wages, led the United States to exclude, by high tariffs, the goods which the world could offer in exchange. In these circumstances how had the illusion of prosperity been so far maintained? The answer has been given with characteristic lucidity by Mr Walter Lippmann.

In 1928, the last full year of prosperity, he says,

we sold about 850 million dollars more goods abroad than we bought. We also had coming to us that year about 200 millions on the war debts, and about 600 millions net return on our foreign investments. How did our foreign consumers and debtors get those 1,650 millions to pay us? They got 660 millions from the tourists. They got 220 millions from immigrants here who sent money home. . . . Where did they get the rest? They got it out of the 970 millions which we loaned to them that year.[2]

This illusory source of payment was already drying up. At this time the whole American population was engaged in a wild orgy of speculation. The money formerly invested in foreign countries was diverted into a new channel. More, the high rate attainable, through the demand for money to gamble with, drew funds from Europe, where they were needed, to America, where they were not. This in itself had a deleterious effect on the industry of the outside world. As loans were no longer available, the debts of Europe had to be paid in gold, which, flowing to a country which had no use for it, was to all intents and purposes returning to the mine. When gold is scarce, prices fall, for a little gold is worth much in goods; prices fell accordingly, even before the American slump came, reducing purchasing power and the capacity of debtors to pay.

---

[1] See address on 'Unemployment in the U.S.A.' by H. B. Butler, *International Affairs*, 1931, p. 184.

[2] Lippmann, W. *Interpretations, 1931-2*. London, Allen & Unwin, 1933, p. 46.

In October 1929 the inevitable collapse began. In one day the value of shares on the New York Stock Exchange broke five billion dollars. There was a temporary recovery, followed in November by another precipitous fall. The stunned speculators were out of action, lending entirely ceased, and all available funds were recalled. As a result the world slipped with a crash from the shoulders of the Atlas who had been sustaining it.

Situation in Germany

During the easy years of the Dawes Plan, on which the Young Committee had based their estimates, American money had been making a kind of circular tour—to Germany, from Germany to the claimants of reparation, and from these back again to the United States in the form of war-debt payments. It is significant that, in the years 1927 and 1928, Germany had borrowed from abroad five times the amount payable in reparation. A glance at the budgets of the Reich for the years in question shows indeed an expansion in revenue, but this had been accompanied by a more than equivalent growth in expenditure, which had left a substantial deficit in every year except the first. The accumulated deficit, when the crash came, amounted to over 1,200 million Reichsmarks. This situation, hitherto masked by the precarious expedient of short-term borrowing, could no longer be dealt with by this simple but dangerous method. It was faced with heroic determination by Dr Brüning, when he took office as Chancellor in 1930, but it was too late, and the stern measures which he was forced to adopt only contributed to his ultimate downfall.

The Failure of the Austrian Credit-Anstalt

The earliest repercussion of the crisis in Europe did not, however, occur in Germany. On 11 May 1931, it was discovered that the Austrian Credit-Anstalt, a private but highly important Viennese concern, which had become an integral part of the financial structure of the world, was threatened with insolvency. Credit was widely shaken, and before the end of May there began an alarming withdrawal of foreign funds from Germany, where a sense of political insecurity added to the suspicions attaching to the economic situation. During the first week in June the alarm was increased on the one hand by Communist riots in the Ruhr, and on the other by the signature of an emergency decree imposing drastic cuts and increases in taxation. By the middle of the month withdrawals of foreign funds from Germany had reached the total of one milliard Reichsmarks. The Austrian situation had meanwhile suffered through the resignation of the Cabinet and the failure of negotiations in Paris for financial support—probably due to an attempt to exert political pressure in relation to the proposal for a customs union with Germany (see p. 342). On 16 June the advance of 150 million schillings by the Bank of England to the Austrian National Bank temporarily saved the situation in this quarter. But by this time the world-wide nature of the crisis was becoming manifest. At this juncture President Hoover came forward as the *deus ex machina* with his proposal, published on 20 June, for a moratorium of one year on all inter-governmental debts.

The Hoover Moratorium

The efficacy of this move on the part of the American President depended on its immediate adoption. Most countries, indeed, were ready to accept the proposal, but France demurred, and France, owing to the volume of the short-term credits held by her citizens in foreign financial centres, occupied a commanding strategic position. Though her objections were met by 6 July, on which date Mr Hoover announced the acceptance of the moratorium by all important creditor Powers, the run upon Germany had meanwhile continued with increasingly disastrous effects. On the very day of the announcement, 100 million marks of foreign exchange were drawn from the Reichsbank, and on the following day that institution drew upon its last disposable reserve. On 13 July the Reichsbank declared its inability to give further support to private banks in Germany, and on the same day the Darmstädter und National-bank, one of the three great joint-stock banks in Germany, closed its doors. Next day the Government declared a two days' emergency bank holiday for all the banks in Germany except the Reichsbank.

The London Conference

On 20 July an influentially composed conference met in London to examine the financial crisis in Germany. This, however, broke down through the intransigence of France, who insisted upon unacceptable political as well as financial guarantees as the terms on which she was prepared to afford the assistance required. As London was by this time *hors de combat*, and New York was unwilling to undertake fresh risks unaccompanied, the French were masters of the situation, and the Conference accordingly proved abortive. All that was achieved was a recommendation to the central banks and private financial houses to adopt palliative measures which they had already to some extent undertaken on their own initiative. On 19 August, following upon the publication of the report of the International Bankers' Committee at Basle (the Layton-Wiggin Report), a Standstill Agreement was initialled by the representatives of the bankers, providing for a six months' prolongation of all banking credits in Germany, expressed in terms of foreign currencies, which were thereby 'frozen'.

The Crisis in Great Britain

In England, meanwhile, the publication of the Macmillan Report on Finance and Industry, on 13 July, had been immediately followed by a serious withdrawal of gold to France and Belgium. During the week ending 25 July bar gold to the value of £21 million was withdrawn, mainly to France. On 31 July the Report of the May Committee on National Expenditure was published, forecasting a budget deficit of nearly £120 million. The run continued, with increased momentum. On 1 August it was announced that the Bank of France and the Federal Reserve Bank of New York had each placed at the disposal of the Bank of England a credit for £25 million, but so serious was the drain that 80 per cent of this large credit was exhausted within four weeks. On 12 August the members of the Cabinet were recalled from their holidays to grapple with the situation, but, under pressure from the Trades Union Council, a number of Ministers refused to face the adoption of the necessary economies. On 23 August the King returned from Balmoral, and on the following day the formation of a

National Government from members of all three political parties was begun.

On 9 September a Bill was introduced in Parliament to effect economies estimated at £70 million, and on the following day Mr Snowden introduced a supplementary budget making provision for balancing that of the coming as well as the current year. These drastic expedients might have successfully achieved their purpose, but on the 15th the news was published of a mutiny among some of the lower naval ratings at Invergordon, who were discontented with the proposed reductions of pay. This was misconstrued abroad into a revolutionary movement of serious importance, and the confidence which the new Government had begun to re-establish was destroyed at a stroke. On 21 September Great Britain, to the consternation of the world, had been forced off the gold standard.

On 6 October Parliament was dissolved and a memorable general election took place, which established in an emphatic way the fundamental common sense of the British electorate. On the one side, that of the Labour 'rump', the very existence of the crisis was questioned, and the events described were dismissed as a 'bankers' ramp'; the necessity of the economies proposed was consequently challenged, and the party candidates were in a position to make most of the usual promises to the electorate. On the other side, there was no programme, and there could be no promises. There were grim references to the necessity for sacrifice as the only prelude to safety. In the result, the National Government, to the embarrassment of some of its candidates, was victorious even in constituencies hitherto regarded as the impregnable stronghold of Socialism, and its opponents were practically annihilated. In the new House of Commons the supporters of the Government numbered 554, while the Labour party returned with only 52 survivors.

The impression on the outside world was immediate and far-reaching. Great Britain regained her prestige, and the value of her now unprotected pound hardly declined below 70 per cent of its previous gold value. It soon became evident, indeed, that it was to the interest of other Powers to follow the British example and the fortunes of sterling by abandoning the gold standard; in the meanwhile the slight depreciation acted as a useful export bonus. A step, the wisdom of which was challenged by most of the orthodox economists, and which led eventually to the secession of many of the Liberal members from the support of the Government, was the abandonment of the traditional free-trade policy of the country. It may be doubted, however, whether Great Britain could any longer afford to remain the one free market in a world of universal tariffs, and in any event the restriction of imports was a temporary necessity. The policy adopted was further justified by its supporters as providing a bargaining weapon by which the worst evils of economic nationalism could be combated, and as a basis of trade agreements, both inter-imperial and with foreign countries, out of which a trustworthy raft could be constructed in the surrounding deluge.

The policy of the National Government was certainly justified by results. Balanced budgets, trade improvement, and a great and steady reduction in the figures of unemployment marked its progress. The return of confidence in the financial stability of the country was exemplified by the success of conversion operations on an unprecedented scale.

The Lausanne Conference

As a consequence of the crisis, the German Government announced, in November 1931, that the future transfer of reparation annuities would endanger the economic life of the country. A special committee was accordingly convened by the Bank of International Settlements to advise on the situation. The advisory committee, which met at Basle on 7 December, reported, towards the end of the month, that the transfer of the conditional annuity for the year beginning in July 1932 would not be possible.

The report concluded by emphasizing the necessity for an adjustment of all inter-governmental debts. In consequence of this report a conference was arranged, which met at Lausanne in June 1932. The date originally proposed had been January, but delay was occasioned by negotiations between Great Britain and France, who had strongly divergent views on the question of Reparation. The United States was precluded from association with the Conference or the preliminary discussions, since Congress in December had passed a resolution that 'it was against the policy of Congress that any of the indebtedness of foreign countries to the United States should be in any manner cancelled or reduced'. Great Britain proposed a six months' moratorium, to be followed by a conference in the autumn, by which time it was hoped that the American view might have been modified. The proposal was unacceptable to France because she thought it meant the end of Reparation, and to Germany because she thought it did not. Discussions, however, continued, and when the Conference met in June a basis of settlement was arrived at. Reparations were abolished, subject to the delivery by Germany to the Bank for International Settlements of 5 per cent redeemable bonds with 1 per cent sinking fund to the amount of RM. 3,000 million or £150 million. The Bank had authority to negotiate any of these bonds by public issues at a price not lower than 90 per cent three years after the date of the agreement, though it was never anticipated that these bonds would be issued in full. But a contemporary agreement signed by the creditor Powers on 2 July made ratification dependent upon a satisfactory settlement between them and their creditors, i.e. with the United States. The questions of Reparations and War-debts were thus once more inextricably linked together, but, so far as the former was concerned, the possibility of its resuscitation was generally regarded as negligible.

War-Debt Negotiations

The centre of interest was now shifted to the United States. The upshot of the conversations held between President Hoover and M. Laval, the French Prime Minister, in October 1931, had been a joint *communiqué* which contained the following passage:

In so far as inter-governmental obligations are concerned we recognize that prior to the expiration of the Hoover year of postponement, some agreement regarding them may be necessary covering the period of business depression, as to the terms and conditions of which the two Governments make all reservations. *The initiative in this matter should be taken at an early date by the European Powers principally concerned* within the framework of the agreements existing prior to 1 July 1931.

This statement it was natural to construe, firstly as an admission that the relationship between War-debts and Reparation was now recognized in America, and secondly as a direct invitation to Europe to take the steps which in fact were taken at Lausanne. Events were, however, to prove that the gulf between what was seen to be economically desirable by instructed opinion and what was politically feasible in a democratically governed country like the United States was far from being bridged. A particular difficulty arose from the fact that the question had become critical on the eve of the American presidential elections, which fell due in November 1932. There was a tacit understanding, indeed, on the European side, that the issue ought not to be raised until the election had taken place. In the American campaign, however, both parties were pledged to oppose cancellation of the debts, and both candidates expressed apprehensions of a united European front in the matter.

Instructed opinion, in the United States as elsewhere, was convinced that complete cancellation would be in the interest of America as well as the rest of the world.[1] Since payment in gold was an expedient which could not be pursued much further, and payment in goods and services had been blocked, it followed that a payment of war-debts to America would be reflected in a diminution of her exports. The loss sustained in the United States through the world-depression was immensely greater than the full amount receivable in respect of war-debts. Since 1928–9 the States had lost about 700 million pounds' worth of exports, as compared with a debt of £40 to £50 million payable to her by the world as a whole. At the same time, it was difficult to get a poor farmer of the Middle West, hard pressed by his creditors, to appreciate the argument that there was any advantage in forgiving a debt to the foreigner which must in that case be discharged by the American tax-payer, and the arguments necessary to persuade him were considered too dangerous to be used by politicians dependent upon his vote.

Immediately after the presidential elections, Notes were almost simultaneously presented by the British and French Governments, asking for a suspension of payment of the instalments due in December, pending discussion of the whole question. The coincidence in date between the two appeals

[1] See Moulton, H. G., and L. Pasvolsky. *War Debts and World Prosperity.* Washington, D.C., Brookings Institution, 1932.

produced a rather unfortunate impression of the united front which had been feared, and the answers returned were unfavourable. This called forth, on 1 December, a British statement of the whole case for remission which is regarded in many quarters as unanswerable, and which should be studied in detail by all who are really interested in the subject.[1] The American Government, however, was unmoved, and refused to consent to the postponement of the instalments due either from France or Great Britain. In these circumstances, the British Government paid the whole instalment in gold, with the proviso that they intended to treat it as a capital payment in any final settlement, but the proposal of the French Government to pursue a similar course was defeated in the Chamber, and France accordingly defaulted on this payment. In order not to reopen or disturb the Lausanne agreement, Great Britain did not make any demand for payment from her own debtors.

Further negotiations were for the moment somewhat impeded by the practical interregnum which intervened before Mr Roosevelt's assumption of office, in March 1933, as the new President. By January, however, it had been tacitly agreed between him and Mr Hoover that the President-Elect should assume the requisite measure of control. An exchange of ideas, particularly desirable in view of the forthcoming World Economic Conference, was thereby rendered possible. Mr Neville Chamberlain, however, made it clear that Great Britain was only prepared to discuss revision of war-debts on condition that the settlement must be final and that the Reparation question must not be reopened. America, on her part, made her attendance at the forthcoming Economic Conference conditional on the exclusion of the war-debt problem from its agenda. The question therefore remained unsettled, and the problem of the next instalment, due on 15 June 1933, was met by a token payment of 10 million dollars in silver. Six of the remaining debtors made no payment, and the only country paying in full was Finland, which discharged its small instalment of $148,592. Similar treatment was applied by Great Britain to the December instalment. But in June 1934 legislation in the United States ruled out token payments as a means

[1] Cmd. 4210 of 1932.

of avoiding default. Faced with the alternative of a full payment, which they described as a policy heading straight for calamity, the British Government, from this time forward, paid nothing.

The World Economic Conference

The World Monetary and Economic Conference, which met in London on 12 June 1933, was the fulfilment of a project suggested at Lausanne, and it was consequently very difficult to dissociate it from the one question on which the completion of the labours of the former Conference depended. As a matter of fact, war-debts were mentioned by Mr Ramsay MacDonald in his opening address, and were referred to as an essential preliminary problem by various other delegates. But this, while it excited some irritation in America, had no important effect upon the fortunes of the Conference. The pivot upon which the whole prospect of a successful issue to the Conference turned was the question of currency stabilization. The importance of this issue had been emphasized by the new American President himself as recently as 16 May, when he had stated that 'the Conference must establish order in place of the present chaos by a stabilization of currencies', and when the United States delegation sailed for England this was the policy to which they were nominally committed. It was also the one important point which united the otherwise divergent views of the gold standard countries and the rest. The event proved that the work of all depended upon the satisfactory settlement of this primary issue. As the hopes of political reconstruction centred upon Versailles were dashed in 1920, so those which hung upon the Economic Conference in London were upset in 1933, by a sudden reversal of policy on the part of the United States.

The economic blizzard which had blown its first gusts on the New York Stock Exchange in the autumn of 1929 had thenceforward grown swiftly to the devastating force of a tornado. On 4 March 1933, when President Roosevelt was sworn in, the whole national banking system appeared to have collapsed, and nearly fifteen million wage-earners were unemployed. On the previous day 116 million dollars in gold were withdrawn from the Federal Reserve Bank. The first step taken by the new President was to proclaim a four days' bank holiday, the next to ask Congress for wide emergency powers which the panic-stricken Americans were only too ready to grant to a leader who was calmly and confidently prepared to take control. On 19 April the United States abandoned the gold standard.

The immediate effect in the rise of dollar prices suggested to the Administration a temptation which revolutionized all the views previously held on the advantages of early stabilization. The decline of the dollar was now regarded as an essential ingredient in recovery. On 22 June the United States delegation announced at the Conference that 'the American Government at Washington finds that measures of temporary stabilization now would be untimely'. On 30 June a formula was found by the five nations of the gold bloc together with Great Britain and the United States, which was designed to restate a belief in the speedy establishment of stability in a generally acceptable form. On Monday 3 July a message was received from President Roosevelt vigorously repudiating it. This message really killed the Conference, which rambled on in an atmosphere of increasing unreality till 27 July and then adjourned with practically nothing of its great task accomplished. It was one of the major disappointments of post-war history. The now habitual oscillation of the United States between interference and isolation had once more played a decisively destructive part.

The New Deal

It is impossible, in the limited space available, to accord more than superficial consideration to the measures promoted by President Roosevelt and his administration with a view to American recovery. It might indeed be urged that the Blue Eagle, the N.R.A., and other much-canvassed associations of initials, belong rather to the internal history of the United States than to that of international affairs. The lesson enforced, however, by the story of the crisis is that in economic matters, even more than in political, the whole world is inevitably affected by the fate and action of any important Power, and particularly by that of the United States. The prospects and extent of American recovery, and the means adopted to promote it, fall, therefore, within the scope of the present work.

It must be recognized at the outset that the aim of the

American President was not simply that of economic recovery. The steps he took had at least a threefold objective: relief, recovery, and reform. The conditions under which industry had developed in the United States were responsible for a deep-seated belief, firstly, that the man who was out of a job deserved his fate, and secondly, that no impassable gulf debarred the able and ambitious workman from promotion to the ranks of the employers. In conformity with the first of these beliefs, no machinery had been constructed for mitigating the sufferings of the unemployed, while the second had delayed the organization of labour, and left the United States far behind other industrialized countries in the province of social reform. America was now confronted with a vast and hungry army of those who, through no fault of their own, were unable to earn their daily bread, and this constituted a pressing problem which it was far beyond the capacity of private charity or local organization to solve. The questions of labour organization and up-to-date social amelioration were, indeed, of a less pressing character, but the unprecedented power which the catastrophe had placed in the hands of the new President, and the desperate submissiveness of the population to anything which might be done, gave him a perhaps irretrievable opportunity of dealing with these overdue reforms. We must therefore be chary of criticism if the steps taken in pursuit of the goals of relief and reform did not in all respects facilitate the task of economic recovery.

Some further inconsistency can be explained by the fact that great haste was essential. The President may be compared to a man who, having no time for a deliberate aim, chooses a shot-gun rather than a rifle for his weapon, in the hope that one or more of a heavy charge of pellets may take effect, in a snap-shot which a single bullet would probably miss. He employed a number of expedients simultaneously, and, no doubt, cannot have expected that all would be equally successful. Unfortunately, however, some of these expedients were not only inconsistent, but mutually destructive. The American policy may therefore be described, in the language of a not unsympathetic observer, as 'a welter of economic experiment'.[1]

The 'New Deal', considered as an instrument of recovery,

[1] *The Round Table*, March 1934, p. 270.

may be divided under the three heads of industrial, agricultural, and financial policy. In the National Industrial Recovery Act (N.I.R.A.), which dealt with the first head, the collateral aims of relief and reform were also prominent. It was intended to absorb into productive industry a large proportion of the unemployed, and attempted, by the inauguration of 'codes' embodying fair conditions of labour, to mitigate such evils as the extensive employment of children, and to give its blessing to the principle of collective bargaining between employer and employed. In these parts of its task it was relatively successful, though so sudden an increase in the power of organized labour was perhaps hardly conducive to that industrial peace upon which prosperity depends. In regard to the purely economic aspects of the Act, it is difficult to be certain how much of such success as it achieved was due to the prescription, and how much to the admirable bedside manner of the physician. The infectious courage and confidence of Mr Roosevelt undoubtedly produced, in the early stages, a psychological effect on the patient which was of incalculable value. There was a quasi-war-time eagerness to sport the 'Blue Eagle'—the emblem of adoption of N.I.R.A. principles. In the hope which its leader had engendered, the stunned economic life of America evinced at least temporary signs of renewed vitality. A country blessed with the monetary wealth, natural resources, and political security of the United States possesses a constitution which not even the most poisonous medicine can permanently impair; its eventual recovery was certain in any event, and the depression was considerably intensified by a loss of self-confidence, for which the President's temperament was a sufficient remedy. The soundness of the economic principles involved is more problematical. The basic idea was the current belief that the road to prosperity lay in the increase of purchasing-power through higher wages. But in an industry whose reserves were depleted by the recent depression, high wages, particularly when associated with shorter hours, could only be provided by raising prices to a point which tended to cancel the effect of the increased number of dollars in the pay-envelope. Moreover, the population of the United States, whose purchasing-power was in question, was by no means confined to the wage-earners who profited by the increased rates of pay in the codes. The feature of N.I.R.A. which specially appealed to the employers was exemption from the provisions of the anti-trust laws which were held responsible for the evils of competitive price-cutting from which they had hitherto suffered. But, relieved from these, prices might again be expected to rise at a faster rate than any increase in purchasing-power could be organized. In order that enhanced wages may operate as a stimulus to industry, it would seem desirable that prices should remain stable, but volume of production increase: this, though it may have been the intention, was hardly the effect of the measures adopted. The ultimate economic consequences of N.I.R.A. remain, however, a mere matter of speculation, for in May 1935 the Act was ruled unconstitutional by a decision of the Supreme Court.

The same fate was to befall, in January 1936, the Administration's parallel effort on behalf of the farming community. The purpose of the Agricultural Adjustment Act (A.A.A.) was, more definitely but more defensibly, to raise prices—those of agricultural products, which had fallen to a ruinous level. This effect was brought about by restricting production, farmers being induced to plough-in part of their crops and otherwise reduce output, in return for compensation financed from taxes levied on those who first processed the raw material—spinners, millers, &c.—the burden ultimately falling, or being designed to fall, on the consumer. This attempt to counteract the unprofitable bounty of nature was confronted with a number of unforeseen difficulties, but did, on the whole, produce the result contemplated, though the gain to the farmer was largely neutralized by the increased price of everything which he had to buy.

The short shrift given to this experiment by the Supreme Court precludes anything like a final pronouncement on its effectiveness. The obstruction to his plans by judicial decision led the President after his triumphant re-election in November 1936 to ask Congress for power to appoint additional judges to the Court to supplement such of its members as elected to continue in office after reaching the age of 70. Since six of the existing nine judges were over this age-limit, the practical effect of the proposal would be to empower the President to pack the court with a majority of his political sympathizers.

Rather incongruously included in the A.A.A. was a provision

conferring upon the President extensive powers of monetary inflation. It was in the financial and monetary sphere that the policy of Mr Roosevelt displayed its most conspicuous inconsistencies. His first acts indicated an intention to tread the hard and narrow path of economy, retrenchment, and a balanced budget. He cut the salaries of Congressmen and federal employees, and had the unexampled courage to apply the same process to the bonuses of war veterans. His treatment of the banks also contributed to the same end, the re-establishment of confidence in the financial soundness of the country. But his economies were almost simultaneously neutralized by the extravagance, however unavoidable, of his relief expenditure, and as early as April 1933, when he voluntarily departed from the gold standard, he set his feet on the alternative road of inflation. The depreciation of the dollar was not, however, aimed at securing an advantage in external trade, but was intended as a contribution to the effort to raise the internal price-level. In October 1933 the President tried to hasten the inflationary process by the purchase of gold at artificially high prices, and in January of the following year he imposed an arbitrary devaluation upon the dollar, to about 59 per cent of its former value.

This aspect of American policy produced a disappointing internal result, while inflicting severe damage upon other nations. As Sir Arthur Salter has pointed out,[1] Mr Roosevelt was, for his intended purpose of internal price-raising, 'using an instrument geared the wrong way; a great (and unintended) external effect was required to secure a lesser effect of the kind intended'. Even worse in this respect was the Silver Purchase Act of May 1934, which, to gratify certain important political interests in the U.S.A., subjected the silver of the world to the same drain which had previously affected its gold, in order to establish a 1 : 3 ratio between the two metals in the monetary stocks of the United States. The effect of this by-path of American policy was peculiarly disastrous to China, a country whose currency was based on silver. Her monetary reserves were depleted, and her currency violently appreciated in the foreign exchange market, with the most deleterious effects on her external trade. In fact, as a result of this policy, against

[1] *Political Quarterly*, October 1937, p. 468.

which she had vainly protested, China was faced with economic difficulties which aroused the gravest concern among other Powers to whom her stability was of importance, and was finally forced to abandon the silver standard, in November 1935. Since the utterances and actions of American statesmen throughout the whole inter-war period testify to their interest in a Pacific balance of power, to which the expansionist aims of Japan were a formidable threat, a policy which thus tended to weaken China's capacity for effective resistance appears to have been extremely short-sighted.

The End of the Gold Bloc

Though the project of stabilization had been killed, at the World Economic Conference, by the attitude of the United States, the adoption of some measures conducive to that end remained essential to any permanent international recovery. The example of Great Britain in severing the pound from gold was rapidly followed by a number of other countries, whose commercial and financial interests were linked with hers. Some European nations, however, moved by lively recollections of the difficulty of controlling devaluation, and of the distress occasioned when the bottom dropped out of a currency, made great efforts to cling to their gold parities.[1] The leader in this policy was France, since the value of the franc had fallen catastrophically in the earlier post-war years. Her principal associates were Belgium, Holland, Luxembourg, and Switzerland. Italy, though ostensibly a member of the group, actually controlled the value of her lira by methods analogous to those of Germany. Poland remained on the gold standard until April 1936, when exchange restrictions were imposed. Czechoslovakia devalued her currency by 16 per cent in 1934, but Belgium was the first fully qualified member of the gold bloc to abandon the struggle, when she reduced the value of the belga in March 1935.

The disadvantages of maintaining gold parities were soon made apparent after 1931. While the indices of industrial production in the sterling bloc countries showed consistent improvement, there was a marked deterioration in the figures of the

---

[1] They had other reasons for this policy, for which it is possible to make out a respectable case, though space does not here permit the elaboration of the argument.

group which adhered to gold. Unemployment increased to a serious extent, the tourist traffic started to abandon Switzerland, and the competitive handicap of relatively over-valued currencies made itself increasingly felt in international trade. When a 'Popular Front' Government of the extreme Left came to power in France, under M. Blum in the early summer of 1936, its programme of social reform portended a further rise in costs injurious to external trade, while the nervousness of capitalists, stimulated by widespread industrial disputes, started a fresh drain on the monetary resources of the country. The advocates of devaluation grew increasingly vocal, and it was convincingly pointed out by a leading economist, M. Charles Rist, that:

The maintenance of the franc at any cost means that the entire French economy is bound more and more by controls and prohibitions at the time when it needs to find fresh initiative, and to re-establish contact with the group of great Anglo-Saxon economies, which are the only prosperous ones today.

It was nevertheless difficult for M. Blum to adopt a policy of devaluation. It was on an anti-devaluation programme that he had come to power, and he had to consider the effect on the *rentier* vote and the hostility of his Communist supporters, who saw in the step the robbery of the working-class, through the consequent rise in the cost of living. Moreover, if France acted alone, she had no security against a further depreciation of competitive currencies, or against an uncontrolled fall in the value of the franc beyond the point intended, occasioned by loss of confidence. Some guarantee of a more general stabilization was essential, and this could only be obtained through international agreement, especially with Great Britain and the United States. The difficulty was met on 26 September 1936, when, as the result of discussion, a joint statement was published by the Governments of France, Great Britain, and the United States. Expressing as their object the restoration of peace and order in international relations, they proposed the establishment of a lasting equilibrium between their currencies, which they pledged themselves individually to avoid disturbing. This involved the readjustment of the French currency, which France simultaneously devalued by between 25 and 34 per cent. The three parties declared their intention of collaborating to maintain stability as far as possible; exchange equalization funds were set up in each country with that object. They further asserted the importance of 'action being taken without delay to relax progressively the present system of quotas and exchange controls with a view to their abolition', and invited the co-operation of other nations.[1]

Though the co-operation requested was not willingly accorded, this *démarche* resulted almost immediately in the whole of the former gold bloc falling into line. Probably the feature of this example of international collaboration which was of the most permanent importance was that it represented a powerful combination directed against that policy of 'autarky' or self-sufficiency, of which the totalitarian dictatorships, and particularly Germany, were the principal exponents.

Effects of the Economic Crisis

In order to enable the reader to grasp the full historical importance of the matters dealt with in this chapter, we may conclude with a brief summary of the political repercussions of the crisis. Most important of all was the part which it played in bringing about the sudden conversion of Germany to National Socialism. Until it came, the political strength of Herr Hitler and his party had remained negligible. But the Nazis had always opposed the settlement worked out in the Young Plan; they had represented its burdens as beyond the capacity of their country to bear; now they seemed to be proved right. Germany had been exhorted, under the Stresemann regime, to persevere in the policy of fulfilment as a stage towards the prosperity which would follow the reconciliation of the nations. They followed this advice, and found themselves and the world plunged in an unprecedented state of adversity. This, they thought, is not the way. The effect of the crisis was, moreover, to place almost insurmountable difficulties in the path of constitutional government. Brüning had to face all the unpopularity which drastic economies entail. He found himself unable to discharge his tasks in the face of parliamentary and popular opposition. He was driven to govern without the

---

[1] A further development of this policy is the main recommendation of the report prepared by the Belgian statesman, M. van Zeeland, at the request of the French and British Governments, which was published in January 1938.

Reichstag, by means of emergency decrees, thus preparing the way for dictatorship. Setting out to defend the constitution of Weimar, he was forced by the pressure of events to demonstrate its weakness. Everywhere, indeed, the exigencies of the situation compelled a degree of State control more compatible with dictatorship than democracy. Everywhere, too, there was a *sauve qui peut* behind national frontiers, with all the friction which the exclusion of the trade of neighbours, looking desperately for markets, entails. It turned the efforts of every nation towards its own independent salvation. And on the top of all this was the danger of internal disturbance to which hard times necessarily give rise. This was not an atmosphere favourable to the peace of the world.

At a later stage, the expedients, such as exchange controls and the conclusion of local trading arrangements, which had been reluctantly adopted in many countries, were turned in Germany, by the ingenuity of Dr Schacht, into a deliberate instrument of political control. By offering the only willing market to most of the countries of south-eastern Europe, exporting less in return, blocking the resultant credits, and offering in exchange for the debt such German manufactures, and especially armaments, as it suited his purpose to supply, he tended to bring this part of the Continent into a position not only of economic but of political dependence on Germany. The same expedients of exchange control and State-directed trading also served to promote the policy of self-sufficiency which the Nazis adopted, less, as it seems, to promote economic recovery than to render it possible for the country to confront the prospect of war.

Outside Germany, the part of Europe where the economic depression exerted its most important political influence was France. The capacity of France to play a strong and decisive part in the destinies of the Continent was adversely affected by the domestic disturbances and the instability of governments which the task of raising revenue, under these unfavourable circumstances, entailed. Her difficulties still persisted, in spite of the collaboration of Great Britain and the United States under the arrangement of September 1936. Her people have a profound disinclination to make personal sacrifices for economic recovery: ministerial crises continued, capital still tended to leave the country, and the franc had to be again devalued at the end of March 1938. But the deleterious effects of the depression upon prospects of peace were not confined to Europe, but may be traced throughout the entire world. For example, the economic crisis, in its earlier phases in 1930, produced an immediate epidemic of revolutions in South America. Among the countries affected were Peru and Bolivia, both of which experienced a sudden change of government. In both cases the new administration was before long engaged in hostilities with a neighbouring country. In the Leticia dispute (see pp. 211–13), while the original disturbance was not the work of the Peruvian Government, yet violent dissatisfaction with the agreement arrived at by its predecessor was not only an important factor in the case, but was definitely the reason for the official support and sympathy which the filibusters subsequently received and which magnified an irresponsible incident into a war. In Bolivia, though the recrudescence of the Chaco dispute with Paraguay preceded the revolution, the rapid deterioration in the relations and behaviour of the two countries seems to date from this event.

Even more clearly, it was the economic crisis which was responsible for the disastrous events which were destined to ensue in the Far East. Here we touch upon a development possibly more responsible for the collapse of world peace than even the troubled situation of Europe—the conversion of Japan and her people to a policy of militarism. There can be no doubt that the motive here was economic, having regard to the decisive control exercised by the highly concentrated power of 'big business' upon the Japanese political parties. The two largest concerns, Mitsui and Mitsubisi, which between them were responsible for more than half of the export trade of the country, completely dominated the Japanese Parliament. But, apart from this, the desperate necessity for economic expansion in order to feed the large and growing population of the country sufficiently explains why, when the methods of peaceful competition failed, a more sinister alternative should be adopted.

Racked by the remorseless turning of the economic screw in the long-drawn-out course of the world depression, the Japanese people at last followed the lead of the Japanese army in reverting from the policy of commercial expansion to the policy of military conquest.

. . . They despaired of continuing the attempt to win their national livelihood in the economic field, in which 'intelligent management' seemed doomed to frustration by inhuman forces beyond human control; and in this mood they returned to the primitive, crude expedient of attempting to hack out a livelihood with the sword, simply because the sword, however rough and clumsy a tool it might be, was at least a tool which the human hand seemed capable of grasping and wielding for the possible attainment of human ends.[1]

In these words of Mr Toynbee's there is summed up not only the situation of Japan, but the world-wide influence of the economic depression as a threat to peace. Other clouds were rising, but this alone was sufficient to cast a shadow upon men's faith and hope in peace and a durable civilization.

Finally, we have to appreciate the difficulties created by the interplay of economic and political developments. Political fears hamper that economic co-operation which is essential for recovery, and the restoration of that confidence which is the necessary prelude to it. The prosperity due to rearmament veiled the persistence of the underlying depression. On the other side, preoccupation with economic difficulties tended to distract the minds of statesmen from the political dangers which threatened, and isolated nation from nation in a way highly prejudicial to that combined effort in which lay the best hope of security.

[1] *Survey of International Affairs*, 1931, p. 403.

XVIII

THE MIDDLE EAST

Growth of Pan-Arab Sentiment

AN increased consciousness of independent strength and impatience of European control have been the common features displayed by the countries of the Middle East in recent years. These were exemplified by the repeated though fruitless claims advanced by Persia, from 1927 onwards, to the sovereignty over Bahrein, and by the more successful efforts made both by the Iraqi and Persian Governments to revise the rights of foreign oil interests to their own advantage in 1931 and 1932–3 respectively. Though the Anglo-Persian oil dispute is not a matter of sufficient importance to warrant further mention in the present work, it was sufficiently serious at the time to necessitate a reference to Geneva. Of more permanent importance, however, was the growing sentiment of solidarity and will to complete independence which characterized the Arab world. The Western ideals of nationalism seem destined to provide a more important rallying-point in the Middle East than is its common adherence to the creed of Islam. Though a strong effort at consolidation on the latter basis was made by the convocation of the Islamic Congress at Jerusalem in December 1931, this body has since shown little sign of renewed activity, and indeed the sectarian differences existing in the Middle East tend materially to lessen the strength of Muslim religion as a unifying force, though perhaps these sectarian differences are being reduced by the growing sense of racial community. On the other hand, a sense of racial community between the various divisions of the Arab world has tended to increase, as was exemplified in the Covenant formulated by the Arab delegates to the Jerusalem Congress at an independent meeting of their number on 13 December. This proclaimed the Arab lands to be an indivisible whole, and laid down that complete and unified independence was the goal to which all Arab efforts were to be directed. Arab solidarity was further demonstrated in the active interest taken and the mediatorial

efforts exerted by the rulers of the three neighbouring Arab
territories on the occasion of the disturbances in Palestine in
1936 (see p. 303). A possible focus for the Pan-Arab movement
was to be found in the powerful kingdom of Saudi Arabia,
under a ruler described by a competent observer as 'the greatest
Arab since the Prophet'.[1] During the period now under consideration Ibn Saud went far to justify this extravagant-sound-
ing encomium by the remarkable statesmanship which he displayed in his relations with his neighbours, as well as by the
vigour with which he repressed both rebellion and external
aggression.

Progress of Saudi Arabia

The first danger with which Ibn Saud had to deal was that
of internal insurrection. In 1932 a revolt of Asiri tribesmen
occurred, at the instigation of the Idrisi Sayyid. This was
quelled by February of the following year, when the Saudi
forces occupied Sabya, and the Idrisi was compelled to flee to
the Yemen. Hardly had this revolt been suppressed when an
incursion occurred from the north, headed by an exiled subject,
Ibn Rifada, who had been taking refuge in Transjordan. The
complicity of the Emir Abdullah in this episode has been, not
unreasonably, suspected. This rebellion was crushed even more
promptly than its predecessor, the leader was killed, and his
followers practically annihilated. Ibn Saud had, however,
immediately to turn his attention to a more formidable antagonist. There had for some time been uneasy relations
between Saudi Arabia and the contiguous territory of the
Yemen, with which the ruler of the former had hitherto dealt
in a remarkably accommodating fashion. Incursions by the
Imam of the Yemen into the Aden Protectorate, which necessitated the interference of British aircraft in 1928, had previously led to strained relations on the southern frontier, but in
February 1934 this tension was relieved by the conclusion of an
Anglo-Yemeni Treaty, and, freed from this preoccupation, the
Imam proceeded to acts of aggression against the territory of
his Arabian neighbour. In fact, these operations had begun in
the previous year, but it was not until February 1934 that
attempts to settle the trouble by negotiation finally broke down.

[1] Captain C. C. Lewis, *International Affairs*, 1933, p. 529.

The war that followed was short and decisive. In April the Imam was suing for peace, and in May a treaty was signed which, from its mild and conciliatory terms, appears to merit its official title—'A Treaty of Islamic Friendship and Arab Brotherhood'.

Having thus effectively disposed of his enemies, at any rate for the time being, Ibn Saud set himself the task of concentrating the prevalent sense of Arab community upon the powerful nucleus which he had created. This policy was inaugurated in January 1936, by the conclusion of a trade and transit agreement with Bahrein, which was immediately followed by a State visit to Kuweit, with the object of bringing to an end, in a conciliatory spirit, an economic conflict between this territory and his own, which had previously strained the friendly relations of the two regions. Having thus laid a promising foundation for the extension of his influence to the shore of the Persian Gulf, he immediately followed up his success by negotiations with Iraq, which resulted, in April 1936, in the conclusion of a treaty of 'Arab brotherhood and alliance', which was left open to the adherence of any other independent Arab State. Of this opportunity the Imam of the Yemen availed himself in the following year. Meantime, on 7 May 1936, a treaty of friendship was concluded with Egypt.

Ibn Saud had thus made considerable progress towards the achievement of his ambition to become the controller and rallying-point of pan-Arab sentiment. The only obstacles to complete success in this direction were the religious differences which distinguish the Wahhabis from the rest of the Arab world, and, more directly, the rivalry and suspicion of the Emir Abdullah of Transjordan. Abdullah had naturally not forgotten the ejection of his family from the Hijaz in 1925 (p 134), and could hardly be expected voluntarily to accommodate himself to Ibn Saud's ambitions. Relations between the two States were, however, considerably improved by the conclusion of a treaty of friendship in 1933.

To Great Britain it is certainly advantageous that so dominant a position in the Arab world should be in the hands of a ruler so well-disposed to her as Ibn Saud. Having regard to the fact that his dominions flank the main routes between Britain and the East both by sea and air, it is essential that they should be in friendly hands, and not exposed to a competitive foreign influence. Such foreign influences can hardly be exercised in a region in which no other nation has important interests, except with the object of creating trouble for Great Britain. The intimate relations cultivated by Italy, from 1926, with the Imam of the Yemen, though possibly innocent in their inception, bore a distinctly suspicious character in 1937, when the Italo-Yemeni treaty was renewed, and the Imam presented with a quantity of armaments of different kinds. Still more obviously hostile was the stream of anti-British propaganda which Italy, about the same time, discharged in Arabic from her broadcasting station at Bari. An attempt to regulate the situation in the Middle East was made in the Anglo-Italian Agreement of 1938, Annexes 3 and 4 (see p. 457). By this agreement, both parties were pledged not to acquire 'a privileged position of a political character' in Saudi Arabia or the Yemen, and they declared it their common interest that no other Power should seek to do so. They promised not to intervene in any internal conflict in this region, and to refrain from propaganda injurious to each other. Having regard to the very unequal degree of legitimate interest which Great Britain and Italy had in this region, the former might be considered to have conceded more than she obtained; the agreement was, however, calculated to promote our interests so long as it was faithfully observed.

The Egyptian Treaty

The deadlock in which negotiations for an Anglo-Egyptian treaty were left after May 1930 (see Chapter XIV) remained unsolved for several years, and this state of things might have continued indefinitely but for an apparently adventitious circumstance, the Italo-Abyssinian war of 1935–6. In Egyptian eyes, the situation in which their country was placed after the adoption of a policy of sanctions against the aggressor rendered the moment particularly opportune for reopening the question of Anglo-Egyptian relations. The popular sympathy for the Abyssinian nation felt throughout Egypt led her, alone among the States who were not members of the League, to adopt the sanctionary measures proposed, and thus exposed her to the danger of an attack by Italy. These circumstances threw a new light on the real advantages to be enjoyed through the continuance of British military protection. On the other hand, the use which Great Britain now proceeded to make of the rights which she had reserved under the declaration of February 1922, for the security of British imperial communications and the defence of Egypt (cf. pp. 137 and 236), opened a prospect for Egypt of becoming an Anglo-Italian battle-field, and accentuated the sense of grievance which the Egyptians had continously entertained against the British military occupation of their country. Such measures as the strengthening of the British forces in Egypt and the removal of the Mediterranean fleet to Alexandria, while they were less unwelcome than they would normally have been, were at the same time difficult to reconcile with the notion of Egyptian independent sovereignty. From the Egyptian standpoint, therefore, the occasion was favourable for placing the relations of the two countries upon a footing more satisfactory to both of them.

British official circles, however, were at first inclined to take an opposite view. The serious preoccupations of the Cabinet in other directions rendered the time, in their eyes, manifestly inopportune for diverting their attention to a matter of secondary importance, especially since the rights which England enjoyed under the existing arrangement gave her a free hand to cope with the main situation. They were inclined to resent, indeed, what they regarded as an attempt to exploit British difficulties for the advantage of Egyptian nationalism, at a time when they were engaged in championing the principles of the Covenant and of world order. But the expression of this point of view had the immediate effect of producing a united front of all parties in Egypt, which unanimously favoured and called insistently for the prompt negotiation of an Anglo-Egyptian treaty. Since one of the principal obstacles to such a step had been the difficulty of finding a party fully representative of Egyptian public opinion with which to negotiate, this development was really favourable; at the same time, agitation for a readjustment of the relations between the two countries was stirred to fresh depths by an episode, to explain which it is necessary to refer in outline to the domestic situation in Egypt.

Stripped of numerous complications which are irrelevant to the matters under consideration, the position was that Egypt had, during the whole period of her existence as a kingdom, been faced with difficulties in working her constitution. Parliamentary government under the Constitution of 1923, at least as amended by Zaghlul in the following year, by the substitution of a direct for an indirect system of election, gave in practice a monopoly of power to the Wafd, which the King only avoided by resort to a 'Palace Government' even more dictatorial: an amended Constitution of 1930, on less Liberal lines, was accused of reducing to a shadow parliamentary control and ministerial responsibility. In these circumstances, the Egyptian Premier, Nessim Pasha, persuaded the King to revoke the new Constitution in November 1934. This step led to an expectation that the Constitution of 1923 was to be restored, and when in the following April a letter from King Fuad was published, expressing a preference for the original Constitution, with any modifications which the representatives might demand, nearly all sections of Egyptian opinion agreed with the Wafd in supporting this solution. Nessim Pasha, however, took no action, having, as he subsequently explained, received from the British Residency advice—which he interpreted as a command—against the restoration of the old Constitution. At this point, when the Egyptian Premier was already the subject of attack on the ground of subservience to British control in internal affairs, Sir Samuel Hoare, in the course of a speech delivered at the Guildhall on Lord Mayor's Day 1935, made the following incidental reference to the Egyptian situation:

It has been alleged that His Majesty's Government wish to use the present situation in order to advance their own at the expense of Egypt's interests. This is not true. . . . Equally untrue are the allegations that we oppose the return in Egypt of a constitutional regime suited to her special requirements. With our traditions we could not and would not do any such thing. When, however, we have been consulted we have advised against the re-enactment of the Constitutions of 1923 and 1930, *since the one was proved unworkable* and the other universally unpopular.

The publication of this utterance, with its definite condemnation of a Constitution the restoration of which was impatiently awaited and demanded by public opinion, was the signal for violent disorders in Egypt, directed impartially against the speaker, the Government of which he was a member, and

Nessim Pasha, and on 5 December Sir Samuel Hoare returned
to the subject with the praiseworthy intention of allaying
the storm by further explanations. Having dealt, however,
with the British attitude to the constitutional question, he
approached the no less burning topic of the proposed Anglo-
Egyptian treaty. As to this he remarked:

His Majesty's Government have no intention of letting the matter
drift, but it is *obviously impossible* for them, in the midst of the pre-
occupations caused by the war in Abyssinia, simultaneously to
engage in negotiations on a matter of such importance.

This, which to English ears sounded as a reasonable and conciliatory request for patience, was taken in Egypt as a crowning
instance of British procrastination in a matter to which the
Abyssinian crisis had given a peculiar relevance and urgency.
There was an immediate revival of disturbance, and a further
consolidation of the united front of Egyptian political parties.
Within a week of the speech, pressure had become so intense
that Nessim Pasha announced his resignation in consequence
of the British attitude to the Egyptian constitutional question.
He was at once informed that the British Government had no
intention of dictating to Egypt the form of its Constitution.
Nessim was thus induced to revoke his decision, and to procure
from King Fuad a rescript re-establishing the Constitution of
1923. At the same time, a note was presented to the British
High Commissioner from the leaders of the United Front,
urging the desirability of immediately reopening negotiations
for an Anglo-Egyptian treaty, and on 20 January 1936, after a
short delay necessitated by the crisis over the Hoare-Laval proposals (see p. 415), the British Government expressed its readiness to enter forthwith into the negotiations which Sir Samuel
Hoare had declared to be 'obviously impossible' in the previous
month.

On the following day the Nessim Cabinet resigned, with the
object of making way for a coalition government of all parties
to deal with the forthcoming negotiations, but the Wafd,
stimulated by the hope of an assured victory in the impending
elections, refused to lend itself to this arrangement, and a
temporary crisis ensued, which was relieved on the 30th by the
formation of a neutral Ministry under Ali Pasha Mahir, and

the appointment of an Egyptian delegation for the negotiations, drawn from all parties under the chairmanship of the Wafd leader, Nahhas Pasha. A further difficulty was created by the fact that the British Government insisted on reopening the military questions on which agreement had been reached in 1930, a course which seemed necessary owing to the change in the strategic situation occasioned by the Italian activities in Africa. Conversations, however, began in Egypt on 2 March. The negotiations were interrupted on 28 April by the death of King Fuad, and in May by the Egyptian elections, which resulted, as anticipated, in a triumph for the Wafd. The military issue gave rise at first to certain difficulties, which necessitated a visit by the High Commissioner, Sir Miles Lampson, to London in June, but in the end a solution was reached which gave to the British forces the right to remain in the neighbourhood of Alexandria for a period of eight years, and secured to them, and to the Air Force in particular, adequate freedom of movement for training, and in case of war or 'apprehended international emergency'. The point in connexion with the Sudan which had proved an obstacle to agreement in 1930 (see p. 236) was met by a provision that Egyptian immigration into the Sudan should be unrestricted except for reasons of public order or health. The principal difficulties having been thus satisfactorily removed, an agreed draft was initialed on 24 July, and the Treaty, which constituted an Anglo-Egyptian alliance, was signed in London on 26 August.

The Franco-Syrian Treaties

The grant of independent sovereignty to Iraq, and its admission to the League of Nations in October 1932 (see p. 233), made it very difficult to defend the continuance of the mandates in Syria and the Lebanon, where the inhabitants were, to say the least, as fitted for autonomy as were the Iraqis. The matter was, however, complicated by the policy of subdivision which the French mandatory authority had pursued in the interests of various compact minorities. The desire of the Syrian Nationalists was for a unified State, corresponding with the whole extent of the Syrian mandate, but the protest of such communities as the Druses of the Jebel ed Druse and the Alawis of Latakia, together with the example of the terrible

fate which had befallen the unprotected Assyrian minority in
Iraq in 1932 (see p. 234), made it difficult for the French to
conclude an arrangement satisfactory to Nationalist aspirations.

In 1933, however, negotiations took place for the conclusion
of a Franco-Syrian treaty on the Anglo-Iraqi model, but the
instrument when drafted raised such a storm among the
Nationalist leaders in Damascus and in the Syrian chamber
that the latter had to be suspended *sine die*, and this attempt at
bringing the mandatory status to an end was temporarily
abandoned. The Nationalists, however, grew increasingly
impatient, and in the first two months of 1936 this impatience
manifested itself in extremely serious disturbances. Under this
pressure, the problem was tackled afresh, and towards the end
of March a Syrian delegation arrived in Paris, charged with the
task of negotiating a treaty.

Progress, which at first was slow, was accelerated by the
accession to power of M. Léon Blum which followed on the
French general elections of 26 April–3 May, and on 9 September 1936 a treaty was finally signed. Like the Anglo-Iraqi
treaty, on which it was closely modelled, this instrument
created an alliance, and was to come into force on the admission of Syria to membership of the League, which was to be
secured within three years of its ratification. France was to have
the right to maintain troops on Syrian soil for a further five
years, i.e. for eight years from the signature of the treaty, and
the interests of the minorities in the Jebel ed Druse and Latakia
were safeguarded by a provision that the troops in question
were to be stationed in these regions, and that the only other
forces there should be locally recruited units under French control. These minorities were to continue to enjoy a special
administrative regime, though the sovereignty over the whole
area was transferred from the mandatary to the Syrian Government.

A similar treaty was concluded with the Lebanon on 13
November 1936, which differed mainly in the absence of
provisions limiting the right of France to station troops in the
territory. For the final liquidation of the mandate it was
necessary to provide for the carrying on of such public services,
e.g. the customs, as had previously been administered in common over both mandates. It was left to negotiation between

the two newly emancipated countries to reach a settlement on this question, which France bound herself to accept.

The Status of Alexandretta

Within the area sovereignty over which was thus transferred to Syria there existed another minority community which was in the fortunate position that its rights were of concern to an important external Power—Turkey. The Sanjak of Alexandretta, comprising a territory of considerable strategic and commercial importance, with an exceptionally fine harbour, was inhabited by a population which was mainly Turkish-speaking, and which contained a large, if not as the Turks maintained a preponderant, Turkish element, amounting, on a conservative estimate, to 40 per cent. Prior to the conclusion of the Franco-Syrian treaty the Sanjak had enjoyed a special regime, by virtue of the Franklin-Bouillon Agreement of 1921 (see p. 120) as confirmed by the Treaty of Lausanne. Under this it enjoyed a large measure of financial autonomy, as well as linguistic and cultural freedom. On the conclusion of the Franco-Syrian treaty, Turkey was not satisfied that the engagements of France in respect of Alexandretta, which were now to be transferred to Syria, would be adequately safeguarded under the new arrangement. The Turks contended that the Sanjak was not an integral part of Syria, and should have been given an independent status, with a direct and separate treaty with France. Such a solution France regarded as *ultra vires*, and the difference between the two points of view threatened at one time to endanger the relations of France and Turkey. It was agreed, however, to refer the matter to the League of Nations, and, after the situation had been studied on the spot by three neutral observers, negotiations were resumed at Geneva in January 1937. With the help of Mr Eden's good offices and those of Mr Sandler of Sweden, a settlement was eventually reached on the 27th. Under this arrangement the Sanjak was to be a separate political entity with a statute and fundamental law of its own, enjoying full internal autonomy: but it was to remain in a customs and monetary union with Syria, and its foreign relations were to be under the control of the Syrian Government. Turkish was to be the principal official language, and the territorial integrity of the Sanjak was to be guaranteed

by France and Turkey in a separate treaty. The conclusion of
this agreement, though disappointing to Syria, was at first
regarded with satisfaction by France and Turkey. In December, however, the Turkish Government formulated certain
objections and reservations to the electoral law drawn up for
the Sanjak. In subsequent discussions at Geneva agreement
appeared to have been reached, and the first elections were
fixed for July 1938. But in May the Turks started a determined effort to obtain control of the local assembly, and the
political feeling aroused by the electoral campaign resulted in
very serious rioting, while the efforts of the French to restore
order were met from Angora with accusations of breach of
faith and of dissemination of anti-Turkish propaganda. Early
in June, after the proclamation of martial law by the Syrian
High Commissioner, relations between France and Turkey
became seriously strained, but as the result of conversations
which then took place, the situation was cleared, on 4 July, by
the initialing of a Franco-Turkish Treaty. The League Commission, whose status Turkey had refused to recognize, was
withdrawn, and the elections postponed. On the understanding
that Turkey made no territorial claims in the area, France
agreed to apply the new status on the basis of the preponderance
of the Turkish element. Two thousand five hundred Turkish
troops were admitted to the Sanjak, to maintain order in co-
operation with an equal French force and 1,000 troops raised
locally. By the Treaty, France and Turkey agreed on a policy
of mutual consultation, and pledged themselves to refrain from
assisting any State guilty of aggression against either of them.
They further agreed not to enter into any political or economic
combination directed against the other party. The conclusion
of the agreement was viewed with alarm by the Armenian
population, and gravely dissatisfied the Syrian Arabs. It was
also criticized for ignoring or superseding the authority of the
League, but it appears to have solved the major issue of Franco-
Turkish relations.

Palestine

In the years immediately following the disturbances of 1929
(see p. 230), though there was a temporary cessation of violent
disorder in Palestine, there was no alleviation of the underlying

causes of the discontent which animated the Arab Nationalists. Indeed, the course of events tended, in a variety of ways, to increase the fears and resentments of the non-Jewish section of the population. The underlying assumption of the mandate was the possibility of creating a 'Palestinian' national sentiment, inspired by which Arabs and Jews could settle down together to an era of co-operative self-government, which would remove the necessity for British tutelage. As this assumption appeared increasingly untenable, the Balfour Declaration and the Jewish National Home were viewed by the Arabs as the one insuperable obstacle to the attainment of that independence on which their aspirations had continuously been fixed. At the same time, all around them, their kinsmen and co-religionists were securing, or rapidly and hopefully approaching, a status of independence from which Palestine remained debarred. Mr Churchill, as early as 1922, had admitted on behalf of the British Government that the people of Palestine were unquestionably no less advanced than their neighbours in Iraq and Syria: it was the redemption of the pledge to the Zionists which alone necessitated the continuation of mandatory control, from which other peoples, no better qualified for self-government, were already, or were soon to be, emancipated.

Yet his claim to independence was asserted by the Palestinian Arab not merely on the ground of an inherent right of self-determination, but on that of an explicit pledge. Though it is true, as stated on p. 133, that the Arab Revolt against the Turks in 1916 was launched without waiting for the conclusion of a treaty, it was begun in reliance upon British promises, embodied in a correspondence between Hussein and Sir Henry Macmahon, and particularly in a letter written by the latter on 24 October 1915. In this document the independence of the Arabs within the territorial limits proposed by the Sherif of Mecca—which indisputably included Palestine—was recognized by Great Britain with the exclusion of 'the districts of Mersina and Alexandretta and the portions of Syria lying to the west of the districts of Damascus, Homs, Hama, and Aleppo', and any parts of the territory included in which Great Britain was not free to act without detriment to the interests of France. Though Mr Churchill, as Secretary of State for the Colonies, contended in 1922 that the first of these reservations excluded from the

pledge the whole of Palestine west of the Jordan, it seems difficult to reconcile such an interpretation with the facts of geography, and it is not surprising that it has never been accepted
by the other party to the transaction.[1] It is true that at the
Peace Conference the policy of the Balfour Declaration was
accepted by the Emir Feisal, in conformity with an agreement
concluded in January 1919 with the Zionist organization. This
agreement was, however, relied on by the Arabs as a recognition
of Feisal's *locus standi* in the matter, and it was accompanied by
a reservation, making its observance conditional on no changes
being made in the claims which he submitted to the Peace
Conference. After his expulsion from Damascus (see p. 129),
'the Feisal-Weizmann Agreement could not operate: the condition attached to it had not been fulfilled'.[2] The 'Macmahon
Pledge' continued therefore to figure prominently in the Arab
argument, and the sense of grievance was unappeased.

Yet, though the continuance of the mandate was resented as
a barrier to independence, there was for a considerable time
no serious fear on the side of the Arabs that they might be
swamped in the tide of Jewish immigration. Restricted by
the Government to the economic absorptive capacity of the
country, the annual flow did not in the earlier years constitute
a threat to the overwhelming numerical preponderance of the
indigenous population. The economic success of the Zionist
experiment was, moreover, for some time in doubt, and there
was a temporary depression during the years 1926–8, characterized by reduced immigration and a flow of disappointed emi-
grants which went far to balance it. In 1928 there were signs
of a return to prosperity, but from that year until 1932 the
annual recorded influx only once slightly exceeded 5,000.
With the coming of the world economic depression, however,
at a time when the Jewish capital invested in the National
Home was steadily growing, the situation was transformed. In
1932 the figure for authorized immigration made a leap to
nearly 5,500 in excess of the previous year, and with the

[1] It appears, however, to have been the intention of the British Government that
Palestine should be excluded from the proposed Arab State, and Sir Henry
Macmahon has publicly stated that the offer in his letter was not intended to
include it. He has further said that he 'had every reason to believe at the time that
the fact that Palestine was not included was well understood by King Hussein'.
[2] Palestine Royal Commission Report, Cmd. 5497, 1937, p. 28.

development of the anti-Semitic policy of Nazi Germany and her imitators from 1933 the pressure on Palestine assumed really formidable proportions. In 1935 there was an official figure of no less than 61,854 Jewish immigrants, while during this period the numbers of those who effected a surreptitious entry into the country was disconcertingly large. A new situation had, moreover, arisen where the restraint of limited absorptive capacity was no longer available. With the growth of industrialism, and a need for new building, the excuse could no longer be put forward that so large an influx could not be accommodated with employment The Arabs were faced with the prospect of an actual Jewish majority within a calculable period, and began not unnaturally to share the anxieties long before expressed by a former inhabitant of their country in a similar predicament: 'Now shall this company lick up all that are round about us, as the ox licketh up the grass of the field.'[1] As the Report of the Palestine Royal Commission puts it (p. 86): 'With almost mathematical precision, the betterment of the economic situation meant the deterioration of the political situation.'

In November 1935 the Arab parties presented the High Commissioner, Sir Arthur Wauchope, with demands for the establishment of democratic government, the prohibition of the transfer of Arab lands to Jews, and the immediate cessation, pending a further inquiry into the true absorptive capacity of the country, of Jewish immigration. In reply to the last two points, the High Commissioner proposed an ordinance forbidding the sale of land unless the owner retained sufficient for the support of himself and his family, and a fresh check on 'absorptive capacity' by a new statistical bureau. In response to the first demand, he submitted to the Jewish and Arab leaders a definite scheme for a Legislative Council, to consist of five official and twenty-three unofficial members, of whom eleven were to be nominated and twelve elected. Of these unofficial members, eleven were to be Muslims, seven Jews, three Christians, and the remainder commercial representatives. This scheme received a measure of reluctant acquiescence from the Arab leaders, but was uncompromisingly rejected by the Zionists.

British parliamentary opinion, voiced in both Houses, gave

[1] Numbers xxii. 4.

it its quietus. The Jewish press was imprudently exultant, claiming the result as 'a great Jewish victory'. This interpretation gave an unwarranted impression of Zionist bias which confirmed suspicions of the dominant influence of Jewry in Britain which the Arabs already entertained. At the same time, the progress of events in the Abyssinian war conveyed an impression, energetically fostered by Italian propaganda, of waning British prestige and power. The success which was being simultaneously achieved by Nationalist agitation in Egypt and Syria (see p. 296) further affected the minds of the Palestinian Arabs, and this combination of adverse circumstances produced a state of unrest which culminated in April 1936. The disturbances which broke out at this time, beginning with isolated murders and progressing to the proclamation of a general strike, rapidly assumed the proportions of a guerrilla war. Large reinforcements were hurried to Palestine, emergency powers were conferred upon military officers, and these measures sufficiently controlled the disorder to induce the Arab Higher Committee to accept the mediatory advice proffered in October by the rulers of Iraq, Transjordan, and Saudi Arabia. By the beginning of November, peace had been sufficiently restored to enable the dispatch of a Royal Commission to investigate the problem.

After hearing the representatives of both sides, the Commission, on its return to England, published a report (see footnote, p. 301, above) in July 1937. In this document the Commissioners, despairing of any ultimate success through the maintenance of the original mandate, proposed a scheme of partition, which, it was hoped, might give sufficient satisfaction to the Nationalist aspirations of both the parties concerned. A Jewish State should be constituted, consisting roughly of northern Palestine as far south as Megiddo, together with the maritime plain to a point about ten miles south of Rehovot, with the exception of a corridor connecting with the sea at Jaffa an enclave designed to include the 'Holy Places'— Jerusalem and Bethlehem—which the Commissioners felt should remain under mandatory control as 'a sacred trust of civilization'. It was suggested that Nazareth and the Sea of Galilee should also be covered by this reduced mandate. The remainder of Palestine should be fused with Transjordan into a single Arab State, and the whole scheme cemented by treaties of alliance between the mandatary, Transjordan, the Palestinian Arabs, and the Zionist Organization. The mandatory Power would support claims for admission to the League of Nations on behalf of the new Jewish and Arab States.

This proposal did not originate with the Royal Commission, a solution on similar lines having been suggested by Mr Amery in the House of Commons, and by others interested in the problem elsewhere. Such a 'judgement of Solomon', however, wise and inevitable though it may have been, could not be expected to escape criticism. The Jews were condemned by it to a Zionism which excluded Zion—the 'Holy Hill' of Jerusalem—and some of the most important creations of their industrial enterprise, such as the hydro-electric power station on the Jordan and the potash plant on the Dead Sea. They also objected to the maintenance of a British mandate indefinitely over Haifa and other towns in Galilee, and to the narrowness of the area allotted to them in the coastal plain. The Arabs complained of severance from their compatriots in Galilee, and from direct access to Mediterranean ports. Neither side was prepared to accept the plan without important modifications. Though the Emir of Transjordan advocated careful consideration of the proposal, the Iraq Government lodged a protest against it with the League of Nations. Debates in the British Parliament revealed an unexpected degree of opposition. At the Zionist Congress, held at Zurich in August 1937, opinion was sharply divided, one section of opinion supporting the principle of partition though rejecting the details of the scheme, while another was more uncompromising. A resolution, however, was finally adopted which favoured further negotiation. The Permanent Mandates Commission of the League, while recognizing the desirability of further examining the idea of partition, considered that a prolongation of the period of mandatory tutelage was essential. In the conclusion of its report it paid a tribute to the efforts of the mandatary, calling the attention of the Jews to the benefits which they owed to Great Britain, and of the Arabs to the origin of their emancipation from Turkish control.

During the latter part of 1937 there began a serious recrudescence of Arab terrorism, which, accompanied by Jewish reprisals, continued to disturb Palestine during 1938. In reporting to the Permanent Mandates Commission on 9 June Sir John Shuckburgh described the situation of the mandatory Power as involving 'incessant war against terrorism, lawlessness, and intimidation'. It was found necessary to begin the erection of a barbed wire barrier along the frontier, known as 'Tegart's wall', from Sir Charles Tegart, who recommended this expedient in his capacity as adviser to the Palestine Government on the question of terrorism. A technical commission, charged to ascertain facts and consider in detail the practical possibilities of a scheme of partition, arrived in Palestine from London on 27 April, and continued its inquiries until August, though greeted without enthusiasm by the Jews and with sullen hostility by the Arabs.

A final settlement of the Palestine question seemed essential if the growing solidarity of the Arab world was not to become a force actively hostile to Great Britain, in an area of great importance to her imperial communications. While the rulers of Arabia, Transjordan, and Iraq were naturally well-disposed to England, the policy of the Balfour Declaration, and its effect in delaying or denying the emancipation of Palestine from foreign control, excited the united and implacable hostility of the whole Arab world. It was, of course, essential that faith should be kept with the Jews, but, unless an acceptable solution could be quickly reached, the prospect for the future was far from reassuring.

XIX

THE FAR EAST

The Question of Extra-territoriality

WITH the formation of a Government which had at least superficial claims to speak for the whole of China, the problem of extra-territoriality naturally acquired a new urgency and importance. As early as December 1926 a British memorandum had expressed willingness to negotiate on this and kindred questions as soon as a Chinese Government existed with which such negotiation was possible. Before the end of 1928 five European countries had agreed to relinquish extra-territoriality as soon as the principal Treaty Powers were prepared to do so. Thus encouraged, the National Government of China reopened the question in a Note addressed to the United States, Great Britain, and others, but found that these were not yet prepared for an immediate abandonment of their treaty rights. In 1929 the State Council issued a mandate unilaterally abrogating such privileges as from January 1930, but in fact the existing situation continued to be recognized, pending the results of further negotiations with the representative of the British Government. In 1931 the issue seemed to be narrowing to the question of a transitory local regime in four treaty ports: Shanghai, Hankow, Canton, and Tientsin. Of these, the problem of Shanghai was the most important, and by far the most complicated. Technically, the question of the rendition of the International Settlement was a matter within the exclusive competence of the Shanghai Municipal Council, and was independent of British policy; in practice, however, the attitude of Great Britain was all-important. In Shanghai, since 1930, an inquiry had been conducted by Mr Justice Feetham, a distinguished South African judge of British origin, at the instance of the Municipal Council. His report was presented in two parts in April and July 1931. While it considered that the ultimate rendition of the Settlement was not only justifiable but necessary, the report maintained that the objections to anything like an immediate adoption of the policy were overwhelming, and that it was 'inevitable that a long transition period should still intervene' before the requisite conditions could be fulfilled. In another passage this period was represented to be one of 'not years, but decades'.

In the meantime, it was becoming increasingly clear that the foundations of such unity as had appeared to exist in China were breaking up, and that a period of political chaos—the duration of which it was impossible to forecast—lay ahead. This difficulty was to some extent recognized even by the Chinese negotiators. But a National Convention was due to meet on 5 May 1931, and, as a bid for domestic support, on the previous day a new mandate was issued from Nanking, announcing the break-down of the negotiations which had been in progress with Great Britain, and the completion of regulations to put in force the provisions of 1929, abolishing extra-territorial privileges, as from 1 January 1932.

Negotiations nevertheless continued, and the statements as to their progress made from time to time by Mr Henderson, the British Foreign Secretary, created an impression that a treaty was on the point of being negotiated. In view of the opinions expressed in the Feetham report, considerable anxiety was felt in many quarters, and this was increased in the course of the summer by the fate of a young Englishman named Thorburn, who had been arrested by Chinese soldiers in June, and had, as subsequently transpired, been shot by their commander.[1] In these circumstances, considerable relief was felt when the operation of the second mandate was further postponed, at the close of the year, and the negotiations with Great Britain allowed to lapse, as a consequence of the international situation brought about by the action of Japan, which will be the main subject for consideration in this chapter.

Recurrence of Anarchy

Indeed, before this date, it had become increasingly evident that the unification of China, which seemed to be approaching by the end of 1930, was neither complete nor durable. The tradition of centuries led the Chinese peoples, as the Lytton Report points out (p. 17), 'to think in terms of family and

[1] He had himself shot a Chinese gendarme.

locality, rather than in terms of the nation, except in periods of acute tension between their own country and foreign Powers'.

In many parts of the country Communism was still in the ascendant. Communist Governments, with their own laws and army, continued to exist in Kiangsi and Fukien. In the central executive itself there was a fundamental cleavage of opinion between those who wished to prolong 'the period of tutelage', prescribed by Sun Yat-sen, and those who were anxious to curtail it, less from any real belief in democracy than from a desire to check the existing power of the politicians in the interests of the military leaders. In February 1931 the protagonist of the former point of view, Hu Han-min, Chairman of the Legislative Yuan, was arrested and interned by Chiang Kai-shek, who carried his point in the constitution adopted by the National Convention in the ensuing May. But the split led to a definite secession in the south, where a rival government was once more set up in Canton. Efforts to deal effectively with the Communists were simultaneously interrupted by a military rebellion in the north, while banditry, flood, and famine added their contributions to the relapse into anarchy with which the country was threatened. At this juncture, the process of disintegration was checked, and the nation once more united, by acute tension with a foreign Power, the necessary factor suggested by the passage from the Lytton Report cited above.

Economic Needs of Japan

In the period of some sixty years, during which Japan had emerged from isolation and obscurity to become a world Power of the first political and economic importance, her population had approximately doubled, and was still increasing at the tremendous rate of about 900,000 a year. The density of the Japanese population stands third in the figures for the world, and, in relation to cultivable area, heads the list. The country is no longer normally self-supporting, nor is the industry on which the support and employment of the people depends independent of outside supplies. Most of the important raw materials required have to be imported from the outside world. Foreign markets, and the prosperity of her international trade, are therefore to Japan a matter of life and death. Emigration affords no solution for the problem, and the grievance created by the restrictive immigration policy of the principal countries to which an outflow might otherwise be directed, while genuinely felt, is sentimental rather than practical.

The normal course of the Japanese export trade has had two main directions: her raw silk has gone to the United States, and her staple manufactures, chiefly cotton textiles, to Asia, especially China. The financial crash in America, which began in the autumn of 1929, had of course disastrous effects upon the disposal of such a luxury product as silk. The Chinese trade of Japan has, on the other hand, been repeatedly interfered with by the application of boycotts of ever-increasing severity, as well as being naturally affected by the anarchic conditions of the country. The economic interdependence between China and Japan which Nature would seem to have prescribed has thus been thwarted by political causes.

A temporary alleviation was provided by the depreciation of the yen, which helped Japan to invade new markets by cutting prices to a level with which no other country could hope to compete, but it is obvious that methods of this kind are only a temporary expedient, which is bound to be met by defensive restrictions in the countries principally affected. It is important, however, for the world to realize that the successful competition of Japan is not merely the result of low wages and a depreciated exchange. The efficiency of her workmen and of the leaders of her industry, the control of which is peculiarly centralized, must also be taken into account, nor must the low wages current in Japan be confused with a low standard of living. Yet the fact remains that the effort to provide for an increasing population by a normal process of expansion of foreign trade appeared to Japan, by the year 1931, to be faced with almost inevitable failure.

Manchuria, the Historical Background

In these circumstances it was natural for Japan to attach increasing importance to the maintenance and extension of the special control which she had acquired in the large, fertile region of Manchuria. As 'the meeting ground of the conflicting needs and policies'[1] of three nations, Russia, China, and Japan, this territory was first an object of contention on political and

---

[1] League of Nations. *Lytton Report*. C.663, M.320, 1932, p. 13.

strategic grounds. The first stage was in 1895, when, as the result of a successful war, a treaty was signed between Japan and China, recognizing the independence of Korea and ceding to Japan Port Arthur and the Liaotung Peninsula. Pressure from Russia, France, and Germany compelled Japan to relinquish these spoils of victory. In 1898 Russia occupied Port Arthur, and in 1901 acquired an effective control of Manchuria, with power to construct and administer a railway from Port Arthur to Harbin, connecting with the Trans-Siberian line. It is usual to assume that this development would have ended in the incorporation of Manchuria and also Korea in the Russian Empire, but this was prevented by the Russo-Japanese War of 1904–5 and the Treaty of Portsmouth, by the terms of which Japan acquired the Russian leasehold rights in the Liaotung Peninsula and the South Manchurian Railway as far north as Changchun, together with the right to maintain a military guard of fifteen soldiers to every kilometre, or an aggregate force of 15,000 men. During the Sino-Japanese Conference held at Peking in December 1905, the Chinese Government promised, though not in any formal document,[1] not to construct any main line 'in the neighbourhood of and parallel to' the South Manchurian Railway, or any branch line which might be prejudicial to its interests. In 1910 Japan annexed Korea.

The next stage was reached in 1915, when Japan confronted China with the famous 'Twenty-one Demands', which bear upon this question inasmuch as by a treaty consequent upon them the Japanese possession of the leased territory and of the railway was extended to ninety-nine years, and the right was conceded to Japanese subjects, which included, in the Japanese view, Koreans, to lease land in South Manchuria, and to travel, reside, and conduct business there. The validity of this treaty has been continuously disputed by the Chinese, but in the partial liquidation of the Twenty-one Demands which was effected at the Washington Conference (see pp. 63–5) these rights were never abandoned by the Japanese.

Japanese Interests in Manchuria

The strategic importance of Manchuria to Japan, both from a defensive and offensive standpoint, is inherent in its situation.

---

[1] League of Nations. *Lytton Report*. C.663, M.320, 1932, p. 44.

Though the Kuomintang, in the later stages of its progress, had turned against its former Russian advisers, 'the likelihood of an alliance between the Communist doctrines in the North and the anti-Japanese propaganda of the Kuomintang in the South' remained a possibility which 'made the desire to impose between the two a Manchuria which should be free from both increasingly felt in Japan'.[1] Economically, Manchuria is mainly of value to Japan as a secure though limited market in a world of shrinking opportunities, and as a basis of supply for some essential raw materials, particularly the soya bean, but also important minerals such as coal and iron, and potentially considerable deposits of oil-shale. A very large amount of Japanese capital has been invested in the country, a fact which makes the preservation of order and the prevention of competitive railway traffic matters of great importance. There is also the possibility of colonization, though in this respect Japan could claim but little success hitherto, the population being overwhelmingly Chinese. It included, however, a considerable number of Koreans, and, if the undisturbed settlement of these Japanese subjects could be promoted, it has been suggested that the pressure in Japan might be indirectly eased by emigration of Japanese to vacated areas in Korea.

Causes of Friction

The question of Korean settlement has proved, however, one of the more serious causes of friction with the Chinese. The Koreans were regarded as 'a vanguard of Japanese penetration and absorption' [2] by the Chinese, their status and rights to acquire land were disputed, they were the victims of oppression and discrimination at the hands of the Chinese authorities, and their protection by the Japanese consular police was resented. On 1 July 1931, a riot was caused by the digging by a group of Koreans of an irrigation ditch, which traversed the land of Chinese cultivators. The rioters were dispersed—without casualties—by rifle fire from the Japanese consular police, but exaggerated reports of the incident led to serious anti-Chinese riots in Korea, in the course of which 127 Chinese are said to have been killed and 393 wounded.

[1] ibid., pp. 36–7. [2] ibid., p. 55.

Study of the history of the Japanese occupation will at once reveal a number of further causes of mutual friction and irritation. The disputed validity of the 1915 treaty, the fact that the construction of parallel competing railway lines by the Chinese was only prohibited by an informal engagement, which, if binding, had certainly been seriously violated, the existence and status of the armed railway guard and of the consular police, had all contributed to increase the tension. As was pointed out in an earlier chapter (p. 253), the approach of the Chinese national forces towards Manchuria and the incorporation of the province in China were matters which immediately aroused Japanese misgiving and protest, and were only reluctantly acquiesced in. In the summer of 1931, in addition to the feeling aroused by the Korean incident, came the murder of Captain Nakamura, a Japanese officer, by Chinese soldiers in the interior of Manchuria. By this time the Japanese claimed that there were 300 incidents outstanding between the two countries and that peaceful methods of settlement had been progressively exhausted.[1]

In fairness to the Japanese attitude it should be recognized that their rights, as claimed, had in fact been persistently infringed and obstructed, the real issue between the parties being the validity of the engagements on which such claims were founded. For example, the Chinese railway construction was deliberately calculated to divert traffic from the South Manchurian Railway. The Chinese, no doubt, claimed that they had a perfect right to act as they did, but, whether this was so or not, their action was highly irritating to Japan and prejudicial to Japanese interests. The Manchurian crisis was, in fact, the final culmination of developments which had been watched with anxiety for years by observers on the spot, though they had perhaps, until recently, attracted too little attention from European Governments. Japan had observed with growing dismay the readiness of Great Britain and other Powers to concede the demands of the Nationalists, and the resultant encouragement to China to feel that she could deal as she pleased with the interests of foreign nations.

---

[1] This claim, according to the *Lytton Report* (p. 66), could not be substantiated, but it was asserted and widely believed.

Growth of Militarism in Japan

Meanwhile the political power in Japan slipped from the hands of the Tokio Government into those of the High Commands of the Japanese army and navy, who began by imposing their will upon the civil executive and went on to make and unmake Cabinets as they chose. The movement, which was accompanied by a series of political assassinations which began in 1930 and became frequent in 1932, had the support of a public opinion rendered desperate by the economic depression and furious by the recurrence of Chinese boycotts and other causes of irritation. Such acts are a usual characteristic of periods of acute political excitement in Japan. Faith in forcible measures directed against the Chinese had been encouraged in 1929, when the seizure of the Chinese Eastern Railway by the Chinese local authorities had resulted in an attack by the Russian Soviet forces, before which the Chinese had ignominiously collapsed. The announcement in Japan, on 17 August, of the murder of Captain Nakamura was followed, on 9 September, by a shower of leaflets, dropped from army aeroplanes, calling on the nation to awaken to the danger threatening Japanese rights in Manchuria. The existence of an extreme state of tension was by this time arousing the concern of the Chinese authorities. On 6 September, a telegram from Marshal Chang Hsueh-liang was received by the garrison in Mukden, which ran as follows:

Our relations with Japan have become very delicate. We must be particularly cautious in our intercourse with them. No matter how they may challenge us, we must be extremely patient and never resort to force, so as to avoid any conflict whatever. You are instructed to issue, secretly and immediately, orders to all the officers, calling their attention to this point.[1]

The Mukden Incident

During the night of 18 September 1931, the inhabitants of Mukden paid little attention to the fact that a loud explosion, followed by sounds of shooting, could be heard. During the previous week the Japanese had been practising manoeuvres

[1] *Lytton Report*, p. 69.

involving vigorous rifle and machine-gun fire in the neighbourhood. In the morning, however, the city was found to be in the
hands of Japanese troops. The alleged occasion for this action
was the blowing-up of a portion of the railway track about
200 yards from a party of Japanese soldiers who were practising
defence exercises. The line had certainly been damaged,
though so slightly that the south-bound train from Changchun
passed over it punctually and without injury to its destination
at Mukden. The perpetrators of the outrage remain uncertain,
though the Japanese patrol alleged that it was fired upon, first
by a small and then by a larger body, without apparently
suffering any casualties at this stage. As the occurrence, according to this account, was altogether unexpected, the brilliance
of the Japanese staff work is undeniably impressive. Not only
were the barracks, containing about 10,000 Chinese soldiers,
immediately occupied with trifling loss, but 'all the forces in
Manchuria, and some of those in Korea, were brought into
action almost simultaneously on the night of 18 September over
the whole area of the South Manchurian Railway from Changchun to Port Arthur'.[1] Two further questions may occur to the
reader. If, as alleged, the Mukden garrison was responsible for
the explosion on the railway, is it not strange that they should
have perpetrated the act in a section where the Japanese troops
were known to be manoeuvring? Secondly, if the garrison was
responsible for the outrage, and for firing on the Japanese patrol,
how is it that the attacking forces encountered so little effective
resistance, and suffered so few casualties at the hands of 10,000
defenders, who must, *ex hypothesi*, have been expecting them?

Planned or not, the first stage of the Japanese operations
placed them in occupation, within some three days, of the
important Chinese towns of Mukden, Changchun, and Kirin,
the last of which lay about sixty-five miles outside the Japanese
railway zone. A further extension rapidly followed, which was
justified by allegations of an increase in banditry—which were
possibly true, though, if so, probably attributable to the withdrawal of Chinese authority—and also by the unfounded
assertion of a Chinese concentration at Chinchow. At the
beginning of October, the Japanese Commander-in-Chief
publicly announced that Marshal Chang Hsueh-liang's Govern-

[1] *Lytton Report*, p. 71.

ment would be no longer recognized. His action was repudiated by the Tokio Government, which had certainly been innocent of complicity in his proceedings, but the Japanese army continued to pursue an independent policy of its own. On 8 October, Japanese aeroplanes dropped bombs on Chinchow, accompanied by leaflets repeating the Commander's declaration, and on the 21st the personal effects of Chang Hsueh-liang were dispatched to Tientsin, as a further hint that his regime in Manchuria was terminated. In November, Japanese forces occupied Tsitsihar, across the Chinese Eastern Railway line to Vladivostok, about three hundred miles from the nearest point in the Japanese railway zone, and, before the end of the month, an advance was threatened against Chinchow, in the south, the only fraction of Manchuria where the Chinese regime still remained. This was temporarily postponed by strong representations from Geneva and from Washington, to which the Tokio authorities were disposed to defer, but on 11 December the Liberal (Minseito) Cabinet fell, and was succeeded by a more Conservative administration. In these circumstances, a reinforcement of the Japanese troops in Manchuria was sanctioned, at the end of December the threatened advance began, and Chinchow, from which the Chinese troops withdrew, was occupied on 3 January 1932. On the following day the Japanese entered Shanhaikwan, at the junction of the Peking–Mukden Railway with the Great Wall, and thus completed their hold over Southern Manchuria.

Reactions in China

The immediate effect of the Japanese intervention was to promote the healing of the breach in the unity of the Chinese Government. Before the end of September representatives of the Nanking and Canton administrations were in conference. Mutual jealousies delayed a settlement, but in November events were hastened through the agency of a large mob of students, who converged, from all parts of China, upon Shanghai and Nanking. In December Chiang Kai-shek and his colleagues were forced into temporary retirement,[1] and

[1] In the opinion of competent authorities Chiang and his fellows intentionally threw into his opponents' hands a situation which he knew they could not handle. Before going the Finance Minister was careful to empty the Treasury.

control was transferred to the Cantonese leaders, until, with the intervention of the Japanese in Shanghai in January 1932, they were discredited, and Chiang Kai-shek resumed control.

A simultaneous result of the Manchurian situation was a great and universal accentuation of the anti-Japanese boycott, accompanied by riots and violence. As early as 21 September 1931, National Anti-Japanese Associations were founded at Nanking, Shanghai, Hankow, and elsewhere. The most stringent rules against relations of any kind with Japanese were drawn up, and a large number of Chinese merchants were stated to have been arrested, fined, imprisoned, and in three cases condemned to death, at the instance of the Shanghai Anti-Japanese Association, for breaches of these regulations. Complaints were also made of maltreatment and insult of Japanese, and the looting of warehouses belonging to Japanese companies.[1] The financial results to Japan were undoubtedly extremely serious. *The Times* correspondent reported from Tokio a startling diminution of the export trade to China by 17 December 1931.

Operations at Shanghai

As a consequence of the friction and disorder thus created, an incident took place in Shanghai, on 18 January 1932, in which five Japanese were attacked by Chinese, two were seriously injured, and one, a Buddhist monk, succumbed a few days later. This led to the dispatch of a communication containing five demands from the Japanese Consul-General to the Chinese mayor of Greater Shanghai. On the 21st naval reinforcements arrived at Shanghai, and on the 24th the Consul-General turned his demands into an ultimatum, expiring on the 28th. On the morning of the 28th Admiral Shiozawa, commanding the Japanese naval forces, intimated that he would take action in default of a satisfactory reply by the following morning. The mayor thereupon accepted all the Japanese demands, but in the meanwhile the Municipal Council had declared a state of emergency, and allocated areas of defence and control to the various contingents. The district allotted to Japan bordered, without any clearly defined boundary, upon the densely populated maze of narrow lanes

---

[1] *League of Nations Official Journal*, December 1931, pp. 2510–11.

and alleys constituting the Chinese area of Chapei, and lay partly outside the limits of the International Settlement. The Chinese do not appear to have been notified of this arrangement. On taking up their positions the Japanese forces met with resistance from Chinese regular troops, and on the early morning of the 29th Japanese seaplanes dropped incendiary bombs on Chapei, which reduced the district to a heap of blazing ruins. A truce was then arranged[1] through the mediation of the British and American Consuls-General, which, however, was never fully observed, and which definitely ended on 2 February. From 3 February what has been described as 'a state of open war' existed; on the 18th an ultimatum, authorized by the Japanese War Office, was delivered, requiring the retirement of the Chinese forces for a distance of twenty kilometres from the boundary of the International Settlement, and on the early morning of the 20th the Japanese forces, which had meanwhile been heavily reinforced, began an attack which continued until 3 March, by which time they had attained their objective after meeting an unexpectedly stubborn resistance. On the same day the League Assembly met in special session to consider the Sino-Japanese dispute. A final armistice agreement was signed by the parties on 5 May as the result of the mediation of Sir Miles Lampson, and at the end of that month the last of the Japanese troops left Shanghai.

Manchukuo

Meanwhile, in Manchuria, an outbreak of local fighting between a Chinese partisan of the Japanese, named Hsi Hsia, and the forces of the Provincial Government of Kirin and Heilungchiang, placed the Japanese and Korean colonies in Harbin in real danger, and a Japanese force was consequently dispatched, which succeeded, on 5 February 1932, in occupying Harbin, a Russian foundation which was the second most important city in Manchuria and the headquarters of the Chinese Eastern Railway. The campaign was then continued against the provincial troops, commanded by General Ma Chan-shan, until August, when the Chinese official forces were temporarily dispersed. Thenceforward the only resistance encountered came from irregulars and bandits until the year was nearly at an end. Meanwhile the Japanese had adopted the policy of setting up provincial governments under Chinese nominees of their own, linked by a 'Self-Government Guiding Board' organized and largely officered by Japanese. Through this organization a conference was staged at Mukden, which decided, on 19 February 1932, to establish an independent republic known as 'Manchukuo' under the Presidency of the ex-Emperor of China, Pu Yi. The new State was inaugurated on 9 March, and received the official recognition of Japan on 15 September, when a treaty was signed between Japan and her protégé. The investigations of the Lytton Commission have made it abundantly clear that the new State was in fact a Japanese creation, which 'cannot be considered to have been called into existence by a genuine and spontaneous independence movement'.[1]

As an alternative to open annexation, the policy pursued by Japan had certain evident advantages. It was tactically sound to give to the affair the colour of an appeal to 'self-determination', since the genuineness of the application of this principle by other Powers had so often been called in question. The burden of disproving the genuineness of the independence movement was thrown on the outside world, whose opinion could always be disputed. The situation was made more generally palatable and defensible in Japan, and finally it has been suggested that the Japanese realized that they could not find anything like the required number of qualified Japanese nationals to staff an all-Japanese administration of the country.

International Reactions

The actions of Japan had, from the first, awakened the concentrated attention of the world. She appeared to be violating not merely her obligations under the Covenant but those of the Kellogg Pact and the Nine Power Treaty safeguarding the territorial integrity of China, which she had signed at Washington in 1922. Not only the members of the League but the United States were therefore interested, while Soviet Russia, though she adopted a policy of patience and forbearance, was perhaps more directly concerned than any other Power. Her anxiety was increased by the refusal of Japan to enter into a non-aggression pact with the Soviet Government, which the

[1] *Lytton Report*, p. 97.

latter had proposed towards the close of 1931. On the other hand, the U.S.S.R. re-established diplomatic relations with China on 12 December 1932, a step which aroused suspicion and resentment in Japan. As early as 21 September 1931, the Sino-Japanese dispute was brought before the League on the appeal of China, under Article 11 of the Covenant, and as early as 14 October the Council expressed the intention of inviting a representative of the United States to sit with them during their consideration of the question. This proposal was carried into effect in spite of the constitutional objections of Japan, and on the 16th Mr Gilbert, the American Consul in Geneva, took his seat with instructions to participate in discussions respecting the Kellogg Pact, but otherwise to act merely as observer. The earlier representations having failed, as already described, to bring about a termination of hostilities, the Japanese representative on the Council proposed the dispatch of a Commission of Inquiry; and on 10 December this proposal was unanimously adopted. The Commission, which was presided over by Lord Lytton, sailed for China in February 1932.

In the meantime the situation had been modified on 29 January, when China invoked Articles 10 and 15 [1] of the Covenant in addition to her original appeal under Article 11. On 12 February the dispute was referred to the Assembly, which met in special session on 3 March. The matter had thus reached a stage when it was likely to be looked on as an acid test of the efficacy of the collective system for the maintenance of peace established in the League Covenant. It was a case, however, where the problem of enforcing sanctions presented such difficulties that the reluctance of the Great Powers to resort to such lengths became increasingly apparent, and the Japanese were encouraged accordingly. Of the three Powers principally interested in the Pacific, neither Russia nor the United States were members of the League, and it appeared that the brunt of any naval operations required would fall exclusively upon Great Britain.

The only contribution which came from America was the

---

[1] Article 10—preservation of territorial integrity of members.

Article 15—submission of dispute to Council or Assembly for report. Article 12 is also involved: no resort to war till three months after such report, and breach of Articles 12 or 15 brings Article 16 (sanctions) into operation.

enunciation, by Mr Stimson, of his celebrated 'Doctrine of Non-recognition', which was published to the world on 7 January 1932. Of this it is sufficient to say that history lends little support to the idea that non-recognition of a *de facto* situation can be permanently maintained, but the doctrine was eagerly grasped and endorsed by other nations anxious to find a safe alternative to the prospect apparently confronting them. For the moment further developments were delayed, pending the publication of the Lytton Report. The Assembly referred the dispute to a Committee of Nineteen, which recommended the extension of the time-limit for its report, and on 1 July the Assembly decided to await the conclusions of the Lytton Commission.

The Reports of the Lytton Commission and of the Assembly

On 2 October 1932, the Lytton Report was published at Geneva. Its findings of fact were generally condemnatory of Japan, but it proposed a settlement which should fully recognize the rights and interests of that country in Manchuria, and should secure to Manchuria a large measure of autonomy under Chinese sovereignty. Internal order was to be secured by an effective local gendarmerie, and all other armed forces should be withdrawn. Economic *rapprochement* between China and Japan was advocated and help in the internal reconstruction of China through international co-operation. The Commission deprecated any attempt to find a solution through a restoration of the *status quo*.

On receipt of the Report the League occupied the next few months in strenuous efforts at conciliation on the lines suggested. But the opening of the New Year destroyed all hopes which may still have been entertained, for on 1 January 1933 the Japanese abandoned all pretence, and launched an attack upon Shanhaikwan, the gateway of the Great Wall; and on 3 January they entered the city. On 11 February the sub-committee entrusted with the task completed a draft report for submission to the League Assembly under Article 15. On 13 February it was approved by the Committee of Nineteen, and on 17 February it was published. On the 21st the Assembly met to consider it, and adjourned for three days in view of the gravity of the situation. On reassembling, it adopted the Report by 42 votes against the single adverse vote of Japan, who, as a party to the dispute, could not affect the validity of the decision.[1] The Japanese delegate at once gave notice of his country's intention to resign from the League.

The Report generally followed the conclusions and recommendations of the Lytton Commission. It declared that the sovereignty over Manchuria belonged to China, that the independence movement could not be recognized as spontaneous, and that the military measures of Japan could not be justified. It recommended the evacuation of the Japanese troops to within the railway zone. The further recommendations for a settlement followed the lines of the Lytton Report.

Invasion of Jehol

Almost simultaneously with the critical vote of the League Assembly, Japan was engaged in a major military operation against the forces of China. The coming of this event had in fact cast its shadow upon the negotiations at Geneva for some time. The territory involved was the province of Jehol, a wedge of mountainous country dividing Manchuria from the Great Wall of China, except for the narrow coastal strip north of Shanhaikwan, containing the central section of the Peking–Mukden railway line. In Jehol Japan had long claimed a special interest, intimating that the maintenance of order there was a matter of internal policy for the Manchurian Government. This claim had now grown into a definite assertion that Jehol formed an integral part of Manchukuo. The local Governor, Tang Yu-lin, had in fact been one of the signatories of the original declaration of Manchurian independence, and had been appointed Vice-Chairman of the new State's Privy Council, but at the end of 1932 he repudiated his allegiance. On 12 January 1933, the War Office in Tokio issued a statement claiming Jehol on behalf of Manchukuo, and from that time forward the outbreak of hostilities was generally recognized as imminent. In the middle of February an ultimatum was delivered to the Nanking Government and to Marshal Chang Hsueh-liang, demanding the evacuation of Chinese troops from the province, and on the 25th the Japanese advance began in

---

[1] Siam abstained from voting.

earnest. It proceeded with unexpected rapidity, the Chinese resistance collapsing, in spite of great numerical superiority. Jehol City (or Cheng-teh) was occupied on 4 March, in advance of the time-table arranged. On the 5th Chiang Kai-shek ordered Marshal Chang Hsueh-liang to resist at all costs, but three days later the young marshal responded by resigning his command. In little more than a fortnight Japan and her protégé were in control of all the passes in the Great Wall.

In April the campaign reached its final stage, when the Japanese troops crossed the Wall in several places, and were soon threatening Peiping (Peking). In these circumstances an armistice was signed at Tangku on 3 May, providing for the demilitarization of an area of 5,000 square miles on the Chinese side of the Great Wall. Since, in the previous December, the Japanese had pushed the Chinese forces remaining in Northern Manchuria over the Russian border, where they were disarmed, Japan now appeared to have attained all the objects which her military adventure was designed to secure. The Nanking Government had, indeed, been taught so stern a lesson that it now adopted a strikingly conciliatory attitude, repressing anti-Japanese boycotts with such energy as to lead to rumours of special understandings and even of a secret treaty for the maintenance of an 'Asiatic Monroe Doctrine'.

Japanese Warning to Foreign Powers

The existence of these suspicions has a special interest in view of the claims put forward by Japan in April 1934, when her Foreign Office spokesman issued a statement which included the following passages:

Any joint operations undertaken by foreign Powers even in the name of technical or financial assistance at this particular moment after Manchurian and Shanghai incidents are bound to acquire political significance. Undertakings of such nature, if carried through to the end, must give rise to complications. . . . Japan therefore must object to such undertakings as a matter of principle. . . . Supplying China with war aeroplanes, building aerodromes in China, and detailing military instructors or military advisers to China or contracting a loan to provide funds for political uses would obviously tend to alienate friendly relations between Japan,

China, and other countries, and to disturb peace and order in Eastern Asia. Japan will oppose such projects.

The rights so claimed were at once made the subject of communications from the United States, France, and Great Britain, and somewhat reassuring statements elicited. It should be recognized, however, that Japan had reason to regard with some anxiety the efforts of Mr T. V. Soong and others to obtain financial assistance for China, the effect of which might well be to increase her ability to oppose Japan: the employment of League of Nations advisers, credited with pronounced anti-Japanese opinions, also aroused not unnatural misgivings in Tokio. The attitude of Japan to this question of foreign economic assistance or advice was tested in 1935, when Sir Frederick Leith-Ross was sent out to China by the British Government to investigate and report upon economic conditions. This move, which was undoubtedly of material assistance to China at a critical period, was received with suspicion and hostility in Japan, where it was believed to be a prelude to a substantial loan to China. Adverse Japanese opinion did not, however, lead to any positive attempt by the Tokio Government to interfere with the British action.

Japanese Action and the Collective System

From the point of view of Japan, action against China seemed to be justified by success, though some of the economic advantages which she hoped to derive from the control of Manchuria could not be fully realized for some time. The expense of the operations was undoubtedly heavy, but this to some extent was set off by the commercial advantage which Japan derived from the heavy depreciation of the yen, which gave a surprising stimulus to her export trade during 1933. It was also evident in 1931, and has become increasingly evident since, that the economic crisis and economic nationalism were driving trade into restricted areas, to the comparative advantage of countries who could establish trading relations with a wide region over which they possessed a special control or influence. Strategically, her control of Manchuria gave Japan a peculiarly valuable base for offensive or defensive operations against either China or the U.S.S.R. From the standpoint of the outside world, too, if the episode could only have been judged by pre-war standards, it might have been regarded as satisfactory in its results. Chinese Nationalism had begun to learn humility, and the preservation of order in the north was probably now in more efficient hands. Few could deny that Japan had been exposed to extreme provocation, and most nations could remember incidents, in their own not very remote past, when their policy had not been dissimilar. In this connexion it is interesting to read Mr Lippmann's characteristically American view, that 'the Japanese Army is, in a word, carrying on not "a war" but an "intervention"', and that the world need not and should not have 'plumped for an interpretation which brought Japan's intervention within the scope of the Kellogg-Briand pact renouncing war'.[1]

On the other hand, judged by post-war standards, the position was this. Japan had not only broken her engagements under the Kellogg Pact and the Nine Power Treaty, but had, in the only sense intelligible to the ordinary man, resorted to war in violation of Articles 12 and 15 of the Covenant, thereby throwing on members of the League the obligation of automatically applying the sanctions of Article 16. Yet nothing had been done, apart from a temporary and unsuccessful effort on the part of Great Britain to apply a limited arms embargo. Everyone felt that while the failure to act might be justified, it necessarily involved the ignoring of the obligations in the Covenant, for if Japan's action was not a 'resort to war', it only escaped the charge through an open conspiracy not to define it so. The shock, therefore, which the incident administered to the whole system of collective security was tremendous, and the only question on which opinion can be divided is as to whether the responsibility for this lies wholly at the door of Japan, or whether it must be shared by those who planned a system which the world was incapable of working. There are, indeed, persons who think that the application of sanctions was practicable, but the difficulties were so great, and the prospect of plunging the world in war so formidable, that the inaction of members of the League must be considered pardonable, if not wholly justified. It is arguable, however, that in such circumstances the intervention of the League, and its expression of an impotent dis-

[1] Lippmann, *Interpretations 1931–2*, pp. 196–7.

approval, was worse than useless, since it tended to consolidate public opinion in Japan behind the militarist aggressors. The 'moral sanction' of an adverse foreign opinion generally produces this result.

Russo-Japanese Relations

The aspect of the question which gave rise to the most immediate threat to general peace was the friction occasioned between Japan and the U.S.S.R. The Japanese control of Manchuria had converted the Russian territory in eastern Siberia, including the port of Vladivostok, into a salient dangerously enveloped by Japan and her sphere of influence. The addition of Jehol to this sphere opened a road into central Asia promising a base of operations against a still longer extent of Russia's vulnerable Siberian frontier. The threat to these Asiatic possessions could not be regarded with indifference by the Soviet Government, since eastern Siberia played a most important part in the Russian schemes for industrial development. During the first Five-Year Plan more money had been invested in this region than the Tsarist Government had devoted to it during the whole of its existence, while the second Five-Year Plan laid down a vast programme of industrial development for this area. Many concessions had been made to its population with the object of attracting settlers, and this policy was threatened with frustration as a result of the alarm occasioned by the Japanese advance and militaristic attitude.

In the nervous atmosphere prevailing, a magnified importance attached to a series of individually trivial incidents which took place in 1933. There were several allegations of violation of Russian territory by Japanese forces, while, on the other side, friction was increased by the shooting of some Japanese fishermen by Russian coastguards in June, and in July a Russian ship was arrested by Japanese authorities for entering Japanese waters in the Kuriles. But the principal cause of tension was the situation with regard to the Chinese Eastern Railway.

Over this system, prior to the Russo-Japanese War of 1904–5, Russia had exercised a virtually complete control, including the southern branch to Port Arthur; this branch south of Changchun had passed to Japan by the Treaty of Portsmouth, but the remainder, since the conclusion of an agreement in 1924, had been under joint Russo-Chinese control until the Chinese authority in Manchuria came to an end. The Russian manager and officials employed under this arrangement now found the Japanese or Manchurian colleagues who had replaced the Chinese considerably more difficult to work with than their predecessors, though their relations with these had not always been harmonious. A dispute also arose concerning the retention of rolling-stock by the U.S.S.R., and in April the Manchurian authorities retaliated by a stoppage of through-traffic at the frontier station. The railway had, indeed, lost most of its value to Russia owing to the construction of competing lines, and in May 1933 the Soviet Government attempted to solve the question by an offer to sell the Chinese Eastern Railway to Japan or her protégé. The matter was complicated by questions of ownership, for while the Manchurian Government contended that it had succeeded to the rights formerly vested in China, and the U.S.S.R. insisted that the Chinese claims had lapsed, China herself protested that the proposed sale was a violation of the 1924 agreement. Further objections were raised by French interests which had contributed a large proportion of the capital employed in the construction of the railway. The negotiations, however, actually broke down over the question of price, that offered by Japan on behalf of her protégé being only about one-tenth of that demanded by Russia. The attitude of the Soviet Government stiffened as a result of its successful conclusion of treaties of non-aggression with its European neighbours, which protected its western frontiers (see p. 374). Japan and Manchukuo, on the other hand, became proportionately intransigent, probably with a view to diminishing the value of the railway in Russian eyes, and thus inducing more favourable terms for purchase. In September 1933 relations were further strained by the arrest of six of the senior members of the Russian railway staff, which the Soviet Government alleged to have been done in pursuance of a deliberate plan for the forcible elimination of Russian control. In support of this allegation documents were published, which were denounced in Japan as forgeries. In October further arrests of Russian employees took place, and complaints were made that the Manchurian railway officials were reducing the administration

of the line to confusion by countermanding all orders issued by
their Russian colleagues. A state of mutual irritation was thus
engendered, which led in both countries and also in the outside
world to a general fear that war between these two nations was
inevitable. On 23 March 1935, however, the tension was for
the moment relieved by the final sale of the Chinese Eastern
Railway to the Government of Manchukuo.

Interlude in 1934

The Tangku Truce in May 1933 (see p. 322) was followed
by a temporary lull. There was no serious fighting in 1934,
and the frontier towns of Shanhaikwan and Koupeikou were
restored to China early in the year. On their side, the Chinese
authorities showed themselves not unwilling, for the moment,
to make concessions. The fact was that neither side was ready
to resume a trial of force. Japan was at first more preoccupied
with the dangers of a collision with Russia which have been
mentioned above, and from the close of 1934, after she had
formally denounced the Naval Treaty of Washington (see
p. 64), she was engaged in the conversations which preceded
the Naval Conference of December 1935. When this Conference met, however, Japan very soon ceased to participate,
retiring as early as 15 January 1936. In July 1934 the Japanese
Government was overthrown by an internal scandal, and was
succeeded by an administration of moderate complexion,
which was mainly concerned to cope with the prevalent
economic depression. China also had her domestic troubles.
The American Silver Purchase Act of August 1934 (see
pp. 282-3) affected her economic position most seriously, and
her capacity for resistance to Japanese pressure was reduced
by the fact that the forces of Chiang Kai-shek were diverted in
a successful effort to destroy the Communist centre of Kiangsi.
As the result of this operation, the 'red' forces were compelled
to retire for a distance of more than 6,000 miles, and to
establish new head-quarters in the western province of Shensi,
where a considerable Communist nucleus already existed.
These pre-occupations induced in the Chinese Government a
conciliatory attitude and a readiness to acquiesce in Japanese
demands.

Renewed Activity in North China

The year 1935, however, saw considerable progress made in the Japanese attempt to separate North China from the control of Nanking, and to extend, by the establishment of a so-called autonomous regime, the influence of Japan as far south as the Yellow River and to Shantung. In January military operations were started in Chahar, on the pretext of an alleged violation of the Tangku truce by the governor of the province, but a temporary settlement of this dispute was almost immediately reached. Trouble, however, started again in May, in consequence of the murder of two Chinese employees of the Japanese in Tientsin, which led to demands for the dismissal of the Governor of Hopei (marked by its earlier name of Chihli on the map on p. 240), the withdrawal of his troops from Tientsin, and the cessation of anti-Japanese activities. Though these demands were at once complied with,[1] the Japanese army continued to seize every excuse for continuing their pressure. For a time they were met in a conciliatory spirit, but in November, by which time the Japanese aim of detaching the northern provinces from the control of the Nanking Government was clearly established, Chiang Kai-shek ordered the suspension of negotiations between the local Chinese authorities and the Japanese military commanders, in order to transfer them to his own hands and those of the Japanese ambassador in Nanking, Mr Ariyoshi. Independently of these negotiations, the Nanking Government, towards the close of the year, appointed a decentralized though not strictly autonomous 'Political Council' for Hopei and Chahar, with the object of forestalling Japanese plans for the establishment of an autonomous regime in all five provinces. Nanking retained its control over Shansi and Shantung, but, on 24 November, Yin Ju-keng, who had Japanese connexions, and who had been appointed administrator of the eastern section of the demilitarized zone in Hopei set up by the Tangku truce, had declared the independent autonomy of his district, and this continued.

---

[1] This was the occasion of the so-called and alleged Ho-Umetsu agreement, to which the Japanese appealed in 1937. The Chinese, however, dispute the existence of this agreement, which has never been published, and the Japanese Chief of Staff denied at the time that any 'demands' were presented.

Internal Tension in Japan

The action of the Chinese Government, in moving the seat of negotiation to Nanking, was prompted by a knowledge of serious differences which at this time separated the army in Japan, or at all events its younger officers, from the constitutional parliamentary Government. The junior military ranks were permeated with the ideology of an anti-democratic movement known as the 'Showa Restoration', which had been spread to some extent through the whole country by means of secret societies and propagandist training camps. In particular, these officers objected to parliamentary control over military policy and expenditure. While the Government at this time tried to attain its ends in China by methods of persuasion, an influential section of the army favoured direct action and the use of force. In the summer of 1935 the removal from his post of the Inspector-General of Military Education led immediately to the murder of a high official of the War Office, General Nagata, by a young officer, who gave as his reason a determination to promote the Showa Restoration and thus free the army from democratic control. His trial for this offence took place in February 1936, immediately after a general election which had considerably strengthened the position of the Government. In these circumstances, a military rising took place on 26 February, characterized by the murder and attempted murder of a number of leading politicians. These actions were condemned by the Emperor, and the leaders of the revolt severely punished, but they managed to attract a measure of public sympathy which did much temporarily to strengthen the power and influence of the army. Towards the end of the year, however, a reaction set in, which tended more than ever to increase the cleavage between the civilian and the military authorities.

Growth of Spirit of Resistance in China

Meanwhile, distaste for continual concession to Japanese demands had been steadily developing in China. The apparent pliancy which had led the Government to such actions as the appointment of the Hopei-Chahar Political Council was highly unpopular. Chiang Kai-shek was suspected of too great readiness to conform to the plans of Mr Hirota, who, in January

1936, enunciated a 'three-point programme' requiring the recognition of Manchukuo, collaboration against Communism, and the cessation of anti-Japanese manifestations. Though the methods of the Japanese had ceased for the time to include military aggression, the end in view was still clearly the virtual severance of a large extent of Chinese territory. Educated public opinion was also outraged by such things as the activities of Japanese and Korean smugglers, through which, on an official estimate, no less than fifty million dollars' worth of duty was evaded in 1936, entailing an extremely serious loss to the Chinese revenue. This 'racket' was quite openly carried on, and was facilitated by the existence of the East Hopei Autonomous Government, which collected a smallduty for itself and then passed the goods through. The Nanking Government was thus faced with the disagreeable alternatives of submitting to spoliation or erecting a customs barrier farther south, which would complete the severance of East Hopei from China, and thus play into the hands of Japan. There was every reason to suspect the encouragement of these illegal proceedings by the Japanese authorities, in furtherance of their policy. Finally, the acceptance by the Hopei-Chahar Council of Japanese diplomatic and economic advisers, in the spring of 1936, and the increase in the Japanese garrison in North China, brought matters to a head.

Early in June, after telegraphic remonstrances against the apparent supineness of the Central Government, a force of Cantonese and Kwangsi troops began to advance northwards, with the object of stimulating resistance to the forward policy of Japan. This 'southern revolt' was soon disposed of, but both the movement itself and the promptitude with which it had been suppressed increased the prestige and strengthened the hands of Chiang Kai-shek. At the same time, the Communist forces in Shensi were making overtures with the object of consolidating a common front against Japanese aggression. In the autumn, during a visit paid to the 'Young Marshal', Chang Hsueh-liang, at Sianfu, Chiang Kai-shek was warned of the prevalent discontent in regard to his policy, and on a later visit, on 12 December, occurred the mysterious incident when he was kidnapped by Chang and his men, and confronted with demands for co-operation with the 'red' forces and positive opposition to Japan. He was released on Christmas Day, the 'Young Marshal' submitted himself to discipline and was quickly condemned and pardoned, and, whatever may be the inner history of this episode, it left the Chinese Generalissimo with undiminished prestige, and in possession of additional evidence of popular support, in the event of his being called on to make a stand against Japanese pretensions. In fact, the Nanking Government received at this time assurances of allegiance and support not only from the provinces under direct control but even from the Hopei-Chahar Political Council. To the combined effect of these occurrences must be added the success achieved by the Chinese Governor of Suiyuan in resisting an invasion of his territory by a mixed force of Manchu-Mongol troops and irregulars, assisted by Japanese officers and material. All these things tended to stimulate the adoption of a more unyielding attitude towards Japanese demands in the future. In fact, the Suiyuan invasion led the Chinese Government to break off negotiations for a general settlement, which it had, during most of the year, been conducting with Japan.

Situation Preceding the War

It will be gathered from the foregoing that by 1937 the trend of events was moving towards a situation where a violent collision was probable. China had achieved an unprecedented degree of unity, and was animated by a new and general resolve to stand firm in resistance to demands prejudicial to the integrity of the country. In Japan, the breach between the ideals of moderates who believed in conciliation and co-operation and those of the section, led by the younger military officers, which believed in force, was becoming wider. The latter saw its only hope in independent action, and its intransigence was encouraged by the success of aggression in other parts of the world, and by the knowledge that the situation in Europe made any interference from that quarter practically out of the question, especially since the expansionist forces of East and West had been linked by the conclusion of the German-Japanese Anti-Comintern Pact of 26 November 1936. At the same time the moderate view was, during the early months of 1937, so strongly pressed upon the Japanese Government, and in particular Mr Sato, the Foreign Minister, that a reduction in the North China garrison was seriously in contemplation. Faced by a danger of this interference with their plans, the garrison and the Japanese forces in Manchuria partially discarded their mutual jealousy, and the extremists, moved by rumours that they were about to be weeded out, may well have decided to create a situation which would force the Japanese people to recognize the necessity of strengthening rather than reducing the forces in China.[1] The political changes in June, when Mr Hirota succeeded Mr Sato, rendered more favourable the chances of producing such an impression.

The Lukouchiao Incident and Outbreak of War

These considerations may be kept in mind in estimating the responsibility for the incident which was the immediate occasion for the outbreak of hostilities which were destined to merge with the world war of 1939–45, and to continue till its termination. For the conduct of successful military penetration into China from the north, the control of the railways converging at Peking is of the first importance. The two lines connecting that city with Hankow and Nanking respectively have a junction at Lukouchiao, thirteen kilometres to the south west; hence strategy would naturally suggest this place as an early objective in a war of aggression. It is significant therefore that, on 7 July 1937, Lukouchiao should have been the scene of the incident which became the pretext for the subsequent hostilities. The immediate responsibility for the clash is a matter on which there is a hopeless conflict of evidence. The Japanese story is that the Chinese first opened fire, apparently mistaking an advance undertaken as a military exercise in the Japanese manoeuvres for a serious attack. On this theory, the Japanese commander would appear to have been at least partially responsible, if, without making the nature of his operations abundantly clear, he chose this vital strategic point as a suitable terrain for sham fighting, and, in any case, the mistake of the Chinese could have been speedily and peacefully rectified. But, according to the Chinese, what happened was that the Japanese, having been refused permission to enter Wanping near Lukouchiao to search for a missing man, at once attacked the place with infantry and artillery. The Japanese forces on the spot

---

[1] See *International Affairs*, November 1937, p. 838.

were within a few days heavily reinforced from Manchuria, and on 15 July the Tokio War Office announced the dispatch of troops from Japan. Two days later, Nanking was officially informed that Japan would not tolerate the entry of Central Government troops into Hopei. On the 19th a local settlement was reported to have been reached, but clashes continued, and the next day Lukouchiao was shelled by the Japanese. By the end of the month, Tientsin and Peking, with the surrounding railway stations and barracks, were in their hands.

From this point, though war was not then or indeed at any time officially declared, it may be considered for all practical purposes to have begun. From the latter part of July a rapid evacuation of Japanese residents from all parts of the country was carried out. Having secured control of the Suiyuan railway to protect their flank, the Japanese advanced along both the railways leading in a southerly direction, and by the end of the year were in control of the greater part of the region enclosed by the Yellow River (Hwang-Ho). In the north west they controlled most of Suiyuan. Meantime a tense situation had been developing in the Shanghai area, where the Chinese on the one hand were determined to prevent the development of a situation similar to that of 1932, when they had been attacked from the shelter of the International Settlement, and the Japanese on the other hand feared for the safety of the large Japanese community at the port. Alarming incidents occurred, including one on 9 August, in which a Japanese naval officer and a seaman had been killed on ignoring—as the Chinese alleged—a warning not to approach a military aerodrome. A member of the Chinese Peace Preservation Corps was stated to have been shot by this officer. The immediate cause of hostilities, however, was the arrival of a large force of Japanese warships, which had been ordered to Shanghai before the date of the incident in question. On 13 August fighting began, with the result that by the end of the year Nanking was in Japanese occupation, and the Yangtse was under their control from Wuhu to the sea.

External Reactions and the Brussels Conference

In September 1937 an appeal which the Chinese Government had addressed to the League of Nations, invoking Articles 10,

11, and 17 of the Covenant, was referred to a Far Eastern Advisory Committee, which reported that the military operations carried on by Japan were out of all proportion to the incident which occasioned the conflict, were in conflict with the Nine-Power treaty of 1922 and the Briand-Kellogg Pact, and could not be justified. It further recommended consultation between the signatories of the Nine-Power Treaty. Its reports were adopted by the Assembly on 6 October, together with a resolution laying down that:

Members of the League should refrain from taking any action which might have the effect of weakening China's power of resistance, and should also consider how far they can individually extend aid to China.

It was hardly likely, however, that any utterance by the League in 1937 would be anything more than a *brutum fulmen*. A conference between the signatories of the Nine-Power Treaty might seem at first sight a more promising expedient, since it would include the United States. The conference duly took place at Brussels in November, though Japan declined the invitation to attend. The U.S.S.R., however, though not an original signatory, accepted an invitation to participate in the conference. But it was soon evident that the time had passed, if it had ever existed, when any of the nations concerned were prepared to go further than words in resistance to aggression, unless their own vital interests appeared to be directly involved. The Brussels Conference consequently produced nothing more useful than a reaffirmation of general principles, while its failure in this respect was one more notice to aggressors that they had nothing to fear from outside parties, whether alone or in combination, whose separate interests were not clearly endangered. It was perhaps significant that the adherence of Italy to the Anti-Comintern Pact between Germany and Japan, which converted the 'Berlin-Rome Axis' into a 'Berlin-Rome-Tokio triangle', took place on 6 November, while the Brussels Conference was in session. The pretext that this arrangement was merely directed against the menace of Bolshevism was completely dropped by Herr Hitler two days later, when he described it as a 'great world-political triangle' which 'consists not of three powerless images but of three States which are prepared and determined to protect decisively *their rights and vital interests*' (cf. p. 442).

The interests of most nations in China were too limited to prompt their intervention. It is true that the operations around Shanghai gave rise to incidents liable to arouse resentment among the nations represented in the International Settlement. On 3 December, in disregard of protests, the Japanese organized a provocative 'Victory March' through the Settlement, and the throwing of a bomb by an incensed Chinese spectator led to the occupation of the neighbouring area by Japanese troops, which were only removed after strong representations from the British commander of the local police. On 12 December two British gunboats were fired on by the Japanese in the Yangtse, while the United States gunboat *Panay* was sunk by a deliberate aerial bombardment, and the survivors were fired on with machine-guns. These incidents led to an exchange of Notes, as a result of which the Japanese Government apologized and agreed to pay compensation, but the general situation was not otherwise affected.

It was, notwithstanding, deeply felt by Great Britain that the forward policy of Japan constituted such a menace to her vital interests as to render interference desirable, if only it were possible. Though the politicians of Japan continued to make reassuring statements as to their intentions with regard to foreign interests, the military, who were obviously the controlling factor, used very different language, some of them speaking openly of a purpose 'to sweep from China the influence of Britain'. Apart from the importance of British commercial interests, and the probability that Hong Kong might be ruined by a Japanese penetration in South China, there existed a body of opinion in Japan which turned covetous eyes to the Pacific islands which flank our imperial communications with Australasia. The adverse effects of a successful and unchecked Japanese expansionism might therefore be not only commercial but strategic. The British Foreign Secretary, therefore, took pains to make it clear that he favoured effective action if adequate support could be obtained, and made, in particular, an unmistakable bid for the co-operation of the United States, whose President, on 5 October, had uttered a strongly worded warning to his people against the illusions of isolation, and had advocated a concerted effort on the part of peace-loving nations 'in opposition to those violations of treaties and those ignorings of humane instincts which are today creating the international anarchy and instability from which there is no escape through mere isolation or neutrality'. In a speech on 1 November, therefore, Mr Eden, after pointing out that nothing effective could be done without the United States, said that though he would not rush on ahead of them neither would he lag behind, and that he would, if necessary, 'go from Melbourne to Alaska' to secure their co-operation. Neither during the Brussels Conference, however, nor indeed for some years after it, did any prospect appear that this co-operation might be forthcoming.

Progress and Prospects of the War

The military aspects of the struggle, which outlasted the rest of the period covered by this history, may be very briefly summarized. During the early part of the year 1938 the Japanese completed their occupation of the region enclosed by the Yellow River, though their authority did not extend far beyond the points actually held by their forces. They were compelled to retain substantial garrisons at all strategic points, and their lengthening communications were constantly menaced by Chinese guerrillas. The main Japanese objectives during the first five months of the year were the two important junctions of Suchow and Chengchow, through which the Lunghai railway provides lateral connexion between the Peking–Hankow and Tientsin–Nanking lines. Suchow was captured towards the end of May, though not before the Japanese had sustained a major reverse at Taierchwang, some sixty miles to the east of it. Having secured this junction, the Japanese forces advanced towards Chengchow, and by 6 June had entered Kaifeng, about fifty miles from their objective. Further progress in this direction was, however, at this point checked by the breaching of the banks of the Yellow River. This caused extensive floods, which temporarily barred the advance and caused considerable loss of life. It was for some time uncertain whether the breaches were cut intentionally by the Chinese, or were an accidental consequence of the Japanese bombardment, but it is now known that the dykes were cut on

the suggestion of the German military advisers of the Chinese.[1]
The main theatre of operations at this stage shifted to the
Yangtse valley, where an advance began towards Hankow, the
seat of the Chinese Government since they were forced to
abandon Nanking. This movement had reached the neighbourhood of Kiukiang by the end of July, and the advance continued, after a brief lull, until it culminated, on 25 October, in
the capture of Hankow. The city was, however, fired by the
retreating Chinese, and the commander, Chiang Kai-shek,
escaped by air just before the entry of the enemy forces.

An even more serious loss was almost simultaneously sustained by the Chinese, on 21 October, in the fall of Canton,
against which the Japanese launched an unexpected offensive
some ten days earlier. Insufficient care had been taken to
strengthen the defences of this important point, since it was not
believed that the enemy would venture on an operation so
provocative to Great Britain, whose interests in Hong Kong
were most seriously prejudiced. It is probable that Japan was
emboldened by the pacific disposition manifested in relation to
the Czechoslovak crisis in September. (See p. 463 et seq.)

This double loss marked an important stage in the progress
of the war, since China was now cut off from all her sea-ports,
and her principal centres of population and of cultural and
industrial life had fallen under enemy control. The seat of
government was removed to Chungking, and effort was concentrated on the defence of a 'Free China', limited to the
comparatively primitive and isolated provinces of the west.

The situation, however, proved less desperate than it
appeared. The remoteness of the new lines of defence gave
them increased protection, and a new sense of national unity
was encouraged by the concentration of energy upon a relatively limited area. The influx of refugees from widely separated
parts of China brought many who had hitherto been strangers
into close contact: the association of members of the cultural
intelligentsia proved of particular value in this respect. Sheer
necessity stimulated tremendous exertions, which achieved
miracles of rapid advance in the transplantation of industry
and the development of communications. Supplies continued
to reach China by the Burma Road, declared open in July 1938

[1] See leading article in *The Times*, 1 September 1938.

and in full operation by the end of the year, as well as by road and rail connexion with Indo-China and by a long road running north west into the territory of the Soviet Union. Thus the year 1939, in spite of continuous fighting, brought about no changes of major strategic importance. The event in the Far East which attracted most attention in the summer of that year, the blockade of the Foreign Concessions in Tientsin, had little direct connexion with the Sino-Japanese struggle, and the situation at the outbreak of the Second World War held prospects of prolonged deadlock.

XX

EUROPE AND THE DISARMAMENT CONFERENCE

The Briand Scheme for European Union

ON the eve of the Disarmament Conference an increasing body of opinion was inclined to the belief that the disappointing state of the problem was largely due to the fact that the post-war system was built on a basis wider than any which the world had in fact attained; a view soon to be strikingly confirmed by the unimpeded resort to war—or war in everything but name—in the Far East and in South America. The nations of Europe still instinctively felt that their true interests were restricted to a narrower area, and their peoples showed no enthusiasm for the idea of crusading for peace in the remoter ends of the earth. The view was reciprocated by the nations external to Europe with regard to the dangers to peace which threatened that continent, and in many quarters there was a feeling that an international organization on a narrower basis would contain more promise of reality. It is significant that one of the earliest utterances in which a leading statesman advocated the idea of European Union strongly emphasized this side of the question. M. Herriot, then Prime Minister of France, made his first reference to the subject as early as October 1924, but in January 1925 he developed the thesis as follows: 'If I have devoted my energies . . . to the League of Nations, I have done so because in this great institution I have seen the first rough draft of the United States of Europe'. To him, even at this date, the desirable consummation was not world but European union; the League was but the means to this end.

It seems to have been in something of the same spirit, if less clearly avowed, that M. Briand, in September 1929, returned to the idea of European union. Professor Toynbee,[1] with his unfailing flair for historical analogies, paints indeed a picture of a Europe 'encircled and overshadowed by a ring of vaster States that had been called into existence by the radiation of European

[1] *Survey of International Affairs*, 1930, p. 133.

civilization into Asia and overseas', and suggests in this the principal reason for a desire for European coalition, a parallel to that which had inspired Machiavelli among the disunited city-States of Italy to project a somewhat similar union, or that which had created the Aetolian and Achaean Leagues among the communities of ancient Greece threatened by the growth of external Powers. Yet it is difficult to believe that this reason was operative, at any rate in the minds of practical statesmen, though it may have been to some extent in the more theoretic propaganda by means of which Count Coudenhove-Kalergi had long been labouring for a similar ideal. The reason for European Union in the eyes of M. Briand seems rather to have been one exactly contrary to this, the feeling, not that the outside world loomed too near and formidable, but that it was inactive and remote. The danger threatening the peace of Europe was, to his mind, not external but from within. International co-operation, to yield a trustworthy security, must be restricted, he thought, to an area sufficiently narrow to appreciate the danger.

In the memorandum in which he developed his views and circulated them to the governments concerned on 17 May 1930, he therefore spoke of a need arising 'from the very conditions of security and well-being of nations whose geographical position already imposes on them in this part of the world a *real* solidarity'. It is further difficult to avoid the inference that he spoke primarily as a Frenchman, and thought, as indeed he was bound to think, above all of French peace and French security. It is true that he strongly emphasized that everything arrived at should be done 'within the framework of the League', but the nations outside Europe were relegated to a mere frame; the picture was a Europe in which France with her allies could exert a commanding influence. The League was indeed a useful card to play, since it enabled M. Briand to reject two awkward participants from his scheme—the U.S.S.R. and Turkey,[1] who were not at this time adherents of the Covenant. In the same spirit he championed the cause of 'absolute sovereignty and entire political independence', which one of his critics, the Netherlands, regarded as inconsistent with any true measure of European federation.

---

[1] Turkey was admitted to membership of the League on 18 July 1932.

In any case, that this suspicion of M. Briand's motives was widely entertained was apparent from the comments received from other European Governments. It is significant that, of the group in alliance with France, the member which was least unqualified in its approval was Belgium, who had always favoured the League as a check on French ascendancy (cf. p. 27). Her other allies, Poland and the States of the Little Entente, were the most enthusiastic supporters of the scheme. Italy, Germany, Bulgaria, and Hungary all advocated the inclusion of the U.S.S.R. and Turkey, and Austria also favoured a close connexion with extra-European Powers. Fear of French dominance was also apparent in the objections of Italy and Bulgaria to the proposed elected committee, and in the emphasis laid by Hungary on the principle of equality. Germany hinted that a new Europe must be based on equality of rights, security for *all*, and peaceful adjustment of natural vital needs, and Italy desired disarmament to precede security, while Hungary openly asserted the necessity of treaty revision as a preliminary.

The replies received from the third group of European States, the comparatively neutral, with whom may be associated Great Britain and the Irish Free State, were also on the whole critical. The sentiments now revealed, in the collection of Foreign Office documents published in 1946,[1] disclose a much more decided hostility to the plan than diplomatic politeness allowed expression at the time. To those who, like the representatives of Great Britain, could approach the proposal with genuine respect and sympathy for its author, but were able to examine it impartially, the principal objection was that the new organization might prove an embarrassing rival to the League of Nations, prejudicial to its work and prestige, or at best would tend uselessly to duplicate its activities. Majority opinion was also unfavourable to the subordination of the economic to the political problem, a point to which M. Briand had attached great importance. This point seemed to surprise and puzzle many of the critics, since M. Briand himself, when first broaching the subject before the Assembly of the League, on 5 September 1929, had stated the association would 'obviously' be primarily economic, and in the sketch of the field of collaboration which

[1] *Documents on British Foreign Policy, 1919–1939*, Series 2, vol. i, chap. 4.

he included in his final memorandum the topics selected seemed to confirm this view. The author of the scheme had, however, come finally to the opinion—natural and consistent for a Frenchman—that 'all chance of progress along the path of economic union was strictly dependent on the question of security'.[1] All the governments consulted expressed, however, agreement with the fundamental idea of the proposal, the need for closer co-operation, which was, indeed, too obvious to be disputed. The question was therefore entrusted for further study to a special Commission of the League, in whose hands it died a natural death. The principal result of the discussion was to bring out once again the main issues on which Europe was divided, the claim of France for security first, the claim of Germany for equality, and of all the discontented Powers for treaty revision. In the light of these, the groupings of Europe appeared no less sinister than before.

The Austro-German Customs Union

During the first discussion in the League Assembly on M. Briand's plan, the Austrian delegate had suggested that regional economic agreements might be a fruitful first step in the required direction. In view of what subsequently occurred this suggestion must be regarded as significant. As early as January 1931, during the second session of the Commission of Inquiry for European Union, the Austrian delegate, Dr Schober, appears to have followed up his idea by entering into discussions with Dr Curtius, the German Foreign Minister, with a view to negotiating an Austro-German customs union. The negotiations, which were conducted with great secrecy, were continued in Vienna in the beginning of March, and on 21 March the world was surprised by the announcement of the conclusion of an agreement for the establishment of such a union, the text of which was published on the 23rd.

This announcement at once aroused a storm of protest. Not only was the step interpreted as a prelude to a political Anschluss of the kind forbidden by the Peace Treaties, but, in the first Protocol for Austrian Reconstruction of October 1922, the Austrian Government had bound itself 'to abstain from any negotiations or from any economic or financial engagement

---

[1] *Documents on British Foreign Policy, 1919–1939*, Series 2, vol. i, chap. 4, p. 320.

calculated directly or indirectly to compromise Austrian independence', and not to 'violate her economic independence by granting to any State a special regime or exclusive advantages calculated to threaten this independence'. The secrecy with which the negotiations had been conducted enhanced the suspicions with which the transaction was immediately regarded.

France, Czechoslovakia, and Italy at once delivered an official protest, as signatories of the Reconstruction Protocol. Great Britain alone retained an attitude of reserve, and deprecated hurried decisions. Mr Arthur Henderson, however, on 25 March, joined in the expression of a hope that, before going further, the parties to the agreement would allow the Council of the League an opportunity of satisfying itself as to the legality of the step proposed. Germany nevertheless showed at first an obstinate and unfortunate reluctance to countenance even this modest precautionary measure. By the end of March, however, a more conciliatory speech by Herr Curtius had somewhat cleared the air, and on 17 April the Austrian Government agreed, in response to diplomatic pressure, to take no further steps pending the forthcoming meeting of the Council.

On 11 May the failure of the Credit-Anstalt (see p. 269) affected the situation by facilitating the exertion of financial pressure by France, which was thenceforth exercised on every opportunity, and by the end of August this pressure had effected its purpose. On 3 September Dr Schober announced the abandonment of the project. This rendered superfluous the decision sought by the Council of the League from the Permanent Court of International Justice as to the legality of the proposed customs union. This had no doubt been the purpose of the French manoeuvres, since the result of the appeal was in fact extremely doubtful. When, two days later, on 5 September, the Court announced its decision, it transpired that the illegality of the course proposed was only established by a narrow majority of eight votes to seven, a fact regarded by many Germans and Austrians as a moral victory for their policy. The incident, however, served to illustrate in a striking way the nervous state of contemporary Europe.

The Franco-Italian Naval Discussions

A further cause for European disquietude was provided by the developments of the naval problem which had been left unsolved in the negotiations resulting in the London Treaty of 22 April 1930. While the Italians claimed that the principle of naval parity had been conceded by France at Washington in 1921–2, this claim had always been repudiated by successive French Governments, and was, in fact, unfounded. M. Briand, indeed, had reluctantly agreed to parity in capital ships, in response to a cable from Mr Hughes to the effect that the recalcitrance of France in this matter would involve the failure of the Conference. But the French reservation in regard to other categories was explicitly and formally maintained.

The policy of Italy was now alternately provocative and conciliatory, a naturally disconcerting state of affairs. On 30 April 1930, the Italians announced the adoption of a competitive building programme, but on 9 May Signor Grandi declared the readiness of his country to resume negotiations. In the same month, however, Signor Mussolini unburdened himself of a series of highly menacing utterances, of which the most striking, delivered on 17 May, has already been quoted in the introductory chapter of this part (see p. 260). The next move was taken on 3 June, when Signor Grandi announced his leader's readiness to suspend the naval construction programme pending negotiations, if France would reciprocate in respect of her own contemplated building. The French response to this overture is open to a charge of rather sharp practice. After a considerable delay M. Briand announced on 7 July that no French keels would be laid down before 1 December, after the 'dispositions already taken'. On the 11th, however, it was revealed that these dispositions included all the new ships in the programme for the current year, so that the offer was in fact deprived of all practical effect. The negotiations, however, continued, with the active mediation of Great Britain and the United States, and in February 1931 Mr Henderson announced that an agreement had been reached in principle, which the author of the *Survey of International Affairs* describes as 'no more readily comprehensible to the lay mind than an astronomical or a theological treatise'. This being so, it is fortunate for the reader, though not for the parties or the world, that it is not necessary for him to master it, since by April it became clear that serious obstacles still impeded agreement, and the negotiations thereafter broke down.

The difficulty arose in connexion with the relative strengths of the parties in light cruisers and destroyers. Italy was prepared to accept the proposed arrangement on the understanding that a considerable proportion of the French margin of superiority, during the currency of the agreement, would be made up of over-age vessels. She was not, therefore, prepared to concur in an interpretation which would give France the right to increase her superiority by laying down tonnage which would be ready to take the place of over-age vessels as soon as the period covered by the agreement had come to an end. The French, on the other hand, laid stress on a provision of the agreement which stated that 'the tonnage of new construction *to be completed* shall not exceed the tonnage which is replaceable in this category before 31 December 1936', and argued, plausibly enough, that ships still under construction at the date prescribed did not fall within the scope of the agreement. Any other interpretation would, it was contended, concede to Italy the parity in this class which France had steadily contested. The misunderstanding, which appears to an outsider to have been perfectly genuine, was not so regarded in Italy, and the recriminations resulting in the press of both countries did not contribute to the restoration of harmonious relations.

Further Causes of European Unrest

Besides these special causes of international friction, and those due to the economic crisis of 1931, there was an outbreak of political disturbances, which in some cases seem to have had no direct connexion with the main stream of events. There was a critical recrudescence of the dispute between Denmark and Norway over the sovereignty of East Greenland, though this was never a threat to peace, and was eventually settled, in favour of Denmark, by a decision of the Permanent Court of International Justice in 1933. Into the complicated issues involved it is impossible to enter in a work of this kind. A revolution occurred in Spain, and something approaching it in Portugal, and in Cyprus there was a serious revolt of the Greek population, which was infected with the universally prevalent virus of self-determination. Malta also gave rise to difficulties in the same *annus terribilis*. The growth in power of the Nazi party in Germany, besides being a major cause of the prevailing uneasiness, had special repercussions upon German-Polish relations, which had temporarily improved as a result of the conclusion of a commercial agreement in 1930 between the two countries. Provocative speeches aroused suspicion, the state of tension in Danzig, which gave rise in April 1931 to the resignation of the Polish Commissioner-General, for a time promised to have serious developments, while the treatment of the German minority in Poland engaged the attention of the Council of the League at the beginning of the year. But the prevalence of disturbance and unrest was by no means confined to the European continent. In South America the revival of the Chaco dispute and its development into a state of war in everything but name occurred also in 1931, while the same year witnessed the resort to force by the Japanese in Manchuria. It was in such unpromising circumstances, when the weapons of war were already beginning to be issued from their armouries, that the Disarmament Conference assembled on 2 February 1932, four days after the guns had started booming in Shanghai and Chapei had been reduced to blazing ruins.

The Disarmament Conference, First Phase

Today, when armaments have once more played their part in a life-and-death struggle, space in a brief general history cannot usefully be devoted to recording in any detail the stillborn proposals of the nations which took part in the Conference. Looking back, we may well agree with Sir Alfred Zimmern that the fate of disarmament was sealed when once 'the enforcement by common action of international obligations' (Covenant, Article 8), not only ceased to be the main use contemplated for national armaments, but even to be a purpose for which any nation was prepared to use its weapons. With everyone left to provide his own security, as Sir Alfred Zimmern has pointed out, 'the discussion of the subject was bound to take place in a spirit not of co-operation but of competition', and 'to expect to arrive at an agreed Disarmament Treaty between fifty States, or between the Great Powers alone, upon a competitive basis of this kind was to expect to succeed in squaring the circle'.[1] The idea of an international force, with which the French were obsessed, apart from the practical difficulties of the project, was not likely to be sympathetically received by nations evincing a growing disinclination to run risks in discharge of their collective obligations. France, indeed, with characteristic logic, continued to link the consideration of disarmament under the auspices of the League with the purpose of arms as defined in the Covenant. The revised French plan, introduced by M. Paul-Boncour on 4 November, still concentrated on making collective security, at any rate to a limited extent, a reality. Its salient feature was a proposal to divide the world into three concentric circles, the outermost of which should comprise all the Powers represented at the Conference. These should undertake to consult together in the event of a breach or threat of a breach of the Kellogg Pact, to abstain from economic or financial relations with an aggressor, and not to recognize a *de facto* situation brought about by the violation of an international undertaking. The second circle was restricted to States members of the League, who were to concur in 'the effective and loyal application of Article 16 of the Covenant'. Finally, for an innermost ring, a special organization was proposed, involving more specific military and political arrangements. Of this plan it is enough at the present time to say that experience in the Abyssinian crisis was to show that the partial and temporary fulfilment of the outermost series of obligations was all that any nation in the world was really prepared to accept.

The British contribution was equally true to type. Great Britain, as represented by Sir John Simon, devoted attention less to the main problem than to a practical attempt to secure such partial limitations as might be acceptable to a non-co-operative and nationalistic world. Sir John's most novel idea was that of 'qualitative disarmament', i.e. the prohibition of weapons which might be regarded as specially aggressive. This proposal was sympathetically received, but broke down, on examination, owing to the inability of the experts to agree on the dividing line between offence and defence. For example, in the British view submarines were essentially aggressive, while

[1] Zimmern, Sir A. *The League of Nations and the Rule of Law.* London, Macmillan, 1936, p. 331.

many nations regarded them as the mainstay of their naval defence. Someone pithily observed that the category to which a weapon could be assigned depended upon the end of it at which one was standing.

On 22 June the President of the United States made one of his periodical contributions to the controversies of Europe by suggesting a plan of his own to a specially summoned meeting of the General Commission. This had the salient characteristics of the American attitude in the matter of naval disarmament, that is to say, it was a simple affair of mathematical proportion which paid but little attention to obstacles of a practical nature. These were described as 'brush' to be cut through. The general idea was to preserve the existing relations of the different national forces, and to cut down the arms of the world, over and above the force needed for internal police duties, by nearly one-third. Though Mr Hoover allowed for 'necessary corrections for Powers having colonial possessions', it may be doubted whether the factor of function was not, as in the previous discussions over the naval treaty, unduly ignored. A small force organized on the British system, under which nearly half the army is strung out in minute garrisons all over the world, while the home forces serve not only for purposes of defence but supply the reliefs for the remainder, is manifestly not comparable with large continental armies: it already represents a practically irreducible minimum, and its aggressive strength is negligible. Similarly, the existing ratios between different countries represent a widely varying capacity for aggression; in some instances, the forces already constitute a minimum defence component, while in others they seem far too large. To reduce all by the same percentage is therefore unscientific. In fact, pure relativity and mathematical subtraction afford far too simple an approach to a highly complex problem. Thus, while the intervention of the American President was politely received, and Italy announced at once her acceptance of the proposals, it did not constitute an important practical advance.

From the first, however, the most insurmountable obstacle to progress was due to the German attitude. As was natural for a nation already disarmed, Germany's concern was less with the extent to which other nations reduced their forces than with the disparity between their position and her own: her object, whether the level adopted were high or low, was to assert her claim to equality. Unless, therefore, the rest of the world was prepared to accept the conditions imposed upon the vanquished at Versailles, what Herr Brüning and his compatriots were demanding for themselves at the Conference was not disarmament at all but rearmament. In these circumstances, the connecting thread perceptible throughout the Conference was the conflict between the French demand for security as an essential preliminary, and the German claim of equality. But for France, who had been preoccupied with her own security even in the days when Germany lay prostrate and impotent, it was practically impossible to feel secure if once her former enemy was released from the bonds of the Peace Treaty.

Germany's insistence on the recognition of her claim to equality grew stronger after Herr Brüning's Cabinet was succeeded by Herr von Papen's 'Cabinet of Barons', in June 1932. On 16 September the German Government notified its withdrawal from the Conference, under existing conditions. Two days later the British Government published a statement of its views, which deprecated the raising of the question of German equality at this stage, and criticized the legal correctness of the interpretation placed by Germany upon the disarmament reference in the Treaty of Versailles and the connected correspondence (see p. 62, n.). It soon became evident, however, that progress was hopeless until this obstacle had been surmounted, and early in December a Five-Power Conference was arranged at Geneva (between France, Great Britain, Germany, Italy, and the United States) to search for an acceptable formula. After five days of intensive labour a declaration was signed on 11 December 1932, which recognized the German claim to 'equality of rights in a system which would provide security for all nations'. The slogans of Germany and France were thus combined in a single phrase, which each was prepared to accept subject to its own interpretation. But though Germany was induced for the moment to resume her seat at the Conference, no verbal ingenuity could touch the substance of the problem.

A student of the Conference cannot fail to be impressed by the small amount of use made of the Draft Convention which had been the sole result of the prolonged debates in the Preparatory Commission. Though formally it remained for some time the framework, in practice it was largely ignored. While it is sad to think of so much wasted effort, this was perhaps no worse fate than it deserved. It was in fact the barest of skeletons, and such decisions as it had managed to achieve were in most cases hedged about with more or less important reservations. But possibly the true reason why the approach to the task of the Conference was a fresh one was that the world of 1932 was no longer that in which the Preparatory Commission had wrestled with the problem. When the Conference terminated the first stage of its labours, on 20 July, by the adoption of a resolution intended, in the words of Sir John Simon, 'to gather such gains as there are, that they may not slip away again', these gains reduced themselves to one concrete decision banning chemical and bacteriological warfare, a matter which, as was trenchantly pointed out by M. Litvinov, had already been substantially agreed upon in the days of the Geneva Protocol. There were general expressions of disappointment, and the U.S.S.R. and Germany carried their disapproval to the length of voting against the resolution. Italy, with seven other States—Afghanistan, Albania, Austria, Bulgaria, China, Hungary, and Turkey—abstained from voting, and the suggestion that Italy might leave the Conference was made in an article in the Italian press, which described the League as 'a limited liability company under the control of England, France, and, indirectly, America'. Signor Mussolini simultaneously published an article eulogizing war, and declaring that Fascists did not believe in the possibility or the advantages of perpetual peace.

Resumption of the Conference—the MacDonald Plan

When the discussions of the General Committee were resumed on 2 February 1933, a new era in European relations had already begun, which was destined speedily to put an end to the last surviving hope of disarmament. On 30 January Adolf Hitler had become Chancellor of the German Reich. On 24 February the outlook for the Conference was made, if possible, gloomier, by Japan's notification of her intention to resign from the League (see p. 321), though her representatives continued to take part in the Conference. Progress had therefore been practically negligible, and a general atmosphere of hopelessness prevailed when, on 16 March, Mr Ramsay MacDonald arrived to make a further effort to inject life and reality into the proceedings. He brought with him as his contribution a new draft convention, which consisted in the main of a collection of all those proposals which had hitherto appeared to stand the best chance of acceptance. It had the advantage over its predecessors of suggesting for the first time definite, though provisional, figures of effectives. The convention was divided into five parts. The first, relating to security, merely provided for conference in the event of a breach or threatened breach of the Kellogg Pact, under conditions which placed the Great Powers in a position of special importance, since their agreement must be unanimous to give validity to a decision, whereas the other participants need only concur by a majority. This, of course, recognized the realities of the situation. Part II proposed the limitation of effectives in accordance with a table included, which set out the proposed numbers for each State as a basis for further discussion. It dealt with material on a qualitative basis, limiting the weight and calibre, though not the numbers, of certain weapons. The naval proposals endeavoured to extend the provisions of the Treaty of London to France and Italy, and to stabilize the situation pending the convening of a special conference in 1935. The numbers of fighting aeroplanes for each country were to be reduced within the period of the convention to specified limits, the complete abolition of military and naval aircraft, with the effective supervision of civil aviation, was recommended as an ultimate goal, and bombing from the air, with a reservation in favour of police purposes in outlying regions, was to be prohibited. Part IV banned chemical and bacteriological warfare, and the final part proposed a Permanent Disarmament Commission with wide powers of inspection and control. These were the main features of the British plan, which was stated to be in substitution, so far as concerned Germany, for the disarmament chapter of the Treaty of Versailles.

In the discussion of the MacDonald plan, which was temporarily interrupted by the negotiations over the Four-Power Pact (see p. 365), a deadlock was soon threatened by the

intransigence of Germany on the point of the proposed stan-
dardization of continental armies on a short-service system, for
the Germans had by this time completely changed their views
on the value of the long-service professional army imposed on
them by the Treaty of Versailles. This principle they now
wished to retain, and their efforts to do so constituted a complete bar to progress. The situation was further complicated,
on 11 May 1933, by the publication in the German press of an
article by Freiherr von Neurath, apparently expressing the
intention of Germany to rearm. This was countered by Lord
Hailsham, in the House of Lords, by a speech in which he
asserted that a refusal by Germany to participate further in the
Conference would leave her bound by the provisions of the
Versailles Treaty, and that any attempt to rearm would justify
the imposition of sanctions. In France, M. Paul-Boncour
echoed the same threat, in the event of German intransigence
leading to a break-down of the Conference. These words were
not without effect. On 13 May, indeed, Herr von Papen
increased the prevailing tension by a speech eulogizing war,
and exhorting German mothers to be prolific, in order that their
sons might perish in adequate numbers on the battle-field. But,
after a further appeal had been addressed to the nations of
Europe by President Roosevelt, the official declaration of policy
made by Herr Hitler on 17 May was unexpectedly conciliatory,
and cleared the air to a marked degree. Within a few days the
German obstructive attitude was abandoned, after which
relatively rapid progress was made with the non-committal
first reading of the draft convention. A favourable impression
was created by a further statement from the United States from
which it appeared that they were prepared to undertake to
refrain from action tending to defeat collective measures against
an aggressor if they agreed with the verdict of the Powers seeking to impose such sanctions. Differences of opinion were still
evident, however, and it was clear that the French requirements
for security were still far from satisfied. On 7 June the Mac-
Donald draft convention was accepted by the General Commission as a basis, and the Conference adjourned until the
autumn.

Germany Withdraws from the Conference

Mr Henderson thereupon proceeded upon a 'disarmament pilgrimage' to the principal European capitals, and independent negotiations were continued. From these it soon transpired that France was unprepared to reduce her forces until the system of control and supervision had been tested, or without adequate guarantees against German rearmament. The idea consequently grew in favour of dividing the period of the Disarmament Convention into two parts, during the first of which the system of supervision would be tested, and there would be limitation but no reduction of armaments on the part of the armed Powers. During the same period, the transformation of continental armies into a standardized short-service system would be carried out, which would involve the gradual growth of the Reichswehr to the figure permitted in the Convention, but there was to be no rearmament by the disarmed Powers. During the second period, the disarmament provisions of the Convention would be put into effect, on a basis of complete equality. When this proposal was laid before Germany, though it was never accepted, her Government was understood to be more concerned to acquire an immediate right to samples of weapons permitted by the Convention but forbidden by the Treaty of Versailles. On being asked, however, to define these 'samples', they delivered a reply which amounted in effect to a claim to substantial rearmament, and as such could not be admitted. As the day fixed for the reopening of the Conference approached, it was felt that agreement, though not reached, was more nearly in sight than at any other time, and no suspicion seems to have been entertained that what actually happened would occur.

On the morning of 14 October 1933, Sir John Simon explained to the Bureau of the Conference the proposals outlined above. They were received with general approbation, and even Freiherr von Rheinbaben, who was representing Germany in the absence of his superiors, gave no hint that any untoward happening was in the wind. It is, however, difficult to resist the conclusion that German policy had in fact been determined at a Cabinet held in Berlin on the previous day. The meeting of the Bureau ended about 12.30 p.m., and by 3 o'clock Mr

Henderson had been informed by telegram of Germany's withdrawal from the Conference. Notice of intention to resign from the League soon followed. Both decisions were announced in the midday papers in Berlin.

With these announcements, all hope that the Disarmament Conference could achieve any real measure of reduction or limitation really faded from the heart of the world. Efforts were thenceforth concentrated on salving anything possible from the wreck, and on preventing the further disaster of an unchecked competition in armaments. On 21 November, the General Commission adjourned, to make way for 'parallel and supplementary efforts'. Before this, Italy had intimated her opinion that the continuance of the Conference was a waste of time, and on 8 December the Fascist Grand Council resolved that 'the continued collaboration of Italy with the League of Nations shall be conditional upon the radical reform of the League in its constitution, organization, and objectives within the shortest possible time'. Any faint hope of repentance on the part of the German Government was speedily removed by the overwhelming support which its action received from the people, in a plebiscite held on 12 November. On 18 December Herr Hitler stated the terms on which he was prepared to resume negotiations. He demanded a conscript army of 300,000 men, which was to be permitted all categories of weapons forbidden under the Versailles Treaty but defined as 'defensive' by the Conference. Civil aviation must be free from supervision or restriction, though the principle of supervision was otherwise accepted. The 'para-military' formations—S.A., S.S., and Stahlhelm—were to be regarded as non-military and to be outside the scope of the Conference. Finally, the immediate return of the Saar territory (see pp. 28, 381) was demanded, as well as negotiation on the subject of the ownership of its coal-mines.

These conditions were uncompromisingly rejected by France on 1 January 1934, but Great Britain and Italy adopted a more realistic attitude. As was clearly pointed out by Comte de Broqueville in the Belgian Senate at a somewhat later date (6 March), Germany could in fact be prevented from rearming only by the adoption of steps which no Power was prepared to undertake. It was, therefore, idle to insist, as did the French, on the manifest fact that the unilateral abrogation of the disarmament clauses of Versailles was being condoned. The proposals of both Italy and Great Britain, therefore, which were simultaneously published at the end of January, accepted a large part of the German claim to rearmament; of the two, Great Britain showed most resistance to them, especially in the matter of aerial armament, where she sought to retain the Versailles restrictions for two years. The main difference between the two proposals was that Italy sought to do no more than stabilize armaments at existing levels, while Great Britain still desired to reach agreement in a convention involving the abandonment of certain classes of weapons. To meet the French demand for security, consultation was proposed between the signatories of the Convention, in the event of an alleged violation of its terms, and the 'inescapable duty' was emphasized of following up such consultation by the necessary action. These suggestions were badly received in France, between whom and Great Britain relations were becoming increasingly strained. To endeavour to bridge the gulf between the parties was now the main aim of British policy. Mr Eden departed on a circular tour of negotiation and explanation, which elicited, on 16 April, some modification of the original German demands,[1] and a Note from France, on 19 March, which brought the British Government squarely up against the problem of whether they were prepared to go further in the matter of guarantees. An inquiry was sent in reply, asking for information as to the nature of the guarantees thought essential. Meantime the situation was affected by the publication of the figures of the German Budget, showing large increases in military expenditure. In the light of these figures, the French Government now made it clear that no guarantees which could be offered would induce them to agree to any immediate measure of German rearmament.

---

[1] In particular, Herr Hitler was ready to accept regulations ensuring the non-military character of the S.A. and S.S. These bodies should possess no arms, nor be trained in their use; they should not be concentrated in military camps, take part in field exercises, or be commanded or instructed by regular officers. It is significant that Captain Röhm, the commander of the S.A., made on 18 April, a speech strongly insisting on the importance of that force, and threatening 'ruthlessly to get rid of' men in official positions who were blind to the socialist side of the Nazi revolution (see p. 379).

The reassembly of the General Committee of the Conference, on 29 May 1934, took place, therefore, in a somewhat hopeless atmosphere. The debate revealed considerable tension, but, at the eleventh hour, a compromise was reached which preserved the Conference in a state of suspended animation. It allotted to committees the further investigation of four questions—regional security pacts, guarantees of execution, air forces, and the manufacture and trade in arms, and recommended the further study, by governments, of a proposal of the U.S.S.R. transforming the Conference into a permanent peace organization of a wholly different character, in which the consideration of disarmament should be postponed to security. But it could hardly be denied that there was a great element of truth in M. Litvinov's criticism, made in putting forward this last suggestion, to the effect that there was a complete lack of agreement on any single concrete proposal, and even on a general formula. In the words of an article in the *Bulletin of International News*,[1]

all hope of disarmament had vanished, that of limitation of armaments had grown tarnished and faded, and the fear of general rearmament and its possible ghastly results had become a threat and a nightmare before the mind of the world.

[1] 2 June 1934.

XXI

EUROPE—THE RESURGENCE OF GERMANY

The Mystery of Hitler

EUROPEAN history, and to some extent that of the entire world, was dominated during most of the period with which the final part of this volume deals, by one fact—the revival of German power under the dictatorship of Adolf Hitler. That Germany could not and ought not to be expected permanently to acquiesce in the conditions imposed on her by the Treaty of Versailles, but must inevitably recover the status of one of the Great Powers of Europe, had, indeed, been generally recognized from the first, even by the French, in spite of their desperate and frequently misguided efforts to postpone the hour of her recovery. But that this recovery should take place under the aegis of National Socialism, and thus restore, in a tenfold accentuated form, the dangers which the world from 1914 to 1918 had fought to remove, came as a sudden and complete surprise to the most competent observers of the international situation. As recently as 1929 Lord D'Abernon, the former British ambassador in Berlin, published the first two volumes of his work, *An Ambassador of Peace*. In this book the only reference to Hitler is a footnote on pp. 51–2, which, after mentioning his arrest and condemnation for participation in the Bavarian rising of 1923, continues thus: 'He was finally released after six months and bound over for the rest of his sentence, thereafter fading into oblivion.' Even later, in December 1932, Professor Toynbee expressed the opinion that 'many things might be obscure, but the one thing you could count on was that the Nazis were on the down-grade'.[1] Forecasts from Germany itself were equally mistaken. Dr Arnold Wolfers, then Director of Studies at the Hochschule für Politik, in an address delivered to the Royal Institute of International Affairs in November 1929, which described in detail the German political parties, never mentioned the name of Hitler, and in a subsequent lecture before the same body in

---

[1] Quoted in *International Affairs*, May 1934, p. 343.

October 1932, after referring to the successes of the Nazi Party in the elections of 1930, and to the consequent 'astonishment, not only of the Germans, but of the whole world', he predicted that 'the threat of dictatorship by one party has, I think, been taken from Germany'.[1] Yet in January 1933 Herr Hitler became Chancellor of the German Reich.

Looking back with the accumulated evidence and experience of the last twelve years of the Führer's career, we are bound to feel some surprise at the incorrectness of contemporary estimates of his capabilities. Superficially, no doubt, if there was any substantial truth in the likeness drawn by those who had the best opportunities of studying his personality, Hitler was the last person whom we should expect to find installed as the accepted and highly successful ruler of a great, intelligent, and cultured people. He was uniformly presented to us as an Austrian of insignificant or ludicrous appearance, a consistent failure in early life, temperamental, emotional, and irresolute, superficially educated and charged with no single new or original idea. But obviously, in the light of what he achieved, and still more of what he came within an ace of achieving, Hitler must have been possessed of many of the qualities of statesmanship, and still more of leadership, to a wholly exceptional degree. If we may ignore his complete lack of the scruples of honesty or humanity, and overlook the few but fatal mistakes which he made, as errors of judgement from which even the wisest are not immune, we can hardly deny to him the attribute of real genius, even if that genius was diabolical rather than divine. No-one without a considerable element of real greatness could have secured the unquestioning obedience and loyalty of soldiers and politicians whose intelligence could hardly be called in question, and his power over the German masses is even less open to dispute.

His lack of originality may perhaps be conceded, but this was by no means necessarily a handicap. There was truth in his own observation that a great theorist is seldom a great leader, and that 'the gift of forming ideas has nothing at all to do with capacity for leadership'.[2] Certainly, the success in Germany of the doctrines on which National Socialism was based was

---

[1] *International Affairs*, January 1930, p. 23, and November 1932, pp. 763, 769.
[2] *Mein Kampf*, p. 650.

assisted by their conspicuous lack of novelty. They corresponded exactly to the long-felt desires and 'wishful thinking' of the German people. The Aryan myth and the Pan-Germanism which flowed from it, together with the quasi-deification of the State on which Nazi power was built, had their roots in the primitive tribal instincts of a remote past, and were culled by the Führer, probably at second or third hand, from the teachings of a long line of German writers and philosophers. Vulnerable as they were to rational attack, they were all too readily acceptable as a religion. The mentality which accepts them has been exemplified at all times when Germany has felt strong and united.

The vague and undefined schemes of Teutonic expansion are but the expression of the deeply rooted feeling that Germany has by the strength and purity of her national purpose, the fervour of her patriotism, . . . the successful pursuit of every branch of public and scientific activity and the elevated character of her philosophy, art, and ethics, established for herself the right to assert the primacy of German national ideals. And as it is an axiom of her political faith that right, in order that it may prevail, must be backed by force, the transition is easy to the belief that the 'good German sword', which plays so large a part in patriotic speech, is there to solve any difficulties that may be in the way of establishing the reign of those ideals in a Germanized world.

So wrote Sir Eyre Crowe more than thirty years ago, in a memorandum [1] the whole of which convincingly demonstrates how little the attitude of Hitlerian Germany is a new phenomenon. When, however, as in Nazi Germany, a Government deliberately exploits these aberrations of national patriotism, and elevates them to the status of an official creed, to criticize which is blasphemy, there arises an obvious danger to the peace of the world. In particular, it is clear that the ideal of peaceful international co-operation, embodied in the League of Nations, was flatly incompatible with that of the world-hegemony of a chosen race—the avowed aim of Hitlerism.[2]

This, however, while it explains the ready and general

[1] Gooch, G. P., and H. Temperley. *British Documents on the Origins of the War.* London, H.M.S.O., 1926–38, vol. iii, p. 397. Also obtainable as a pamphlet issued by 'Friends of Europe', No. 16.

[2] Cf. *Mein Kampf*, p. 438: 'das siegreiche Schwert eines die Welt in den Dienst einer höheren Kultur nehmenden Herrenvolkes.'

acceptance of the principles of *Mein Kampf*, once its author had attained to power, does not altogether provide a reason for this sudden and unexpected achievement. Professor Toynbee has recorded how, as shortly before the Nazi triumph as November 1932, 'his eye fell, at every street corner, upon dejected-looking young men, in brown shirts, rattling money-boxes timidly, and without response, in the faces of unheeding passers-by'.[1] It is dangerously inaccurate and superficial to adopt the theory, which long enjoyed some popularity in this country, that Hitler could simply be explained as a product of the injustices, whether alleged or actual, of the Versailles Treaty, and that consequently the menace of his regime might be expected to disappear with the removal of its legitimate grievances. The theory utterly fails to account for the suddenness of his success, after years of futile fulminations against the 'Diktat' of Versailles had left him still despised and discredited. The rise in the number of his supporters was more immediately connected, as has been elsewhere suggested (see p. 285), with the disappointment associated with the economic crisis, and the introduction of undemocratic methods of government which it forced upon his immediate predecessors in office. But the final triumph is not, even so, fully and satisfactorily explained. It is really attributable to a quality characteristic of statesmanship which Herr Hitler undoubtedly possessed—an apparently intuitive capacity for the accurate computation of risks, and an uncanny perception of the psychological moment for instantaneous and ruthless action.

The general election of November 1932 had shown a marked decrease in the Nazi vote since the previous July, and when, on 30 January 1933, Herr Hitler became Chancellor, his appointment was a political manoeuvre engineered by Herr von Papen. The idea was either to tame him by running him in the double harness of a coalition, or to discredit him by entrusting him with responsibility divested of power. His party only held 196 seats in a Reichstag of 584, and, even including the Nationalists with whom he was temporarily allied, could not achieve a majority. But, having attained to power, the Nazi leader was quite determined not to leave go. The first steps were at once taken by Hitler's Lieutenant, Captain Göring, who made sure

[1] *Survey of International Affairs*, 1933, p. 143.

of the police and the provincial officials in Prussia. Something further seemed to be needed to ensure the requisite success of the elections which had been timed for 5 March 1933, and mysterious warnings were soon current of some remarkable occurrence in the days immediately preceding this event.[1] These turned out to be well founded, or at least destined to be confirmed by a remarkable coincidence. On 27 February at 10 p.m., the Reichstag building was seen to be on fire. It is fair to point out that the incendiarism was, according to his own confession, the act of an apparently half-demented Dutchman, who professed Communist tenets, but it is none the less true that by 2 a.m. in the same night a special edict 'for the protection of the Reich against the Communist danger' was issued in printed form,[2] the drastic provisions of which were put into force so promptly that in the course of the next day all the Communist deputies in the Reichstag were under lock and key, in company with their political confrères in the Prussian Landtag. Within the next few days hundreds of leading 'Marxists', including Social-Democrats as well as Communists, had been arrested throughout the country. The Reichstag fire was evidently an event as disastrous to the Communists as it was opportune for the Nazis. In these circumstances, it is somewhat surprising that the victory of Hitler's supporters in the ensuing election was not even more sweeping than it was, for the moderate parties maintained their strength, and Nazis and Nationalists together could only muster a majority of 33 seats (Nazi 288, Nationalist 52, in a Reichstag of 647). This, however, was sufficient for its purpose, for on 23 March parliamentary government was terminated for four years by the passage of an Enabling Bill which secured for that period dictatorial powers to the Nazi party and its leader, while, by an even earlier date, power was centralized by the *Gleichschaltung*, under emergency decree, of the different provincial governments, and by 11 July the revolution had been completed by the suppression of some opposition parties and the quasi-voluntary liquidation of the rest. The revolting persecution and ejection of the Jews, which accompanied and followed

---

[1] See J. W. Wheeler-Bennett, 'The New Régime in Germany', in *International Affairs*, 1933, p. 315.

[2] Wheeler-Bennett, loc. cit.

these events, while it shocked the outside world, was the reverse of unpopular among 'Aryan' circles in Germany.

'Mein Kampf' and the Nazi Programme

In the official programme of the National Socialist party, adopted in 1920, the first three points express the aims of its external policy. They are the following:

1. The union of all people of German race by the right of self-determination in one Great-Germany.
2. The cancellation of the Peace Treaties of Versailles and St Germain.
3. The acquisition of further territory for the support of the people and the settlement of the surplus population.

These are also the broad lines of Herr Hitler's foreign policy as elaborated in *Mein Kampf*, though he goes further. Point 3 is localized in 'Russia and the border-States dependent on it', and the final objective is 'world-power or nothing', to which the preliminary expansion is only ancillary, since 'for world-power that size is needed which gives it at the present time its importance, and supplies life for its citizens'.[1] As to the Treaty of Versailles, the propaganda value of the grievance seemed, in Herr Hitler's mind, the essential point, and the use to be made of it was to kindle a desire for arms, not for defence or security, but to gratify hate.

What a use could be made of the Peace Treaty of Versailles! . . . How each one of these points could be branded into the brain and senses of this people, till at last in sixty million heads of men and women the common feeling of shame and hate became a single fiery sea of flame, from which furnace there issued a tempered will of steel, and a cry was wrung from it—'We will have arms again!' [2]

As to Point 1, there is a significant exception, where the fulfilment of the programme might stand in the way of a useful alliance. The South Tyrol is 'a special hobby-horse which the Jew in these times rides with extraordinary skill' (p. 707). Herr Hitler thus leaves the worst-treated of German minorities to its fate, with the comment that 'Jews and Hapsburg Legitimists

---

[1] *Mein Kampf*, p. 742.
[2] ibid., pp. 714–15. Note the alliterative slogan form of the cry, 'Wir wollen wieder Waffen!'

have the greatest interest in hindering a policy of alliance for Germany' (p. 709), and states that:

the winning back of the lost territories of a country is in the first place the question of winning back the political independence and power of the mother country. To make this possible, and to secure it through an adroit policy of alliance is the first task for a vigorous direction of our foreign policy.[1]

Herr Hitler sums up the foreign policy of *Mein Kampf* thus, in what he describes as a 'political testament':

Never allow the rise of two continental Powers in Europe. See in every attempt to organize a second military Power on the German frontier, even if it is only in the form of creating a State capable of military power, an attack upon Germany, and see in it not only the right but the duty, by all means, up to recourse to arms, to check the rise of such a state, or to smash it up again if it already exists.[2]

It is clear that such a policy is directly opposed, not only to the post-war system of the League of Nations, but to the pre-war system of a multiple balance of power. If, therefore, *Mein Kampf* represented the real aims and intentions of Herr Hitler, it became impossible to fit him into any scheme yet devised for the preservation of peace and order in Europe. Herein lay the crucial difficulty of the situation.

There existed, however a school of thought, especially in this country, which discounted *Mein Kampf* as the tacitly abandoned indiscretion of a period when its author was an irresponsible agitator, and which also regarded the programme of 1920 as an out-of-date vote-catching manifesto, which need no longer be taken very seriously. No one could deny that many of the Führer's later utterances were in irreconcilable conflict with the principles proclaimed in his book; the question, therefore, arose—which represented the true lines of German foreign policy under the Nazi regime? The fact that *Mein Kampf* continued to be circulated in Germany as the basis of the national *Weltanschauung* did not perhaps conclusively answer the question: all canonical scriptures are allowed, as time goes on, to be interpreted with considerable freedom, and it cannot be denied that history holds many examples of the

[1] ibid., p. 711. The same point is repeated on p. 688.
[2] ibid., p. 754.

moderating effects of practical responsibility upon the earlier programmes of agitators. As Tom Moore observed:

> Our Whigs, when in office a short year or two,
> By a *lusus naturae* all turn into Tories.

The difficulty of deciding between these two interpretations may be illustrated from the story of Germany's departure from the League and the Disarmament Conference, as given in a previous chapter (see pp. 353–4), though it will be found constantly recurring at later stages. Assuming the aims of German policy to be anything like those of *Mein Kampf* and the Nazi programme, it was obvious that they could not be realized by peaceful methods. Herr Hitler himself entertained no illusions upon this point.

> The oppressed lands [he said] are not to be brought back into the bosom of a common Reich by flaming protests, but by a sword strong to smite (*schlagkräftiges*). To forge this sword is the object of a people's government in its internal policy: to safeguard the work of forging it and to seek for partners in arms (*Waffengenossen*) is the task of its foreign policy.[1]

This view was constantly repeated, e.g. on p. 708—'nur durch Waffengewalt', and p. 741—'nur die Gewalt eines siegreichen Schwertes'. On this assumption we should have expected *a priori* an early break-away from an institution so opposed to the use of lawless force as the League of Nations, and an attempt to wreck the Disarmament Conference, since only in conditions of unrestricted competition could Germany rearm to a point where her strength could be used effectively in power politics. At the same time, we should not anticipate that the mask would be completely discarded at first; on the contrary, an attempt would probably be made to throw the blame for these proceedings upon other shoulders.

The *Mein Kampf* school pointed out that this was the exact situation which resulted from Herr Hitler's policy in the first year of his regime. Its opponents appealed to the favourable and moderate offers made by the leader in the months which followed; and, assuming the correctness of their interpretation, and the sincerity of his offers, they were undoubtedly right to blame M. Barthou, and in a lesser degree the British Government,

[1] *Mein Kampf*, p. 689.

for failure to grasp a golden and never to be repeated opportunity. On the other hand, if the real Hitler stood revealed in his autobiography, it might be replied that the Führer knew that he had to deal with M. Barthou and the legalistic and suspicious mind of France; the refusal, therefore, may well have been expected, and, even if this expectation had been disappointed, it would not have been difficult to find a pretext for departing from these pledges, of the same kind as Herr Hitler used for such a purpose on many subsequent occasions. Anyhow, the situation actually produced was that which the author of *Mein Kampf* might be supposed to desire. In this connexion, a speech by Herr Hess, the Führer's deputy, delivered on 19 June 1938, is perhaps significant:

It had not [he said] been possible under the old democratic system to rearm secretly in defiance of the Treaty of Versailles, because pacifists . . . were always ready to reveal these designs to the world. After National Socialism had put these traitors in concentration camps, where they belonged, and with a National Socialist people behind him, the Führer had however dared to rearm, at first secretly and then openly, to restore conscription, to march into the Rhineland, and fortify the western frontier.

Hitler's real aims and policy are now, of course, no longer open to controversy. The evidence produced at the Nuremberg trial and elsewhere since the war has thrown a flood of light upon them, in which they stand clearly revealed. But at the stage with which we are here concerned, and indeed considerably later, the existence of two opposed interpretations of the Führer's intentions must be recorded as a historical fact, of enormous importance in its effects upon subsequent international policy.

Reactions in Europe

1. *The Four-Power Pact*

It was natural that the reappearance of a Germany supposed to be animated by the ideals of *Mein Kampf* and the Nazi programme should produce immediate reactions in Europe. The most important of these took the form of the surprising reorientation of Continental affiliations which marked the first two years of Herr Hitler's regime. At an even earlier stage, however, there was a striking indication that the effect which German resurgence was likely to have on the organization of Europe was quickly realized. On 18 March 1933, during an interlude in the Disarmament Conference, Signor Mussolini laid before Mr Ramsay MacDonald and Sir John Simon in Rome a new project which had for some time been germinating in his fertile brain. It may indeed be questioned whether the discussion which then took place had much more than a fortuitous connexion with the change of government in Germany. It was characteristic of the Duce to believe in drawing a very definite line between the class of Great Powers, in which Italy had established her hard-won status, and the common herd: as a Fascist, he had no real belief in such a principle as the equality of nations. The League, in his opinion, was paralysed for action by the necessity for unanimous agreement between over fifty member States: in the matter of disarmament, such agreement struck him as not only difficult of attainment, but superfluous. A trustworthy pact between the four Great European Powers, either in respect of the maintenance of peace or with regard to their armaments, was likely to be a more easily realized and at least an equally effective method of warding off the only sort of war which really threatened world civilization. This view he had put forward, in a speech at Turin, as early as October 1932, and so far it was probably shared in large measure by the other Powers in the same class.

But Italy was also convinced, particularly after the resurrection of a Germany under Nazi control, that the maintenance of peace depended on the revision of the Peace Treaties. Her advocacy of revision was genuinely founded, at this time, on a desire for peace—peace especially between France and Germany, a contest between whom would raise awkward problems of alliance. With this motive, the scope of the contemplated revision was narrowed; as involving an immediate risk of war, neither the grievances of Hungary, Austria, nor Bulgaria were really vital. The revision in Signor Mussolini's mind was primarily revision in the interests of Germany, and this in a particular direction, since the last thing that the Duce wanted was to concede the South Tyrol, or to bring Germany in contact with the Brenner Pass by an Anschluss with Austria. It is important to grasp this point, for it meant in practice that the real threat of the proposed policy was in the direction farthest removed from Italy, and therefore affected one nation only— Poland, in relation to the Corridor and to Polish Silesia.

It might seem that the required hegemony of the Great Powers was sufficiently maintained through the dominant position which such Powers occupied upon the Council of the League. But in regard to treaty revision at Poland's expense, a discussion in the Council had the obvious disadvantage that it would be conducted in the presence of the principal opponent, whose consent would be as essential as it would be unobtainable. Such seem to have been the leading ideas in the Duce's mind in proposing a pact between France, Germany, Italy, and Great Britain, which had 'as its general purpose, peace, and as its big and almost only detail the revision of treaties'.[1] Such a consultative body would have, in Signor Mussolini's view, the great advantage that on it France would be separated from her anti-revisionist allies, and confronted by two definitely re-visionist Powers, and would be dependent for support in her opposition on Great Britain alone, whose views on the subject were at best not whole-heartedly in favour of Poland. It might seem, in such circumstances, that the prospects of French con-currence in the plan were not bright—which was possibly why a separate approach was first made to British politicians—but France could hardly return a blunt 'No' to the proposal, thus risking a definitely hostile association between Italy and Germany.

If the aim of the Italian plan was international appease-ment, the reactions to his suggestion must have been dis-appointing to the inventor. It aroused an acute and immediate storm, the more bitter because authentic details of the scheme were at the time unobtainable, and a wide margin for specula-tion was therefore left open. The permanent Council of the Little Entente issued an outspoken protest, which was echoed in still plainer language by the press not only of these three countries but also of Poland and France. The British statesmen at once insisted that the proposals were wholly unacceptable in their original form, and M. Daladier, though unexpectedly calm and polite, raised similar objections on behalf of France. In these circumstances, the pact was emasculated in a way

[1] Mr Ramsay MacDonald, House of Commons, 23 March 1933.

which, if it rendered it harmless, deprived it of all real purpose
or significance; thus amended, it satisfied the objections of the
Little Entente, as well as of the proposed parties, who initialed
it on 6 June.

2. *Poland*

It seems certain, however, that the suspicions which this proposal had aroused in the mind of Poland, and which were not
completely allayed, played an important part in bringing
about the first of the reorientations to which reference has been
made. On 26 January 1934, the world was surprised by the
announcement of a pact between Poland and Germany,
wherein, for a period of ten years, the parties renounced the
use of force in the settlement of their differences. It was soon
evident that this agreement was taken seriously in Poland, in
spite of the fact that its terms merely limited in time the engagements already entered into by both nations as signatories of the
Kellogg Pact. This unexpected development led at first to a
suspicion, in some quarters, that a secret understanding had
been concluded, under which one party or both might be compensated for territorial modifications at the expense of neighbouring countries.[1] It is now possible, however, to form a less
sinister view of the probable forces at work. Up to the time of
Herr Hitler's assumption of power, Poland's two most probable
enemies—Germany and the Soviet Union—had been on the
same side continuously since the Treaty of Rapallo in 1922
(see pp. 95, 103). The territory occupied by post-war Poland
was mainly created out of the former possessions of Germany
and Russia, and a hostile combination of these two Powers
involved a danger that the whole country might be dissolved
into its original components. In these circumstances, the only
possible line for Polish policy was to cling to the French alliance,
and such security as the League of Nations might provide, however distasteful such dependence might be to the national pride.
With the appearance of a violently anti-Bolshevik Germany,
whose expansionist designs on 'Russia and the border-States'
were openly proclaimed, the situation was revolutionized, and

[1] This suspicion was temporarily revived in March 1938, when Poland presented an ultimatum to Lithuania. But it was evidently ill-founded.

the danger was of an entirely different character. Apart from the direct threat to Poland from German irredentism, it was clear that a clash between Germany and the U.S.S.R. involved the use of Polish territory as a battle-ground. On the other hand, it was now possible to play off one powerful and potentially hostile neighbour against the other, and the friendship of France, while it need not be wholly abandoned as a reinsurance, was of less vital importance, particularly since France was now much weaker than in the earlier post-war years. Since the expansionist aims of Germany could not all be pursued simultaneously, it was worth while to obtain, if possible, the temporary immunity promised by Polyphemus to Ulysses—of being the last to be eaten. Such an arrangement was also acceptable to Germany, as lessening the likelihood of a preventive war, for which she was still quite unready: though her ultimate aims were unattainable without aggression, she could make a beginning without it, since the return of the Saar into the German fold was more likely if she kept quiet, and the temporary reassurance of Poland left her hands free for the more promising task of fishing, with the bait of self-determination, in the troubled waters of the Danube. Poland was also relieved from some of her fears by Germany's retirement from the Council of the League, and, having already secured a similar understanding with her eastern neighbour, felt that the new agreement offered the best security obtainable for the moment, and that there was no harm in alarming France as to the safety of her alliance, an object which was certainly achieved by the publication of the pact. The misgivings aroused in France were, indeed, not without justification. Though it realized that the Corridor question was only 'in cold storage', and periodically emphasized the continued existence of the French alliance, public opinion in Poland soon began to show signs of becoming increasingly pro-German and anti-French, a tendency encouraged by local anti-Semitism and the character of the Polish Government. We may, in fact, trace from this date the inception of the Polish policy, soon to be professed, of the 'barrier of peace', i.e. of preferring the role of a neutral buffer State between Germany and Russia to the obligations of collective security under the Covenant of the League.

3. *The Little Entente*

The rise of Nazi Germany had a naturally weakening effect upon the solidarity of the Little Entente. This organization, as will be remembered, was primarily constituted as a barrier to Austro-Hungarian revisionism, in which alone all three partners had an equal interest. German expansion was a direct threat to Czechoslovakia only; to the other two partners the increase in German power might be to some extent welcome, as a balance to that of two potential enemies which they respectively had cause to dread. The question of Bessarabia left the Soviet Union a perpetual source of disquiet to Roumania, who could accordingly find some consolation in the thought that, in opposition to Russia, her interests and those of Germany now coincided. Yugoslavia had seen with alarm and hostility the extension of Italian influence in the Danube basin, and the intimately protective relations of Italy with Austria and Hungary. To her, therefore, a prospect of the extension of German influence to the Brenner was not altogether unwelcome. The three partners in the Entente, indeed, lost no opportunity of reiterating their solidarity, but these exaggerated protestations failed to carry conviction in the outside world. The common front seemed no longer to be based on a clear common interest.

4. *France*

Considerations based on the foregoing European realinements, together with the reorientation of Russian policy which is dealt with below, stimulated the French Foreign Minister, M. Barthou, to strenuous efforts towards strengthening the existing defences of his country and constructing fresh ones. The first part of his programme he endeavoured to put into effect by a series of visits to Warsaw, Prague, Bucharest, and Belgrade in the early summer of 1934. The second part took the form of a proposal for an Eastern Pact of Mutual Guarantee, on the lines of the Locarno agreements, which it was hoped would be followed by the conclusion of similar regional agreements in other parts of the Continent. The proposed parties to the Eastern Pact were Soviet Russia, the Baltic States, Poland, Czechoslovakia, and Germany, and it was an integral part of the scheme that the U.S.S.R. should accept and be admitted to membership of the League of Nations. Russia was also to be connected up with the existing Locarno treaties, in return for a French guarantee of the Russian frontiers.

M. Barthou may well have derived inspiration and encouragement from the fact that another, though less important, pact of mutual guarantee had recently come into existence. On 9 February 1934, a treaty was signed in Athens by the representatives of Greece, Yugoslavia, Roumania, and Turkey, under which the parties agreed mutually to guarantee their Balkan frontiers, to consult together on measures affecting their interests, not to embark on any political action towards a non-signatory Balkan country without previous discussion, and not to assume political obligations towards such countries without the general consent of the signatories. The effect of this Balkan Pact was definitely anti-revisionist at the expense of Bulgaria, which therefore refused to adhere, while the absence of Albania was probably to be explained as the result of Italian dissatisfaction with an arrangement calculated to impede revision, and in particular to preclude the realization of Bulgarian claims to which Italy was sympathetic. By thus leading Bulgaria to look elsewhere for support, the pact may be thought to have frustrated its main ostensible object, namely the liberation of south-eastern Europe from dependence upon any of the Great Powers.[1] Nevertheless, it was a case in being of the kind of regional agreement on which M. Barthou had set his heart.

The French project was favourably received by Great Britain and Italy, on the assumption of its strict mutuality, though both these nations refused to assume any fresh commitments of their own. It broke down, however, through the opposition of Poland and Germany. To Poland, temporarily reassured by her German agreement, it seemed to increase her obligations without materially adding to her security, and it seemed likely to

---

[1] At a later stage this main object became paramount. On 31 July 1938, an agreement was concluded between Bulgaria and the Balkan Entente which went far towards the inclusion of Bulgaria in the pact, and by releasing that country from the military restrictions of the Peace Treaty of Neuilly, demonstrated that it was no longer Bulgarian aggression which was feared in the Balkans. The fear of German domination had a similarly beneficial result in improving the relations between the Little Entente and Hungary, who entered into an agreement on 23 August 1938, renouncing force, while permitting the rearmament of Hungary.

involve the passage either of German or Russian troops across her territory, a prospect which she was determined to avert. Germany consistently refused, since the advent of Herr Hitler, to be a party to multilateral treaties of the kind proposed, while professing her willingness to enter into bilateral agreements on the Polish model. This attitude might be interpreted in different ways, according to the view held of Nazi foreign policy in general. Germany was probably quite right in mistrusting the alleged mutuality of the pact. It was not easy to imagine the U.S.S.R. or Czechoslovakia fighting on the side of a Nazi Germany. On the other hand, it was difficult to picture Germany as the victim of aggression from these quarters. Russia was preoccupied with her internal development, which required a long period of peace, and, so far as she still was likely to interfere with other countries, her weapon was subversive propaganda rather than armed force. Possessing already a territory of continental dimensions, she seemed to have no temptation to covet that of any other nation. As for the other proposed partners, their pacific intentions could not reasonably be questioned. The proposed pact might be compared to one between a wolf, some sheep, and a buffalo; the reluctance of the first to join might no doubt be explained by the fact that he could hardly derive any positive advantage from it, but, assuming that his carnivorous nature was unreformed, he would also clearly prefer bilateral pacts, which would depend merely on his own good faith, and would isolate one victim from another in the event of his deciding to break his promise.

M. Barthou thus found himself unable to realize his scheme for the defensive encirclement of Germany. In the later part of the year, indeed, he had a vision of an even more promising alternative, when the events in Austria which are recorded later (see p. 388) brought for a time into the anti-German camp the formidable strength of Italy. But this reorientation threatened seriously to strain the loyalty of one of the earlier allies of France—Yugoslavia. As a choice of evils, German hegemony in the Danubian region seemed preferable in the eyes of the Yugoslavs to that of France and Italy. It was to the problem of reconciling these discordant alliances that M. Barthou was devoting his attention in the autumn of 1934. On 9 October King Alexander of Yugoslavia landed at Marseilles, with the object of pursuing the required negotiations. He was met by M. Barthou, and a few minutes later both men had met their deaths at the hands of a Croatian assassin. This unexpected act of terrorism might easily have proved fatal to the peace of Europe. The passions which it aroused led to serious tension between Yugoslavia and both Hungary and Italy, both of which countries were credibly suspected of sheltering, if not encouraging, terrorist organizations of the type to which the criminal belonged. Fortunately the gravity of the danger was quickly realized. When the matter came before the League of Nations in December, any part played by Italy was, by common consent, kept out of the picture, while Hungary was induced, largely through the tactful handling of the dispute by Mr Eden, to accept a limited censure sufficient to appease Yugoslav sensibilities.

5. *The Soviet Union*

All that remained of M. Barthou's ambitious plans for the organization of Europe was the *rapprochement* between France and Soviet Russia. The change in the Russian attitude was perhaps the most surprising of the reorientations to which the rise of Nazi Germany gave occasion. In the early years after the war, ostracized and actively opposed by the victor Powers, the Soviet Government was naturally drawn towards Germany, in a friendship of which the first signs were seen in the Treaty of Rapallo in 1922. An estrangement from France was also the natural consequence of the alliance of that nation with Poland and with Roumania, both of whom were in possession of territory which exposed them to a risk, or fear, of Russian hostility. A further reason for tension between France and Russia lay in the large proportion of anti-revolutionary *émigrés* who had found asylum in the former country. During the discussions of the Preparatory Commission on Disarmament, and even in the earlier phases of the Conference itself, the policy of Germany and of the U.S.S.R. found common ground in the effort to bring about a substantial reduction in the armaments of the victor Powers; at this stage the French thesis, which postponed disarmament to security, met with the most outspoken criticism from the lips of the Russian delegation. Even more embittered had been the language and attitude of the Soviet Union towards the League of Nations, which it regarded as an abominable and dangerous alliance of the forces of world-capitalism. Yet so true it is that 'circumstances alter cases' that Russia was destined, soon after Herr Hitler's rise to power, to become for a time France's closest and most powerful ally, and not merely a member of the League, but the most eloquent advocate of its principles.

The change was attributable to three main factors, two of them new, and one a few years older. The two new factors were the threat of war from Japan and the rise of Herr Hitler. The risk of an attack in the Far East naturally suggested an effort to secure the western frontiers of Russia by pacific agreements with all her neighbours. In these circumstances, a series of treaties of neutrality and non-aggression were concluded by the U.S.S.R. in 1931 and 1932 with France, Poland, Estonia, Finland, and Latvia. The Bessarabian question still precluded, at this stage, a similar agreement with Roumania. These treaties had quite a different motive from the earlier series of pacts of neutrality and non-aggression, which the U.S.S.R. succeeded in negotiating between December 1925 and October 1927, since these were primarily intended to set up a rival system, centred upon Moscow, to counteract the influence of the Locarno Agreements. The easier obligation of neutrality was substituted for that of active assistance to the victim of aggression. The first treaty of this class to be concluded was signed by the representatives of the Soviet Union and Turkey on 17 December 1925. In the following year similar agreements were signed with Germany, Afghanistan, and Lithuania. Persia was included in the system in October 1927. The duration of the European treaties was for five, and of the Asiatic for three years.

A second stage was reached in the negotiations for adherence to the Litvinov Protocol of 1929 (see p. 183), which was mainly intended to forestall the efforts of Polish diplomacy by bringing the Baltic States to the acceptance of the Kellogg Pact under the aegis of the U.S.S.R. rather than that of Poland. The intention was partially frustrated when the Protocol was signed simultaneously by Poland, her Baltic neighbours, and Roumania. M. Litvinov's diplomacy achieved, however, a measure of success in obtaining the accession of these countries to his protocol. But even at this stage, as in the first, there was no real sign of willingness on the part of Russia to co-operate in the working of a European system.

It needed a threat from Europe to override the antipathies and suspicions dividing France and the League from the Soviet Union. So long as the danger of war came from Japan alone, pledges of neutrality and non-aggression might serve Russia's need. With the rise in Germany of the man who had publicly indicated Russia as a field for German expansion, there came a desire for active support. The new orientation of Soviet policy became apparent as early as May 1933, when M. Radek, in a series of articles in *Isvestia,* pronounced decisively against treaty revision, stating that:

> The way to revision of the predatory Versailles Peace leads through a new world war. Discussion of revision is the smoke-screen behind which Imperialism prepares the most terrible and ruthless war that the human brain can conceive.[1]

At this date, therefore, the Soviet Union was already ranged definitely in the anti-revisionist camp. The Russian desire for support was reciprocated in France. The direction in which her mind was turning was already perceptible during the debate in the French Chamber preceding the ratification of the treaty of 1932. In recommending the acceptance of the treaty, M. Herriot claimed that it—and by implication far more than it— was in line with traditional French policy:

> Remember how Francis I allied himself with Turkey not only in the face of, but actually against, the whole of Christendom, because this was what the interests of France required.

The relevance of this historical precedent was more close to a military alliance than to a mere declaration of neutrality. Both to France and to the U.S.S.R., the use of the arms of each in a common defence quickly became the undisguised aim of a closer *rapprochement.*

The final factor in the reorientation of the Soviet Union was the change in the attitude of her Government to the world-revolution, to which the establishment of Communism in Russia had originally been regarded as merely preliminary. This development may be said to date from the expulsion of

[1] *Bulletin of International News,* vol. 10, no. 4, 17 August 1933.

Trotsky and Zinoviev from the Central Committee of the Russian Communist Party in June 1927 (see p. 109). Trotsky and his associates had steadily maintained that Communism could only be permanently achieved on a world-wide basis, and had thus striven to foster and encourage revolution everywhere: Stalin, on the other hand, whose views became from this time triumphant, expressed belief in the possibility of developing a socialist State independently, within the vast boundaries of Russian territory. Which party was right need not concern us; there seem to be elements of truth on both sides: but the practical effect of a Stalinist policy concentrated on the huge task of internal development was doubly beneficial to the outside world; firstly, it reduced to insignificant proportions the danger of active interference in the internal affairs of other countries, and secondly, since prolonged peace was essential to the success of the policy, it ranged the Soviet Union, on grounds of self-interest, on the side of those countries which were concerned to prevent the outbreak of war in Europe. Thus, though the series of political trials which attracted attention to Russia during the last few years preceding the Second World War may be criticized from the standpoint of justice, and remain in many respects perplexing to the Western mind, in their international aspect they were regarded as welcome signs, since the offence of which most of their victims were accused was adherence to the creed of Trotsky.

The first stage in the realinement of the Soviet Union was reached in September 1934, when it was admitted to membership of the League of Nations, with a permanent seat on the Council, on the initiative of France, Great Britain, and Italy. The final consummation was reached by the conclusion of a treaty of mutual assistance between France and the U.S.S.R., with a supplementary treaty between the latter and Czechoslovakia, contingent for its operation on the active intervention of France in a case of aggression. The first of these treaties was signed on 2 May 1935, the second on the 16th of the same month. The French treaty was ratified by the Chamber of Deputies on 27 February 1936, and by the Senate on 12 March. Final exchange of ratifications took place on 27 March. These dates will be found in the sequel to be of considerable importance. Too much importance should not, however, be attached to these apparent indications of a change in Soviet policy. Experience acquired since the termination of the Second World War suggests that the improvement in the Russian attitude was more apparent than real. While, from the days of Lenin's New Economic Policy onwards, the political *tactics* of the Soviet Government have been variable and opportunist, their closest observers perceive and emphasize a remarkable consistency in the *strategy* which they have pursued in furtherance of their Marxian ideology. A whole generation of Russians has now been trained to accept as an unquestionable and immutable article of faith the view that the ultimate triumph of world Communism is inevitable, but that, owing to the resistance to be expected from the forces of capitalism, it will not be realized without armed conflict. The Russian mentality is peculiarly uncompromising, and temporary modifications of policy should be regarded rather as applications of the principle *reculer pour mieux sauter* than as evidence of any permanent change of heart.

XXII

NATIONAL SOCIALISM IN ACTION

The Party Purge of 30 June 1934

As a result of the vigilance which the arrival of Herr Hitler on the scene had aroused in all the countries of Europe, the Führer found himself, at the beginning of his second year of office, with no striking successes to show in the carrying out of his external programme. It was, indeed, unreasonable to expect anything better, until German rearmament was more advanced. The first morsel which was likely to be provided to satisfy German appetites was the recovery of the Saar, the fate of which was due to be decided by plebiscite, in accordance with the Treaty of Versailles, in the beginning of 1935. It would be very difficult for Herr Hitler to present the return of the Saar in the light of a resounding victory, seeing that, until the rise of the Nazi regime, this had been regarded as a foregone conclusion, and the excesses of National Socialism were the only elements in the situation which might affect the voting adversely. The Saar, in fact, while it would fall into Germany's mouth like a ripe plum if affairs were left to take their normal course, might possibly be lost by an exhibition of violence. It was necessary to remain quiet. Elsewhere, the prospects of immediate progress seemed little better. Herr Hitler's references to the Polish Pact, in a speech delivered on 30 January 1934, were met with a significant lack of applause, and his statement on the same occasion, that 'the German Reich has during this year endeavoured to cultivate its friendly relations with Russia', was not likely to be enthusiastically received by his old supporters. The same speech was the occasion for the first of a series of pledges, now of merely historical interest, in regard to Austria. The Anschluss was apparently to wait on the voluntary self-determination of the Austrian people.

The assertion that the German Reich intends to violate the Austrian State is absurd, and cannot be substantiated. . . . I must categorically deny the further assertion of the Austrian Government that an attack will be made on the Austrian State or is even being planned by the Reich.

The enforced postponement, in fact, of the external policy of National Socialism, in all its aspects, removed from the Nazi party most of the ground on which it was really united. The party was driven back to consider domestic aspects of its policy as to which considerably less unanimity prevailed. As the expectations of the National element were disappointed, those of the Socialist side began to be impatiently emphasized. A prominent supporter of the view of this left section of the party was Captain Röhm, Chief of Staff of the Nazi private army, the brown-clad S.A. or Sturm-Abteilungen. He was credited with contemplating a socialistic programme of a drastic kind, highly obnoxious to the Junker and industrial interests from whom at this time Herr Hitler derived essential support. The only successes which the Führer might hitherto be said to have achieved, the annihilation of internal opposition and the opening of a prospect of German rearmament, tended to deprive a 'private army' of its *raison d'être*. There were no domestic foes to defeat, and the defeat of external enemies was the function of professional soldiers. The old friends whose violent methods had sustained their leader in his long struggle for power were becoming as inconvenient as poor relations. The S.A. had in fact become something of a nuisance and even a menace to Herr Hitler, which may account for his willingness, expressed in his offer of 16 April, to deprive the force of its arms and forbid its participation in military exercises (see p. 355, n). Röhm, on the other hand, kept pressing for the wholesale incorporation of his storm-troopers, as units under their own officers, in the Reichswehr, and endeavoured to exalt the importance of the S.A. in every possible way. According to the official story, Captain Röhm and his associates are reported to have gone further, and to have entered into an intrigue with General von Schleicher and an unspecified representative of a foreign Power, the leading idea of which is declared to have been that Röhm should be appointed to the effective control of the regular army as well as of such 'patriotic associations' as the S.A., and that General von Schleicher should replace Herr von Papen in the Vice-Chancellorship. The arrest of Herr Hitler was asserted by the Führer himself to have been an integral part of the plot, which was said to be planned for four o'clock on the afternoon of 30 June.

All that is certain is that, the Brownshirts having been ordered a holiday for the whole of July, the alleged conspirators were scattered in places, and engaged in occupations, strangely inappropriate to their supposed design. In the early morning of 30 June, Röhm and a few other prominent leaders of the S.A. were asleep in a lake-side villa some distance from Munich; later in the same day, Karl Ernst, the Berlin leader, who had been recently married, was starting from Bremerhaven on a honeymoon trip to Majorca; General von Schleicher was rusticating with his wife in his home at Neubabelsberg, near Potsdam, some twenty miles from Berlin. There is more evidence of preparation on the other side. According to a statement made by General Göring, the Führer had given him orders some days previously to strike whenever he gave the word, and had entrusted him with summary powers for the purpose. The Reichswehr seems also to have received warning of the impending *coup*. At 2 a.m. in the morning of 30 June, Herr Hitler, accompanied by Dr Goebbels and two others, left Bonn by aeroplane for Munich, which they reached two hours later. Here they collected several cars filled with police, and drove to Wiessee, where Röhm and his companions were surprised in their beds and shot. Göring in Berlin, and Major Buch in Munich, were acting simultaneously. A large number of arrests were made in both places, and the victims—one at least of whom was a victim of mistaken identity—were put to death without trial. Ernst, caught as he was starting on his holiday, suffered the same fate, and both General von Schleicher and his wife were murdered in their home, at almost the exact moment at which, according to the official story, the S.A. revolt was timed to occur. 'In these twenty-four hours', said Herr Hitler, 'I was the supreme court of the nation in my own person.' In other words, personal enemies were disposed of at the sole will of the Dictator, without any pretence at a judicial inquiry.

His faithful henchman, Herr Hess, speaking on 8 July, compared what was done to the ancient Roman punishment by decimation. When the fate of the nation was at stake, the degree of guilt of the individual could not be too meticulously judged.

Severe though it might be, there was yet a deep significance in the old system of crushing mutinies by shooting every tenth soldier, without putting the smallest question about his guilt or innocence.[1]

The parallel is hardly an exact one, since the object of decimation was to limit the number of victims in a case where the guilt of the whole body was established, but it may be taken as a convincing admission of the lawless barbarism of the proceedings. The number of those done to death in this way was officially given as 77, but it is certain that the list was a much longer one, since the firing which was heard continued for a long time: an estimate of over 200 victims has been given, and is probably not much above the mark. A crowning touch of meanness was given to these revolting proceedings by the vilification of the deceased on moral grounds, since however vicious the private lives of some of them may have been, this was quite irrelevant to the issue on which they suffered.

The Saar

As indicated earlier in this chapter, under the Treaty of Versailles the ultimate fate of the Saar territory was to be determined in 1935, by a plebiscite of the inhabitants resident on 28 June 1919. Their vote was to decide between three alternatives, in respect of the whole or part of the territory:

(a) Maintenance of the Treaty regime.
(b) Return to Germany.
(c) Transfer to France.

The third alternative had never had any popular support, and, until the accession to power of the Nazi regime, it was generally felt that the decision would be in favour of the return of the whole territory to Germany by an overwhelming vote. Prior to 1933, however, the predominant parties in the Saar were the Catholic Centre, the Social Democrats, and the Communists, and though the members of the first seemed mostly to have joined the local Nazi organization known as the 'Deutsche Front', the two latter had organized a strenuous anti-Nazi propaganda. Since the ultimate attitude of the Catholic vote might be affected by Herr Hitler's relations with the Vatican, there seemed to be a certain risk that parts, at any rate, of

[1] *Bulletin of International News*, 19 July 1934.

the territory might decide to continue under the existing regime.

In these circumstances, the Nazi party embarked upon a campaign of threats and terrorism which gave rise to complaints not only on the part of anti-Nazi refugees and residents, but on that of the Chairman of the Commission, Mr Knox, in official reports and correspondence. In a letter published on 8 May Mr Knox expressed fears of a *coup de main* directed against the Commission, while his reports to the League referred to Nazi endeavours to set up a *de facto* government side by side with the local administration. The Nazis, in fact, regarded as traitors to Germany all who were prepared to oppose reunion with the Reich, and the danger of reprisals directed against such persons, whether voters or refugees of a later date, weighed heavily in inducing French opposition to a plebiscite which, it was maintained, would be 'une dérision du plébiscite qui serait en quelque sorte criminelle'.[1] The French Foreign Minister, in fact, conceived it his duty to assure the safety not only of voters but of refugees. In his speech on 25 May, above referred to, he mentioned a case where the Socialist leader in the Saar had been hanged in effigy, and added, to universal applause:

If I had delivered this man and the other inhabitants who are not voters to eventual and too certain reprisals, could I have presented myself before this Assembly (the Chamber), which I know is dominated by respect for rights and liberties of every kind?

The tension at the end of May was thus peculiarly acute, and there existed considerable fear that an incident might occur leading to a clash between France and Germany which might have far-reaching consequences. Great relief was accordingly occasioned by the announcement, on 2 June, of an agreement by which the French and German Governments bound themselves:[2]

1. To abstain from pressure or reprisals, and to prevent and punish any action by their nationals contrary to these undertakings.
2. To maintain for a transitional period, of one year from the establishment of the final regime, a supreme Tribunal,

---

[1] M. Barthou in the French Chamber, 25 May 1934.

[2] These undertakings only applied to those who had the right to vote, but all inhabitants of the Saar were to have the right to appeal to the League Council against any form of maltreatment.

to hear complaints of any such reprisals and to award appropriate reparation.

3. To refer any difference between them regarding the application of these undertakings to the Permanent Court of Arbitration.

The Council of the League, on 4 June, adopted the report embodying this agreement and reserved its right to extend to non-voters the protection it provided for the electorate. It also fixed the date of the plebiscite on 13 January 1935, and adopted provisions, outlined in the agreement, for the organization and conduct of the plebiscite. But the hopes that the conclusion of this agreement would lead to a discontinuance of Nazi interference in the affairs of the Saar were not fulfilled. On the contrary, during July and August the 'Deutsche Front' intensified its campaign on behalf of Germany, carried on a system of espionage, and maintained close relations with the Secret Police in Berlin. In these circumstances, the fears of France that the plebiscite might be affected by intimidation or coercion were by no means allayed, and in the latter days of October there were reports of French military preparations on the Saar border. To French military intervention, even in the interests of free voting and for the maintenance of order, Germany was, however, inexorably opposed. It was argued that this would be an act of aggression comparable to the invasion of the Ruhr, and a violation of the Locarno Treaty. On the other hand, the German Government showed at this stage a praiseworthy desire to maintain order, and to restrain the irresponsible enthusiasm of their supporters.

The difficulty of ensuring a satisfactory plebiscite was happily solved on 5 December, when Mr Eden, at a meeting of the League Council, offered to contribute British troops to an *ad hoc* international force, provided that other countries would make a similar contribution, and that both Germany and France accepted the proposal. The suggestion was enthusiastically received, and the necessary force was accordingly composed from detachments provided by Great Britain, Italy, the Netherlands, and Sweden. It reached the Saar on 22 December, and under its control the plebiscite passed off quietly on 13 January 1935. It resulted in a vote of over 90 per cent in favour of reunion with Germany, and with this not unexpected solution the question of the Saar passed from the scene of international controversy.

National Socialism in Danzig

Until the military power of Germany had had time to grow to formidable proportions, it was evident that the best chance of external success in the programme laid down for National Socialism was to be found in the encouragement of independent activity on the part of unredeemed German populations. This was soon in evidence wherever such populations existed, even in Denmark, in spite of the admirable forbearance shown in the Danish claims put forward after the war.[1] A place where such a policy promised exceptional opportunities was the Free City of Danzig, since there, so far from being a minority, the German element was numerically dominant. The pursuit of this policy was, however, a matter of some delicacy, from the time when Herr Hitler decided to postpone his settlement of accounts with Poland. While encouraging the capture of power by the local Nazis, he had not infrequently to restrain their exuberance for fear of international complications.

Such a complication threatened at a very early stage in Herr Hitler's career as Chancellor. The Poles had, within the area assigned to the Free City of Danzig, a munitions depot on the Westerplatte peninsula. By a decision of the League Council in December 1925, the guard which the Poles were entitled to maintain on this spot was limited to 88 men, though the number might be increased with the consent of the High Commissioner. An arrangement whereby the Danzig Senate had placed at the disposal of the Harbour Board a body of special police was revoked in February 1933, with the result that there was no longer any satisfactory guarantee for the protection of Polish property in the port. In these circumstances, on 6 March 1933, the Poles increased their guard to 200 men, without previous reference to the High Commissioner. There is no doubt that they thus placed themselves legally in the wrong. The matter came up for consideration before the League of Nations, but a conciliatory disposition was evinced on both sides, and the dispute was satisfactorily settled by the reinstatement of the

[1] See on this an interesting brochure by Nicolas Blaedel. *Er vor Sydgraense truet?* Copenhagen, 1935.

Harbour Police and the withdrawal of the Polish reinforcements.

At the time when this crisis first occurred, the strength of National Socialism in Danzig had not reached formidable proportions. In the early part of 1933 a coalition Government was in office, and the Danzig Volkstag only contained 13 Nazi members in a House of 72. In April, however, the Nazis forced a dissolution, and in the ensuing elections they contrived to obtain an absolute majority of 4, though they were still far short of the two-thirds majority requisite if the Constitution were to be amended. Under a National Socialist Government Danzig at once completely changed its appearance.

Anyone who revisited Danzig in the autumn of 1933 after a year's absence must have been bewildered by the change which it had undergone. The outward symbol of that change was the swastika flag which waved over every public building and hung out of innumerable private windows. . . . A stranger visiting Danzig for the first time from Germany could not have possibly known that he was not treading on German soil.[1]

It must be agreed that, in anticipation of the *rapprochement* between Germany and Poland, the relations between Poland and the Free City underwent a positive improvement, and negotiations relating to the apportionment of trade between Danzig and Gdynia led to a satisfactory agreement in September 1933. But the Government was practically controlled by a German *Gauleiter*, Herr Förster, who was not even a Danzig citizen, and discrimination against Jews and political opponents, combined with arbitrary arrests, led to complaints of unconstitutional action which came before the League of Nations as early as January 1934. The assurances given by Dr Rauschning, the new President of the Danzig Senate, were, however, satisfactory, and, though his unusual moderation led to his enforced resignation in the following November, a comparatively tranquil period followed. In February 1935, however, a new dissolution took place, since the Nazi rulers were anxious to exploit the success recently obtained in the Saar, and entertained hopes of gaining the coveted two-thirds majority which would entitle them to approach the amendment of the Constitution.

[1] Morrow, I. F. D. *The Peace Settlement in the German Polish Borderlands.* London, Oxford University Press for Royal Institute of International Affairs, 1936, p. 470.

But, in spite of acts of violence and intimidation, the result of the election was disappointing. Only 43 Nazi members were returned, and these numbers were reduced to 39 by proved charges of electoral irregularity. Herr Greiser, however, the Nazi President of the Senate, continued to behave in an intransigent manner, insulted the High Commissioner, Mr Sean Lester, and overrode the Constitution in various ways.

The financial straits to which his policy reduced the Free City also gave rise to trouble during the ensuing summer. In May the currency was devalued without previous consultation with the Polish authorities, who were aggrieved by the repercussions of this step on the competitive prosperity of Gdynia. On 18 July the Polish Finance Minister ordered that Polish imports through Danzig could be released from the customs only by Polish officials in Polish territory. In retaliation, Herr Greiser ordered the admission of foodstuffs and necessaries into Danzig from Germany duty-free, thus going far towards constituting a virtual customs union with Germany. But at this stage the desire not to prejudice German-Polish relations led Germany to exercise a mediating influence, as a result of which the crisis was settled by the cancellation of the obnoxious steps taken by each side.

The irregularities of the Nazi regime were, however, a recurrent item on the agenda of the Council of the League, and the Nazification of Danzig had by this time gone so far that parliamentary discussion in the Volkstag was reduced to a farce. 'In a parliamentary sitting, the Opposition parties' time allowance was: Social Democrat Party, 5 minutes: Centre Party, 4 minutes: German National, Polish and Communist Groups, each one minute.' [1]

There seemed to be a promise of some improvement when Herr Greiser appeared before the Council of the League in January 1936. At this time, while the League was still enforcing sanctions against a delinquent Great Power, the Council enjoyed a special prestige, and its firm handling of Herr Greiser brought about his temporary capitulation. The Senate agreed to modify certain legislative measures which had been declared unconstitutional, and this was done on 20 February. All went fairly well for some months, and Mr Lester, on being re-

[1] High Commissioner's Report for 1935.

appointed to the post of High Commissioner, was the recipient of courteously expressed congratulations from Herr Greiser.

In June, however, an abrupt change occurred. By this time the prestige of the League had sunk to zero. Italian aggression in Abyssinia had been crowned with success, the Emperor was in exile, and sanctions were about to be abandoned. Germany had reoccupied the Rhineland without interference, and was engaged in cementing close relations with Italy. Since these necessitated for the moment an abandonment of the Austrian Anschluss project, a display of minor aggressiveness elsewhere would be not only harmless but even timely. Accordingly, disturbances broke out in June 1936, one of which gave Herr Förster, the *Gauleiter*, occasion to announce publicly that he was responsible to no-one for his actions in Danzig, except to the Führer in Germany. Towards the end of the month a visit by the German cruiser, *Leipzig*, was made the occasion for a deliberate insult to the League's High Commissioner. July consequently saw Herr Greiser again in Geneva, where he delivered two intransigent and defiant speeches, and, on passing the press gallery on his way out, 'cocked a snook' and put out his tongue.

From this time forward the League appears to have abandoned the effort to exercise any effective control in Danzig. In September it withdrew Mr Lester from the High Commissionership, by the expedient of appointing him Deputy Secretary-General of the League. An undisguised campaign for the complete suppression of all opposition parties, accompanied by wholesale arrests, began in October, and continued unchecked. In January 1937 the Council adopted a report, drawn up by Poland, to whom the matter had been referred, which, in Professor Toynbee's words, 'meant in practice the renunciation by the League of Nations of its right to intervene on behalf of the Opposition in Danzig, whose fate was thereby finally sealed'.[1] It was therefore of less significance than it might otherwise have been that in May 1937 the Nazis at last succeeded in obtaining the coveted two-thirds majority, thanks to defections, under pressure, from the Social Democrat and Centre Parties, and the dissolution of the German National Party, whose members joined the ranks of the Nazis.

[1] *Survey of International Affairs*, 1936, p. 571.

Austria

At the beginning of 1934 there was perhaps some truth in
Herr Hitler's repudiation of an intention to absorb Austria by
direct aggression (see p. 378). For the Anschluss differed from
other Pan-German or expansionist projects in the Nazi programme, in that it presented an objective which might be
reached without the use of force. In the days immediately
following the Armistice of 1918 a wish for union with Germany
had been general in Austria, and, at any time previous to the
triumph of National Socialism, there would probably have been
a large majority of the Austrian people who favoured the
Anschluss. The proposal for an Austro-German customs union,
put forward in 1931 (see p. 342), had been opposed by France
and other nations mainly through fear that it would prove to
be a prelude to a voluntary political union between the sister
nations. Objections to an Austro-German union were indeed
very strong, and an attempt to bring it about might easily, it
was felt, lead to war; but, unlike other schemes for the aggrandizement of Germany, it did not necessarily put that country
into the position of an aggressor; on the contrary, it thrust upon
other nations the onus of preventing, in the last resort by forcible
measures, a union between the two peoples at the expressed
desire of both of them; in other words, resistance to such a
union gave the principle of the balance of power, which
the Peace Conference had ostensibly repudiated, precedence
over that of self-determination, on which the Treaties were
mainly based. The object in view might, moreover, be attained
by stages so gradual that opposition to each successive move
would be rendered difficult. To encourage, therefore, the
growth of National Socialism in Austria seemed the most promising line of approach to the realization of an important part
of Herr Hitler's political aims.

To do this necessitated, however, the overthrow of the existing Austrian Government, presided over by Dr Dollfuss, and
a constant stream of criticism directed to this end, and combined with collaboration with the Austrian Nazis, was poured
from Germany from the first moment when Herr Hitler
attained to power, firstly by the machinations of German
agents in Austria itself, and later, when these had been ejected,

in June 1933, through the use of the more elusive weapon of wireless broadcasting. On 17 February 1934, the dangers inherent in this situation were met by the publication of a joint declaration by the Governments of France, Great Britain, and Italy, stating that they took 'a common view of the necessity of maintaining Austria's independence and integrity in accordance with the relevant treaties'. A British *aide-mémoire*, published a few days earlier, further clarified the attitude of this country:

The integrity and independence of Austria are an object of British policy, and while His Majesty's Government have no intention whatever of interfering in the internal affairs of another country, they fully recognize the right of Austria to demand that there should be no interference with her internal affairs from any other quarter.[1]

Italy, at this time, aspired to a quasi-protective relation with both Austria and Hungary, and concluded with these countries, on 17 March, a treaty comprised in three protocols (the Rome Protocols), which had the effect of drawing the other parties still more intimately into the Italian orbit. Dr Dollfuss, the Austrian Chancellor, occupied at this time a somewhat precarious position, engaged as he was in a simultaneous domestic contest on two fronts, against Nazis and against Socialists. His situation, indeed, might have been untenable under a parliamentary regime, but the providential resignation of the President and Vice-Presidents of the National Council, almost exactly at the moment of the German elections which had consolidated the Nazi power, had enabled the Chancellor to dispense with parliamentary government, and to assume a position of virtual dictatorship. He was thus enabled to take energetic measures to suppress the terrorist activities of the Austrian Nazis, but he was handicapped by the fact that his principal supporters had Fascist leanings, which rendered them more concerned to repress Marxism than Nazism, with many of the ideals of which they were in obvious sympathy. His leading coadjutors, Prince Starhemberg and Major Fey, were leaders of the Heimwehr, an armed organization originally formed to combat Socialism, and, while Major Fey was induced to pronounce definitely against the Nazi party, Prince Star-

[1] Read by Sir John Simon to the House of Commons, 13 February 1934.

hemberg's objections to it were mainly confined to the personnel of its German leaders, while many of the rank and file of the Heimwehr were known to have Nazi proclivities. Dr Dollfuss was therefore forced to humour his supporters, and this led, on 12 February 1934, to extremely drastic action against the Austrian Socialists, who were provoked into armed resistance and then ruthlessly suppressed by the use of artillery, with a loss of many hundred lives. There are grounds for believing that this step was taken under pressure from Italy, or at least at her suggestion. This sanguinary policy probably tended still further to discredit the Government, and to provide the Nazis of Austria with many new recruits.

During the week beginning 22 July 1934, exceptional activity was observed among the Austrian Nazi legionaries quartered in Germany in and about Munich. Lorries loaded with armed Austrians passed every night towards the frontier and returned empty to Munich. On the 25th a large party of armed men broke into the Chancellery in Vienna and made temporary captives of the ministers there present. There was to have been a full cabinet meeting at the time, but, owing to a warning received, it had been postponed. The Chancellor, Dr Dollfuss, was separated from his colleagues and shot. Simultaneously, another group of Nazi conspirators entered the Vienna broadcasting station, and announced to the world the resignation of the Chancellor. This was probably intended as a signal for a general rising in other parts of the country, which indeed broke out in several places, especially in Styria and Carinthia, but order was restored in a few days after some heavy fighting. The rebels in the Chancellery, on being confronted with the forces of order, released their prisoners and were eventually promised permission to retire to Germany under a safe conduct to which the German Minister in Vienna seems to have been a party. It was subsequently contended, however, that this arrangement had been conditional on the avoidance of bloodshed, and this condition having been violated, the protection was withdrawn and the conspirators arrested. The German Government, too, repudiated the action of their Minister, and recalled him in disgrace for having entered into such an arrangement without authority from Berlin. A further result was the dismissal of Herr Habicht, the German 'inspector for

Austria', stationed in Munich, whose broadcast attacks upon the Dollfuss Government had been for a long time notorious. Except for the elimination of the Austrian Chancellor himself, the *coup* seemed to have failed, while the indignation universally aroused in other countries by the outrage was everywhere manifest. Signor Mussolini, indeed, went so far as immediately to move troops to the Austrian frontier, and he declared, in a message to Prince Starhemberg, which significantly referred to 'those involved from afar', that the independence of Austria would be defended by Italy even more strenuously than before. In these circumstances the correctness and moderation of the official German attitude are readily intelligible. The pronouncements of the Nazi press were, however, less guarded: several papers endeavoured to represent the *coup* as a natural explosion of the popular will, and 'a warning to all who think they can trample on the right of a people to determine its own destiny'.[1] Most striking was a statement issued on the day of the *coup* by the official *Deutsches Nachrichtenbüro*, and hurriedly withdrawn immediately afterwards. This represented the rising as 'a revolt of the whole people in Austria' against 'their gaolers, torturers and oppressors'. Imprudently assuming the success of the movement, it added, 'the triumph over the Government of Dollfuss is being hailed by Germanism. . . . The new Government will see to it that . . . Pan-Germanism is given a home also in German Austria'. The appearance of this statement may suggest a doubt whether the attitude of Germany would have been the same if the *coup* had been successful. If, however, as the evidence now available appears to render certain, Herr Hitler was responsible, the Austrian *putsch* of 1934 must be reckoned among his failures. Its only effect was to increase the strength of the European combination opposed to his designs. For the time being, though this reorientation was not destined to last for long, Italy was reconciled with France and ranged decisively in the anti-German camp.

[1] *Völkischer Beobachter*, 26 July 1934.

XXIII

ITALY AND ABYSSINIA

The Franco-Italian Agreements

THE first event of international importance in the year 1935 was an endeavour on the part of France to consolidate her newly won friendship with Italy. During practically the whole of the post-war period down to July 1934, a variety of causes had subjected Franco-Italian relations to considerable tension (see Chapter X), and the policy of Italy had been on the whole extremely sympathetic to Germany. M. Barthou had been succeeded as French Foreign Minister by a man whose character and personality were destined to exert so decisive an influence on the events recorded in this chapter that he merits a few words of introduction. M. Pierre Laval, the individual in question, has been pungently described by Lord Vansittart, who had first-rate opportunities of studying him at close quarters, as—in the category of 'rotters'—'one of the few in whom the microscope has revealed nothing but more teeming decomposition'.[1] Nature, in casting him for the role of a crook and a traitor, seemed to have overdone the make-up. In spite, however, of a reptilian countenance calculated to inspire the liveliest mistrust, M. Laval succeeded, over a number of years, in playing the part most competently. Lord Vansittart suggests that as early as 1935 he was already prepared to betray his country's interests both to Hitler and Mussolini.[2] But it is proposed here to give him the benefit of the doubt, and to interpret his actions on the hypothesis that his aims at this stage may have been those of a patriotic but narrow-minded Frenchman, though the means by which he sought to achieve them were completely unscrupulous and dishonest. M. Laval lost no time in attempting to exploit the favourable circumstances which had brought about the reorientation of so important a European Power. Immediately after the New Year he set out for Rome, where, in the course of three days, agreement was

---

[1] Vansittart, Lord. *Lessons of my Life.* London, Hutchinson, 1943, p. 45.
[2] ibid.

reached on a number of outstanding questions. A concession of further territory in Africa, considerable in extent though of small value, was made by France to Italy in supplementary and final redemption of her pledge in the Treaty of London, 1915 (see p. 162). Further compensations to Italy in Africa took the form of an arrangement for a transfer of some 2,500 shares in the French-owned Djibouti–Addis Ababa railway, through which the trade of Abyssinia was connected with the sea in French Somaliland. On the Tunisian issue (see p. 163), a settlement was arrived at whereby children born of Italian parents in that colony before 1945 should retain Italian nationality, and those born in the ensuing twenty years should have a right of option. After 1965 the French common law was to prevail.

In reference to the European situation, both parties agreed to act in concert in the event of a unilateral repudiation by any country of its armaments obligations, and recognized the principle that no such unilateral action was permissible. They reaffirmed the obligation to respect the independence and territorial integrity of other States, and recommended the conclusion of a convention for reciprocal non-intervention between Austria and other 'particularly interested States'. Superficially, it appeared that Italy had derived few advantages from this bargain. The willingness of France to co-operate in opposition to German interference with Austria seemed a foregone conclusion in any case, for which no payment was required; the Tunisian arrangements involved on the whole a relaxation of the claims previously made by Italy, and the territorial gains in Africa amounted to no more than a number of square miles of thinly populated desert. Having regard to the sequel, there can be little doubt that the aspect of the Franco-Italian settlement to which Signor Mussolini attached the greatest importance was that it would clear the way for a project, plans for which had been for some time in preparation—the conquest of Abyssinia. Hitherto, an Italian forward policy in this region would have been met by the jealous opposition of France, but, at the present juncture, as the very fact of the negotiations tended to prove, the situation arising from the resurgence of Germany made her inclined to subordinate all other interests to the paramount aim of organizing a common front against the European peril. In the Rome conversations Signor Mussolini obtained at least an assurance that the direct interests of France would not stand in the way of the establishment by Italy of a predominant economic influence in Abyssinia, and, though M. Laval was perhaps truthful in asserting that 'nothing in the Rome Agreements tampers with the sovereignty, independence, and territorial integrity of Ethiopia',[1] and in repudiating the charge that he had given *carte blanche* in advance to Italian aggression, the Duce appears to have concluded, rightly in the light of what followed, that if French interests were no bar to his plans, Ethiopian interests were not a matter in which France would be greatly concerned.

The First Repudiation of the Versailles Treaty

Meanwhile, Herr Hitler was realizing the advisability of some sensational stroke of policy to vindicate his claim to be the destined leader to bring his nation from the Egyptian bondage of the Peace Treaty into the Promised Land of German hegemony. Progress had so far been slow and unimpressive. The Anschluss seemed farther off than ever, and the main result of the Austrian *putsch* had been to turn a probable ally into an active opponent. It was true that the work of rearming Germany had already surreptitiously begun, but it seemed probable that it might be robbed of dramatic interest by the acquiescence of the other Powers, so long as it was not too defiantly advertised. From the conversations between France and Great Britain which took place in London at the beginning of February 1935, it was apparent that both Governments were prepared, conditionally, to abrogate the disarmament clauses of Versailles. The condition which France was most anxious to impose was the adherence of Germany to the system of mutual guarantee projected by M. Barthou, and this idea found expression in the communiqué issued at the conclusion of the London conversations, where it was coupled with a new proposal for an 'air Locarno', under which the Western Powers would mutually undertake to give the immediate assistance of their air forces to whichever of them might be the victim of unprovoked aerial aggression by another of the contracting parties.

[1] Speech in the French Senate, 26 March 1935.

These proposals were presented to Germany as an integral whole, since the point on which British opinion was most insistent was the attainment of a general settlement; in Germany, however, they were considered separately and met with different receptions. The air-pact, which, as General Göring later pointed out, implied the existence of the air force denied by the Peace Treaty to Germany, was decidedly welcomed; to refuse such a proposal would merely be to deprive Germany of the contingent benefits of an arrangement which the other parties were quite capable of concluding between themselves, but Germany maintained her objections to entering into multilateral pacts in eastern Europe. Still, the prospects seemed sufficiently favourable to warrant an invitation to Sir John Simon to visit Berlin on 7 March. Three days, however, before the date proposed, the British Government published a parliamentary paper relating to the question of defence.[1] This drew attention to the 'fact that Germany was . . . rearming openly on a large scale, despite the provisions of Part V of the Treaty of Versailles', and recognized 'that not only the forces but the spirit in which the population, and especially the youth of the country, are being organized lend colour to, and substantiate, the general feeling of insecurity which has already been incontestably generated'.

Whether in consequence of this outspoken publication, as was generally assumed at the time, or from other causes, Herr Hitler immediately developed 'a cold', which necessitated the postponement of the British visit until towards the end of the month. His recovery from this diplomatic ailment was further jeopardized by a decision of the French Cabinet, on 12 March, to make up the serious deficiency in available conscripts which faced them during the years 1935–9, owing to the fall in the French birth-rate during the Great War. This end they proposed to attain by doubling the period of service and reducing the age of enlistment. Though this would not result in an expansion of the French forces, but was merely designed to maintain them at the normal level of about 350,000 men, it supplied the Führer with a convenient pretext for a step which he may already have contemplated. It was by this time evident that the policy both of France and Great Britain contemplated,

[1] Cmd. 4827 of 1935.

as inevitable, an increase in the armed forces of Germany; it was therefore a safe conjecture that neither of them would proceed to extremities, however flagrantly Herr Hitler chose to repudiate his obligations under Part V of the Peace Treaty. In these circumstances, he was presented with the opportunity for a dramatic *coup*.

On Saturday, 9 March, foreign Governments were officially notified of the existence, in spite of the Treaty, of a German air force. This date is of importance as marking the first open repudiation by Germany of her treaty obligations, but the essential fact had for some time been common property, and the announcement, therefore, while it may have been intended as a *ballon d'essai*, fell comparatively flat. On the 13th Sir John Simon stated, in the House of Commons, that the postponed Anglo-German discussions would take place on the 25th, and that he and Mr Eden would leave for Berlin on the previous day. The next week-end was, however, more sensational. On 16 March the Government of the Reich published a decree reintroducing conscription in Germany, and placing the peace-strength of the German army at twelve corps and thirty-six divisions, or, as Herr Hitler subsequently paraphrased it, about 550,000 men. As a force of this size nearly doubled the figure which Herr Hitler had previously proposed as adequate, and was overwhelmingly in excess of the normal peace-strength of the French army in Europe, the announcement aroused general consternation. As the British Government hastened to point out in an official protest, it gravely impaired, if it did not finally destroy, the prospects of a 'general settlement freely negotiated', which had hitherto been the accepted objective of European diplomacy:

The attainment of a comprehensive agreement, which by common consent would take the place of treaty provisions, cannot be facilitated by putting forward, as a decision already arrived at, strengths for military effectives greatly exceeding any before suggested—strengths, moreover, which, if maintained unaltered, must make more difficult, if not impossible, the agreement of other Powers vitally concerned.[1]

The French and Italian Governments also protested, and the former lodged an immediate appeal with the Secretary-General

[1] Cmd. 4848 of 1935.

of the League. An extraordinary meeting of the League Council was summoned, to be preceded by a conference between the representatives of France, Great Britain, and Italy, at Stresa, on 11 April, to consider the attitude of these three Powers to the new situation.

The Stresa Conference and the Proceedings at Geneva

The visit of the British Ministers to Berlin took place, as arranged, on 25 March, but achieved little more than the disclosure of a stubborn and recalcitrant attitude on the part of Herr Hitler. It was followed by the visit of Mr Eden to Moscow, Warsaw, and Prague, and by the meeting of the Stresa Conference on 11 April. This was mainly an attempt to demonstrate a common front. The three Governments

regretfully recognized that the method of unilateral repudiation adopted by the German Government, at a moment when steps were being taken to promote a freely negotiated settlement of the question of armaments, had undermined public confidence in the security of a peaceful order.[1]

They reaffirmed their loyalty to the Locarno Treaty, and, recurring to the subject of Austria,

confirmed the Anglo-Franco-Italian declarations of the 17th February and the 27th September, 1934, in which the three Governments recognized that the necessity of maintaining the independence and integrity of Austria would continue to inspire their common policy.[2]

It was, perhaps, significant that Signor Mussolini issued on the morning of the Conference a warning to the Italian people not to expect too much from its deliberations. At this time his mind was already occupied with a project subversive of peace and fatal to collaboration, to which, by a conspiracy of silence, no allusion was made at the Conference by any of the parties.

The subsequent proceedings of the Council of the League, which deliberated at Geneva from 15–17 April, resulted in a declaration that:

[1] Cmd. 4880 of 1935.
[2] *League of Nations Official Journal*, May 1935, p. 551.

Germany has failed in the obligation which lies upon all the members of the international community to respect the under-taking which they have contracted,[1]

and in a hint that verbal reproof might be supplemented by positive action, if any further actions of the kind condemned were to take place.

In this connexion it was decided that repudation of the kind of which Germany had been judged guilty should, 'in the event of its having relation to undertakings concerning the security of peoples and the maintenance of peace *in Europe*', call into play appropriate measures, and a committee was requested

to propose for this purpose measures to render the Covenant more effective in the organization of collective security, and to define in particular the economic and financial measures which might be applied should, in the future, a State, whether a member of the League of Nations or not, endanger peace by the unilateral repudia-tion of its international obligations.[1]

The rather strange limitation to 'the security of peoples and the maintenance of peace *in Europe*' attracted some attention at the time, and more later. It was evidently deliberate, for an attempt by M. Litvinov to widen the scope of the resolution was keenly resisted, but it might be justified in that the aim was to devise a new sanction for something not expressly dealt with in the Covenant, and that in instituting fresh punitive legisla-tion it was advisable not to propose anything which might not command general approval. It seems clearly mistaken to read into the words a hidden reference to the Abyssinian situation, which, if it resulted in aggression, was already covered by Article 16.

Herr Hitler's Speech of 21 May 1935

Those who adopted the more favourable view of Herr Hitler's intentions and policy could at this stage cite in support of their thesis the reasonableness and moderation of his attitude as expressed in an important speech which he delivered on 21 May. It is important, in view of subsequent developments, to remember that this exhaustive and deliberate pronounce-ment on German foreign policy was uttered immediately after

---

[1] *League of Nations Official Journal*, May 1935, p. 551.

the signature of the French and Czechoslovak pacts with the
Soviet Union, which, indeed, it treated as a factor in the
situation, since it stated that:

as a result of *the military alliance between France and Russia*, an element
of legal insecurity has been brought into the Locarno Pact,

and accordingly—

the German Government would be specially grateful for an authentic
interpretation of the retrospective and future effects of *the Franco-
Russian military alliance* on the contractual obligations of the single
parties who signed the Locarno Pact.

It was therefore with a full recognition of this treaty as a *fait
accompli* that Herr Hitler, while justifying his unilateral repudiation of the imposed Treaty of Versailles, especially since, on his
interpretation, the understanding as to disarmament had been
previously broken by the other parties, gave an assurance that
he would faithfully observe international obligations voluntarily assumed, and in particular the Locarno Treaty, including
its provisions with regard to the demilitarized zone in the
Rhineland. On this subject he spoke as follows:

In particular they (the German Government) will uphold and
fulfil all obligations arising out of the Locarno Treaty so long as the
other partners on their side are ready to stand by that pact. In
respecting the demilitarized zone the German Government consider
their action as a contribution to the appeasement of Europe, which
contribution is of an unheard-of hardness for a sovereign State.

While this sentence may possibly now be interpreted as conceal-
ing a means of escape from the policy which it proclaimed, it
can hardly be regarded as an honest indication that the pledge
could not, in fact, be relied on.

Even more specific was the declaration made in the same
speech with regard to Austria:

Germany neither intends nor wishes to interfere in the internal
affairs of Austria, to annex Austria, or to conclude an Anschluss.

With regard to the rearmament of Germany, Herr Hitler
was equally modest and reassuring. He would in no circumstances depart from the scale announced, and was ready at any

time to limit the forces of Germany to any extent equally adopted by the other Powers. In the air, he claimed no more than parity with the Western European nations, and at sea he was willing to limit the German navy to 35 per cent of the British, and disclaimed any intention to approach naval rearmament in a competitive spirit. Finally, he protested against 'irresponsible propaganda', and urged the desirability of an international agreement to exclude external interference with the domestic affairs of any nation.

Strangely as some passages in this speech may read in the light of subsequent events, it produced at the time a satisfactory impression of pacific intentions and not unreasonable demands. Those, however, who doubted the sincerity of the speaker could point out that some reassurance to the troubled mind of Europe was urgently called for in the circumstances. The *fait accompli* of 16 March had resulted in a defensive consolidation of all the remaining Great Powers of Europe, for to the three participants at Stresa the Franco-Russian treaty had now linked the Soviet Union. In addition to this the League of Nations had been induced seriously to consider the planning of effective steps to prevent the repetition of such a *coup*. Nothing further could be gained by truculence, and existing gains might be jeopardized. The most Machiavellian statesman might be expected in these conditions to resort to fair words and specious promises, to lull the suspicions which had been aroused, while losing no opportunity of attempting to sow dissension in the ranks now arrayed against him. Proposals such as the Führer now put forward were calculated to bring into conflict the sceptical legalism of France and the British predilection for compromise; the widespread unpopularity of the Franco-Soviet Pact was a source of discord which might be profitably exploited, but the distinction drawn between armament by sea and land was also a promising instrument to serve the same purpose.

The Anglo-German Naval Agreement

The sincerity of Herr Hitler's offer in regard to naval armament seemed less open to question than that of any other part of his proposals. In *Mein Kampf* he shows a clear perception of the folly of following a 'Drang nach Osten' with an antagonized England in the rear:

Only with England was it possible, with the rear protected, to begin the new German advance. . . . No sacrifice should have been too great to win England's favour.[1]

Among the necessary sacrifices enumerated in the above passage he included the 'renunciation of a German navy'. Later on, with the revival of designs upon a colonial empire, this programme might be revised, but, so long as the objectives were expansion in the east and the destruction of French hegemony, Herr Hitler would be ready enough to reassure the misgivings of the predominant maritime Power. The British Government was therefore quite justified in believing that the naval part of the German offer was genuine and trustworthy.

True to the British spirit of compromise, they hastened to make sure of the half loaf obtainable. On 4 June negotiations were begun, and on the 18th an agreement was completed. The ratio of 35:100 which had been offered by Herr Hitler was adhered to in this document, though Germany also acquired the right to a submarine tonnage equal to the total in this category possessed by the entire British Commonwealth, so long as the arrangement as to total tonnage was not transgressed. There is no doubt that naval construction at least up to these limits would in any case have been undertaken, and had, indeed, already begun. As far back as 26 April the German Government had announced to Great Britain the construction of a number of submarines, in clear contravention of Article 191 of the Peace Treaty. As early as 8 July a German naval building programme was published, comprising two 26,000-ton battleships, two 10,000-ton cruisers, sixteen destroyers of 1,625 tons each, and twenty submarines, and there is good reason to believe that some progress had been made with this programme before 18 June. Considered in isolation, from the British point of view, there was everything to be said for the policy of imposing, while the opportunity was open, some agreed limit upon the naval rearmament of Germany. If the agreement had been concluded in collaboration with France and Italy, it would have been unobjectionable.[2]

None the less, what was done amounted to a condonation by Great Britain alone of a further breach of a treaty obligation.

[1] *Mein Kampf*, p. 154.
[2] This would, however, have been difficult, and might have proved impossible.

By England's action, the common diplomatic front agreed on at Stresa had been broken. Equally, what was done was a departure from the standpoint agreed on by France and Great Britain in February, that German release from the restrictions of Versailles should only be conceded as part of a general settlement. France and Italy showed clear signs of dissatisfaction. England appeared in their eyes too readily to have swallowed a bait artfully dangled before her by the German dictator. If the primary purpose of Herr Hitler's offer had been to shake the solidarity of the 'Stresa Front', it had certainly achieved its object.

The Italo-Abyssinian War

This solidarity was, however, much more seriously threatened by the Italian determination to engage in war with Abyssinia, which was by this time beginning to be generally apprehended. It is now known, thanks to the candid disclosures of Marshal Emilio de Bono,[1] that this determination had been irrevocably formed at least as far back as the autumn of 1933, and that from this point forward Italy had been working energetically, against time, to prepare for war by a date which would allow the affair to be settled no later than 1936. Much had to be done in a short time, but by entrusting the preparations and the command in the coming campaign to de Bono, a man already 67 years of age in 1933, the Duce ensured that everything possible would be done to avoid postponement of the date arranged. A year or two later the General would be too old to realize his cherished ambition of ending his military career with a high command on active service. It was originally contemplated that this planned act of aggression should be camouflaged either as intervention in an internal rebellion in Abyssinia, or what the Marshal suggestively calls a 'manoeuvred defence followed by a counter-offensive'.[2] Energetic efforts were therefore made from the first to subvert, by intrigue and bribery, the loyalty of the subordinate Ethiopian chiefs, a policy which, though it never got so far as to supply a pretext for intervention, proved of considerable value in the subsequent campaign.

[1] *La Preparazione e le Prime Operazioni*, English translation, Anno XIV.
[2] 'Difensiva manovrata seguita da controffensiva', ibid., p. 81.

The important thing to understand is this: that from the very outset of the campaign there were signs of the results of this disintegrating political action, and that it deprived our enemy of at least 200,000 men.[1]

The alternative pretext broke down through the refusal of the victim to be provoked into offensive action, and his disconcerting readiness to afford satisfaction for any 'incidents'. Hence, when the prearranged moment arrived, all attempt at disguise had to be abandoned.

From the plan of a manoeuvred defensive followed by a counter-offensive we were obliged to change over to the plan of an offensive action.[2]

The grounds of the Duce's decision, taken in 1933, immediately after the accession of Herr Hitler to power in Germany, may be assumed to have been approximately the following. Italy's need for expansion was a fundamental postulate of Fascist policy (cf. p. 162). Asia Minor having been ruled out, first by the Peace Conference and finally by the resurgence of Turkey, there remained two alternative possibilities—'pacific expansion towards the east' (see p. 164), converting the whole Danubian and Balkan region so far as possible into an Italian protectorate or sphere of influence, or the acquisition of increased colonial territory in Africa. In this region, however, whatever may have been Signor Mussolini's ultimate dreams of Mediterranean hegemony, there was only one piece of territory the acquisition of which did not involve direct collision with a rival European Power. This was the Empire of Ethiopia, a region where the temptation to a forward policy was peculiarly strong, firstly, because of its potential wealth and resources, but also because, by the Treaty of Ucciali in 1889, the Italians had once before believed themselves to have acquired a protectorate over it, until the denunciation of the treaty by Menelik in 1893, and the disastrous defeat at Adowa in 1896, temporarily destroyed these hopes, and left only a rankling and vindictive memory. But, although the other European Powers concerned, Great Britain and France, had

---

[1] ibid., Italian, p. 36; translation, p. 54.
[2] ibid., Italian, p. 81; translation, p. 119.

long recognized a wide sphere of Italian interest in the Ethiopian
Empire, until the European situation was modified by the
arrival of Herr Hitler any further possibilities of colonial
expansion here, as elsewhere in Africa, were liable to meet with
the opposition of France, if not of England. Both these Powers,
together with Italy, were in fact bound by the Tripartite
Agreement of 1906 to make every effort to preserve the integrity of Ethiopia. French opposition had therefore hitherto
barred the complete realization of either of the alternative
schemes for Italian expansion; in south-east Europe, through
the relations of France with the Little Entente, and in Africa,
because of competing French interests in all of the coveted
regions. In the event of Germany, under the new dispensation,
growing strong enough to pursue the declared plans of the
Führer, Italian predominance on the Danube was equally
barred, but these plans were at least equally prejudicial to
French interests, and it might in these circumstances be
possible to play upon the European fears of France sufficiently
to disinterest her in the fate of Abyssinia. Having regard to the
European situation, and the attitude hitherto adopted by the
League towards extra-European wars (e.g. the Manchurian
affair and the struggle between Bolivia and Paraguay), the
project of aggression against Abyssinia seemed to be a relatively
safe speculation.

It was true that, in the earlier post-war years, an endeavour
had been made to establish Italian influence in Abyssinia by
peaceful and co-operative methods; it was largely on the Italian
recommendation that Abyssinia had been admitted to membership of the League in 1923, against the inclination of Great
Britain; but the use which Abyssinia had made of her new status
was not encouraging from the Italian standpoint, since an
attempt in 1925 by Italy and Great Britain to apportion
Abyssinian spheres of influence without consulting the third
party affected had been met, and partially frustrated, by an
Ethiopian appeal to the League. In 1928 a final effort to secure
Italian interests by peaceful means took the form of an Italo-
Abyssinian treaty, by which, *inter alia*, the parties pledged
themselves not to take action detrimental to the independence
of each other, and to submit all disputes to conciliation and
arbitration, without resorting to armed force.

With the rise of the Nazi menace, however, it now appeared safe to pursue Italian ends by more vigorous and far-reaching action.

Though the unruliness of the border tribes had undoubtedly given constant trouble to all Abyssinia's neighbours, none of them had hitherto thought of making these periodical acts of irresponsible banditry an excuse for punitive action against the Empire, whose ruler, Ras Tafari, who succeeded as Haile Selassie I in November 1930, was an Ethiopian of exceptional enlightenment, and animated by a sincere spirit of reform. The first warning of serious trouble impending between Italy and Abyssinia occurred on 5 December 1934, when a clash occurred between some Italian and Abyssinian forces in the neighbourhood of Walwal, as a result of which 30 Italian native soldiers were killed and 100 wounded, while the casualties on the other side were considerably heavier. Having regard to what is now known of the Italian intentions, and to the fact that the subsequent decision of the Conciliation Commission (on 3 September 1925) exonerated both sides, the merits of the Walwal dispute are now a matter of minor importance. The Italians consistently refused to allow the discussion of the preliminary question—whether the attack took place in Italian or Abyssinian territory; though the frontier was undefined, there is a strong case for deciding that Walwal lay some sixty miles within the Ethiopian border. The area had, however, been under Italian control, not officially recognized by the Abyssinians, since 1928, and permanently occupied since 1930. It is impossible to be certain which side fired the first shot.

The Walwal incident was, however, the occasion whereby the Italo-Abyssinian crisis first came within the purview of the League. On 14 December the Italian Government had refused a proposal by the Abyssinians to refer the dispute to arbitration under the treaty of 1928, on the ground that the facts were indisputable, and on the same day the Ethiopian Government accordingly telegraphed to the Secretary-General of the League, informing him of the situation and alleging further Italian acts of aggression. But it was not until 3 January 1935, that they lodged a formal appeal to Article 11 of the Covenant.

From the point of view of the European Powers, and especi-

ally of France, this development could hardly have taken place
at a more inconvenient moment. It practically synchronized
with the visit of M. Laval to Rome, in an attempt to effect
a close and durable *rapprochement* with Italy (see p. 392). In
these circumstances, the Italian Government was persuaded to
accept the suggestion of settling the incident by arbitration
under the 1928 treaty, and the appeal was consequently withdrawn from the League agenda. In the following month, however, the military preparations of Italy were so formidably
apparent that from this date little doubt remained, in the mind
of anyone not troubled by diplomatic considerations, as to her
aggressive intentions. At the same time, the proposed arbitral
proceedings were brought to deadlock by a fundamental
divergence as to the scope of the inquiry, and on 17 March the
Abyssinian Government formally appealed to the League under
Article 15.

This date was once more a peculiarly unfortunate one, since
it coincided exactly with Herr Hitler's unilateral repudiation
of the disarmament provisions of Versailles (see p. 396).
Though, as early as February, the British Ambassador in Rome
had warned Signor Mussolini 'of the possible reactions of
Italian policy on British public opinion and on Anglo-Italian
relations',[1] it appeared at this stage regrettably tactless to hint
that the promising new recruit to the police force enrolled for the
control of Germany was contemplating an independent act of
gangsterism of his own. The League accordingly welcomed the
leisurely and obstructed progress of the negotiations for settlement, in spite of protests from the Ethiopians that these delays
were merely facilitating the perfection of Italian military
preparations.[2] The Stresa Conference (see p. 397) drew further
attention to the importance of consolidating the anti-German
front, and the Council, in its ensuing extraordinary session,
postponed consideration of the Italo-Abyssinian dispute till the
following month. On 25 May the Council left the settlement
of the dispute still in the hands of the two parties, with the
proviso that it would meet again to consider the matter if the

[1] Speech of Mr Eden, House of Commons, 23 October 1935.

[2] Marshal de Bono's book makes it clear that the necessary preparations
demanded every moment of the time available before the date prearranged, at the
conclusion of the rainy season, for the commencement of hostilities.

final arbitrator had not been selected by 25 July, or if the settlement had not been concluded by the same day of the following month.

The first contingency was duly brought about by the breakdown of the Commission on 9 July, but in the meantime the British Government had made an independent effort at mediation. On a visit to Rome in the latter part of June, Mr Eden suggested to the Duce the cession to Italy by Abyssinia of a portion of the Ogaden, in return for an outlet to the sea at Zeila in British Somaliland. In reporting his refusal to entertain this proposal to Marshal de Bono, Signor Mussolini wrote: 'You can imagine my reply. . . . The English attitude has helped instead of injuring. . . . You have then only 120 days in which to get ready.' 'Actually', records the Marshal, 'I had less.' [1]

The extraordinary meeting of the Council occasioned by the breakdown of the Commission took place on 31 July. It now succeeded in getting the Commission of Inquiry into the Walwal incident really going, with the result that, as already stated, a finding was returned on 3 September, exonerating both parties. It further decided to meet again on 4 September to undertake the general examination of Italo-Ethiopian relations, and in the meantime delegated the negotiations on the major issue to a Three-Power Conference, consisting of Italy, France, and Great Britain. This Conference resulted in the submission of further proposals for a compromise to Signor Mussolini, which were summarily rejected by him on 18 August, and on the 21st Marshal de Bono received this laconic message: 'Conferenza niente concluso; c'è Ginevra che concluderà lo stesso. Concludi.' [2] When the Council met again on 4 September, the aggressive intentions of Italy were apparent to all. From this date until the outbreak of hostilities on 3 October, the proceedings at Geneva were practically continuous. On 11 September the British Foreign Secretary, Sir Samuel Hoare, made his memorable declaration of the intention of his country to fulfil its obligations under the Covenant. With the proviso that:

---

[1] De Bono, op. cit., translation, pp. 170-1.
[2] 'Conference settled nothing; Geneva will settle the same. Settle it.' op. cit., p. 129. Cf. translation, p. 190.

If risks for peace are to be run, they must be run by all. The
security of the many cannot be assured solely by the efforts of a few,
however powerful they may be,

he proceeded:

In conformity with its precise and explicit obligations the League
stands, and my country stands with it, for the collective maintenance
of the Covenant in its entirety, and particularly for steady and
collective resistance to all acts of unprovoked aggression. The
attitude of the British nation in the last few weeks has clearly
demonstrated the fact that this is no variable and unreliable sentiment, but a principle of international conduct to which they and
their Government hold with firm, enduring and universal persistence.

The demonstration of the attitude of the British people here
referred to seems to be an allusion to an attempt to secure a
pronouncement of public opinion on the question of the League
and kindred matters, which had been organized, under the
somewhat question-begging name of the 'Peace Ballot', in the
latter part of 1934. In this the public was asked to record its
vote on the following questionnaire:

1. Should Great Britain remain a member of the League of
   Nations?
2. Are you in favour of an all-round reduction in armaments by
   international agreement?
3. Are you in favour of an all-round abolition of national military
   and naval aircraft by international agreement?
4. Should the manufacture and sale of armaments for private
   profit be prohibited by international agreement?
5. Do you consider that, if a nation insists on attacking another,
   the other nations should combine to compel it to stop by
   (a) Economic and non-military measures?
   (b) If necessary, military measures?

The implication in the title—that an affirmative vote was for
peace, and presumably a negative one for war—is perhaps
deserving of criticism, and all the questions except the first
postulated the existence of a degree of international agreement
and collaboration, the difficulty of ensuring which was in fact
the crux of the whole problem. Granted 'international agreement', and the combination of 'the other nations' on which
question 5 depended, British statesmen of all parties, whether

in 1935 or later, could with a clear conscience have returned an affirmative answer to every question except the fourth, which was more controversial and open to objection, but does not concern us here. The fifth question may be further criticized on the ground that it assumes the possibility of applying economic sanctions without an ultimate willingness to back them with force.[1]

On 27 June 1935, the results were announced. The total votes cast reached the impressive figure of 11,559,165. Over eleven million answered the first question affirmatively. Over ten million did the same for questions 2, 4, and 5 *a*, while the affirmative vote on No. 3 was not much lower. There was, however, a highly significant drop in the answers to 5 *b*, and those who approved military sanctions were only 6,784,368, though even this showed a striking majority over the negative vote of 2,351,981. Regarded, therefore, in the light of a mandate to the British Government, on a critical occasion, the voice of the plebiscite may fairly be said to have been: 'Go as far as you can, in combination with other members, to secure and observe loyalty to the Covenant, and to resist aggression; but do all you can to keep out of war, even in company with other member-States; and we give no support at all to military measures which will fall exclusively or preponderantly on British shoulders.' The policy subsequently followed by the British Government is exposed to criticism from a number of standpoints, especially from that of its intrinsic soundness as a way of dealing with the situation, but there is a good case for saying that it conformed closely to the above prescription. By treating the sanctions dealt with in question 5 as an open question independent of No. 1, the 'Peace Ballot' clearly drew a distinction, whether rightly or wrongly, between remaining a member of the League of Nations and remaining bound by the obligations of the Covenant. Its promoters are therefore estopped from relying on a breach of Article 10—an issue which they never laid before the public—or from insisting on

---

[1] This point was effectively taken by Colonel Herbert, Chairman of the Executive Committee of the National Union of Conservative and Unionist Associations: 'The impression which is given is that it might be quite possible for a nation to impose an economic blockade with certainty that it would not lead to war. This is, in fact, not the case. . . . In fact, it would in reality be impossible to vote for (*a*) without being ready also to vote for (*b*). Yet this is not explained.'

the letter of the law as laid down in Article 16. The 'Peace Ballot' is merely mentioned here as a fact in the history of the Abyssinian crisis, indicating the current trend of British opinion: it should not, in the writer's opinion, be regarded, as it has been, as something which the National Government, in the ensuing election in November, accepted and then betrayed.

On 3 October 1935, the expected act of Italian aggression took place, and on the 7th the Council of the League, its members voting individually by roll-call, unanimously except for the vote of the delinquent, adopted a report declaring that Italy had resorted to war in breach of the Covenant. In the ensuing meeting of the Assembly, on 11 October, fifty States members concurred in the view adopted by the Council, Switzerland made a reservation with regard to its participation in sanctions, while Austria, Hungary, and Albania, owing to their special relations with the transgressor, declared their dissent. The problem of recommending and co-ordinating the sanctions to be imposed was entrusted to a committee, and it was immediately decided to raise the arms embargo previously imposed by some nations upon Abyssinia and to impose a similar embargo against Italy (Proposal 1). A comprehensive financial sanction was also at once imposed (Proposal 2), and the acceptance of imports from Italy was immediately afterwards prohibited (Proposal 3). Finally, a very limited embargo on the export to Italy of certain important supplies came into force on 18 November.[1] From this the most important omission was oil, which was excluded ostensibly on the ground that the list was confined to commodities controlled by League Powers.

Though some surprise was expressed at the fact that the rusty sanctions machinery of the League had at last been set in motion, the most that was done fell lamentably short of the complete and general boycott visualized by the founders of the League, or indeed of the minimum obligations under the letter of the Covenant. For by Article 16 all members of the League

undertake *immediately* to subject (the delinquent State) to the severance of *all* trade or financial relations, *the prohibition of all intercourse between their nationals and the nationals of the Covenant-breaking*

---

[1] Though the effect was as stated, technically all these decisions were merely proposals, for the consideration of the individual governments concerned.

State, and the *prevention of all financial, commercial or personal intercourse between the nationals of the Covenant-breaking State and the nationals of any other State, whether a Member of the League or not.*

Very little of this was done. It must be remembered, however, that the leading Powers concerned—England and France— were determined from the first to avoid putting such pressure upon Italy as might involve them in war. On the day preceding his historic speech at Geneva Sir Samuel Hoare had consulted with M. Laval, with a result which the latter professed to understand as follows:

> We found ourselves instantaneously in agreement upon ruling out military sanctions, not adopting any measure of naval blockade, never contemplating the closure of the Suez Canal—in a word, ruling out everything that might lead to war.[1]

Though this interpretation was incorrect, and Sir Samuel at no time pledged himself permanently to exclude military sanctions, the obvious unwillingness of France to co-operate to such an extent placed at once practically the whole burden of any such measures upon Great Britain, and threatened to convert collective into individual action. The situation with which both of these Powers were confronted was, in fact, a very difficult one. Italy had thrown down a challenge to the League, the non-acceptance of which might be fatal to its continued existence, and would in any case be a most serious blow to its prestige. To France the League had always been an instrument of *European* security and organization (cf. p. 339). To most English statesmen the League was an institution almost essential, under present-day conditions, for carrying on the traditional lines of British foreign policy in regard to Europe. The course marked out for Great Britain in Europe has almost always been a combination of the mediatory role for which her external position fits her, with the preservation of a multiple balance of power nearly incompatible with fixed alliances. Isolation, if ever practicable, is regarded in all responsible quarters as impossible today; with isolation and fixed alliances thus ruled out, England turned naturally to the support of an institution which, like herself, promoted a multiple balance and opposed the steps leading to the hegemony of a single Power,

---

[1] Statement to the French Chamber of Deputies, December 1935.

while at the same time it afforded unrivalled facilities for mediation. The view, generally entertained on the Continent, that in the Abyssinian crisis Great Britain was manipulating the League in her own special interests, was of course quite unfounded in the sense in which the imputation was made, but it is none the less true that, in wishing to preserve the League against the dangers now threatening it, England was not actuated by a vague and altruistic idealism, but by a most realistic desire to maintain an instrument vital to her own traditional policy.

But there were some considerations which militated against firm action in the situation which had now arisen. The first was the military and naval weakness of Great Britain, owing to the extent to which she had disarmed. A second was the necessity of correlating British policy with that of France. A third was the advisability of retaining as large a combination as possible to control the actions of Germany. And finally, there was the fact that the League was a means to an end, that end being above all things the prevention of a general war, such as is almost inevitable when war breaks out between the Great Powers of Europe. To use the means of the League, *à outrance*, for the defence of Abyssinian integrity, involved the only conceivable immediate risk of the precise catastrophe which the League was created to avert.

It was in this dilemma that the policy adopted in the Abyssinian crisis fell hopelessly between two stools and met with complete disaster. There was something to be said for a 'European' attitude which refused to intervene at all, and frankly explained why. There was much to be said for a resolve to save Abyssinia—and the League—at all costs. There was little enough to be said for the imposition of innocuous sanctions, which the aggressor, though none the less irritated, could modify at his pleasure by the threat of war.

This might well have been evident but for an erroneous estimate of the Italian prospects. The preponderant expert opinion of soldiers and travellers was inclined to believe that the difficulties of climate and terrain would prove insuperable to the Italian forces, and that Italy was either faced with defeat or at any rate with a long war, in which even the mildest sanctions might have time to play a decisive part. Mr

Chamberlain, who at this time was among the members of the Cabinet most heartily in support of a vigorous policy, went even farther, and recorded in his private diary, on 8 December, the view that: 'by putting his great army the other side the Suez Canal, Mussolini has tied a noose round his own neck, and left the end hanging out for anyone with a Navy to pull.'[1] This belief affected different categories of opinion in different ways. The British public rejoiced, and was not in the least inclined to do anything to extricate Signor Mussolini from what they took to be his awkward predicament. To the French, on the other hand, the defeat of the Italians meant simply ruining the prestige and permanently estranging the sympathies of a hardly won and valued ally. They could not in the least understand the apparently new-born enthusiasm of England for this particular experiment in collective security. For years they had implored Great Britain to play an effective part in the only security which mattered in their estimation, and to pledge herself unmistakably to maintain the integrity of their friends in eastern Europe. All in vain. But just when, at a most critical juncture, Italy had been won over into the camp of the faithful, England chose to direct against precisely that country a hitherto unsuspected zeal for the policy she had previously refused to promote. France could not appreciate the distinction, so important to the British mind, between a concrete case and an abstract principle. For herself, the present crisis left her torn between rival anxieties. None valued the security side of the Covenant—for use in Europe *bien entendu*—more than she; it was all to the good that the determination of the League to resort to sanctions should be demonstrated, but, now that the demonstration had been made, she wanted to save the face and keep the favour of her new ally as well. Let there be a happy ending—a settlement by mutual consent. Let the husks of the sanctionist regime induce just sufficient hunger in the prodigal to tempt him home to a liberal provision of some one else's fatted calf. Thus a grateful and not altogether discredited Mussolini could restore his support to a League which would have established a useful precedent of at least partial victory to deter future and more dangerous aggressors.

[1] Feiling, Keith. *The Life of Neville Chamberlain*. London, Macmillan, 1946, p. 273.

As for Sir Samuel Hoare, he found himself in the position of the leader of a charge exposed in no-man's land with his troop refusing to follow. If Italy were faced with defeat, she would rather go down fighting the champions of the League than face the ignominy of a second Adowa, brought about by a shortage of supplies. And, when she turned to look for the League's forces in the field, she would find only those of Great Britain.

We alone have taken these military precautions. There is the British fleet in the Mediterranean, there are the British reinforcements in Egypt, in Malta and Aden. Not a ship, not a machine, not a man has been moved by any other member State.[1]

The hollow pretence, as Sir Samuel viewed it, of collective resistance would be exposed when the struggle turned into a duel between just two nations. In these circumstances, after the apparent failure of his original trumpet call, he was induced, in common with the League as a whole, to adopt M. Laval's specious argument that it was the duty of that institution, after as well as before the act of Italian aggression, to pursue the policies of coercion and mediation simultaneously. The argument was indeed more characteristic of British than it was of French thought, since it was as a forum of international negotiation rather than a potential alliance marshalled against aggressors that the League had from the first been valued by British politicians, and it was probably accepted with more sincerity by Sir Samuel than by M. Laval. In view of current misconceptions of British Government policy, it should be emphasized that there is no reason to doubt the sincerity of Sir Samuel's conviction that the step which he was about to take was that best calculated to preserve the influence and prestige of the League itself, and that this was his main objective. In his own words:

We had no fear as a nation of any Italian threats. . . . What was in our mind was something very different, that an isolated attack of this kind launched upon one Power without . . . the full support of the other Powers would, it seemed to me, almost inevitably lead to the dissolution of the League.[2]

In the light of what actually occurred, we have all grown so used to attributing the death of the League to a flagrant

---

[1] Sir Samuel Hoare, House of Commons, 19 December 1935.
[2] Speech of Sir Samuel Hoare, loc. cit.

sacrifice of principle in its endeavour to achieve a settlement that we are apt to forget that it was equally possible, as Sir Samuel contended, for its authority to be finally destroyed by a situation which revealed unmistakably the pasteboard composition of the Don Quixote's helmet of military sanctions. There was also, no doubt, a secondary consideration. We could defeat Italy, but what if another enemy seized the opportunity of exploiting the reduced and battered condition of our navy?

The reader may observe, as a further possible point in extenuation of British Government policy, the strength of the bargaining position occupied by M. Laval. In complaining of the isolated situation of Great Britain, Sir Samuel obviously implied, in particular, the defection or hesitation of France, on whom, as the only other Great Power capable of affording effective naval assistance in the Mediterranean, Great Britain primarily relied in the event of a trial of force. With French co-operation, his argument clearly lost its validity. The weakness of our situation really lay in the necessity for keeping step with France, a circumstance which gave M. Laval an invaluable lever in his task of exacting British acquiescence in his schemes.

Such was the background of the notorious Laval-Hoare 'peace proposal' of December 1935. The urgent necessity, in the opinion of the authors, for such a plan was due to the imminence of a proposal for the imposition of an 'oil-sanction'. It was the view of Sir Samuel Hoare that if

the non-member states took an effective part in it, the oil embargo might have such an effect upon the hostilities as to force their termination.[1]

The co-operation of the United States at least seemed at this time a possibility, and, in spite of the blocking and procrastinating tactics of M. Laval, the project was shortly due to come up for final consideration, and the orator of 11 September

did not feel . . . justified in proposing any postponement of the embargo, unless it could be shown to the League that negotiations had actually started.[2]

He was on the point of seeking a much-needed holiday in Switzerland when M. Laval, on 7 December, secured his

[1] ibid.   [2] ibid.

approval of a plan which, stripped of its euphemistic clothing as an 'Exchange of Territories' and a 'Zone of Economic Expansion and Settlement', meant the buying off of Signor Mussolini by conceding to him territory and virtual control of far wider extent than he had so far won by the sword. As an attempt to rescue Abyssinia from complete annihilation, it might perhaps have been justified, but in fact it was put forward at a time when no such débâcle was anticipated. Sir Samuel himself predicted a long and indecisive struggle, followed by a compromised settlement. The proposal was obviously put forward in the interests of Powers pledged to the maintenance of Ethiopian integrity, rather than in those of Abyssinia. It was in fact a 'peace plan' on the lines of that for which the Great Powers had been satirized by an Oxford poet towards the end of the nineteenth century:

> Be it yours to assuage for inadequate wage our unseemly contentions and quarrels;
> Be it yours to maintain your respectable reign in the sphere of Political Morals;
> And, relying no more on the shedding of gore or the rule of torpedoes and sabres,
> Make beneficent plots for dividing in lots the domains of your paralysed neighbours! [1]

Having thus provisionally agreed to what he regarded as a proposal ripe for further consideration by the British Cabinet and the League, Sir Samuel dispatched the results of his conference to London and proceeded on his holiday to Switzerland. The understanding was that the plan should remain a profound secret until such further consideration had taken place, but in fact it was immediately disclosed to the French press through what we may now confidently attribute to a deliberate breach of faith on the part of M. Laval. He felt, no doubt, that such premature disclosure would force the hand of the British Cabinet by bringing into play their loyalty to an absent colleague, and this calculation proved correct. Though admittedly unhappy and dissatisfied about the terms, the Cabinet gave the project a reluctant assent, and on 10 December a telegram was sent to Addis Ababa, urging the Emperor 'to give careful and favourable consideration to these proposals and on

[1] A. D. Godley, *Lyra Frivola*, 1899, p. 67.

no account to lightly reject them'. That the terms were not regarded as final is indicated by the fact that the message further spoke of 'the opportunity of negotiation which they afford'.

But M. Laval had not reckoned with the force of British public opinion. The plan, thus disclosed, and illustrated in the press by a map showing that apparently two-thirds of Ethiopia were to be awarded to the aggressor, was immediately met with a storm of indignant protest from the British public and the newly elected rank and file of Government supporters. In the recent electoral campaign the latter had constantly and sincerely repudiated the forecast of Government intentions expressed in a work hastily brought out for the occasion by a band of opposition students of international affairs:

> They reckon on the General Election definitely giving them the upper hand in the Conservative Party, with a blank cheque to arm to the teeth as well as freeing them from the fear of public opinion. *Then they will do a deal with their friend Mussolini,* and after that launch out on the 'new foreign policy' about which the Government Press have been hinting for some time. That policy in their view is either to say that the League has failed altogether or that it needs drastic reform by dropping Articles 10 and 16 from the Covenant, and in either case to plunge with a vengeance into the game of alliances and power politics.[1]

In the light of what had now transpired, they felt, with shame, that they had won the election under false pretences. The Government bent to the storm, and Sir Samuel Hoare was replaced at the Foreign Office by Mr Eden. The plan was dead, but its ghost continued to haunt the nations who had hitherto reposed confidence in the protection of the League. The harm was irrevocably done.

In any case, the pessimistic view of the Italian prospects proved to be mistaken. Unable to secure adequate supplies of arms, subjected from the air to a rain of mustard gas against which they were altogether unprotected, and defective in their strategy and tactics, the Abyssinian forces met with much earlier and more decisive defeat than anyone had anticipated. On 2 May 1936, the Emperor left the country, and three days later the Italian forces were in occupation of his capital. In the

---

[1] 'Vigilantes' (K. Zilliacus), *Inquest on Peace.* London, Gollancz, 1935, p. 281.

following month there was a very general movement for the abandonment of sanctions, in which policy the British Government met with no perceptible opposition from the public opinion of the country. On 6 July the Co-ordinating Committee of the League recommended that sanctions should be dropped as from 15 July. The experiment in practical collective security had finally broken down.

Some days earlier, the seven States of the so-called Oslo group—Sweden, Norway, Denmark, Finland, Holland, Belgium, and Luxembourg—had drawn from the situation the conclusion, which they embodied in a joint communiqué, that, so long as conditions remained as at present, they would not consider themselves bound by the provisions of Article 16 of the Covenant, and from this point the Scandinavians at any rate swung back to their traditional policy of neutrality.

The Abyssinian crisis may perhaps be thought to have been given an amount of space disproportionate to a work of this description. The justification lies in the fact that it marks a crucial turning-point in post-war history. The triumph of Italian aggression, naked and unashamed, affected the whole world with fundamental consequences. To England, it meant the virtual destruction of the institution which successive Governments, of different parties, had proclaimed to be the keystone of their foreign policy. To France, as will appear in the next chapter, it meant that the enemy of whom she stood most in terror was encouraged to fresh audacity and rescued from his previous isolation. And finally, to the Italian transgressor, by an act of poetic justice, it was destined to mean the extinction of his influence on the Danube, and the arrival of German forces on the Brenner.

XXIV

THE BERLIN-ROME AXIS

The Remilitarization of the Rhineland

THE discordance between the League Powers and Italy, brought about by the act of aggression against Abyssinia, left Germany in the position of a *tertius gaudens*, who could wait upon events in the hope of deriving material advantages from the victory of either side. If Italy were defeated, the most determined opponent of Germany's Austrian ambitions would be discredited and weakened; but if France, Great Britain, and the minor League Powers were to prove themselves incapable of dealing triumphantly with this act of aggression, their effective resistance to any further lawlessness on the part of the Nazi Government was proportionately less probable. In either case, Germany stood an excellent chance of escaping from her isolated position; for Italy, beaten or victorious, was alienated from her Stresa partners, and, if the Austrian obstacle could be temporarily surmounted or removed, could be drawn into the opposite camp by a blend of inclination and interest. At the turn of the year, 1935-6, the issue of the Abyssinian war was still doubtful, but from the middle of February 1936 the Italian progress was impressively rapid. At the worst, from Herr Hitler's standpoint, the attention of France and Great Britain was, at this stage, effectually diverted, and the risk of forcible interference with his plans small enough to be disregarded. In these circumstances, the Führer embarked upon a second *coup*, success in which was calculated to add enormously to the relative power of Germany in Europe.

So long as the Rhineland frontier was demilitarized and unfortified, France could without difficulty exert effective pressure on behalf of any of her protégés in Eastern Europe; but, faced with a formidable barrier in this quarter, she would be unlikely to interfere with any moves in the east which did not involve so clear a threat to her own security as to warrant the awful step of engaging in a full-scale European war.

It was not, indeed, contemplated either in France or Great

that the provision in the Peace Treaty for the demili-
tion of the Rhineland zone could endure for ever, but it
assumed that it would eventually be modified by negotia-
/s, in which this would merely be one of the questions to
be simultaneously solved in a general European settlement.
Negotiations between the Governments of France, Germany,
and Great Britain, directed to such a settlement, and in
particular to the conclusion of the air-pact projected in
February 1935 (see p. 394), were in fact almost continuously
in progress up to 6 March 1936, on which day Mr Eden had an
important discussion on the subject with the German ambassador in London. In view of what was about to happen, it
should be realized that the existence of an agreement between
France and Soviet Russia was assumed by Germany in the
course of the negotiations. Thus, in an interview between Herr
Hitler and the British Ambassador in Berlin, as early as 13
December 1935, the former 'declared that the Franco-Soviet
"military alliance" directed against Germany had rendered any
Air Pact out of the question'.[1] But whatever may have been the
feelings of dislike with which the Führer regarded the Russian
agreement, he was full of most disarming professions of friendship for France, even after the pact had been laid before the
French Chamber for ratification, on 11 February 1936. A week
before this ratification was finally approved, Herr Hitler
granted an interview to a French journalist, the whole burden
of which was devoted to the theme that enmity between France
and Germany was an absurdity. When the interviewer
delicately insinuated that this attitude was difficult to reconcile
with a number of passages in *Mein Kampf*, he received the reply
that this book dated from the occupation of the Ruhr, and that,
in bringing about a Franco-German *rapprochement*, its author
would 'enter his correction in the great book of History'.
This answer ignored the fact that the most hostile references
to France occur in the second volume of *Mein Kampf*, published after the conclusion of Locarno and the acceptance of
Germany as a member of the League of Nations, but it was
at all events calculated to remove any suspicion that a major

---

[1] Cmd. 5143 of 1936, Document 46. Cf. also the German memorandum of
7 March 1936: 'A diplomatic conversation has even revealed that France already
regards herself as bound by her signature of this pact on the 2nd May, 1935.'

step towards the diminution of French power was in immediate contemplation.

Such, however, proved to be the fact. Immediately after the publication of the interview, the French Ambassador in Berlin was instructed to ask Herr Hitler to explain further the suggested basis of the proposed *rapprochement*, and received the reply that detailed proposals were in preparation. But the next communication from Germany to France was of a very different character. On the morning of Saturday, 7 March, the representatives of Belgium, France, Great Britain, and Italy, were informed that German troops were at that moment marching into the demilitarized zone.

The pretext for this *coup* was the Franco-Soviet Pact, and its alleged incompatibility with the Locarno Treaty. The pact had been approved for ratification by the Chamber of Deputies on 27 February, though it had still to be passed by the Senate when Herr Hitler took the step described. The view that the agreement was inconsistent with Locarno was not shared by any of the other parties to that treaty, and M. Flandin had publicly offered to submit the question to the Permanent Court of International Justice, and to abide by its decision. By his action Herr Hitler had indisputably created a *casus foederis* under Article 2 of the Locarno Treaty, by a sudden and direct breach of Articles 42 and 43 of the Treaty of Versailles, which if construed as flagrant, would have justified, and indeed required, immediate military action by the other signatories. The seriousness of the offence is brought out in Article 44 of the Versailles Treaty:

In case Germany violates in any manner whatever the provision of Articles 42 and 43, she shall be regarded as committing a hostile act against the Powers signatory of the present Treaty and as calculated to disturb the peace of the world.

It seems, indeed, to have been anticipated, in the highest military circles of Germany, that the reoccupation of the Rhineland would be met by immediate and combined resistance, to which the invading force would have no alternative but to submit. Herr Hitler had, however, more correctly judged the temper of the Powers affected. The suddenness of his action brought into play, to his advantage, the time-lag in public opinion. He accompanied his act of unilateral repudiation with a memorandum in which he offered a western non-aggression pact for twenty-five years, the conclusion of the air-pact, and bilateral pacts with his eastern neighbours, and ended by expressing the willingness of Germany, if certain conditions were satisfied, to rejoin the League of Nations. In spite of Herr Hitler's fresh demonstration of the way in which he regarded treaty obligations, a large section of the British public was inclined to pay more attention to his specious projects for the future than to the manner in which he had torn up the pledges of the past. Ignoring alike the method and the danger, many people saw no more than the introduction by a sovereign nation of troops into a portion of its own territory from which they had been unjustly excluded. Even *The Times* hailed the impact of this charge of explosive upon the fabric of international confidence with a leader entitled 'A Chance to Rebuild'—a comment which no doubt applies in a sense to any devastated area, provided the foundations have not been irremediably shaken.

It was left to Mr Eden, in his speech in the House of Commons on 9 March, to bring England to a just appreciation of the gravity of the affair, to point out that 'one of the main foundations of the peace of Western Europe has been cut away', and to reiterate his country's continued loyalty to its obligations to France and Belgium under the broken treaty. The British Government, however, was determined that the case should not be interpreted as a 'flagrant breach', with the consequences set out in Article 4 (3) of the Locarno Rhineland Treaty. As Mr Chamberlain's biographer has put it, 'By treaty we were guarantors, but from the first we made ourselves mediators, and though we had led in imposing sanctions on Italy, we led also in refusing to impose them on the Germans'.[1] For inaction in this crisis it is now clear that Great Britain must shoulder the main responsibility. M. Sarraut, the French Premier, and his Foreign Minister, M. Flandin, favoured the simultaneous mobilization of the combined forces of Britain and France, and M. Flandin arrived in England on 11 March to advocate such a policy. Even if M. Flandin's own account of these discussions

---

[1] Feiling, Keith. *The Life of Neville Chamberlain.* London, Macmillan, 1946, p. 279.

is not altogether to be trusted,[1] there can be little doubt that the British Government found considerable difficulty in persuading the French representative to adopt a milder course, or that with any hope of British support and co-operation M. Flandin would have persisted.[2] But in the end all that was done was to 'bring the question at once before the Council of the League of Nations', in accordance with subsection (1) of the Article above referred to.

At an earlier stage of the inter-war period, there can be little doubt that France would have been more resolutely militant in her attitude. A very large part, if not the whole, of French foreign policy between the wars was inspired by the desire to escape from the nightmare of another German invasion of the soil of France. It was as a measure promoting security from this that French statesmen had originally clamoured and schemed for a natural defensive frontier on the Rhine: the alliances of France with eastern European countries were similarly assumed in the interests of French security from German aggression, and French interest in the League of Nations was equally concentrated on its potentialities as a further reinforcement against the same danger. But by this time, the importance of some of these measures in the eyes of French public opinion—and therefore to some extent in the eyes of French statesmen dependent on that opinion—had been considerably reduced by a further expedient which had been adopted in the interests of national security. As an alternative to the natural defensive frontier of which she had been disappointed, France had long contemplated, and from 1929 had been actively engaged in constructing, an artificial substitute which it was hoped might prove even more effective. The wonders of this 'Maginot Line', covering the whole length of the Franco-German frontier, had been extensively advertised, and as the last word in up-to-date and elaborate fortification it was commonly regarded as impregnable—which indeed to a direct frontal attack it may possibly have been. But in proportion as the average Frenchman was thus relieved from fears of a renewed experience of German

---

[1] Flandin, P. E. *Politique française 1919-40.* Paris, Editions Nouvelles, 1947, pp. 207-8.
[2] See Mr Churchill's account, in *The Gathering Storm.* London, Cassell, 1948, pp. 150-4.

invasion, he tended to grow indifferent to those aspects of French strategic policy which involved anything more than passive defence. To this new 'Maginot-minded' France, the reinforcement of the barrier between herself and Germany by a corresponding German line of fortification did not appear of alarming importance, in spite of the manifest obstacle which it created to the supply of contingent military assistance to her allies in Eastern Europe.[1] This change in mentality was destined, in the sequel, to be of considerable importance.

There was, however, a considerable divergence between the desire of Great Britain to embark on the negotiations suggested by the proposals of the German memorandum, and the French determination that nothing should be done to condone this further example of unilateral treaty-repudiation. In these circumstances, the Council of the League, which met in London on 14 March, did little more than record its verdict declaring Germany guilty of a breach of her international obligations, and the subsequent negotiations were left in the hands of the Locarno Powers. These had, by 19 March, drawn up a long list of proposals, in the course of which they invited the German Government to accept a decision of the Permanent Court on the alleged incompatibility of the Franco-Soviet Pact and the Locarno Treaty, and, pending the conclusion of negotiations on the new German proposals, to limit the forces introduced into the Rhineland to innocuous proportions, and to refrain from constructing fortifications or aerodromes. A proposal to form and station an international force in the zone was included, but soon tacitly dropped.

On 31 March the German Government, which had meanwhile been encouraged by an almost unanimous vote of confidence on the part of their nation, submitted counter-proposals under nineteen heads, which were mainly an expansion of the memorandum of 7 March, and were significantly silent on the subject of fortification. This document was subjected to severe criticism by the French, who dwelt upon the lack of effective guarantees against breaches of the proposed arrangement, and pointed out that simple bilateral agreements for non-aggression added nothing in the way either of sanctity or security to the obligations of the parties under the Kellogg

---

[1] Cf. M. Tardieu's argument of 1919, quoted on p. 54.

Pact. At a meeting of the Locarno Powers which followed on 10 April, the French representatives were only restrained from abandoning all further idea of negotiation by an undertaking on the part of the British to submit to Germany an elucidating questionnaire. France was at this juncture temporarily paralysed by the defeat of her Government in the elections of 2 May, since the retiring administration had, under French procedure, to remain in office, without real authority, for another month. The task of drafting interrogatories fell, therefore, inevitably on Great Britain, whose Government submitted its questions to Germany on 7 May. To these, however, Herr Hitler's Government, assuming an affronted pose, vouchsafed no reply. It went on with its work of consolidation, with the result that the construction of an effectively fortified line was admitted during the anniversary celebrations of March 1937.

The demilitarized zone was important to France as the one remaining element of the compromise whereby she had been induced at the Peace Conference to abandon her insistent demand that Germany west of the Rhine should be separated from the authority of Berlin. It might therefore be regarded as the most important part of the price at which Germany was permitted to retain her transrhenane territory. Moreover, the Locarno Treaty, which Herr Hitler had thus torn up, so far from being imposed on Germany, was initiated at her suggestion, and it was from the German side that the proposal first came to include in its guarantees the maintenance of the demilitarized zone.

In the same sense, the Treaty States could guarantee in this pact the fulfilment of the obligation to demilitarize the Rhineland which Germany has undertaken in Articles 42 and 43 of the Treaty of Versailles.[1]

The wrong to Belgium was even more flagrant and less capable of justification. To Belgium, the existence of the zone had been the principal guarantee of her security from a repetition of the outrage of 1914, and the remilitarization of the territory along her frontier lacked even the slender pretext which the ratification of the Franco-Soviet agreement afforded. Herr Hitler's

---

[1] German memorandum communicated to M. Herriot, 9 February 1925. Cmd. 2435 of 1925.

act also destroyed the only condition which justified, in Belgian eyes, the abandonment of her pre-war status of neutrality. In the new situation she was forced to revert to something which appeared very like it. The first hint of this change was given in a speech by King Leopold on 14 October 1936, in which he said: 'We must follow a policy exclusively and entirely Belgian. That policy should aim resolutely at placing us outside any disputes of our neighbours.' These words created some consternation in France, but it was later explained that they did not go so far as to imply a repudiation of the duties incumbent on Belgium as a member of the League of Nations. They did express, however, the view that it was no longer possible for Belgium actively to participate in the guarantees of the Locarno system. This view was accepted by France and Great Britain, in a joint declaration by the two Powers on 24 April 1937. In return for an undertaking by Belgium greatly to strengthen the defences of her own frontier, they agreed to release her from the obligations of Locarno, while maintaining, from their side, the guarantees of Belgian security from aggression embodied in that treaty.

The Montreux Conference

The reoccupation of the Rhineland by the forces of Germany was very quickly followed by the release from its treaty restrictions of another demilitarized zone—that of the Black Sea Straits (see p. 122). The circumstances in which this occurred were, however, strikingly different. In place of a fresh instance of unilateral repudiation, the Montreux Conference provided a welcome precedent for treaty revision by the general and deliberate consent of the parties. For this reason, the request which Turkey put forward, not for the first time, in April 1936, for the modification of the Straits Convention embodied in the Treaty of Lausanne, won the approval of revisionist and *status quo* Powers alike; of the former because of the end, and of the latter because of the means. The principle of the sanctity of treaties was upheld, while at the same time the provisions of this particular instrument were subjected to 'peaceful change'.

Demilitarization was only a subsidiary part of the arrangements made at Lausanne which now came up for reconsideration. The Straits Convention regulated, under the auspices of an international commission, the passage of ships of war and commerce through the Straits in times of war and peace, and demilitarized the adjacent shores and islands; though this provision was not absolute, but subject to modification by Turkey in time of war, on notice to the other signatory Powers. The freedom of the Straits and the security of the demilitarized areas were covered by the guarantee of the signatory Powers.

From the time when the prospects of disarmament and of peace began to be shaken by the revival of Nazi Germany, Turkey, who had been admitted to the League of Nations in July 1932, continually raised the question of the remilitarization of the Straits. Her arguments were based on the diminished value of international guarantees, and the general rearmament which was in process of taking place. But little attention had been paid to these Turkish claims, until the successful aggression of Italy and Hitler's violation of the demilitarized zone in the Rhineland created a general state of mind more favourable to the reconsideration of the question, when Turkey once more raised it, in April 1936.

In the first place, there was reason to fear that, if revision by mutual consent was refused, Turkey would take a leaf out of Herr Hitler's book. Secondly, there was no longer any harm in creating a precedent for remilitarization, as there might have been before the German *coup*. Thirdly, the apparent trend of Italian policy led Great Britain to welcome the strengthening of a friendly Power in the Mediterranean, while France saw in the proposal a chance of improving the position of her new ally, Russia. Italy, the only important signatory Power likely to object, was temporarily in the position of a discredited outlaw. But above all, the whole idea of revision by mutual consent presented a refreshing contrast to the process of compulsory or unilateral change which seemed the fashionable alternative.

Turkey, therefore, succeeded by the end of April in securing the consent of all the Powers signatory to the Treaty of Lausanne, except Italy, to the proposed Conference, which accordingly met at Montreux on 22 June 1936, and produced an agreed amendment of the Straits Convention within a month from that date. There were, however, some tense and critical moments before this conclusion was reached. It had not been originally contemplated that the Conference would be called on to modify any provisions of the 1923 Convention except those relating to demilitarization and the international guarantee. Even this limited modification might no doubt have made the *de jure* freedom of transit for the ships of all nations somewhat illusory, since it would be subject to the *de facto* control of the rearmed riparian Power, but it had not been anticipated that there would be any attempt to depart undisguisedly from the principle of the freedom of the Straits as an international waterway which animated the original Convention. When the Conference met, however, it was confronted with Turkish proposals which made no mention of the principle of the freedom of the Straits, but substituted for it that of the security of Turkey. The draft went on to modify the original Convention in the interests, as it seemed, less of Turkey than of Russia, by drastically restricting ingress to the Black Sea, while allowing freedom to the fleet of any riparian Power to pass out into the Mediterranean. This unexpected development in the negotiations led to a conflict between the views of the U.S.S.R., which had the sympathy of most of the nations participating, and those of Great Britain. Put shortly, the questions were whether the Black Sea should be treated as part of the high seas, or accorded a special regime in the interest of the security of its riparian Powers, and alternatively, if such special privileges were accorded, whether they should be granted on a principle of reciprocity, which placed corresponding restrictions upon the egress of Black Sea fleets into the Mediterranean. It was the contention of the British Government that the Straits should be equally open or equally closed to all, and that Russia should not be enabled to fight in the Mediterranean and then retreat into a position where her fleet was completely immune from attack. The British negotiators, in adopting this attitude, were probably not so much concerned with any direct danger to which her navy might be exposed through the institution of such a system of 'one-way traffic', as with the possible effects upon the Anglo-German naval agreement which might be produced if such an advantage were conceded to the maritime strength of the Soviet Union. To this extent there may have been a grain of truth in the charge hinted by some of the participants in the Conference, that we were fighting the battle of Germany.

The matter was eventually settled by a compromise in which the Black Sea Powers retained substantial advantages. The case which had aroused most controversy was that of a war in which Turkey was non-belligerent. In such case it was agreed that the warships of belligerent Powers should not pass the Straits in either direction except in fulfilment of obligations under the Covenant, or to give help to the victim of aggression in virtue of a treaty of mutual assistance binding Turkey and concluded within the framework of the Covenant.

The remaining provisions of the new Convention need not be dealt with here. As already hinted, much of the controversy seems academic, in view of the real power of control which passed into the hands of Turkey with the remilitarization of the coasts and islands. This part of the new arrangement came into force immediately after the signature of the new Convention by the Conference Powers, on 20 July, which was followed the same night by the introduction of 30,000 Turkish troops into the former demilitarized zone.

The Austro-German Agreement

The conclusion of the Montreux Conference was greeted with expressions of dissatisfaction by Germany and Italy, who were the two States most likely to be adversely affected by the new arrangements. By this time it was evident that a close *rapprochement* between the Governments of these two countries was in process of being effected. This might have been expected from the similarity of their methods and political ideals; indeed, it was no more than a reversion to the attitude which had characterized their relations during most of the inter-war period. For some months the policy of each had played into the hands of the other. The diversion which Germany had created in the Rhineland made the rigorous prosecution of a sanctions policy against Italy more difficult, and, conversely, Germany could hardly have ventured to embark on such risks if the Stresa front had remained intact, and if the Abyssinian war had not engaged much of the attention of Europe. The one obstacle to the construction of a 'Berlin-Rome Axis' was the problem of Austria, and this was now satisfactorily shelved for the time being by the conclusion of an Austro-German agreement on 11 July 1936, which had been disclosed to and approved by Signor Mussolini more than a month earlier. In view of what was to happen within the next two years, the terms of the official communiqué announcing this arrangement should be quoted:

(1) Following on the declarations made by the Führer and Chancellor on 21 May 1935, the Government of the German Reich recognizes the full sovereignty of the Austrian Federal State.

(2) Each of the two Governments considers the internal political structure of the other country, including the question of Austrian National Socialism, as part of the internal affairs of that country, over which they will exercise no influence, whether directly or indirectly.

(3) The policy of the Austrian Federal Government, both in general and towards the German Reich in particular, shall always be based on principles which correspond to the fact that Austria has acknowledged herself to be a German State. This will not affect the Rome Protocols of 1934 and the supplementary agreements of 1936, or the position of Austria in relation to Italy and Hungary as her partners in these protocols.[1]

The agreement brought Austria into a willing partnership with Germany, and appeared to secure most of the advantages of an Anschluss without alienating those sections of opinion which were opposed to it. These included, apart from Italy, the supporters of the Austrian Government and a large number of persons who, however friendly to Germany, valued the historic independence of their country and disliked the Nazi regime. In particular, there was the Catholic Church, and a large body of influential opinion, both in Austria and Hungary, which still looked to a Habsburg restoration as the best and ultimate solution. Thus the agreement served the purpose of bringing not only Italy and Austria but Hungary closer to the orbit of German policy, and it went far to reconstruct the Triple Alliance of pre-war days, though of course the Austro-Hungarian contribution to the power of the group could have for some time little of its old military importance. But it was mainly conceived as a method of allaying the fears and suspicions of Italy, who, from this time forward, was obviously working in close consultation and collaboration with Germany,

---

[1] Broadcast by Dr Goebbels, German Minister of Propaganda.

though the existence of a 'Berlin-Rome Axis' was not publicly proclaimed until November.

The Spanish Civil War

The new-formed alliance was strengthened, almost simultaneously with the conclusion of the Austro-German agreement, by the outbreak, on 17 July, of civil war in Spain, intervention in which offered a promising field for a co-operative Italo-German policy. It is this aspect of the Spanish struggle which gives international importance to what was primarily a domestic matter with which a history of international affairs would have had no concern. During the post-war period there had, in fact, been a number of important internal changes in Spain, which have not hitherto seemed relevant, but of which it may now be necessary to say something.

Spain has always been a peculiarly unfavourable soil for the growth of parliamentary methods of government. With a proportion of illiteracy higher than 45 per cent in 1931, with the existence of disruptive regional loyalties antagonistic to the Central Government, and of such *imperia in imperio* as the Army, the Catholic Church, and Labour organizations under the conflicting inspirations of Marx and Bakunin, and finally with a national temperament fundamentally averse from compromise, Spain has never possessed the requisites without which democratic government is suppressed by dictators or dissolves in anarchy. The customary *deus ex machina* for resolving an impossible situation has been an army general, leading a revolt or issuing a military *pronunciamiento*. The earlier history of the nineteenth century, from 1820 to 1874, is punctuated with incursions of the army into the political arena. Sometimes this expedient has introduced a period of exceptionally stable and successful government. In 1874 it was a military *pronunicamiento* which brought about the restoration of the Bourbons. It was the same device which inaugurated the dictatorship of General Primo de Rivera, in 1923, which lasted till 1930. General Franco's *coup*, in July 1936, was intended as a further use of the same time-honoured expedient, which is almost entitled to be regarded, in Spain, as a recognized instrument for the achievement of constitutional changes.

Government by such methods as those of Primo de Rivera,

however, too often produces merely a deceptive appearance of tranquillity by a process of 'sitting on the safety-valve'. The pent-up forces of discontent accumulate to a dangerous degree. Primo's withdrawal in 1930 was followed, in little more than a year, by the flight of King Alfonso in April 1931. The republic was suddenly born, and its fate entrusted to men of extremely divergent ideas, whose main qualification for government, in the eyes of the public, was that they had been imprisoned on political grounds under the previous regime. They included Monarchists and Catholics, Liberal Free-thinkers and Republican Socialists. The result was made the subject of an amusing comparison by Señor José Castillejo, in a lecture delivered in October 1936:[1]

> In the first days of the railway in Spain, a farmer entered a train going in the direction of Madrid from Barcelona. Since there was only one track, the trains had to stop at various stations until those going in the opposite direction had passed. The farmer went to have a drink, and when he returned his train had left for Madrid and the train in the station was going in the contrary direction. He entered the train and found another man sitting there, and he asked him, 'Where are you going?' The other man replied, 'I am going to Barcelona.' 'Oh,' said the farmer, 'what a wonderful invention! You are going to Barcelona and I am going to Madrid, and we are both in the same car!' And that was the situation of the Ministers in the first years of the Republic.

The new Constitution was thus found to be unworkable without the exclusion or imprisonment of political opponents. There were continual reversals of policy, and progress with much-needed reforms was slow and intermittent. The impatient proletariat started to act in anticipation of legislative measures not yet carried into effect. A general sense of insecurity increased the discontents of labour, since employers and landlords hesitated to embark on any undertaking not urgently necessary, thus increasing unemployment. The one thing clear was that the victory of political opponents meant disaster to the minority, whether it were of the Right or the Left. Such a vital interest in the triumph of one or the other extreme naturally tended to eliminate moderate opinion. Instead of true parliamentary government there was from the

---

[1] Unpublished: quoted in *International Affairs*, May 1937, p. 408.

first a contest between mutually irreconcilable factions. The essence of all good government is the preservation of order and the securing of a 'square deal' for all sections of the population. These essentials were lacking from the first under the Spanish Republic. A sort of civil war prevailed almost from the outset. There was a revolt of Military Royalists as early as August 1932. In January 1933 an Anarcho-Syndicalist rebellion had to be crushed. When the elections of December 1933 resulted in a swing towards the Right, there were immediate threats of revolt from the leaders of the opposition, which culminated in the serious Asturias rising of October 1934.

The elections of February 1936 produced a situation in which the Centre was almost eliminated, and the forces of Right and Left were evenly balanced. The Right polled over 4,570,000 votes, the Left 4,356,000, but in seats the Left achieved a majority of 57 over all other parties. This victory was gained through the formation of a 'Popular Front' coalition of all Left groups, ranging from mild Liberals to Communists and Anarchists. Though the Communists polled no more than 50,000 votes over the whole of Spain, the intervention of the Anarcho-Syndicalists was important; thus, a parliamentary triumph was largely due to a force whose tenets were opposed to parliamentary government. It was known, too, that the formation of the *Frente Popular* was in line with the policy laid down by the Comintern at their Congress of August 1935. Though there may have been little risk, in a country so individualistic and regionally minded as Spain, of the establishment of a centralized dictatorship of the proletariat on the Russian model, there were evidently elements in the Popular Front which were bent on securing their ends by means the reverse of constitutional. This fact naturally created acute alarm among the classes threatened by such elements.

The victory of the Left, narrow though it was, immediately encouraged a feeling among their extremists that the hour of revolution had arrived. In France, where a similar Popular Front had come to power, there was at first a similar reaction, but the Government of M. Léon Blum was strong enough to restore and maintain order. In Spain there was never a hope of any such relief. A state of intolerable anarchy immediately prevailed. No doubt many of the outrages must be laid at the door of the extremists of the Right, but the impotence of the Government cannot be denied. Between the elections and the outbreak of General Franco's revolt, 251 churches were burnt, 324 newspaper offices, political clubs, and private houses were attacked—of which 79 were completely destroyed, 339 persons were murdered, 1,287 were wounded. Robbery was rife, and there were 331 strikes.

On 13 July Señor Calvo Sotelo, the ablest political figure on the Right, was assassinated, and this event is often represented as the cause of General Franco's insurrection. There is ample evidence, however, that the plans were already complete, and the only part which this occurrence can have played may have been slightly to advance the date originally fixed for the outbreak. In fact, rumours of an impending military *coup d'état* were mentioned at a meeting in Chatham House as early as May.[1] The Spanish statesman, Señor Lerroux, was informed of the conspiracy on the day following the death of Sotelo. Even more significantly, some Italian airmen who made forced landings in French territory on 30 July are reported to have testified that they were recruited for their mission to General Franco three days before the outbreak of the revolt, i.e. as early as 14 July. This evidence is of particular importance as indicating Italy's complicity in the plot.

Considered, therefore, apart from foreign intervention, what happened in Spain on the night of 17–18 July was the repetition of a domestic event of constant occurrence in modern Spanish history, under circumstances which rendered something of the sort almost inevitable, and it was a matter in which no other country had good reason to be concerned. In actual fact, neither side deserved to enlist the sympathies of democractic nations. The really powerful elements on both sides 'sought to use the difficulties in which the republic found itself in 1936 as an opportunity to overthrow liberal institutions and to capture the Spanish State'.[2] Towards such a situation an attitude of strict non-intervention by Great Britain was in line with her traditional policy. The arguments justifying such an attitude may be read in a State Paper composed by Lord Castlereagh, in remarkably similar circumstances, as long ago as 1820. A

[1] *International Affairs*, September 1936, p. 667.
[2] *The Round Table*, June 1938, p. 443.

victory for General Franco might augur ill for the Spanish working community, and the triumph of those extreme elements in the *Frente Popular* which had from the first regarded it as a 'stepping stone' to a proletarian revolution held prospects of terror for the propertied classes of Spain. But it was probably as true in 1936 as in 1820 that

> there is no portion of Europe of equal magnitude in which such a revolution could have happened less likely to menace other States with that direct and imminent danger which has always been regarded—at least in this country—as alone constituting the case which would justify external interference.[1]

The British Government, therefore, readily responded to an appeal issued by M. Blum on 1 August, for 'the rapid adoption and immediate observance of an agreed arrangement for non-intervention in Spain'. Favourable replies were also received from Belgium, Poland, and Soviet Russia, and the policy was soon accepted in principle by Portugal, Germany, and Italy, though the adherence of the last-named was at first subject to the inclusion of special provisions preventing the departure of volunteers and the raising of subscriptions, and to adequate international supervision. By the end of August the principal European Powers, including Italy, Germany, and the U.S.S.R., had signed a non-intervention agreement; France, Germany, Great Britain, Belgium, and Portugal had prohibited the export to Spain or her possessions of specified arms and war material—including aircraft—and the French proposal had been accepted in principle by fifteen other European States. An international non-intervention committee began work in London on 9 September.

But the verbal acquiescence of certain European Powers in the policy thus inaugurated did not correspond to their actions. Italy clearly, and Germany probably, was privy to the military revolt, which had been expected to succeed at once, as a sudden *coup d'état*. This expectation was disappointed. The Spanish Government retained control of the east and the centre of the country—a connected area corresponding to the old provinces of Catalonia (with parts of Aragon), Valencia, Murcia with Almeria, and New Castile: Malaga and Badajoz

---

[1] Lord Castlereagh, loc. cit.

also opposed the revolt, though the latter fell in the middle of August, and in the north the Basque provinces, with the district between the mountains and the sea nearly as far westwards as Oviedo, but excluding it, constituted another island of territory where the *coup* had failed. The situation therefore was that so long as General Franco could hope for success with the forces at his disposal and the supplies which he had already received, it was to the interest of his backers to stop the reinforcement of the Spanish Government, for whose benefit large levies were being made upon the workers of Russia, while they were also receiving war material and aeroplanes from many quarters, especially the Soviet Union. But when the affair assumed the proportions of a civil war, the supporters of each side were anxious to maintain and increase their contributions. The earliest meetings of the Non-Intervention Committee heard repeated charges of intervention brought by Russia against Germany, Italy, and Portugal, and before the end of October the Soviet Government declared itself unable to remain bound by the agreement to a greater extent than any of the remaining participants. By this time, the help given by Russia was assuming important proportions, and on 19 November Mr Eden stated in the House of Commons that 'there are other Governments more to blame than either Germany or Italy'. The opinion expressed by a British visitor to Spain may probably be accepted, that but for German and Italian assistance the revolt would have failed in the first few weeks, but that without the help received from the Soviet Union in October the Spanish Government would have been quickly defeated.

Almost from the first, therefore, the agreement for non-intervention was seriously infringed by the foreign supporters of both the contending forces. The pretext on both sides was ideological. Many of the sympathizers with the Spanish Government were no doubt sincerely actuated by such considerations, but it is open to question how far they represented the true motive for intervention on the part of Italy, Germany, or Russia. For the last-named, the intention seems largely to have been to prevent an important accession of power to the Nazi-Fascist combination, which it was the primary object of Germany and Italy to secure. Anarcho-Syndicalism, the prevalent political doctrine of 'red' Spain, had closer affinities with

the earlier faith of Signor Mussolini than with that of Marx or
Lenin, and its triumph in a remote corner of Europe was not
calculated to contribute directly to the spread of international
Communism. Nor did the victory of such a faith threaten
serious dangers either to Italy or to Germany, in both of which
countries the strength of proletarian revolutionary movements
was negligible. Herr Hitler, indeed, was so obsessed by the
Russian peril that his pose as an ideological crusader may have
had some elements of sincerity. But in regard to Signor Mussolini, his past attitude seems to forbid any such conclusion. In
the days before Stalin came to power, while the dread of international Bolshevism was generally and reasonably felt, Fascist
Italy had been among the very first European Powers to accord
official recognition to the Soviet Government (see p. 107).
Throughout the sessions of the Disarmament Conference, the
collaboration between Italy and Soviet Russia had been
noticeably cordial, and as recently as September 1933, Signor
Mussolini had concluded a new treaty of amity and non-
aggression with the U.S.S.R. under which, *inter alia*, each
country undertook not to enter into any agreements or any
combination directed against the other party. The peril of
Bolshevism was at least no more formidable now than then, and
neither for Italy nor Germany was the victory or defeat of any
of the varied political faiths arrayed on both sides in the
Spanish struggle sufficiently important to explain convincingly
a serious expenditure of money, material, and man-power on
behalf of either antagonist.

There were, however, obvious strategic advantages to be
sought. The establishment through Nazi and Fascist assistance
of a protégé in power in Spain would mean to Herr Hitler that
on every important frontier France would have to keep watch
on a government sympathetic to Germany. To Italy it would
offer a prospect of disputing French and British control of the
western Mediterranean through facilities offered by a friendly
regime. In time of war, such a Power would have bases to offer
in European and African Spain, in the Balearic Islands, and in
the Canaries, which would go far to neutralize if not to destroy
the British grip on the Straits of Gibraltar and seriously to
interfere with the supply of soldiers to France from her North
African colonies. These advantages could be secured, or at

least rendered so probable as to immobilize large forces in the west, without any overt transfer of territory or grant of acknowledged treaty privileges. They were clearly worth an effort to secure, when the real aims of that effort could be disguised as a holy war against Communism, a device which served simultaneously to weaken the solidarity of resistance in democratic countries by an appeal to the sympathies and fears of large sections of their population.

In September, knowledge that the island of Majorca was under the *de facto* control of the Italian Count Rossi caused representations to be made to Rome as to the close concern which would be felt by the British Government at any alteration of the *status quo* in the western Mediterranean. On 18 November the German and Italian Governments announced in almost identical terms their official recognition of General Franco's Government. Between this date and Christmas 1936 large numbers of German troops continued to arrive in Spain, totalling, on a conservative estimate, not less than 20,000 men. According to a German journalist in the part of Spain in Franco's control, the method of selecting these men in Germany was not to call for volunteers, but to detail whole units for service and then announce that anyone who objected might remain behind. On Christmas Eve the British and French Governments, acting in concert, issued an appeal to Berlin, Lisbon, Moscow, and Rome urging the need of putting an end to the foreign supplies of man-power to the Spanish forces. The replies received were favourable, but the influx continued.

On 2 January 1937, what was generally though inappropriately known as a 'Gentleman's Agreement' was concluded in Rome between Great Britain and Italy, which recognized the interests of the two countries in the Mediterranean, and in which both parties disclaimed any desire to modify or see modified the *status quo* with respect to national sovereignty in the Mediterranean area, and agreed to discourage any activities liable to impair their good relations. On the same day reports reached Gibraltar that 4,000 Italians had landed at Cadiz, and the flow continued up to nearly the end of February, by which time the Italian troops in Spain amounted to a minimum of some 40,000 men, serving in four divisions, each commanded by a general of the Italian regular army. About a fortnight later the

Italian press expressed the view, which was confirmed by the Duce, that the establishment of a Bolshevist Government in Spain would be a modification of the *status quo* within the meaning of the 'Gentleman's Agreement', and as such could not be tolerated. Anti-British propaganda also continued.

Meanwhile, diversions had been created by two incidents. On Christmas Day the German ship *Palos* was seized by Spanish Government warships on the high seas. She was released in a few days, but part of her cargo was confiscated and a prisoner detained. Germany retaliated with reprisals, seizing the Spanish ship *Aragon* and disposing of her to General Franco. The action of each side in this episode appears to have been of doubtful legality. On 8 January France was disturbed by a report of the impending arrival of large numbers of German troops in Spanish Morocco. Since such an occurrence would have been a violation of the Franco-Spanish Treaty of 1912, immediate and energetic representations were made, which were met by a denial that any such step was in contemplation, and an invitation to investigate on the spot. The result of this investigation was reassuring, but an impression was left in many minds that the firmness of France on this occasion had been neither uncalled-for nor useless.

During the whole of this period the negotiations for stopping 'volunteers' had continued, with the result that a decree was promulgated in Italy on 15 February, with effect from the 20th, prohibiting Italians from leaving to serve in Spain. Reports of the arrival of Italian reinforcements at Cadiz continued till 7 March, but it seems probable that the decree was substantially obeyed at this stage from the date laid down. By this time the Italo-German contribution to General Franco's forces seems to have been considered adequate to ensure his success, or alternatively as much as could be afforded for the object in view, and the Non-Intervention Committee managed to agree upon the institution of a naval patrol and a system of frontier supervision, which began to operate from 19 April. On 29 May, however, the German battleship *Deutschland* was bombed by Spanish Government aircraft in the roadstead of Iviza, and in retaliation for this the town of Almeria was bombarded by a German cruiser and four destroyers two days later. On 19 June Berlin announced that the German cruiser *Leipzig* had been attacked by submarines, and, though this was denied, the refusal of France and Great Britain to take part in a joint demonstration led to the withdrawal of Germany and Italy from the patrol. Portugal withdrew facilities for the observation of her frontier, and on 10 July supervision of the Pyrenean frontier was suspended by France. The measures of control so far taken to ensure non-intervention were thus materially interfered with.

On 14 July, therefore, the British representatives on the Non-Intervention Committee came forward with a new proposal, in the nature of a compromise, whereby—

1. The naval patrol should be withdrawn and observers established in Spanish ports, while the supervision of land frontiers should be resumed.
2. Commissions should be constituted to superintend the withdrawal of foreign nationals from the forces of both sides.
3. After substantial progress with the withdrawals had been reported, both sides should be recognized as belligerents, and granted the rights accorded to that status by international law.

After a series of apparent deadlocks, in which the Soviet Union played perhaps the most obstructive part, a scheme on these lines was agreed to by the whole Non-Intervention Committee almost exactly a year later. This development belongs, however, to the next chapter, and much had happened in the interval.

In the opinion of the British Government, the deterioration in Anglo-Italian relations, which was responsible not only for the Italian attitude in the Spanish war but for the active and incessant campaign of anti-British propaganda carried on by Italy in other regions, was primarily due to fear. Signor Mussolini regarded the League's opposition to his aggression in Abyssinia as a purely British move, inspired by consideration of exclusively national interests, and his triumph over that opposition as a defeat not so much of the League as of Great Britain. He considered, in Mr Chamberlain's view, that 'we were engaged in a Machiavellian design to lull the Italians into inactivity while we completed our rearmament, with the intention presently of taking our revenge for the Italian conquest of Abyssinia'.[1] The British Prime Minister, in pursuit of his consistent policy of general appeasement, consequently exerted himself to dispel these suspicions, and on 27 July 1937, in response to an oral message delivered by Count Grandi, he wrote Signor Mussolini a conciliatory letter, to which he received a reply couched in friendly terms.

Almost simultaneously, however, reports began to be received of piratical attacks upon neutral and Spanish Government shipping by submarines of unknown nationality, operating in the Mediterranean. Since the beginning of the year there had, indeed, been numerous attacks of a similar illegal character upon shipping in the vicinity of Spain, but these had hitherto been carried out by aeroplanes. Owing to General Franco's known lack of submarines, the new phase of piracy was generally attributed to Italian agency, which, indeed, was openly alleged by the Spanish and Russian Governments. The fact that some of these incidents took place in the eastern Mediterranean, at a great distance from Spanish waters, tended to convert this suspicion into virtual certainty in the minds of many people. Mr Chamberlain himself seems to have shared this suspicion, since he stated that, immediately before September, 'certain incidents took place in the Mediterranean which, in our opinion, rendered it impossible that conversations at that time could have any chance of success'.[2] On 17 August orders were issued through the Admiralty enjoining immediate counter-attack in any case of an attack without warning by submarines upon British ships. A fortnight later these orders were carried into effect when the British destroyer *Havock* was unsuccessfully attacked by a submarine between Alicante and Valencia. In these circumstances a suggestion from the French Government was accepted for the holding of a conference of the Mediterranean Powers to consider the best method of coping with the new menace. The conference accordingly met at Nyon on 10 September. Nyon had been chosen in preference to Geneva in order to secure Italian participation; this, however, was refused. The conference succeeded in making arrangements for a patrol of the main trade routes and territorial waters by the British and French fleets,

[1] Mr Neville Chamberlain, House of Commons, 2 February 1938.
[2] Mr Chamberlain, loc. cit.

assisted in the eastern Mediterranean by the local participating Powers. On 30 September an agreement was reached with Italy, under which she was allotted a patrol zone in the Tyrrhenian, Adriatic, and Ionian seas, and in the neighbourhood of Sicily and the Dodecanese islands. Taking warning by these precautions, the piratical submarines at once desisted from further operations.

In other respects, however, the situation in regard to the 'Axis' Powers grew worse instead of better. In September and October large reinforcements, for which no very convincing explanation was forthcoming, were sent from Italy to Libya, and during October the presence of 40,000 Italian troops in Spain was officially admitted. On 29 October a still more authoritative recognition of Italian intervention was given, when Signor Mussolini himself presented medals to the relations of legionaries killed in Spain, and a casualty list was published, giving a total of 763 killed and 2,675 wounded. The 'Axis' was further consolidated by an official visit of the Duce to Germany in September, and by a speech in October in which he supported the claims of Germany to the return of her former colonies—a pronouncement which called forth a sarcastic rejoinder from Mr Eden. On 6 November Italy adhered to the Anti-Comintern Pact previously concluded between Germany and Japan, and this step was hailed by Herr Hitler in a speech which laid little stress on the Communist danger, but applauded the combination as 'suited to us and to our interests', and as putting an end to isolation. Finally, on 12 December, Signor Mussolini announced the decision of his country to withdraw from membership of the League.

Details of military operations in a civil war are hardly the concern of a history of international relations. But this chapter may perhaps fittingly conclude with a brief summary of the leading phases of the struggle down to the close of 1937. It was carried on with extreme ferocity by both sides. The brunt of the insurgent offensive during 1936 was concentrated in a vain effort to capture Madrid. In these operations the relief by General Franco's forces of the heroic defenders of the Alcazar of Toledo deserves special mention. Malaga fell to the insurgents in February 1937, and in the late summer and autumn of that year they completed the conquest of the Basque and other northern territory which had remained loyal to the Government. But at the close of 1937 the eastern and central portions of Spain still remained in the hands of the Government, and its forces even succeeded, on 21 December, in temporarily regaining Teruel, the nearest point to the Valencian coast which had hitherto been in the possession of the Nationalists. Connected with the rest of the territory held by General Franco by a narrow salient, it had been in his hands from the earliest stages of the revolution.

XXV

EUROPE IN 1938

The Second Purge in the Nazi Organization

JANUARY 30th, the anniversary of Herr Hitler's appointment as Chancellor of the German Reich, had normally been made by him the occasion for an important public pronouncement. It had therefore been expected that the Reichstag would be summoned on that day in 1938, in order to listen to the Führer's report of progress and commentary on the general situation. On the previous anniversary Herr Hitler had taken occasion to announce that 'the period of so-called surprises is at an end', and indeed it looked for a time as if 14 November 1936 had ended, with a comparatively innocuous gesture of unilateral repudiation, those interferences with weekend rest and recreation which Foreign Office employees had come to expect from Germany. On that date the section of the Treaty of Versailles relating to the internationalization of certain German waterways had been suddenly denounced by the Führer, but during the whole of 1937 his January announcement corresponded to the facts. Some such respite was, indeed, required, or the surprises would cease to surprise, for Herr Hitler's predilection for Saturday shocks had become so notorious that, to adopt a sporting metaphor, the batsmen were all set for that fast and tricky ball at the end of the over. To deliver an important speech on 30 January was another of the Führer's regular habits, and some attention, not unmixed with uneasiness, was therefore aroused when the date for the customary address to the Reichstag was postponed to 20 February.

It has been suggested that there was a connexion between this change of plans and an event which took place a few days earlier, on 26 January, when Dr Tavs, a leading Austrian Nazi, was arrested in Vienna, and the plot for an impending *coup* disclosed and temporarily frustrated. It is alleged that the intention was to bring this conspiracy to a successful conclusion in time for the anniversary celebrations on 30 January. It is also said that the intervention by German forces on which the scheme depended was opposed in influential Reichswehr circles, and particularly by the Commander-in-Chief, General von Fritsch, who is even believed to have given his word that the troops under his control should not be used for such a purpose.[1] This story does not materially conflict with the reasons for the postponement of his speech subsequently given by Herr Hitler:

> In the first place, I wished to make a number of changes in important posts and it seemed to me fitting to make them after, rather than before, 30 January; while in the second place I deemed it advisable to effect a further and very necessary understanding in a certain department of foreign affairs before addressing you.[2]

The men of Herr Hitler's entourage prominent in Nazi counsels had, from the first, tended to fall into two groups, one of which had favoured and advocated a much more daring and active foreign policy than the other. The more cautious element was particularly associated with the Reichswehr. Since the purge of 1934 the regular army had adopted an increasingly independent attitude; many of its officers not only disapproved of such hazardous steps as the reoccupation of the Rhineland and of the wastage of military strength through intervention in Spain, but had shown a certain distaste for the emphasis laid on ideological differences, and were believed to hanker secretly for a return to better relations with the great military power of Russia. They also disapproved of the treatment to which all branches of the Christian Church had been subjected under the Nazi regime. Broadly speaking, the Reichswehr exercised a conservative and restraining influence in Nazi counsels.

Field-Marshal von Blomberg, the Minister of War, had recently contracted a marriage which was regarded in army circles as socially undesirable. General von Fritsch, the Commander-in-Chief, found in this circumstance an occasion for the Reichswehr to assert itself. Basing himself on the traditions of the German officer caste, he now demanded of Herr Hitler the resignation of Marshal von Blomberg, a demand which seemed to place the Führer in something of a difficulty, since he had been induced to grace the wedding with his presence. The demand was, however, conceded, but the trial of strength was

---

[1] See article by M. Fodor in *Foreign Affairs*, July 1938, p. 587.
[2] Speech to the Reichstag, 20 February 1938.

not allowed to terminate in the anticipated triumph of the Reichswehr group. On the contrary, Herr Hitler seized the opportunity for a reshuffle which would put the too independent spirits of the German army into what he conceived to be their proper place. On 4 February General von Fritsch and thirteen other senior officers were removed from their posts, and a decree was issued vesting the immediate command over the armed forces in the Führer himself. A second decree set up a Cabinet Council in which the Ministry for Foreign Affairs was entrusted to Herr von Ribbentrop, an adherent of the more dashing and hazardous school, while the more moderate and diplomatic Freiherr von Neurath was delicately put on the shelf by being appointed President of the Council. On the whole, these changes, together with the simultaneous recall of Herr von Papen from the Austrian Embassy, led the outside world to anticipate a fresh outbreak of startling developments in the near future.

The Resignation of Mr Eden

The world had not long to wait, for before 20 February, the date arranged for the assembly of the Reichstag, Herr Hitler had to carry through the second part of his programme, and 'effect a further and very necessary understanding in a certain department of foreign affairs'. On 12 February Dr Schuschnigg and Herr Hitler met at Berchtesgaden, in response to the invitation or summons of the latter. According to the official communiqué issued in Germany, the aim of the discussion between the German and Austrian Chancellors was to clarify difficulties which had arisen in the working of the Austro-German Agreement of 1936. 'It was agreed that both parties are resolved to keep to the principles of that agreement.' The sequel to the interview was difficult to reconcile with this statement. It will be recalled that the first clause of the 1936 agreement recognized the full sovereignty of Austria, and the second promised non-interference by each country in the internal affairs of the other, under which heading the question of Austrian National Socialism was expressly included. Yet the immediate results of the Berchtesgaden discussions were the appointment of Dr Seyss-Inquart, a man of Sudeten origin and Nazi sympathies, to the key position of Minister of the Interior with control of the Austrian police, the admission to the Cabinet of a number of new ministers of pronounced German leanings, the release of political prisoners and the legalization of Nazi activities within the confines of Austria. These things suggested the fruits of a German ultimatum rather than voluntary concessions by Dr Schuschnigg induced by peaceful persuasion.

Signor Mussolini was quick to grasp the trend of events. Indeed, his first perception of them seems to have preceded the Berchtesgaden interview, and to have arisen immediately after the political rearrangements in Germany. It was on 10 February that the first fresh overtures to Great Britain are said to have been made. But the desirability of reconciling old antagonisms became much more obvious and urgent after Dr Schuschnigg's return to Austria. As a matter of fact, it was already too late to save the situation, but at any rate accelerated action seemed called for. For the 'Axis' was now assuming the appearance of a mechanism binding Italy to the triumphant chariot wheels of Germany, and carrying her whither she would not. The British Prime Minister and the majority of his Cabinet also saw in what was occurring a golden opportunity for realizing that policy of reconciliation on which their hearts were set.

Mr Eden saw the situation differently. He, no less than Mr Chamberlain and his colleagues, had desired and worked for better relations with Italy, but he saw no value in professions of friendship which Signor Mussolini belied by his every action. The 'Gentleman's Agreement' had been immediately followed by a reinforcement of the Italian troops in Spain, of which Mr Eden said, 'It may be held that this was not a breach of the letter of our understanding, but no-one, I think, surely will contend that it did not run counter to its spirit.' [1] Adverse propaganda, though expressly renounced in the agreement, 'was scarcely dimmed for an instant'.[2] The amicable correspondence between his leader and the Duce had been immediately followed by the submarine incidents in the Mediterranean. At the moment, from 5 February, the forces of General Franco in Spain were engaged in a rapid and triumphant advance from the Teruel sector to the sea, which the *Popolo d'Italia* and other organs of Mussolini's press were almost daily applauding as a predominantly if not exclusively Italian exploit. In these cir-

[1] House of Commons, 21 February 1938.   [2] ibid.

cumstances, Mr Eden was unwilling to pay a price for professions of friendship unvouched by performance.

> It is my contention [he said] that before His Majesty's Govern-
> ment open official conversations in Rome . . . we must make further
> progress with the Spanish problem; we must agree not only on the
> need for withdrawal and on the conditions of withdrawal . . . but we
> must go further and show the world not only promise but achieve-
> ment. The withdrawal must have begun in earnest before those
> conversations in Rome can be held on a really solid basis of good will,
> which is essential to success.[1]

The British Foreign Secretary no doubt realized as well as
everyone else that the new situation between Italy and Germany might give to Signor Mussolini's professed desire for English
friendship a new sincerity, but in that case, was not this desire
a valuable lever with which to adjust the Spanish difficulty?
In Mr Eden's view, the matter might be urgent from the Italian
standpoint, but for England it was not a case of now or never,
and it was

> a moment for this country to stand firm, not to plunge into negotia-
> tions unprepared, with the full knowledge that the chief obstacle to
> their success has not been resolved.[2]

Matters were brought to a head on Friday, 18 February,
when Mr Chamberlain and Mr Eden together held a long
conference with the Italian ambassador, Count Grandi. The
ambassador emphasized the earnest desire of his country for
an early start of conversations with a view to an agreement. He
was understood by Mr Eden to convey an intimation, in the
nature of a threat, that it was 'now or never'. This interpretation was vigorously contested by Mr Chamberlain, but he
seems to have considered the matter one of exceptional urgency,
since the unusual step was taken of summoning a Cabinet
meeting on Saturday afternoon, which reassembled on Sunday
and settled the whole matter without waiting for the reply to a
question which Mr Chamberlain himself had asked—whether
the Italian Government was prepared to accept the British
formula for the withdrawal of volunteers from Spain. An
affirmative reply to this question was received from Italy by
Count Grandi on the morning of Sunday, 20 February, and

---

[1] House of Commons, 21 February 1938.   [2] ibid.

communicated to the Prime Minister on the following morning. In the meantime, the whole issue had been fought out in the Cabinet, and Mr Eden's resignation was in Mr Chamberlain's hands on Sunday evening. He was accompanied into retirement by the Parliamentary Under-Secretary, Lord Cranborne. If there was no suggestion of 'now or never', the intense activity and rapid conclusion are difficult to understand.

It seems clear, however, that the retirement of the Foreign Secretary was merely the culminating point in a conflict between two opposed points of view which had for some time been dividing the Cabinet. Rumours of a coming split had been constantly appearing in the press both of this and other countries. The fundamental cleavage had been hinted by Mr Eden in a speech which he delivered to the Junior Imperial League on 12 February, in which he said that peace for the younger generation meant that

in any agreement made today there must be no sacrifice of principles and no shirking of responsibilities merely to obtain quick results. . . . We offer friendship to all but on equal terms. For it is not by seeking to buy temporary good will that peace is made, but on a basis of frank reciprocity with mutual respect.

The contrasted view of the opposing school may be conveniently illustrated from the speech delivered by Mr Eden's successor, Lord Halifax, at Geneva on 12 May.

Where two ideals are in conflict: that of devotion, unflinching but unpractical, to some high purpose, and that of a practical victory for peace, I cannot doubt that the stronger claim is that of peace.

This conception would be criticized not only by those idealists who feel that peace *should not* be bought by a sacrifice of principle, but by others of a more realistic outlook who, like Mr Eden, believed that in the existing situation peace *could not* be so purchased, and that the assumption that the two ideals were actually in conflict was therefore fallacious.

But, apart from any question of principle, there was a divergent interpretation of the facts. Both parties were in agreement as to the vital importance of achieving, if possible, a trustworthy reconciliation with Italy: no-one in the National Government was deterred by ideological prejudice from attempting the task. But that section of Conservative opinion which supported the Prime Minister assumed that the interests of Italy predisposed her far more to friendship with England than with Germany; this led them to be sanguine of success, and they saw in a situation which subjected the Berlin-Rome Axis to strain a peculiarly opportune moment for a fresh effort at negotiation. In the Spanish struggle the natural sympathies of many of them were with General Franco: they could see dangers, no doubt, to British interests if the insurgents won with the help of an Italy hostile to England, but if once Anglo-Italian relations could resume their old friendly footing this conflict between their sympathy and their interest would disappear. In the Prime Minister's opinion, a fresh rebuff to the Italian advances might exacerbate anti-British feeling in Italy to the point of war. In any case, no permanent pacification of Europe was possible so long as it was ranged in two mutually hostile camps, and no opportunity should be neglected which held promise of reconciliation. Finally, if conversations were initiated, the presence of Mr Eden would be more of a hindrance than a help, for his diplomacy was thought to be lacking in tact, and the Italian and German dictators and their press made it abundantly clear that he was not a *persona grata* to them. On the very day of the crisis Herr Hitler was indulging in sarcastic personal references to the British Foreign Secretary, and in the previous week Signor Farinacci, in the *Regime Fascista*, had declared: 'There can be no improvement in the relations between Italy and Great Britain so long as the British foreign policy is directed by Mr Eden.'

This last point was seized by Mr Chamberlain's opponents and converted into an argument on the other side. The dictators say 'Eden must go', and he goes, they said: what will be the effects upon British prestige? Mr Eden himself, however, was inclined to agree that, if negotiations were to be begun, he was not the man to conduct them. But he considered the time inappropriate, and the method ineffective. The recent victory of the more incautious and intransigent elements in Germany, and Italy's unconcealed glorification of her intervention in Spain, made it, in his view, essentially a moment for firmness rather than concession. Moreover, from the moment when the British Government embarked, unprepared, upon the suggested conversations, they staked everything on achieving a satisfactory agreement. If this failed, Anglo-Italian relations must inevitably deteriorate, and the prestige of the Government in England would equally inevitably suffer. This placed the British negotiators in a position where the agreement might be more necessary to them than to Italy, and thus transferred the bargaining power to the wrong hands. If the real designs of Italy were more sinister than Conservative opinion supposed, she could almost compel the British Government to turn a blind eye to reinforcements in Spain or other actions inimical to our interests, by the threat of breaking off the negotiations.

The issue really turned upon the correct diagnosis of Italian intentions, upon the best prescription for the treatment of dictators, and upon the suitability of the occasion. An attempt has here been made to indicate both points of view, but time alone could show which judgement was the more correct one. There is no doubt that both opinions were sincerely supported by men of great political experience and unimpeachable character.

The Rape of Austria

In some quarters there have been attempts to trace a connexion between the resignation of Mr Eden, with the effects upon British prestige attributed to it by the opponents of the Government, and the violent annexation of Austria to Germany which was the next sensation of the year 1938. Thus, the editor of the *Fortnightly Review*, after quoting Mr Chamberlain's warning against the risk of starting an avalanche by an incautious move or a sudden exclamation, continued:

> By his own clumsy gesture in dislodging the Eden boulder he has now set in motion just such an avalanche: the snows, long perilously poised, have begun to move, and the shout of jubilation that went up from the enemies of democracy has determined its momentum.[1]

It does not seem possible, however, that the later event was actually affected by the British ministerial crisis. The evidence of careful preparation for the Austrian *coup* suggests that the fate of that country was in fact sealed after the Berchtesgaden interview of 12 February, and it is now clear that the decision

[1] *Fortnightly Review*, April 1938.

to carry this policy into effect had been taken considerably earlier. It was with the object of consummating the Anschluss that Herr Hitler had insisted on giving the control of order to Dr Seyss-Inquart, and granting to Nazi agitation in Austria what amounted to a free hand. Once this was done, in one way or another the pretext for German intervention was bound to arise, and the troops and police could move to their allotted quarters in Vienna.[1] From the first, the tragedy moved steadily to its dénouement on the lines which were planned. On 18 February the Austrian Cabinet announced that the Nazis 'will have the possibility of legal activity, but only on the basis of the Constitution, which now as heretofore precludes political agitation'. This restriction was at no time more than a dead letter. By the 21st, continuous Nazi demonstrations in all the principal centres of Austria had forced the Government to ban all meetings and processions and to forbid the wearing of Nazi emblems. Notwithstanding this, at Graz, on the 24th, large crowds of Nazis interrupted the broadcast of a speech by Dr Schuschnigg, demanded the hoisting of the swastika flag on the town hall, and forced the town officials to stop the broadcast when the Chancellor spoke of Austrian independence. Vienna rang continuously with cries of 'ein Volk, ein Reich!' At Graz, on 1 March, Dr Seyss-Inquart, who had visited Herr Hitler in Berlin immediately after his appointment in February, was greeted with a Nazi torchlight procession and the strains of the *Horst Wessel Lied*. Here, as at Linz four days later, the Minister of the Interior looked on with smiles and without protest while his official instructions were openly and flagrantly disregarded.

It was in these difficult circumstances that Dr Schuschnigg, on 9 March, prepared to play his trump card in the game for which the survival of his nation was the stake. He announced that he would hold, on the following Sunday, a plebiscite, to demonstrate, against the clamour of a vocal minority, the strength of the public opinion supporting him on the issue of Austrian independence. The question for popular decision was framed as follows:

---

[1] The actual moment chosen for this final stage may, however, have been affected by the fall of the French Government on 10 March, as a result of which France was without a Government on the critical days, 11 and 12 March.

Are you for a free and German Austria, independent and socially
harmonious (*soziales*), Christian and united; for peace and employment, and the equality of all who profess their faith in the people and
the Fatherland? [1]

Although the rhetorical phrasing of the question may be
criticized, it was well understood that the issue to be determined was that of independence versus Anschluss, and it is
the opinion of those best qualified to judge that the Chancellor
would have secured, in the answers to his question, a majority
of from 60 to 80 per cent. Even among Austrians generally
sympathetic to National Socialism there were many who
desired to retain at least the nominal independence and sovereignty of their country.

Herr Hitler himself was evidently apprehensive as to the real
state of Austrian public opinion. He would not allow his project to be subjected to such a test. The next day was spent in
consultations and arrangements, and on 11 March an ultimatum was presented to Dr Schuschnigg demanding the postponement of the plebiscite. To this the Chancellor is understood to have agreed, on condition that the Nazis should in
future refrain from disturbing order. By 6 p.m. or somewhat
earlier it was announced that the plebiscite had been postponed.
The respite was short. A second ultimatum, expiring at 7.30,
was presented, demanding the resignation of Dr Schuschnigg
in favour of Dr Seyss-Inquart, the allocation of two-thirds of
the Cabinet seats to Nazis, the grant of unrestricted freedom to
the Nazi party, and the return to Vienna of the Austrian legionaries, who had remained in exile since the *putsch* of 1934.
Almost simultaneously it became known that German troops
were massing on the frontier. At 7.30 p.m. listeners on the
radio were addressed for the last time by the Chancellor. He
announced that the march of German troops into Austria had
been threatened 'for this hour' unless he and the Government
resigned, and unless the President appointed a Cabinet nominated by Germany. He was not prepared in this terrible situation to shed blood, and had therefore yielded to force and

[1] 'Für ein freies und deutsches, unabhängiges und soziales, für ein christliches
und einiges Österreich. Für Frieden und Arbeit und die Gleichberechtigung aller,
die sich zu Volk und Vaterland bekennen.'

ordered the Austrian troops to withdraw without resistance. He concluded:

I declare before the world that the reports issued concerning disorders created by the workers and the shedding of streams of blood, and the assertion that the situation has got out of the control of the Government, are lies from A to Z. I take my leave with a German word and a German wish—God guard Austria!

If it was his intention to save Austria from a German invasion his sacrifice was made in vain. At 8.15 Dr Seyss-Inquart broadcast the intelligence that the German army was already on its way to Vienna. He is understood to have invited them to come and preserve order, but the pretext is hardly convincing, in view of the fact that by this time the only disturbers of the peace were the triumphant Nazis, who immediately swarmed into the streets, while the railway stations filled with departing refugees. At 10 p.m. mechanized units crossed the frontier, before seven o'clock on the following morning German aeroplanes were showering on the capital large printed leaflets in which Germany conveyed her greeting to 'Her National Socialist Austria and the new National Socialist Government', and very shortly afterwards about 1,000 German troops were in occupation of the capital. As an eyewitness points out, Seyss-Inquart's Government had only been in existence about five hours, and he pertinently inquires, 'Could those leaflets have been printed in that time, distributed to the air squadrons, brought to Vienna and dropped there?'[1] Once more, a Saturday found Europe suddenly confronted with a Hitlerian *fait accompli*. Evidently, 'the period of so-called surprises' was not, as the Führer had declared, 'at an end'.

There were reports of mechanical break-downs,[2] but observers on the spot were impressed by the evidence of thorough and careful organization.

Reflect [says the eyewitness already cited] that in two days they sent seven hundred aeroplanes into Austria . . . and that this vast air force landed in Austria as surely as birds homing to their nest, every detail of shelter, ground organization, fuel supply, billeting, and repairs having been thought out long in advance. . . . Reflect

---

[1] Douglas Reed, *Insanity Fair*. London, Cape, 1938, p. 396.

[2] There is no doubt that a number of tanks, lorries, &c., broke down on the advance.

that Germany sent something like 200,000 troops of all arms into Austria in the course of a long week-end, and that every man went to his appointed post and billet as if the invasion had been rehearsed a dozen times. Consider that food and fodder and fuel for every man and horse and tank and tractor of this great army . . . were available without the slightest hitch.[1]

At the frontier, the examining officials were provided with—

a thumb-indexed volume containing thousands of names and descriptions of people who were to be stopped; prepared by the dreaded German secret police, these volumes appeared in the hands of Nazi inquisitors at the frontier a few hours after the ultimatum.[2]

About 6 p.m. on that eventful Saturday, Herr Hitler arrived at Linz, where, in acknowledging the welcome of Dr Seyss-Inquart, he declared:

When I first set out from this town I felt in the depth of my soul that it was my vocation and my mission given to me by destiny that I should bring my home country back to the great German Reich. I have believed in this mission and I have fulfilled it.

While it is impossible to be certain whether the conception was actually formed at so distant a date, we may agree that this final declaration on the Austrian question was a closer approach to the truth than any of the Führer's utterances on this subject during the previous four years (cf. pp. 378, 399, and 330). The legalization of the union to which he alluded was not, however, completed until the next day, when it was announced that a new law had been decreed, the first and only important article of which declared Austria to be a *land* of the German Reich. *Finis Austriae.*

No attempt was made to conciliate national sensibilities. Austria was at once treated as a conquered country. Vienna was put in charge of some thousands of German police, who made wholesale arrests, and transferred to concentration camps all suspected opponents of the new regime. Herr Bürckel, the Governor of the Saar, was commissioned to reorganize the Nazi party. The Austrian National Bank was taken over by the Reichsbank, and the removal from Austria of more than 20 schillings in any month, or the equivalent of 30 schillings in foreign currency, was prohibited. Major Fey, the former Vice-

[1] Reed, op. cit., p. 397.　　[2] ibid., p. 416.

Chancellor, with his wife and son, together with other prominent persons, were reported to have committed suicide. Major Fey's dog appears also to have been shot. The Austrian Jews were subjected to every kind of ignominy, insult, and persecution. In these circumstances, few will be inclined to attach much importance to the plebiscite held on 10 April, which resulted, as anticipated, in a percentage of 99·73 votes endorsing the *de facto* situation.[1]

By the annexation of Austria the programme of *Mein Kampf* was brought considerably nearer realization through the acquisition of important strategic and economic advantages. Direct contact was established with Italy, Hungary, and Yugoslavia. A wedge was driven deeply into the heart of the Little Entente, and the Bohemian and Moravian districts of Czechoslovakia were enclosed as between the jaws of a pair of pincers. As was pointed out by Mr Churchill in the House of Commons, 'mastery of Vienna gives to Nazi Germany military and economic control of the whole of the communications of south-eastern Europe, by road, by river, and by rail'. There was an increase in the available man-power of the German army, attained by augmenting the population of the Reich by some $6\frac{3}{4}$ millions. Besides these direct additions to the military strength of Germany, her internal resources were increased, and her self-sufficiency developed, by the acquisition of the enormous and easily worked iron ore deposits of the Alpin-Montan Gesellschaft, of magnesite, for aeroplane manufacture, sufficient for all the present needs of the nation, and of a supply of timber adequate for half the German requirements, which were heavy, owing to the use of pulp and cellulose in making substitutes for materials not available at home. The seizure of the Austrian bank gave Germany control of some £20,000,000 worth of additional gold and foreign exchange. Herr Hitler had also enormously increased his economic control of neighbouring countries. The proportion of Hungarian foreign trade dependent on Germany rose from 20 per cent to 43 per cent in imports, and from 12 per cent to 44 per cent in exports. In Yugoslavia, the proportion in imports grew from 16 per cent to 44 per cent. About one-third of the total foreign trade of Roumania now

---

[1] The vote was taken over the whole Reich, and Austrian opinion was therefore, in any case, swamped. Apart from spoilt papers, there were 452,180 negative votes.

became dependent on Germany, and similar considerations apply to Greece and Turkey. The provisions of the Treaty of Versailles forbidding the Anschluss were perhaps not so iniquitous or unreasonable as has sometimes been contended.

Among those who drew grave conclusions from the situation were the Scandinavian States, who considered that the time had now arrived to declare their policy in the event of war. At a meeting of the foreign Ministers of these countries in Oslo on 5–6 April, a communiqué was prepared and issued, declaring that these northern States would in all circumstances keep out of war, without regard for possible obligations under Article 16 of the Covenant. This decision, which was ratified by the Norwegian Storting on 31 May, was reported by Dr Koht, the Foreign Minister of Norway, to the League Assembly in the following September.

The Anglo-Italian Agreement

Herr Hitler evinced some natural nervousness as to the possible reactions of his Austrian *coup* on the mind of Signor Mussolini. On 11 March he had written him a reassuring letter, in which he reminded the Duce that 'at a critical hour for Italy, I demonstrated the strength of my sentiments for you. Do not doubt that in the future also nothing will be changed in this respect'. He added that the Italian frontiers were henceforth as safe from German encroachment as those of France, and, less ambiguously, that they 'would never be touched or questioned'. A telegram which he dispatched on the 13th, 'Mussolini, I will never forget you for this!' suggests, however, an almost hysterical relief that the Italian attitude of 1934 had not been resumed. Indeed, the general public in Italy were extremely disquieted and perplexed at their leader's apparent indifference to a step which he had hitherto taught them to regard as disastrous to Italian security. In these circumstances Signor Mussolini became naturally eager to conclude an Anglo-Italian agreement which he could represent as a valuable diplomatic success. On the other hand, indifference on the Brenner and in the Danubian region might be thought to indicate an intention to pursue a course in the Mediterranean which might entail conflict with the interests of Great Britain; it is therefore not surprising that the negotiations following upon Mr Eden's resignation made rapid progress, and were, in the words of the British Prime Minister, 'carried on in a spirit of mutual accommodation and good will', with the result that the agreement was signed in Rome on 16 April.

After a protocol recording a desire for permanently friendly relations, and the attainment of general peace and security, and providing for subsequent negotiations in conjunction with the Egyptian Government on frontier delimitations in Africa, the terms of the agreement were embodied in eight annexes and an exchange of notes.[1] The first annex was a reaffirmation of the 'Gentleman's Agreement' of January 1937. The second provided for an exchange of information as to the movements of armed forces in overseas Mediterranean territories, the Red Sea, the Gulf of Aden, Egypt, and African territories including northern Tanganyika, but apparently excluding western and central Libya. The parties agreed not to construct new naval or air bases east of longitude 19 E. in the Mediterranean or the Red Sea without notification. In this part of the agreement the balance of advantage apparently rested with Italy, since she was a Power geographically situated in the Mediterranean, and was placed under no obligation to disclose anything with regard to herself, Sicily, or Sardinia; this annex has also been criticized as impeding the construction of an adequate base in Cyprus. The third annex regulated the position with regard to Arabia and certain islands in the Red Sea; treating Italian and British interests in this region on an equal footing, and declaring it to be in the common interest of both parties that neither they nor any other Power should acquire sovereignty or a 'privileged position of a political character' over the territories of Saudi Arabia or the Yemen.

The three succeeding annexes reaffirmed:

1. The ban on injurious propaganda.
2. Italian assurances as to the waters of Lake Tsana in Abyssinia as a source of water-supply to the Anglo-Egyptian Sudan.
3. The assurance previously given to the League, that natives in Italian East Africa should not be compelled to undertake military duties other than local policing and territorial defence.

[1] Cmd. 5726 of 1938.

The seventh annex dealt with the status of British religious bodies in Italian East Africa, and, finally, the eighth re-affirmed the intention of both parties to abide by the Convention of 1888, guaranteeing free use of the Suez Canal in peace and war.

The accompanying exchange of letters announced an immediate reduction of the Italian forces in Libya, and the intention of Italy to accede to the London Naval Treaty of 1936. The more important matters dealt with in this part of the agreement were, however, Spain and Abyssinia. Great Britain repeated that a settlement of the Spanish question must precede the entry into force of the agreement, but announced her intention of taking steps at the forthcoming League Council to clarify the situation of member States with regard to the recognition of the Italian conquest of Abyssinia—in other words, to remove an obstacle to such a recognition by herself. Italy confirmed her adherence to the British compromise proposal for the evacuation of foreign volunteers for Spain, and repeated her disclaimer of seeking a territorial, political, or privileged economic position in Spanish mainland or overseas possessions. She undertook in any case at the close of the Spanish war to withdraw forthwith all Italian troops and war material.

The Opposition did not fail to point out the extent to which the whole agreement consisted of reaffirmations of previously disregarded undertakings, but it was generally felt that it served the purpose of allaying any possible suspicions on the part of Italy that England harboured unfriendly or vindictive intentions, while its assumptions of Italian good faith, if rather optimistic, were sufficiently safeguarded by the proviso that it should not come into force before a 'settlement of the Spanish question'. On 16 April, when the agreement was signed, a settlement of a kind acceptable to Italy seemed an immediate prospect. On the previous day the forces of General Franco had reached the sea, severing the land connexion between Barcelona and Valencia, and thus cutting the territory retained by the Spanish Government into two separate portions. On the 19th the insurgent commander, in a broadcast from Saragossa, declared, 'The war is over. Our glorious soldiers, sailors and airmen are now experiencing the last days of the reconquest.' The advance of General Franco's army over the whole north-eastern front had, indeed, been so rapid during March and April as to suggest that the Government defence was finally collapsing. In these circumstances, the condition precedent to enforcing the agreement did not seem likely to cause any considerable delay. When, however, at this point, the pace of the advance slackened, and the expected end of the war receded into a remoter future, the condition assumed a new importance. Its existence, if firmly insisted on, forced the Italians to choose between the British Agreement and the continuance of their intervention in Spain.

They may not, indeed, have expected that the fulfilment of the condition would be rigorously enforced. On 21 February Mr Chamberlain had informed the House of Commons that he had told Count Grandi

it was essential that it should not be possible, if we went to the League to recommend the approval of the agreement, for it to be said that the situation in Spain during the conversations had been materially altered by Italy, either by sending fresh reinforcements to Franco or by failing to implement the arrangements contemplated by the British formula.

During the whole of General Franco's spring offensive, though the repeated allegations of the arrival of fresh Italian reinforcements may not have been sustained by adequate proof,[1] there could be no dispute whatever as to the indebtedness of the Spanish insurgents to their Italian allies. This was loudly proclaimed in the Italian press, and on 23 March the National Directorate of the Fascist Party had publicly stressed 'with pride . . . the valour of the legionaries, who are once again an essential factor in the victory in Spain.' This frankness, which forced the British Prime Minister to meet Opposition criticism with rather fine-spun distinctions between an essential factor and a material alteration, tended to revive suspicions that Anglo-Italian reconciliation was now less valued by Signor Mussolini than by Mr Chamberlain, and that the negotiations were assisting rather than impeding Italian intervention in Spain. In these circumstances, if we may judge from his subsequent impatience, Signor Mussolini seems to have expected that

[1] The arrival of Italian reinforcements does not now seem to be denied.

the stipulated 'settlement of the Spanish question', which Mr Chamberlain refrained from closely defining, would either be waived or subjected to an agreeably elastic interpretation; but in this he was disappointed. With the support of all parties, the British Government continued to insist on the Spanish settlement as a *sine qua non.*

In fact their main object, the demonstration of a friendly intention, had been achieved by the signature of the agreement, particularly after Lord Halifax, the new Foreign Secretary, at the meeting of the League Council on 12 May, had made it clear that Great Britain was really prepared, as part of a policy of general appeasement, to recognize the Italian conquest of Abyssinia. Any hope of a simultaneous reconciliation with Germany had been removed by Herr Hitler's action in Austria, and if there had originally been a design of breaking the Berlin-Rome Axis the impracticability of any such achievement was made clear by Herr Hitler's reception in Italy at the beginning of May. There was therefore, from the British standpoint, no longer any hurry about bringing the agreement into force; the matter of immediate urgency was to succeed in putting into effect the plan for the withdrawal of foreign assistance from Spain: for this purpose, insistence on the condition attached to the agreement was a useful lever.

Progress on the Non-Intervention Committee

The practical adoption of the withdrawal scheme was rendered desirable not only because of the danger of international conflict inherent in the presence of foreign elements on both sides in the Spanish civil war, or from the strain to which the Anglo-Italian Agreement was exposed so long as the Italians were likely to yield to the temptation to intervene in a way which could not be camouflaged or ignored, but also because of the inconveniences arising from the fact that the belligerent rights of the two Spanish parties were not internationally recognized. General Franco and his supporters, deprived as they were of the right to establish a recognized blockade or to visit and search neutral shipping in the war-zone, had endeavoured to get out of their difficulty by methods which were clearly illegal, and yet calculated to establish a dangerous precedent. The submarine outrages of 1937, leading to the

Nyon Conference, have already been mentioned: after some
respite, a fresh instance of this lawless behaviour occurred on
31 January, when the British steamer *Endymion* was torpedoed
by a submarine off Cartagena, and sank in four minutes.
Instructions were thereupon issued to attack any submarine
found submerged in the western Mediterranean. But this did
not prevent a variant of the same procedure, which was so
commonly practised during May and June as to raise a very
serious problem. This consisted in bombing and in many
instances machine-gunning from the air ships in Spanish
Government harbours, under circumstances which left no doubt
that the offence was deliberate, and not the accidental result of
operations against the ports in question. In some instances,
similar outrages took place outside territorial waters, but here
it was possible for the British navy to afford some protection.
Ships in harbour could not, however, be so defended without
incurring a charge of active intervention. A further complication was due to the fact, or well-grounded suspicion, that most
of the attacks were the work of Italian airmen, operating from
a base in Majorca. It was very difficult to induce the British
public to believe that such conduct was consistent with the
idea of Anglo-Italian friendliness which it was desirable to
foster. The quotation seemed appropriate:

> Perhaps it was right to dissemble your love,
> But—why did you kick me downstairs?

To place General Franco in the position of a recognized belligerent would remove even the shadow of the plea of necessity
under which such behaviour was extenuated. It was therefore increasingly urgent to proceed with the British compromise plan (see p. 440).

An argument enabling progress to be obstructed lay in the
fact that the French had for some time more or less admittedly
opened their frontier for the passage of war-supplies to the
Spanish Government. This was treated as a serious grievance
by the foreign interveners on the other side. There is reason to
think that this difficulty was rather forcibly pointed out by
Great Britain to France, though the exercise of actual pressure,
widely alleged and universally believed by the French, was
denied by the British Government. Whether spontaneously or

otherwise, the French Government on 13 June took steps securely to close the Pyrenean frontier. After this, the Non-Intervention Committee made rapid progress, and on 5 July a resolution was adopted providing a detailed scheme for the application of the British plan of 14 July 1937. Commissions having been sent to Spain to count the foreign elements on both sides, evacuation of these volunteers was gradually to be completed by the hundredth day from final adoption of the resolution and its acceptance by both the Spanish parties. Belligerent rights with certain specified restrictions were to be accorded when 10,000 volunteers had been evacuated from the side found to possess the smaller number, and a proportionately larger number from the other side. Provisions were laid down for observation by land, at sea, and in the air. Finally, there were financial provisions covering the cost of implementing the scheme. At the meeting of 5 July, the representatives of France, Great Britain, Germany, and Italy paid over a sum of £50,000 towards the initial cost. At the time it was impossible, in view of previous disappointments, to describe this progress otherwise than in the cautious language used by *The Times*, as 'the uphill path, scarcely yet begun, that may lead to a Spanish settlement,' and General Franco's refusal, published on 22 August, to accept the plan, which the Spanish Government had approved, with minor reservations, almost a month earlier, justified the cautious pessimism of this estimate.

The Czechoslovakian Crisis

Almost from the time of Herr Hitler's advent to power in 1933, and certainly from the date of his reoccupation of the Rhineland, observers of the European situation were inclined to regard Czechoslovakia as the most serious danger-point on the Continent. After the absorption of Austria, no one could entertain the smallest doubt as to the critical nature of the situation.

The existence of such a State as Czechoslovakia is extremely difficult to justify if the sole criterion applied is the principle of self-determination. It reproduced in miniature the racial jig-saw of the pre-war Austro-Hungarian Empire. According to the census figures of 1930, its composition, in round numbers, was as follows:

Czechs	7,447,000
Germans	3,231,600
Slovaks	2,309,000
Magyars	691,900
Ruthenians	549,000
Poles	81,700

Thus the Czechs could claim the position of a dominant majority only by treating the Slovaks as identical with themselves: these, however, though racially similar, had a separate history under Hungarian rule from the eleventh to the twentieth century, and there existed among them a by no means negligible movement for home rule.

The different races catalogued above, though distributed in a way which made the construction of separate administrative boundaries difficult if not impossible, were, broadly speaking, not blended but in occupation of portions of territory capable of fairly precise definition. If we dissect the tadpole form which the state assumed on the map, the head, corresponding to Bohemia and Moravia, was a Czech brain with a German rash on its face and skin, and a virulent but isolated patch in the back of the neck, to the south of Silesia. The body was Slovak, with a Polish infection of the spine and a belly full of indigestible Magyars. The slender tail was Ruthenian. To Germany, the position of Bohemia and Moravia, the parts of the country in which she was interested, was not that of a Czech majority and a German minority, but of a small Czech island in an immense Teutonic ocean. After the Anschluss with Austria, that island was almost surrounded by the rising tide of Nazidom.

The application of the principle of racial self-determination to Czechoslovakia was therefore bound to involve its complete disintegration. Even Czech and Slovak could only cling precariously to each other by one slender arm, and the districts which they would retain would be neither strategically nor economically viable. Nor did it seem any longer possible to establish a cantonal system on the Swiss model, as was suggested by some of the founders of the State at the time of the Peace Conference. This solution would in any case have been difficult owing to the shape and distribution of the administrative units, but after the rise of German National Socialism conflicting theories of government, and the existence of external ties incompatible with internal loyalty, made any such system clearly unworkable. The centrifugal forces would greatly have exceeded the centripetal.

Looked at, however, from the standpoint of the European balance of power, with an eye influenced by strategic considerations, the picture became a very different one. Czechoslovakia then assumed the appearance of an important bulwark against the threat of German hegemony. The words attributed to Bismarck might be recalled—'Who holds Bohemia is master of Europe'. If she succumbed, it might be difficult indeed to escape the nightmare of European diplomats, the domination of the whole Continent by a single Power. To France in particular the friendly democracy of Czechoslovakia was the one element in her post-war alliances which remained trustworthy: she was a most important link in Franco-Soviet co-operation, and an invaluable centre, in the event of war, for a radiating attack by air upon the principal nerve-centres of eastern Germany. France, therefore, as she repeatedly and emphatically declared, must be expected to intervene for the defence of Czecho-Slovakian integrity: since the reoccupation of the Rhineland she could only do this by enlarging the struggle to the scale of a European war: it seemed therefore a vital interest of Great Britain, as a country involved in the fate of France, as a country threatened by a Germany dominating Europe and reinforced by the products and munitions of Bohemia, and as a country desirous of peace, to do her best to ensure that no attack upon Czechoslovakian independence took place. Her obligations under the Covenant, for what they were worth, involved a similar policy. Since it was generally assumed that the Czechs themselves would not surrender without a struggle, any attack upon their country entailed the overwhelming probability of a general war. Czechoslovakia might well be the Serbia of a coming struggle.

On the other hand, intervention in Czechoslovakia seemed in many ways to be precisely the sort of risk which Nazi Germany was likely to take. The obstacle which the existence of this State imposed to the path of Germany's eastward expansion or domination, and the facilities which she provided as a base for hostile air attack, made it unlikely that Hitlerian Germany could ever be permanently reconciled to the independence of so embarrassing a neighbour. By his refortification of the Rhineland Herr Hitler had made it extremely difficult for France to come effectively to the rescue. The 'barrier' policy of Poland and Roumania stood in the way of assistance to the victim from Soviet Russia. Great Britain had made it clear that she was for peace at almost any price. The chances of League intervention seemed negligible. Except at the tip of her Ruthenian tail, where Czechoslovakia marched with Roumania, she was surrounded by indifferent or unfriendly neighbours. Finally, the grievances of the German minority could at almost any time be made a pretext for intervention sufficiently plausible to divide and weaken external sympathies. Czechoslovakia was a tempting field for another sudden *fait accompli*.

It is therefore not surprising that in almost every quarter the immediate reaction to the Austro-German Anschluss was— 'Czechoslovakia next!' As early as 24 March, Mr Chamberlain, though refusing to give a specific guarantee, uttered an impressive warning as to the probable consequences of aggression in that quarter:

If war broke out, it would be unlikely to be confined to those who have assumed such obligations. . . . It would be well within the bounds of probability that other countries, besides those which were parties to the original dispute, would almost immediately become involved. This is especially true in the case of two countries like Great Britain and France, with long associations of friendship, with interests closely interwoven, devoted to the same ideals of democratic liberty, and determined to uphold them.

In quarters subject to Nazi influence there was the same expectation with a different emphasis. Sudeten Germans greeted one another with the watchword—'Im Mai die Tschechoslowakei!' Speaking at Carlsbad on 23 April, Herr Henlein, the leader of the Sudeten German Party, put forward eight demands, which he presented as a minimum. Among these were full autonomy for the German areas, with complete liberty to profess German nationality and political philosophy. He also demanded a 'complete revision of Czech foreign policy' with special reference to the Russian alliance, and openly declared that his policy was inspired by the principles and ideas of National Socialism. The German press simultaneously assumed a hostile and minatory tone.

Before the end of April, the accumulating evidence of the danger of the situation led to conversations between the representatives of the British and French Governments, who met in London on 28 and 29 April. Here, as on the occasion of the Rhineland crisis, the voice of France advocated a resolute stand against further German aggression, while that of the British Government counselled caution and restraint. In M. Daladier's opinion, 'war could only be avoided if Great Britain and France made their determination quite clear to maintain the peace of Europe by respecting the liberties and the rights of independent peoples. . . . If, however, we were once again to capitulate when faced by another threat, we should then have prepared the way for the very war we wished to avoid'. He desired that both countries should at once make a firm declaration to Germany that, while prepared to urge Czechoslovakia to make all reasonable concessions, they were determined to support the Czechoslovak Government and prevent the dismemberment of Czechoslovakia. M. Bonnet considered that in the view of the Führer and his immediate entourage ' it was simply a question of removing Czechoslovakia from the map of Europe', they would not therefore be satisfied by any legitimate alleviation of Sudeten grievances. France must respect her engagement with Czechoslovakia, though 'if France remained alone, the situation must be uncertain; but if solidarity existed between France and Great Britain they could ensure the success of their views'. The policy advocated by M. Daladier was described by Mr Chamberlain as 'bluff':

One had only to look at the map. Czechoslovakia was surrounded by German territory on three sides. . . . In such circumstances, how would it be possible to save Czechoslovakia? In such a situation, were we to say to Germany that we would not tolerate her continued progress in Europe and that the moment had come to call a halt; and that, if Germany were to take certain steps, we would then declare war?

Were we sufficiently powerful to make victory certain? 'Frankly he did not think we were . . . At this moment he was certain public opinion in Great Britain would not allow His Majesty's Government to take such a risk.'

Lord Halifax took the same line:

If he had rightly understood M. Bonnet, the latter had asked whether, after Dr Beneš had informed His Majesty's Government of the concessions which he was prepared to make, and the latter had found them reasonable, His Majesty's Government would then be prepared, in the event of the rejection of these concessions by Germany and of a German attack on Czechoslovakia to accept an obligation to defend Czechoslovakia against the results of such German aggression. If this was M. Bonnet's question, he could only answer that, for the reasons already given, it would be impossible to accept such a commitment.

In these circumstances, the discussion could only reveal a fundamental divergence between French and British views on policy and leave France uncertain of British support in the event of being called upon to fulfil her treaty obligations towards Czechoslovakia.[1]

On 20–21 May, on the eve of the Czechoslovak municipal elections, the tension reached a critical climax. There were reports of disquieting movements of German troops on the frontier, as to which reassuring explanations were given to the British ambassador in Berlin on the 20th; but these seem to have failed to carry complete conviction, since they had to be repeated in response to a further inquiry on the following day. In Czech circles there was a general conviction that a *putsch* was imminent, and a partial mobilization was ordered which is believed to have helped to save the situation. The tension was increased by an incident on 21 May, in which two Sudeten Germans were shot dead while attempting to pass a frontier post without halting in response to a challenge. The French Government announced that its obligations in the event of aggression would be fulfilled up to the hilt, and Great Britain was understood to have adopted an attitude of equal firmness. In these circumstances, this crisis, and the ensuing elections, passed off without disturbance, but a general impression prevailed that a most serious situation was very narrowly averted. These suspicions were not dispelled by subsequent German utterances, in particular by a speech addressed to a huge audience by Dr Goebbels on 21 June, in which he said: 'We

---

[1] For a full report of these Anglo-French conversations, see Woodward, E. L., and R. Butler. *Documents on British Foreign Policy*, Third Series, vol. i, 1938. London, H.M.S.O., 1949, pp. 212–32.

will not look on much longer while 3,500,000 Germans are maltreated. We saw in Austria that one race cannot be separated into two countries, *and we shall soon see it somewhere else.*'

By the month of August the attention of all concerned was concentrated upon the task of achieving a satisfactory solution of the minorities problem, especially that of the German minority. The Czechoslovak Government were busy with the preparation of a 'Nationalities Statute', in which they professed to have gone as far as was compatible with national security and independence (some say even farther), to satisfy legitimate grievances. The Sudeten Germans retaliated with a memorandum of fourteen points, and it was evident that a gap of formmidable dimensions still separated the two sides. To assist in bridging this gap, or to defer a crisis by keeping negotiations alive as long as possible, the British Government dispatched Lord Runciman to Prague, a diplomatic move which was very generally approved. There remained, however, a doubt in many minds as to whether the Sudeten question was the major Czechoslovak problem. In the opinion of a very wise observer of the international scene,

It was never a major problem, and it is less than ever a major problem today. So far as the larger issues are concerned, the grievances of the German minority in the Historic Provinces are simply a pretext. If they did not exist they would have needed to be created or invented.[1]

If this diagnosis was true, the most admirable settlement which Lord Runciman might assist in arranging could effect no more than a temporary alleviation. The external danger would recur at any moment when the statesmen of Europe were lacking in wisdom, in vigilance, or in courage.

During August and September the atmosphere of the Czechoslovak situation became charged with ever-increasing tension. As Lord Lloyd stated in the House of Lords, there was considerable evidence that the German Government were determined from the first to foment and exploit the discontent of the Sudetens, and to bring the crisis to a head about the date when this actually occurred. This has now been placed beyond doubt by the public admission of Herr Hitler and his associates. The

[1] Sir Alfred Zimmern, *International Affairs*, July 1938, p. 467.

Czechoslovak Government made great and continuous efforts to meet the claims of their German minority in an accommodating spirit, but the latter showed no disposition whatever to compromise. In the meanwhile the prevailing uneasiness was increased by German army manoeuvres on an unprecedented scale—involving the mobilization of over a million men—and by the conscription of labour for intensive work on the Rhineland fortifications. The controlled German press simultaneously did all in its power to exacerbate the situation by emphasizing, exaggerating, and inventing 'incidents' in Czechoslovakia, and by persistent vituperation of the Czech Government. On 27 August Sir John Simon, at Lanark, reiterated Mr Chamberlain's warning of 24 March (see p. 466). On 1 September Herr Henlein, the Sudeten leader, visited Herr Hitler at Berchtesgaden. Five days later, Dr Beneš handed to the Sudeten leaders an amended plan, which, in Lord Runciman's opinion, and in that of the more responsible Sudeten leaders, 'embodied almost all the requirements of the Carlsbad eight points, and with a little clarification and extension could have been made to cover them in their entirety'.[1] However, 'the very fact that they were so favourable operated against their chances, with the more extreme members of the Sudeten German party'.[1] On 7 September an incident at Moravska Ostrava, in which a Sudeten deputy was struck by a Czech policeman, and some minor clashes between German demonstrators and the authorities led to some temporary arrests, was made the pretext by the Sudeten party for suspending if not breaking off negotiations, though disciplinary action against the police was promised by the Czech Government. Negotiations were resumed on 10 September, and agreement was very nearly reached, but a speech by Herr Hitler at the Nuremberg party rally on 12 September was the signal for immediate outbreaks of disorder, amounting in effect to a revolution in the Eger-Asch district. The emergency measures decreed by the Czechoslovak Government were met by an ultimatum from Herr Henlein. Some fighting ensued, with loss of life on both sides, and Lord Runciman decided that his functions as a mediator were at an end, since 'the connexion between the chief Sudeten leader and the Government of the

[1] Cmd. 5847 of 1938, p. 4.

Reich had become the dominant factor in the situation; the dispute was no longer an internal one'.

Prospects of European peace became at once extremely precarious, and on 15 September Mr Chamberlain flew to Germany and interviewed the Führer at Berchtesgaden. By this time Lord Runciman, according to his report written on 21 September, had become convinced that, though at the time of his arrival the more moderate Sudeten leaders still desired a settlement within the frontiers of the Czechoslovak State, 'those frontier districts between Czechoslovakia and Germany where the Sudeten population is in an *important* majority should be given full right of self-determination at once'.[1] But for territory where the German majority was not so important he advocated a solution on the lines of the amended plan of the Czechoslovak Government. After listening to Herr Hitler, however, Mr Chamberlain favoured a more drastic solution. A conference was held in London with M. Daladier and M. Bonnet, at which the British and French statesmen agreed to support a proposal that all districts containing over 50 per cent of German inhabitants (i.e. any absolute majority) should be directly transferred to Germany without plebiscite. The dangers and practical difficulties of plebiscites in the existing situation were so great that they met with no support in well-informed and responsible quarters. The divergence from Lord Runciman's proposal is not without importance, for whereas the transfer of an *important* majority could be justified as conforming to the principle of self-determination, a bare majority of German inhabitants, many of whom were opposed to union with the Reich, meant presumably an absolute majority of the population which did not desire the course proposed. In other respects, however, the proposal conformed to Lord Runciman's recommendations. Czechoslovakia's existing treaties of alliance were to be replaced by an international guarantee of her reduced frontiers against unprovoked aggression, which the French and British Governments recognized that the Czechoslovak Government was justified in demanding, and in which they declared themselves prepared to join. To these proposals the Czechoslovak Government was requested on Sunday the 18th to give a reply not later than the following Wednesday.

[1] Cmd. 5847 of 1938, p. 6.

The recipients of this message at first demurred, but, in spite of what they regarded as the 'many unworkable features' of the plan, they were eventually persuaded to accept it, being led to understand that they would otherwise stand alone in the event of war, but that it was the end of the demands to be made upon them, and that 'it followed from the Anglo-French pressure that these two Powers would accept responsibility for our reduced frontiers and would guarantee us their support in the event of our being feloniously attacked'.[1]

French public opinion is said generally to have accepted this solution as a 'shameful necessity', though three members of M. Daladier's Government were gravely dissatisfied and were reported to have tendered their resignations, and General Faucher, a distinguished French soldier, repudiated his nationality and asked to be accepted as a Czechoslovak citizen.[2] M. Hodza's Government in Czechoslovakia resigned after accepting the terms proposed, and was succeeded by a new one under General Sirovy, which, however, declared itself bound by the decision of its predecessor. Perhaps the most important effect of the step taken was to encourage Hungary and Poland to prefer their claims to a share in the partition. Representatives of these countries at once conferred with Herr Hitler, and when Mr Chamberlain once more flew over for a further interview with the Führer at Godesberg he found to his surprise that Herr Hitler was now demanding much more onerous terms. He had now espoused the cause of Polish and Hungarian 'self-determination', and in a memorandum in the nature of an ultimatum which he gave to Mr Chamberlain on 23 September to forward to Prague, he now made the following demands:

1. Withdrawal of all Czech forces, including police and customs officials, from an area defined in an attached map and roughly corresponding to the whole area to be ceded, and the cession of this area to Germany on 1 October.

2. The territory to be handed over in its existing state, with all fortifications and commercial installations, railway rolling-stock, &c., and without the removal of foodstuffs, cattle, or raw materials.

---

[1] Cmd. 5847 of 1938, pp. 16, 17.
[2] General Faucher had been head of the French military mission to Czechoslovakia, and had lived there for many years.

3. The discharge of all Sudeten Germans serving in the Czechoslovak military or police forces and of all German political prisoners.

4. Final delimitation to be decided by a plebiscite under the control of an international commission and settled by a German-Czech or an international commission.

These terms were rejected by the Czechoslovak Government as 'absolutely and unconditionally unacceptable'. They also shocked the British Prime Minister, who 'bitterly reproached' the Führer, and

declared that the language and manner of the document . . . would profoundly shock public opinion in neutral countries.

He further said:

I am sure that an attempt to occupy forthwith by German troops areas which will become part of the Reich at once in principle, and very shortly afterwards by formal delimitation, would be condemned as an unnecessary display of force. . . . The Czech Government cannot, of course, withdraw their forces . . . so long as they are faced with the prospect of forcible invasion.

The Godesberg Conference accordingly broke down, and with Mr Chamberlain's return England and other countries prepared for inevitable and imminent war. The fleet was mobilized, and anti-aircraft territorials were called up for service. Whether as a result of this demonstration of firmness or of a request now put forward by Signor Mussolini, Herr Hitler, however, now modified his attitude to the point of agreeing to a Four-Power Conference of the representatives of France, Great Britain, Germany, and Italy, to be held in Munich on 29 September, and this Conference succeeded for the time being in preserving peace by an agreement arrived at and signed in the course of that day. The Munich Agreement, which was accompanied by an Anglo-German declaration renouncing war in the settlement of their differences, succeeded in modifying in certain respects the conditions of the Godesberg memorandum. Herr Hitler was allowed his military occupation, but in five instalments spread between 1 and 10 October instead of simultaneously on 1 October over the whole of the territory to be ceded. It must be noted, however, that the shrift given to the Czechs was not very materially longer between 29 September and 10 October than between 23 September (date of the Godesberg memorandum) and 1 October, and portions of the occupation took place on much shorter notice. The final line of German occupation was to be fixed, not by Herr Hitler's map, but by an international commission. This commission, however, consisted of representatives of the two Axis Powers, of Great Britain and France, whose will to defend Czechoslovak interests had not proved conspicuous, and of Czechoslovakia herself in a minority of one. In these circumstances it is hardly surprising that the correspondence between the boundary claimed by the Führer and that fixed by the commission was so close that the differences are not readily apparent. The condition that the territory was to be handed over as it stood was modified to the extent of permitting the removal of foodstuffs, cattle, or raw material, if the owners could find time or opportunity to do so. More reasonable terms were agreed upon for the plebiscite areas, though the idea of holding plebiscites was almost immediately abandoned. Finally the agreement provided for a right of option into and out of the transferred territories, and the exchange of populations. On the whole, however, the divergences from the original Anglo-French proposals were more striking than the differences from the Godesberg memorandum.

The Governments of France and Great Britain reiterated their willingness to enter into an international guarantee of the new frontiers of Czechoslovakia against unprovoked aggression, in which Germany and Italy professed themselves willing to join when the question of the Polish and Hungarian minorities had been settled. Meanwhile the Poles occupied Teschen by a successful threat of invasion, and no country interfered with them. Hungary at the same time put forward extensive revisionist claims in a more decent manner. It did not seem likely that the mangled remains of Czechoslovakia would offer such temptation to an aggressor as to call into operation the international guarantee. *Cantabit vacuus coram latrone viator.*

In recognition of her sacrifices, Czechoslovakia asked for a loan and was offered by Great Britain an immediate advance of £10 million. While no more could reasonably be asked of this country, the losses sustained under the Munich terms were, of course, immeasurably heavier.

There can be no doubt that the steps taken by Mr Chamberlain and M. Daladier for the preservation of peace were in accord with the overwhelming sentiment of public opinion in their two countries. Majority opinion, at any rate at the moment, probably endorsed the view of *The Times* that 'No conqueror returning from a victory on the battlefield has come home adorned with nobler laurels than Mr Chamberlain from Munich yesterday'. In fact, except for the Czechoslovak State, whose sacrifice was consummated by the resignation of her President, Dr Beneš, all the parties had solid grounds for satisfaction. Signor Mussolini had the pleasure of seeing the affairs of Europe regulated by his cherished Four-Power Pact. As for Herr Hitler, unless his conscience pricked him with the recollection of his assurance on 13 March that he had no designs against the integrity of Czechoslovakia, he might congratulate himself on achieving his masterpiece in the accurate computation of risks, when once more a Saturday saw his armies marching unresisted into an extension of German territory.[1]

[1] The extent to which the optimistic diagnosis of the situation, widely prevalent at the time, differed from the reality has now been made clear by the revelation, in the Nuremberg trial, of Hitler's remarks to his supreme commanders at a secret meeting held on 23 November 1939:

'It was clear to me from the first moment that I could not be satisfied with the Sudeten German territory. That was only a partial solution. The decision to march into Bohemia was made. Then followed the erection of the Protectorate and with that the basis of the action against Poland was laid.'

Further light on the realities of the Czechoslovak situation is shed by the following passage from the Nuremberg judgement (Cmd. 6964 of 1946, p. 20):

'On 28 May 1938, Hitler ordered that preparations should be made for military action against Czechoslovakia by 2 October. . . . On 30 May 1938, a directive signed by Hitler declared his "unalterable decision to smash Czechoslovakia by military action in the near future".'

A feature of the situation unrealized at the time is the pessimism as to the prospects of this policy entertained by the highest military authorities in Germany. General Beck, in particular, the Chief of the General Staff, in a memorandum drawn up in July, urged that Hitler 'should be made to stop the preparations he has ordered for war. . . . For the present I consider it hopeless, and this view is shared by all my Quartermasters General and departmental chiefs of the General Staff who would have to deal with the preparation and execution of a war against Czechoslovakia.'

XXVI

THE LAST YEAR OF PEACE

The Policy of Appeasement

THE policy of 'appeasement', of which Munich was the culminating and final expression, has suffered such debasement of meaning in the light of events that it is the more necessary for the student to make a serious effort to appreciate fairly the reasons which prompted it. He should realize that, whether right or wrong, it was a definite and deliberate policy, and not, as many would-be defenders of the Munich agreement have represented, a mere subterfuge necessitated by the inadequate state of the British preparations for war. It is indeed astonishing that this explanation should have been so popular with many of Mr Chamberlain's unofficial supporters. If their case were true, as to which most of them had no accurate means of knowledge, it hardly amounted to a defence of a Government which had held the reins of office securely during all, and more than all, the time during which Germany was raising her armed strength practically from zero. But in fact, whatever the state of the British forces in 1938, their weakness can hardly have been the determining ground of the policy pursued. It is clear that, after the meeting in Godesberg, Great Britain was expecting to fight, and irrevocably committed, if Hitler failed to modify the attitude which he had, at this stage, taken up. This left the question of peace or war out of our own control, and it is difficult to believe that the Government would have placed itself in this situation had it felt altogether unprepared to fight. It is, moreover, doubtful whether the forces which eventually took the field against Germany in 1939, in spite of any additions made to the strength of Great Britain, were more formidable than those available at the time of Munich, when they would have included not only the thirty to forty finely equipped divisions of Czechoslovakia, but, according to its declared intentions, the power of the Soviet Union as well.

It is only fair to Mr Chamberlain to suggest that the motives which actuated him were quite different. The whole course of the negotiations shows him, while comparatively indifferent to the conditions of the settlement, firmly resolved that it should be brought about through the machinery of conference, and not as a concession to naked force. This he considered that he had achieved at Munich. In his repeated insistence on 'carrying out the principles already agreed upon in an orderly fashion and free from the threat of force' lies the real clue to his policy. To secure a conference of the Great Powers of Europe, settling their differences round a table, Mr Chamberlain was willing to pay a very high price. Even if he had unquestionably been in control of overwhelming military strength, the policy which he pursued would probably have been on the same lines, though he would doubtless have driven a harder bargain. Throughout his whole tenure of office, down to March 1939, he followed, with obstinate sincerity, a consistent even if a mistaken line. He was a man singularly free from political opportunism, and he undoubtedly felt complete conviction as to the rightness of the course which he pursued.

That course was an endeavour to escape from the real 'international anarchy' following on the collapse of the League system, by a return to the earlier alternative of a Concert of the Great European Powers. It is true that this alternative was no more available than the other, if the dictators were as unscrupulous and faithless as Mr Chamberlain's opponents considered them, or their ambitions as unlimited as was suspected. But, on this hypothesis, the dismal alternatives seemed to be: continued international anarchy culminating in war, or a prospect of war in the immediate future. Mr Chamberlain's mind revolted from what he called 'this bleak and barren policy of the inevitability of war'. He preferred to act on the assumption, which also had numerous and distinguished supporters in England, that both Hitler's and Mussolini's aspirations were confined to the redressal of certain limited grievances, and that, if these were satisfied, they could be brought to sit round a conference table in the traditional way, and that a general and peaceful European settlement might thus be achieved. The policy which he consequently adopted was, in its general lines, unexceptionable, assuming the correctness of the diagnosis on which it was based, and the situation was

certainly such as to make an effort of the kind desirable, provided that, in view of the obvious probability of war, important
strategic bastions were not successively surrendered, or the
prestige and honour of the nation jeopardized. It was in fact
in its diagnosis and in its application rather than its principles
that the policy of 'appeasement' was most open to criticism.
Such criticism was certainly aroused by the Czechoslovakian
settlement.

England after Munich

After the burst of natural, but perhaps rather hysterical,
enthusiasm with which Great Britain hailed the unexpected
respite provided by the Munich agreement, public opinion
showed itself to be sharply and even acrimoniously divided.
Wherever two or three were gathered together, the merits of
the settlement were sure to be discussed, and old friendships
were strained and long-standing ties of party allegiance
broken to an extent seldom experienced in this country. A
large majority still defended the agreement, though the need
for intensified defence preparation was generally recognized,
and the numbers of those who expressed unqualified approval
or even pride in the achievement, though still considerable,
tended to diminish.

Regarded qualitatively, the critics of Munich were more
impressive. Those whom the public had learnt to regard as
experts on the conditions of central or south-eastern Europe—
the foreign correspondents of the press and other publicists—
were mostly to be found in their ranks, and the authorities of
Chatham House, seeking, as always, to preserve a just balance
in their discussions, found an almost if not quite insuperable
difficulty in securing an effective unofficial champion of
Government policy. In the House of Commons debate on the
Munich settlement, the critics, apart from members of the
regular opposition, included Mr Duff Cooper, who resigned his
office as First Lord of the Admiralty, Mr Churchill, Mr Eden,
Lord Cranborne, Mr Amery, and Mr Harold Nicolson, but it
would perhaps be invidious to institute a comparison of these
names with the list of those who defended the agreement.

The dissatisfied minority further compensated for its numerical inferiority by greater confidence and conviction. From the

nature of the case the supporters of the Munich agreement were
on far less certain ground, and forced, for the most part, to
adopt a defensive attitude. Hitler's gains were patent, and the
sacrifice of Czechoslovakia was an undeniable fact, but Mr
Chamberlain's claim to have achieved 'peace for our time'
remained a matter of personal opinion which only the future
could confirm or refute. Indeed, in the House of Commons, the
Prime Minister almost immediately qualified the optimism of
his forecast by admitting that—'we have only laid the foundations of peace. The superstructure is not even begun', and by
urging the intensification of national rearmament. The most
prominent supporter of his policy, Sir John Simon, was even
less positive.

It can only be for history [he said] to decide hereafter whether the
things that were done at Munich the other day lead, as we all of us
everywhere in this House hope they will, to better things, or whether
the prognostications of increasing evil will prove to be justified,

and he concluded by urging the Commons, in the words of
Shelley,

to hope till Hope creates
From its own wreck the thing it contemplates;

a quotation which does not seem to provide a very firm
foundation for confidence. Mr Churchill, on the other hand,
was able roundly to describe the situation as 'a disaster of the
first magnitude', and indeed, with a prescience shared at the
time by very few, to prophesy: 'I think you will find that in a
period of time which may be measured by years, but may be
measured only by months, Czechoslovakia will be engulfed in
the Nazi regime'.

Mr Amery suggested that the settlement represented 'the
triumph of sheer, naked force', which might figure in history
as 'the greatest—and the cheapest—victory ever won by aggressive militarism'. Critics outside Parliament were no less
emphatic on the strategic defeat incurred, and even more
inclined to dwell on the moral aspects of the question; their
attitude being well exemplified in Professor Toynbee's remark,
'So far, all the bars to our peace-medal have been cast out of
other people's coin'. Two books, issued at the time by com-

petent journalistic observers—Mr Gedye's *Fallen Bastions* and
Mr Douglas Reed's *Disgrace Abounding*—enshrined in their titles
the strategic and ethical lines of attack respectively.

Herr Hitler, in the meantime, did nothing to encourage a
favourable view of his own intentions or of British policy. He
took not the slightest trouble to play convincingly the character
assigned to him by the 'appeasers'. His harsh voice continued
to scream out threats and insults directed at England and her
statesmen, and, while Mr Chamberlain was contending that the
settlement was an instance of the use of discussion rather than of
force, the German leader and the press which he controlled
continued unhelpfully to draw the exactly opposite conclusion.
Little credit could be given to the Führer's statement to Mr
Chamberlain that the acquisition of the German districts of
Czechoslovakia was the last of his territorial claims in Europe,
since it was a repetition in identical terms of assurances previously
made in a different context, only to be falsified by his subsequent action. Some humorist remarked that the phrase would
be an appropriate epitaph to engrave on the Führer's tomb-
stone, where it would for the first time be a truthful statement.
The result was to render comparatively unimportant the bitter
divisions which undoubtedly existed on the merits of past
policy, since there was complete agreement as to the course
marked out for the immediate future—an unrelaxing and
energetic concentration on the needs of national defence. The
state of public opinion is well reflected in a *Punch* cartoon for
12 October 1938, which showed a child indicating to its
parent a vast array of recruiting posters on the wall of a railway
station, and demanding, 'What are you going to do in the
Great Peace, Daddy?' In the same issue of the paper a poet
conveys the same idea:

> It's peace!
> The gas-masks are distributed.
> It's peace!
> Ten millions are contributed.
> We've dug up lots of trenches in everybody's garden,
> We've commandeered the underground without your leave or
>   pardon;
> Father's a balloon-barrage, mother's an air-warden.
> It's peace! It's peace!

Resurgence of Optimism

During the remainder of the winter, however, a brief respite was enjoyed. 'The boa constrictor', in the candid and illuminating metaphor of Dr Goebbels in his speech of 22 October, 'needed to digest all it had eaten before it started again.' Feeling against the Nazis was indeed exacerbated by the brutal outburst of organized anti-Semitism which followed the death of the third secretary of the German Embassy in Paris at the hands of a misguided young Jewish refugee, on 7 November. Attacks on Jewish property, so synchronized as to destroy any real semblance of spontaneity, broke out three days later in most of the large towns of Germany, and, though these were officially deprecated, the innocent victims were immediately subjected to the severest disabilities and penalties, including a fine of a billion marks imposed collectively on the whole community. At the same time, while the rioters went unpunished, extensive arrests of Jews were made all over the Reich, amounting, according to a trustworthy estimate, to some 35,000 persons.

The first cloud on the international horizon came not from Germany but from Italy, on 30 November, when an allusion to 'the interests and natural aspirations of the Italian people', in an otherwise unprovocative speech by Count Ciano in the Chamber, was received with cries of 'Tunis! Nice! Corsica!' Such a demonstration in a State subject to totalitarian discipline was suspicious, and it was followed by a campaign in the Fascist press which went far to confirm the misgivings aroused by the incident. But the cloud passed sufficiently to allow of an official visit by Mr Chamberlain and Lord Halifax to Italy on 11 January, and at the turn of the year the most probable danger-spot seemed to be the Ukraine, in the Polish and Carpathian districts of which autonomist agitation appeared to be being fomented and directed from Germany. The elections in Memel in December, which were accompanied by demonstrations demanding a return to the Reich, and brought into power the Nazi German party in overwhelming strength, also caused some moments of temporary anxiety, but led, for the time being, to no more serious developments. On 6 December the international outlook was lightened by the signature in Paris of a

Franco-German declaration in similar terms to that signed by Mr Chamberlain and Herr Hitler at Munich.

The hopes of the New Year were further encouraged by a prospect of the early termination of the Spanish Civil War. The surrender of Barcelona to the forces of General Franco on 26 January was the signal for the almost immediate flight of many of the opposing leaders to France; by the end of February the outcome was sufficiently certain to allow of the recognition of the victorious Government by Great Britain and France; after which, interest so dwindled that the actual termination of hostilities at the end of March passed almost unnoticed in the midst of the more exciting developments which by that time were distracting attention elsewhere.

In these circumstances a more optimistic spirit was apparent during the first two months of 1939, and Herr Hitler's profession, in his speech to the Reichstag on 30 January, of his belief in a long peace, was in many quarters accepted as more than cancelling the truculent tone of other passages. In view of what was to happen before the end of the year, the Führer's reference, on this occasion, to his non-aggression pact with Poland deserves to be recorded.

There can scarcely be any difference of opinion today among the true friends of peace with regard to the value of this agreement. One only needs to ask oneself what might have happened to Europe if this agreement, which brought such relief, had not been entered into five years ago. In signing it, the great Polish marshal and patriot rendered his people as great a service as the leaders of the National Socialist State rendered the German people. During the troubled months of the past year, the friendship between Germany and Poland was one of the reassuring factors in the political life of Europe.

In the early days of March the spirit of optimism reached its final culmination, when forthcoming visits to Germany by the President of the Board of Trade, the Secretary to the Department of Overseas Trade, and representatives of the Federation of British Industries were announced, which were to initiate financial discussions. On 10 March the Home Secretary, Sir Samuel Hoare, who had previously condemned the alarmists as 'jitterbugs', delivered a speech hinting at the possible return to disarmament and a 'golden age', as the result of the friendly collaboration of the European Great Powers. Misled by these signs of hopefulness in high quarters, *Punch* for once turned the laugh against itself by publishing what events were to make the most inappropriate cartoon possible, rather ominously entitled 'The Ides of March'. It represented a relieved John Bull, waking up to see the nightmare figure of the war-scare flying out of his window, and remarking, 'thank goodness that's over!' Below the drawing, the fact was recorded that pessimists 'predicted another major crisis in the middle of March'. This was issued on 15 March, the exact date, by an unfortunate coincidence, of the next episode in the international tragedy, for which the stage had meanwhile been prepared.

The Destruction of Czechoslovakia

In a desperate effort to enlist the support of all elements in the preservation of what remained of the Czechoslovak Republic, a great concession had been promised, early in October 1938, to separatist sentiment. By legislation passed on 19 November, Czechoslovakia was converted into a Federal State, with full autonomy for the Diets of Slovakia and Ruthenia, subject to the reservation to the Central Parliament of foreign policy, defence and other matters of national interest and application, and under Prime Ministers nominated by the President of the Republic. In spite of these concessions, tension, in which the hand of Germany can clearly be traced, continued to grow between the central Government in Prague and the two units to the east of it. In Ruthenia separatist Ukranian propaganda was carried on with German help and approval, while the Slovak Premier, Father Tiso, continued, in defiance of the new constitution, to maintain an independent foreign policy, by separate contact with the Reich and other foreign Governments.

On 9 March an acute crisis developed. The Slovak Government were understood to have presented a virtual ultimatum to Prague, in which they refused to issue a declaration of loyalty to the Republic, and demanded a loan, the formation of an independent Slovak army, and separate diplomatic representation. Failing the acceptance of these terms, they were suspected of contemplating a proclamation of the complete independence of Slovakia. On the following day President Hacha, acting under the powers conferred on him by the federal constitution, and, as has since been divulged, after consultation with Berlin, dismissed the Slovak Premier, Father Tiso, and most of his Ministers, ordered the arrest of several Separatist leaders, and sent Czech troops to Bratislava and other Slovak towns, where martial law was proclaimed. Dr Durčansky, one of the dismissed members of the Slovak Government, escaped to Vienna, where he began hostile broadcasts from the German station.

On 11 March an attempt was made from Prague to come to an understanding with a new Slovak Government, under M. Sidor, as a result of which the Czech forces were withdrawn on the following day. But on 13 March Father Tiso escaped from surveillance over the frontier to Germany, where he was received by Herr Hitler. A large body of German troops simultaneously concentrated near the frontier, and on the following day it was officially announced that they had crossed it, occupying Moravska Ostrava, Vitkovice, and Frydek in the north, and the Moravian capital of Brno. Father Tiso had meanwhile returned, resumed office, and carried in the Diet a declaration of Slovak independence. As Lord Halifax observed in a masterly summary of the case, in the House of Lords on 20 March, it was 'impossible to believe that the sudden decision of certain Slovak leaders to break off from Prague, which was followed so closely by their appeal for protection to the German Reich, was reached independently of outside influence'.

In this critical situation, the Czechoslovak President, Dr Hacha, left for Berlin to appeal to Hitler, who received him at 1.10 a.m. on the 15th, and extracted from him under duress his signature to a document consenting to place the country under the 'protection' of the German Reich, thus purporting to cover, *ex post facto*, the invasion of Czech territory which had already begun. This meanwhile continued and Prague was occupied at 9 a.m. It was on the same day that Father Tiso, who was as above suggested obviously acting in collusion with the German Führer, asked that Slovakia also should be placed under the protection of Germany, and naturally received an immediate consent. Hitler at once proceeded to Prague, where he slept the night in the historic Hradčany Palace, consummating on the next day his renewed act of aggression against the now helpless

Republic by the issue of a formal proclamation. In this, after asserting that Bohemia and Moravia had for thousands of years belonged to the German *lebensraum,* he established a protectorate over these regions, which were stated to belong thenceforward to the territory of the Reich. The Gestapo at once set to work, and a concentration camp for their victims was established at Milovice.

The dissolution of the Czechoslovak Republic was meanwhile completed by the action of the Hungarians towards Ruthenia, which they forcibly occupied, without objection from Germany, on 15 and 16 March, thenceforth incorporating it in Hungary.

Revolution in British Policy

These sudden events produced a tremendous shock: in fact, it is hardly too much to say that the school of thought which had hitherto believed in the possibility of a negotiated settlement with Germany was converted overnight. The scales fell from Mr Chamberlain's eyes, and he voiced the general revulsion of feeling in a speech which he delivered in Birmingham on 17 March. Hitler, as he pointed out, had violated his own declared principles by including in the Reich a people of non-German race. He had manifestly departed both from his assurances at Munich, as to the extent and nature of his claims, and from his undertaking to deal with any further questions in consultation with Great Britain. 'Is this', asked the Prime Minister, 'the end of an old adventure, or is it the beginning of a new? . . . Is this, in fact, a step in the direction of an attempt to dominate the world by force?'

The answer to these questions could hardly be in doubt. In addition, therefore, to the immediate step of cancelling the projected visit of the President of the Board of Trade and the Secretary of the Department of Overseas Trade to Berlin, the whole foreign policy of Great Britain underwent, from this point, a drastic and revolutionary change. This change marked, in fact, the realization that the days of peace were numbered, or that at least the only faint hope lay in confronting force with force, since force was the only argument which the German Führer recognized.

The traditional foreign policy of Great Britain in Europe, as has already been pointed out, is best served by maintaining freedom to mediate impartially, and by a consequent abstention from permanent attachments. All through the period covered by this history, we have seen a steady refusal on our part to undertake responsibilities towards the countries of eastern Europe, and indeed, a determination to confine to the minimum any military obligations on the Continent. When, therefore, the reader observes, in the ensuing pages, the bestowal of military guarantees on one eastern European country after another, he may at first be baffled by the apparent inconsistency. It is, he may think, as if an insurance company, which had hitherto refused all risks in a particular locality, were suddenly to begin insuring every house in the district, at a moment when serious conflagrations had already begun to break out. The explanation is that the traditional policy is only appropriate so long as negotiation is possible: faced with the threat of war, England, like any other Great Power, has always sought to confront her prospective antagonist with as formidable a combination as possible. The change in British policy had, in fact, already been forecast by Mr Chamberlain in the debate on the Munich agreement on 6 October 1938. On the hypothesis of inevitable war, which he then rejected, he had admitted that 'clearly we must make military alliances with any other Powers whom we can get to work with us'. He thus drew a sharp distinction between the policy which he considered appropriate for England in pursuit of the objective of peace, and that to be followed if war were felt to be inevitable. Within a few days the probability of the latter assumption, which was by this time widely held, was immensely increased.

Memel and Roumania

On 22 March, in response to a virtual ultimatum conveyed by the German Minister in Kovno, the Lithuanian Government signed an agreement ceding the Memelland to Germany, and the real nature of the transaction was emphasized, on the following day, by the arrival in Memel harbour of the Führer in person, with the whole German battle-fleet. The 23rd March was further rendered notable by the signature of a trade agreement between Germany and Roumania, which went far to suggest that the tentacles of the Reich were now stretched out to control yet another important area of south-eastern Europe. This agreement, though falling short of the full aims of which Germany was suspected, probably as a result of the popular reaction to a premature disclosure, nevertheless established an ominous degree of German control over the economic life of the country. The exploitation of the mineral wealth and especially the important oil supplies of Roumania was entrusted to mixed Roumano-German companies, and it was clearly indicated that the function of the purely native population was to revert to agriculture and produce food for the German 'herrenvolk'. It was not the kind of agreement likely to have been concluded by a nation which felt itself really free and independent.

The Guarantee to Poland

The sinister implications of what had so far taken place can be appreciated by a glance at the map of eastern Europe (see p. 78). After the occupation of Memel, Lithuania was subjected to German domination, through the control of her only port by the Reich. To the west of it, along the northern boundary of Poland, lay East Prussia and the now almost completely Nazified town and territory of Danzig. To the south of Poland there now lay a German-controlled Moravia and Slovakia, a Hungary owing her contiguity to an accession of territory achieved through German acquiescence, and a Roumania which had just proved susceptible to German influence by the conclusion of the trade agreement. On every frontier, therefore, except that bordering on the Soviet Union, the jaws of the German pincers were visibly placed in position around the body of Poland. Meantime, the preliminaries of a German offensive were clearly perceptible. On 21 March von Ribbentrop had conveyed to the Polish Minister in Berlin a proposal that Danzig should be returned to the Reich, and that Germany should be granted in addition a route through the Corridor with full extra-territorial status, in return for the following concessions:

1. Recognition of Polish economic rights and the retention of a free harbour in Danzig, and an assurance that the existing frontier between Germany and Poland should be recognized as permanent.
2. A 25-year non-aggression treaty.

As described by Herr Hitler on 28 April, the proposal also included a Polish share, with Hungary and Germany, in a sort of condominium over Slovakia, but this comparatively unimportant inducement was not, according to the Polish Foreign Minister, Colonel Beck, mentioned by Herr von Ribbentrop when the matter was first mooted.

The obvious reflection in considering this proposal is that while the advantages to Germany were concrete and definite, the value of the consideration offered to Poland depended entirely on the trustworthiness of assurances from a Government which had just given additional and emphatic proof of the worthlessness of its undertakings. It might also be observed, with reference to the proposed non-aggression pact, that about five years of the similar agreement, already in force, were still to run, so that the immediate situation was unaffected by it. Under the arrangement suggested, Poland's future security and independence would depend almost entirely on the good faith and good will of Nazi Germany.

Poland, however, in her desire to maintain friendly relations with Germany, though unable to accept the solution proposed, was willing to continue negotiations, and, in this spirit, her Government submitted, on 26 March, a counter-proposal in writing, to the effect that—

1. The separate character of the Free City of Danzig should be the subject of a joint guarantee by Germany and Poland.
2. Facilities for transit across Poland should be examined and conceded to any extent short of the transfer of sovereignty over the belt of territory involved.

To this conciliatory answer, however, no reply was vouchsafed, and the next to be heard on the subject was a reference in a speech by the German Chancellor, a month later, from which it appeared that the submission of alternative proposals was treated as tantamount to rejection of terms which Germany regarded as irreducible and final.

Though these negotiations were not publicly disclosed until later, the existence of danger to Poland was generally recognized at the time. In the Commons Debate on 3 April, Dr Dalton stated on the authority of a recent arrival from Prague, that German soldiers were saying in every tavern: 'We shall not be here long; we shall soon be going on—*going on to Poland.*' During the last days of March the barrage of calumny discharged against that country by the German press was interpreted as the now familiar prelude to a fresh offensive. On 31 March, therefore, Mr Chamberlain took occasion to inaugurate his new policy by announcing to Parliament that consultations were proceeding with 'other Governments', and that in the meanwhile Great Britain would promise Poland all the support in her power 'in the event of any action which clearly threatened Polish independence, and which the Polish Government accordingly considered it vital to resist', while the French Government had authorized him to say that they adopted the same position. These guarantees were given a reciprocal character after the arrival of Colonel Beck in London, in the beginning of April.

Italy and Albania

Though the announcement of the Franco-British guarantee to Poland produced an immediate reaction from Herr Hitler, in a speech which he delivered in Wilhelmshaven on the following day (1 April), he had not yet had time to consider his policy fully in the light of this new development. He contented himself with rather scornful invective directed against what he described as a new attempt at the 'encirclement' of Germany, and the only positive indication which he gave of his intentions was a hint that the Anglo-German Naval Agreement of 1935 had perhaps been fulfilled long enough. He asserted, however, in the same speech, that 'Germany does not dream of attacking other nations', and expressed his intention of calling the forthcoming party rally 'the Party Rally of Peace'.

For the moment, though the events of this crowded year followed one another so rapidly that a purely chronological treatment is impossible, attention was almost immediately diverted by a fresh act of aggression, this time committed by the other partner to the Axis. On Good Friday, 7 April, Italian troops suddenly invaded Albania, expelled King Zog after a very brief and of course hopeless resistance, and occupied the country, over which Italy assumed control on the following day. The pretexts advanced for this act of aggression need not be seriously considered. They may be set off against the equally false official broadcast issued from Bari only three days previously, stating that:

At the explicit request of the King of Albania conversations are in progress for the reinforcement of the defensive alliance between the two countries. It is not in the intention of the Italian Government to make an attempt against the independence and integrity of Albania.

It is obvious that neither Italy nor any other country had anything to fear from this Lilliputian kingdom. What is clear is that by his action Mussolini violated not only the Treaty of Tirana of 1926, but the Anglo-Italian Agreements of 1937 and 1938, as to respecting 'the *status quo* as regards national sovereignty of territory in the Mediterranean area'. The true motive was presumably to stake out a claim while there was yet time, in view of the growing extension of the conception of German *lebensraum*, and to re-establish the prestige of the Duce, which was becoming over-shadowed by that of his Axis partner, by a cheap and easy piece of banditry.

The incident acquires more importance if considered in relation to the combined strategy of the Axis. Thus regarded, it represented an additional stranglehold on the Balkan peninsula, by which the independence of every country in that region was seriously affected. Greece, indeed, felt immediately and directly threatened, in spite of assurances, and it is not surprising that the next application of Mr Chamberlain's new policy of guarantees was to that country. The guarantee to Greece was announced on 13 April, simultaneously with a similar declaration in regard to Roumania, which was probably included at this time more or less by coincidence, since she was one of the Powers with whom conversations had been going on since the inception of the new policy. Turkey was known to be another, and her association in the system of guarantees was already generally expected, though no agreement was in fact concluded till a month later. On 12 May a reciprocal Anglo-Turkish declaration was announced, pledging mutual aid and co-operation in the event of an act of aggression leading to war in the Mediterranean area.

The American Démarche

The cumulative menace represented by two acts of aggression perpetrated in such rapid succession by the rulers of Italy and Germany was at once grasped by the President of the United States. On 14 April, addressing the Board of the Pan-American Union, Mr Roosevelt summed up the situation as follows:

The issue is really whether our civilization is to be dragged into the tragic vortex of unending militarism, punctuated by periodic wars, or whether we shall be able to maintain the ideal of peace, individuality and civilization as the fabric of our lives. We have the right to say that there shall not be an organization of world affairs which permits us no choice but to turn our countries into barracks, unless we be the vassals of some conquering Empire.

Next day he followed up this pronouncement by a note addressed to the two dictators, challenging them to give assurances that twenty-nine independent nations, which he specified, ranging from Finland to Iran, would not be the object of aggression by their armed forces, for a minimum period of ten years, or preferably twenty-five. He promised to transmit any such assurance to the nation concerned, and to request a reciprocal assurance in return. This *démarche* was received with a chorus of abuse and derision by the controlled press of Germany and Italy.

Herr Hitler's Reichstag Speech

Mr Roosevelt was not alone in the grave view which he took of the situation. Indeed, most people in England had before this abandoned any hope that peace could be permanently preserved, but the sands now seemed to be running out with alarming rapidity. On 26 April, Mr Chamberlain announced in Parliament the Government's intention to introduce a Bill for compulsory military service. In doing so, he frankly admitted that he had given a pledge that such a measure would not be laid before the existing Parliament in time of peace, but, he urged in justification, 'no-one can pretend that this is peacetime in any sense in which the term could fairly be used'. This assertion could not be seriously challenged, although the passage of two more days was to see the world still further advanced along its precipitous progress into actual war.

On 28 April Herr Hitler addressed a speech to the German Reichstag, which had been specially summoned to hear his reply to the American President's communication. This matter, however, he postponed to the concluding stage of his address, the crucial importance of which lies much more in the decisions which he announced as a result of the Anglo-Polish guarantee. Disclosing publicly for the first time the proposals submitted verbally to Poland on 21 March (see p. 487), he described them as 'the greatest imaginable concession in the interests of European peace', and the attitude of Poland in failing to accept them without modification or discussion as 'incomprehensible'. He did not explain how the existing situation endangered the maintenance of peace from any quarter except Germany. Danzig, he said, was a German city and wished to belong to Germany, and the question had sooner or later to be solved. The acceptance of the English guarantee he interpreted as inconsistent with the German-Polish agreement of 1934, which, owing to this 'unilateral infringement', had ceased to exist.

In a memorandum of the same date, acquainting the Polish Government with this decision, he attempted to forestall the argument that the agreement of 1934 had not been held incompatible with the continuance of the Franco-Polish alliance, by drawing a distinction between agreements already in existence and those contracted subsequently. The guarantee pact was described as 'an alliance directed against Germany', in furtherance of a policy of encirclement, and was quite unjustifiably interpreted as showing the intention of Poland to co-operate actively with England 'in the event of aggression against Germany'. The memorandum also recurred to the question of Danzig, describing the March proposals as 'the very minimum which must be demanded' and which could not be renounced.

With regard to the relations between Germany and Great Britain, the Führer, in his speech, after a complimentary reference to the British Empire, and an assurance that he still adhered to the wish and conviction that a war between the two countries would never again be possible, declared that a war against Germany was nevertheless taken for granted in Great Britain, and that he had decided, in consequence, to denounce the Anglo-German naval pact. A note embodying this decision had in fact been sent to the British Government on the previous day.

Turning, finally, to President Roosevelt's communication, he read, in scornful tones, the negative replies received from the greater number of the States which it had specified, to a direct enquiry whether they felt themselves threatened. The best comment on this part of the speech was embodied in a cartoon by David Low, representing a diminutive Yugoslavia, seated between the immense and menacing armed figures of Hitler and Mussolini, and appending, at their demand, a tremulous signature to the required declaration of confidence. The President's *démarche* did, however, have the effect of inducing Germany to offer non-aggression pacts to her Baltic and Scandinavian neighbours, except Lithuania, the existence of negotiations being announced on 18 May. The offer was accepted by Estonia, Latvia, and Denmark, but declined by the others. The fate of Denmark less than a year later seems to afford an appropriate commentary on the value of these agreements.

Negotiations with Russia

After the deterioration produced in the political outlook by this speech and the positive measures which accompanied it, the task of constructing the strongest possible combination against the ill-concealed aggressive designs of Germany became increasingly urgent. This urgency became even more evident when, on 7 May, it was announced that a political and military pact between Germany and Italy was in process of formulation, and still more on 22 May, when this pact materialized as a treaty of alliance, providing for full mutual military support in the event of either party 'becoming involved in warlike complications'.

In the defensive combination which was being organized as a counterweight, there was a manifest and serious gap. As early as the parliamentary debate of 3 April, a number of speakers, notably Mr Lloyd George, had urged the importance of securing the adhesion of the Soviet Union. The desirability of this was freely acknowledged by the Government, but was not equally apparent to some of the other parties to the peace-front, particularly Poland, who retained a deep and intelligible suspicion of her Russian neighbour. Notwithstanding this obstacle, negotiations were in fact started in the middle of April, between M. Litvinov and the British Ambassador in Moscow, Sir William Seeds. Such approaches, however, were somewhat impeded by the ominous fall from power of M. Litvinov on 3 May, and his replacement by M. Molotov as Commissar for Foreign Affairs. During M. Litvinov's tenure of office, there had seemed to be little doubt that the policy of the Soviet Union would lead it to collaborate against German aggression. Although the desire to attract the Axis Powers to a conference had prevented any attempt to include Russia in the Munich negotiations, the U.S.S.R. had at that time given assurances of its intention to fulfil its obligations under the pact with Czechoslovakia, in the event of France granting that country military assistance. The interests of the Soviet Union appeared so strongly opposed to the aggrandizement of Germany that it did not seem probable that this policy would be modified, though it was noticed that, in his speech on 28 April, Hitler refrained from his customary abuse of Bolshevism. The replacement of M. Litvinov by M. Molotov was the first sign that any reversal of Soviet policy might be contemplated.

In spite of this, negotiations continued, but there now appeared a fresh obstacle. In the early days of the Bolshevik regime, while its hopes were fixed on international revolution, little importance was attached by Moscow to the independent status acquired by the Baltic Provinces and Finland, and the Soviet Union paid lip-service to the principle of self-determination on which the separation of these countries from Russia was based. The Bolshevik movement, at this stage, disregarded national frontiers, but, in the situation now developing, strategic considerations acquired a new importance. The fact that the Baltic ports were no longer under Russian control obviously weakened the position of the Soviet Union in the event of war with Germany. In particular the security of Leningrad was seriously affected by the fact that both sides of the Gulf of Finland and most of the islands within it were in the hands of foreign countries none too favourably disposed towards the Soviet regime. The frontier of Finland, moreover, was only separated from Leningrad by about fifteen miles. Such handicaps had not existed during the war of 1914-18, when Russia was fighting Germany. In considering, therefore, the question of association with an anti-German combination, the Russian negotiators were now impressed with the desirability of forcing the Baltic States and Finland to participate in the contemplated 'peace-front', or alternatively to concede facilities for Russian forces in the event of war. The countries in question were, however, strongly opposed to either alternative, and it seemed quite impossible for the British Government to go beyond persuasion in trying to induce these independent States to accept them.

The difficulty was indicated in a speech delivered by M. Molotov on 31 May, but, in view of the repeatedly declared antagonism of Herr Hitler to the Soviet Government, it was not expected to lead to a breakdown in the negotiations. Indeed, as late as 30 July, the Soviet paper *Isvestia* asserted that the Soviet Government 'stand for the creation of a general peace front capable of halting the further development of Fascist aggression', and on the following day Mr Chamberlain announced in Parliament a decision to send French and British military missions to Moscow, while political discussions were to continue concurrently, 'with a view to reaching a final conclusion on the terms of the political agreement'. Staff talks actually began in the Soviet capital on 12 August.

On 15 August, however, Baron von Weizsäcker, the German State Secretary at the Ministry for Foreign Affairs, made the significant remark to Sir Nevile Henderson, not only that he believed that Russian assistance would be negligible, but that the U.S.S.R. would in the end share in the spoils of Poland. Four days later, the prospects of a satisfactory agreement were disturbed by the conclusion of a trade and credit agreement between the Soviet Union and Germany, and on 23 August all hope was suddenly and finally removed by the signature in Moscow of a Russo-German non-aggression pact, in which the parties agreed to withhold all support from a State with which one of them might become engaged in war, and not to participate in any grouping of Powers aimed, directly or indirectly, against either of them. It is now clear that the price paid for this agreement was not only the swallowing by Herr Hitler of all his utterances on the subject of Bolshevist Russia from the days of *Mein Kampf* inclusive, and the abandonment of the principle upon which the Nazi regime was based, but also recognition of the right, which the British Government had been too scrupulous to concede, for Russia to secure strategic advantages, by force if necessary, from the Baltic States and Finland. The lack of principle involved in this transaction is perhaps less surprising than the apparent willingness to allow the U.S.S.R. to take steps obviously conceived in contemplation of an ultimate clash with the Reich, since the enemy against whom Russia was thus seeking to strengthen herself in the Baltic was clearly no other than Germany. Nothing could better demonstrate Hitler's complete confidence in Stalin's desire to avoid war and to maintain a purely defensive attitude. Some persons have credited him with thinking that this sudden interference with the British plan, coming at a most critical moment, might induce a second Munich, and permit the conquest of further territory without a serious recourse to war, though he had been repeatedly and authoritatively warned against harbouring such a delusion. Against this possibility must be set the apparent determination of Hitler, throughout the Polish crisis, to reject every opportunity of a settlement by conference, and to bring matters to the arbitrament of force. More probably, he hoped, in the war on which he had by this time decided, to hold off attack from the one quarter which could render direct assistance to his intended victim, and to escape that simultaneous war on two fronts against first-class Powers which had proved fatal to his country on the previous occasion.

The Final Crisis

The course of the negotiations with Soviet Russia has, in the preceding section, been carried down to the final denouement, within but a few days of the actual outbreak of war. It is now necessary to go back, and to trace the development of the final crisis. From the date of Hitler's Reichstag speech on 28 April, in which he had definitely declared that the question of Danzig must be solved, and described his own unilateral solution as a minimum claim which could not be renounced, the situation in and around the Free City had been giving rise to continuous anxiety.

Danzig was by this time so completely Nazified that its policy

could be assumed to be controlled and directed from Berlin
The periodic ebb and flow of political tension there could
generally be seen to correspond to the requirements of German
policy. An instrument was thus placed in the hands of Hitler
which enabled him, if he so desired, to produce at any moment
a pretext for launching his armies. Yet the situation in Danzig
in 1939 did not essentially differ from that of a year earlier,
when the Führer had publicly expressed his satisfaction with it.
Even assuming the necessity for an ultimate settlement, there
was nothing to make this an urgent problem. As late as the
second half of July the Nazi *Gauleiter* for Danzig, Herr Förster,
returning from a visit to Hitler in Berlin, stated that the question could wait for a year or more. There was, indeed, an
apparent deadlock, after the Führer's categorical insistence on
his minimum claims had been answered by the objections of the
Polish Government on 5 May, but there was at no time unwillingness, on the Polish side, to enter into further negotiations.

Throughout the whole period of crisis, however, the reader
may observe how the German Government not only refused to
initiate fresh discussions but seemed resolved that no attempt to
settle the questions at issue by the method of conference should
be made. The conclusion seems almost inescapable that Herr
Hitler was by this time determined upon war, and was careful
to preserve, against the most favourable moment, the pretext
for action which the situation in Danzig could at any time be
made to provide. At the same time he was anxious if possible
to throw upon Poland the responsibility for the first shot, and
the Nazis, under the encouragement and direction of the Reich,
consequently embarked on an almost continuous policy of
provocation.

On 12 May a mob destroyed Polish property in the Free City,
and tore down flags flown in commemoration of Marshal
Pilsudski on the anniversary of his death. On the 20th a frontier
post occupied by Polish customs officials at Kalthof, on the
East Prussian borders of the territory, was attacked by Germans
led by men in Nazi uniform, shots were fired, and the building
sacked. The chauffeur of the Polish Deputy-Commissioner,
who arrived to investigate, finding his car attacked, fired a shot
which caused the death of a Danzig citizen named Grübner.
This incident gave rise to an acrimonious exchange of claims

and counterclaims between the Polish Government and the Senate of Danzig. At the same time, an extensive smuggling of arms into the Free City was in progress, and early in June the arrival was reported of S.A. men in large numbers. A demand by Herr Greiser, the President of the Danzig Senate, for the diminution of the number of Polish customs officials accompanied by a threat to restrict their activities, was rejected by the Polish Government on 10 June. On the following day a Polish customs inspector, M. Lipinski, was arrested by the Gestapo and subjected to brutal treatment by members of the S.S. On 23 June, following the return of the *Gauleiter*, Herr Förster, from a visit to Berlin, the formation of a *Frei-Korps* in Danzig was understood to have begun, and at the end of the month the acting British Consul-General reported extensive military preparations, which, however, he did not consider to be intended for use before August. The attitude of the Polish Government to these developments was vigilant but calm.

Meantime the German population of Danzig was treated to inflammatory speeches by Dr Goebbels and others, and the local Nazi press admitted openly that the German aim was not merely the recovery of Danzig, but the annexation of the Polish Corridor, which was described as 'a key position indispensable to Germany'. The flood of men and munitions continued, and on 3 July German owners of house-property were instructed to get rid of their Polish tenants. On 15 July motorized units of the German army were reported to have arrived in Danzig, and the strength of the military formations in the territory was estimated at 14,000. Five days later, another frontier incident occurred, in which a Polish customs officer was shot dead.

On 31 July M. Chodacki, the Polish Commissioner-General, informed the Senate that, as a reprisal against interference with Polish customs inspectors, the produce of certain Danzig factories with an export trade in Poland would be treated as foreign and subjected to duties; the Senate threatened counter-reprisals, and proceeded to inform a number of Polish customs inspectors that they would not be permitted to continue their functions.

To this open challenge of their rights the Polish Government reacted with firmness, but, on the testimony of the British

Ambassador, Sir H. Kennard, with studious moderation. On 4 August they delivered a note to the Senate, offering to stop the economic reprisals in exchange for a pledge that there would be no further interference with their officials, but at the same time issuing a serious warning as to the consequences which might be expected to follow further encroachments upon the rights of Poland. The Senate immediately revoked the notices given to the Polish officials, and on 7 August delivered a formal reply of an equally satisfactory character.

In the meantime, however, the *Gauleiter*, Herr Förster, left for Berchtesgaden to discuss the situation with the Führer. By this time Herr Hitler considered the time ripe for the final moves in the game. On 9 August, accordingly, the German Government intervened in the already settled controversy, with a note sharply rebuking the Polish Government for having addressed to the Danzig Senate the communication of 4 August. The Polish reply questioned the juridical basis of this intervention, and warned the German Government that any interference by it with the rights and interests of Poland in Danzig would be considered an act of aggression.

The audacity of this answer provided the Führer with the required pretext for declaring his patience exhausted, and from this time forward a stream of accusations of Polish atrocities towards German subjects poured from the press of the Reich, and the charges were repeated in even more exaggerated terms by Hitler himself. German military preparations reached a state of complete readiness for war, and, about 20 August, an ominous concentration of force began to approach the Polish frontiers. The crisis was at once generally recognized to be acute, and the danger became even more pressing when, two days later, the Russo-German agreement was known to be imminent. On 23 August the Danzig Senate still further exacerbated the situation by a decree appointing *Gauleiter* Förster the head of the State in Danzig.

On 22 August Mr Chamberlain made a desperate effort to appeal to Herr Hitler through the medium of a personal letter, proposing a relaxation of tension to render possible the resumption of peaceful negotiations between Poland and Germany; to this the Führer returned an uncompromising reply, repeating his accusations of Polish atrocities and declaring that 'the question of the Corridor and of Danzig must and shall be solved'. President Roosevelt also intervened with a note to the King of Italy, appealing for his mediation, and with communications to Herr Hitler and the President of Poland, urging an attempt to solve their differences by peaceful methods. Appeals to the same effect were broadcast by the Pope, and by the King of the Belgians in the name of the 'Oslo' group of Powers, and correspondence on similar lines also passed between M. Daladier and the German Chancellor.

On 25 August Herr Hitler made a curiously characteristic attempt to isolate his intended victim, in a message delivered verbally to Sir Nevile Henderson. Poland's provocation he described as intolerable: he was determined to abolish these 'Macedonian conditions' and to solve—in his own way—the German-Polish problem, that of Danzig and the Corridor. But, as 'a man of great decisions', he was ready to make an offer to Great Britain, after the solution of these questions. He would pledge himself personally to the continuance of the British Empire, and even guarantee it German assistance should this be necessary. He was also prepared, after agreements to this effect had been concluded, to 'accept a reasonable limitation of armaments', and he declared that he was disinterested in the frontiers of Western Europe. The conditions for this transaction were to be the continuance of Germany's association with Italy, and the satisfaction, by peaceful methods, of 'limited' colonial demands. A point in the communication now perhaps of special interest is its expression of 'the irrevocable determination of Germany never again to enter into conflict with Russia'.

This attempt to induce Great Britain to break her solemn engagements towards Poland was answered the same day, when the British guarantee was emphasized by the conclusion of a formal Anglo-Polish agreement for mutual assistance in case of aggression.

On 28 August the British Government made a last effort to achieve a peaceful solution of the crisis. They proposed the initiation of direct discussions between Poland and Germany, with a view to a negotiated settlement, safeguarded by international guarantees in which Great Britain was willing to participate. This proposal provided a crucial test of Herr

Hitler's real intentions. If a just settlement of the differences between Germany and Poland was all that he desired, he could have no objection to adopting the course proposed. If, on the other hand, the present crisis was merely engineered as a pretext for immediate and general war, by rejecting the offer he would expose his want of sincerity.

Faced by this dilemma the German Chancellor took the course of purporting to accept, under conditions which ensured that the suggestion could never be put into practice. On the evening of 29 August a reply was handed to Sir Nevile Henderson in Berlin, requiring the dispatch from Warsaw, by the following evening, of a Polish emissary with full powers to accept proposals which the German Government would in the meantime formulate. These proposals would thus not be the subject of discussion or modification, and they were in fact never presented to the Polish Government; what was in form the acceptance of a proposal for a negotiated solution was thus converted into an ultimatum with a time-limit.

To this travesty of the British suggestion Lord Halifax replied on the 30th that he could not advise the Polish Government to comply with the procedure indicated, which was wholly unreasonable. The British Government, however, urged normal contact on both sides, and received from Poland an acceptance of the principle of direct discussion. But when the British Ambassador approached Herr von Ribbentrop with the same suggestion at midnight on the 30th, his reply was to read 'at top speed' the terms proposed by Germany, and to refuse to supply a copy of the text, on the ground that the time fixed for the arrival of the Polish plenipotentiary had already expired. In spite of this, the Polish Ambassador in Berlin was instructed to establish contact, and carried out his instructions at 6.30 p.m. on the 31st, but his efforts were unavailing, and at dawn on 1 September, without any preliminary declaration of war, the German forces began their invasion of Poland.

Even under these circumstances, the participation of Great Britain and France, in accordance with their obligations, was delayed for two days more, in response to an eleventh-hour intervention by Signor Mussolini. Poland's allies, however, naturally insisted on a withdrawal of the invading forces as a condition of any further delay, and at 11 a.m. on 3 September a British ultimatum insisting upon such withdrawal having expired without reply, this country was declared to be at war with Germany, while France followed her example by the same evening, and the period of peace which this history has attempted to cover thus came to an end.

XXVII

EPILOGUE

Causes of Failure

As I finish the revision of a work which has hitherto continued to express, substantially, the viewpoint of some sixteen years ago, I feel that a painstaking critic will probably still be able to find vestiges of opinions and hopes which experience has modified or destroyed. The spirit in which I wrote in 1934 cannot be altogether obliterated from these pages by any amount of verbal correction. We live and learn; the study of history would be a barren occupation if it had no lessons to impart for our future guidance, and mistakes of judgement are peculiarly inevitable when, as in this instance, the events recorded in the later chapters were still hidden in an inscrutable future when the earlier pages were printed. It seems, therefore, appropriate to make some attempt, in conclusion, to draw a moral from the record of frustrated aspiration which has here been attempted. My personal analysis is bound to be both subjective and incomplete, but it may none the less serve, in a modest way, to stimulate that process of hard and realistic thinking which our critical situation most urgently demands.

Looked at broadly, the history covered by the present volume is that of an unsuccessful attempt, made by at least an impressive majority of the peoples of the civilized world, to eliminate war from international relations. It can hardly be disputed that this objective was—and indeed still is—in accord with the wishes and sympathies of an overwhelming preponderance of the human race. We have seen how, more than twenty years ago, there was an 'almost universal repudiation of war as an instrument of policy' (p. 183). Yet the passage of another ten years was sufficient to see the commencement of a world war even more calamitous than its predecessor, and the attempt to avoid such a catastrophe had ended in apparently complete and disastrous failure. The main problem for us all must be to discover what went wrong,—how it was that the hopes and aims of the vast majority of mankind could be ruined by the actions of comparatively few. Are we to accept the humiliating conclusion that the task attempted was beyond human power?

Withdrawal of the United States

Some of the contributory impediments to the successful solution of the problem are obvious and generally appreciated. Chief of these was the repudiation by the United States of a settlement of which their President was the principal architect. It cannot be denied that this defection was a most serious hindrance to the effective application of the machinery devised for the maintenance of peace. The League of Nations was deprived, almost at birth, of a large proportion of the military and economic power on which its authority ultimately depended. This deprivation, however, was not and cannot be regarded as necessarily fatal to the working of the system. There was no fear that American power and influence might be used to augment the resources of potential violators of the Covenant. The prevalent view at the time was that expressed by a writer in the *History of the Peace Conference* (vol. vi, pp. 525–6), that 'the fifty-one nations, including as they do four of the Great Powers, with a fifth as at worst a benevolent neutral, control such an enormous proportion of the world's resources that their ability to enforce any policy upon which they are agreed and prepared to act will hardly be disputed'. More unfortunate, perhaps, was the resultant abrogation of the Anglo-American guarantee to France, on the strength of which she had been reluctantly persuaded to abandon her demand for the removal of the west bank of the Rhine from German control. The breakdown of this arrangement inevitably created a feeling of insecurity, for which the French endeavoured to compensate by the pursuit of an independent policy of a highly provocative character, by which the whole subsequent development of European relations was prejudiced.

Infidelity to Undertakings

Apart from these direct effects, the withdrawal of the United States undoubtedly helped to initiate one of the most disastrous features of the period—a really appalling disregard for the

sanctity of international obligations. An infant had been abandoned on the doorstep of Europe whose every feature unmistakably proclaimed its transatlantic paternity. It was left to
the care of foster-parents who inevitably compared it rather
unfavourably with the child which they considered themselves
capable of producing. It is indeed possible to argue, on some
of the lines suggested in the opening chapter of this work, that
their misgivings were justified. None the less, they had willingly
undertaken the responsibilities of adoption, and were under a
binding pledge to do their duty by the waif, *in loco parentis*, to
the best of their ability. To drop the metaphor,—it may well
be disputed whether certain of the obligations of the Covenant
were wise or unwise, but they certainly remained obligations
by which the whole membership of the League was solemnly
bound. In the absence, however, of the author of these provisions, the case went by default, and while the obligations in
respect of them were never expressly repudiated they were
tacitly ignored. There is irony in the reflexion that the crucial
obstacle to the acceptance of the Covenant by the United
States was the guarantee included in Article 10, which President
Wilson regarded as the keystone of the whole structure. America
need not have worried; as early as 1923 this article was a dead
letter. The provisions of Article 16 were almost as completely
and generally evaded. The point here is not whether, as policy,
these evasions were right or wrong, but they certainly promoted
an attitude of mind which soon learnt to treat all international
agreements with equal laxity. International good faith, in fact,
fell to so low a level that there remained no expectation that
engagements would be honoured if the circumstances of the
moment rendered their fulfilment inconvenient. In such conditions, aggression cannot be kept in check by the conclusion
of defensive treaties or by the warnings of statesmen; the wrong-
doer will simply estimate his chances of impunity from the
general facts of the situation, and may readily decide that his
chances of 'getting away with it' are favourable.

The dictum of Hobbes—that we are in the condition of war
when men do not observe their covenants—has already been
quoted (p. 261); if this is accepted, we have not far to look for
a prime cause of the failure to maintain peace. During the
period under consideration, there are few nations against whom

a charge of infidelity to their solemn undertakings cannot be substantiated.

The increased influence of public opinion in modern democracies must bear some of the responsibility for this fatal development. In old days, when treaties represented the promises of individual monarchs or aristocratic oligarchies, their repudiation carried a personal stigma, the fear of which created a substantial guarantee of their probable fulfilment. In a modern democracy, the responsibility is diffused almost to vanishing point; no individual feels that his personal honour is engaged; if a pledge is broken, the blame does not apparently lie with him. A duty nevertheless rests upon the public to react strongly and certainly against any lowering of international standards on the part of its Ministers; at present there is no consistency; the storm raised by the Hoare-Laval proposals contrasts with the approval generally bestowed at the time on the transactions of Munich. If the spectre of war is to be exorcised, the first desideratum is a recovery of a standard of international morality at least sufficient to encourage a general expectation that undertakings will be honoured.

The Handicap of Pacifism

A further source of weakness in the diplomacy of the peace-loving Powers lay, paradoxically enough, in the discredit which had now become attached to the use of force as an instrument of policy. There can be no doubt that the discouragement of aggression was, as a rule, a far simpler task in the days when 'an unfriendly act', even of a preliminary character, was liable to involve an immediate prospect of war,— when the threat 'we will fight if you do it' was a normal diplomatic card to play. Confronted by a world which stigmatized war as a crime, the aggressor could proceed with the early stages of his plans with a comfortable sense of certainty that his opponents would not proceed to extremities.

One of the points most likely to perplex future historians is the way in which German military power was developed in the course of a few years, practically from zero, by successive stages, none of which were interfered with by nations obviously possessing the power to do so. In the days when war was generally accepted as a legitimate if extreme instrument of policy, it would probably have been impossible for any State to defy obviously superior power by such actions as the repudiation of the disarmament clauses of the Versailles Treaty in 1935, or the reoccupation of the demilitarized Rhineland in 1936. Any such attempt, at a date prior to 1914, would almost inevitably have been met with a peremptory demand for its abandonment, followed, in case of recalcitrance, by a use of force which could hardly in the circumstances have amounted to much more than a police operation, which the transgressor was not in a position to resist. As recently as the Agadir crisis of 1911, it proved possible to nip a serious incipient crisis in the bud by a mere hint, in a speech by Mr Lloyd George, that peace, at a certain price, 'would be a humiliation intolerable for a great country like ours to endure'.[1] Such methods, or the expedient frequently resorted to in the past of a naval or military demonstration, had now been rendered far more difficult to adopt, by the disrepute attaching in the public mind to the use of force in international negotiation. The support of public opinion, always an important consideration in a democracy, was more than ever essential in an age when war was no longer the business of professional soldiers, but something with which every man, woman, and child in a nation was intimately concerned. But a populace educated to regard war as a crime, while it had developed an almost embarrassing interest in international affairs, tended to be strangely blind to their strategic aspects, which would, of course, have been irrelevant in the warless world of its wishful thinking. Actually, in each successive stage of Hitler's progress, the strategic considerations were the vital ones. If these were ignored, a public afflicted—like Ibsen's Master-Builder—with a conscience lacking in 'robustness', and disposed to be critical of the supposed iniquities of the peace settlement, saw a certain amount of justice in the German claims. Why, it was asked, should not Germans station their own troops in their own territory? Why should they submit to a permanent inferiority of armament to neighbours who had not themselves disarmed? Was not an Austro-German Anschluss a logical application of the right of self-determination? Why should Sudeten Germans be subjected to Czech sovereignty? On the

---

[1] Grey of Fallodon (1st Viscount). *Twenty-Five Years*. London, Hodder & Stoughton, 1925, vol. i, p. 225.

assumption of perpetual peace and an effective League of Nations, such questions might well have been difficult to deal with; the true answer in each case lay in the strategic implications, and these were not immediately apparent to a people trained by a sedulous propaganda to regard the maxim *Si vis pacem para bellum* not merely as a paradox but as an almost blasphemous falsehood.

Attitude to Disarmament

The attitude of mind which rejected this maxim was also responsible for the importance attached, both in the Peace Treaties and subsequently, to the question of disarmament. The prevalent opinion on this subject was an instance of a dangerous and fallacious generalization from the special experience of the First World War. In the circumstances of 1914, there was something to be said for the view—enshrined in Article 8 of the Covenant—that armaments in themselves are a danger to peace. When two Great Powers, or groups of Powers, engage in a competition in armaments, each step taken by one side tends to arouse the fear, resentment, and suspicion of the other, defensive moves are interpreted as offensive, and a vicious circle is thus created which increases the dangerous tension. As the burden grows heavier, there may come a point when the risk of being passed in the race may tempt a nation to try conclusions while success in war is still considered probable. Yet even in such a case the competition originates in a pre-existing state of tension, of which the armaments are a symptom rather than a cause. Moreover, the temptation to strike before it is too late is not induced by the growth of armaments alone, but by any prospect of a diminution in relative power. It may be questioned whether the Central Powers would have embarked on war in 1914 but for the manifest signs of decay in the strength of the Austro-Hungarian Empire. Similarly, the fear and suspicion aroused by increases in armaments are stimulated to an even greater degree by other steps, such as the formation of a new alliance or entente, which the advocates of disarmament rarely object to, and which were recognized as legitimate throughout the inter-war period.

But quite different considerations arise when, as in the circumstances in which the Disarmament Conference was prepared, the armed strength of one Power is plainly not directed against another. A nation which does not fear aggression from a neighbour is usually quite unperturbed by the state of the latter's armed forces. Normally, the growth of armaments is merely an indication of an inflamed international situation; to seek a remedy in a general reduction of forces is like breaking a thermometer with the object of curing a fever. Granted complete confidence in a system of collective security, every nation not actively contemplating aggression would automatically comply with the first requirement of Article 8, 'reduction of national armaments to the lowest point consistent with national safety'. Its reluctance to do so arises merely from a lack of faith in the security offered. The governments of modern democracies especially, faced with a popular demand for increasingly heavy expenditure on measures of social amelioration, are all too ready to lend an ear to arguments in favour of reducing the burden of their armed forces. But when the second criterion of the Article in the Covenant—enforcement by common action of international obligations—is shirked or ignored, as it manifestly was by most of the membership of the League, 'the lowest point consistent with national safety' inevitably comes to mean a point where each nation is stronger than every potential opponent, a situation which creates an obvious *reductio ad absurdum*. Hence, as has already been suggested (p. 346), the attempt to achieve the mathematically impossible was at best a waste of time and energy, but actually the effects of these long and hopeless negotiations were positively harmful.

In the first place, negotiations for disarmament on a competitive basis create precisely the same situation as any other competition in armaments. Suspicions are aroused, as nation *A* asks why nation *B* is so obstinate in its efforts to retain an existing advantage. International friction is stimulated. Secondly, the attempt led precisely those nations which were most genuinely peace-loving—notably our own country—to seek to promote the cause of disarmament by unilateral example, based on an over-sanguine estimate of the prospects of peace. As has been pointed out (p. 346), when the Disarmament Conference started in 1932 the outlook was already so clouded as to call for increased defensive precautions, but such nations were deterred from taking them by fear of the effect of such steps on the policy to which they were at that time committed. The most serious effect, however, was that which was produced on public opinion. Taught to identify the cause of disarmament with that of peace, and disposed in any case to fear a deflexion of expenditure from 'butter' to 'guns', i.e. from social amenities to national defence, a democratic electorate grew so opposed to the least hint of rearmament that when this policy became urgently necessary, a British Prime Minister was deterred from advocating it by the fear of losing an election.[1] Such an attitude, however reprehensible and open to the imputation of moral cowardice, was the logical result of many years of intense disarmament propaganda. In the speeches and writings of leftward politicians especially, any demand for a standard of armament on which the deterrence of aggression really depended was represented as a betrayal of the League, and its supporters denounced as unprincipled war-mongers. Looking back, we may now question whether the best possible guarantee of peace in these troubled years might not have been found in a resolute determination by the victor Powers to retain a vast preponderance of armed force.

Fallacious Generalizations from the First World War

The inherent defects of the system designed at the Peace Conference, I suggest, may, as in the attitude to disarmament, for the most part be traced to the operation of a single factor,— the extraordinary impact of the First World War upon contemporary thought. In the opening chapter of this book, attention has been called to the influence of this unprecedented and world-shaking event in revolutionizing the general attitude to war as an institution. The lesson was no doubt a salutary one, but at the same time the shock of this terrific experience had the disadvantage that it seems to have rendered the world incapable of thinking out the problem except in terms of that experience. The special and more or less accidental circumstances of 1914 appear to have been so indelibly

---

[1] Mr (subsequently Lord) Baldwin, House of Commons, 12 November 1936: 'Supposing I had gone to the country and said that Germany was rearming and that we must rearm, does anybody think that this pacific democracy would have rallied to that cry at that moment? I cannot think of anything that would have made the loss of the election from my point of view more certain'. Mr Baldwin himself described this admission as 'appalling frankness'.

impressed on the minds of those responsible for the League system that the conditions of future recourse to war were assumed to be identical.

Everyone tended to think too narrowly in terms of that unique experience and of that alone. To illustrate this point, we may recall the special conditions under which the war of 1914 began. The development of the crisis was sudden. Its immediate cause was an unpredictable incident—the assassination of an Austrian archduke by a Serbian nationalist. It appeared to contemporary statesmen that the outrage had produced a hasty and ill-considered reaction on the part of Austria, which opportunity for mature reflexion would have avoided. Hence the stress laid on a 'cooling-off period' and the delay associated with international conference. The notion of deliberate aggression, long planned and slowly prepared, such as that which culminated in the Second World War, seems hardly to have occurred to anyone. Yet in fact war, on the scale which alone constitutes a general threat to world-stability, must normally call for years of preparation, and the immediate occasion is a mere pretext, which can easily be provided about the date previously determined by the aggressor.

On a rather longer view, the first war might be regarded as the fruit of that 'trouble in the Balkans' which had long been a proverbial preoccupation of European diplomacy. Looked at superficially, this trouble was due to the presence in that region of a number of turbulent and insufficiently civilized small nations. Hence the view, expressed in Mr Lloyd George's memorandum quoted on page 61, that the main problem was to control the pugnacity of minor States, and to stamp out sparks of war which might otherwise spread disastrously. Yet, on a more searching analysis, it is clear that the Balkan danger really arose from the rivalries of the Great Powers in that region, which rendered probable their intervention in squabbles which in other circumstances and in other parts of the world they could have ignored. In most regions of the world, the clashes between small Powers constitute no danger to the general peace, and can be most effectively dealt with by the old expedient of isolating the conflict.

This preoccupation with a conception of war as a sudden explosion resulting from hot temper provoked by some more or less fortuitous incident made the machinery of the League strangely inappropriate to deal with cases of planned and deliberate aggression. In such cases, the aggressor, *ex hypothesi*, is prepared to violate the Covenant at the moment which suits him. The dilatory procedure of Article 15 need not delay him for an instant. It is all to his advantage to keep discussion and negotiation in progress until the pre-determined hour for his blow. If he has any case at all, he may even, as at Munich, obtain his object without fighting. However plain his intention, until, in the rigid formula of Article 16, he 'resorts to war', he is immune from the risk of any kind of forcible interference. Even after the first shots are fired, he may be able to play for time with a plea that his conduct does not amount to actual warfare. His prospective victim, on the other hand, cannot transfer the choice of time and occasion to himself without plainly violating the Covenant. If he forestalls the attack at a moment more favourable to himself, he will probably be condemned as an aggressor. He must submit his case to the arbitrament of judges possibly more intent on the maintenance of peace then the administration of ideal justice.

Prevention better than Cure

It followed, moreover, from the same conception of war as a sudden explosion of temper which could be allayed by the dilatory methods of international conference, so that the ultimate sanctions of the Covenant were not available till the actual outbreak of war, that a far greater preponderance of force was necessary than would otherwise have been sufficient. In fact, as we shall see as we proceed, the apparent superiority of the force theoretically at the disposal of the League was somewhat illusory, yet it is probable that a League which retained anything like its original prestige, and whose members showed a conscientious determination to fulfil their obligations, would have given pause to the boldest and strongest aggressor, if the problem had been one of prevention and not merely of cure. For the former task, no great preponderance is necessary. While the choice of time and occasion remains in its hands, no nation is likely to resort to war while success, in its own estimation, is a matter of doubt. The question asked at this stage is not 'am I hopelessly weaker' but 'am I certainly stronger than any combination I may possibly have to face?' The power of the League, whether real or imaginary, would probably have been adequate as a deterrent, if the nation contemplating aggression had had reason to fear it in the earlier stages of its plans. The risk of forcible intervention should have been a factor in the aggressor's calculations from the embryo stage of his preparations. As it was, the rigid criterion 'resort to war' left him nothing to fear till they were complete. On the other hand, to stop a war which had already begun required a real and substantial superiority of force, used in a way which could not be differentiated from precisely that type of warfare which it was the essential function of the system to eliminate. It was, in fact, a serious defect of that system that the element of power was reserved till too late a stage.

Illusory Strength of the League

The coercive machinery of the League was also much less adequate to its formidable task than was at the time supposed. Nearly sixty nations were solemnly pledged to support the Covenant. It was no doubt realized from the first that the contribution of a large proportion of this imposing array of States could only be of an economic character, however clear it might be to all thoughtful persons that 'the effectual enforcement of all sanctions against a Great Power must, in the last resort, depend upon the will and the power to employ military force'.[1] Yet, when all allowances were made, it still appeared to most people that, granted the will, the power was more than sufficient. The obvious fact that from an early stage the will was conspicuously lacking was generally attributed to a want of the spirit of international co-operation; the force available nevertheless appeared too overwhelming to be challenged.

But one of the most striking lessons inculcated by the Second World War is the negligible capacity for resistance possessed by any States below the rank of a Great Power, in opposition to a nation in the higher category. So long as war was thought of in terms of 1914–18, where a few hundred yards of ground were slowly gained at a bloody cost, in spite of great superiority on the side of the attacker, it was felt that a comparatively weak

[1] *International Sanctions: a Report by a Group of Members of the Royal Institute of International Affairs*, p. 115.

force, suitably entrenched, could probably delay an aggressor long enough to permit of reinforcement. The 'blitzkrieg' has now taught us a very different lesson, which—it is safe to say—was hardly anywhere appreciated before 1940. It is now clear that a first-class Power can knock out little nations, one after the other, almost as quickly and easily as a grown man might dispose of a number of children. Poland, for example, a country of large extent, with impressive natural resources, possessed of a population of the highest fighting capacity not greatly inferior in numbers to that of France or Italy (34 millions as compared with 42), collapsed in a single month before the onslaught of Germany. In this instance, moreover, the aggressor could not claim the advantage of surprise. Holland capitulated in five days (10 to 15 May), Belgium, invaded simultaneously, was defeated by 27 May. Greece, with British assistance, made a better showing in opposition to Italy, but when invaded by Germany on 6 April 1941, admitted her incapacity to resist further in fifteen days, and was finally occupied before the end of the month; Yugoslavia, attacked at the same time, was almost immediately brushed aside, apart from the action of guerillas. Except for the few countries which were permitted to remain neutral, the whole European continent had lost its independence by the middle of 1941, in spite of Germany's simultaneous preoccupation with the main struggle. The moral of all this seems to be that, against the aggression of a first-class Power, only the opposition of other Great Powers need be taken into serious consideration.

Once this is realized, a glaring defect in the power of the League is at once apparent. As planned, this organization included at the outset five Great Powers, but this number was at once reduced to four by the defection of the United States. There remained Great Britain, France, Italy, and Japan, of whom the two last were destined to rank among the most flagrant violators of the Covenant. The validity of Italy's claim to first-class status is, moreover, open to question. Outside the League were the United States, the Soviet Union—during most of the inter-war period an outspoken opponent of the Covenant, —and the arch-aggressor, Germany. Fear of the last-named brought the Soviet Union into the League in 1934, by which time Germany, admitted in 1926, had resigned her membership, but the genuineness or permanence of Russian adherence to the principles of the Covenant is rendered doubtful not only by the previous attitude of the Soviet Government, but by the pact with Germany in August 1939, participation in the dismemberment of Poland, and the flagrant act of aggression against Finland which led to the expulsion of the U.S.S.R. from the League in December. It should be clear from the above that 'collective security' against the aggression of a Great Power, in which consisted the only real danger to general peace, amounted in substance to little more than the strength of an Anglo-French alliance. No doubt, since this defect was at the time imperfectly realized, there existed also for some time the deterrent effect of the *apparent* strength of the League, but this was soon impaired by the obvious and growing reluctance of its membership as a whole to fulfil their plighted obligations. Strong leadership by the real possessors of military power was urgently needed.

The provision of this leadership was impeded by the fact that France and Britain entertained widely divergent conceptions of the proper function of the League, neither of which was wholly satisfactory. Each saw in this institution an instrument for the pursuit of its traditional national policy. France leant, indeed, to the coercive side, but to her the League was simply a wide system of alliance for her own protection against the menace of a reviving Germany. This safeguard she sought to reinforce by resort to other alliances of a more traditional character, and she was disposed to turn a very blind eye to breaches of the peace by any of her friends or protégés (Poland in the earlier stages; Italy in 1935). Outside this narrow function of the League as an anti-German alliance, and especially outside the confines of Europe, France was plainly and almost admittedly uninterested. The British view had, perhaps naturally, the merit of greater universality, since the interests of Great Britain were of a much more world-wide character, but she maintained her traditional dislike of automatic and far-reaching commitment to military action, and valued the Covenant mainly for the opportunities which it afforded for the solution of international problems by conference and negotiation. So far as possible, Great Britain sought to limit her coercive obligations to the protection of her time-honoured interests, the safeguarding of the Channel ports and opposition to the domination of the neighbouring Continent by any single Power. While whole-heartedly anxious to preserve peace by every other means, it was for these national interests only that she was plainly prepared to resort to force. In these circumstances a situation which depended so much on the collaboration of these two Powers was beset with peculiar difficulty.

Failure to Discriminate Between Types of War

It follows as a corollary from the negligible military strength of all but the few Powers of really first-class status that it is from such Powers alone that threats to the general peace are to be feared. In fact, a conflict on the scale of that which, between 1914 and 1918, had revolutionized the general attitude to war as an institutiôn, can only be conducted by States with the very highest military and industrial potential. Even today, however, it does not seem to have been grasped that the real problem confronting the world is the elimination of such war as is a universal catastrophe, and that this means concentrating on the aggressive tendencies of Great Powers alone. If these could be controlled, the petty clashes of small nations would not greatly matter—the situation would not differ materially from that in which wars were generally tolerated down to 1914. Conversely, no collective peace system can be really effective which leaves—as the United Nations Charter appears to do— the Great Powers in the position of 'chartered libertines'. This lack of discrimination between different types of war was perhaps the most striking respect in which the unique experience of the First World War misled the architects of the Covenant.

A system of collective security, like a system of alliance, necessarily rests, on ultimate analysis, on a coincidence of national interests. Rightly or wrongly, we have not reached a stage of civilization when nations will face the risks, exertions, and sacrifices demanded of them from a purely moral desire to prevent or punish any action, however criminal, by which they do not deem themselves affected. The designers of the Covenant saw such a common interest in the task of preventing a repetition of the experience from which the world had just emerged. And indeed to abolish *such* wars was clearly a well-nigh universal interest, since their injurious effects are so extensive as to be practically world-wide. It was overlooked, however, that this type of war was a unique example in human history, and was still likely to be the exception rather than the rule. To wage it, as has already been pointed out, was in fact within the capacity of only a very few of the greatest Powers. Ignoring this point, the Covenant drew no distinction between fundamentally different types of war. By Article XI, 'any war' was declared 'a matter of concern to the whole League', and the method devised in the last resort for dealing with it depended in fact on the general acceptance of this highly disputable proposition. It involved an obligation, in case arising, by the entire membership of the League to participate in military action, or at least to impose a drastic boycott which entailed a risk of forcible reprisals. But in many, perhaps in most, wars, no common interest to intervene was perceptible. Wars between belligerents with any but the highest military and industrial potential were still incapable of producing the world-shaking results which had shocked the conscience of mankind. In relation to them, the pre-1914 attitude to war was still tenable, and was in fact subsconsciously prevalent. Hitherto, the principle applied to such minor and local outbreaks in the interests of general peace had been to isolate the struggle and to ensure that the Great Powers should abstain from extending its scope by participation. The policy most conducive to general tranquillity had been held to be the exact opposite of that voiced in Article XI. It consisted in persuading the States not directly involved that this was *not* their concern. In my opinion, this alternative policy of isolation and non-intervention should still have been retained, and frankly applied, in such cases. For the new method which it was now proposed to apply involved in effect the conversion of a local and relatively unimportant contest into precisely the type of war which it was the real object of the Covenant to prevent—a world war in which all the Great Powers in the League must participate. When this issue was presented in a concrete form, the common sense of the community revolted. But the consequent breakdown of the League's machinery in face of a series of practical tests contributed more than anything else to destroying the prestige on which depended its efficacy as a deterrent of war. If, while that prestige was still high, the first challenge had come from a situation involving a risk of the type of war which alone had inspired the system, the response—and the result—might well have been different.   Principle, in fact, here as in other features of the peace settlement, was too rigidly applied and pressed to unreasonable lengths, and the system might well have been more effective if it had been more elastic.

It may, perhaps, be urged that such a discretionary power as is here suggested might provide too ready an excuse for evading the obligation to apply the ultimate sanction of combined force, even in a case where this was the appropriate remedy, and also that it would not always be easy to judge in which category of warfare a particular case actually lay.   There is, no doubt, some force in these objections; probably no system could be made absolutely watertight.   To the first point, however, it may be replied that where the war which threatens is in the 1914 or 1939 class, the existence of a common interest in its suppression should be clear to all, and that, provided the right had existed to bring the available force into play at the preventive stage, when the danger first became apparent, instead of waiting for the moment of 'resort to war', the members of the League would have been more willing to fulfil their international obligations.   As to the second point, it would in most cases be easily within the capacity of such a body as the League Council to determine in which category a given breach of the peace, whether threatened or actual, really lay.   The real danger of a world conflagration, which there is a common interest to prevent, is for the most part confined to the Continent of Europe, and can, as already argued, only arise from the aggressive intentions of a *Great* Power.   There are of course borderline cases, but most instances of resort to war lie definitely on one side or other of the line.   A League constituted on more elastic principles might, no doubt, have been less attractive to a multiplicity of little States who were the 'consumers' rather than the 'producers' of its illusory guarantee of security, but its efficiency as a preventative of the catastrophe of world war would probably have been increased.

The Federal Utopia

The foregoing argument is frankly based on the assumption that a system of collective security rests on a coincidence of national interests.   To many students of international relations, however, this dependence on the will of separate sovereign nations is the vitiating factor of the whole situation. Federalism, they maintain, or some form of supreme international executive entrusted with forces of its own, is the true and only remedy. As a utopian theory, this view can be supported by almost irrefutable arguments. But the practical applicability of the remedy really depends on the price which we are prepared to pay for peace. If mankind actually valued peace above all things, the problem could be simply solved on the lines of complete pacifism and non-resistance. But in fact, whatever it may imagine, it does not. The whole world, with negligible exceptions, makes a reservation in favour of national defence. What does this mean? It is important to recognize that the right thus reserved is essentially different from that of personal self-defence, such as the law accepts as a justification for the private use of violence. An individual using weapons with such a justification is protecting his life, or at least his property. A nation engaged in national defence is doing nothing of the kind. The lives and indeed the property of its citizens are actually exposed to dangers which they would escape by complete and immediate capitulation. The individual members of a conquered State, even if its territory is annexed or occupied, are able as a rule to keep their lives and their possessions, though under alien sovereignty or control. When men fight in defence of their country, the thing defended is in fact the right of the nation to a sovereignty independent of foreign interference. Experience, particularly that of the Second World War, shows that the determination to preserve this right is among the strongest and most universal of human instincts. To satisfy this instinct, men will cheerfully sacrifice their lives and property. They will face hopeless odds to resist an invader, and when they are defeated and their territory occupied they will still face prison, torture, the gallows or the firing squad rather than submit to the rule of the conqueror. The comparative merits of that rule are irrelevant. As Chesterton has put it:

> I knew no harm of Bonaparte and plenty of the Squire,
> And for to fight the Frenchmen I did not much desire;
> But I did bash their baggonets because they came arrayed
> To straighten out the crooked road an English drunkard made.

Similarly, the aspirants to national self-determination are often ready to admit that the Government against which they are in revolt is superior to anything which they are likely to put in its place; they clamour, none the less, to be allowed to make their own mistakes without alien interference. The advocates, therefore, of any form of international super-State, or of a federation which can override the discretion of the individual nations composing it, may be right in saying that peace on these terms is obtainable, but the price demanded is the surrender of the very thing which mankind as a whole values still more highly. Men will give much for peace and security, but the one cause for which they are prepared to fight to the death is the sovereign independence of their country. Any system which ignores the force of nationalism is doomed to failure as surely as a man who tries to swim up the falls of Niagara.

Problem of Ideological Warfare

But there is an even more cogent reason why the spirit of nationalism should not be dethroned, or discredited—in the severe language of Professor Toynbee—as 'the arch-enemy of the human race'.[1] The casting out of this devil, if devil it be, would open the door to other spirits no less certainly destructive of human liberty and justice. Recent experience has shown with ever-increasing clarity that the elimination of war would not by itself deliver mankind from the risk of conquest and tyranny. A new school of aggression has discovered a technique independent of guns and bombs by which to achieve its aims— the method of ideological warfare. In the defence against this new form of hostile penetration a vigorous spirit of national patriotism seems to be the most essential element.

The phenomenon with which we are here concerned has been one of the most striking developments of the period covered by this history. Until quite lately, the clumsy and sinister word 'Ideology' was unfamiliar in its modern sense to English ears. The 1934 edition of the Concise Oxford Dictionary gets no nearer to its present meaning than 'visionary speculation'. Down to the close of the First World War, it was usually found

[1] Toynbee. A. J. *A Study of History.* London, Oxford University Press for the Royal Institute of International Affairs, 1934–9, vol. iv, p. 221.

easy for perfectly harmonious relations to exist between nations, quite irrespective of the theory or practice of government which they exemplified. Republics, limited monarchies and despotisms of all kinds lived in amity side by side and even concluded alliances; indeed, it was considered wrong to interfere with the internal politics of another country, even in revolution, unless it was held—in the words of Castlereagh—'to menace other States with a direct and imminent danger', a criterion really identical with the traditional motive of national defence. The door was perhaps opened to the use of what is now known as ideological warfare by so sincere a democrat as President Wilson, when he insisted on the adoption of a particular theory of government as a condition of peace. The real inventors of this new technique, however, were the Russian Bolsheviks. In their hands, the policy pursued was strictly logical. The world conquest at which they aimed was at first genuinely in the realm of opinion. They were for the most part men in whom long periods of proscription and exile had destroyed almost every spark of national feeling. Since in all countries they and their supporters formed but an insignificant minority, they were necessarily hostile to democracy with its system of free majority voting. Their weapons had to be ideological rather than physical, their tactics the seizure of key-points by a handful of sympathetic and suitably de-nationalized citizens of the country attacked. They were—and are—adepts in apparently accepting for a time coalition with the leftward parties of a genuine democracy, with the ultimate intention of ruthlessly evicting such bedfellows and appropriating their power, as a young cuckoo ejects its fellow nestlings.

Employed against a democracy, these methods could be extremely effective. The nation exposed to them was placed in the dilemma of either being utterly defenceless or belying its fundamental tenets by the suppression of free speech and opinion. It was open to infiltration by disciplined and fanatical disciples of Marx and Moscow, ready to subordinate all national loyalty to the dictates of their alien teachers. It was debarred from reprisals in kind, since in Russia, as in any totalitarian country, a rigid uniformity of political faith was imposed, and speech and opinion subject to an iron control. It was soon evident that similar methods could be made to serve the ends of purely national aggrandizement. Fascists and Nazis, though ostensibly ultra-nationalistic, found no difficulty in adapting the Russian example. Though the rival movements to some extent neutralized one another, both depleted the ranks of democracy, as fear and hatred of one extreme drove fresh recruits into the arms of its opponents. The supporters of Communism responded with automatic docility to every turn of the helm, however sudden and inconsistent, in Russian policy. In almost all countries there also grew up Fascist nuclei, whose enthusiasm for their imported creed overrode every consideration of national loyalty. Where democracy survived relatively unscathed, this was mainly due to the existence of a strong moderate opinion with a healthy tradition of national patriotism. But the exacerbation of political antagonisms was inevitably injurious to a system of free government whose efficiency largely depends on the possibility of compromise and mutual toleration, and weakening to the nations so governed, through the dissolution of national solidarity. 'Every kingdom divided against itself is brought to desolation.'

The effects of the new development were well exemplified in the Spanish civil war, itself an instance of the destructive clash of irreconcilable opinions. While the totalitarian States could freely use the territory of Spain for a dress-rehearsal of the coming world war, democratic policy was seriously paralysed by a cleavage of public sympathies, important sections of opinion espousing the cause of each side with an equally uncritical enthusiasm. Everyone was infected with some form of ideological bacillus. So much so that on the outbreak of war in 1939 the real justification of British policy was never clearly stated. There can be little doubt that future historians, looking back dispassionately on the two great wars from which we have recently emerged, will regard both of them as contests fought with the time-honoured motive of preventing the domination of Europe—and incidentally of the world—by a single Power. This motive has hitherto been the most consistent element in British foreign policy, and has been considered the most unimpeachable, indeed almost the only, reason justifying British intervention in a European war. But, in the prevailing atmosphere, this reason was never pleaded; in its place ideological

considerations of a far more questionable character were substituted. We were fighting, it was explained, for democracy,
and for the overthrow of totalitarianism. These propositions
will not stand impartial examination. There was no ideological
colour whatever in the friendships sought by Mr Chamberlain
when war appeared to him to be imminent. The Government
of Poland was certainly not democratic; the Soviet Union,
though apparently opposed to Hitler, was clearly the exponent
of a rival totalitarianism. Turkey was still under an authoritarian regime; Greece was subject to the dictatorship of General Metaxas; Roumania, from February 1938, was virtually
an autocratic monarchy. It is surely undeniable, too, that Nazi
Germany, with which diplomatic relations persisted down to
the act of aggression against Poland, and even slightly beyond
it, would have been left in peace but for its leader's bid for
European domination. The equally totalitarian regime in
Italy was left completely—and carefully—undisturbed until
Mussolini declared war in June 1940. In 1939, the intervention
of the Western Allies was plainly and abundantly justified, not
only as the fulfilment of a treaty obligation, but as resistance
to an attempt at European domination which threatened the
independence both of themselves and of the other nations of
the continent. Nevertheless, it was found necessary to overlay
this real reason with an ideological camouflage for which there
was really much less to be said.

These remarks may perhaps be considered a departure from
the theme of this chapter—the reasons for the failure of the
attempt to abolish war. But the crisis of democracy created by
the new instrument of ideological warfare raises perhaps the
most formidable problem with which the planners of true peace
are confronted. If the elimination of armed force from international relations were all, our outlook today might be a great
deal more hopeful than it is. In spite of the apparent failure of
the League of Nations, and of the criticisms which I have
attempted to make of certain of its causes, we may, I think,
agree that a gigantic stride has in fact been made towards the
end which it had in view. Little more was really needed for
success than a greater measure of elasticity and a broader and
truer appreciation of the nature of the problem. Some of the
defects have already been realized and amended, and we may

even feel that, with all its faults, a more propitious combination of circumstances might have enabled the system to survive and to gather strength and experience for its own amendment. The experiment of 1919 came much nearer to success than some of us are disposed to recognize.

At present the world sees more clearly than ever before the incompatibility of modern total war with the survival of civilization. All this is to the good; no Great Power in the world will today enter upon war with the light-hearted alacrity of earlier historical periods. But we cannot afford to lay aside our arms while to do so is to leave defenceless those principles of freedom and justice which the best of us value more highly than mere immunity from physical danger. Ideological disarmament and the rediscovery of mutual tolerance are the crying needs of the hour. Till this problem is solved, the motive behind our efforts for peace is basically nothing but fear, and a world which seeks peace with no higher motive than this is perhaps ripe for annihilation by the atomic bomb.

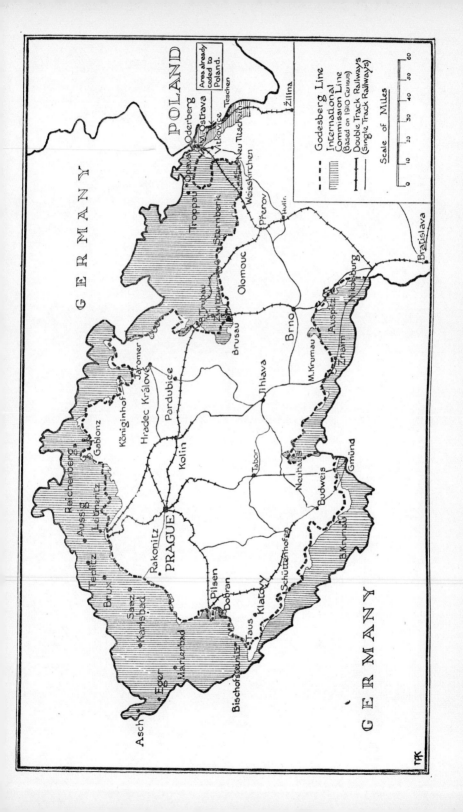

POLAND

GERMANY

GERMANY

PRAGUE

Godesberg Line

International Commission Line (Based on 1910 Census)

Area already ceded to Poland.

Double Track Railways

Single Track Railways

Scale of Miles

0 10 20 30 40 50 60

Asch
Eger
Asch
Karlsbad
Marienbad
Saaz
Brüx
Teplitz
Aussig
Leitmeritz
Reichenberg
Gablonz
Königinhof
Jaromer
Hradec Králové
Pardubice
Rakonitz
Kolin
Pilsen
Dobran
Taus
Bischofsteinitz
Klatovy
Schüttenhofen
Tabor
Jihlava
B.Krumau
Budweis
Neuhaus
Gmünd
M.Krumau
Znaim
Auspitz
Nikolsburg
Brno
Brusau
Olomouc
Mähr. Trübau
Landskron
Sternberk
Prerov
Holic
Weisskirchen
Neu Tisschein
Troppau
Jägerndorf
Oderberg
Mähr.Ostrava
Witkovice
Teschen
Žillna
Bratislava

INDEX